THE OXFORD HANDBOOK OF

THE NEW PRIVATE LAW

THE OXFORD HANDBOOK OF

THE NEW

PRIVATE LAW

Edited by
ANDREW S. GOLD,
JOHN C.P. GOLDBERG,
DANIEL B. KELLY,
EMILY SHERWIN,
and
HENRY E. SMITH

OXFORD
UNIVERSITY PRESS

OXFORD
UNIVERSITY PRESS

Oxford University Press is a department of the University of Oxford. It furthers
the University's objective of excellence in research, scholarship, and education
by publishing worldwide. Oxford is a registered trade mark of Oxford University
Press in the UK and certain other countries.

Published in the United States of America by Oxford University Press
198 Madison Avenue, New York, NY 10016, United States of America.

Library of Congress Cataloging-in-Publication Data
Names: Gold, Andrew S., 1973- editor.
Title: The Oxford handbook of the new private law / edited by
Andrew S. Gold, John C.P. Goldberg, Daniel B. Kelly, Emily Sherwin, and Henry E. Smith.
Description: New York : Oxford University Press, 2021
Identifiers: LCCN 2020018595 (print) | LCCN 2020018596 (ebook) |
ISBN 9780190919665 (hardback) | ISBN 9780190919689 (epub) | ISBN 9780190919696
Subjects: LCSH: Civil law. | Natural law. | Law and economics. | Trusts and trustees.
Classification: LCC K600 .O94 2021 (print) | LCC K600 (ebook) | DDC 346—dc23
LC record available at https://lccn.loc.gov/2020018595
LC ebook record available at https://lccn.loc.gov/2020018596

1 3 5 7 9 8 6 4 2

Printed by Sheridan Books, Inc., United States of America

This volume is dedicated to our friend and colleague John Gardner.

CONTENTS

PART II CORE FIELDS OF PRIVATE LAW

PART III CORE PRINCIPLES
OF PRIVATE LAW

About the Editors

Andrew S. Gold is Professor of Law at Brooklyn Law School and is Associate Director of the Center for the Study of Business Law and Regulation. Professor Gold's primary research interests address private law theory, fiduciary law, and the law of corporations. He has recently published a monograph on private law theory, *The Right of Redress* (Oxford University Press, 2020). He is also a co-editor of multiple books on fiduciary theory, including *Fiduciary Government* (Cambridge University Press, 2018), *Contract, Status, and Fiduciary Law* (Oxford University Press, 2017), and *Philosophical Foundations of Fiduciary Law* (Oxford University Press, 2014). Professor Gold previously was the Bruce W. Nichols Visiting Professor at Harvard Law School; an HLA Hart Visiting Fellow at the University of Oxford; and a Fulbright Visiting Research Chair at McGill University.

John C.P. Goldberg is Deputy Dean and Carter Professor of General Jurisprudence at Harvard Law School. An expert in tort law, tort theory, and political philosophy, he previously taught at Vanderbilt Law School, where he served as Associate Dean for Research (2006–2008). He is co-author of *Recognizing Wrongs* (Harvard University Press, 2020) (with Benjamin Zipursky), *Tort Law: Responsibilities and Redress* (4th ed. 2016) (with Anthony Sebok and Benjamin Zipursky), and *The Oxford Introductions to U.S. Law: Torts* (2010) (with Benjamin Zipursky).

Daniel B. Kelly is Professor of Law, Director of the Program in Law and Economics, and Director of the Fitzgerald Institute for Real Estate at the University of Notre Dame. He has been a Visiting Professor of Law at the University of Chicago Law School and Harvard Law School. His primary research and teaching areas include property, real estate, and trusts and estates.

Emily Sherwin is Frank B. Ingersol Professor of Law at Cornell Law School. She is the author of *The Rule of Rules: Morality, Rules, and the Dilemmas of Law* (Duke University Press, 2001) (with Larry Alexander); *Demystifying Legal Reasoning* (Cambridge University Press, 2008) (with Larry Alexander); *Ames, Chafee, and Re on Remedies, Cases and Materials* (Foundation Press, 2012, 2018, 2019) (with various others).

Henry E. Smith is Fessenden Professor of Law and the Director of the Project on the Foundations of Private Law at Harvard Law School. Previously, he taught at the Northwestern University School of Law and was the Fred A. Johnston Professor of Property and Environmental Law at Yale Law School. He has written extensively on property, equity, remedies, and private law theory. In 2014 the American Law Institute named him Reporter for the *Restatement (Fourth) of Property*. With Professor Thomas Merrill of Columbia Law School he is the co-author of *The Oxford Introductions to U.S. Law: Property* (Oxford University Press, 2010) and *Property: Principles and Policies* (Foundation Press, 3d ed. 2017).

Contributors

Kenneth S. Abraham, University of Virginia

Lisa M. Austin, University of Toronto

Aditi Bagchi, Fordham University

Anita Bernstein, Brooklyn Law School

Samuel L. Bray, University of Notre Dame

Margaret F. Brinig, University of Notre Dame

Richard R.W. Brooks, New York University

Andrew Burrows, Lord Burrows, Justice of the Supreme Court of the United Kingdom

Hanoch Dagan, Tel Aviv University

Mark P. Gergen, University of California, Berkeley

Joshua Getzler, University of Oxford & University of New South Wales

Andrew S. Gold, Brooklyn Law School

John C.P. Goldberg, Harvard University

Gregory C. Keating, University of Southern California

Daniel B. Kelly, University of Notre Dame

Gregory Klass, Georgetown University

Dennis Klimchuk, Western University

Daniel Markovits, Yale University

Ben McFarlane, University of Oxford

Thomas W. Merrill, Columbia University

Paul B. Miller, University of Notre Dame

John D. Morley, Yale University

Ruth L. Okediji, Harvard University

Nathan B. Oman, College of William & Mary

J.E. Penner, National University of Singapore

Barak Richman, Duke University

Arthur Ripstein, University of Toronto

Alan Schwartz, Yale University

Emily Sherwin, Cornell University

Robert H. Sitkoff, Harvard University

Henry E. Smith, Harvard University

Lionel Smith, McGill University & University of Oxford

Robert Stevens, University of Oxford

Molly Shaffer Van Houweling, University of California, Berkeley

W. Bradley Wendel, Cornell University

Tess Wilkinson-Ryan, University of Pennsylvania

Benjamin C. Zipursky, Fordham University

INTRODUCTION

ANDREW S. GOLD, JOHN C.P. GOLDBERG,
DANIEL B. KELLY, EMILY SHERWIN,
AND HENRY E. SMITH

The New Private Law (NPL) is an exciting development in private law theory. Yet NPL is such a new movement that its open embrace can sometimes seem too open. This *Handbook* aims to change that. The chapters in this volume are authored by leading private law theorists interested in the NPL approach. Many offer groundbreaking examples of NPL scholarship, while others explain the workings of NPL methodology or critically engage with its implications. In combination, these works offer a fresh perspective on the private law.

Given the breadth of coverage, it is not a simple task to explain what unifies the material in this *Handbook*. This breadth, however, is itself a testament to important aspects of NPL, including its attention to private law subjects that have suffered neglect, and its desire to illuminate private law with theory without thereby reducing law to some other subject or discipline. The New Private Law takes law seriously on its own terms; it recognizes a distinct sphere for private law; and it also shows an openness to new methodologies, insights, and subject areas. Several broad themes cut across both the *Handbook* and the movement itself. These include the incorporation of both internal and external approaches to analyzing law, a commitment to reconstructive engagement with the concepts and categories of private law, and a recognition of the breadth and diversity of private law.

A major theme in NPL work is its openness to considering both internal and external points of view in analyzing the law. Classic law-and-economics or Legal Realist accounts of private law often eschew the internal point of view in favor of an external, functionalist perspective. While not an inevitable feature of these approaches, they tend to treat legal concepts as epiphenomenal. Much work in private law theory over the past few decades has moved in the opposite direction. It has emphasized the internal point of view to the exclusion of external perspectives, sometimes suggesting that the latter are simply to be avoided. NPL scholarship often combines internal and external perspectives.

The second major theme is related to the first one: NPL takes private law concepts and categories seriously. Scholarship in this vein generally understands rights, duties, powers, liabilities, and remedies as distinctive concepts that hang together more or less coherently. NPL scholarship also starts from the premise that distinctions among established private law categories (contract, property, tort, unjust enrichment, fiduciary law, etc.), while potentially subject to critique, are intelligible and pragmatically warranted. There is accordingly great value in scholarship that aims to identify their respective domains, and the ways in which they interact.[1] NPL likewise respects differences between private law and public regulation, notwithstanding the import of the state's role in shaping private law and its enforcement. Although the NPL approach enables substantial reconceptualization and criticism, it starts from a distinctive, anti-skeptical premise about law and its departments. This starting point in turn dampens standard academic divides between consequentialist or welfarist approaches, on the one hand, and deontological or rights-based approaches, on the other.[2]

A third major NPL theme concerns subject matter coverage. Contemporary work in private law theory has tended to focus on tort, contract, property, and unjust enrichment. While other fields—for example, fiduciary law—receive occasional attention, the tendency to emphasize the "core" topics over others is evident. While by no means inattentive to core fields, NPL devotes substantial attention to others that are sometimes seen as peripheral, or that sit on the borders of private and public law. The materials in this *Handbook* are no exception. For example, it contains important contributions to our understanding of corporate law, employment law, false advertising law, intellectual property law, family law, and law governing the ownership of traditional knowledge.

Indeed, the diversity of subject matters covered by this volume extends beyond basic questions regarding specific private law categories. In keeping with NPL's recognition that private law is a complex system, it invites attention to system effects. Evolutionary perspectives, common law theory, and an interest in local understandings of private law are among the topics that fall within this description. In some cases, the NPL approach also puts pressure on the unity of private law fields. NPL is not always pluralist, but pluralist accounts find a comfortable home within it.

The chapters in this volume offer cutting-edge examples of NPL scholarship, while also serving as an introduction to the NPL approach. Coverage ranges from methodology, to the classic private law categories, to new subject areas and related disciplines. Authors discuss the differences between public and private law, between common law and civil law, and between local and more general private law perspectives. With these subject areas in mind, this volume is divided into three broad categories: Theoretical Perspectives; Core Fields of Private Law; and Core Principles of Private Law. We turn now to an overview of the chapters themselves.

*   *   *

---

[1] See John C.P Goldberg, *Introduction: Pragmatism and Private Law*, 125 HARV. L. REV. 1640, 1654 (2012).

[2] *Id.* at 1662.

PART I: THEORETICAL PERSPECTIVES

The first set of chapters begins with theoretical perspectives. As previously suggested, NPL often combines multiple approaches to private law theory, and it may even call for reconceptualizing private law fields. The first set of chapters thus delves into the range of theoretical perspectives that NPL employs, in addition to offering theoretical perspectives on NPL itself.

An initial concern is the New Private Law's methodology. As Andrew S. Gold argues in his chapter, NPL scholarship is distinctive for the way it builds on both internal and external perspectives. In some cases, an NPL approach is concerned with making sense of a private law field from the external point of view (for example, it seeks to understand what makes contract law economically efficient), yet it incorporates legal concepts on their own terms as part of that endeavor. This type of "Inclusive Functionalism" is a classic example of an NPL perspective. In other cases, NPL seeks to ascertain the internal point of view, yet it draws on social science insights and methodologies in doing so. And, finally, some NPL approaches are hybrids, blending both internal and external points of view. For example, this occurs when a theory is concerned with the internal point of view at the ground level of legal reasoning and an external point of view at the level of institutional justification. In other cases, a theory uses concepts that are recognizably "legal," yet these concepts are not precisely the ones used by the courts themselves.

Dennis Klimchuk's chapter argues for the continued relevance of the natural law tradition for private law theory, including the New Private Law approach. Klimchuk focuses in particular on a natural law perspective that begins with Grotius and ends with Kant. Theorists in this vein are concerned with nonconventional principles to which our conventions must conform if they are to claim legitimacy. Klimchuk then raises two potential objections: first, that the natural law tradition may be too metaphysical; and second, that the natural law tradition may not be metaphysical enough: that is, that the natural lawyers deployed the idea of laws of nature as a mere instrument in the service of morally objectionable ends. Using Grotius, Locke, and Pufendorf as examples, Klimchuk argues against these objections. On Klimchuk's view, Grotius, for example, understands the original community of property as a representation of how we stand with respect to one another in a world abstracted from the institutions that administer private property. In turn, the moral aspect of that standing can be understood in terms of nonconventional principles that protect the natural rights of equals.

Corrective justice is often taken to be the central focus of private law. Gregory C. Keating's chapter puts pressure on several leading accounts of corrective justice's role, using tort law as an illustration. As Keating indicates, corrective justice can be taken to be a subordinate feature of private law. For economic accounts, the corrective justice in tort law may be part of the data to be explained. Alternatively, corrective justice can be taken as sovereign, in which case it is both instantiated in the institution of tort law and a justification for that institution. Keating notes that economic accounts which treat tort law as forward-looking offer an implausible account of tort adjudication as a forward-looking search for cheapest cost-avoiders. The traditional understanding of tort adjudication as a backward-looking exercise in attempting to determine whether the defendant wronged the plaintiff is much more persuasive than the revisionist account offered by economic analysis. Furthermore, economic accounts struggle to make sense of central substantive concepts within tort law (e.g., duty, harm, cause, and repair). Yet corrective justice theories face another challenge. On Keating's view, primary responsibilities are antecedent to and more important than secondary, remedial responsibilities. As he argues, the wrongs that tort law recognizes and specifies are the heart of tort law.

Depending on one's view, civil recourse may be either an alternative to a corrective justice theory or a component of such a theory. Benjamin C. Zipursky's chapter clarifies the role and meaning of civil recourse theory in private law. As developed by Zipursky and John Goldberg, civil recourse began as a response to theories of corrective justice, focusing on plaintiffs' legal power to demand recourse for wrongs rather than wrongdoers' moral duty to repair wrongs. A plaintiff's right to demand a remedy is a right against the state, rather than a right that grows out of the defendant's moral duty to pay. Correspondingly, the defendant has a liability to pay if sued, rather than a duty to right the wrong. Accordingly, the state plays a central role in private law, both as the source of rules governing private interaction and as the entity that is obligated to empower, and does empower, victims to obtain recourse. Civil recourse theory is thus a *political* theory of the structure and ends of tort law and other branches of private law, a theory that has both an interpretive and a normative (or prescriptive) dimension.

In his chapter, Arthur Ripstein examines the relationship between Kantian morality and private law. Within a Kantian understanding of law, the rules and categories of private law reflect basic norms of human interaction, and in particular the norm of individual self-determination. Rights to property, contract rights, and parental or fiduciary rights and duties all follow from the same conception of equal personal right. At the same time, the "organizing structure" of private law and private adjudication is necessary to give manageable content to private rights. As Ripstein argues, this approach shows how a theory of private law can be both conceptually coherent and normatively compelling.

Law and economics offers an important and distinctive perspective for both NPL and private law theory generally. Daniel B. Kelly examines how law and economics influences private law, and how New Private Law is influencing law and economics. Economic analysis of law has had a profound effect on almost every field of private law, including property, contracts, torts, and business associations. Kelly distinguishes three waves of scholarship within law and economics, surveys the major ideas that economic analysis has contributed to private law, and highlights recent research within NPL that attempts to take seriously both the law and its effects. Going forward, he suggests, there will be potential synergies between law and economics and NPL in theoretical, empirical, experimental, and institutional analysis.

The New Private Law shares some intellectual antecedents and methodological similarities with New Institutional Economics (NIE), and Barak Richman's chapter explores how appreciating the overlap of both approaches can expand our understanding of each. He observes that NPL and NIE share methodological orientations and scholarly priorities, including interdisciplinarity, a rejection of orthodoxy, and an attention to real-world phenomena. Richman contends that, just as NIE—in part as a rejection of orthodox economics—pursues a nuanced understanding of human behavior, NPL is more multifaceted and pluralistic than its precursors in the legal academy (e.g., law and economics or critical legal studies). Likewise, both fields are circumspect to the complexity of social institutions. He draws a parallel between NIE's reverential approach to social norms and NPL's deference to legal doctrine, and he observes that recent scholarship in the "New Formalism" in contract and property theory illustrates the collective influence of NIE and NPL. Richman elaborates on various settings in which NIE has helped explain and expand private law fields, and he argues that these approaches have motivated and reinforced each other. Lastly, Richman indicates fruitful paths forward for NPL in light of NIE insights.

Turning to law and psychology, Tess Wilkinson-Ryan offers a framework for understanding the contributions of psychological methods and insights for private law. She argues that psychological analysis of legal decision-making challenges the predominant conception of choice and preference in private law, especially in the wake of the law and economics movement. Unlike economists, psychologists almost never talk about preferences; they talk about decisions, choices, beliefs, and attitudes. One of the interventions of psychology in the NPL is to reject simplistic accounts of preferences. Focusing on cognitive and social psychology, Wilkinson-Ryan explores how each choice entails a series of considerations: doing the math (calculation), understanding self-interest (motivation), reckoning with the visceral experience of being a human (emotion), internalizing social norms (social influence), and conducting a moral audit (moral values). In doing so, Wilkinson-Ryan outlines the case for taking behavior and cognition seriously in the NPL.

Henry E. Smith then considers how systems theory might bear on private law. Within a complex system, properties of the system are "emergent": they cannot be inferred from properties of the system's individual parts. Instead, they result from the ways in which particular components of the law work together. When areas of private law are viewed as systems in this sense, reductionist approaches, such as the "bundle-of-rights" approach to property law, prove to be seriously inadequate to an understanding of the law. Conventional analysis is overly reductive in that it assumes that the attributes of the whole bundle are the additive sum of the attributes of the "sticks" in the bundle taken individually. Theoretically and empirically this aggregative approach is not as accurate as one based on "organized complexity," corresponding to a rugged fitness landscape from evolutionary models. Smith then shows how systems theory leads to a better and more unified account of the bundle of rights, standardization in property, possession, title, and equity. Systems theory also promises to mitigate some of the dichotomies in private law, such as holism versus reductionism, homogeneity versus specialization, formalism versus contextualism, and the publicness of private law.

Private law theory often assumes a single subject matter across fields like contract law or tort law. Nathan B. Oman's chapter suggests private law fields are more localized. As Oman notes, both the private law and common law fit awkwardly with theoretical models that emphasize regulation and social control by the state. But the private law and common law also pose due process challenges to the extent their doctrines are applied retroactively. A solution from classical common law theory is to understand common law doctrines as "discovered"—as there all along—rather than genuinely new. Such a view naturally draws objections, but Oman argues that they can be resolved if the common law is able to draw on custom and practice. Unfortunately, some neoformalist accounts of private law cannot so readily turn to this solution: they suffer from incompleteness and placelessness. Oman contends that private law theory should thus take into account the local, even parochial, features of the common law.

Private law pluralism suggests a distinct but overlapping set of concerns. Hanoch Dagan argues that private law contributes to autonomy by enabling individuals to interact with one another from a baseline of recognizable private right. Because private law confers powers, it must also be limited in ways that respect each participant's right to self-determination. Specifically, according to Dagan, private law should be "structurally pluralist," meaning that it should recognize a variety of ends. It also should provide for a right to exit from legal commitments and should limit the kind and extent of commitments that actors can make to one another. Private law provides "types" that frame and support interaction, but these types should also protect personal choice over time.

Note, however, that private law theory can also adopt critical perspectives. In her chapter, Anita Bernstein argues that private law is structurally designed to benefit those who have been socialized to assert rights and make demands, at the expense of those who have been socialized to support others and make sacrifices. It places legal rights in the hands of those who both possess entitlements and choose to press their rights rather than compromise. Bernstein further contends the "modal female person" is taught to submit to others and refrain from making demands. The result is a large-scale unjust enrichment of those who are trained to be assertive, at the expense of those who are trained to be supportive.

Joshua Getzler's chapter considers how New Private Law can draw on the history of classical jurisprudence and, in particular, its roots in ancient Rome. Getzler contends that it is valuable not merely to understand present-day doctrinal reasoning; it is valuable to know the deep intellectual history of that doctrine. To that end, he indicates the significance of various legal heuristics the Romans adopted. Getzler also develops a further point: classicism has not always been a conservative, limiting factor—the classical tradition can also liberate judges who seek to experiment with the law or engage in programs of reform. Indeed, the classical tradition is a powerful mechanism for state formation. Getzler's chapter offers insights on these subjects that range from Gaius' legal taxonomy, through the development of the common law, and ultimately to the New Private Law itself.

Roman law forms the basis of the civilian tradition, and Lionel Smith's chapter offers insights on New Private Law from the perspective of the civil law. He begins with an analysis of what makes a civilian perspective, and he concludes that it involves more than just a basis in a civil code. Rather, there is a civilian mindset that draws on abstract concepts and categories. By way of contrast, common law approaches are more pragmatic and use casuistic reasoning. Next, Smith considers the domain of private law. For the civilian, he argues that private law is not so much concerned with a type of justice as with a field of justice, the field that covers justice between citizens. In the common law tradition, he argues, most theorists of private law understand it in much narrower terms (potentially excluding topics like family law). Smith then analyzes a specific private law subject—trust law—to show what a civilian perspective can offer for both "Old" and "New" private law approaches.

PART II: CORE FIELDS OF PRIVATE LAW

While not everyone will agree on the core fields of private law, certain fields are long-standing subjects of interest for private law theory. These include contract, tort, property, and unjust enrichment. Private law theory also incorporates equitable fields like trust and fiduciary law, and it likewise assesses corporations and intellectual property. This volume devotes substantial attention to each of these fields, while also covering additional legal spheres, from employment law and false advertising to family law and insurance. The next set of chapters shows the richness of the NPL approach in its treatment of these diverse subject areas.

In their chapter on contract law, Alan Schwartz and Daniel Markovits outline two accounts of contract law: a functionalist account focused on outcomes and a formalist account focused on doctrines. They conclude, after analyzing a series of examples, that there is a striking convergence of function and form in contract law. Rather than opposing each other, as they often do in other fields, functionalism and formalism operate more nearly as complements than as competitors. The explanation for this convergence in contract law, they argue, is that functionalists and formalists share a basic understanding of what a contract is—namely, a legal relation that creates and shares surplus produced through mutually beneficial, free exchange. Functionalist and formalist accounts of contract complement each other because the two camps, in spite of their differences, address the same basic legal relation.

John C.P. Goldberg's chapter argues that tort law "identifies and enjoins the commission of certain injurious wrongs, and empowers victims of such wrongs to obtain redress through the courts." Tort law, on this view, is both substantive and remedial, and torts are both distinctively legal wrongs yet nonetheless closely track moral wrongs. Goldberg argues that the rise to prominence of economic accounts of tort law—emblemized by ubiquitous invocations of the Hand Formula, the cheapest cost avoider, and the liability rule/property rule distinction—is both understandable and misguided.

It is understandable because these concepts reflect important features of tort law, including its distinctively legal standards of wrongdoing. It is misguided because it gives an implausibly reductive cast to these same features. An alternative, nonreductive "New Private Law" interpretation of tort law can better account for its content and structure without the distortions introduced by economic interpretations.

J.E. Penner argues forcefully against the disintegration of "property" as a legal category. Historically, the category of property was subject to attack for most of the twentieth century. Penner notes how a type of "nominalism" about property has had an impact in U.S. case law. But, he argues, it is not a helpful view to take as a property theorist. Instead, there are high-level abstractions about property that are necessary for understanding property rights and doctrine. Penner explains why attempts to define property as a "bundle of rights" do not assist us in making sense of these abstractions. He concludes that property has the character of "alienable exclusivity" because ownership comprises the right to immediate, exclusive possession, plus powers to deal with that right. In contrast to the Kantians, instrumentalists view property rights as serving some interest or advantage beyond property, whether coordinating activities and resolving conflicts over external resources through exclusion and governance strategies or engaging with moral norms as a part of our nature as rational beings.

In his chapter, Andrew Burrows begins by offering an Anglo-American comparative discussion of the law of unjust enrichment and restitution. He notes a recent surge of interest in unjust enrichment among courts and scholars in England and Wales, in comparison to a seeming loss of interest in the United States. Burrows attributes the difference in levels of engagement with unjust enrichment to an American preoccupation with constitutional and administrative law, greater attention to doctrine among English scholars, and the influence of Legal Realism on courts and legal scholars in the United States. He goes on to examine different approaches that are being taken by English scholars to a central question, that has recently been considered by the U.K. Supreme Court and goes to the heart of the law of unjust enrichment, which is what is meant by "at the expense of the claimant." He suggests that New Private Law could lead to a revival of interest in unjust enrichment among American scholars, while increasing attention to normative considerations affecting this area of the law among scholars in England and Wales.

W. Bradley Wendel's chapter considers the challenges that interpretive theories face when assessing fiduciary relationships, obligations, and remedies. Drawing on lawyer-client settings, Wendel notes that discretion-focused accounts of fiduciary relationships may fit awkwardly in such contexts. Turning to fiduciary duties of loyalty and care, he notes the degree of controversy over specific applications (notwithstanding consensus on these duties at a high level of generality). Indeed, the justification for fiduciary relationships is likewise debated. Instrumentalist accounts may be in tension with private law theory understandings, yet Wendel notes that such accounts have been influential in some jurisdictions. Wendel emphasizes, however, that fiduciary law has developed over time through analogical reasoning, or the common law method. He concludes that insistence on too much coherence may conflict with a central private law theory commitment—that is, that the law should be taken seriously as it is.

John D. Morley and Robert H. Sitkoff identify the ways in which the law of trusts, which sits at the heart of Anglo-American private law, has been used as an instrument of private ordering. In providing a legal and functional taxonomy of American trust law, they show that the law of trusts has branched into two distinct categories, donative trusts (which further divides into revocable, irrevocable, and charitable trusts) and commercial trusts. This branching, which is evident in both formal law and the norms and customs of practice, reflects underlying differences in facilitating private ordering in service of freedom of disposition versus freedom of contract. By explaining the logic of this branching in both practical function and doctrinal form, Morley and Sitkoff show that the law of trusts is a fruitful field in which to employ the tools of the New Private Law. Trust law is replete with categories that scholars can take seriously as theoretical and doctrinal constructions, even as scholars explore their functions in facilitating private ordering.

Corporations pose unique challenges for private law theory, including NPL. Paul B. Miller's chapter notes that most interpretive theories tend to simplify legal concepts in order to illuminate their core or essential features, but in the case of corporate law he contends that there is a significant risk of oversimplification. While private law fields often involve irreducible forms of interaction, corporate law regularly involves compound forms of interaction. Miller's argument elaborates on various leading theories of corporate law (e.g., the nexus of contracts theory and the team production theory), demonstrating how each simplifies the corporation. He proposes an integrative theory of the corporation that avoids treating the corporation in reductive terms. Focusing on four concepts that are central to the corporate form—corporate personality, agency, purpose, and fiduciary duty—he then offers a range of insights into the corporation and into long-standing debates about corporate law.

Aditi Bagchi notes that our relationship with our employer is one of the most formative and consequential private relationships in our lives. She distinguishes between two types of purposes of employment law, public and private. First, employment law is a kind of economic policy that aims to regulate wage and employment levels and to ensure public safety. On this public side, the law constrains what employees can agree to in significant part to advance the interests of others, usually other employees. Second, employment law governs a bilateral relationship between employer and employee. It aims to promote the justice of that relationship in ways that are familiar from the private law regimes of contract and tort. Within these private law purposes, there are some rights and restrictions that help to realize or preserve free choice for each employee and employer, and these rights and restrictions embody the first-order commitment to private ordering that underpins employment law. Other rights and restrictions can be understood to prohibit interpersonal treatment that we collectively reject as incompatible with human flourishing, in ways that resemble elements of tort law. Bagchi offers an interpretive scheme that identifies the ways in which employment law promotes justice between employees and employers, while also advancing broader public objectives.

In turn, Margaret F. Brinig explores the public and private law dimensions of family law. In attempting to explain and justify family law, legal scholars have typically used a framework based on contract. Brinig contends that a more apt analogy, and one that can help explain the public/private division in family law, is covenant. While lawyers may think of covenants as especially serious contracts, historically in the family context covenant has meant more than that. The idea of covenant depends upon support from the outside: extended family, religious community, and the state or God. Although family law deals with some of the most private aspects of life, concepts appropriate for other private transactions are inadequate. Brinig maintains that explaining trust, intimacy, and flourishing requires a new vocabulary of love, gift, and covenant. By emphasizing this idea of covenant, Brinig adds to the work of the New Private Law theorists who have set forth unifying theories that account for, explain, and systematize many fields of law.

False advertising law is a new topic in private law theory. Gregory Klass's chapter shows why it should be of great interest to private law scholars. As he indicates, false advertising law draws heavily on statutes and regulations, but it also has another unusual feature: this sphere of law adopts one duty owed to two distinct categories of persons. The law imposes a single obligation that is owed to both consumers and competitors. Klass also suggests that there are features of false advertising law's duties that pose practical challenges for traditional private law enforcement doctrine. For various reasons, it is difficult to compensate consumer victims under traditional approaches. Yet, as Klass concludes, the remedies and adjudicative mechanisms of the classic private law fields were designed to address practical problems in particular social contexts. The practical problems are different in the false advertising context, but Klass argues that while false advertising law makes use of distinctive enforcement techniques, it can still be traced to private law roots.

Molly Shaffer Van Houweling observes that a hallmark of the New Private Law is appreciation of legal concepts and categories including common law categories. For scholars interested in intellectual property (IP), common law categories can be used to describe patent, copyright, trademark, and other IP fields as more or less "property-like" or "tort-like." Van Houweling investigates both the property- and tort-like features of IP to understand the circumstances under which one set of features tends to dominate and why. She surveys copyright doctrines that demonstrate how courts move along the property/tort continuum depending on the nature of the copyrighted work at issue, including how well the work's protected contours are defined. She concludes that the techniques for navigating along the property/tort continuum are not unique to the IP field; they are familiar to scholars of tangible property, where courts similarly tend to soften property rules and remedies when rights are claimed in connection with unclear, novel, or otherwise problematic subject matter.

Traditional knowledge is also a new topic for private law theory. Ruth L. Okediji considers possible roles for private law in protection of traditional forms of knowledge developed and maintained within indigenous groups. Knowledge of this type is generated collectively over time and is subject to norms and rules internal to the community. As a result, intellectual property regimes established by legislation or treaty are often a poor fit. Okediji reviews the harms that follow from failure to provide adequate protection for traditional knowledge, including harm to the relationships that constitute indigenous communities, harm to collective identity, and harm to community development.

She then considers a variety of possible private law solutions, such as extension of privacy protection to communities, support for knowledge databases, enlargement of the concept of fiduciary duty, and modified versions of contract and trade secret law. She concludes that while private law mechanisms hold some promise, they might also cause damage to community values if applied ad hoc.

In his chapter, Kenneth S. Abraham analyzes the field of insurance law and explores its connection to New Private Law. One principle of the NPL is that legal doctrine should be taken seriously. In insurance law, a corollary of that principle is that legal doctrine should take insurance policy language seriously. Abraham maintains that insurance law and insurance law scholarship are largely—though not always—consistent with both the principle and its corollary. By analyzing varies types of insurance coverage disputes, Abraham concludes that insurance law takes common law doctrine seriously, and in doing so takes insurance policy language seriously. In general, he concludes, insurance law doctrine and interpretation are not covert vehicles for the judicial achievement of regulatory goals, such as protecting policyholders or promoting risk-spreading more generally. Instead, they reflect the courts' effort to apply the principles underlying insurance law with integrity and in an even-handed fashion.

PART III: CORE PRINCIPLES OF PRIVATE LAW

Private law principles are a fertile ground for NPL research. Topics range from abstract features of the law (such as formalism and the rule of law) to more specific doctrinal features that cut across private law fields (such as privity doctrine and remedies). This last section offers new research into the content and significance of the principles at work in private law.

NPL scholarship offers new perspectives on the relation between formalism and American Legal Realism. In her chapter on formalism and realism in private law, Emily Sherwin offers a qualified defense of strict rule-following. In a number of private law contexts, consistent application of rules according to their terms can yield significant benefits. These benefits can be obtained when following a rule will produce a better set of outcomes overall than would case-by-case evaluation. These "good" rules can only produce their benefits if followed without deviation over the run of cases. The difficulty is that it may not be rational for judges to follow rules in what appear to be recalcitrant cases, and apparent ways out of the dilemma, like generalized exceptions and presumptive rules, will lead to unraveling of the rule itself and the dissipation of its benefits. Traditionally, equitable defenses have offered a way out in hard cases, with only limited effect on the general practice of rule-following. Legal Realism, however, has upset the delicate balance between rules and equity that once prevailed in private law.

As noted, privity doctrine plays a role in multiple private law fields. Mark P. Gergen's chapter traces the functions that privity rules play throughout private law. The set of privity rules extends far beyond the well-known limit on tort liability to parties to downstream contracts, the rejection of which has called the notion itself into doubt. Instead, privity rules manage the information costs and liberty implications of causes of action and keep areas of law within their proper spheres. More precisely, privity rules perform a "partitioning" function, by limiting the extent to which actors are responsible for transactions in which they are not directly involved. And privity rules also perform a "boundary drawing" function that protects zones of private ordering. Gergen traces the functions of privity rules through the areas of contract, property, torts, and restitution and suggests that privity rules are most easily justified when they limit the effect of contracts to the contracting parties, and to a lesser extent when they protect the freedom of action of actors. As to the decline of privity in tort law, one can see the emphasis on the rule disallowing negligence liability for pure economic loss as serving the partitioning and boundary-drawing functions of privity rules. Privity rules also protect the contracting process when they prevent courts from displacing contractual solutions, even indirect chains of contracts indirectly connecting actors.

Richard R.W. Brooks explores the doctrine of good faith in contractual exchanges. Good faith is incorporated in national legal regimes, international law, and transnational legal orders. Yet its meaning remains ambiguous and indeterminate. Brooks maintains that, although good faith protects contracting parties, its principal aim is to protect the practice of contracting. By interpreting contracts to prevent holdups and others bad-faith uses, courts provide assurance to parties engaging in the institution of contracts. Brooks discusses two competing views of the doctrine of good faith. Consensual rationality restricts good faith to expectations derived from the parties, and cooperative norms are internal to the agreement. Contractual morality, in contrast, expands the legal bounds of good faith to include external standards and norms established outside of any agreement between the parties. Under both views, courts are encouraged to avoid an interpretation that would allow one side to exploit another in an unanticipated manner. Finally, Brooks argues, efforts to remove morality from the doctrine of good faith are futile. Even if it were possible to eliminate morality, a good-faith doctrine that was devoid of morality would be less able to bring about an efficient legal and economic order.

The linkage between private law and the rule of law has recently drawn significant attention. Lisa M. Austin's chapter focuses on how private law and public law concerns can be intertwined. She asks whether the rule of law applies to interpersonal norms that regulate relations between private individuals, and she likewise considers whether the rule of law can tell us something important about private liberties and the private law system that protects them. On the view adopted in her chapter, Austin sees the rule of law as something that renders power nonarbitrary. Austin then notes that state power in the twenty-first century is tied to information, and that in this regard the private sector may enable rather than constrain state power. Indeed, major private actors can exercise significant power as a consequence of their data practices. Rule-of-law features can provide a means to assess private law doctrines respecting private domination. In Austin's view, we should also be focusing on concerns about arbitrary power in the global private sector.

Defenses are another feature of private law of broad significance across the field. In his chapter, Robert Stevens examines the general role of defenses in private law. Stevens suggests that defenses follow patterns that are largely consistent across the various substantive grounds for private law claims. For example, defenses may take the form of justifications, which negate duties, or excuses, which leave duties in place but negate liability. Defenses also respond to normative considerations that are distinct from the normative grounds for liability. Accordingly, defenses should be studied in their own right, as a distinct component of private law.

Ben McFarlane argues that recent work on equity not only exemplifies the New Private Law but is also vital to justifying the distinctiveness of equitable principles. The most promising approach to identifying what is special about equity accepts equity's second-order role of adjusting the position that would otherwise arise through the operation of first-order law. Equity not only mitigates the risk of injustice, as between specific parties, arising from the operation of particular private law rules; it also mitigates the risk of injustice, as between specific parties, arising from having a system of private law at all. In addition, equity plays a role in providing parties with further means of structuring their legal relations. In some cases, the assistance is indirect; the "safety valve" offered by equity permits first-order legal rules to operate in a clear, stable manner that facilitates planning and transactions. In other cases, the role of equity is direct, for example, the creation of the trust, which offers parties a flexible and highly customizable means of both managing wealth and structuring commercial transactions.

Remedies have long been central to both private law theory and doctrine. Samuel L. Bray makes a number of observations about remedies, their objectives, their relation to private law, and the role of equity in enforcing private rights. He suggests that, although private remedies may have the effect of reducing social costs, they do not reliably track deterrent goals and are best explained as means for restoring or vindicating the plaintiff's rightful position. Similarly, although remedies vary among fields of law, their variations reflect contextual differences in the courts' conception of the rightful position. Bray also discusses the roles that equitable remedies play in law. In areas that were once subject to the concurrent jurisdiction of law and equity courts, equitable remedies tend to be supplemental remedies that address deficiencies in the default remedy of damages by shaping the outcome more closely to the facts. In areas that developed initially in equity, equitable remedies use the special powers historically associated with equity to enforce fiduciary duties.

Lastly, Thomas W. Merrill observes that, in the American legal system, judges are at pains to preserve a domain for private law, notwithstanding their inability to articulate a general case for its functional importance. An incompatible layering of legal theory has left judges without a clear conception of the distinction between private and public law. But judges retain a realm for private law because the distinction is critical in many contexts. As Merrill argues, both law and economics and the human rights tradition often overlook the role that private law plays in facilitating private ordering. Private law allows individuals to shape their affairs, exercise initiative, and plan for the future. But to perform this role, private law needs to be stable and predictable, and the content of private law should be developed from the bottom up, reflecting existing social norms, rather than top down, dictated by administrative "experts" or judges acting as moral authorities. The task of the New Private Law is to develop a defense of private law that is at once pragmatic but at the same time more doctrinal and conceptual than either economists or human rights lawyers would have it be.

*   *   *

As we hope this volume will show, the New Private Law is a novel and important development for private law theory. As an approach to private law inquiry, NPL is also attractive for more than one reason. The NPL movement takes doctrine seriously on its own terms, while also showing openness to new methodologies. NPL considers the law at the local level of two-party interactions, while also adopting insights about how complex systems work as a whole. And NPL seeks insights into core private law fields (such as contract, tort, or property), while also analyzing fields that have only recently been subjects for private law theory. In combination, these features open up multiple avenues for new research. This *Handbook*, we hope, provides a valuable introduction to New Private Law and to the insights it offers.

PART I

THEORETICAL PERSPECTIVES

CHAPTER 1

....

INTERNAL AND EXTERNAL PERSPECTIVES

On the New Private Law Methodology

....

ANDREW S. GOLD

I. INTRODUCTION

....

KARL Llewellyn faced a difficult challenge in trying to explain what Legal Realism was. Llewellyn noted that Legal Realism was not a school of thought, but a movement—and indeed a sufficiently broad movement that it included people who did not self-identify as Legal Realists.[1] The same challenge faces efforts to explain the New Private Law: there is no specific doctrine that must be accepted, no precise methodology that adherents need to adopt. And, while various scholars qualify as participants, it is not because they all profess to be members. New Private Law scholarship shows certain tendencies of thought, but it is not a school so much as a loosely defined movement.[2]

If there is a common feature that cuts across New Private Law scholarship, it is an interest in the internal point of view.[3] Theorists want to better understand what is sometimes called private law's self-understanding, and they seek to grasp private law concepts from that perspective. In pursuing this end, their theories focus on the way that

---

[1] See Karl Llewellyn, *Some Realism About Realism—Responding to Dean Pound*, 44 HARV. L. REV. 1222, 1233–1234 (1931).

[2] See John C.P. Goldberg, *Introduction: Pragmatism and Private Law*, 125 HARV. L. REV. 1640 (2012).

[3] See, e.g., John C.P. Goldberg & Benjamin C. Zipursky, *Seeing Tort Law from the Internal Point of View: Holmes and Hart on Legal Duties*, 75 FORDHAM L. REV. 1563 (2006); Stephen A. Smith, *Contract Theory* 7–32 (2004). The significance of the internal point of view, and the merits of explaining legal fields from this perspective, are the subject of a larger debate. See Charles L. Barzun, *Inside-Out: Beyond the Internal/External Distinction in Legal Scholarship*, 101 VA. L. REV. 1203 (2015).

judges and lawyers talk and reason. In practice, these theories also tend to take the language of the law at face value, rather than treating that language as code for other concepts. Yet this does not quite capture the spirit of the New Private Law, as private law theory has been focused on the internal point of view for decades. Many of the classic works in the 1980s and 1990s also emphasize the internal point of view.[4]

It may help to compare external perspectives on private law. Such perspectives take a wide variety of forms, but they often focus on what law does (rather than what law is), and they often care about how judges or other legal actors behave in practice (rather than how judicial opinions express judges' public reasoning). Such theories include functional accounts that emphasize some external objective the law is thought to accomplish. They may also include explanations of private law that suggest court opinions lack transparency or reflect a false consciousness; they regularly treat legal concepts in a reductive fashion. New Private Law theory clearly differs from many leading external accounts, for it takes legal concepts and reasoning to be central to the law rather than epiphenomenal.

Yet in various ways New Private Law scholarship adopts insights and methodologies associated with externalist legal analysis. A thread that runs throughout New Private Law theory is an interest in the internal point of view that is combined with an interest in empirical research, functional analysis, or the practical effects of legal doctrine. These additional features often begin with an interest in the internal perspective, but they incorporate approaches developed elsewhere. For example, research in social psychology may help theorists to ascertain the internal point of view, even though such social science approaches are commonly associated with an external legal analysis. The goal is to understand the internal perspective, yet the method of reaching that goal is commonly associated with an externalist mode of inquiry.

New Private Law scholarship also includes external perspectives that incorporate the internal point of view. Inclusive functionalism is a good illustration.[5] An inclusive functionalist approach to private law seeks to understand law's function in light of the concepts that are immanent in private law reasoning. For example, a theory of tort law that draws on the modularity of tort law's concepts will take seriously the ways that rights, duties, wrongs, and remedies are conceptually linked in adjudication.[6] To see how these concepts limit information costs or delineation costs requires appreciating how they are understood from the legal perspective. The internal point of view thus makes clear how tort law's concepts can play a functional role.

Bearing in mind the difficulties in defining what should count as New Private Law, this chapter will review several recent themes in New Private Law scholarship in an effort to show the distinctiveness and richness of the movement's general approach. Notably, internal and external perspectives and associated methodologies often

---

[4] See, e.g., Ernest J. Weinrib, *The Idea of Private Law* (1995); Jules Coleman, *Risks and Wrongs* (1992).

[5] For an elaboration of this approach, see Andrew S. Gold & Henry E. Smith, *Sizing Up Private Law* (forthcoming, University of Toronto Law Journal), https://ssrn.com/abstract=2821354.

[6] See, e.g., Henry E. Smith, *Modularity and Morality in the Law of Torts*, 4 J. TORT L. 1 (2011).

converge in New Private Law theory. The result is a type of private law scholarship that takes private law concepts seriously on their own terms, while simultaneously seeking to understand how those concepts fit in with other considerations—including functional considerations that extend well beyond private law. As will be developed, this intertwining of internal and external is also justified, given the insights that each perspective can offer to the other.

Section II will discuss several ways that New Private Law theory makes use of the internal point of view in support of an external legal analysis. Section III will consider how external perspectives and associated methodologies offer insights for inquiries into the internal point of view. Among other things, this section discusses how interpretive criteria are an important part of the picture. New Private Law theorists tend to adopt moderate interpretive criteria, and as a consequence external perspectives and empirical analysis are, or can be, more likely to affect their inquiries. Section IV recognizes an additional possibility: a hybrid approach that incorporates features of both internal and external perspectives. Such approaches are increasingly common, and they may be particularly relevant where stare decisis and precedent are factors in legal analysis.

II. External Approaches that Draw on the Internal Point of View

A. Inclusive Functionalism

Some private law theorists believe that private law should be explained in light of a single principle, such as corrective justice. On a strict version of this view, teleological accounts are to be avoided, and if private law is understood in functional terms, it is a mistake. In contrast, New Private Law theories often see the internal point of view as something we should take seriously precisely because the concepts that are immanent in private law may have functional benefits. A variety of recent contributions see private law concepts as a desirable part of a functional account, even when those concepts are taken on their own terms.

For example, Stephen Smith has argued that the normativity of private law should matter to efficiency theorists because, as a practical matter, legal duties motivate individual actors to comply with the law.[7] If efficiency theorists focus on sanctions to the detriment of private law's guidance function, they will fail to understand fully the ways in which private law incentivizes the parties it regulates. As he notes, many individuals comply with legal directives "simply because they are legal rules and not because of the incentives that the law offers for compliance."[8] While some individuals are motivated by

---

[7] See Stephen A. Smith, *The Normativity of Private Law*, 31 Oxford J. Legal Stud. 215 (2011).
[8] *Id.* at 216.

the risk of sanctions, others are driven by the view that they have a moral obligation to obey the law.[9] Functionalists with an interest in the behavioral consequences of legal rules should therefore pay attention to this latter perspective.[10]

Similarly, Rebecca Stone has argued for an understanding of contract law that takes proper account of "internalizers" and not just "externalizers."[11] Internalizers take legal rules as guides for conduct even when this is not in their self-interest, while externalizers think like the Holmesian "bad man." As Stone indicates: "[T]he internalizer's behavior will depend on how she resolves a prior interpretative question: What exactly is the legal norm that governs the perform-breach decision?"[12] Again, the implications matter for purposes of efficiency reasoning, and it turns out that an efficient contract law will look different if it is assumed that the population includes internalizers.

There is also another reason for functionalist authors to take the internal point of view into account. Research in social psychology suggests that the moral credibility of legal norms affects compliance with those norms.[13] Accordingly, it could matter what understanding of duties is contained within a private law field. Consider the distinction that John Goldberg and Benjamin Zipursky have drawn between instrumentalist conceptions of legal duties and relational conceptions. As they explain, a relational conception is noninstrumental, "in that it rejects a reductive-instrumentalist account of 'duty' in terms of pros and cons of liability rules, and takes seriously the idea that duty [in negligence law] refers to a kind of obligation."[14] In Goldberg and Zipursky's view, a relational conception "reflect[s] ordinary moral judgments about duties owed to others,"[15] and the relational conception is embedded in negligence law.[16]

If Goldberg and Zipursky are right, instrumentalist conceptions of legal duties may not be the best approach to achieving functional aims.[17] A relational conception may better induce compliance than an instrumentalist conception, in part because the relational understanding is "more easily internalized, guides citizens more reliably and with less enforcement, and commands greater respect."[18] In other words, to the extent that moral concepts in private law are consistent with prevailing conceptions of interpersonal morality, these moral concepts may increase the likelihood of compliance with private law rules. Again, this is a possibility which

---

[9] See *id.* at 223 & n.21 (citing Tom R. Tyler, *Why People Obey the Law* (1990)).

[10] *Id.* at 242.

[11] See Rebecca Stone, *Economic Analysis of Contract Law from the Internal Point of View*, 116 COLUM. L. REV. 2005 (2016).

[12] See *id.* at 2009.

[13] See Paul H. Robinson & John M. Darley, *The Utility of Desert*, 91 NW. U. L. REV. 453, 468–488 (1997) (developing arguments on this basis in the criminal law setting); Janice Nadler, *Flouting the Law*, 83 TEX. L. REV. 1399 (2005) (indicating that individuals may flout the law if there is a divergence between the individual's common-sense understanding of justice and the understanding that the individual sees enshrined in the law).

[14] John C.P. Goldberg & Benjamin C. Zipursky, *The Moral of* MacPherson, 146 U. PA. L. REV. 1733, 1826 (1995).

[15] See *id.*   [16] See *id.* at 1826–1827.   [17] See *id.* at 1841.   [18] *Id.*

should interest functionalists,[19] but in order to assess this possibility we need to know which norms are internal to each private law field. Such inquiries fall within a New Private Law rubric.

B. External Perspectives Concerning the Development and Impact of the Internal Point of View

Theorists may also be interested in understanding the historical path of the law, and this goal offers another reason for internal and external to interrelate. Suppose we want to understand why private law concepts have the features that they do, for functional reasons or otherwise. What events influenced the development of one set of concepts within the law rather than another? This kind of analysis requires us to take seriously whatever the internal point of view happens to be, but it also requires an understanding of how legal institutions work in practice, of what fact patterns affect judicial psychology, and of which cognitive biases or heuristics are in play. Theorists may also need to incorporate the problem of system effects, which can likewise shape legal analysis as courts struggle to avoid intractable complexity.[20]

Indeed, historical or sociological investigations may help to predict the path of the law going forward, while still being concerned with the law's self-understanding. For example, one might ask: What is the law's self-understanding likely to become?[21] Assuming we would like to see the law's self-understanding move in a different direction from its probable path, which factors are likely to impact that result? Understanding the legal perspective is an important part of this kind of inquiry, but it is necessarily only a component. We cannot readily figure out where the internal point of view will end up without also determining where it currently is. Such analysis can ultimately contribute to an external point of view, but it will need to incorporate knowledge of the internal point of view along the way.

A related puzzle concerns the mechanisms by which external perspectives are incorporated into the internal point of view, or otherwise affect its content. What is the interface between external and internal? In some cases, judges may read the latest scholarship on a given subject area and draw on it in their opinions, but that is probably not the dominant pattern. In other cases, clients may express their legal concerns to an attorney, who in turn translates these concerns into language that a court will find convincing. A range of further interfaces and pathways may exist. Analysis of how and when inputs of information alter the internal point of view is, again, a matter for classically externalist approaches.

---

[19] Indeed, compliance-related questions have generated a sophisticated literature from within the law and economics camp. See, e.g., Steven Shavell, *When Is Compliance with the Law Socially Desirable?*, 41 J. LEGAL STUD. 1 (2012).

[20] See Gold & Smith, *supra* note 5.

[21] For example, emergent properties and modularity may affect the ways in which property law evolves. For helpful discussion, see Henry E. Smith, this volume.

In addition, even if a focus on the internal point of view is taken as a given, there is a reasonable basis for an external analysis regarding its effects. As John Gardner indicates, theories of tort law that focus on corrective justice must still take into account the possibility that a legal norm of corrective justice will be self-defeating.[22] Do legal norms of corrective justice—as understood from the law's perspective—effectively produce compliance by the regulated parties? To what extent do such norms deter future wrongings? Which institutions are most effective at providing corrective justice, and among which groups of litigants? Such inquiries usually fall within an analysis from an external perspective, but they may still presuppose the internal perspective as a subject of study.

These questions are focused on the internal point of view (whatever its content may be), yet they require analysis of the law's practical consequences in light of that point of view. Perhaps moral norms of corrective justice are less readily complied with when legal norms of corrective justice are consistently enforced. Perhaps there is a crowding out effect where the regulated parties feel content to rely on the law's pronouncements rather than their own sense of extralegal obligation. Such possibilities may be of interest precisely because the internal point of view is taken seriously on its own terms, and yet they fit within an external analysis of how law operates.

Finally, understanding the internal point of view may provide a basis for an externalist critique. For example, the internal point of view might have aggregate effects that consistently disadvantage a particular subset of a society's population. In this volume, Anita Bernstein suggests that tort law systematically disadvantages women by rewarding forms of self-assertion that have long been associated with masculinity.[23] Rather than indicate a functionalist benefit, critical accounts may show that there is something problematic about the internal point of view that is in need of reform. As part of making that type of critical argument, however, it may also be necessary to capture the internal perspective.

III. Internal Perspectives that Adopt Insights from External Legal Analyses

While the previous discussion focuses on external perspectives that look to internal perspectives for insight, New Private Law approaches may also work in the reverse direction. In part, this is because social science methodologies can provide information as to what the internal perspective is on a particular doctrinal topic. For example, social psychology can tell us something about how legal actors perceive the law regarding a specific type of wrong. It is also because external perspectives can help in determining what criteria are appropriate for a successful interpretation of the internal point of view.

---

[22] John Gardner, *What Is Tort Law For? Part 1: The Place of Corrective Justice*, 30 LAW & PHIL. 1, 20–22 (2011).

[23] See Anita Bernstein, this volume.

Furthermore, the application of a chosen set of interpretive criteria may lead to theories that incorporate substantive insights commonly associated with external legal analysis. Each possibility will be discussed below.

A. Empirical Analysis of the Internal Perspective

There are important points of intersection between the methods common to external analysis and the search for an accurate account of the internal perspective. Some scholars are now testing the perspectives of legal actors to see if they actually perceive the law in the way that theorists assume that they do. To use contracts as an example, it may be an empirically testable question how contracting parties understand a breach of contract. Scholars can research whether such parties see a contract breach as a wrong, and they can test what kind of a wrong it is perceived to be. It is also possible to test whether contracting parties feel that contractual promises are disjunctive promises to either perform a service or pay damages—a key component of some scholarly accounts of contract law.[24]

Context can matter for such questions as well, for different kinds of contract breaches may have different types of significance to a disappointed promisee. As Tess Wilkinson-Ryan and David Hoffman have found: "Breach creates an injury distinct from the economic loss created in tort-like cases. Breaches for gain are perceived as worse than breaches to avoid loss. And the degree of control and intention exhibited by the promisor matters to perceptions of harm."[25] Torts likewise present a wide range of distinctive puzzles about how various types of wrongings are perceived by their victims.

To the extent an internalist theory is particularly concerned with the judicial perspective, it will also be worth knowing how judges are likely to see particular kinds of wrongs and private law relationships—beyond what is expressed in their published opinions. Do judges make use of cognitive schemas? Of heuristics? Which cognitive biases affect their decision-making? If lawyers are the legal actors at issue, the same point carries over into this realm. Do practicing attorneys understand the deontological concepts in tort law or contract law the same way as legal academics? Various techniques might assist in these inquiries, including not only survey results but also quantitative case studies and corpus linguistics approaches.[26]

Notice also that judgments as to which legal participants are those whose views constitute the internal point of view may increase the relevance and helpfulness of externalist methodologies. Thus, if the legal participants whose internal perspective is under

---

[24] Cf. Daphna Lewinsohn-Zamir, *Can't Buy Me Love: Monetary versus In-Kind Remedies*, 2013 U. Ill. L. Rev. 151 (assessing whether contracting parties prefer in-kind or monetary remedies).

[25] See Tess Wilkinson-Ryan & David A. Hoffman, *Breach Is for Suckers*, 63 Vand. L. Rev. 1003, 1045 (2010).

[26] Corpus linguistics scholarship makes use of databases to assess patterns of word use within collections of texts. For an example of the approach applied to the statutory interpretation setting, see Thomas R. Lee & Stephen C. Mouritsen, *Judging Ordinary Meaning*, 127 Yale L.J. 788 (2018).

consideration are the individuals who draft contracts—rather than just the courts or legal practitioners—this will have bearing on both the import and accessibility of empirical data. Prior determinations of what counts as the internal point of view bear on the degree to which externalist approaches can add further insights for internalist inquiries.

B. The Adoption of Interpretive Criteria

New Private Law scholars tend to adopt moderately demanding criteria ("moderate criteria") for what will count as a satisfactory interpretation of some doctrine or body of law, and choices among these criteria will bear on several of the aforementioned topics. Importantly, moderate interpretive criteria allow for accounts that accept the possibility of judicial error. Such criteria can also make room for multiple objectives to be included in an internal account, and some of these objectives may track the content of external explanations. In addition, the moderate criteria themselves may be justified by external considerations, such as findings in social psychology or sociology that offer insights into the likelihood that a given view really is the internal point of view.

Standard criteria invoked in private law theory for assessing interpretive accounts of law are fit, morality, transparency, and coherence.[27] Several additional criteria have been elaborated in recent work, including consilience, simplicity, justice, determinacy, and predictive force.[28] (Elegance has also been mentioned, but that has not been actively pursued as a criterion.[29]) For space reasons, the primary focus here will be on fit, transparency, morality, and coherence, with an emphasis on the moderate versions of each. Each will be developed with an aim to showing how external approaches to understanding private law can affect internal approaches. As we will see, both the selection of criteria and their application invite analysis that is ordinarily associated with external perspectives on private law.

1. *The Fit Criterion*

An account of a private law field cannot be a successful account unless it fits the data it purports to cover. All theorists accept that a fit criterion of some sort is fundamental for determining whether an interpretive theory of private law is a successful one. That said, while a fit criterion is uncontroversial, its application is a matter of dispute. The determination of what data a theory must fit will sometimes require application of the type of

---

[27] Influential accounts of these four criteria are developed in Stephen Smith's contract theory work. See Smith, *supra* note 3, at 7–32.

[28] On consilience and private law, see Jules Coleman, *The Practice of Principle* 38–40 (2001); on simplicity, see Gold & Smith, *supra* note 5; on justice, see Andrew S. Gold, *The Right of Redress* (2020); on determinacy, see Jody S. Kraus, *Transparency and Determinacy in Common Law Adjudication: A Philosophical Defense of Explanatory Economic Analysis*, 93 VA. L. REV. 287 (2007).

[29] See W. Bradley Wendell, *Explanation in Legal Scholarship: The Inferential Structure of Doctrinal Legal Analysis*, 96 CORNELL L. REV. 1035, 1050–1051 (2011); Coleman, *supra* note 28, at 38.

social science techniques developed by scholars who employ external legal perspectives. In addition, the criterion of fit that a theorist adopts may allow for at least some substantive convergence with external perspectives, depending on the type of fit that is demanded.

One major concern is with the boundaries of a private law field. For example, should some estoppel doctrines count as part of contract law? The answer to this question may depend on how judges understand the boundaries of contract law. A promising approach is to focus on consensus among legal actors, to the extent a consensus can be discerned.[30] We may, however, wish to allow for definitions of private law fields that deviate from that consensus—particularly if doing so offers a more perspicuous account of the underlying legal doctrine. In a given case, this boundary question has significant import for the ease of showing doctrinal fit.

Another concern is with the definition of "core features." Within the accepted boundaries of a field, private law theorists often seek to explain the core features of that field, but the assessment of what is at the core is frequently contentious.[31] Must a theory of tort law be able to make sense of nominal damages? Punitive damages? If a subset of a field is commonly resolved through statutes instead of the common law, is this statutory component something that must be included in a successful account? The answer may again be determined by consensus among legal actors,[32] but it is as often determined in light of a theorist's other interpretive commitments.

A variant on these issues arises when theorists wish to avoid a troubling precedent. The theorist's focus is often on the precedents that are thought to matter more, or to have been correctly decided. Up to a point, this move is widely seen as legitimate, but at some stage it raises interpretive concerns. For example, tort theorists might wonder if it is acceptable to disregard aspects of defamation law unique to the United States when interpreting the law of torts.[33] Perhaps it is—but a choice to excise that much doctrine is inevitably going to meet resistance.

Whether our concern is with legal consensus, or instead with practical importance, the selection of a field's boundaries or a field's core principles is contingent on the types of investigations that external accounts emphasize. For example, figuring out what qualifies as a consensus understanding might call for survey results or other forms of empirical analysis. And, likewise, practical importance might require an analysis of compliance effects, or economic impact, or citation rates. Such questions could be resolved through moral reasoning or conceptual analysis, but in many cases social science tools will be relevant to solving the fit criterion puzzle. In addition, while New

---

[30] See Stephen A. Smith, *Taking Law Seriously*, 50 U. TORONTO L.J. 241 (2000).

[31] For helpful discussion of the challenges, see William Lucy, *Method and Fit: Two Problems for Contemporary Philosophies of Tort Law*, 52 McGILL L.J. 605 (2007).

[32] See Smith, *supra* note 3, at 9 (suggesting that what is "core" is determined by consensus).

[33] See Arthur Ripstein, *Private Wrongs* 190 (2016) (suggesting that the distinctive rules of U.S. defamation law are sufficiently anomalous that they need not be accounted for within an interpretive theory of tort law).

Private Law scholarship varies in the type of fit that it expects of a successful theory, at least some approaches are amenable to insights from external legal analysis.[34]

2. *The Transparency Criterion*

The transparency criterion is concerned with the internal understanding of the law. If law is transparent, that internal perspective is accurately expressed: "[l]aw is transparent to the extent that the reasons legal actors give for doing what they do are their real reasons."[35] Stephen Smith has offered one of the more influential accounts of the interpretive criteria in private law theory. He rightly notes that law claims to be transparent, and a transparency criterion accordingly calls for a legal theory that will explain the reasons judges give for their decisions (and by implication, that lawyers invoke in their arguments).

As Smith suggests, a strong transparency criterion "holds that a good theory of law will portray legal practice as in fact transparent."[36] A weak criterion means something much less stringent: "it is enough that a theory explain why legal actors might claim, sincerely or not, that the law is transparent."[37] A moderate criterion "holds that a good theory must explain the law in a way that shows how legal officials could sincerely, even if erroneously, believe the law is transparent."[38]

The transparency criterion can be understood as a component of the fit criterion.[39] It requires theorists to take into account certain facts about the underlying legal phenomena to be explained.[40] As indicated earlier, theorists may decide that fit concerns need only extend to core features, and it is possible to think that a court's legal reasoning is not a core feature of the data to be explained. Yet this latter option is hard to square with an emphasis on law's self-understanding as a goal of interpretation—a transparency criterion thus makes sense for the kind of theory that New Private Law theorists ordinarily seek.

Importantly, Smith's view allows for the acceptability of concepts that differ from those that courts employ. As he argues, one may:

> explain the law using concepts that are recognizably "legal" (or at least using concepts that, though more abstract than standard legal concepts, work through recognizably legal concepts in their explanation of particular rules and decisions) even if those concepts are not the same legal concepts that were employed by judges.[41]

---

[34] Note that differences on which features a theory must fit may be a dividing line between external and internal accounts. Cf. Jody Kraus, "Philosophy of Contract Law," in *The Oxford Handbook of Jurisprudence & Philosophy of Law* 687, 694 (Jules Coleman & Scott Shapiro eds., 2002) ("[T]he criterion of fit with outcomes provides the dispositive constraint on legal interpretation for economic analysts, whereas the criterion of fit with stated judicial reasoning provides the dispositive constraint for deontic theorists.").

[35] *See* Smith, *supra* note 3, at 24.   [36] *See id.* at 25.   [37] *See id.*   [38] *See id.*

[39] *See id.* at 7 n.8.

[40] *See also* Ernest Weinrib, *The Idea of Private Law* 16 (1995) ("Because legal concepts and institutions are indicia of the law's self-understanding, an internal account attempts to make sense of them on their own terms by allowing them to have the meaning they have in juristic thought.").

[41] *See* Smith, *supra* note 3, at 28.

Thus, a broadly legal realist approach to contract theory like the one espoused by Lon Fuller and William Perdue can meet this criterion. They view expectation damages as a proxy for reliance—a view which is arguably in tension with the concepts courts actually employ—but their remedial picture makes use of recognizably legal concepts.[42] Their account passes a moderate version of the transparency criterion.

The benefit of the moderate transparency criterion is that it allows for mistaken judicial judgments.[43] Just as judges can be mistaken about what is moral, they can also be mistaken about how to explain the law. Smith's key precondition is this: "a false, but sincere, claim is perfectly intelligible so long as a plausible (i.e., non-conspiracy-based) explanation is given for that claim."[44] If the real reasons for a judicial decision plausibly differ from what judges think they are, there is no difficulty under this criterion. This flexibility, however, makes room for some efficiency and other functionalist analyses that are often barred by more stringent interpretive criteria.

Once again, there are also empirical questions. How are we to determine what cluster of concepts is in the right ballpark? This inquiry invites the type of research program that is characteristic of external legal analysis (even if it is not an externalist inquiry per se). Again, the question at hand is what should be seen as recognizably legal, and that question may call for reference to the views of actual judges or actual lawyers. Psychological and other social science research realistically bears on this inquiry.

3. *The Morality Criterion*

The morality criterion can likewise be understood as a component of the fit criterion.[45] The morality criterion is also said to follow from law's claim to authority. In other words, the morality criterion is thought to reflect another feature of the legal practice being explained. Except in a very limited sense, this claim-based view is doubtful: there is probably not a useful morality criterion to be derived from what law claims. Yet this shortfall does not mean that a moderate morality criterion is undesirable. Instead, its justification should come from a different source, and its most plausible basis invites empirical research into judicial reasoning.

As Smith suggests, a moderate morality criterion "holds that a good legal theory should explain the law in a way that shows how the law *might be thought to be* justified even if it is not justified."[46] On his view, such a criterion makes law's claim to authority intelligible:

> Insofar as the law is, or could be thought to be, supported by recognizably moral principles, law's claim to authority is intelligible. It is intelligible because we have satisfactorily explained why legal actors might claim the law is morally justified. The explanation is that the actors believe the relevant principles both fit the law and morally justify.[47]

---

[42] See Lon Fuller & William Perdue, *The Reliance Interest in Contract Damages*, 46 YALE L.J. 53 (1936).

[43] See Smith, *supra* note 3, at 29.   [44] See *id.* at 28.

[45] See *id.* at 7 n.8.   [46] See *id.* at 18.   [47] See *id.* at 20.

Such a criterion also allows for legal error without opening the door for conspiracy theories or false consciousness accounts. The moderate morality criterion assesses interpretive theories based on the extent to which the principles that they recognize in contract, tort, or other fields are morally justified or at least plausible enough that legal actors could think they are morally justified (even if they are mistaken).[48]

Yet there is a substantial stumbling block that confronts the internalist at this point. There is a major difficulty with the authority-based argument for a moderate morality criterion: the law's claim to authority may not indicate that the law's content is (or is thought to be) morally justified. A recent paper by John Gardner illustrates the difficulty.[49]

Gardner's argument responds to Robert Alexy's contention that the law claims to be both just and moral. If Gardner is right, law still makes a moral claim, and it still makes a claim to authority. But the law's claims are different from Alexy's apparent understanding.[50] Law claims to be morally *binding*, and that is not the same thing as a claim to be just or morally correct.[51] Judges often feel that they must follow statutes and precedents even if they think those statutes and precedents are gravely mistaken. Judges may still contend that such holdings bind the parties, and even that they morally bind them. As Gardner emphasizes: "moral authority is such that abiding by it is morally correct even though the exercise of it was morally incorrect."[52]

If this view of law's claims is accepted, where does that leave the morality criterion? Recall that the moderate version of the morality criterion "holds that a good theory should explain the law in a way that shows how the law *might be thought to be* justified even if it is not justified."[53] Depending on how we apply it, this morality criterion is now open to doubt. Courts could very reasonably determine that some private law doctrines are morally binding given their origins in legitimate precedent, while simultaneously concluding that those doctrines ought to be changed because they are not justified.

This is not to say that morality criteria should drop out of the picture, and there are good reasons to adopt a moderate morality criterion even so. For example, judicial language and predictable features of judicial psychology may support a moderate morality criterion. Supposing that law only claims to be morally binding, it can still make sense to think that a good theory will explain the law in a way that shows how private law principles are justified or might be thought to be morally justified. Judges frequently talk as if the principles described in their opinions are morally justified, and it is not unreasonable to think that—as a matter of psychology—they are drawn to readings of precedent that will square with their sense of what is morally correct. We nonetheless must turn to social science methodologies if that view on judicial thinking is to be tested.

---

[48] Note that a theorist who adopted a stronger morality criterion—one that looked to the moral *correctness* of a theory—might still engage in NPL scholarship in other respects.

[49] See John Gardner, "How Law Claims, What Law Claims," in *Law as a Leap of Faith* 125 (2012).

[50] Gardner suggests some ambiguity in Alexy's argument. See *id.* at 140 n.33.   [51] See *id.*

[52] See *id.* at 143.   [53] See Smith, *supra* note 3, at 18.

4. *The Coherence Criterion*

Coherence is also a fundamental concern for private law theorists, including New Private Law theorists. Yet, while theorists characteristically seek coherence when they interpret private law fields, proponents offer more than one basis for adopting a coherence criterion. For example, a coherence criterion is commonly adopted because it will advance the theorist's objective of rendering the social practice of private law intelligible.[54] Alternatively, coherence is adopted as a criterion because, as Ernest Weinrib notes: "those who think about private law in its own terms must include the law's pervasive impulse toward coherence within their purview."[55] These are not identical reasons for caring about coherence, and agreement breaks down once we try to determine the type of coherence criterion that private law theorists should follow.

How much coherence a successful theory should demonstrate is a matter of debate. Arguably, it is enough for a legal theory to show the law to be noncontradictory.[56] Alternatively, a theorist might seek a theory that explains a legal field in terms of a single unifying principle.[57] This is a substantially more difficult standard to meet, and if we require a fit between theory and doctrine, it may be impossible for any theory to attain this level of coherence.[58]

There are also intermediate positions on coherence. In his work in contract theory, Smith suggests a moderate coherence criterion. In his view: "a good theory must show that *most* of the core elements of contract law can be traced to, or are closely related to, a single principle."[59] As Smith adds: "[u]nless one assumes (as few people do) that all reasons for acting can, in the end, be reduced to a single master principle, it is accepted as perfectly intelligible, indeed appropriate, that people act for different reasons in different situations."[60]

Still, it is unclear why we should need most of the core elements of a field to be traceable, or closely related to, a single principle in order to render them intelligible. Intelligibility is not so high a hurdle. Perhaps this view can be grounded on evidence suggesting legal actors see a field in a comparatively unified way.[61] Still, this argument makes the basis for a moderate coherence criterion contingent on something other than intelligibility. The justification has now shifted to contextual evidence for the law's self-understanding. And that brings us back to empirical questions that are the bread and butter of external legal analysis.

[54] See *id.* at 13–14 (suggesting a link between coherence and the intelligibility of the features of private law).

[55] See Weinrib, *supra* note 40, at 13–14.

[56] Cf. John Gardner, "What Is Tort Law For? Part 2. The Place of Distributive Justice," in *Philosophical Foundations of the Law of Torts* 335, 338 n.11 (John Oberdiek ed., 2014) ("Any justification has to be coherent in the thin sense of intelligible. But Weinribian unity (or Dworkinian integrity) is not, in my eyes, any kind of plus. Reality, including moral reality, is fragmentary.").

[57] See Smith, *supra* note 3, at 11.

[58] That said, an abstract unifying principle may call for pluralism at the ground level of legal doctrine. See, e.g., Hanoch Dagan, *Pluralism and Perfectionism in Private Law*, 112 COLUM. L. REV. 1409 (2012).

[59] See Smith, *supra* note 3, at 13.   [60] See *id.* at 12.

[61] See *id.* (emphasizing the way that lawyers refer to "contract law" as a field).

What then of an argument based on law's pervasive impulse toward coherence? As Joseph Raz's work indicates, there are several reasons why global coherence across the law may be doubtful. For example, Raz notes: "the existence of a plurality of inconsistent views on moral, religious, social, and political issues in democratic (and in many other) societies, is likely to be reflected in a society's law."[62] This variation can generate pockets of coherence without global consistency. Furthermore, there may be choices legislatures and courts face that involve conflicts of values, with no particular solution to these conflicts holding superiority over the others.[63] Once made, adherence to a given choice can then readily result in local coherence in the law.[64]

Substantial shifts in legal doctrine or philosophy are also a good reason to predict local coherence, particularly given that systems of precedent encourage piecemeal changes in legal doctrine.[65] In times of legal change, some *incoherence* might even be anticipated. Legal transitions may be incomplete when imposed by statute, and an incomplete change is more likely when elaborated through judicial opinions in multiple jurisdictions and subfields. Whatever the merits of a coherence criterion in general, context should matter for the adoption of interpretive criteria, and some private law settings may not be congenial for coherent doctrine at a given point in time.

Once we allow for local coherence in this way, we are allowing for parts of a private law field to be explained in terms that track standard internalist accounts, while other parts are potentially explained in terms that track standard externalist accounts. To give an example, tort law duties of care might match a deontological picture, while proximate cause doctrines might incorporate at least some efficiency analysis. That is not to say that tort law is best explained through showing pockets of local coherence, but it could be so explained without violating a reasonable coherence criterion. Again, selection of interpretive criteria can open up space for internalist New Private Law accounts that accept insights developed by the externalist camp. Strictly speaking, such accounts may only be interested in the internal point of view, but the substantive theories they accept may share features in common with classic external perspectives.

IV. Hybrid Accounts

The flexibility of the fit and transparency criteria described earlier suggests another potential relation between internal and external accounts: these accounts may be blended together in a hybrid form. It is possible for certain abstract concepts, such as the

---

[62] See *id.* at 316.   [63] See *id.* at 317.   [64] See *id.* at 318.

[65] *See* Andrew S. Gold, "Interpreting Fiduciary Law," in *Research Handbook on Fiduciary Law* 37, 47 (D. Gordon Smith & Andrew S. Gold eds., 2018) (suggesting this type of change may have occurred for fiduciary loyalty obligations); Gold, *The Right of Redress, supra* note 28 (developing this account). Cf. Jeremy Waldron, *"Transcendental Nonsense" and System in the Law*, 100 COLUM. L. REV. 16, 42 (2000) (describing a legislative process under which "the law becomes a 'checkerboard' ").

concept of a wrong, to be understood from the internal point of view, while other concepts are explained in terms that diverge considerably from the internal point of view. An interpretation of a private law field that adopts this tack is a *tertium quid*—neither fully internal or external.

Recall that there is room under a moderate transparency criterion for accounts like Fuller and Perdue's account: these are accounts that are "in the right ballpark." Such accounts take seriously a major component of the internal point of view—for example, the legal perspective on what wrongs and remedies are—while diverging in certain key respects from the exact concepts that courts employ in deciding cases. Thus, Fuller and Perdue see the expectation remedy in reliance terms, yet they still understand conventional contract law remedies more generally in the way that remedies are seen by courts of law.

Such accounts are best seen as *quasi-internal*, for they are internal with respect to certain more abstract private law concepts while external with respect to the content that renders those concepts determinate.[66] These accounts are accordingly hybrid accounts, with substantive features that are both internal and external. Such accounts are also valuable, for they can suggest pathways to legal reform that do not require a dramatic break from precedent or from private law's conceptual structure. They can also suggest ways for a private law that is only locally coherent to become more globally coherent—assuming that more globally coherent doctrine is a desirable goal.

There is also a subtler way that external and internal perspectives can overlap in New Private Law theory, with consequent hybrid features. New Private Law scholars have sometimes separated the justifications for legal institutions (such as tort law or contract law) from the legal reasoning that operates within those legal institutions. In these cases, the justification may track an external perspective while the conceptual analysis it supports may track an internal perspective.

A good example of this possibility is found in Henry Smith's argument that much of tort law can be explained by the practicalities of implementing it. On his account, what grounds tort law remains an open question, even where the modular structures of tort law are explained in terms of concepts from everyday morality.[67] This perspective allows for ground-level deontological analysis while allowing for higher level, institutional justifications that are consequentialist or otherwise unconnected to the conceptual inferences located in judicial opinions.[68]

---

[66] For another variant, consider theories that recognize a set of private law concepts and then simplify them for explanatory purposes. This approach is discussed in Paul B. Miller, this volume.

[67] Smith, *supra* note 6, at 31. The point is elaborated further in Gold & Smith, *supra* note 5.

[68] Cf. Liam Murphy, "Purely Formal Wrongs," in *Civil Wrongs and the Justice in Private Law* (Paul B. Miller & John Oberdiek eds., 2020) (raising the possibility that the internal normative order of private law may not express its purpose); see also Coleman, *supra* note 28, at 36 n.20 (describing "a hybrid account in which efficiency or utility maximization enters at the grand level of political theory").

V. CONCLUSION

Internal and external perspectives on private law share a common subject matter, but they often seem to share little else. Much late-twentieth-century private law theory is aimed at showing how an internal viewpoint offers a better way to explain private law than leading external rivals, such as efficiency analysis. New Private Law theory generally rejects reductive accounts of private law concepts, but it is otherwise much more open to the external point of view. In part, this is because New Private Law scholarship makes use of social science methodologies, including empirical analysis, that are often associated with externalist research. There are, however, additional areas of overlap between the internal and external.

Some New Private Law scholarship is functionalist at its core, yet it makes use of the internal point of view to show how private law can function successfully. Understanding the internal point of view on doctrinal categories and concepts can help to clarify how those categories and concepts are useful. Such inclusive functionalist theories may show how private law's deontological concepts motivate regulated parties, or how their modularity permits law to address problems of complexity. Indeed, nonfunctionalist approaches may also show an external orientation while taking the internal point of view as a starting point. Scholars interested in the historical path of the law, or in prediction of its future content, or even in analysis of its efficacy as a source of corrective justice, may engage in external analysis of the law's operation while simultaneously including the internal point of view as a needed contribution.

Other New Private Law scholarship is interested exclusively in providing correct understandings of law from the internal point of view. Such internalist accounts may nonetheless draw from external perspectives and methods in an effort to develop adequate interpretive criteria. Moreover, the application of these interpretive criteria may lead to substantive theories of tort, contract, fiduciary relationships, or property that are partly comprised of classically functionalist understandings. It may be, for example, that a subset of contract law is best seen in efficiency terms, from the internal point of view—and this conclusion could follow from a straightforward application of criteria designed to give an internalist interpretation.

Interestingly, New Private Law theory also incorporates hybrid accounts. These mixed approaches take different forms. A good example is the kind of theory permitted by a moderate transparency criterion: a theory that is "in the right ballpark." Such a theory may take private law's understanding of a wrong or a remedy seriously, while filling in the particular details using concepts that the courts may not actually employ (e.g., by seeing contract law's expectation remedy as a proxy for a reliance remedy). A different kind of hybrid theory may leave each private law concept intact, while justifying private law as an institution along separate lines. Private law fields like torts might be understood to incorporate deontological, nonutilitarian concepts yet ultimately be justified on utilitarian grounds. This kind of hybrid theory likewise uses internal and external perspectives in combination, but the external perspective is invisible at the ground level of legal reasoning.

These multiple approaches—each developing alongside each other, sometimes in the work of a single author—represent a genuine flowering of private law theory as a field of inquiry. They also provide an opportunity for seemingly opposed methodological camps to reconcile, at least in some areas of inquiry. The New Private Law offers an opportunity for scholars of internalist and externalist tendencies to find points of convergence, and also for them to understand better their points of divergence.

ACKNOWLEDGMENTS

I am grateful to Julian Arato, Aditi Bagchi, Hanoch Dagan, Evan Fox-Decent, John Gardner, John Goldberg, Matthew Harding, Dan Kelly, Greg Klass, Tom Merrill, Paul Miller, Steven Schaus, Henry Smith, and Steve Smith for helpful comments on ideas in this chapter. I am also grateful to participants at the Landscape of Private Law conference, held at Harvard Law School. Any errors are my own.

CHAPTER 2

··

NATURAL RIGHTS AND
NATURAL LAW

··

DENNIS KLIMCHUK

My aim in this chapter is to make a case for the continued relevance of what I will call the natural law tradition to inquiry into the philosophical foundations of private law. I say "what I will call . . . " because more than one idea answers to the name "natural law." One is a view in general jurisprudence, associated with, for example, Aquinas and Blackstone. In its classic form, natural law theory in this sense is the view according to which a condition of a rule's claim to be law is its conformity with substantive principles of morality or justice that have as their object the conduct the rule aims to govern. A second idea associated with "natural law" is the view according to which conformity with human nature and securing the conditions of its proper realization are the guiding ideals of moral and political life. Aquinas represents this tradition as well; the classic formulation is in Aristotle.

I don't mean to refer to either of these. The tradition I have in mind is the arc in the history of political philosophy that starts in Grotius and ends in Kant. Not everyone in this tradition was a social contract theorist, but even those who were skeptical of the explanatory and justificatory value of the idea of a social contract agreed that political and legal authority was, in part, a matter of convention. Only in part, though: they were natural lawyers because they held that there were nonconventional principles—laws of nature—to which our conventions must conform if they are to claim legitimacy.[1] My goal here is to suggest a way of reading this tradition that brings out its enduring relevance. I'll begin by considering the case against the very idea.

---

[1] Some were natural lawyers in one or both of the other senses. This is not a historical accident; nor is it a conceptual necessity.

I. Natural Law Skepticism

In an introduction to an earlier symposium on the theme, John Goldberg characterized the New Private Law as set against a jurisprudential orientation he called "brass tacks pragmatism," according to which "being pragmatic in one's thinking [as one ought to be] involves getting past mere appearances to what is 'really' going on in the law."[2] A particularly stark expression of brass tacks pragmatism is the view, most closely associated with Holmes but also counted by Llewellyn as among the points of departure common among the realists,[3] that, in Holmes's words, the object of the study of law is "the prediction of the incidence of the public force through the instrumentality of the courts."[4] This formulation makes a compelling case for Goldberg's claim that a kind of private law skepticism is implicit in brass tacks pragmatism. On the view that courts are instruments though which public force is exercised, a complete account of private law would explain away, rather than explain, its doctrines and concepts.

It is pretty clear that, on an approach to law according to which (again in Holmes's words) "[t]he primary rights and duties with which jurisprudence [busies] itself . . . are nothing but prophecies,"[5] and bear only accidental points of correspondence with the extralegal senses in which "right" and "duty" are used, the idea that the natural law tradition has something to offer to the study of private law would likely get little sympathetic hearing. A more friendly audience might be expected in the New Private Law. But even that audience, and readers of this *Handbook*, might regard the natural law tradition with suspicion. The main worries can, I think, be collected into two groups.

First, you might think that, even from the perspective of the inclusive pragmatism that (on Goldberg's account) characterizes the jurisprudential stance of the New Private Law, theorists in the natural law tradition are too metaphysical, too theological in their foundations, and too foundational in their aspirations. The second worry is the mirror image of the first: that the natural lawyers were, if anything, not metaphysical enough; that their accounts were mere instruments in the service of morally objectionable ends.

The first worry can, I think, be answered fairly easily. While the language of natural law and natural rights has an ontologically audacious ring to it—there is a Thomistic air to, for example, Hobbes's claim that "the laws of nature are immutable and eternal"[6]—the early modern political philosophers' understanding of natural laws was metaphysically quite deflationary: Hobbes continued, "for [acting in breach of the laws of nature] can never be made lawful. For it can never be that war shall preserve life, and peace destroy it."[7] And while many philosophers in this tradition refer to scripture and infer God's intentions from the structure of the natural world as they saw it, for the most part their claims were that reason and scripture are alternative, consistent, and equally authoritative grounds of

[2] John C.P. Goldberg, *Pragmatism and Private Law*, 125 HARV. L. REV. 1640, 1645 (2012).
[3] Karl Llewellyn, *Some Realism About Realism*, 44 HARV. L. REV. 1222, 1237 (1931).
[4] Oliver Wendell Holmes, *The Path of the Law*, 10 HARV. L. REV. 457, 461 (1897).   [5] *Id.* at 162.
[6] Thomas Hobbes, *Leviathan* 99 (Edwin Curely ed., 1994) (1651).   [7] *Id.* at 100.

justification.[8] The independence was most starkly and (in)famously cast by Grotius when he wrote that "what we have said here would still have great weight, even if we were to grant, what we cannot grant without wickedness, that there is no God, or that he bestows no regard in human affairs."[9] And as a general point, I think there is much to be said in favor of readers of the early modern tradition who argue that the evidently nonpolitical premises on which philosophers such as Hobbes represented their argument as having been built are, and would have been received by their audiences as, really political.[10]

The second ground of natural law skepticism, that the natural lawyers deployed the idea of laws of nature as mere instruments in the service of morally objectionable ends, is not quite so easily dismissed. Grotius's first treatment of property, for example, was in a work[11] commissioned by the directors of the United Dutch East India Company (VOC), who asked Grotius to provide a brief in defense of the seizure of the Portuguese ship *Santa Catarina* in the straights of Singapore by Jakob van Heemskerk, a Dutch admiral acting in service of the United Amsterdam Company (a precursor of the VOC). It is not particularly conspiratorial to see his accounts of private law as resources deployed in the service of the vindication of Dutch commercial expansion in the Indies, and of violent means taken to that end. Similarly, James Tully has argued that "the central sections on labour, value, and commodities" in Locke's treatment of property

> are designed to legitimate and to celebrate the superiority of English colonial market agriculture over the Amerindian hunting, gathering, and replacement agriculture that it forcibly displaced. The destruction of centuries-old native American socio-economic organizations and the imperial imposition of commercial agriculture is made to appear as an inevitable and justifiable historical development.[12]

While I am not sure we can draw the inference Tully does about Locke's ultimate ends from the ways in which his account could be deployed as means to them with quite the confidence he does, there's no doubt that this is something troubling here. And Locke's hands were elsewhere unclean, for example, when it came to American slavery.[13]

---

[8] If there is an exception here, it is probably Locke, for whom, a case can be made, theology is not easily disentangled from philosophy. See Jeremy Waldron, *God, Locke and Equality: Christian Foundations in Locke's Political Thought* (2002). My view, implicit in the reading of Locke's account of property outlined later is that we can start with Locke's egalitarianism, without having to engage the question of its foundations.

[9] Hugo Grotius, *The Rights of War and Peace, Preliminary Remarks* xxvii (William Whewell ed., 1853) (1625).

[10] See Don Herzog, *As Many as Six Impossible Things Before Breakfast*, 75 CAL. L. REV. 609 (1987); Arthur Ripstein, *Foundationalism in Political Theory*, 16 PHIL & PUB. AFF. 115 (1987). Hobbes himself suggests this understanding, in the preface to *De Cive*, where he reports that while it represents the final part of a projected three part work—the first planned to discuss "body and its general properties" and the second "Man and his particular faculties and passions"—he decided to publish it before completing the first and second because the political times called for it, and "especially as I saw it did not need the proceeding parts, since it rests upon its own principles known by reason."

[11] Hugo Grotius, *De Jure Praedae Commentarius*, translated as *Commentary on the Law of Prize and Booty* 316 (Martine Julia van Ittersum ed., 2006) (1868).

[12] James Tully, *An Approach to Political Philosophy: Locke in Contexts* 162 (1993).

[13] See Wayne Glausser, *Three Approaches to Locke and the Slave Trade*, 51 J. HIST. IDEAS 199 (1990).

Further stock for this second ground of natural law skepticism can be found in many examples of the use to which the ideas of natural rights and law were put by lawyers and judges. In R.H. Helmholz's careful study, *Natural Law in Court*, for example, we learn that in England natural law was invoked to deny legal status to adoption[14] and to deny that a son-in-law had any duty to support his wife's impecunious parents.[15] While not on the immoral order of defending colonialism, arguments such as these could reasonably enough lead one to be doubtful that there is much to be gained, morally, from reaching back to the natural law tradition.[16] These judicial examples and the broad variety of doctrines for which the law of nature has been invoked in support might suggest a third worry: that "natural law" is an empty idea, a placeholder whose substantive content is filled with particular, contingent moral judgments of particular, contingent moral communities.

Against this I will argue that among the philosophers in the natural law tradition we find a set of commitments and concerns that, if particular and contingent, are nonetheless shared by us. Philosophers such as Grotius, Pufendorf, and Locke presented their accounts as freestanding arguments from principle and observation. I propose to take them as thus represented and see what we find—to ask what they were arguing and arguing about, independently of the political motivations we may find they had in reaching the conclusions they did. I will focus on private property, in particular on arguments about its foundations and limit in the right of necessity, both for the sake of space and because private property was a special preoccupation among philosophers in the early modern period. Even within these limits, I will have to be selective. My aim is neither to provide a comprehensive survey nor to defend any substantive view in particular. Instead what I hope to make a case for is a way to read the tradition and a view about what was at stake in the debates that characterized approaches to property in it, and I will do so by example rather than by a general argument. What I hope to show is that, understood this way, the natural law tradition provides a rich set of conceptual resources for the New Private Law, or, indeed, any approach to private law that takes it deontic vocabulary at face value.

But first, to set the stage, a (true) story.

II. THE LEVELLERS AND THE DIGGERS

On October 23, 1647, the Council of the New Model Army met in the church in Putney to discuss "The Case of the Army Truly Stated," a pamphlet co-authored by members of a group of Army officers and civilians who would soon come to be known as the Levellers, some of whom had been invited to participate. "The Case" raised concerns about the terms on which Army leadership seemed prepared to accept Charles I's return

---

[14] R.H. Helmholz, *Natural Law in Court* 96 (2015).   [15] *Id.* at 104.
[16] On the other hand, Helmholz recounts the deployment of natural law in judicial arguments against slavery, in both English and American law (*id.* at 108–109, 161–165), drawing on an association between natural law and equality that I will argue is at the heart of the natural law tradition.

to power. On the day before the meeting, however, another pamphlet was circulated called "An Agreement of the People," and it was that document that was the subject of what we now call the Putney Debates. The "Agreement" contained a draft of a proposed written constitution outlining the freedoms many soldiers thought they had been fighting to secure.

The second day began with a reading through of the document and then again the first article, which begins:

> That the people of England being at this day very unequally distributed by counties, cities and boroughs for the election of the deputies in parliament, how to be more indifferently proportionate according to the number of the inhabitants...

Here, before it could be finished,[17] Commisary-General Henry Ireton (Oliver Cromwell's son-in-law) interrupted. His worry was that with "according to the number of inhabitants" the drafters smuggled in a controversial bit of franchise reform, by implication abolishing the requirement that only persons with property worth a minimum of forty shillings could vote. And indeed that was their intention. Colonel Thomas Rainborough famously replied:

> [R]eally I think the poorest he that is in England has a life to live as the greatest he; and therefore truly, sir, I think it's clear that every man that is to live under government ought first by his own consent to put himself under that government, and I do think that the poorest man in England is not at all bound in the strict sense to that government that he has not had a voice to put himself under.[18]

If *that* is what is meant by "according to the number of the inhabitants," Ireton replied in turn, then to justify it "you must fly for refuge to an absolutely natural right and you must deny all civil right."[19] He justified the traditional, conventional, rule on two grounds.[20] First, only persons with a permanent interest in England could be expected to vote with the long-term good of the nation in view. If the property-less could vote, why not foreign visitors? Second, with property came independence. Indeed, even some Levellers were persuaded that servants should not vote, because they would vote as their employers asked.[21] The property requirement, Ireton emphasized, treated everyone who passed its threshold equally. Abolishing it would have the effect of increasing the influence of the wealthy. Rainborough was unmoved: "I'm a poor man, therefore I must be oppressed? If I have no interest in the kingdom, I must suffer by all their laws—be they right or wrong?"[22]

---

[17] The proceedings were recorded in remarkable detail.

[18] Extract from the debates at the General Council of the Army, Putney, in *The English Levellers* 103 (Andrew Sharp ed., 1998).

[19] *Id.* at 103.   [20] *Id.* at 108.

[21] *Id.* at 130.   [22] *Id.* at 102.

Ireton and Rainborough, then, were not in disagreement over whether equality is a governing substantive ideal in a just constitutional structure. They were disagreeing about what respecting it requires, and doing so, in part, through the question of the relationship between natural and positive law. My suggestion is that this is a (I'm tempted to say *the*) central theme running through the natural law tradition. Arguments about natural law and what it requires are really just arguments about what nonconventional principles constrain the arrangements we enter into through adopting the laws by which we govern ourselves. The principal substantive constraint is our moral equality, the starting point of the early modern tradition in political philosophy.[23]

So far this is about the fundamental constitutional principles. A link to private law is drawn by what Ireton presents as a *reductio* of the Leveller position. "If you will hold forth [natural law] as your ground" (and Ireton thought there could be no other basis for the Levellers' bid for franchise reform),

> then I think you must deny all property too, and this is my reason. For thus: by that same right of nature (whatever it be) that you pretend, by which you can say that one man has an equal right with another to the choosing of him that shall govern him—by same right of nature he has the same equal right in any goods he sees: meat, drinks, clothes, to take and use them for his sustenance. He has a freedom to the land, to take the ground, to exercise it, till it; he has the same freedom to anything that anyone does account himself to have any propriety in.[24]

The Levellers were quick to deny this (in the Debates, by appeal to natural law in another sense: Rainborough replied to Ireton that to draw his interference is to forget the Law of God, which commands that Thou shalt not steal).

The *True* Levellers, as a group we now call the Diggers called themselves, however, embraced Ireton's inference. The Diggers were radical egalitarians and communists who occupied and cultivated a number of small tracts of waste land, land privately owned but left unused by its owners. Their most prolific and celebrated spokesperson was Gerrard Winstanley. Among his writings were a series of pamphlets published as the first group of Diggers settled on a plot of land at St. George's Hill in 1649.

What I will call Winstanley's challenge[25] is expressed in an argument he makes in the first of these pamphlets, "The True Levellers Standard." There he argues that God is "mightily dishonoured" by the state of affairs in which the world is held by a few who buy and sell it among themselves, "as if he were a respecter of persons, delighting in the comfortable livelihood of some, and rejoicing in the miserable poverty and straits of others."[26] God is dishonored because this inequitable state of material affairs is

---

[23] Equality sets the problem for which the social contract is a solution: if by nature I have no reason to defer to your judgment, nor you to mine, how can we settle our disputes?

[24] Sharp ed., *supra* note 18, at 108.

[25] I am drawing here, and in the first part of the next section, on my earlier work in Dennis Klimchuk, *Property and Necessity, Philosophical Foundations of Property Law* (James Penner & Henry E. Smith eds., 2015).

[26] *Winstanley: "The Law of Freedom" and Other Writings* 78 (Christopher Hill ed., 1983).

inconsistent with our moral equality. On Winstanley's account, furthermore, relations of domination are not a contingent effect of private property, but instead are essentially bound up with it. "In the beginning of time," Winstanley says,

> the great creator Reason, made the earth to be a common treasury, to preserve beasts, birds, fishes, and man, the lord that was to govern this Creation; for man had domination given to him, over the beasts, birds, and fishes; but not one word was spoken in the beginning, that one branch of mankind should rule over another.[27]

It follows from each of us having been created as a "teacher and ruler within himself," that is, not naturally subject to anyone else's authority, that the world is held in common.

Winstanley's critique of private properly is expressed through a set of robustly theological and teleological claims. But we can extract from Winstanley's account a metaphysically neutral challenge to private ownership. The challenge is that equality, understood in a particular way, seems inconsistent with private property. For Winstanley, we are equals in the sense that no one is naturally subject to another's authority. By claiming ownership of, say, a piece of land, I claim the right to exclude others from it even when I am not using it: that is, to unilaterally subject them to my authority. But that seems inconsistent with our being equals. That is Winstanley's challenge. The understanding of equality implicit in Winstanley's account is shared by Grotius and Locke. So we can fairly ask how they answer his challenge.

III. Grotius and Locke on the Foundations of Private Property

On Winstanley's view, no one can show that she has a special claim to a particular part of the world, to the exclusion of all others with whom she shares it.[28] Grotius, I imagine, would have replied: ownership does not really amount to a claim *to* a piece of the earth. It is rather a claim against others, pursuant to an arrangement we make among ourselves, to have exclusive rights to use a part of our common world. On Grotius's account, we start in a state of common ownership in the limited sense that each of us has a right to the resources of the world, and no one has a right to prevent us from using them. Working out from the exclusion implicit in use we came, through our practices, to recognize a right to exclude free of the requirement of actual, present possession.[29]

The regime of private property, on this understanding, is an arrangement governing use that arises by tacit agreement. As David Lewis suggested, a tacit agreement is really

---

[27] *Id.* at 77.
[28] I am generalizing a point made by Winstanley in "An Appeal to the House of Commons," *id.* at 120.
[29] See Grotius, *Commentary on the Law of Prize and Booty, supra* note 11, at 316.

just a convention[30] and need not involve anyone's explicitly agreeing with anyone. Lewis's model of a convention was Hume's: "[T]wo men pull the oars of a boat by common convention, for common interest, without any promise or contract; thus gold and silver are made the measures of exchange: Thus speech and words and language are fixed by human convention and agreement."[31] Hume himself licenses interpolating this understanding of the conventionality of property into Grotius's account, remarking at one point that his account of property is "in the main, the same with that hinted at and adopted by Grotius."[32]

On this account, the conventionality of property is a fact, and perhaps saying property is conventional in this way does not justify private rights of ownership. But this is arguably not an objection to Grotius, at least on his own understanding of what an account of property must do. The theory of property, as Grotius develops it, does not bear the burden of justifying the adoption of private property. What it does, rather, is explain how it is possible and set the conditions under which it is permissible. Put another way, for Grotius the question whether we ought to adopt private property is a question about the good, and the theory of property, strictly speaking, concerns the right but not the good.

Though the conventionality of property, understood this way, does not justify private rights of ownership—it does not aim to—it goes some way to answering Winstanley's challenge. If the regime of private property comprises a convention among ourselves setting the conditions of exclusive use, its adoption is a permissible departure from the original community of ownership even if one holds, as arguably Winstanley did, that each of us has an inalienable right to the common ownership of the world.[33]

Indeed, it is a crucial element of Grotius's account that there is a sense in which the right to common ownership survives the adoption of private property: you might even say that on his account, too, it is inalienable. While private property exists as a convention, there are constraints on the forms it may take. Some consist in first-order substantive rules, such as the law against theft. Others, such as the right of necessity, derive from a second-order principle that I will call the foundational presumption, according to which "we must consider what was the intention of those who introduced private property: which we must suppose to have been, to recede as little as possible from natural equity."[34] On what I believe to be the best interpretation of the text, "natural equity" refers not to the original use right directly but rather to the equality to which it gave expression.[35] In holding that neither you nor I need the other's permission to use the world's resources in a state before the institution of private property Grotius represents

[30] David Lewis, *Convention* 35 (1969).

[31] David Hume, "An Enquiry Concerning the Principles of Morals," in *Hume's Enquiries* 306 (P.H. Nidditch ed., 3d ed. 1975).

[32] *Id.* at 307.

[33] I owe the idea that we can think of Winstanley's view this way to Sarah Bittman.

[34] Grotius, *The Rights of War and Peace, supra* note 9, at 72.

[35] I defend this interpretation in Dennis Klimchuk, *Grotius on Property and the Right of Necessity*, 56 J. HIST. PHIL. 239 (2018).

the idea that we enjoy the kind of moral independence from one another that I suggested forced Winstanley's challenge. It is from this state that we must suppose that those who introduced private property intended to recede as little as possible. We must suppose this because it is a condition of the legitimacy of conventions we adopt.

Grotius's idea is this: whatever form private property takes, it must respect the moral equality we enjoyed before its introduction (as expressed in the original use right), and as a condition of doing so, the right to exclude may extend only so far as is necessary to realize the ends for the sake of which we adopt private property. This entails, for example, the right of necessity because we can achieve the material benefits private ownership makes possible without enjoying a right to exclude that makes into trespasses others' life-saving uses of our property.

Grotius's answer to Winstanley's challenge is that when the institution of private property respects the foundational presumption, it makes that institution consistent with our equality in the sense that he shares with Winstanley and Locke.

Locke, however, would have rejected the idea that private property rights arise merely as a matter of a convention. If the consent of all others was necessary before I could consume anything, Locke argued, then "Man had starved, notwithstanding the Plenty God had given him."[36] Thus Locke sought a nonconventional account of the right of original acquisition. Because in the second chapter of that volume Locke argues that we are all equal in that we are subject only to the law of nature and not, by nature, to any else's authority (§ 4), we can think of Locke as trying to answer Winstanley's challenge on its own terms.

And so here appears the account for which Chapter Five of the second *Treatise of Government* is most famous: anyone may gain ownership over something in the commons by mixing one's labor with it, subject to the limitations that enough and as good is left for others and that what one takes does not spoil before one can use it. We can divide this into two components: an account of the *ground* of original acquisition and an account of its *limits*. The ground of the right of original acquisition is the mixing of one's labor with the object of ownership. This makes an unowned thing one's own because each of us already has property in our persons and so, Locke argues, in our labor and in the work of our hands. The limits are the rules that one leave enough and good for others and that what one takes does not spoil before one can use it.

Gopal Sreenivasan argues that we can find a second account later in Chapter Five.[37] This account in effect promotes what counts as a limit to original acquisition in the first to a freestanding basis for it. "[H]e that leaves as much as another can make use of," Locke argues (we could add on his behalf "and as good"), "does as good as taking nothing at all" (§ 33). In other words, original acquisition is permissible when and because it leaves things no different for others.

Each account seems vulnerable to important objections. The first invokes a sequence of ideas that seem mysterious: that my relationship to my person is a kind of ownership,

---

[36] John Locke, *Two Treatises of Government* 228 (Peter Laslett ed., 1960).
[37] Gopal Sreenivasan, *The Limits of Lockean Rights in Property* 47–50 (1995).

that from that I gain title to my labor and its products, and that in mixing something I own with something I do not, I gain ownership of the latter (rather than losing ownership of the former).[38] More basically, it is not clear how the argument does not assume what it aims to show. No amount of your laboring on my garden will make the fruits of your labor your property unless I have made that arrangement with you. Why is original acquisition different? Similarly, if the costlessness of your use of my property does not thereby make it permissible, it is not clear how one can infer a right of ownership from the fact of the material nonconsequences of the possession from which that right is purported to follow.

I think that there is a way to read Locke that unifies these two accounts and goes some way to answering these objections, by suggesting that they are based on misunderstandings. The first step is to be cautious in what we find in Locke's claim that each of us has a property in our persons. I think by having a property in something Locke means having a right in rem to it, and by having a property in our persons he means nothing more mysterious than that our persons cannot be deployed by others without our permission. We get to property, to things other than our persons, by a link suggested by what I represented as the second account. Just after the passage quoted earlier, Locke continues:

> He that had as good left for his improvement, as was already taken up, needed not complain, ought not to meddle with what was already improved by another's labour: if he did, it is plain he desired the benefit of another's pains, which he had no right to.[39]

If without my permission you pick the fruit from my orchard I've grown, you are an advantage-taker; you are, in effect, retroactively deploying my person without my permission. A violation of my property rights, on this view, is thus a failure to treat me as an equal in just the same way that a wrong to my person is. Locke's answer to Winstanley is that acquisition that respects the limits Locke imposes on it respects the terms of equality that Winstanley thought rendered private ownership impermissible.

By putting Grotius and Locke on the same page this way, you may think I have obscured a crucial difference between the two, namely, that Grotius held that property arises as a matter of convention and Locke as a matter of natural right. But wait. For Grotius, the problem that Locke found with the idea that property was a matter of convention—that if it was necessary to secure consent before consuming any resources "Man had starved, notwithstanding the Plenty God had given him"—does not arise, for two reasons. The first is that, as we saw, Grotius allows that tacit consent is sufficient to put a regime of private property in place. The second, and deeper point, is that for Grotius, the concept of private property is required to do less work than it is on Locke's account. What it does is explain how I can be wronged by another's interference with land or a

[38] See the discussions in Sreenivasan, *id.* at 59–92, and A. John Simmons, *The Lockean Theory of Rights* 236–277 (1992).

[39] Locke, *supra* note 36, at 291.

thing, though I am not currently in possession of it. But it is not (and need not be) invoked when I exercise the right to use the world's resources prior to the adoption of a regime of private property. That I have a natural right to, as Locke, too, insists I must. On this, then, they agree. What they part ways on is when "property" begins. This, and their other differences, should not distract us from appreciating they were engaged in the common undertaking of determining which nonconventional constraints need to be imposed on the conventions we adopt to render the regime of property consistent with our equality.

IV. GROTIUS AND PUFENDORF ON NECESSITY

On Grotius's account, the right of necessity is, in effect, a property right. In using your property to save myself, I am exercising a right I have to its use, which correlates to a limit on your right to exclude. Here a puzzle arises: if the property is mine to use, why do I owe you compensation for any damage I cause (as I do, on Grotius's account)? Grotius's answer is that "more is not to be taken than it [the necessity] requires; that is, if keeping the thing is sufficient, it is not to be used; if using it is sufficient, it is not to be destroyed; if destroying it is requisite, the price is to be repaid."[40] His argument is that damaging and not repairing when I am able to set things right is just like keeping when all I needed to do is borrow. It is taking more than I have a claim to—it is to recede further from natural equity than is required. In reply to Grotius, Pufendorf argued that the simpler explanation is that I owed you compensation because the right of necessity is not a property right but rather a right against another to the use of her property. It is interesting to isolate on just what their disagreement turned.

For Pufendorf, as for Grotius, private property exists by convention, permitted but not established by natural law. The most important reasons advanced for its adoption, on his telling, are that by instituting private property, the quarrels arising from the original community are avoided and that "the industry of men is thereby increased."[41] More important for our purposes is that on Pufendorf's account, "[c]ertainly property was not distinguished with the purpose of allowing a man to avoid using it in the service of others, and to brood in solitude over his hoard of riches."[42] Instead, we all have a duty to help those in need whether enduring or, as in necessity, fleeting. That said, "such is the force of ownership," Pufendorf says, that I may dispose even of property I owe another, and she cannot simply come and take it from me even though I am under an obligation to transfer ownership to her. "If, however"—and here we see the foundation for Pufendorf's account of the right of necessity being laid—"the owner refuses of his own accord to meet his obligation, the power of ownership is by no means so great that

---

[40] Grotius, *The Rights of War and Peace, supra* note 9, at 400.

[41] Samuel Pufendorf, *The Rights of Nature and of Nations* 301 (C. H. Oldfather & W. A. Oldfather eds., 1934) (1672).

[42] *Id.*

property owed another may not be taken from an unwilling owner, through the authority of a judge in commonwealths, or, in the state of natural liberty, by the might of war."[43]

Now, "from the point of view of mere natural right," Pufendorf tells us, "a man is expected only on the basis of an imperfect obligation, in so far as it arises from the virtue of humanity, to aid another in the latter's extreme necessity."[44] It is permissible for a polity to strengthen this obligation into a perfect one by civil law, for example, by compelling contributions to the poor. What, however, if the obligation does not exist by positive law? Pufendorf answers with two rhetorical questions:

> [I]f such a precaution is not taken for the poor in some particular commonwealths, and if the obduracy of men of means cannot be overcome by prayers, while there is no means whereby a person may come to the aid of the man who is in want either of money or assistance, would you have him die of hunger? Can any human institution have such power that, if another neglects to do his duty toward me, I must perish rather than depart from the customary and usual manner of procedure?[45]

The (implicit) answer is no. He continues:

> I should not feel, therefore, that a man has made himself guilty of the crime of theft if when he has, through no fault of his own, fallen into extreme want of food necessary to maintain life, or of clothing to protect his body from the bite of cold, and has been unable either by entreaties, or money, or the offer of his services, to get other in easy circumstances, and even in luxury, to give them to him of their own accord, he should make away with them by violence of by stealth; and especially so if he intends to make good their value whenever a kindlier fortune may smile upon him.[46]

Let's call the man Pufendorf describes in his example the "needful taker." Left unexplained by Pufendorf is precisely how the needful taker's circumstances, conjoined with the property owner's refusal to aid, make it that he would not wrong the owner by seizing his land. This needs explaining because the owner's duty is imperfect and Pufendorf states often that those to whom an imperfect duty is owed cannot compel its performance by force or through the law. One answer would be that the needful taker's circumstances, conjoined with the property owner's refusal to aid, somehow perfects the latter's duty. That gives the needful taker a perfect right to possession or use of the property (as the facts require) and, we might say, the urgency gives him authority to execute the right. But this transformation is rather mysterious, and, while Pufendorf is quite elliptical in this passage, it strikes me that he is careful not to say this. I think there is a better way to reconstruct Pufendorf's argument on this point. It rests on a particular claim about imperfect duties.

Pufendorf tells us that the imperfect duty to aid is owed "on grounds of humanity" and that with it a person is given the opportunity to show that "his mind is intent upon voluntarily doing his duty."[47] One who refuses another aid in necessitous circumstances,

[43] *Id.* at 302.   [44] *Id.*   [45] *Id.*   [46] *Id.*   [47] *Id.* at 305.

he continues, reveals that he considers such an attitude superfluous. Ordinarily, one has discretion in how to discharge an imperfect duty. Pufendorf's thought seems to be that in some circumstances, that is not so. Let's say that in such circumstances an imperfect duty becomes determinate.

The idea can be helpfully explicated in the terms with which Kant explains imperfect duties.[48] On Kant's account, an imperfect duty is a duty to adopt a particular end. In contrast, perfect duties require that one act or forbear from acting in particular ways. It is a perfect duty to pay one's taxes, for example, but an imperfect one to be beneficent. One discharges the imperfect duty of beneficence by adopting among one's ends the happiness of others. Doing so entails no action in particular, but—and this is key—if one does nothing, then one has not, in fact, made others' happiness one's end. Put another way, one does not make others' happiness one's end merely by wishing them well (that is mere benevolence) or even just by planning to help them.

What makes the best sense of Pufendorf's argument is adding the next step (which is not explicitly in Kant, but I think he would accept): circumstances sometimes make it that there is an action that no one who has made others' happiness her end could refrain from doing. Put another way: there are circumstances in which I could not refrain from helping a particular person in a particular way and it be true that I have made others' happiness my end. This is not to say that in those circumstances the duty to which I am subject has been perfected, because neither its foundation nor basic structure have been altered. Rather it has been made determinate.

If the distinction between an imperfect duty made determinate and a perfect duty is sound, then arguably it vindicates the care Pufendorf took not to claim that the needful taker gains a right to the owner's property but rather to claim that she does not wrong him in seizing it. The former seems possible only if the duty is perfected. The latter, we might say, is the correlative of the property owner's imperfect duty to aid having been made determinate.

So while for Grotius the right of necessity is a property right, for Pufendorf it is personal. It is a right that another allow one to use her property. That right correlates to the property owner's imperfect duty to aid, which duty has been made determinate by the necessitous circumstances. On what does their disagreement turn?

To start, note again that for Pufendorf, a property owner's right to exclude in an important sense does *not* run out at the point of necessity. While, on his account, as we saw earlier, "property was not distinguished with the purpose of allowing a man to avoid using it in the service of others, and to brood in solitude over his hoard of riches,"[49] in choosing to thus avoid and so brood, one would be acting within one's rights as an owner. The needful taker's claim is a claim that another exercise his (the other's) rights to a particular end. By contrast, for Grotius the needful taker exercises her (the needful taker's) right to the property. Her claim is exercised in a normative space that marks one limit to the owner's right to exclude.

---

[48] Immanuel Kant, *The Metaphysics of Morals* 153 (Mary Gregor ed., 1996) (1797).

[49] Pufendorf, *supra* note 41, at 301.

Grotius and Pufendorf were in agreement as to the measure by which the scope of the right to exclude is determined. Their disagreement was in its application. On Pufendorf's account, the introduction of property provides persons the means "of making a richer display of humanity and kindness to others, while before that time they could aid others only by their own personal service."[50] His claim is not just that in fact among the goods of private property is that it expands the means by which we can discharge the imperfect duty of beneficence. It is that part of what justifies the adoption of private property is that it does so. Property owners have the right to exclude the imperiled trespasser precisely so that they have the opportunity to waive its exercise in fulfillment of a duty of humanity.

So we can find implicit in Pufendorf's argument his endorsement of the principle on which I argued Grotius's account of necessity rested, namely, that the right to exclude may only be as strong as is necessary to secure the benefits of a regime of private property. What they disagree on is what benefits we ought to seek to secure. For Grotius, the list stops short of providing greater opportunities for the cultivation of virtue, and so for him the scope of the right to exclude is commensurately narrower than it is for Pufendorf.

This disagreement, in turn, rests on two issues. *First*: here we see Pufendorf endorse the Aristotelian view that it is among the responsibilities of the state to enable its citizens to cultivate virtue, that among the goods whose realization justifies the adoption of private property is that it affords greater opportunities to act virtuously than does communal ownership, and that the scope of property rights ought to be set with an eye to this end (among others).[51] While he does not address the question explicitly, Grotius's rejection of this view is implicit in his account, which we might therefore say is more classically liberal on at least one measure. We might think this feature of his account tells us something about Grotius's conception of the good or of what sorts of goods he thinks are aptly pursued through legal institutions. More consonant with his account, I would suggest, is attributing to him the view that to the extent that Pufendorf's account leaves the needful taker's fate in another's hands, morally speaking, it fails to respect natural equity.

Second: Implicit in each of Pufendorf's and Grotius's accounts is the claim that the right of necessity is required by equality, but they disagree as to what equality requires, or, perhaps, at what point it imposes its obligations. For Pufendorf, property rights are subordinate to a regime of virtue that is essentially egalitarian. The person who broods in solitude over his riches fails to discharge a duty owed to others simply because they are persons like him. The duty of beneficence is, in his words, a duty of humanity.

For Grotius, by contrast, rights of private property are limited by the condition that they be in conformity with the equality upheld by the original use right. Here we see the heart of his account of the right of necessity. On Grotius's account, in short, the world is each of ours, and there is a sense in which it remains so even after we have adopted a regime of private property: our equality, once expressed in common ownership, now limits the ways in which we can, through the institutions we adopt, make ourselves vulnerable to being excluded by others from the world we share.

---

[50] *Id.* at 302.   [51] See Aristotle, *Politics* 26–27 (Stephen Everson ed., 1988).

V. CONCLUSION

It is not unreasonable to think that a political and intellectual world in which the starting point of thinking about property is the original community of ownership in an anarchic state of nature is a world at some distance from ours. The classic social contract theorists thought they were, in part, describing the actual world, which appeared to them still significantly unowned, in point of fact and of right. There is every reason to take moral issue with this idea and, furthermore, to wonder whether much light is likely to be shed on the structure and content of ownership in our world by accounts of the original acquisition of land.

In answer to both worries, consider Grotius's claim that certain distinctions lawyers draw among kinds of ownership

> will be very easily explained if, in imitation of the method employed by all the poets since the days of Hesiod as well as by the ancient philosophers and jurists, we draw a chronological distinction between things which are perhaps not differentiated from one another by any considerable interval of time, but which do indeed differ in certain underlying principles and by their very nature.[52]

While Grotius casts the steps taken away from it as a series of events in history, the original community of property on his account and throughout the early modern tradition is really—or at least is also—a conceptual starting point, a representation of how we stand with respect to one another in the world abstracted from the institutions through which we administer the regime of private property.

Grotius and others in the natural law tradition cast the moral aspect of that standing in terms of the natural laws that protected the natural rights of equals. I've tried to answer the mirror-image worries that this language expresses an approach in one sense, too, and in another, insufficiently, metaphysical for modern sensibilities, by suggesting a way of reading two debates that are, I think, exemplary of the tradition. As I have reconstructed them, Grotius's and Locke's disagreements about the foundations of property rights and Grotius's and Pufendorf's about the foundations of the right of necessity are, at their core, disagreements about how to render private ownership consistent with equality. The common ground against which these disagreements is framed is the view that through its doctrines the institution of private property inevitably expresses some view on this question, and in this way reveals its connection to the rest of our moral lives. If this is right, and can be generalized to private law more broadly, then perhaps we can see the natural lawyers as fellow travelers with those who hold that, in undertaking to get down to brass tacks, the realists were obscuring rather than illuminating what private law is really about.

---

[52] Grotius, *Commentary on the Law of Prize and Booty*, *supra* note 11, at 315.

CHAPTER 3

....

CORRECTIVE JUSTICE

Sovereign or Subordinate?

....

GREGORY C. KEATING

THE concept of corrective justice has been at the heart of much recent scholarship on the law of torts in particular and private law more generally. On the face of it, this is both surprising and unsurprising. Unsurprising, because the term "corrective justice" is at least as old as Aristotle and private law is its natural habitat. Competing conceptions of private law remedies are generally thought to share the premise that the "primary" role of such remedies "is [to] restor[e] the plaintiff to his rightful position."[1] Surprising, because everyday examples suggest that corrective justice is common sense—not an opaque concept in need of theoretical clarification. Suppose I walk past your stand at a farmers market and see a mouthwatering array of fresh fruit. I pick up a basket of raspberries and consume them on the spot—they're delicious. Suddenly, you appear and make it clear that you are the owner of the farm stand. You had run off on an errand, and I had mistakenly thought your berries were just there for the taking—a gift to passersby. You let me know that the berries I've just eaten were only available for purchase. My thinking otherwise was silly and mistaken, but not malicious. I now owe you an obligation of reparation. I've taken and consumed something that belonged to you. I am unable to return the raspberries, and I owe you recompense for the loss that I've inflicted on you, at least if you choose to stand on your rights. That *I* am the person who must make reparation seems as evident as the fact that *reparation* is what I owe to you. This paired obligation and relation is what Aristotle called "corrective justice"[2] and Locke called the obligation of "reparation."[3] It is intuitive that this kind of obligation is fundamental not just to tort but to private law in general. And so it is.

Notwithstanding its familiarity, ancient origin, and apparent universal acceptance, the concept of corrective justice has spawned a remarkable number of distinct

---

[1] Samuel L. Bray, Chapter 34 of this volume.
[2] Aristotle, *Nicomachean Ethics* 85–86 (Roger Crisp ed. & trans., 2000).
[3] John Locke, *Second Treatise on Government* 11 (C.B. Macpherson ed., 1980) (1690).

conceptions and has stirred up major controversies. For at least a generation, corrective justice stood at the center of the argument between contending conceptions of tort. For legal economists, corrective justice was an aspect of the institution of tort law. It was part of the data that needed to be explained and justified in economic terms. Corrective justice was *subordinate*. It was a feature of—not a justification for—the institution of tort law. For legal philosophers Ernest Weinrib and Jules Coleman—who championed corrective justice as the countertheory to economic analysis—corrective justice was *sovereign*. It was both instantiated in the institution of tort law and the justification for the institution. It was incipiently normative. And the justification it supplied was formal, not instrumental. The aim of this chapter is to explain and analyze corrective justice in light of this history, in the hope that this will set the stage for tort theory to move forward. What this history teaches, I think, is that tort law's remedial norms are parasitic on its primary ones. Tort theory should therefore attend more to tort law's primary norms.

I. Theorizing Corrective Justice

For the tort theorists who have marched beneath the banner of corrective justice in the past few decades, corrective justice is defined in contradistinction to distributive justice and in terms of a relationship between the parties. Distributive justice has to do with the justice of holdings, with the distribution of wealth, income, rights, and property. Persons who participate in the same institutions of distributive justice have their claims against one another mediated by those institutions. Claims in distributive justice are not direct claims on other persons. We may have a claim in distributive justice to some particular share of wealth and income, but we do not have a claim in distributive justice against another private person for that share. Corrective justice, by contrast, involves the relationship between the parties to a claim. It requires a "wrong" or a "rights-violation." That wrong must relate the parties directly to one another, so that it gives rise to an obligation of reparation owed by the wrongdoer to the victim. "Corrective justice," Ernest Weinrib tells us, "treats the wrong, and transfer of resources that undoes it, as a single nexus of activity and passivity where actor and victim are defined in relation to each other." "Corrective justice joins the parties directly, through the harm that one of them inflicts on the other." It involves "the correlativity of doing and suffering harm."[4]

Weinrib's emphasis on the "unity of doing and suffering"—with the "doing" being the infliction of the suffering by violating the "abstract equality of free purposive beings

---

[4] Ernest J. Weinrib, *The Idea of Private Law* 56, 71, 77, 142 (1995); see also *id.* at 213 ("Corrective justice represents the integrated unity of doer and sufferer."). The idea originates with Aristotle: "For it makes no difference whether it is a good person who has defrauded a bad or a bad person a good. . . . The law looks only to the difference made by the injury, and treats the parties as equals, if one is committing injustice, and the other suffering it—that is, if one has harmed, and the other has been harmed." Aristotle, *supra* note 2, at 87.

under the Kantian conception of right"[5]—articulates a particular conception of corrective justice. The general concept is broader. Richard Epstein's theory of tort also marches under the banner of corrective justice, but it articulates a form of liability where cause is central and "wrong" is attenuated.[6] George Fletcher, for his part, applies the term to a theory of liability for nonreciprocal risk imposition.[7] Catherine Wells argues that it involves providing an appropriate process for determining whether the defendant is responsible for the plaintiff's loss.[8] Jules Coleman asserts that the principle of corrective justice "states that individuals who are responsible for the wrongful losses of others have a duty to repair [those] losses."[9] Arthur Ripstein identifies corrective justice with "the unity of right and remedy" and with the fact that both must be understood relationally.[10] Scott Hershovitz explains the gist of corrective justice theory by remarking that "according to corrective justice theorists, tort law enforces duties of repair that arise in response to wrongdoing."[11]

These conceptions differ in diverse ways. Jules Coleman, for example, identifies corrective justice with wrongful losses. Others identify corrective justice with "wrongs" instead of "wrongful losses" or with "allocation back."[12] These distinctions make a difference. For example, theories which identify corrective justice with "wrongs" instead of with "wrongful losses" have an easier time encompassing violations of rights that do not involve losses (e.g., some trespasses and batteries). Identifying corrective justice with "allocation back" includes "gains-based" measures of recovery (e.g., for unjust enrichment) within corrective justice. Of course, broadening the scope of corrective justice may also diminish its explanatory power by casting the concept as more formal and less substantive. For our purposes, these differences and the issues they raise can be put to one side. The important division is the division between theories that take corrective justice to be a subordinate aspect of tort law and those that take it to be the paramount principle of the legal field. This distinction captures the central issue contested

---

[5] Weinrib, *supra* note 4, at 58.

[6] See Richard A. Epstein, *A Theory of Strict Liability: Toward a Reformulation of Tort Law* (1980). Compare Robert Nozick, *Anarchy, State and Utopia* 54–87 (1974).

[7] George P. Fletcher, *Fairness and Utility in Tort Theory*, 85 HARV. L. REV. 537 (1972).

[8] Catherine Pierce Wells, *Tort Law as Corrective Justice: A Pragmatic Justification for Jury Adjudication*, 88 MICH. L. REV. 2348 (1990).

[9] Jules Coleman, *The Practice of Principle* 15, 36 (2001).

[10] Arthur Ripstein, *Private Wrongs* 7 (2016).

[11] Scott Hershovitz, *Corrective Justice for Civil Recourse Theorists*, 39 FLA. ST. U. L. REV. 107, 108 (2011). Other conceptions can also be found in the literature. See, e.g., Christopher Schroeder, *Corrective Justice and Liability for Increasing Risks*, 37 UCLA L. REV. 439, 449–450 (1990) (identifying corrective justice theory with three requirements: "action-based responsibility," "just compensation," and "internal financing of compensation").

[12] Ripstein, *supra* note 10, and Weinrib, *supra* note 4, identify corrective justice with rights and wrongs. John Gardner, *What Is Tort Law For? Part 1: The Place of Corrective Justice*, 30 LAW & PHIL. 1 (2011), identifies corrective justice with "allocating back." Tony Honoré remarks that "[o]n a wide view [corrective justice] requires those who have without justification harmed others by their conduct to put the matter right." Tony Honoré, *Responsibility and Fault* 73 (1999). Note that harming "without justification" is not necessarily the same as "wronging" or "harming wrongfully."

by economic theories of tort and their philosophical challengers over the course of the past several decades.

On a subordinate account, corrective justice is an aspect of tort—perhaps even a necessary and defining feature of the institution—but it does not play a fundamental role in explaining or justifying tort law. Instead, the justifications for tort law—say, minimizing the combined costs of preventing and paying for accidents—call for corrective justice as a feature of the institution. Accounts which treat corrective justice as the sovereign principle of tort work the other way around. Rather than being required by other, more basic, justifications for tort, corrective justice justifies tort law as an institution and shapes its design. If corrective justice is the fundamental principle on which tort law rests and if, as Jules Coleman argues, corrective justice requires repairing wrongful losses, then tort liability must attach to losses generated by *wrongful conduct*.[13] Justice governs claims that persons have against one another, and one person has a claim in corrective justice against another when the wrongful conduct of the latter has inflicted a loss on the former. The wrongfulness of the conduct makes the loss it inflicts a wrongful one. On this account, then, corrective justice is an independent principle to which the law of torts answers, and it imposes significant constraints on tort law's primary norms. Because corrective justice requires that those responsible for wrongful losses repair them, if tort law does corrective justice, its primary norms must proscribe conduct which begets such losses.

A. Corrective Justice as Subordinate

An oversimplified version of a libertarian theory of tort is useful for understanding how corrective justice might be a subordinate principle of justice in tort. Suppose that everyone has a natural right to liberty and that, therefore, "[a] line (hyper-plane) circumscribes an area in moral space around an individual."[14] Accidental harms constitute impermissible crossings of this line and thus violate the victim's natural right to the liberty and integrity of her person, unless consent to the risk imposition that resulted in the crossing has been given in advance. "Voluntary consent opens the border for crossings."[15] Absent such consent, the infliction of accidental injury constitutes a wrong. When a wrong has been done, the person whose rights were violated acquires a derivative right to redress against the person who violated her rights. These rights to redress are claims of corrective justice. When we honor them by requiring the wrongdoer to

---

[13] Coleman, *supra* note 9, at 32–34 (suggesting "assault and battery" as a paradigm case of the kind of wrong that gives rise to a duty of repair). Coleman's emphasis on "wrongful conduct," like his emphasis on "wrongful losses," stakes out a contested position in a debate. To flesh out the difference between sovereign and subordinate conceptions of corrective justice, we need an account of sovereign corrective justice that takes a position on these issues and so puts flesh on the bones of the concept. More than anyone else, perhaps, Coleman championed the view that corrective justice was the conceptual key which unlocked the law of torts.

[14] Nozick, *supra* note 6, at 57.   [15] *Id.* at 58.

rectify the harm done by her violation of the victim's right, we do justice in the specific form of corrective justice. The work of determining when a boundary has been wrongly crossed and when, therefore, a rights-violation must be repaired, is done by principles of distributive justice. Libertarian principles of *distributive* justice specify initial entitlements and a procedure for altering them. Initially, each person has a natural right to liberty encompassing the physical integrity of her person. The boundaries that define and protect that right may only be altered by consensual agreement. When consent has not been given, boundary crossings are not permissible and harm that results from them is wrongly inflicted. Corrective justice comes into play because *principles of distributive justice* identify some boundary-crossings as unjust. Libertarian principles of distributive justice and permissible transfer do the real work. They determine what people are and are not entitled to. Corrective justice is the handmaiden of distributive justice; it undoes illegitimate alterations of entitlements.

Many different accounts of tort liability may incorporate corrective justice as a subordinate principle of tort justice. Richard Epstein's theory of tort liability, for example, incorporates corrective justice in this subordinate sense, but rests (in its original formulation) on a natural right to liberty.[16] That right is violated when harms are caused in various paradigmatic ways. Wrongful conduct—fault—is not necessary. George Fletcher's influential fairness conception of tort law also incorporates corrective justice in a subordinate way. Fletcher's conception takes a Rawlsian view of tort as a realm of equal freedom and so founds tort on a conception of distributively just risk imposition.[17] Reciprocity of risk identifies a fair distribution of risks of accidental harm and guides the substantive criteria of tort liability—determining the choice between negligence and strict liability, for instance. Within Fletcher's theory, corrective justice operates in the same subordinate way that it does in our stylized libertarian theory. It restores a distributively just state of affairs by requiring reparation for harm done when tortious harms issue from distributively unfair risk impositions.

B. Corrective Justice as Sovereign

For theorists like Coleman and Weinrib, corrective justice is the *sovereign* principle of tort law. Coleman claims that "tort law is best explained by corrective justice" because "at its core tort law seeks to repair wrongful losses."[18] For this claim to be significant, "wrongful losses" must be a concept which does some work and which has some constraining content. It must identify a class of losses to which a duty of repair properly attaches. Coleman thus argues that corrective justice is concerned with responsibility for wrongful losses, harms, or rights-violations. Losses are wrongful when they are

---

[16] See Epstein, *supra* note 6.

[17] Fletcher, *supra* note 7 (invoking Rawls's first principle of justice as the parent of his principle of reciprocal risk imposition).

[18] Coleman, *supra* note 9, at 36.

attributable to wrongful conduct.[19] Such conduct gives rise to liability in corrective *justice* because it is *wrongful*, not because it disrupts a preexisting pattern of just holdings. Disruptions that are not wrongful do not give rise to claims of corrective justice. Corrective justice is thus separated from distributive justice, and the criteria of wrongfulness that corrective justice places at the center of tort law do the work of determining when liability in tort is justified.

The proposition that corrective justice involves both the infliction of harm or the violation of a right *and conduct that is in some way wrong* establishes the *independence* of corrective justice from distributive justice, but it does not establish the *importance* of corrective justice, or show that it explains the law of torts. Richard Posner drove these points home in an important paper. Posner argued that "[o]nce the concept of corrective justice is given its correct Aristotelian meaning, it becomes possible to show that it is not only compatible with, but required by, the economic theory of law."[20] Starting from the premise that corrective justice in its robust sense requires wrongful conduct, Posner argued first that economics could supply the requisite standard of conduct, and second, that an economic conception of tort *required* corrective justice:

> [For an economic theory,] law is a means of bringing about an efficient (in the sense of wealth-maximizing) allocation of resources by correcting externalities and other distortions in the market's allocation of resources. The idea of rectification in the Aristotelian sense is implicit in this theory. If A fails to take precautions that would cost less than their expected benefits in accident avoidance, thus causing an accident in which B is injured, and nothing is done to rectify this wrong, the concept of justice as efficiency will be violated. . . . Since A does not bear the cost (or the full cost) of his careless behavior, he will have no incentive to take precautions in the future, and there will be more accidents than is optimal. Since B receives no compensation for his injury, he may be induced to adopt in the future precautions which by hypothesis . . . are more costly than the precautions that A failed to take.[21]

Corrective justice can, in short, take a standard of efficient precaution as the criterion of wrongful conduct that it requires. For its part, economics requires that corrective justice be done if tort is to induce efficient precautions.

When corrective justice is conceived of as compatible with economics in this way, however, it is neither sovereign nor justificatory. Corrective justice is a feature of tort law: it helps to constitute the institution that we have and it therefore requires economic explanation and justification. It is not a justification but an aspect of tort law that needs to be justified. For Posner, the principle of wealth maximization supplies the necessary

---

[19] See Jules Coleman, *The Practice of Corrective Justice, in Philosophical Foundations of Tort Law* 53, 56–57 (David G. Owen ed., 1995) (explaining that corrective justice imposes a duty on an injurer to repair a victim's loss when the injurer is responsible for having brought the loss about by virtue of the injurer's wrongful conduct).

[20] Richard A. Posner, *The Concept of Corrective Justice in Recent Theories of Tort Law*, 10 J. LEGAL STUD. 187, 201 (1981).

[21] *Id.*

justification. When tort law is a society's principal mechanism for addressing accidents—and is otherwise efficient—corrective justice is necessary to ensure that the law of torts as a whole induces efficient precautions. By accepting the proposition that corrective justice involves not just the restoration of a prior, distributively just regime—but liability for wrongful conduct—Posner's account both incorporates a robust idea of corrective justice and makes corrective justice a subordinate principle of tort liability. The reasons that we have for corrective justice reduce to the reasons that we have for deploying tort law in the first place and, for Posner, those are reasons of efficiency. Wrongful losses—meaning losses inflicted by inefficient conduct—must be shifted back onto the parties responsible for them, or else neither injurers nor victims will have the right incentives. Posner's theory pours the substance of efficiency into the form of corrective justice.

This union is surprising. Corrective justice and the economic theory of tort appear to be rival conceptions. The economic conception of tort law is forward-looking, and it takes as its touchstone the attainment of a state of the world where wealth is maximized.[22] The rights and duties of plaintiffs and defendants with respect to one another matter only insofar as they may be deployed as instruments to the realization of this end. Corrective justice theory, by contrast, is backward-looking. It aims to repair past wrongs. It places the rights and wrongs of plaintiffs and defendants at the very center of its account and focuses on who has done what to whom. Tort is about the obligations of wrongdoers to repair the wrongful losses that they have inflicted on their victims. The total amount of value in various states of the world is immaterial.[23]

C. Corrective Justice as a Practice of Principle

Tort theorists who march under the banner of corrective justice reject the conclusion that it is merely a feature of tort law to be explained and justified, claiming that corrective justice is the principle that does the explaining and justifying. "Corrective justice," Coleman asserts, "expresses the principle that holds together and makes sense of tort law."[24] The principle that wrongful losses should be repaired is a *morally* authoritative norm in its own right. Within the domain of tort law that principle is sovereign, not subordinate. The economic theory of tort is both the target of, and the foil for, the claim that corrective justice is the master principle of tort law. The nerve of the argument is that the economic theory of tort is instrumental, and instrumentalism does and must look forward. Corrective justice, however, does and must look backward. Consequently, it cannot be adequately explained by instrumentalism.

---

[22] The standard criterion is the one usually attributed to Guido Calabresi, *The Costs of Accidents: A Legal and Economic Analysis* 26 (1970) ("I take it as axiomatic that the principal function of accident law is to reduce the sum of the costs of accidents and the costs of avoiding accidents.").

[23] The economic theory of tort is an "end-state" theory whereas corrective justice is an "historical" theory of tort justice. See Nozick, *supra* note 6, at 153–160.

[24] Coleman, *supra* note 9, at 62.

For Coleman and Weinrib, the relation between tort and corrective justice is one of instantiation. For Weinrib, tort adjudication appears to be an entirely autonomous institution. Its principles are given by the form of tort law—as embodied in the traditional, bipolar (P v. D) tort lawsuit—and they neither need nor have any further justification.[25] For Coleman, the principle of corrective justice and the practice it sustains can be explained and justified by reference to more abstract and fundamental principles, such as the principle that the costs of life's misfortune should be allocated fairly.[26] Tort adjudication cannot, however, be conceived of as a means to an independently valuable end. Instead, it must be understood to enforce claims that persons have the standing to assert against one another in their own names. On Coleman's account, because corrective justice rests on the sound moral *principle* that wrongfully inflicted losses should be repaired, it is not an instrument for the realization of an end but the specification of a morally authoritative principle of responsibility. It is *fair* to hold people responsible for repairing the wrongful losses that they inflict on others. This gives corrective justice a dual relation to tort practice. On the one hand, the principle of corrective justice grounds the practice. On the other hand, the practice puts flesh on the bare bones of the principle.[27]

Wrongful exercises of human agency, correlativity, and repair lie at the core of both tort law and corrective justice.[28] That tort law is about agency is evident enough to the pre-theoretic eye, but obscured by the theoretical apparatus of economics, with its emphasis on achieving states of the world where value is maximized. The thesis that losses are more easily borne when they are widely dispersed, for example, gives us reason to be as concerned with concentrated losses caused by natural disasters as with concentrated losses caused by human malfeasance. Yet tort law denies this equivalence: it is about malfeasance, not misfortune.[29] In this respect, the law of tort taps into deep moral sentiments, constitutive of the sense of justice itself. We have reason to resent mistreatment by others, but it is anthropomorphic nonsense to complain of mistreatment by

---

[25] Weinrib famously analogizes private law to love. "Explaining love in terms of extrinsic ends is necessarily a mistake, because love does not shine in our lives with the borrowed light of an external end. Love is its own end. My contention is that, in this respect, private law is just like love." Weinrib, *supra* note 4, at 6.

[26] Coleman, *supra* note 9, at xiii, 4, 5, 8, 9–10, 43, 55, 58. At page 28, Coleman writes: "Anglo-American tort law *expresses, embodies, or articulates* corrective justice. Tort law is an institutional realization of principle, not an instrument in the pursuit of an external and hidden goal."

[27] *Id.* at 62.

[28] *Id.* at 58 ("[C]orrective justice requires that the costs of misfortune owing to human agency be imposed on the person (if any) whose wrongful conduct is responsible for those costs. The losses are made his by imposing on him an enforceable duty of repair.").

[29] "There is a basic pre-theoretic distinction between misfortunes owing to human agency and those that are attributable to no one's agency. The traditional philosophical distinction between corrective and distributive justice reflects, among other things, this pre-theoretic distinction among kinds of misfortune." *Id.* at 44 (footnote omitted).

Mother Nature.[30] Wrongfulness explains why the distinction between malfeasance and misfortune is intuitively basic. The wrongfulness of someone's action is a reason to hold that person responsible for a loss that conduct inflicts on someone else. Last, wrongful conduct figures very prominently in the law of torts itself. Both intentional and negligent torts involve wrongful conduct.

Correlativity is central to tort because "[t]he claims of corrective justice are limited ... to parties who bear some normatively important relationship to one another. A person does not ... have a claim in corrective justice to repair in the air, against no one in particular. It is a claim against someone in particular."[31] The bilateral (or bipolar) structure of tort adjudication, which itself mirrors the underlying interaction of a tortious wrong, is the institutional incarnation of correlativity. For Coleman (and also for Weinrib), the bilateral relationship of plaintiff and defendant is "the most basic relationship in our actual institution of tort law."[32] Tort law's core is represented by case-by-case adjudication in which particular victims seek redress for certain losses from those whom they claim are responsible.[33] Having a wronged plaintiff seek reparation from the wrongdoer who has injured him is the most natural way to give institutional expression to the principle that persons who are responsible for wrongly injuring others ought to repair the harm they have done.[34]

Here the payoff from taking the formal structure of tort law seriously becomes visible. Coleman and Weinrib offer a convincing explanation for the form of a tort lawsuit, whereas economic analysis offers an implausible one. Tort adjudication presents itself as a backward-looking practice concerned with repairing harm wrongly done. Economists take it to be a forward-looking regulatory mechanism concerned with minimizing the combined costs of accidents and their prevention going forward. Tort adjudication's true target is not wrongdoers but "cheapest cost avoiders"—parties best positioned to minimize *future* accident costs. Because it is only contingently the case that the particular defendants responsible for the injuries before the court are the cheapest cost-avoiders with respect to the general classes into which those injuries fall, the orthodox economic

---

[30] "The nature of things does not madden us, only ill-will does." Jean Jacques Rousseau, *Émile* 320 (Bernard Gagnebin trans., 1969). P.F. Strawson, "Freedom and Resentment," in *Studies in the Philosophy of Thought and Action* 71 (1968) (showing that "reactive attitudes" such as resentment are fundamental to our sensibilities and cannot be accounted for by instrumentalism).

[31] Coleman, *supra* note 19, at 66–67.

[32] Jules Coleman, Scott Hershovitz, & Gabriel Mendlow, *Theories of the Common Law of Torts*, STAN. ENCYCLOPEDIA PHIL. (Edward N. Zalta ed., 2015), https://plato.stanford.edu/archives/win2015/entries/tort-theories/; Weinrib, *supra* note 4, at 10.

[33] Coleman, *supra* note 9, at 16. Cf. Coleman et al., *supra* note 32 (giving "[t]he bilateral structure of a tort suit—the fact that victims sue those they identify as their injurers and do not instead seek repair from a common pool of resources [as is the case in New Zealand]" as an example of a structural feature of tort law).

[34] For Weinrib, this relationship expresses the "unity of doing and suffering," the intrinsic moral salience of the doer of harm as presumptively responsible for the harm that she has wrongly done. Weinrib, *supra* note 4, at 142.

analysis of tort has to work hard to explain why plaintiffs always have rights against and only against those who have wronged them. Economic analysis explains this by asserting that the law of tort enlists plaintiffs as private attorney generals and holds wrongdoers liable in order to induce efficient accident prevention going forward. Coleman and Weinrib rightly find this hypothesis strained and unconvincing. Coleman writes:

> In the absence of any explanatory theory, our intuition is that a victim is entitled to sue *because* he makes a cognizable claim that the injurer has wrongfully harmed him; that the victim must present arguments in support of that claim *because* the harm and the wrong are recognized by the law as pertinent to the outcome of the lawsuit; and that if the victim's claims are vindicated, he recovers against his injurer because the law recognizes wrongful harm as grounds for such recovery. The economic theory tells us, however, that each of these intuitions is wrong; that the apparently transparent purpose of the law of tort in each case is not the real purpose; and that the real purpose, efficiency, has nothing at all to do with the fact that the injurer may have wrongfully harmed the victim. If the fact of the harm has any significance at all, it is epistemic. . . . [T]he economic analysis asserts that in the absence of search, administrative, and other transaction costs, these structural features of tort law would be incomprehensible.[35]

The implausibility of the economic account of tort adjudication is compounded by the weakness of its explanation of the central substantive concepts of tort law—duty, "harm, cause, repair, fault and the like."[36] These concepts hang together to articulate a relationship of right and responsibility between victim and injurer.[37] Orthodox economic analysis, however, dismisses these concepts as a kind of false consciousness. It denies that they operate as *reasons* for the imposition of liability in tort. For the law of negligence, breach of duty is a *reason* for the imposition of liability. Duty specifies an obligatory standard of conduct. In conjunction with the other elements of a negligence claim, failure to conform to that standard of conduct is a reason to hold a defendant responsible for harm done to a victim by that failure. Tort law looks backward toward the past interactions of the parties in order to determine if the defendant should be held responsible for the plaintiff's injury. The basic concepts of negligence law are the ground of liability for negligence. Defendants are liable to plaintiffs not only *when* they breach duties owed to them but *because* they breach those duties. A secondary obligation to repair a tortiously inflicted injury arises from and *because of* a failure to comply with a primary obligation of harm avoidance.

For orthodox economic analysis, liability is not imposed because the defendant breached a duty of care and was the actual and proximate cause of harm done. Liability is imposed when and because we rightly conclude that the imposition of liability for past

[35] Coleman, *supra* note 9, at 21 (footnote omitted). Compare Ernest J. Weinrib, *Understanding Tort Law*, 23 VAL. U. L. REV. 485 (1989); Weinrib, *supra* note 4, at 37–38, 142, 212–213.

[36] Coleman, *supra* note 9, at 9–10; see also Jules Coleman, *The Economic Structure of Tort Law*, 97 YALE L.J. 1233 (1988).

[37] Coleman, *supra* note 9, at 23.

harm will induce optimal prevention of accidental harm going forward. For economics, the concepts of duty, breach, actual and proximate cause, and harm are not the real grounds of liability.[38] Judges say that they are imposing liability in negligence because duty, breach, actual and proximate cause, and injury are present, but standard economic analysis takes them to be justified in what they are doing only if they are engaged in a transaction cost-minimizing search for cheapest cost-avoiders. Duty, breach, actual and proximate cause, and injury are not reasons for the imposition of liability. They are evidentiary markers that do a respectable job of identifying cheapest cost-avoiders going forward.

Sovereign corrective justice theory thus argues persuasively that the basic structural features and main concepts of tort adjudication instantiate the principle of corrective justice. The bilateral form of the lawsuit tracks the substantive responsibility of a wrongdoer for the wrongful losses that she has inflicted. The retrospective character of tort adjudication reflects the fact that the wrongful infliction of harm is the reason why tortfeasors must repair the losses that they have inflicted. Duty and breach articulate criteria of wrongfulness. If tort regularly enjoined repair of losses attributable to innocent conduct, it could not be said that the law of tort institutes the principle "that individuals who are responsible for the wrongful losses of others have a duty to repair them."[39] Causation connects the wrongdoer to the loss wrongfully suffered by the victim and so plays an essential role in establishing the special responsibility of the wrongdoer for that loss. Corrective justice thus gives each of the elements of a typical tort suit a natural, unforced justification. The institutional practice of tort law fleshes out the abstract moral principle of corrective justice.[40]

II. Turning Tort Law Upside Down

It is commonplace to distinguish between primary (or substantive) responsibilities and secondary (or remedial) ones.[41] In tort, primary responsibilities are grounded in the rights of those they protect and the responsibilities that they articulate are diverse: to avoid harming others in various ways, to avoid violating certain of their rights even when no harm is thereby done, and in certain circumstances, to repair harm reasonably inflicted.[42] Remedial responsibilities are responsibilities of repair, triggered by the

---

[38] *Id.* at 34–36.   [39] See, e.g., *id.* at 15, 36.

[40] *Id.* at 62. Compare Benjamin C. Zipursky, *Pragmatic Conceptualism*, 6 L. Theory 457 (2000) (offering a similar account of this debate).

[41] See Henry M. Hart & Albert M. Sacks, *The Legal Process: Basic Problems in the Making and Application of Law* 122–124 (William Eskridge Jr. & Philip Frickey eds., 1994). Perhaps because tort has had to fend off the charge that it is not a freestanding body of law but a remedial appendage to other bodies of law, the distinction has loomed especially large in tort theory. See, e.g., Thomas C. Grey, *Accidental Torts*, 54 Vand. L. Rev. 1225, 1242–1244 (2001).

[42] See Gregory C. Keating, *The Priority of Respect Over Repair*, 18 Legal. Theory 293, 308 (2012).

breach of various primary obligations. When the distinction between these two kinds or responsibilities is marked, it is natural to think that primary responsibilities are, well, primary—that is, antecedent to and more important than secondary ones. In part, the priority is logical. Remedial responsibilities arise out of breach of antecedent primary duties.[43] But the priority of primary responsibilities is also normative.[44] Remedial responsibilities are second-best ways of complying with obligations that are best honored by discharging primary responsibilities.

Secondary, remedial responsibilities express the persisting normative pull of undischarged primary obligations. Remedies are, as Arthur Ripstein says, "the continuation of the right that was violated."[45] Breach of a primary obligation does not relieve the breaching party of her responsibility to comply with that obligation; it simply makes it impossible for the breaching party to comply fully with that obligation. That conjunction of continuing obligation and factual impossibility requires doing the next-best thing: repair the harm wrongly done. Breach of a primary obligation is the circumstance that calls corrective justice into play, and the undischarged primary obligation is the reason why corrective justice must be done. Right and reparation form a unity within which right has priority. The first-best way of complying with tort law's obligations is not to harm anyone or violate their rights in ways that tort law proscribes. Repairing harm done by failing to fulfill that responsibility is the next-best way of respecting that right. Corrective justice has an important place in the law of torts, but that place is subordinate.

In tort law, as elsewhere, remedies exist to enforce and to restore rights.[46] The prospect of a remedy helps to assure a right holder that she can enforce her right if necessary and by so doing gives others reason to respect her right. The enforcement of a remedy when a right has been violated serves to restore the right. Even though rights and

---

[43] See Coleman, *supra* note 9, at 32 ("Someone does not incur a second order duty of repair unless he has failed to discharge some first-order duty.").

[44] See Neil MacCormick, *The Obligation of Reparation, in Legal Right and Social Democracy* 212 (1981); Joseph Raz, *Personal Practical Conflicts, in Practical Conflicts: New Philosophical Essays* 182 (Peter Baumann & Monica Betzler eds., 2004).

[45] Arthur Ripstein, Chapter 5 of this volume.

[46] See, e.g., Smothers v. Gresham Transfer, Inc., 23 P.2d 333, 348, 356 (Or. 1999); Hart & Sacks, *supra* note 41. Because remedies exist to enforce as well as to restore rights, the relation between right and remedy is more varied and complex than the corrective justice literature suggests. For example, tort actions often enforce property rights (as trespass, conversion, and nuisance do), yet those rights are also enforced by property doctrines (e.g., actions to quiet title and to evict) and by public law doctrines (e.g., applications of constitutional Takings clauses). Tort's own history includes actions which mixed public and private remedies. The action for "amercement" under medieval trespass included penalties payable to the state among its remedies. Even today, restitution is often matched with criminal punishment and, in our not very distant past, there was a burgeoning debate over whether and when tort actions should be preempted by or implied from regulatory statutes. See, e.g., Richard B. Stewart & Cass R. Sunstein, *Public Programs and Private Rights*, 95 HARV. L. REV. 1193 (1982). On amercement, see Calvin R. Massey, *The Excessive Fines Clause and Punitive Damages: Some Lessons From History*, 40 VAND. L. REV. 1233, 1251–1252 (1987). For a brief but acute explanation of the relation of all of this to the emergence of tort, see Grey, *supra* note 41, at 1230–1239.

remedies are reciprocal—and even though remedies are partially constitutive of rights—remedies are the servants of rights, not their masters. Thinking about the content and the contours of a remedy ought to begin by attempting to determine what the enforcement or the restoration of the right requires. In tort, the remedy fixed upon by corrective justice theorists—the duty to repair a loss—is preeminent because tort is preoccupied with physical harm.[47] Physical harms leave their victims with injuries to be repaired, if their right to the physical integrity of their persons is to be restored.

When the right violated is not one whose violation leaves the victim in an impaired condition the presumptively appropriate remedy is different. For example, when the underlying right is exclusive control or dominion over real property, and the violation is the denial of that control, injunctive relief is presumptively appropriate. Injunctive relief is routinely available in cases of recurring or ongoing trespass because injunctive relief vindicates the right of control.[48] Remedying harmless trespasses by requiring merely that the wrongdoer repair the harm that he has done would not vindicate the right. It would, indeed, enable those whose trespasses inflict no injury to do so as long as they were prepared to pay nominal damages.[49] In both trespass cases and wrongful physical injury cases, the remedy is governed by the right. The lesson of these examples is that remedies are prominent in tort, but they are prominent because rights are fundamental to tort and there is a unity of right and remedy. Remedies enforce rights and repair their violation.

Overemphasizing corrective justice distorts our understanding of torts in a second, subtler way. By mistakenly identifying tort and tort alone with responsibilities of repair, sovereign corrective justice theories misconceive tort law's relation to the rest of private law.[50] Rightly, remedial theories recognize that tort law enforces and restores rights in a particular way. It does so by enabling the victims of tortious wrongdoing to obtain redress for the wrongs done them from those who have done them wrong. This, however, is a distinctive feature of *private law in general*, not a distinctive feature of the law of torts in particular. Contract, property, and restitution also enforce rights by empowering those whose rights have been violated to seek redress from those who have done the violating. If a duty of *repair* is more characteristic of tort than it is of contract or restitution, that is because primary tort rights differ from primary contract, or restitutionary

[47] *Restatement (Second) of Torts* § 1 cmts. *b* and *d* (1965) describe the law of torts as treating the interest in "bodily security" as a "right" and protecting it in diverse ways: "the interest in bodily security is protected against not only intentional invasion but against negligent invasion or invasion by the mischances inseparable from an abnormally dangerous activity."

[48] "Generally an injunction will lie to restrain repeated trespasses. . . ." Planned Parenthood of Mid-Iowa v. Maki, 478 N.W.2d 637, 639 (Iowa 1991). See generally Dan B. Dobbs, *Law of Remedies* ch. 5 (2d ed. 1993) (noting, inter alia, that a plaintiff may be entitled to an injunction prohibiting a recurring trespass).

[49] The award of punitive damages in Jacque v. Steenberg Homes, Inc., 563 N.W.2d 154 (1997), enforces the right to exclusive control by stripping the one-shot, harmless trespass in that case of the economic advantage that rendered its commission by the defendant instrumentally rational.

[50] This criticism does not apply to Ernest Weinrib's view, which identifies private law in general with corrective justice.

rights, and those differences are reflected in the corresponding remedies. We lose sight of the fact that private law *in general* has a distinctive relation to rights when we identify responsibilities of repair, broadly conceived, with tort and tort alone. And we fail entirely to see that tort is distinguished from other private law subjects by the character of the primary rights and obligations it enforces.

Step back and consider the natural extension of the principle that wrongful losses ought to be repaired by those responsible for their infliction. That principle is *formal*: it does not contain within itself any criterion of wrongfulness. It latches onto many torts because we have independent reasons for thinking of torts as wrongs, and many tortious wrongs cause losses. We supply the content that the principle requires. Without that provision of content, the principle of corrective justice would wander the law looking for wrongful losses to repair. Furthermore, when we supply content we are likely to find wrongs requiring correction both within and beyond the private law of torts. Much depends on how broadly or narrowly the principle is stated. For example, when we interpret corrective justice as having to do with the repair of wrongful *loss*, restitution is not corrective justice because it undoes wrongful *gain*. On a broader interpretation of corrective justice the undoing of wrongful gain might be as much a matter of corrective justice as the repair of wrongful loss.[51]

Similar issues arise with respect to contract law. If contract is really about reliance—as Lon Fuller thought—then breach of contract results in wrongful loss and contract damages do corrective justice on a narrow interpretation of the principle. If, however, contract is about expectation damages then contract damages are about being put in the position that one would have occupied had the contract been performed.[52] That counts as corrective justice only if corrective justice is construed more broadly. When corrective justice is construed that broadly, however, it can no longer be presented as the paramount principle of liability in tort. It is now at least a principle of private law in general, and it may well be a general principle of law, full stop.

Just how broadly to state the principle of corrective justice is, fortunately, a problem we can leave to others. For our purposes, the point is that wrongful loss is not unique to tort and corrective justice is therefore not distinctive of tort. Wrongful loss crops up across the legal landscape.

Calling the repair of wrongful losses the "overarching ambition or purpose" of tort law[53] is a mistake. This theory of tort goes wrong in the way that retributivism goes wrong as a theory of criminal law. Just as we do not have the criminal law in order to

---

[51] Weinrib takes this broader view of the matter, because he thinks of correlativity of right and duty as the essence of corrective justice. See Weinrib, *supra* note 4, at 122–126. Restitution and contract damages both do corrective justice because they involve breaches of duty correlative to rights. *Id.* at 136–140, 140–141, 197–198. Similarly, on Gardner's or Honoré's views, restitution is an instance of corrective justice. See *supra* note 12.

[52] See Lon L. Fuller & William R. Perdue Jr., *The Reliance Interest in Contract Damages (pt. 1)*, 46 YALE L.J. 52 (1936); cf. Daniel Friedmann, *The Performance Interest in Contract Damages*, 111 L.Q. REV. 628 (1995).

[53] Jules Coleman, *Risks and Wrongs* 395 (2002).

punish the wicked, so too we do not have the law of torts in order to repair wrongful losses. Corrective justice is a secondary part of tort, not the heart of the subject. The wrongs that tort law recognizes and specifies are the heart of the subject. Tort obligations are discharged most fully when wrongs are not committed and harm is not done—when persons' sovereignty over their physical selves and their property is respected in the first instance, not when harm wrongly done is repaired after the fact. Given the choice between a law of torts which effects perfect compliance with its obligations of repair and one which effects perfect compliance with its primary responsibilities, there is no choice to be made. When the primary norms of the law of torts are perfectly complied with, there is no work left for its remedial norms to do.

The role of tort law's primary norms is to articulate certain obligations to others, obligations grounded in interests of persons urgent enough to count as rights and imposed irrespective of voluntary agreement or ownership of external objects. The wrongs that tort law recognizes spell out an important part of what we owe to each other in the way of coercively enforceable responsibilities. Those rights and responsibilities of respect have to do, for the most part, with liberty and security, broadly construed. Because tort law is fundamentally concerned with the question of what we may reasonably demand from each other as a matter of right with respect to our liberty and the security of our persons and property, tort is basically concerned with *justice*, but the justice that lies at the base of tort law is *not corrective*. Committing battery is wrong not because it fails to correct a prior wrongful interaction but because it violates a primary obligation of harm avoidance. That primary obligation is, in turn, grounded in the victim's right to the physical integrity of his or her person. Torts—fraud, battery, intentional infliction of emotional distress, negligent infliction of physical injury, and the like—are wrongs which presuppose rights. It is wrong to batter someone because it violates their right to physical integrity. It is wrong to defraud someone because it makes their mind the unwitting instrument of wrongdoer's will, undermining their right to be the master of their own life. It is wrong to imprison someone falsely because it violates their right to liberty. It is wrong to injure someone negligently because it violates their right to reasonable security. And so on.

The question of what rights people have is not a question of corrective justice. If anything, the question of what rights people have is a question of distributive justice.[54] Taxonomy aside, the substantive point is this: tort law is fundamentally about wrongs and wrongs are grounded in rights. Corrective justice broadly construed is *an essential aspect of tort* because legal rights generally require remedies and private law remedies

[54] Theorists are split on this point, but prominent usages of the term "distributive justice" include within its domain the question of what rights people have on the ground that this is one kind of question about the distribution of entitlements. See John Rawls, *A Theory of Justice* 54 (rev. ed. 1999) ("[T]he basic structure of society distributes certain primary goods . . . the chief primary goods *at the disposition of society* are rights, liberties, and opportunities, and income and wealth.") (emphasis added). For an example of distributive justice being used in this broader sense in connection with private law, see Peter Cane, *Corrective Justice and Correlativity in Private Law*, 16 Oxford J. Legal Stud. 471, 481 (1996).

requiring making right one's wrong.[55] But the core of tort consists of the primary rights and responsibilities that its remedial norms enforce.

Sovereign conceptions of corrective justice are thus fundamentally correct to emphasize what is now called the "continuity thesis."[56] Practical reason exhibits a fundamental unity. Duties of repair have their roots in the same normative material that primary rights and responsibilities do. The rights or duties or reasons that figure centrally in the justification and explanation of primary rights and responsibilities also figure centrally in the justification and explanation of remedial rights and responsibilities. Rights, as Jeremy Waldron has argued, "generate[] waves of duties."[57] The right to the physical integrity of one's person generates primary duties of harm avoidance, secondary duties of repair, powers of civil recourse, and duties on the part of all of us to support the institutions which enable these rights to be enforced and realized. Where sovereign corrective justice theory goes wrong is not in emphasizing the continuity of obligations of repair with primary wrongs but in putting the cart before the horse. The law of torts does require repair, but it enjoins repair of wrongs. Remedial responsibilities are parasitic on primary ones. Philosophically inclined theorists of tort need to turn their attention toward the field's primary norms, and the reasons and values that either succeed or fail in justifying them.

For their part, economic analysts of tort have been right to argue that obligations of repair are subordinate to the justification of the institution as a whole, but the relentlessly forward-looking theory they have offered can account for the backward-looking obligations of repair that tort law enforces only by claiming that tort is not at all what it seems to be. For economics, the way forward may be to follow in the footsteps of economic analyses of property, which now give the concept of property itself its due and deploy the concept of efficiency indirectly to justify the institution as whole.[58]

ACKNOWLEDGMENTS

I am grateful to participants in the conference for helpful comments and suggestions and to Joseph Harper and Taiyee Chien for excellent editorial and research assistance.

[55] As Tony Honoré says, *supra* note 12.
[56] For recent, illuminating discussion, see Sandy Steel, *Compensation and Continuity*, Oxford Legal Stud. Res. Paper (July 18, 2019), https://papers.ssrn.com/sol3/papers.cfm?abstract_id=3422418.
[57] Jeremy Waldron, *Rights in Conflict*, 99 ETHICS 503, 510 (1989).
[58] See, e.g., Thomas W. Merrill & Henry E. Smith, *What Happened to Property in Law and Economics?*, 111 YALE L.J. 357 (2001).

CHAPTER 4

··

CIVIL RECOURSE THEORY

··

BENJAMIN C. ZIPURSKY

I. INTRODUCTION

THE phrase "civil recourse theory" has, I believe, developed two connotations, suggesting: (1) a structural theory of the normative underpinnings of private law liability placing primary emphasis on a plaintiff's right of redress and the role of the state in affording plaintiffs the power to exact damages from those who have violated the plaintiff's legal rights; and (2) a distinctive, overarching tort theory that emphasizes a plaintiff's right of redress while simultaneously emphasizing relational duty in negligence law and torts as legal wrongs. Both are principally associated with myself[1] and Goldberg,[2] and both are recognized as simultaneously claiming distinctiveness from corrective justice theory, yet sharing so many of its features that corrective justice theorists[3] (as well as those who reject philosophical tort theory more generally) are inclined to dismiss the alleged differences. Conversely, some scholars—Andrew Gold[4] and Nathan Oman[5] most notably—have been sufficiently attracted to civil recourse theory (understood along the lines of (1)) that they have developed distinctive versions of it and suggested that it nicely illuminates the law of contracts.

---

[1] Benjamin C. Zipursky, *Rights, Wrongs, and Recourse in the Law of Torts*, 51 VAND. L. REV. 1 (1998) [hereinafter RWR]; Benjamin C. Zipursky, *Civil Recourse, Not Corrective Justice*, 91 GEO. L.J. 695 (2003) [hereinafter CRNCJ].

[2] John C.P. Goldberg, *The Constitutional Status of Tort Law: Due Process and the Right to a Law for the Redress of Wrongs*, 115 YALE L.J. 524 (2005).

[3] Ernest J. Weinrib, *Civil Recourse and Corrective Justice*, 39 FLA. ST. U. L. REV. 273 (2011).

[4] Andrew S. Gold, *The Taxonomy of Civil Recourse*, 39 FLA. ST. U. L. REV. 65 (2011); Andrew S. Gold, *A Moral Rights Theory of Private Law*, 52 WM. & MARY L. REV. 1873 (2011); Andrew S. Gold, *On Selling Civil Recourse*, 63 DEPAUL L. REV. 485 (2014).

[5] Nathan B. Oman, *Why There Is No Duty to Pay Damages: Powers, Duties, and Private Law*, 39 FLA. ST. U. L. REV. 137, 139 (2011); Nathan B. Oman, *The Honor of Private Law*, 80 FORDHAM L. REV. 31 (2011).

The inconsistency of connotation has led to confusion and to an inadequate grasp of both the theory more narrowly conceived and the overall Goldberg-Zipursky view of tort law. In this chapter, I aim to clarify the meaning I have intended for "civil recourse theory" and the scope of propositions I have intended it to cover—far closer to (1) than to (2). Doing so will allow for the identification of several other views that Goldberg and I have developed in connection with civil recourse theory but were meant to stand apart from it. The thesis that negligence law's duty of care is relational is among them;[6] so too is the thesis that tort law consists of specifications of legal wrongs, that these wrongs are defined in relatively strict manner, and that plaintiffs must have an injury to prevail on a tort claim.[7] It is entirely possible that someone who rejects civil recourse theory will want to adopt these or other propositions we affirm. Indeed, that is one of the reasons many are inclined to doubt the difference between civil recourse theory and corrective justice theory, for many of our substantive views about duties, rights, and wrongs are shared by corrective justice theorists.

A second reason for focusing on this task of clarification is that one of the most popular criticisms of civil recourse theory derives from an equivocation between these two meanings. John Gardner and others have complained that, while the notion of a right to recourse for legal wrongs may indeed be important, it is not distinctive to tort law and therefore not well suited to a theory of the distinctiveness of tort law.[8] We agree, but insofar as "civil recourse theory" has been used loosely to name the Goldberg-Zipursky view of *torts*, it goes far beyond the notion of a right to recourse and always has. Our account of the nature of wrongs within tort law is a critical component of our overall view, and it is one that complements civil recourse theory in the narrower sense, rather than being part of it.

A third reason flows quite naturally from the prior two. Civil recourse theory can be and has been utilized as a part of the theory of private law beyond torts, including in contract, equity, and constitutional torts, and I have elsewhere suggested there are aspects of the private/public distinction that civil recourse theory illuminates.[9]

Finally, Goldberg and I have not always been clear enough about the relation among descriptive, interpretive, normative, evaluative, and prescriptive aspects of our account, and the task of doing so is facilitated by clearly separating out the idea of civil recourse from various other aspects of our account of tort law. Deploying the narrower conception of civil recourse theory, this chapter defends the principle of civil recourse as a matter of political morality and depicts the place of private rights of action in the basic structure of a just liberal democracy.

---

[6] John C.P. Goldberg & Benjamin C. Zipursky, *The Moral of MacPherson*, 146 U. PA. L. REV. 1733 (1998).

[7] John C.P. Goldberg & Benjamin C. Zipursky, *Torts as Wrongs*, 88 TEX. L. REV. 917 (2010).

[8] John Gardner, *Torts and Other Wrongs*, 39 FLA. ST. U. L. REV. 43 (2011).

[9] Benjamin C. Zipursky, *Civil Recourse and the Plurality of Wrongs: Why Torts are Different*, 2014 NEW ZEALAND L. REV. 145; Benjamin C. Zipursky, "Philosophy of Private Law," in *The Oxford Handbook of Jurisprudence and Philosophy of Law* 623 (Jules Coleman & Scott Shapiro eds., 2002).

II. Civil Recourse and the Interpretive Critique of Corrective Justice Theory in Torts

Philosophical legal scholarship of the late twentieth century made several interventions in tort theory, but its structural critique was the most important of all. The significance of that critique is best understood alongside of the contrary ideas of the law and economics scholars whose contributions began in the 1960s and early 1970s. For Coase, Calabresi, and Posner, the phenomena to be explained in tort theory were various occasions of *liability for damages*. And from a normative point of view, the kind of legal scheme to be evaluated or proposed was a liability scheme. Tort law assigns costs to certain actors. The interpretive question was what is the rationale and set of goals behind the pattern of liability imposition; the normative challenge was to ascertain which pattern of liability imposition is best justified. To answer these questions, law and economics scholars developed theories of how rational actors respond to ex ante knowledge of a certain risk of liability imposition. This, in turn, required saying how the prospect of liability in one scenario rather than another would alter conduct.

Ernest Weinrib and Jules Coleman provided a formidable methodological critique of these scholars' work, insofar as it purported to be interpretive theory.[10] They contended that the phenomena to be explained were different. Tort law involves *duties owed by actors to members of a class of potential victims*. Of course, legal economists understood perfectly well that tort liability, in the first instance, involves injurers paying victims, and they offered interesting accounts of why this part of the legal system relies on this particular "enforcement mechanism." But on the issue of what the phenomena to be explained actually are, the economists simply missed the boat. Weinrib argued that defendants have duties of repair that run to plaintiffs; that tort liabilities are not mere sanctions but compensatory payments to injured plaintiffs. Moreover, correlative to the defendant's duty of repair is the plaintiff's right to be paid.

In comparison to law and economics, corrective justice theory more accurately characterized the phenomena to be explained, and then actually provided a more successful explanation. It deems the foundation of the law of torts to be the state's commitment to enforcing a set of rights and duties as between private parties, such that violations of right entail that defendants have duties to rectify the rights violations—duties that run to plaintiffs in particular. In seeing to it that such rights and duties are institutionally realized through law, tort law is enabling corrective justice to be done.

Civil recourse theory emerged from a critique of corrective justice theory that was analogous to the corrective-justice critique of law and economic theories. Though closer to the mark than the economists, corrective justice theorists had the phenomena

---

[10] Ernest J. Weinrib, *The Idea of Private Law* (1994); Jules L. Coleman, *Risks and Wrongs* (1992).

wrong, too. They were right to point out that there is a relationality wired into the structure of tort law—defendants' are required to pay plaintiffs, not simply to pay. But they were wrong to characterize tort law as enforcing defendants' duties of repair to plaintiffs.[11] On this, the economic theorists were closer to the mark. Tort law involves, at a structural level, defendant liabilities to plaintiffs; it does not *enforce* legal duties of repair but generates them. Moreover, what is correlative to a defendant's duty of repair is not a plaintiff's claim right to be paid but a plaintiff's legal power to demand payment (one that emerges without dependence on a claim right to be paid). Insofar as a plaintiff (post-tort) has a claim right that is correlative to a duty, it is a claim right against the state to provide a legal power against the defendant tortfeasor. The principle of civil recourse states that those who have been wronged are entitled to some avenue of civil recourse against the wrongdoer. The central interpretive contention of civil recourse theory, in torts, is that the state's provision of private rights of action in tort through the common law is best understood as a commitment to the principle of civil recourse.

Several kinds of arguments support (and were used to defend) the critique of corrective justice theory sketched in the prior paragraph.

A. Misclassification

Let us stipulate that D has acted in such a manner, and with such results for P, that in the relevant jurisdiction P would be entitled to prevail in a tort claim against D were she to choose to bring one. A corrective justice theorist would assert that D, having so acted and with such results, owes a secondary legal duty to P. The starkest claim supporting civil recourse theory is that it is a legal mistake to characterize D's commission of the tort as giving rise to such a duty. The correct analysis is that the commission of the tort gives rise to a liability to P, but the liability does not do so via an intermediating legal duty of repair.[12] To the contrary, the legal duty of the defendant, in tort, only arises when a court enters judgment. The liability is the vulnerability to being successfully sued and being subject to a judgment, *should such a claim be brought*. For the past decade or so (and in a forthcoming book), Stephen Smith has defended this analytic claim in detailed and rigorous work spanning private law.[13]

Let us call the foregoing "the misclassification thesis." Three kinds of arguments have been used to support it: (a) formal, (b) contrastive, and (c) internalist. (a) The formal argument is principally that legal duties are systematically connected with certain features—either a duty-imposing legal rule or an authoritative injunctive order in a binding legal document or an authoritative injunctive order from a legal official—and that none of these springs from the commission of a tort as such.

---

[11] Zipursky, RWR, *supra* note 1, at 80.   [12] Zipursky, CRNCJ, *supra* note 1.
[13] Stephen A. Smith, *Duties, Liability, and Damages*, 125 HARV. L. REV. 1727, 1727–1728 (2012); Stephen A. Smith, *Why Courts Make Orders (And What This Tells Us About Damages)*, 64 CURRENT LEGAL PROBS. 51, 82–83 (2011); Stephen A. Smith, *Rights, Wrongs, and Injustices: The Structure of Remedial Law* (2020).

(b) A second argument in favor of the misclassification thesis is that an alleged tort-feasor's position can be contrasted sharply with the position of certain other kinds of legal actors who do in fact have duties to pay certain other legal actors, and not just liabilities. Consider a buyer under a contract who has had delivered (by a seller) the goods under a contract according to which the buyer has a duty of payment. The failure to pay for the goods that have been delivered leaves the buyer with a duty to pay the seller. If the seller sues the buyer for the money due under the contract, the reason for liability is, quite plausibly, that there is a duty to pay the money that is owed. The duty comes from the contract and the fact that the delivery of goods by the seller triggers a duty to pay. Similarly, a government agency that provides benefits to those who satisfy certain conditions (e.g., Social Security, Disability) has a duty to provide such benefits to those who qualify because the law requires that such payments be made. To be sure, beneficiaries typically are required to prove that they are among those to whom a duty of payment is required. But the duty stems from the statutory or regulatory qualifications, and it is not a liability. In the tort case, by contrast, the legal claim is not predicated on a preexisting but unfulfilled legal duty, but on the injury or invasion brought about through the tort-feasor's tort. The liability stems from the wrongful conduct and ensuing injury.

(c) What I am calling here an "internalist" argument might be called "phenomeno-logical" or "Hartian." Its basic idea is that the experience of needing to pay because one has committed a tort is understood differently (than failure to perform a contract one has breached) by a fully socialized and prototypical member of the legal community, including by a Hartian actor who takes the internal point of view on the law. Let's call this figure "the internalist." I have argued elsewhere that the internalist understands herself or himself to have a legal duty to pay in the contract example, when goods have been delivered, and if he fails to do so and breaches, he continues to have a legal duty to pay. Moreover, such a person would regard herself as having a duty to pay before being sued; indeed (as suggested previously), it would be normal to understand the contractual liability for the debt as in fact stemming from the prior legal duty to pay it. Like Hart, I do not regard the internalist as a bizarre goody-goody, but as a willing participant in the system—for example, a largely successful businessperson who wishes to be known for conventionality and law-abidingness in the commerce of society, broadly speaking.

The internalist takes an importantly different attitude toward tort liability. She does not typically make a point of voluntarily—without litigation or a threat of litigation—paying others the amount she would be required to pay were they successfully to sue. She does not regard herself as have a duty of payment that matches what tort liability would be, which springs from having committed a tort. She may indeed be cooperative in the sense of trying to settle lawsuits against her that are meritorious by paying reasonable compensation. When such cooperation occurs early and in a reasonable form, it is rarely for what the full amount of compensation would be and without a written release of liability. In either case, judgment (or settlement) is prior to legal duty.

Defenders of a pre-litigation legal duty of repair, as against this objection, have replied that the failure of proactive payment simply reflects the indeterminacy of the damages prior to litigation or a claim being brought. But if the internalist believed there was a duty but its content needed specification, she would often be proactive in seeking information so that she could carry out the duty. Rarely do we find such proactive inquiry by tortfeasors, or those who might be aware or become aware that they have committed a tort.

The internalist point, while subtle, comes into clearer focus when we recognize that the law contains other examples of liabilities that do not stem from duties—criminal law is a clear example. One does not have a legal duty to offer up self-incarceration at the appropriate level, even if one might have a duty to be cooperative with a legal system undertaking a prosecution, and even if one sometimes might have a duty to turn oneself into authorities. Prior to a conviction and an entry of judgment, one does not have a duty to serve time. It is a liability, not a duty.

B. Standing

On the most intuitively appealing forms of corrective justice theory, the tortfeasor's secondary duty to the victim is a duty of repair. Jules Coleman and Stephen Perry, in the 1990s, advanced corrective justice theories according to which tort law understood a plaintiff's loss as the responsibility of the defendant who wrongfully caused it, and the duty of repair flowed from this relationship of responsibility.[14] If the foregoing account is correct, then a plaintiff should be able to recover compensation for an injury from the one who caused it by tortious wrongdoing, so long as there is a proper causal connection between the injury and the wrongdoing. And, it seems, what should determine whether the plaintiff's injury is properly connected is a matter of the connective glue of negligence law—foreseeability, because responsibility turns on foreseeability.

Plaintiff standing does not work this way in tort law. Not all foreseeable victims of the wrong are properly situated. It is critical that the wrong committed by the defendant was a wrong relative to the plaintiff. I have called this a "substantive standing" rule, and students of American negligence law know that it lies at the heart of Cardozo's *Palsgraf* opinion. Although *Palsgraf* is less clear than it might have been (because both substantive standing *and* foreseeability were missing, on the facts of the case), liability is denied in negligence cases even where there is foreseeability, if no breach of a duty to the plaintiff is established. Indeed, a version of the same point can be found in every tort.[15] Where courts must choose between *having been wronged by defendant* and *having been foreseeably injured by defendant through conduct that was wrongful, but not wrongful relative to the plaintiff*, courts choose the former. That is powerful evidence that the right to bring a right of action stems from having been wronged, and does not do so via the intermediary of a duty of repair.[16]

---

[14] Coleman, supra note 10; Stephen R. Perry, *The Moral Foundations of Tort Law*, 77 Iowa L. Rev. 427 (1992).

[15] Palsgraf v. Long Island R.R. Co., 162 N.E. 99 (N.Y. 1928).

[16] It should be said that some important forms of corrective justice theory—Weinrib's and Ripstein's—are indeed capable of accommodating substantive standing, and certainly agree with the characterization of the doctrine.

C. Remedies

Tort law contains a variety of remedies and, indeed, separates the issue of whether a plaintiff has a right of action at all from the issue of what remedy ought to be supplied if she does. Apart from damages, there is injunctive relief and declaratory relief. And within damages, compensatory damages are only one kind: restitution, punitive damages, and nominal damages are possible. Even within compensatory damages, it is far from clear that pecuniary and nonpecuniary compensatory damages really work the same way.[17]

Corrective justice theory fails to capture the breadth of remedies and the underlying separateness of remedies and rights of action. Those versions that are loss-based (for example, Coleman's) are especially vulnerable to this criticism, as the very idea of liability stems from there being responsibility for the loss in question. But even wrongs-based accounts, such as Weinrib's, present difficulties, because the notion of rectification is central and there is an insistence on the continuity between the primary right of the plaintiff and the right to a remedy. Restitution remedies and punitive damages, for example, indicate that the law sometimes abandons the requirement of a match between the loss suffered and the remedy required. Civil recourse theory is more supple; it recognizes that courts treat make-whole as a default rule of remedies,[18] but also permit a plaintiff who can prove willfulness or wantonness or intentional wrongdoing a degree and kind of redress that is typically unavailable.[19]

III. *Ubi Jus* and the Conduct-Rule Theory of Rights

The maxim *ubi jus, ibi remedium*—where there is a right, there is a remedy—fits nicely with civil recourse theory. Recognizing its fit with civil recourse theory may appear to be a curse, but it is in fact a blessing. It might appear to be a curse because of a worry about circularity: in torts, one might think, for there to be a right is simply for there to be a remedy. Yet this putative problem actually forces one to provide a nonvacuous model of what a legal rights invasion is, and then an account of what a remedy or a right of action is, and then an account of why a rights invasion generates a remedy. And this turns out to be the core of civil recourse theory.

---

[17] See, e.g., Benjamin C. Zipursky, *Substantive Standing, Civil Recourse, and Corrective Justice*, 39 FLA. ST. UNIV. L. REV. 299, 319–320 (2011).

[18] See John C.P. Goldberg, *Two Conceptions of Tort Damages: Fair v. Full Compensation*, 55 DEPAUL L. REV. 435 (2006).

[19] Benjamin C. Zipursky, *A Theory of Punitive Damages*, 84 TEX. L. REV. 105 (2005); Benjamin C. Zipursky, *Palsgraf, Punitive Damages, and Preemption*, 125 HARV. L. REV. 1757 (2012).

In my introduction of civil recourse theory in 1998, I identified a parallel problem and provided an analytical apparatus to solve it.[20] The problem was to explain what I called the "substantive standing rule": a person does not have a common law tort claim against a putative tortfeasor unless she proves that she herself was wronged (under the tort in question) by that tortfeasor. I argued that this was equivalent to the principle that a person does not have a right of action in tort against someone who committed tort T, unless her right to be free of tort T was violated by that tortfeasor. This remains so (as a doctrinal matter), I argued, even if the person in question was injured by the person who committed tort T and even if that injury was foreseeable. The principle is that where there is no right, there is no remedy. This is the converse to the *ubi jus* principle. It is problematic for a similar reason: if, analytically or definitionally, part of what it is for there to be a right is that it provides the basis for a right of action, then it is vacuous to say that there is no basis for a right of action where there is no right.

The solution was to provide a conception of the notion of right that is independent of the notion of a right of action. I claimed that for c to have a legal right against b that b not do A to c is:

(1) for there to exist a relational legal directive of the form "For all x, and for all y, if x is a member of set S1 and y is a member of S2, then x shall not do A to y", and

(2) for b to be a member of S1 and c to be a member of S2.

This is also what it means for a b to have a duty to c not to A c.

In that initial article, and to a greater extent in subsequent co-authored articles with John Goldberg, I set forth what it means for there to exist a relational legal directive of the form just described analytically.[21] Principally, it is for there to exist a norm of conduct and guidance rule that is picked out by the secondary rules (rules of recognition and related rules) of the relevant legal community. Such legal norms have the force of enjoining persons not to mistreat other persons in certain ways, or to treat them in certain ways. If there is such a directive and b does mistreat c in that manner, then b has wronged c and committed a tort against c.

Goldberg and I have, both individually and jointly, continued to argue in several articles and two books that such relational legal directives exist in American jurisdictions and more generally in common law jurisdictions, and we have provided arguments that the claim for their existence does not, intrinsically, presuppose the existence of rights of action in tort.[22] If those arguments are sound, then there exist such legal rights—rights not to be tortiously mistreated by being battered, assaulted, negligently injured, defrauded, libeled, slandered, falsely imprisoned, and so on. Relatedly, battering, assaulting, negligently injuring, and so forth are legal wrongs or torts.

---

[20] Zipursky, RWR, *supra* note 1.

[21] John C.P. Goldberg & Benjamin C. Zipursky, *Seeing Tort Law from the Internal Point of View: Holmes and Hart on Legal Duties*, 75 FORDHAM L. REV. 1563 (2006).

[22] See especially John C.P. Goldberg & Benjamin C. Zipursky, *Recognizing Wrongs* (2020); see also John C.P. Goldberg & Benjamin C. Zipursky, *The Oxford Introductions to U.S. Law: Torts* (2010).

Recall that the project of setting forth such an argument is rooted in the view that it is not vacuous to say that where there is a right, there is a right of action. Indeed, it is part of civil recourse theory to identify in our legal system a substantive commitment by the state to the maxim that where there has been a rights invasion, there shall be a right of action. As mentioned, the converse of the principle is that where a plaintiff claims a right of action despite failing to establish a rights invasion, she is *not* entitled to the state's assistance in demanding redress from another.

The principle of civil recourse states that a person who has suffered a rights invasion is entitled to an avenue of civil recourse against the one who invaded her right. The state's commitment to the maxim that there shall be a right of action against one who invaded one's right constitutes the practical form of its commitment to the principle of civil recourse.

The focus on the principle of civil recourse as a substantive principle of political morality has in the aforementioned ways led to a reconceptualization of the structure of rights and duties within the common law of torts. Two other benefits flow from recognizing the central role of the principle of civil recourse in the law of torts. As John Goldberg has demonstrated most forcefully, the idea of civil recourse—like the maxim *ubi jus*—is deeply entrenched in the common law tradition.[23] While corrective justice theorists may point to Aristotle and to Kant, civil recourse theorists point to Hale, Locke, Blackstone, and the framers of the U.S. Constitution. The idea of an entitlement to access to courts to redress a private wrong is front and center in Book 3 of Blackstone's Commentaries, fittingly titled "Private Wrongs." The point is not, of course, to rely upon the moral authority of these figures; the point is rather to emphasize a remarkably strong historical foundation in English and American legal history for the contention that the common law of torts relies upon a substantive conception of the political right to redress wrongs.

Finally, numerous scholars of other fields have come to recognize that the right to a remedy for a wrong characterizes fields beyond the law of torts. We see this as only an advantage. Nate Oman and Andrew Gold,[24] among others, have argued that contract law generates a right to recourse for the wrong of breach of contract. More particularly, they have contended that the principle of civil recourse provides a clearer elucidation of contract doctrine than corrective justice theory. Michael Wells has described the illumination that civil recourse brings to 1983 actions and *Bivens* claims.[25] In numerous places, John Goldberg and I have developed and defended the notion of an implied right of action in civil rights law[26] and in the law of securities fraud.[27] None of this is to say that a

---

[23] See Goldberg, *supra* note 2.

[24] See, e.g., Gold, *A Moral Rights Theory of Private Law*, *supra* note 4; Gold, *The Taxonomy of Civil Recourse*, *supra* note 4.

[25] Michael Wells, *Civil Recourse, Damages-As-Redress, and Constitutional Torts*, 46 GA. L. REV. 1003 (2012).

[26] See, e.g., Goldberg & Zipursky, *Recognizing Wrongs*, *supra* note 21, chs. 1, 3, 4.

[27] John C.P. Goldberg & Benjamin C. Zipursky, *The Fraud-on-the-Market Tort*, 66 VAND. L. REV. 1755 (2013); John C.P. Goldberg, Anthony J. Sebok, & Benjamin C. Zipursky, *The Place of Reliance in Fraud*, 48 ARIZ. L. REV. 1001 (2006).

right of access to courts is the same in all of these areas or that all of these areas involve wrongs in the same sense. To the contrary, civil recourse theory sheds light on both the similarities and the differences among these areas of law.

IV. Wrongs, Positivity, and Normative Guidance

Perhaps unsurprisingly, the founders of law and economics have given civil recourse theory the back of the hand. Posner deems the theory to be a form moral intuitionism;[28] Calabresi says it is circular.[29] These comments stem from the same mistake. Civil recourse theory provides part of an interpretive and positive theory of tort law, in the first instance; it is not a theory that invites morally insightful judges to make tort law what it ought to be. Its implications will be most relevant to judges who take it to be their job to apply the law that is there, in the first instance.

Here is a much gentler critical observation along similar lines: *judges, students, and scholars can only go so far with the insights of civil recourse theory without an account of what the wrongs of tort law are, and civil recourse theory itself does not supply such an account. Moreover, any such account will itself face challenges and areas of incompleteness. It is part of what one would hope tort theorists would do to supply theoretical guidance on what holds the set of wrongs in tort law together, and how they should be expanded or reduced, revised or rejected, explained and critiqued. Civil recourse theory does not do this.*

The short answer is that it is not a shortcoming of a theory that it explains only what it sets out to explain, if what it sets out to explain is substantial and important. The longer point, however, is that those who have principally advanced civil recourse theory in torts—myself and John Goldberg—have indeed said a great deal about what the wrongs of tort law are, and how to think about them in contexts where guidance is needed. While some of this work does fall within the fold of civil recourse theory as such, much of it does not. A theorist explaining why there are tort claims at all should not, qua defender of such a theory, be required to set out what should and should not or does and does not count as a tort. And if she or he does so offer such explanations, it is enough that they do not clash with the theory of liability. To suppose otherwise is to ignore the fact that a basic move in the design of civil recourse theory is to separate the existence of legal wrongs and rights from the availability of rights of action and liability for their commission, and a basic argument provided for civil recourse theory is the coherence of a such a separation.

Our account of the wrongs of tort law is usefully divided into three parts: structural, doctrinal, and jurisprudential. As section III indicated, at least one aspect of our theory

---

[28] Richard A. Posner, *Instrumental and Noninstrumental Theories of Tort Law*, 88 Ind. L.J. 469, 473 (2013).

[29] Guido Calabresi, *Civil Recourse Theory's Reductionism*, 88 Ind. L.J. 449, 452 (2013).

of legal wrongs is not independent of civil recourse theory. Civil recourse theory presupposes a conduct-based theory of legal rights that analyzes their existence through the notion of relational legal directives. Violations of those legal directives are wrongs, the wrongs of tort law. Hence, *relationality* is one of the structural features of those legal wrongs that counts as torts. This is, of course, what Chief Judge Cardozo was saying about the tort of negligence; negligence in the air (rather than to anyone) is not a possibility.

Another feature of our account of wrongs, also indicated previously, is that torts are *legal* wrongs. This means that there are grounds in a legal system for deeming them to be wrongs or proscribed conduct. It does not mean that moral standards may not be used to identify or classify the conduct as wrongs: it means only that if they are so used, they are used because a legal standard demands the incorporation of the moral standard. Whether right or wrong, the New York Court of Appeals' 1902 decision in *Roberson v. Rochester Folding Box Co.*[30] that invasion of privacy was not a tort was predicated on its view that the legal sources of New York law, properly understood, did not include or generate such a wrong.

A third feature of our account is that torts are *injury-inclusive* wrongs. A tort has not been committed unless some person or legal person has endured an injury. The injury need not be harm as such; it could be a rights invasion. Torts must be, as John Goldberg and I have called them, "realized" wrongs and cannot be "unrealized" wrongs.[31] Unlike crimes, torts cannot be inchoate. Carelessly driving toward someone is not a tort, unless it injures them (although creating a risky environment or scaring someone could, for various reasons). Moreover, it is not enough that the wrong be realized in some way: a person who promises to provide a gift to another, and then fails to fulfill the promise, has not committed a tort because what is realized is in no sense a harm, rights invasion, setback, or untoward interference with interest. Exposure-only toxic tort claims, when rejected (which is usually) are rejected on this ground.

Finally, the wrongs of tort law are what might be called "agency-engaging." The easiest way to see this point is through analysis of the nature of the legal directives whose violation counts as a wrong. A legal directive is agency-engaging if its injunction, when normally understood, directs a course of conduct that an actor could intend to perform or undertake to perform. A kind of wrong is agency-engaging if the legal directive that generates it is agency-engaging. The legal directive "Do not bring about harm" is not agency-engaging in the requisite sense.

All four of these structural attributes of tort law go along with civil recourse theory, but do not presuppose it and are not part of it, strictly speaking. Torts are relational because otherwise there would not be an affront to the plaintiff, and an affront to the plaintiff is part of why there is an avenue of civil recourse. Similarly, a plaintiff does not sue as a private attorney general, in the law of torts. She has standing to bring a claim because it is she who was wrongfully injured. Vulnerability to another private party's

---

[30] Roberson v. Rochester Folding Box Co., 64 N.E. 442 (N.Y. 1902).
[31] John C.P. Goldberg & Benjamin C. Zipursky, *Unrealized Torts*, 88 VA. L. REV. 1625 (2002).

decision to bring a claim for damages is significant. It only exists when the plaintiff can prove she really was injured. The defendant end of tort law has corresponding features. A defendant's vulnerability hinges on whether the defendant (or someone for whose conduct the defendant is responsible) violated a legal norm of conduct, not whether social mores or divine injunctions were contravened. Moreover, tort law speaks to how one is or is not expected to conduct or oneself or act. That is why tort directives are agency-engaging.

Civil recourse theory thus supplies structural constraints on what can count as a tort. Nonetheless, these constraints leave plenty of room for variations in substantive tort law. The largest part of our tort scholarship that is not civil recourse theory is the actual explanation and legal analysis of the content of the wrongs as fleshed out in tort doctrine. It is not part of civil recourse theory to show how the standard of care in negligence law works, what sorts of duties lawyers and physicians owe to persons who are not their clients or patients, how intent plays into the tort of battery, or how to understand different forms of strict liability. However, when civil recourse theory, as an account of why there are private rights of action at all, is combined with a systematic account of the nature of legal wrongs and an actual doctrinal account of tort law, the resulting combination defeats Posner's gibe that we have nothing to say about what counts as a tort except that we know it when we see it.

Most importantly, Goldberg and I have combined with all of the foregoing a jurisprudential account—both interpretive and normative—of the character of common law legal reasoning regarding what counts as a legal wrong. Since our first co-authored article, *The Moral of* MacPherson, we have recognized that one can conjoin civil recourse theory (narrowly conceived) with a non-instrumentalist but constructive judicial methodology for articulating, criticizing, and revising legal wrongs.[32] Similarly, one can identify both in legal scholarship and in judicial reasoning a strain that is at once pragmatic and conceptualistic.[33]

Tort law—elaborated and applied through a constructivist methodology—has at least two kinds of virtues. It provides a guidance function with regard to how natural and artificial persons how must treat others and also how they may expect to be treated. In a moment of pluralistic weakness of will, we once referred to the first conjunct as "internal deterrence."[34] The larger point—elaborated in Goldberg's "Torts" chapter in this *Handbook*[35]—is that tort law, developed by a constructivist methodology and applied through private rights of action, sustains and generates conceptions of duty and responsibility that exist in social practices, commonly taught social mores, and institutions.

The first guidance function is problematically labeled a "virtue" without the second virtue, for the second is importantly political. The nature of the methodology of common law adjudication and its (largely subordinate) connection to the legislative process

[32] Goldberg & Zipursky, *The Moral of MacPherson, supra* note 6.
[33] Benjamin C. Zipursky, *Pragmatic Conceptualism*, 6 LEGAL THEORY 457 (2000).
[34] John C.P. Goldberg & Benjamin C. Zipursky, *Accidents of the Great Society*, 4 MD. L. REV. 1463 (2005).
[35] John C.P. Goldberg[link], this volume.

generate and comprise a set of rule-of-law virtues that are special to private law. Legitimacy is provided by stare decisis, the conventionalistic basis of the resources for interpreting the law, and the constraints that standing rules and legislative superiority place on common law appellate courts. If there is "moralizing" in the common law of torts—and to some extent there is—it is structured and bounded in a manner that permits it to retain the virtues of law while nonetheless sustaining norms of mutual care.[36]

V. Equality, Liberty, and Civil Recourse

The content of section IV perhaps seems inappropriate in light of the avowed goal of this chapter to separate civil recourse theory as such from Goldberg-Zipursky tort theory more broadly. It is all about the part of our tort theory that is not really civil recourse theory as such. The reason, however, is that doing so will help us to focus upon what has probably been the most pervasive complaint about civil recourse theory and its most pressing challenge. Scholars ranging from John Finnis to Arthur Ripstein, John Oberdiek, and Andrew Gold have pressed us to go beyond the interpretive or positive. They want us to say not only what principles are entrenched within our system of tort law but why those principles merit allegiance and stand as normatively defensible. That is what this section and the next do, condensing prior work and our recent monograph, *Recognizing Wrongs*. We have argued here and elsewhere that among the reasons to regard tort law as normatively justifiable are many—such as those laid out in section IV—that relate to the theory of torts as legal wrongs. We stand by those claims, but emphasize in what follows that there are grounds for deeming tort law justifiable that relate to civil recourse more narrowly conceived.

It is useful to begin by noting that the principle of civil recourse was introduced as a justification for an institutional structure in which those who are wrongfully injured by another (under the law) are provided with a right of action against the other for damages. What needs to be justified, in significant part, is the vulnerability of certain persons to the power of others to demand compensation or other remedies. The power and the correlative vulnerability only exist by virtue of the state's willingness to empower individuals who succeed in proving that the right sort of relational directive was violated as to them. The principle of civil recourse deems such persons to be entitled to the state's provision of a legal power. A justification of the principle of civil recourse will, in turn, require an explanation of why persons so situated are entitled to this private power.

---

[36] Benjamin C. Zipursky, "Torts and the Rule of Law," in *Private Law and the Rule of Law* (L. Austin & D. Klimchuk eds., 2014); Benjamin C. Zipursky, *The Inner Morality of Private Law*, 8 Am. J. Juris. 27 (2013).

Like Gregory Keating's theoretical view,[37] but in a manifestly different way, our account is in broad outline contractarian. The legitimacy of empowerment and correlative liability is best understood in terms of two alternatives: *no accountability or answerability at all* for those who violate the relevant relational directives, or *accountability but not within the control of the victim*. The contractarian argument for the principle of civil recourse stems from the claim that neither of these alternatives is acceptable in a liberal democracy like ours.

No accountability at all renders each of us too vulnerable to the actions of others. It undermines the status of the protection of the state as a right. If others face no accountability for mistreating me, I do not in fact have protection and arguably I do not have a legal right. Leaving aside whether I have a right at all, there plainly are reasons for not agreeing to a set of duties not to mistreat others without also insisting on a right to enforce the same norms against others who mistreat me. Problems of equality, insecurity, and lack of autonomy are profound. This is the core of Locke's argument in the *Second Treatise*.

It is plain to see that the foregoing argument does not actually entail the necessity or legitimacy or value of private rights of action. Criminal law, regulation, top-down enforcement, or enforcement by a variety of different parties other than oneself present the possibility of accountability and deterrence and a set of genuine legal rights. Yet, for two different sorts of reasons—each quite broad and deep—individuals in a liberal democratic state such as ours would reasonably reject this option. The first relates to equality, and the second to liberty. Both relate to distrust of the government and of centralization of power.

A central problem with the pure public law option is that individuals' protection of their rights against others would be entirely dependent on state discretion, were this the law. It would always be the state's choice whether to pursue the wrongdoer who injured them, the state's choice whether to demand that the wrongdoer provide compensation, and the state's choice how much to demand. Such dependency on the state—in the real world or in any set of circumstances remotely like our own—would render individual protection extraordinarily vulnerable to the influence of the rich, powerful, and well connected, as against the poor, powerless, and unconnected. Courts may be obligated under the law to follow rules and principles in ascertaining who is the winner in litigation battles between individuals or between individuals and the state. But where only the state has the legal power to bring an action, the state is empowered to decide whether it is worthwhile to do so. The right to be provided with a private right of action against a wrongdoer gives this discretion to the person whose right was allegedly invaded.

---

[37] Gregory C. Keating, "A Social Contract Conception of the Tort Law of Accidents," in *Philosophy and the Law of Torts* (G. Postema ed., 2001). Keating's body of Rawlsian-influenced tort theory is at this stage quite broad and deep. See, e.g., Gregory C. Keating, *Reasonableness and Rationality in Negligence Theory*, 48 STAN. L. REV. 311 (1996); Gregory C. Keating, *Rawlsian Fairness and Regime Choice in the Law of Accidents*, 72 FORDHAM L. REV. 1857 (2004); Gregory C. Keating, "Strict Liability Wrongs," in *Philosophical Foundations of the Law of Torts* (J. Oberdiek ed., 2014).

Potential wrongdoers know the difference, and the difference is an equalizing force. The entitlement to a power to hold others responsible to oneself is in this way a matter of equality.[38]

A second reason for rejecting the pure public option complements the first, in the sense that it pertains to the possibility each of us must confront (in a social contract framework) that we might be the putative wrongdoer. A world of the pure public option is one in which all of our legal duties generate a legal vulnerability to prosecution or enforcement by the state. An extreme version of this is one in which all of the things that are today possible grounds of tort liability would be possible grounds of criminal liability. Such a pervasive vulnerability is inconsistent with the liberty we rightly demand in a liberal democracy. This liberty would be imperiled by any form of regulatory power that was similarly all-encompassing.

The foregoing discussion can be removed, if one wants, from the social contract framework and stated more plainly. Having enforceable legal rights and relational legal duties is critical to the protection of our security and dignity.[39] The principle of civil recourse flows from the recognition that equality precludes the state's keeping the power of enforcement all to itself, and demands that individuals be empowered to enforce their own rights. Decentralization of enforcement power also sounds in a post-Enlightenment recognition that too much power creates a world of peril inconsistent with our civil society.

VI. Justice and Civil Recourse

In an important paper, Andrew Gold criticizes civil recourse theory as developed by myself and Goldberg:

> For civil recourse theorists, it is…problematic to reject a conceptual link between civil recourse and justice. The civil recourse theorist may recognize that justice is sometimes achieved by private law remedies or that a perceived correlation between private law and justice is beneficial. He or she may conclude that these features are socially desirable. The problem, however, is conceptual: from the legal perspective,

---

[38] Jason Solomon has played a substantial role in explaining the centrality of equality to the normative defensibility of the principle of civil recourse. Jason M. Solomon, *Civil Recourse as Social Equality*, 39 FLA. ST. U. L. REV. 243, 267 (2011); Jason M. Solomon, *Equal Accountability Through Tort Law*, 103 NW. U. L. REV. 1765, 1813–1814 (2009).

[39] Both Scott Hershovitz and Anthony Sebok have emphasized equality and dignity as values central to tort law, and both have stayed cautiously around the edges of civil recourse theory—Hershovitz by endorsing expressivism and pushing corrective justice theory in the direction of plaintiff empowerment, Scott Hershovitz, *Treating Wrongs as Wrongs: An Expressive Argument for Tort Law*, 10 J. TORT L. 1 (2017), and Sebok by restricting his recourse-oriented work to punitive damages, Anthony J. Sebok, *Punitive Damages: from Myth to Theory*, 92 IOWA L. REV. 957 (2007).

a properly functioning private law remedy brings about a form of justice between the parties to a dispute.[40]

Gold offers what he understandably regards as a friendly elaboration,[41] and a very deep one at that. The mistake of corrective justice theory, as he sees it, is its too-narrow focus on *justice being done by the defendant's performance of reparative duties*. Much of tort law involves, instead, *justice being done by the plaintiff's redressing an injustice done to him or her*. If the first is called "corrective justice," the second could be called "redressive justice." The insights of civil recourse theory help to understand private law at many levels, he argues. One of the most important is that by focusing on a defendant's liability and a plaintiff's right to redress a wrong, we have brought to light the importance of redressive justice. He therefore suggests that Goldberg and I can have our cake and eat it too. We can recognize the importance of the right to civil recourse and also the normative significance of the state's playing a role in doing justice by permitting redress of wrongs to happen through its court system.

There may be good reasons to accept Gold's suggestions about the existence and value of redressive justice, but finding *some* way to connect civil recourse with justice is not one of them (nor does Gold mean to suggest that it is). Our view, laid out in greater detail in *Recognizing Wrongs*, is that civil recourse theory plays an important part in understanding the preconditions for a just liberal democracy. As Samuel Scheffler argued in his 2014 Hart lecture and as Arthur Ripstein has made clear in both of his books in tort theory,[42] it is implausible that a theory of the basic structure of a just society would have nothing to say about private law.

As argued in section V, states, in supplying private rights of action to enforce relational duties and protect rights, play a role in constructing and securing a form of equality and in shielding a domain of liberty from the state. It is not an exaggeration to say that recourse to the courts as a source of empowerment—both against the government and against private parties—is part of the structure of our constitutional democracy. What civil recourse theory suggests goes beyond this. It suggests that nonviolent, civilly mediated power against others affects our relations with others both prior to wrongful injury and posterior to it. Indeed, there is great importance to the state's being there not only as purveyor of norms of conduct but also as an entity that empowers victims of rights violation. This is fundamental in the structure of interaction between persons and in how they stand as against one another and as against the state. In these respects, it is plausible to suggest that having an avenue of civil recourse is part of the basic structure of a just society. Private power to enforce rights—if part of the basic structure—cuts across many areas of private law.

---

[40] Andrew S. Gold, *A Theory of Redressive Justice*, 54 U. TORONTO L. REV. 159, 183 (2014).

[41] *Id.* at 204.

[42] Arthur Ripstein, *Private Wrongs* (2016); Arthur Ripstein, *Equality, Responsibility and the Law* (1998).

....

CHAPTER 5

KANTIAN PERSPECTIVES
ON PRIVATE LAW

....

ARTHUR RIPSTEIN

PRIVATE law presents itself as a system of norms governing relations between private persons. The corrosive effects of utilitarianism and American legal realism have made private law seem much more puzzling than it is. The Kantian approach to private law restores the familiarity of the naïve picture and shows how a system of norms for private legal relations can be conceptually coherent and normatively compelling.[1] It does so by articulating the organizing principle of private law, demonstrating the ways in which it frames legal issues, and explaining the role of courts and positive law in bringing these ideas to bear on particular interactions and disputes.

This chapter is organized into five sections. It begins with an overview that explains the aims and ambitions of Kantian legal philosophy more generally, in particular, introducing the Kantian idea that a particular form of thought is appropriate to a particular domain of inquiry or conduct. The second section situates the Kantian view within a broad natural law tradition. For the part of that tradition that Kant develops, the moral structure of natural law is animated by a conception of personal interaction that is so familiar as to be almost invisible. Despite its centrality to both morality and law, in the absence of legal institutions, this natural law is inadequate to its own principles. It requires legal institutions to render it fully determinate and its application consistent with everyone's independence. It also requires public institutions of adjudication. Section III looks to Kant's "division" of private rights, distinguishing first, between the innate right that everyone has simply in virtue of being human, and acquired rights that require an affirmative act to establish them. It then goes through the Kantian division of the titles of private right, situating them in relation to the distinction between persons and things. Acquired rights also differ in their respective modes of acquisition. Section IV articulates the Kantian account of what might be called the naïve theory of remedies, that is,

---

[1] Immanuel Kant, *The Doctrine of Right,* the first part of the *Metaphysics of Morals* (1797), in Kant, *Practical Philosophy* (Mary Gregor trans., 1996).

that the remedy is an imperfect continuation of the right that was violated. Section V concludes by bringing the earlier account of the need for legal institutions to complete natural law to bear on issues of adjudication and enforcement of private rights.

I. Category-based Reasoning

Lawyers arguing cases in private law, and judges deciding them, frame the issues and introduce particular facts through a structured sequence of legal categories. In a contract dispute, for example, questions of whether a contract was formed, what its terms are, and whether a particular consequence was within the scope of those terms are examined in an ordered sequence. In processing a tort claim, the plaintiff must establish each of the elements of the specific tort alleged. The legal parts of the inquiry precede the consideration of any factual questions.

These unremarkable features of private law adjudication figure in the teaching of private law subjects, but are strikingly absent in many prominent approaches to legal scholarship. American legal realism began with the claim that the available legal materials permit a court to reach whatever result the judge thinks best overall. Legal realism's progeny provide narrower readings of the space within which judges reach their decisions, but agree that the doctrinal structure occupies very little of it: economic analysts of law purport to provide social-scientific explanations of the decisions that judges actually reach; critical legal scholars contend that legal categories are a façade for decisions that are ultimately political. Any acknowledgment of the role of legal categories in such accounts represents them as bright-line rules, proxies for messier underlying policy decisions. On all of these views, the factors that do and should guide decision-making have a fundamentally different structure than the law's category-based reasoning.

The Kantian approach understands private law's category-based thinking in a fundamentally different way. The realists and their heirs suppose that categories introduce sharp divisions in a reality that is marked by multiple and perhaps incommensurable continuities; the Kantian contends that the categories capture normatively distinctive forms of interaction and thereby articulate a distinctive way of framing it. The realist supposes that the point of using legal categories is to facilitate a straightforward classification of particulars; the Kantian, by contrast, supposes that the relevant categories do not, on their own, make the classification of particulars easy. As we shall see, the categories are morally and conceptually prior to legal doctrine, but require articulation and development in legal doctrine to bring them to bear on particulars.

These contrasting conceptions of categorical thinking manifest themselves in very different conceptions of rules. For utilitarians and realists, rules are a remedy for the limits of human knowledge and the natural human tendency to self-preference. They solve information and coordination problems, so that people can reliably plan their affairs, secure in the knowledge that their course of action is likely to bring about the best consequences overall.[2] Law provides information about the rules and incentives for compliance. Non-utilitarian writers share this view; Joseph Raz writes that rules occupy an "intermediate" level of practical reasoning, mediating between concrete decisions and deeper considerations, and in so doing enable agents with incomplete or imperfect information to do what is most likely to be in conformity with the reasons that apply to them independently of those rules.[3]

The Kantian treatment of rules is fundamentally different. Kant sees the fundamental morality of human interaction as organized around two sets of rules: norms of conduct (keep your promises; don't interfere with other people's bodies or property, etc.), which in turn reflect deeper questions of the form "who gets to decide about this question?" The reason that you may not run your fingers through someone else's hair without that person's permission is because it is up to that person, not you, whether you touch them; so, too, the reason you must keep your promises is that it is up to the person to whom you have made the promise whether to release you from it; you cannot release yourself. The reason you need to be careful around other people is that it is not up to you to determine how much risk they must endure. None of these familiar moral thoughts enters the Kantian account as a summary of received wisdom about what is most likely to bring about good consequences, or as a generalization about the non-rule-governed reasons that are likely to apply to people. Your say-so about whether I may run my fingers through your hair does not track reasons that apply *to me* independently of what you happen to say; what you say goes, because it is up to you whether I touch you. These relational moral ideas are, then, primitive in the Kantian account; the basic form of an interpersonal moral norm is the one that says something like "that is not up to you."

II. THE RULE-BASED STRUCTURE OF INTERPERSONAL MORALITY

This Kantian picture of interpersonal morality is so familiar as to be easy to overlook. Many of its basic norms are clearly articulated in kindergarten. Such norms as "don't run with scissors," "keep your hands to yourself," "if you do not have something nice to say don't say anything at all," and "that is not yours" or "because you promised," are fundamental features of a normal moral repertoire. It is no surprise that the same familiar ideas show up in private law in the basic norm of negligence, the basic norm of battery, the rule against defamation, and the basic norms of property and contract. So, too, with the basic remedial norm, "give it back!" All of these ideas require instantiation, articulation, and specification in legal doctrine. But for all that, none of them is mysterious, and the ability of legal officials to deploy these concepts is completely unremarkable. In their

---

[2] For a clear and forceful articulation of this view, see Richard A. Epstein, *Simple Rules for a Complex World* (1995). See also Emily Sherwin, this volume (making similar arguments).

[3] Joseph Raz, *The Morality of Freedom* 58 (1986).

legal use they become highly technical, but that does not remove them from their order-ing moral structure.

The significance of these categories for private law can be articulated from two differ-ent directions. Ernest Weinrib's pioneering work on private law begins with the organiz-ing structure of a private law action: the plaintiff comes before a court and demands a remedy on the ground that this very defendant in particular has wronged the very plain-tiff who complains of the defendant's conduct.[4] The entire proceeding is structured around the transaction between the plaintiff and the defendant: the plaintiff objects to what the defendant did to the plaintiff; the defendant's defense consists in disputing the claim that the defendant wronged the plaintiff. Weinrib's argument is not that the only reason the plaintiff would be allowed to initiate an action in private law would be if its point were to vindicate the plaintiff's rights.[5] Perhaps an ideal ruler would find it useful to induce people who have suffered losses to act as a sort of "private attorneys general," bringing actions the aim of which are, for example, to regulate safety or to reduce inefficient conduct. Weinrib's point is not to deny this possibility; the point instead is that private law is a system of binary adjudication, such that each element of a private law action concerns the single transaction between the two parties before the court. It does not look to the expected effects of a finding of liability on parties not before the court.

Kant's own presentation of his account proceeds in the opposite direction, beginning with structuring ideas of human interaction—the most basic of which is that each person is entitled to be independent of all others and entitled to make claims in his or her own right.[6] This idea is irreducibly relational: the only thing that can compromise your independence is the deed of another. Only beings capable of determining their own purposes can stand in these relations; only they can have their independence violated, and only such beings could interfere with the independence of others. But your right to independence is not in the service of seeing to it that you are capable of or successful in setting and pursuing pur-poses. That is the sense in which it is irreducibly relational: the basic form of wrongdoing is the subordination of one person's capacity for choice to that of another.

Kant works up this concept of independence to generate norms of conduct governing relations between such beings, and progressively introduces additional forms of interac-tion, based on the introduction of additional respects in which one person's independence might be compromised by the deeds of another.

III. The Three Types of Private Law Rights

The idea that each person is entitled to be independent of others generates the main division of private law. Every person has what Kant calls an "innate right of humanity"

---

[4] Ernest J. Weinrib, *The Idea of Private Law* (1995).

[5] As some think is suggested by Jules L. Coleman, *The Practice of Principle* (2001).

[6] Kant, *supra* note 1, at 393–394.

in his or her own person.[7] The right is innate because nothing has to be done to acquire it. It is the right to be independent of another's determining choice; others wrong you if they interfere with your person, either by interfering with your body (by failing to keep their hands to themselves) or by injuring you (for example, by running with scissors). If someone wrongs you in either of these ways, you are entitled to make a claim of right in your own name, for a wrong personal to you.[8] By contrast, they do not wrong you if they fail to assist you or fail to provide you with the context that is best suited to whatever purposes you have set for yourself. Notoriously, most legal systems deny a private law duty to rescue;[9] this is an instance of the more general absence of any private law duty to order your affairs in the way that best suits another person's particular purposes. Any such duty would be inconsistent with the independence of persons, requiring one to subordinate his or her purposes to those of another. Your innate right also includes what Kant calls the "right to be beyond reproach," that is, the right to not be held to account for anything unless another person has proved that you have indeed done wrong; the same right undergirds the tort of defamation, which entitles you to demand that anyone who has accused you of doing wrong either prove their allegation or withdraw it.[10]

Your right to your own person is a right as against other people, and it sets out a system of reciprocal limits on independence; it describes a system of equal freedom, not in the sense that there is something called freedom of which everyone has an equal amount, but rather in the sense that no person is superior, and so no one is the subordinate of another.

A. Acquired Rights

If there are things other than your own body that you can use in setting and pursuing purposes, and you can do so in a way that does not interfere with any other person's independence, then there must be some way in which you can have rights over those other things.[11] This structure is easiest to see in the case of property: from the standpoint of right it is contingent whether embodied rational beings are able to use any things

---

[7] Kant, *supra* note 1, at 393ff.

[8] In Palsgraf v. Long Island Railroad Co., 248 N.Y. 339, 342 (1928), Judge Cardozo notes that to prevail in a tort action, "[t]he plaintiff sues in her own right for a wrong personal to her"; H.L.A. Hart points to the defects of a system that enforced "the refusal, to all alike, of compensation for injuries which it was morally wrong to inflict on others. The crudest case of such unjust refusal of redress would be a system in which no one could obtain damages for physical harm wantonly inflicted. It is worth observing that this injustice would still remain even if the criminal law prohibited such assaults under penalty." H.L.A. Hart, *The Concept of Law* 164 (1961). In the context of international law, Sir Hersch Lauterpacht remarks, "[i]t would appear that, apart from physical or similar incapacity, the right to bring a claim is of the essence of juridical personality." Hersch Lauterpacht, *The Development of International Law by the International Court* 178 (1982).

[9] See, e.g., Buch v. Amory Mfg. Co., 44 A. 809, 811 (N.H. 1897).

[10] See generally Richard Parkes et al., *Gatley on Libel and Slander* (2013).

[11] Kant, *supra* note 1, at 404.

other than their own bodies as means for achieving their freely chosen purposes. The universal principle of right requires only that *if* there are objects that can be subject to our choice, we must be entitled to have them formally, that is, independently of the particular ends for which we are using them. You can only have rights to objects (property) or the choices of others (contract) materially if you can have them formally.

The second step in Kant's derivation generates the three titles of private right: property, contract, and status.[12] The division reflects the different ways in which free beings can interact, that is, independently (property); interdependently and consensually (contract); and interdependently and nonconsensually (status). The same division of acquired rights can be generated by applying the distinction between persons and things to itself to generate the three titles of private right: a right to a thing (property), a right against a person (contract), and what Kant calls a "right to a person akin to a right to a thing," which includes the broad category of fiduciary relationships, in which one person is charged with managing some aspect of another's affairs.[13] The fourth member of the division produced by applying the person/thing distinction to itself (a right against a thing akin to a right against a person), is empty because only persons can be under duties.[14]

Your rights with respect to your property are broadly parallel to your rights with respect to your own body, not because your property is an extension of your body, but rather because the form of your right—the way in which it constrains the conduct of others—is the same. You, rather than anyone else, are the one who gets to decide the purposes for which your property will be used. Property ownership determines the "who" question about such things, because the owner is the one who gets to decide the purposes for which the thing will be used. But the entitlement to make this decision is formal, and so your entitlement to decide the purposes for which it will be used includes using it for no purpose whatsoever, or, what comes to the same thing, for the vacuous purpose of keeping it in case you think of something. Property rights thus borrow the structure of your right to your own body and apply it to things outside of it.

Contract right gives one person the entitlement to have another person's action available for the first person's purposes. Because it is a right against a person, it can apply only to the particular deed; it is one person's entitlement to determine (that is, demand or compel) a particular action from another, rather than a more general entitlement to compel that other person to serve the purposes of the first.

A right to a person akin to a right to a thing is different from both a property right and a contractual right. This class of rights entitles one person to demand the general services or loyalty of another. The simplest case on Kant's account is the duty of a parent to his or her child. As Kant puts it, parents bring their children into the world "of their own initiative and without the consent of the children."[15] The child is also not in a position to refuse subsequent consent, and so the parent must act on the child's behalf. Rather than

---

[12] Kant, *supra* note 1, at 402ff.   [13] *Id.* at 402.

[14] Or rather, that would be slavery, which is morally impossible.

[15] Kant, *supra* note 1, at 428.

a voluntary undertaking, whose terms might be varied by the parties, this is a mandatory form of interaction, generated by the inability of the child to give or refuse consent. It provides the model for other fiduciary-like obligations, in which the trustee is required to act on behalf of the beneficiary. In many of these circumstances, ranging from simple bailments through complex corporate structures to physician-patient relationships, the obligations are entered into via contract, but even in these cases, the relationship is asymmetrical, and it has a mandatory structure, precluding the fiduciary from using the powers for personal advantage.

The three divisions of acquired rights differ in their form, based on the type of relation in which the right holder and duty bearer stand. A property right puts all others under a system of negative duties of non-interference to avoid interfering with the thing that is the object of the right. A contract right puts the promisor alone under a duty to the promisee to perform a particular act. Fiduciary-like obligations prohibit the fiduciary from managing the beneficiary's affairs for the fiduciary's own purposes.

The three titles of private right are specified in the first instance through the type of relation between one person's choice and another's, rather than in terms of their modes of acquisition. That form of relation, in turn, determines its mode of acquisition. Modes of acquisition are relevant when rights are in dispute, because the only way of establishing a claim of right is to establish either that your right is innate and does not require further proof, such as your right to bodily integrity or, even more fundamentally, your right to be beyond reproach, or that you acquired it in the right way. In cases of dispute about acquired right, the standard way of establishing a superior claim is by demonstrating how you came to have the object in question.

If I want to contest your title to a horse, I must establish that I have superior title, something I can only do by showing that I acquired title in the right way, either from another or by taking control of a previously unowned horse. To do so I do not need to show that no other person has better title than I do; pointing to the manner in which I acquired it shows that my title is better than yours, which is the only issue that can be in dispute between us. So, too, if I claim that you have failed to perform under our contract, I must first establish that there was a contract between us, and that its terms required you to do the act in question. These are both legal requirements, antecedent to the burden that lies with me of proving that, as a matter of fact, you did not perform.[16] And if I contend that you breached your fiduciary obligation to me, I must first establish that we stand in the relevant relationship and show that what you did falls within its scope. Only then do the particulars of your conduct come into juridical focus. That is, modes of acquisition matter to private law because they are the ways in which people come to stand in specific instances of standard types of legal relationships.

---

[16] *Id.* at 394.

B. Some Contrasts

It is worth contrasting this conception of private legal relations with another with which it is sometimes confused, that is, the "historical" theory of justice defended by Robert Nozick in his book *Anarchy, State, and Utopia*.[17] For Nozick, and those who follow him, the categories of private law are part of a more general theory of justice in holdings, which has three parts: a theory of acquisition, a theory of transfer, and a theory of rectification. On this view, someone has a claim to some object if, and only if, he or she acquired it from an unowned condition by mixing labor with it, or alternatively, acquired it from some other person who had valid title to it, either through a valid contract, a gift, or as (part of) the rectification of a wrong that someone with good title had done. On Nozick's view, then, the categories of private law apply to things that are validly owned. His libertarian opposition to economic redistribution follows from the related supposition that there are no other legitimate ways in which something can be taken from one person and given to another.

Despite the fact that both speak of property and contract, however, the Kantian view and the libertarian view share no structuring features.[18] The Kantian account of private right is exclusively relational, concerned only with how things stand between one person and another. If I contract with you to deliver to you something to which I lack good title, you still have a valid claim against me; if I wrongfully damage stolen property that is in your possession, you have a claim against me which is not called into doubt by the defects in your title. As between us, I have wronged you, either by failing to perform a contract or by depriving you of things that, as against me, you were entitled to have securely. The law's treatment of such examples reflects its exclusive focus on the particular transaction between the parties. The libertarian view, as Nozick develops it, attaches priority to good title, and so could at most treat such examples as derivative, ones in which whatever cause of action you had somehow piggybacked on the fact that in what it treats as the central class of cases there is an interference with the transfer or security of good title. Second, the Kantian view does not attempt to ground the theory of property in the theory of acquisition; it identifies the form of property, and from that generates the naïve theory of acquisition—taking something out of an unowned condition is the way in which that thing makes its way into the system of property. Further, the Kantian account entails that property rights are only binding in a condition of public law. The most striking difference between the Kantian view and the libertarian one follows from this: the libertarian supposes that private rights are complete in a "state of nature," that is, in the absence of legal institutions. By contrast, on the Kantian view they are fundamentally incomplete in a state of nature, not only in the sense of being partially

---

[17] Robert Nozick, *Anarchy, State, and Utopia* (1974).

[18] They also differ in that Nozick's fundamental concepts all rest on ideas of benefit and burden that have no place in a Kantian account: his justification of property in terms of the claim that appropriation does not disadvantage others, and his view that being prohibited from doing as you wish generates a basis for compensation, both of which are assessed in terms of their welfare effects.

indeterminate but, more strikingly, in that they are not enforceable even in clear and determinate cases.

IV. THE ROLE OF PUBLIC
LEGAL INSTITUTIONS

Kant uses the seventeenth- and eighteenth-century vocabulary of a "state of nature" to explain why concepts of private right require instantiation in positive law and legal institutions.[19] Where earlier writers such as Hobbes and Locke drew attention to empirical challenges—lack of assurance, imperfect information, and partiality—Kant argues that in the absence of legal institutions, the concepts of private right would be inadequate to their own *normative* demands. Kant offers three related lines of argument. First, he shows that the acquisition of property can only be consistent with everyone's freedom if it is governed by publicly authorized procedures. Without such procedures, others would not be bound by one person's acquisition of an object through his or her own initiative. Second, he argues that people do not need to refrain from interfering with the acquired rights of others unless they have assurance that others will refrain from interfering with theirs. In this, acquired rights differ from your innate right to your own body. Third, and most immediately relevant to adjudication, private rights only form a system of freedom if there is a public standpoint from which disputes can be resolved. I will focus on this third argument, because it is most directly related to the structure of private law adjudication.

Recall that for Kant concepts of right are highly abstract and partially indeterminate in their application. This is obviously true in the case of the acquisition of property. Although there are cases in which taking control of a thing is straightforward—such as wrapping my hand around an apple—in many other cases, including the central case of the acquisition of land, what counts as taking control of it is in part indeterminate. This point applies more generally to the familiar concepts that figure in private law. For example, the law of negligence demands "reasonable care" and although the normative impetus of this demand is clear enough—reasonable care is the amount of care that reasonable people take toward each other's safety when they are being careful[20]—most attempts to articulate any such standard border on platitudes. Worse, they seem like the kind of platitudes on which people agree only because everyone will apply them differently. So, too, with the question of whether an offer has been accepted in contract and the purely legal question of what does and does not fall within the scope of a negligent wrong or within the terms of a contract, or of when title passes in a sale.

---

[19] Kant, *supra* note 1, at 450.
[20] E.g., Blyth v. Birmingham Waterworks Co. (1856) 11 Ex. Ch. 781, 783.

Utilitarians and legal realists sometimes suggest that such indeterminacy shows that the core concepts of private law cannot mean what they say, they must just be either an approximation of or a façade[21] for some other way of guiding conduct or resolving disputes.[22] Neither the approximation nor the façade model can make sense of these concepts, particularly because they are so open-ended that it is difficult to see how they could be making things more rather than less determinate (as an approximation is supposed to do). Nor is it easy to see how they could be a façade; disagreements about their application reflect the fact that everyone knows exactly what they require if they apply, but disagree about whether they do.

Instead, the Kantian view is that legal concepts are open-ended because they are abstract. As Martin Stone has argued, this sort of indeterminacy is pervasive in other aspects of practical life.[23] The demands of friendship may explain why I will help my friend move a couch, though perhaps not a body. The category of friendship provides a way of framing the inquiry about what to do without providing anything like an algorithm for determining what to do. That is, the concept of friendship requires judgment; any explication of it is likely to seem circular or question-begging; and, unlike the principle of utility, even perfect information would be insufficient to tell you what exactly you should now do.

The concept of right requires not just a determinate application but a shared one. The boundaries between our respective rights are also the limits of our respective authority as against each other, because they determine the things for which we must seek another's permission. The metaphor of boundaries is straightforward in the purely spatial case of our rights to body and property, but the same point applies to contracts and fiduciary relations. Whether I need your permission to do something depends on how things stand as between us. Precisely because we are independent, neither of us needs to defer to the other about where, precisely, those boundaries are or the details of how things stand between us. Instead, we require a common answer. But the concepts that get us started in thinking of ourselves as each being independent are, as we have seen, open-ended and indeterminate, and so both demand a common solution and fail to provide one. For that, we require public legal institutions, that is, a body capable of specifying the law and applying it to particular disputes in a way that is binding on both parties to the dispute.[24]

In a state of nature, then, private rights are inadequate to their own normative basis. The solution to this inadequacy is to set up institutions that make, apply, and enforce law. The absence of these institutions poses a further problem, however. As we saw, every person has an innate entitlement to demand that anyone who alleges that they have done wrong establish their wrong before anything can be done. That same right requires that

---

[21] E.g., Joseph William Singer, *The Player and the Cards: Nihilism and Legal Theory*, 94 YALE L.J. 1 (1984).

[22] E.g., Richard A. Posner, *A Theory of Negligence*, 1 J. LEGAL STUD. 29 (1972).

[23] Martin J. Stone, *Legal Positivism as an Idea about Morality*, 61 U. TORONTO L.J. 313, 314ff (2011).

[24] Kant, *supra* note 1, at 451.

law-applying institutions be structured so that the burden of establishing wrongdoing lies with the person who alleges it.

Rightful dispute resolution requires further that the tribunal charged with determining whether wrong has been done be capable of binding both parties to it. You and I can resolve our dispute by accepting the determination of an arbitrator. But if we cannot agree on which arbitrator, or on what procedures the arbitrator will use, we cannot resolve that dispute about how to resolve our dispute. A public court is fundamentally different from an arbitrator, because in cases in which rights are in dispute, one party can compel the other to submit to the court's procedures (the relevant compulsion consists in the fact that if a party refuses to appear, the court can issue a binding judgment in that party's absence).

The development and codification of legal doctrine in positive law play a further essential role in bringing concepts of private right into conformity with their own normative basis. Positive law makes the requirements of right public in a specific sense: to ensure that everyone can enjoy their rights by making private rights members of a system of rights. This sort of publicity is importantly different from the epistemic sense of publicity that has figured in a variety of different approaches to private law, on which law provides rules with low information costs that are easy for ordinary citizens to follow.[25] On the epistemic interpretation of publicity, clear public rules guide behavior by providing readily accessible markers. Conformity with those markers will bring about an outcome the point of which makes no reference to those rules, either directly or through a division of labor between simple rules for individuals and more complex ones for tax and transfer institutions.

The Kantian view sees things differently; it need not deny the advantages of clear demarcations, but it also recognizes that although the basic rules of interpersonal morality are simple, their application may be complex, and can be difficult even for lawyers to understand or apply. Doctrine is public through the existence of a public procedure through which it can be applied. Positive law and institutions charged with the authoritative application of it make private rights members of a consistent set.

A. Remedies

Some writers insist that private law is not really a system of rights at all, but rather exclusively a system of remedies, which does not aim to direct conduct but only to tell people what will happen if they do certain things. Others see remedies as a form of recourse, designed to give satisfaction to those whose rights are violated and triggered by the fact

---

[25] See, e.g., Epstein, *supra* note 2; Frederick Hayek, *The Road to Serfdom* (1944); John Rawls, "The Basic Structure as Subject," in *Political Liberalism* (1993); Henry E. Smith, *Property as the Law of Things*, 125 HARV. L. REV. 1691 (2012).

of violation but at most incidental to the specific right violated.[26] The Kantian approach sees the purpose of remedies in a fundamentally different way, as the continuation of the right that was violated.[27] It is easy to find this suggestion puzzling, especially in the case of tort damages for serious personal injury, the loss of a child, or an egregious invasion of privacy. Nobody thinks that any sum of money can make up for such losses, let alone that the sum of money is some kind of equivalent, such that the plaintiff is, or ought to be, indifferent between the wrong never having happened and receiving the relevant sum of money.

The Kantian claim is not that the remedy is an equivalent of the right; it is the claim that the rationale for the remedy is completely exhausted by the content of the right. That thought reflects a more general conception of the nature of juridical norms. Norms of right specify how things properly stand between the right holder and others. A wrong is a violation of such a right, but it does not change how things rightfully stand between the parties. The basic norm of property has this familiar feature: if I wrongfully take your coat, it does not thereby stop being your coat. You are still entitled, as against me, that I forbear from using or interfering with it without your permission. So, too, if I am supposed to cut your lawn next Wednesday and fail to do so, your entitlement to compel me to do so is intact, even in the face of my nonperformance. It is not that you have a right that I do something impossible—change the past—but that you are still entitled to constrain my conduct with respect to how things stand between us. What survives is this normative relation between us.[28] If I owe you a sum of money and fail to pay, my obligation to you does not disappear but persists, because the obligation governs how things are supposed to stand between us. If I am a trustee, I am not allowed to use the trust for my own purposes. If I do, my doing so does not change my duty to you, thereby making my wrong retroactively permissible. Instead, any proceeds of my misappropriation of what is yours continues to be properly yours. In each of these examples, I wrong you, but your right survives.

The basic form of your remedy is, then, your entitlement to be in the position—in relation to me—in which you would have been if not for the wrong. For example, I have to return your coat (even if in the meantime someone has given you a new coat that you prefer) because, as against me, it is still your coat. I have to pay the agreed sum, not as a kind of second-order monetization of the obligation that I owed to you,[29] but rather

---

[26] This was the position once taken by John C.P. Goldberg & Benjamin C. Zipursky. Their forthcoming book, *Recognizing Wrongs* (forthcoming 2020), takes an approach that is closer to the Kantian one.

[27] I explain this point in more detail in Arthur Ripstein, *Private Wrongs* ch. 8 (2016).

[28] Thus the Kantian approach contrasts with John Gardner's claim that reasons for action, rather than rights and duties, survive. For Gardner, rights and duties are not normatively basic, but rather middle-level concepts of practical reasoning. Thus he concludes that a duty must require a specific action, such as a Wednesday lawn-cutting, rather than, as the Kantian view frames it, a normative relation between the parties. See John Gardner, *What Is Tort Law For? Part 1. The Place of Corrective Justice*, 30 LAW & PHIL. 1, 28 (2011).

[29] See the discussion in Robert Hadley Stevens, "Private Rights and Public Wrongs," in *Unravelling Tort and Crime* 130 (Matthew Dyson ed., 2014).

because that is the obligation I owed to you. I need to disgorge the misappropriated funds because the funds properly belong to you.

In the case of cutting your lawn next Wednesday, things may look different; courts hesitate to compel performance of personal services and are more likely to award a damage remedy. But even here, money damages serve as a substitute for the act that I failed to perform. They may be an excellent substitute because there are lots of other people who will quickly and efficiently cut your lawn, or they may be a terrible one because the person you had hoped to impress was already dismayed by your overgrown yard. But the measure of the money damages is always tied to what I was supposed to do or omit. That is the sense in which they are a substitute. There will be some cases in which no substitute is anywhere close to adequate; many cases of bodily injury and wrongful death are like this. But the inevitable inadequacy of the substitute does not change the rationale for requiring one.

V. THE ROLE OF A COURT

The Kantian approach requires positive law and public legal institutions to give effect to private rights. In this concluding section, I want to say something more about the role of one type of institution in particular, that is, a court. In private law, a court is charged with resolving a dispute between the parties to it. As we have seen, it must do so exclusively on the basis of the transaction or alleged transaction between those parties. In processing the claim, however, it must not only be governed by the substance of the rights of the parties; it must also be governed by the form of those rights. That is, a court is not necessary merely in order to make claims of right more determinate. In addition, a court is required in order to make binding determinations that are consistent with the rights of the parties before it as right holders.

The most basic of these rights, as we have seen, is what Kant calls the "right to be beyond reproach."[30] In the absence of a court, the fact that one person has wronged another is not sufficient to give the other juridical standing to enforce a remedy against the wrongdoer. Instead, everyone is entitled to be presumed to have done no wrong, simply in virtue of being a person. Anyone who acts in contravention of that presumption does wrong, even if doing so to retaliate or to seek a remedy for some past wrong. The court itself needs to be structured by that same right and so must place the burden on the plaintiff who alleges that another has done wrong. For the same reason, the traditional law of defamation requires only that the defendant has accused the plaintiff of doing wrong; having established that, the burden then lies with the defendant to either withdraw the accusation or prove that it was true or privileged in a way that makes it turn out not to have been a wrongful accusation.

---

[30] Kant, *supra* note 1, at 394.

The role of a court deepens the explanation of the relation between right and remedy. Although the rationale for the remedy is continuation of the right, and in some cases, such as the payment of an agreed sum, the remedy is identical to the object of the right, the remedy is juridically distinct from the right in that it must be ordered by a court in order for the plaintiff to enforce it. There is a perfectly natural sense in which we can say that the defendant is under an obligation to compensate the plaintiff because the defendant breached their contract; but the plaintiff can only enforce that obligation after proving before a court that there was indeed a contract and that the defendant breached it, and establishing the quantum of damages. If the facts are straightforward, the defendant would do well to settle with the plaintiff and save them both the bother of litigating uncontroversial matters. But because right always includes the authority to coerce, the plaintiff's entitlement to the remedy is incomplete until proven before the court.

We also saw in section II that the legal order is required to resolve the inherent indeterminacy in the application of concepts of right to particulars. In characterizing this indeterminacy, the Kantian approach does not represent every resolution of it as as good as any other one, as though the role of the court is to pick one among the possible resolutions. To put it that way is to mischaracterize the nature of the indeterminacy, as well as the distinctive role of a judge. Questions of whether a particular injury was within the ambit of the risk in a negligence action, whether a consequential loss was within the terms of a shipping contract, or whether someone has taken possession of some unowned or abandoned object are not fully determined by the relevant juridical concepts. But that does not make them entirely open-ended either: the court must exercise judgment with respect to the application of those categories, rather than pursuing some other purpose, external to the transaction between the parties.

Outcomes may be determined further by the development of positive legal doctrine in two ways. First of all, explicit codification can narrow the range of application of concepts, particularly by specifying a procedure through which things can be determined. The procedure's application to particulars will still require the exercise of judgment, but not in the open-ended way imagined by the objection. Second, in a casuistical system such as the common law, judges decide cases by looking for analogies between cases that have already been decided and the case before them. Sometimes the same issues arose on analogous facts in a settled case, which is sufficient to decide the issue; other times there are multiple analogies and the judge must develop some of them but not others. This development can be done in different ways—that is the sense in which it is an exercise of judgment—and its product is in a formal sense chosen, that is, positive, law. Had the judge developed it differently, the result would have been different. But that does not mean that the judge is somehow in equipoise between two equally good possible ways of doing it and might consult some third principle, perhaps such as utilitarianism, in order to come up with a solution.

Rather than looking outside the relation between the parties, part of what happens when lawyers argue a case is that each of them has analogies to offer, trying to make the case at hand look more like one group of settled cases and less like another. The plaintiff's counsel will choose one set of analogies, the defendant's another, and the judge will judge which is more compelling. Settled cases enter in as available specifications or determinations of the relevant transaction. Further, on some questions the court will need to apply such open-ended terms as "reasonable" or "careful." In applying those concepts to the particulars before it, common understandings about such things as what careful people do when they are being careful instruct the finder of fact on how to frame the inquiry, directing them away from cost-benefit analysis or a determination of what, all things considered, the person should have done in this circumstance. The fact that a different finder of fact given the same assignment could come up with a different answer only looks like a problem if the court is seen as a reliable mechanism for producing a result that is entirely independent of its existence and procedures. But the court's role is fundamentally different: as with all exercises of authority, the question of its entitlement to decide the case is not exclusively a matter of correctness or reliability, but rather of standing. The highest court's decision is final because it is charged with deciding on behalf of both parties to the dispute. Its authority is to resolve the dispute in accordance with the law, to bring abstract legal categories and more specific doctrines to bear on the particulars before it. Its authority thus derives from the fact that it is the body charged with doing so. Judges or jurors are required to carry out the task carefully and conscientiously.

VI. Conclusion

The Kantian claim is that private law can be taken more or less at face value, rather than as a convoluted attempt to accomplish something other than the upholding of the rights as between the parties to a particular transaction. It begins with the idea of individuals having rights against each other. Those rights specify acceptable modes of interaction, consistent with every person's independence of every other person. Beginning with the right that each of us has to our own person, the account expands to include rights with respect to other things: objects that exist apart from you (including land), another person's future actions, via contract, and the management of some aspect of another person's affairs. The broad structure of these rights is familiar both in law and in interpersonal morality; giving full effect to them, consistent with the freedom of everyone, requires the creation of a public legal order, which must have powers different from the private rights that private individuals have as against each other. By relating the organizing structure of private law to moral ideas, and to a philosophical characterization of freedom as independence, the Kantian account both shows how private law can be taken at face value and, at the same time, shows that it has a fundamental role in constituting your distinctive moral and juridical standing, both to be treated as an independent human being, who is neither the superior nor the subordinate of any other and also, when things go wrong, to demand a remedy in your own name, for a wrong that is personal to you.

CHAPTER 6

··

LAW AND ECONOMICS

··

DANIEL B. KELLY

I. INTRODUCTION

··

THE economic analysis of law, or law and economics, has emerged as the predominant school of thought for analyzing legal policy and institutions over the last half century.[1] Today, law and economics plays an important role in debates in almost every area of substantive law. Law and economics has had a significant impact on foundational private law subjects—property, contracts, and torts—as well as advanced private law areas. This chapter analyzes how law and economics influences private law and how (new) private law is influencing law and economics.

The chapter focuses on three generations or "waves" within law and economics and how they approach private law. In the first generation, many scholars took the law as a starting point and attempted to use economic insights to explain, justify, or reform legal doctrines, institutions, and structures. In the second generation, the "law" at times became secondary, with more focus on theory and less focus on doctrines, institutions, and structures. But this generation also relied increasingly on empirical analysis. In the third generation, which includes scholars in the New Private Law (NPL), there has been a resurgence of interest in the law and legal institutions. To be sure, NPL scholars analyze the law using various approaches, with some more and some less predisposed to economic analysis. However, economic analysis will continue to be a major force on private law, including the New Private Law, for the foreseeable future.

This chapter analyzes the influence of law and economics on private law in general and specific substantive areas in private law. Section II provides background on law and economics. Section III focuses on three foundational private law areas: property,

[1] See generally A. Mitchell Polinsky, *An Introduction to Law and Economics* (5th ed. 2019); Richard A. Posner, *Economic Analysis of Law* (9th ed. 2014); Steven Shavell, *Foundations of Economic Analysis of Law* (2004) see also *The Oxford Handbook of Law and Economics* (Francesco Parisi ed., 2017).

contracts, and torts. For each area, this section distinguishes three generations of scholarship in law and economics, discusses the major ideas that economic analysis has contributed to private law, and surveys contributions of the NPL. Section IV briefly discusses the impact of law and economics on advanced private law areas such as business associations, trusts and estates, and intellectual property. Section V concludes by focusing on future directions in NPL and economics, including recent scholarship that takes seriously both the law and the effects of law.

II. Background on Economic Analysis

The origins of modern law and economics date back to two articles by Ronald Coase.[2] In "The Nature of the Firm" (1937), Coase studied why some business activities occur within the "firm" while others occur in the "market" and developed a transactions costs theory of the firm.[3] In "The Problem of Social Cost" (1960), Coase pointed out that neighbors may resolve social costs via bargaining: if transaction costs are zero, parties will reach the same outcome, irrespective of which party holds the initial legal entitlement, and that outcome will be socially optimal.[4] Coase was an economist, not a legal scholar. But legal scholars, including NPL scholars, have noted that this article has become "the most frequently cited work in all of legal scholarship."[5]

The 1970s and 1980s witnessed the rise of law and economics. Guido Calabresi (Yale) published *The Costs of Accidents* (1970), an important book applying the economic approach to tort theory, and "Property Rules, Liability Rules, and Inalienability: One View of the Cathedral" (1972), an influential article on the modes of protecting legal

---

[2] Much of the early work applying economic insights to legal institutions focused not on private law but on criminal law and public law. See, e.g., Cesare Beccaria, *On Crimes and Punishments, and Other Writings* (1767); Jeremy Bentham, *An Introduction to the Principles of Morals and Legislation* (1789). On Adam Smith's role in the development of law and economics, see Paul G. Mahoney, *Adam Smith, Prophet of Law and Economics*, 46 J. Legal Stud. 207 (2017).

[3] Ronald H. Coase, *The Nature of the Firm*, 4 Economica 386 (1937); see also Adolf Berle & Gardiner Means, *The Modern Corporation and Private Property* (1932).

[4] Ronald H. Coase, *The Problem of Social Cost*, 3 J.L. & Econ. 1 (1960); see also Richard A. Posner & Francesco Parisi, *The Coase Theorem* (2012). Commentators have identified and distinguished multiple versions of the "Coase theorem," including the "efficiency" version and "invariance" version. Also, as a number of commentators have pointed out, Coase does not focus on distributional concerns or the parties' roles as consumers in his model, but the initial allocation of entitlements may affect the ultimate distribution of entitlements.

[5] Thomas W. Merrill & Henry E. Smith, *Property: Principles and Policies* 32 (3d ed. 2017). Other pioneers include Armen Alchian, Harold Demsetz, Aaron Director, William Landes, Henry Manne, and several scholars noted later. Many scholars, including James Buchanan, Anthony Downs, Mancur Olson, Elinor Ostrom, Vernon Smith, George Stilger, and Gordon Tullock, also used economic insights to understand government through public choice theory.

entitlements.[6] Richard Posner (University of Chicago) applied the economic approach to nearly every legal area in *Economic Analysis of Law* (1973), which continues to be the field's leading treatise. The "Chicago School" of economics influenced the analysis of both market activities, in fields such as antitrust,[7] corporate law,[8] and intellectual property,[9] and nonmarket activities, in fields such as family law.[10] The 1980s also witnessed seminal work by several of the movement's leading scholars, including Robert Ellickson (Yale),[11] Mitchell Polinsky (Stanford),[12] and Steven Shavell (Harvard),[13] each of whom has continued to generate pathbreaking scholarship over several decades.[14]

The spread of law and economics in the 1990s and 2000s was driven by a number of key developments. In 1990, several scholars founded the American Law and Economics Association (ALEA),[15] an organization dedicated to promoting research in law and economics. The John M. Olin Foundation also established Olin Centers at top law schools to generate and disseminate scholarship in law, economics, and business.[16] Moreover, rigorous empirical research soon became a distinguishing feature of law and economics.[17] Later, behavioral law and economics, which incorporates insights from experimental economics and psychology, would broaden the movement's scope and influence even further.[18]

The law and economics movement also influenced legal policy. For example, in 1981, President Ronald Reagan issued an executive order incorporating cost-benefit analysis into federal regulations.[19] Fewer than three decades later, executive officials working for

---

[6] See Guido Calabresi & A. Douglas Melamed, *Property Rules, Liability Rules, and Inalienability: One View of the Cathedral*, 85 Harv. L. Rev. 1089 (1972); see also Keith N. Hylton, *Calabresi and the Intellectual History of Law and Economics*, 64 Md. L. Rev. 85 (2005).

[7] Robert Bork, *The Antitrust Paradox* (1978).

[8] Henry Manne, *Mergers and the Market for Corporate Control* (1965); Frank Easterbrook & Daniel Fischel, *The Economic Structure of Corporate Law* (1991).

[9] William M. Landes & Richard A. Posner, *The Economic Structure of Intellectual Property Law* (2003).

[10] Gary Becker, *The Economic Approach to Human Behavior* (1976); Gary Becker, *A Treatise on the Family* (1981).

[11] Robert C. Ellickson, *Of Coase and Cattle: Dispute Resolution Among Neighbors in Shasta County*, 38 Stan. L. Rev. 623 (1986); see also Robert C. Ellickson, *Property in Land*, 102 Yale L.J. 1315 (1993).

[12] A. Mitchell Polinsky, *An Introduction to Law and Economics* (1983); A. Mitchel Polinsky, *Private versus Public Enforcement of Fines*, 9 J. Legal Stud. 105 (1980).

[13] Steven M. Shavell, *Economic Analysis of Accident Law* (1987); Steven M. Shavell, *Strict Liability versus Negligence*, 9 J. Legal Stud. 1 (1980).

[14] Polinsky, *supra* note 1; Shavell, *supra* note 1; *Handbook of Law and Economics* (A. Mitchell Polinsky & Steven Shavell eds., 2007); Robert C. Ellickson, *The Household: Informal Order around the Hearth* (2008); Robert C. Ellickson, Order Without Law: How Neighbors Settle Disputes (1991).

[15] See http://www.amlecon.org/.

[16] See Steven M. Teles, *The Rise of the Conservative Legal Movement: The Battle for Control of the Law* 183–207 (2010).

[17] Shavell, *supra* note 1, at 4 (noting that the use of stylized models and statistical, empirical tests of theory distinguishes economic analysis from other types of legal analysis).

[18] *Behavioral Law & Economics* (Cass R. Sunstein ed., 2000); *The Oxford Handbook of Behavioral Economics and the Law* (Eyal Zamir & Doron Teichman eds., 2014).

[19] Exec. Order No. 12291, 3 C.F.R. 127 (1982).

President Barack Obama were implementing cost-benefit analysis throughout federal agencies.[20] The role of cost-benefit analysis across time, including both Republican and Democratic administrations, suggests the movement's influence on administrative and public law. Law and economics also has influenced the development of private law, including property, contracts, and torts.

III. Foundational Private Law Subjects

A. Property Law

John Locke in the seventeenth century and William Blackstone in the eighteenth century both emphasized the role of private property in a modern liberal economy.[21] Likewise, the protection of property rights was central to the U.S. constitutional order.[22] Over the centuries, property law crystallized into formal doctrines. The advent of legal realism was a reaction to this formalism; accordingly, realism also ushered in an era of skepticism about property rights.[23]

Ronald Coase helped to revive interest in property rights. In "The Problem of Social Cost," Coase compared private ordering to government solutions for dealing with social costs.[24] With his famous illustration of a farmer and rancher, Coase showed how parties may have an incentive to bargain around an allocation of rights. As noted previously, Coase argued that, in the absence of bargaining frictions, the parties would reach the same outcome and that this outcome would be socially optimal, regardless of the initial allocation of legal entitlements. Coase arrived at this counterintuitive result after analyzing two concrete issues: the resolution of nuisance cases in English common law and the allocation of broadcast spectrum by the FCC.[25] His focus on legal cases and institutions led to a result that diverged from the then-prevailing wisdom on corrective taxes and subsidies. Building on Coase, the "first generation" of law and economics scholars

---

[20] Cass R. Sunstein, *The Real World of Cost-Benefit Analysis: Thirty Six Questions (and Almost as Many Answers)*, 114 COLUM. L. REV. 167 (2014).

[21] See Eric R. Claeys, *The Private Society and Public Good in John Locke's Thought*, 21 SOC. PHIL. & POL'Y 201 (2008); Albert W. Alschuler, *Rediscovering Blackstone*, 145 U. PA. L. REV. 1, 28–36 (1996).

[22] James W. Ely Jr., *The Guardian of Every Other Right: A Constitutional History of Property Rights* (3d ed. 2008).

[23] See Thomas C. Grey, "The Disintegration of Property," in *NOMOS XXII: Property* 69 (J. Roland Pennock & John W. Chapman eds., 1980). On the realist conception of property as a "bundle of rights," Thomas W. Merrill & Henry E. Smith, *What Happened to Property in Law and Economics?*, 111 YALE L.J. 357, 365 (2001).

[24] Coase, *supra* note 4.

[25] See *id.* at 8–15, 19–39; Ronald H. Coase, *Federal Communications Commission*, 2 J.L. & ECON. 1 (1959).

emphasized the importance of property rights and often investigated the functions of various property doctrines.[26]

The "second generation" of property scholars in law and economics focused less on legal doctrines, institutions, and structures. Coase, in addition to analyzing English nuisance law cases, suggested that "[s]atisfactory views on policy can only come from a patient study of how, in practice, the market, firms and governments handle the problem of harmful effects."[27] The second generation, while perhaps focusing less on how legal doctrines and institutions work in practice, often relied on empirical analysis to analyze the effects of property rights.

At the end of the twentieth century, a number of NPL scholars, including Thomas Merrill, James Penner, and Henry Smith, have helped to revitalize the field of property law. While some of this work in NPL is philosophical,[28] a significant portion of it is part of a "third generation" of law and economics scholarship. This third generation has focused on the underlying structure of property law. But it also has challenged conventional thinking on several subjects, including nuisance, transfer, and trespass.

1. *Nuisance*

Nuisance law is one way of dealing with externalities among neighbors, the external effects that one party's actions have on another. Coase suggests the problem is a reciprocal one: just as a factory may be imposing costs on a nearby homeowner, the homeowner is imposing costs on the factory.[29] Modern nuisance law explicitly adopts a basic tool of law and economics: cost-benefit analysis. Specifically, in analyzing intentional nuisances under the *Restatement (Second) of Property*, which a majority of states have adopted, a court must decide whether an intentional activity that substantially interferes with the use and enjoyment of a neighbor's property is "unreasonable." The test for unreasonableness is based on whether the gravity of the harm outweighs the social value of the activity.[30] Nuisance law also relies on baseline norms about the type of activities that are consistent with a neighborhood. But it would be difficult to understand nuisance law without incorporating cost-benefit analysis to evaluate conflicting land uses.[31]

However, in deciding nuisance cases, courts rarely engage explicitly in rigorous cost-benefit analysis. This is true even in jurisdictions that have adopted the *Restatement* and

---

[26] See Robert C. Ellickson, *Alternatives to Zoning: Covenants, Nuisance Rules, and Fines as Land Use Controls*, 40 U. CHI. L. REV. 681 (1973) (analyzing zoning and land use regulations); Jeffrey E. Stake, *Darwin, Donations, and the Illusion of Dead Hand Control*, 64 TUL. L. REV. 905 (1990) (analyzing Rule Against Perpetuities).

[27] See Coase, *supra* note 4, at 18.   [28] See James Penner, *The Idea of Property in Law* (1997).

[29] Coase, *supra* note 4, at 2. For Coase, it would be erroneous to claim that the factory is "causing" the harm to the homeowner because social costs arise only because of the location of both the factory and the homeowner. If the homeowner did not locate near the factory, there would be no conflict. Therefore, according to Coase, the homeowner is just as responsible for these social costs.

[30] *Restatement (Second) of Torts* §§ 826–828 (1979).

[31] See Keith N. Hylton, "The Economics of Nuisance Law," in *Research Handbook on the Economics of Property Law* 323 (Kenneth Ayotte & Henry E. Smith eds., 2011).

apply its cost-benefit approach.[32] The divergence between theory and practice illustrates the relevance of actual cases, doctrines, and institutions, and it suggests that there may be functional issues that an idealized cost-benefit analysis might overlook. Perhaps the additional decision costs of expert witnesses and statistical studies outweigh any improvements in accuracy; perhaps litigants or courts are not competent institutionally to generate and evaluate this type of statistical analysis; or perhaps courts are inclined to use certain social norms as a proxy for what types of uses are "efficient" in a given time and place.

2. *Transfer*

Coase emphasizes that parties can bargain to rearrange their property rights. Coase's point is not to suggest that bargaining is a panacea but to highlight the importance of transaction costs in the real world. Transaction costs are any costs that parties may incur in bargaining or resolving disputes over the allocation of resources,[33] including the costs of delineating, enforcing, and monitoring property rights.[34]

Building on Coase, Calabresi and Melamed ask not only to whom the law should award an entitlement but also how law should protect an entitlement, the classic "property rules" versus "liability rules" distinction.[35] Under *property-rule* protection, the law requires an owner's consent before a transfer of property can take place at a bargained-for price. The law may ensure property-rule protection through injunctions, punitive damages, or criminal sanctions. By contrast, under *liability-rule* protection, the law allows a non-owner to force a transfer of property without the owner's consent if the non-owner pays the "fair market value" to the owner. The law typically provides liability-rule protection through compensatory damages or an equivalent remedy.[36]

The debate over property rules and liability rules raises the question of under what circumstances voluntary versus involuntary exchange is superior.[37] Some proposals in the literature, including certain auction mechanisms and "optional law" instruments,[38] have become divorced from the realities of most transfers. In addition to problems with valuation (e.g., subjective versus objective valuation), liability rules also may entail high assessment costs and rent-seeking.[39] These costs are not always apparent without examining how legal systems actually employ liability rules.

Moreover, in analyzing property rules versus liability rules, the Calabresi-Melamed framework presents a stylized two-party model. As is generally true with stylized

---

[32] See, e.g., Hendricks v. Stalnaker, 380 S.E.2d 198 (W. Va. 1989).

[33] Polinsky, *supra* note 1, at 14.

[34] Douglas W. Allen, "Transaction Costs," in *Encyclopedia of Law and Economics, Volume 1: The History and Methodology of Law and Economics* (Boudewijn Bouckaert & Gerrit De Geest eds., 2000).

[35] Calabresi & Melamed, *supra* note 6.   [36] See *id.* at 1093, 1106–1107.

[37] Louis Kaplow & Steven Shavell, *Property Rules Versus Liability Rules: An Economic Analysis*, 109 HARV. L. REV. 713 (1996); James E. Krier & Stewart J. Schwab, *Property Rules and Liability Rules: The Cathedral in Another Light*, 70 N.Y.U. L. RE Stewart v. 440 (1995).

[38] See, e.g., Ian Ayres, *Optional Law: The Structure of Legal Entitlements* (2005).

[39] See Krier & Schwab, *supra* note 37.

models, the simplicity of the model can be illuminating.[40] But there are problems with this stylized world, especially in property law. The stylized model involves two parties, just as litigation does. But, in reality, the structure of property law involves more than two players. Because property is a right to a thing that is "good against the world," property transfers affect many people and parcels, and may entail information-cost externalities.[41] A more complete economic analysis that includes these transaction costs suggests that the stylized model is incomplete and potentially misleading.

3. *Trespass*

The ability of an owner to use or transfer property depends on the owner's ability to exclude others. Without the ability to exclude others from property and determine how to use property, owners will have little incentive to invest, manage, and use their property for beneficial ends. Thus, trespass law plays a critical function in supporting the right to exclude.

Some courts and commentators have proposed shifting trespass law to a "standard" that balances the reason for excluding and reason for entry.[42] At first glance, such an approach seems consistent with maximizing welfare in individual cases. However, one of the contributions of the "third generation" of law and economics in property law has been to focus on information costs. Information costs help to explain why property, unlike contract, comes in a limited number of standardized forms.[43] Information costs also provide a rationale for why defining property as a collection of use rights ("bundle of rights"), any one of which a court may limit or remove, can be problematic. Early law and economics scholars appear to adopt this conception of property.[44] However, viewing property as a right to a thing that is good against the world and that includes the right to exclude may be more consistent with maximizing social welfare.[45]

Overall, an analysis of property law, including the rights to use, transfer, and exclude, suggests the influence of the economic perspective. In focusing on doctrines and institutions, economic analysis has generated insights into the structure of property law by

---

[40] See, e.g., Spur Industries v. Del E. Webb Development Co., 494 P.2d 700 (Ariz. 1972) ("Rule 4"). But cf. Samuel L. Bray, *Remedies, Meet Economics; Economics, Meet Remedies*, 38 OXFORD J. L. STUD. 71 (2018) (criticizing the *Cathedral* for its representation of remedies and showing the long history of conditional relief in equity).

[41] Thomas W. Merrill & Henry E. Smith, *Optimal Standardization in the Law of Property: The Numerus Clausus Principle*, 110 YALE L.J. 1 (2000). Calabresi and Melamed do consider third parties in discussing inalienability, and one of their justifications for inalienability rules is that certain two-party deals may impose costs on third parties with whom contracting is infeasible. See Lee Anne Fennell, *Adjusting Alienability*, 122 HARV. L. REV. 1403 (2009).

[42] See, e.g., State v. Shack, 277 A.2d 369 (N.J. 1971); see also Gregory S. Alexander, *The Social-Obligation Norm in American Property Law*, 94 CORNELL L. REV. 745 (2009).

[43] Merrill & Smith, *supra* note 41; see also Thomas W. Merrill & Henry E. Smith, *The Property/Contract Interface*, 101 COLUM. L. REV. 773 (2001).

[44] Merrill & Smith, *supra* note 23.

[45] See Thomas W. Merrill & Henry E. Smith, *Making Coasean Property More Coasean*, 54 J.L. & ECON. S77 (2011); see also Jonathan Klick & Gideon Parchomovsky, *The Value of the Right to Exclude: An Empirical Assessment*, 165 U. PA. L. REV. 917 (2016).

incorporating cost-benefit analysis (nuisance law), transaction costs (transfer), and information costs (trespass law).

B. Contracts

Nineteenth-century jurists, including Christopher Columbus Langdell, contributed to an age of formalism in contract law.[46] This formalism was based on deductive legal reasoning and generally eschewed functional analysis. In the early twentieth century, scholars such as Oliver Wendell Holmes, Arthur Corbin, and Karl Llewellyn "rejected the classical aspiration to formality and dismantled ruthlessly the deductive system that the classicists had constructed."[47] The movement known as legal realism arguably cleared a path for law and economics,[48] including economic analysis contract law,[49] but more recent scholars within law and economics have questioned some of its premises and conclusions.

The first generation of law and economics scholars focused on a number of issues, including the remedies for breach. Posner originally emphasized that expectation damages are socially desirable because "they induce performance if and only if the cost of performance is relatively low."[50] Shavell pointed out that expectation damages are mutually desirable for the contracting parties themselves, that damages measures are implicit substitutes for more complete contracts, and that damage measures will affect incentives to rely.[51] Schwartz investigated specific performance, arguing that it should be as routine as damages.[52] The second generation of economic analysis of contracts also included research on incomplete contracts, contractual holdup, and remedies for breach.

However, some contract scholars in law and economics have rejected several of the law reforms of the legal realists. For example, the realists incorporated the legal enforcement of custom into Article 2 of the Uniform Commercial Code and the *Restatement*

---

[46] See Bruce A. Kimball, *Langdell on Contracts and Legal Reasoning: Correcting the Holmesian Caricature*, 25 LAW & HIST. REV. 345 (2007).

[47] David Charny, *The New Formalism in Contract*, 66 U. CHI. L. REV. 842, 842 (1999).

[48] Richard A. Posner, "The Law and Economics Movement: From Bentham to Becker," in *The Origins of Law and Economics* 328, 344–345 (Francesco Parisi & Charles K. Rowley eds., 2005).

[49] Alan Schwartz, "Karl Llewellyn and the Early Law and Economics of Contract," in 2 *The New Palgrave Dictionary of Economics and the Law* 421 (Peter Newman ed., 1998).

[50] Shavell, *supra* note 1, at 311 (citing Richard A. Posner, *Economic Analysis of Law* (1973)); see also Robert L. Birmingham, *Breach of Contract, Damage Measures, and Economic Efficiency*, 24 RUTGERS L. REV. 273 (1970).

[51] See Shavell, *supra* note 1, at 312 (citing Steven Shavell, *Damage Measures for Breach of Contract*, 11 BELL J. ECON. 466 (1980)); Steven Shavell, *The Design of Contracts and Remedies for Breach*, 99 Q.J. ECON. 121 (1984).

[52] Alan Schwartz, *The Case for Specific Performance*, 89 YALE L.J. 271 (1979); Alan Schwartz, *The Myth That Promisees Prefer Supracompensatory Remedies: An Analysis of Contracting for Damage Measures*, 100 YALE L.J. 369 (1990).

(Second) of Contracts. But, from an economic perspective, the realists' incorporation of custom is questionable.[53] For one thing, the norms and practices that contracting parties adhere to during a contractual relationship might be different from the provisions the parties would like a court to apply following breach after a contractual relationship has ended. Many law and economics scholars embrace a "new formalism"[54] based on functional justifications.[55] This new formalism posits that a textual, rather than contextual, interpretation of contracts between sophisticated commercial parties is socially desirable; these parties incur costs to formalize their obligations in writing, which permits a party to stand on its rights under the written contract, improves incentives to invest in the deal, and reduces litigation costs.[56]

This renewed focus on doctrines, institutions, and practices is striking because, unlike classical formalists, who thought and wrote as lawyers, contemporary formalists tend to be economists and other social scientists. These scholars have advanced our understanding of contracts through the application of economic principles. But there is a risk that "social scientists are not likely to spend their careers parsing judicial decisions and building doctrinal superstructures; they are not likely to value the intuitive judgments of practitioners."[57] Economists and economically oriented legal scholars within the New Private Law aim to maintain the "comparative advantage" of relying on "experts trained in law and legal institutions,"[58] while also analyzing the law from an economic perspective, including issues of contract formation, interpretation, and breach.

Doctrines affecting contract formation are important because the law of contracts is concerned with facilitating mutually beneficial transactions.[59] Law and economics scholars generally endorse freedom of contract. Limited public policy exceptions may apply in situations in which a party may not have agreed to enter into a contract voluntarily, for example, because of duress or incapacity,[60] or if the contract imposes significant external costs on third parties, for example, a collusive agreement that harms consumers. But, in general, the parties should be able to form

---

[53] Lisa Bernstein, *The Questionable Empirical Basis of Article 2's Incorporation Strategy: A Preliminary Study*, 66 U. CHI. L. REV. 710 (1999); David Charny, *Nonlegal Sanctions in Commercial Transactions*, 104 HARV. L. REV. 373 (1990); Alan Schwartz, *Relational Contracts in the Courts: An Analysis of Incomplete Agreements and Judicial Strategies*, 21 J. LEGAL STUD. 271 (1992); Robert E. Scott, *Conflict and Cooperation in Long-Term Contracts*, 75 CAL. L. REV. 2005 (1987).

[54] Charny, *supra* note 47, at 842.

[55] On the convergence of formalism and functionalism in contract law, see Alan Schwartz & Daniel Markovits, this volume.

[56] Alan Schwartz & Robert E. Scott, *Contract Theory and the Limits of Contract Law*, 113 YALE L.J. 541 (2003); Alan Schwartz & Robert E. Scott, *Contract Interpretation Redux*, 119 YALE L.J. 926 (2010); Alan Schwartz & Robert E. Scott, *The Common Law of Contract and the Default Rule Project*, 102 VA. L. REV. 1523 (2016).

[57] Mark L. Movsesian, *Formalism in American Contract Law: Classical and Contemporary*, 12 Ius Gentium 115, 144 (2006).

[58] *Id.* at 144.

[59] See Shavell, *supra* note 1; see also Charles J. Goetz & Robert E. Scott, *Enforcing Promises: An Examination of the Basis of Contract*, 89 YALE L.J. 1261 (1980).

[60] Steven Shavell, *Contractual Holdup and Legal Intervention*, 36 J. LEGAL STUD. 325 (2007).

a contract for any purpose without judicial intervention or review of the agreement's substantive provisions.

Law and economics scholars also have provided key insights on contract interpretation, especially for incomplete contracts.[61] In contract settings, parties can negotiate before a dispute arises. So, one question is: Why have contract law? The answer, going back to Coase, is transaction costs, defined broadly to include imperfect information. It would be prohibitively costly, and likely impossible, to negotiate and draft a provision for every possible contingency.[62] Due to unforeseen and unprovided-for contingences, contracts are incomplete. Contract law aims to fill in the "gaps," that is, to provide default rules for what parties would have specified if they could have bargained with complete information and without transaction costs.[63] Under these circumstances, parties would select terms to maximize the parties' joint interests. The literature on incomplete contracts is immense,[64] A including how these gaps affect contract design,[65] interpretation,[66] and breach.

Finally, as noted previously, law and economics has analyzed the optimal remedy for breach of contract, particularly the choice between damages and specific performance.[67] In a complete contract in which all contingencies are specified, remedies would be unnecessary because breach would not occur. However, the existence of transaction costs and imperfect information mean that parties will not specify contingences that are of low probability or value. In addition to discouraging breach when breach is inefficient, remedies should encourage parties to rely on contracts when doing so is efficient. However, as scholars have shown, none of the remedies is efficient with respect to both breach and reliance.[68] Thus, which remedy is optimal depends on which decision—breach or reliance—is more important. In addition, scholars continue to debate the merits of expectation damages versus specific performance.[69]

[61] Alan Schwartz, "Incomplete Contracts," in 2 *The New Palgrave Dictionary of Economics and the Law* 277 (Peter Newman ed., 1998); see also Shavell, *supra* note 1, at 299–304.

[62] Polinsky, *supra* note 1.

[63] See Ian Ayres & Robert Gertner, *Filling Gaps in Incomplete Contracts: An Economic Theory of Default Rules*, 99 YALE L.J. 87 (1989); Frank H. Easterbrook & Daniel R. Fischel, *Contract and Fiduciary Duty*, 36 J.L. & ECON. 425 (1993); Robert E. Scott, *A Relational Theory of Default Rules for Commercial Contracts*, 19 J. LEGAL STUD. 597 (1990). The law and economics literature also distinguishes between different types of default rules, including majoritarian, penalty, and sticky defaults.

[64] See Oliver Hart, *Incomplete Contracts and Control*, 107 AM. ECON. REV. 1731 (2017); Eric Maskin & Jean Tirole, *Unforeseen Contingencies and Incomplete Contracts*, 66 REV. ECON. STUD. 83 (1999).

[65] See Robert E. Scott & George G. Triantis, *Incomplete Contracts and the Theory of Contract Design*, 56 CASE W. RESERVE L. REV. 1 (2006).

[66] See Alan Schwartz & Joel Watson, *Conceptualizing Contractual Interpretation*, 42 J. LEGAL STUD. 1 (2013).

[67] See *supra* notes 50–52 and accompanying text. On the remedy of specific performance, see Samuel L. Bray, this volume.

[68] See Polinsky, *supra* note 1.

[69] Schwartz, *supra* note 52; Steven Shavell, *Specific Performance Versus Damages for Breach of Contract: An Economic Analysis*, 84 TEX. L. REV. 831 (2006).

Recent scholarship that intersects with NPL tackles several of these issues, from remedies based on specific performance and self-help to the idea of "efficient breach."[70]

Overall, an analysis of contract doctrine, including rules for formation, interpretation, and breach, suggests the influence of the economic perspective. Law and economics has generated insights into the content and structure of contract law by focusing on mutually beneficial transactions (formation), incomplete contracts (interpretation), and optimal remedies (breach).

C. Torts

Tort law has been central to American legal practice and legal thought since America's founding.[71] During the Industrial Revolution, tort law went through dramatic changes, including a shift from strict liability to negligence.[72] Then, during the 1920s and 1930s, legal realists attacked the idea of "fault" in connection with accidents; many realists argued that the function of tort law was to provide insurance, not deter accidents.[73]

The first generation of law and economics scholarship began with Coase's article on "The Problem of Social Cost" and Calabresi's first article on tort law.[74] As Posner and Landes state: "An initially neglected aspect of Coase's article was his examination of actual English nuisance cases and his suggestion that the English courts had displayed a better (intuitive) grasp of the economics of the problem than had economists in the Pigovian tradition."[75] By contrast, "Calabresi was interested in constructing an efficient system of accident law from first principles rather than in appraising the operations of the existing system of accident law."[76] Thus, even early law and economics scholars had different views about the role of doctrine and structure.

A decade later, Calabresi published *The Costs of Accidents: A Legal and Economic Analysis*, and Posner published several articles on strict liability and negligence.[77] Since then, Landes, Posner, Shavell, and others in both the first and second generations of law

---

[70] Yonathan A. Arbel, *Contract Remedies in Action: Specific Performance*, 118 W. VA. L. REV. 100 (2015); Mark P. Gergen, *A Theory of Self-Help Remedies in Contract*, 89 B.U. L. REV. 1397 (2009); Daniel Markovits & Alan Schwartz, *The Myth of Efficient Breach: New Defenses of the Expectation Interest*, 97 VA. L. REV. 1939 (2011).

[71] John C. Goldberg, *Tort Law at the Founding*, 39 FLA. ST. U. L. REV. 85 (2011).

[72] See Morton J. Horwitz, *The Transformation of American Law, 1780–1860* (1977). But cf. Robert J. Kaczorowski, *The Common-Law Background of Nineteenth-Century Tort Law*, 51 OHIO ST. L.J. 1127 (1990).

[73] See Richard A. Posner & William M. Landes, *The Positive Economic Theory of Tort Law*, 15 GA. L. REV. 851, 853 (1980).

[74] Coase, *supra* note 4; Guido Calabresi, *Some Thoughts on Risk Distribution and the Law of Torts*, 70 YALE L.J. (1961).

[75] Posner & Landes, *supra* note 73, at 854.   [76] *Id.* at 854–855.

[77] Richard A. Posner, *A Theory of Negligence*, 1 J. LEGAL STUD. 29 (1972); Richard A. Posner, *Strict Liability: A Comment*, 2 J. LEGAL STUD. 205 (1973).

and economics have investigated tort issues from an economic perspective.[78] In addition, the second and third generations of law and economics include empirical studies of tort issues, from no-fault accidents to medical malpractice.[79] While many NPL tort scholars have not focused on economic or functional concerns, including the influential civil recourse theory,[80] other scholars have used economic insights to examine various aspects of tort law,[81] including nuisance law,[82] as well as liability for accidents, insurance, and products liability.

In analyzing the liability for accidents, economic scholars focus on which rule of liability will maximize the joint interests of the parties. In both nuisance law (see section III.A.1) and breach of contract (see section III.B), bargaining can lead to an efficient solution. However, in accidents, the parties do not know in advance with whom to bargain. Nevertheless, Coase's work remains relevant: the efficient rule should be based on what the parties would have chosen if they could have negotiated costlessly before the accident.[83]

In comparing strict liability versus negligence, law and economics emphasizes levels of care and activity levels for unilateral and bilateral accidents. If the only issue is how to induce an injurer to take appropriate care, both strict liability and negligence are efficient, provided that liability equals damages under strict liability or the standard of care corresponds to the efficient outcome under negligence. If the problem is to induce both the injurer and victim to take care, either strict liability plus contributory negligence or negligence is efficient.[84]

---

[78] William M. Landes & Richard A. Posner, *The Economic Structure of Tort Law* (1987); Shavell, *supra* note 13; A. Mitchell Polinsky, *Strict Liability vs. Negligence in a Market Setting*, 70 Am. Econ. Rev. 363 (1980).

[79] For early studies, see, e.g., Elisabeth M. Landes, *Insurance, Liability, and Accidents: A Theoretical and Empirical Investigation of the Effect of No-fault Accidents*, 25 J.L. & Econ. 49 (1982); Patricia M. Danzon, *Medical Malpractice: Theory, Evidence, and Public Policy* (1985). More recently, several chapters in the *Research Handbook on the Economics of Torts* (Jennifer H. Arlen ed., 2013) focus on empirical issues in tort law, including Michael Heise, "Empirical Analysis of Civil Litigation: Tort Trials in State Courts," at 11; W. Kip Viscusi, "Empirical Analysis of Tort Damages," at 460; Catherine M. Sharkey, "Economic Analysis of Punitive Damages: Theory, Empirics, and Doctrine," at 486; Theodore Eisenberg, "The Empirical Effects of Tort Reform," at 513, and Kathryn Zeiler & Lorian Hardcastle, "Do Damage Caps Reduce Medical Malpractice Insurance Premiums? A Systematic Review of Estimates and the Methods Used to Produce Them," at 551.

[80] See John C.P. Goldberg, this volume; see also John C.P. Goldberg & Benjamin C. Zipursky, "Rights and Responsibility in the Law of Torts," in *Rights and Private Law* 251 (D. Nolan & A. Robertson eds., 2012); Benjamin C. Zipursky & John C.P. Goldberg, *Torts as Wrongs*, 88 Tex. L. Rev. 917 (2010).

[81] Keith N. Hylton, *New Private Law Theory and Tort Law: A Comment*, 125 Harv. L. Rev. F. 173 (2012).

[82] See *supra* section III.A.1; see also Hylton, *supra* note 31.

[83] Polinsky, *supra* note 1; see also United States v. Carroll Towing Co., 159 F.2d 169 (2d Cir. 1947) (providing basis for the "Hand" formula, a balancing test for determining the standard of care in negligence).

[84] Polinsky, *supra* note 1.

However, expected accident losses depend not only on the level of care by the parties but also on the parties' activity levels. Thus, in general, the problem is how to induce both parties to take appropriate care and to engage in the activity to an appropriate extent. In situations in which the problem is to induce the injurer both to take appropriate care and to engage in the correct level of the activity, strict liability is efficient, while negligence is not. Under a negligence rule, the injurer will engage in the activity excessively, unless the standard of care encompasses activity levels.[85]

This analysis assumes that the parties are risk-neutral. But, often, individuals are risk-averse. One of the contributions of law and economics is to incorporate systematically the idea that individuals are often risk-averse.[86] A common way of mitigating or eliminating risk is insurance. However, by eliminating risk, insurance may have an undesirable effect: the problem of moral hazard,[87] which arises when the insured party lacks sufficient incentive to take precautions.[88]

Finally, in products liability cases, tort law uses a rule of strict liability. Recently, Polinsky and Shavell have argued that the case for products liability is weak for a range of products that consumers may purchase.[89] Their claim is based on the idea that firms worry about their reputations even in the absence of legal liability and that the litigation costs of the tort system are very high. Therefore, they argue, the use of products liability may not be warranted, especially for products in which both market forces and regulations are strong.[90]

Overall, this brief analysis of tort law suggests the influence of the economic perspective. Law and economics has generated insights into the structure of tort law by emphasizing the idea of deterrence and incorporating care and activity levels (liability for accidents), risk and moral hazard (insurance), and reputation and litigation costs (products liability).

IV. ADVANCED PRIVATE LAW SUBJECTS

A. Business Associations

As in welfare economics more generally, the economic analysis of law focuses on *welfare*-maximization, not *wealth*-maximization. Nevertheless, modern law and economics also addresses a number of subjects involving high financial stakes,

---

[85] *Id.*   [86] In contrast to many individuals, firms may be risk-neutral.

[87] George A. Akerlof, *The Market for "Lemons": Quality Uncertainty and the Market Mechanism*, 84 Q.J. ECON. 488 (1970).

[88] Polinsky, *supra* note 1.

[89] A. Mitchell Polinsky & Steven M. Shavell, *The Uneasy Case for Product Liability*, 123 HARV. L. REV. 1436 (2010).

[90] *Id.* But cf. Benjamin C. Zipursky & John C.P. Goldberg, *The Easy Case for Products Liability Law: A Response to Professors Polinsky and Shavell*, 123 HARV. L. REV. 1919 (2010).

including business associations. For example, in "The Nature of the Firm," Coase asked why some business activities occur within the "firm," while others occur in the "market."[91]

A number of theories seek to explain corporations and other business associations, including their existence, organization, and functions. Coase provided a transactions costs theory of the firm: individuals organize production in firms when the costs of coordinating production through market exchange are greater than the costs of organizing production within the firm. Other economists focus on managerial theories of the firm; they emphasize that managers may seek to maximize their own utility and shareholders cannot costlessly monitor how these managers are behaving.[92] Other economists, most notably Oliver Williamson, as well as scholars in New Institutional Economics, argue that the existence of firms derives from "asset specificity" in production and other institutional factors.[93] Indeed, Grossman, Hart, & More have developed a "property rights approach" to the theory of the firm: if contracts are incomplete and cannot identify what to do in every possible contingency, then property rights and firm boundaries, that is, institutions, matter.[94]

In addition, the agency costs that arise because of the different interests of shareholders and managers have raised thorny questions regarding corporate governance. As Jensen and Meckling illustrated, a principal-agent problem arises because shareholders, the principal, seek to maximize profits but managers, their agents, have incentives that may diverge.[95] On the other hand, shareholders may have an incentive to be too "short-termist" and prevent managers from investing in long-term projects that may increase firm value. The extent to which the law should increase shareholder rights or protect managers and directors remains highly contested.[96]

Like property, contract, and tort law, the economic analysis of business associations evolved over three generations of law and economics scholarship. In the first generation, many scholars focused on economic explanations for existing doctrines and

[91] Coase, *supra* note 4.
[92] See William J. Baumol, *On the Theory of Expansion of the Firm*, 52 AM. ECON. REV. 1078 (1962); see also Armen A. Alchian & Harold Demsetz, *Production, Information Costs, and Economic Organization*, 62 AM. ECON. REV. 777 (1972); Yoram Barzel, *Measurement Cost and the Organization of Markets*, 25 J.L. & ECON. 27 (1982).
[93] Oliver E. Williamson, *Markets and Hierarchies: Analysis and Antitrust Implications* (1975); see also Barak Richman, this volume.
[94] Oliver Hart, *Firms, Contracts, and Financial Structure* (1995); Sanford J. Grossman & Oliver D. Hart, *The Costs and Benefits of Ownership: A Theory of Vertical and Lateral Integration*, 94 J. POL. ECON. 691 (1986); Oliver Hart & John Moore, *Property Rights and the Nature of the Firm*, 98 J. POL. ECON. 1119 (1990).
[95] Michael C. Jensen & William H. Meckling, *Theory of the Firm: Managerial Behavior, Agency Costs and Ownership Structure*, 3 J. FIN. ECON. 305 (1976).
[96] Compare Lucian Arye Bebchuk, *The Case for Increasing Shareholder Power*, 118 HARV. L. REV. 833 (2005), with K.J. Martijn Cremers & Simone Sepe, *The Shareholder Value of Empowered Boards*, 68 STAN. L. REV. 67 (2016).

institutions.[97] In the second generation, corporate law and economics scholarship focused less on law and more on policy. This generation included a surge of empirical studies in corporate law.[98] In the third generation, many scholars have adopted a renewed focus on the relevance of law and institutions.[99]

B. Trusts and Estates

Until recently, law and economics has had relatively little to say about donative transfers, including the donative side of trust law.[100] Unlike business associations, trusts and estates does not deal primarily with firms and markets. Instead, trusts and estates focuses on altruistic individuals and gifts. However, the economic analysis of donative transfers has resulted in significant law reforms. Moreover, recent scholarship has incorporated agency costs and various economic insights in analyzing trustees and other fiduciaries.

First, law and economics generally assumes that individuals are rational and self-interested. But this notion of self-interest is capacious: it includes altruistic motivations, as a donor's utility function may include a donee's utility as well.[101] Accordingly, economic analysis of wills, trusts, and estates also includes foundational work on the bequest motive,[102] including attempts to control the behavior of children.[103]

Second, the handful of trusts and estates scholars writing from an economic perspective have focused on legal doctrines.[104] An early example of this attention to law reform was the application of modern portfolio theory to trust investment law. Richard Posner, one of the founders of law and economics, and John Langbein, a leading scholar of trusts and estates, collaborated on a series of articles on the prudent

[97] Berle & Means, *supra* note 3; Coase, *supra* note 3; Jensen & Meckling, *supra* note 95; Henry G. Manne, *Some Theoretical Aspects of Share Voting*, 64 COLUM. L. REV. 1427 (1964); Ralph K. Winter Jr., *State Law, Shareholder Protection, and the Theory of the Corporation*, 6 J. LEGAL STUD. 251 (1977).

[98] Sanjai Bhagat & Roberta Romano, "Empirical Studies of Corporate Law," in *Handbook of Law and Economics*, Vol. 2 (A. Mitchell Polinsky & Steven Shavell eds., 2007).

[99] See, e.g., Gabriel Rauterberg & Eric Talley, *Contracting Out of the Fiduciary Duty of Loyalty: An Empirical Analysis of Corporate Opportunity Waivers*, 117 COLUM. L. REV. 1075 (2017).

[100] John D. Morley & Robert H. Sitkoff, this volume; see also Gordon Tullock, *Inheritance Justified*, 14 J.L. & ECON. 465, 465 (1971) ("I have not been able to turn up any serious effort to apply welfare economics to the problem.").

[101] Shavell, *supra* note 1, at 58.

[102] Douglas B. Bernheim, *How Strong Are Bequest Motives? Evidence Based on Estimates of the Demand for Life Insurance and Annuities*, 99 J. POL. ECON. 899 (1991); Kathleen McGarry, *Inter Vivos Transfers and Intended Bequests*, 73 J. PUB. ECON. 321 (1999).

[103] Douglas B. Bernheim, Andrei Shleifer, & Lawrence Summers, *The Strategic Bequest Motive*, 93 J. POL. ECON. 1045 (1985); Audrey Light & Kathleen McGarry, *Why Parents Play Favorites: Explanations for Unequal Bequests*, 94 AM. ECON. REV. 1669 (2004).

[104] Daniel B. Kelly, *Toward Economic Analysis of the Uniform Probate Code*, 45 U. MICH. J.L. REFORM 855 (2012); Robert H. Sitkoff, *An Agency Costs Theory of Trust Law*, 89 CORNELL L. REV. 621 (2004).

investor rule.[105] Their work on trust investment law has led to law reform that all 50 states have adopted.[106]

Third, more property now passes outside of probate, through revocable trusts and other nonprobate transfers, than in probate, via intestate succession and wills.[107] As a result, the use of trusts has become increasingly important.[108] A trust is a mechanism that provides managerial intermediation: a settlor transfers trust property to a trustee who invests, manages, and distributes the property for the benefit of the trust beneficiaries. For this reason, like corporate law, trust law involves principal-agent problems. Applying agency costs theory to trust law, Robert Sitkoff has discussed how trust and fiduciary law rely on fiduciary duties to mitigate these costs.[109] Thus, trusts and estates scholars are increasingly incorporating economic insights into their analyses of legal rules and institutions.

C. Intellectual Property

Under the U.S. Constitution's Intellectual Property (IP) Clause, Congress has the power "To promote the progress of science and useful arts, by securing for limited times to authors and inventors the exclusive right to their respective writings and discoveries."[110] As commentators have noted: "This language is understood by most courts and scholars to entail a utilitarian or consequentialist approach to IP law. The possibility of obtaining copyrights and patents encourages creators to produce new innovations that ultimately redound to the public good."[111] Intellectual property law arguably involves a mixture of both private and public law. But economic analysis serves to highlight the justifications and limitations of intellectual property, including the social benefits of providing incentives to create information and the social costs of monopolies.

In private law, real property and intellectual property are similar in certain ways. For example, protecting a landowner's right to exclude through trespass law may be socially beneficial because it allows the owner to use his or her property without interference from others with certain exceptions and limitations such as necessity and

[105] See John H. Langbein & Richard A. Posner, *The Revolution in Trust Investment Law*, 62 A.B.A.J. 887 (1976).

[106] See Uniform Prudent Investor Act; see also Max M. Schanzenbach & Robert H. Sitkoff, *Did Reform of Prudent Trust Investment Laws Change Trust Portfolio Allocation?*, 50 J.L. & ECON. 681 (2007).

[107] Robert H. Sitkoff & Jesse Dukeminier, *Wills, Trusts, and Estates* 40 & n.66 (10th ed. 2017); John H. Langbein, *Curing Execution Errors and Mistaken Terms in Wills*, 18 PROB. & PROP. 28, 30 (2004).

[108] On the structure of trust law, see John D. Morley & Robert H. Sitkoff, this volume.

[109] Sitkoff, *supra* note 104; Robert H. Sitkoff, *The Economic Structure of Fiduciary Law*, 91 B.U. L. REV. 1039 (2011).

[110] U.S. CONST. art. I, sec. 8, cl. 8.

[111] Christopher Buccafusco & Jonathan S. Masur, "Intellectual Property Law and the Promotion of Welfare," in *Research Handbook on the Economics of Intellectual Property Law* 98 (Ben Depoorter & Peter Menell eds., 2019); see also Landes & Posner, *supra* note 9.

antidiscrimination laws.[112] Similarly, protecting an IP owner's right to exclude through an injunction for patent or copyright infringement may be beneficial as it allows the owner to use his or her intellectual property without copying by others with certain exceptions and limitations such as fair use.[113] However, the underlying justification for property rights differs for tangible versus intangible property.

The justification for property rights in tangible property is relatively straightforward. Property rights in tangible things (land, cars, jewelry, etc.) allow parties to invest in and use their property in various ways. In addition, property rights in tangible things allow people to exchange things so that scarce resources can be allocated efficiently among potential users. Thus, property rights promote the optimal investment, use, and transfer of tangible property.

But there is a different justification for property rights in information or intangible things (inventions, drugs, movies, etc.). Because information is a "nonrival" good, one party's use of the information does not preclude its use by another. Thus, the socially optimal allocation of information, once it is created, is to share the information with everyone, or at least everyone for whom the private benefits exceed the costs of copying. However, information can be costly to produce. Consider a firm that is deciding to invest in the development of a new drug with R&D costs of several billion dollars and a high risk of failure. Without the possibility of an exclusive right, inventors (or their investors), knowing that others would be able to copy their ideas, might have an inadequate incentive to create. An economic approach suggests "the primary reason for creating property rights in information is to provide incentives for producing more of it, not to assure that it is allocated efficiently among potential users."[114]

However, an IP right essentially gives the owner a monopoly right. When the law awards an IP right over information, the holder of a patent or copyright has the exclusive right to use this information and may exclude others, including its competitors, from using the IP, if the owner meets certain prerequisites for injunctive relief. As a result, this owner can charge a monopoly price, in which some users will not have access to the information even though their private benefit from the property exceeds the competitive price. This monopoly price creates a deadweight loss. While IP rights may be necessary to provide incentives for producing information (or commercializing inventions and new works), this deadweight loss is a social cost. For this reason, IP law gives authors and inventors only "time-limited" property rights, after which time the IP rights expire and anyone is able to use the information as part of the public domain.

---

[112] See *supra* section III.A.3.

[113] See Henry E. Smith, *Intellectual Property as Property: Delineating Entitlements in Information*, 116 YALE L.J. 1742 (2007).

[114] Merrill & Smith, *supra* note 5; see also Ronald A. Cass & Keith N. Hylton, *Laws of Creation: Property Rights in the World of Ideas* (2013). In addition to this "reward" theory, another economic justification for intellectual property is based on "commercialization" theories, which also tend to point to the use of private law concepts and property rights protection. See, e.g., Edmund W. Kitch, *The Nature and Function of the Patent System*, 20 J.L. & ECON. 265 (1977); Robert Merges, *Commercial Success and Patent Standards: Economic Perspectives on Innovation*, 76 CAL. L. REV. 803 (1988); Stephen Yelderman, *Coordination-Focused Patent Policy*, 96 B.U. L. REV. 1565 (2016).

The economic approach has long been influential in IP law, and recent scholars, including scholars in NPL, also have analyzed the economic justifications and effects of IP's legal doctrines and institutions.[115]

V. Conclusion

The economic analysis of law has had a profound effect on private law over three generations of law and economics scholarship. In the first generation, many scholars used economic insights to explain, justify, or reform legal doctrines, institutions, and structures. In the second generation, the "law" at times became secondary, with less focus on doctrines, institutions, and structures, but greater assessment of empirical issues. In the third generation, there has been a resurgence of interest in the law and legal institutions, including a number of NPL scholars writing from an economic perspective. These scholars have contributed insights about the economic structure of property, contracts, and torts, as well as business associations, trusts and estates, and intellectual property.

Going forward, there is the potential for a great synergy between law and economics and New Private Law in theoretical, empirical, experimental, and institutional analysis. For example, just as Merrill and Smith use economic analysis to provide a deeper understanding of the structure of property law, NPL scholars can engage in theoretical analyses in fields such as contract and tort law. Furthermore, NPL can inform empirical studies by emphasizing the importance of doctrines and institutions in designing empirical projects and collecting and coding data. Likewise, NPL can inform experimental work in law and the social sciences.[116] And, given their mutual interest in legal institutions and structures, there is a natural synergy between NPL and New Institutional Economics.[117] Overall, there are many opportunities for future generations of scholars in the economic analysis of private law.

Acknowledgments

Thanks to Samuel Bray, Erik Hovenkamp, Alan Schwartz, Emily Sherwin, Henry Smith, and participants at the Landscape of Private Law conference at Harvard Law School for their helpful comments and suggestions.

[115] See, e.g., Cass & Hylton, *supra* note 114; Smith, *supra* note 113; see also Robert P. Merges, "Philosophical Foundations of IP Law: The Law and Economics Paradigm," in *Research Handbook on the Economics of Intellectual Property Law* 72 (Ben Depoorter & Peter Menell eds., 2019). On the intersection of intellectual property and New Private Law, see Molly Van Houweling, this volume.

[116] See, e.g., Tess Wilkinson-Ryan, *Incentives to Breach*, 17 Am. L. & Econ. Rev. 290 (2015); Tess Wilkinson-Ryan, *Do Liquidated Damages Encourage Breach? A Psychological Experiment*, 108 Mich. L. Rev. 633 (2010); Tess-Wilkinson-Ryan, this volume.

[117] See Barak Richman, this volume; see also Richard A. Posner, *The New Institutional Economics Meets Law and Economics*, 149 J. Inst. & Theoretical Econ. 73 (1993).

CHAPTER 7

......

NEW INSTITUTIONAL ECONOMICS

......

BARAK RICHMAN

I. Introduction

THE architects of this volume on the New Private Law (NPL) are prescient in asking for a chapter on New Institutional Economics (NIE). Those unfamiliar with NPL, aside from noting that both fields begin with the word "New," would wonder why an encyclopedia on a budding movement in legal scholarship would be associated with a particular subfield of economics. Those familiar would not. NPL and NIE share methodological orientations; they share scholarly priorities; they have influenced each other; and they offer parallel paths ahead.

I begin this entry by describing my own understanding of the NPL. I do not expect my understanding to be too different from the other contributors to this volume, but it is fruitful to use my own words to describe this emerging field. I then offer a brief introduction to NIE and its intersection with the study of legal doctrines and institutions. In this second section, I pay particular attention to NIE scholarship's focus on subjects related to private law and, reciprocally, how legal scholarship illustrates how the law reflects the teachings of NIE. Lastly, in an effort to identify common principles that sustain both academic movements, I discuss how both NPL and NIE exhibit the hallmarks of interdisciplinary, scholarly pluralism, and an inquisitive focus on real-world, tractable problems. I conclude with some thoughts about the future of NPL, and in particular the lessons it can take from NIE's successes.

II. The New Private Law

A provocateur would say that the New Private Law is not new, not private, and not law. There is some truth to the provocation. In spite of the *new* moniker, NPL looks backward, rescuing old doctrines more than creating new ones. Henry Smith, illustrating how NPL can correct some excesses in prevailing legal realism, has remarked that "traditional baselines [are] very worthy of explanation and a good deal of respect."[1] Although NPL focuses on fields that conventionally have been categorized as *private law* (contract, property, and tort), the normative motivations of NPL are very public oriented. John Goldberg addresses the conflation of private law with public motives directly, noting that while some assert that "all law is public law," private law—not just through courts—plays a public purpose specifically because it "enable[s] individuals and entities to define their relationships and to assert and demand the resolution of claims against others."[2] And it could be said that NPL is less *law* than a way of operationalizing the law to achieve normative ends. Although Benjamin Zipursky observed that NPL requires one to "think and theorize like lawyers," he emphasized that the field recognizes "a pragmatism that is sensitive to which functions the law serves, critical as to how well it is serving those functions, and open-minded about how it might better serve them."[3]

Regardless of its label, NPL describes a discernable scholarly movement.[4] Or better yet, it reflects some identifiable areas of scholarly emphasis. Although these points of emphasis reflect both methodological and normative diversity, the emerging field is more than an assembly of remotely related concepts. I aim in this opening section to describe the core elements of (my understanding of) the New Private Law.

A. Interdisciplinary, Multinormative Functionalism

The predominant feature of New Private Law is its broad commitment to functionalism, that is, its objective is to assess and understand the law from a normative foundation.[5] NPL embraces the enduring tradition of the realists insofar as it continues the "law and" pursuit to employ nonlegal disciplines to assess and understand the law. At the same time, NPL embraces a broader, more nuanced, and more intertwined functionalism than the realists.

---

[1] Henry E. Smith, *Property as the Law of Things*, 125 HARV. L. REV. 1691, 1692 (2012).

[2] John C.P. Goldberg, *Introduction: Pragmatism and Private Law*, 125 HARV. L. REV. 1640, 1640 (2012).

[3] Benjamin C. Zipursky, Palsgraf, *Punitive Damages, and Preemption*, 125 HARV. L. REV. 1757, 1757 (2012).

[4] This New Private Law movement, despite what a provocateur might say, is very aptly named. And it should be distinguished from the "New Private Law" described in a 1996 symposium of the *Denver Law Review*, which is defined therein as a movement toward "deregulation, decentralization, privatization, and contractualization" in public policymaking that "prefers the ordering of the private market to that of public decision-makers." See Julie A. Nice, *The New Private Law: An Introduction*, 73 Denver L. Rev., 993 (1996).

[5] In his role as one of the editors of this *Handbook*, and thus one of the editors of this chapter, Andrew Gold remarked that some NPL scholarship is dedicated to the interpretation of the law's concepts, rather than the pursuit of normative approaches. See, e.g., Benjamin C. Zipursky, *Pragmatic Conceptualism*, 6 LEGAL THEORY 457 (2000). I would argue that conceptual approaches at least overlap with normative approaches, but I see Professor Gold's point that the two objectives could be distinct, and thus there at least is a debate as to whether all of NPL scholarship is functionalist.

If one could draw a (flexible) straight line from legal realism to law and economics, and perhaps another flexible (and nearly parallel) line from legal realism to critical legal studies, both lines would lead to New Private Law. This is because NPL embraces the structural critiques and outside perspectives exhibited by both prior movements. But NPL is also decidedly broader than either. The normative motivations underlying both law and economics and critical legal studies are parsimonious, whereas NPL's normative foundations are deliberately multifaceted and pluralistic. NPL scholarship includes, for example, utilitarianism exhibited in Tom Merrill and Henry Smith's assessment of property law through the lens of economizing on information and transaction costs;[6] virtue ethics exhibited by Nate Oman's impressive *Dignity of Commerce*;[7] and corrective justice in Andrew Gold's many works in tort law.[8] In some fields, these works would be at cross-purposes with each other, but in NPL, they are deliberately co-located within a broad normative tent.

Yet while remaining distinctively normative, fully centered within the "law and" scholarly world, NPL scholarship is also meaningfully integrated into and integrative with traditional legal analysis. While realism and, especially, the "law and" world that it spawned tended to eschew and resist doctrinal reasoning and other interpretative strategies that typify the traditional legal method, NPL is in many ways quintessential legal scholarship. Judicial reasoning is part of the fabric of NPL, not merely a means to a desired end. Legal categories, such as law versus equity, or questions of intent, are often central rather than instrumental to the NPL approach. Far from being determined to supplant traditional thinking, NPL is eager to embrace the common law method. Thus, while NPL is committed to functionalism, and certainly is not confined to operating purely within the legal framework, it offers a less confrontational approach than its predecessors.

The diversity and richness—and perhaps messiness—of NPL's partly normative, partly traditional framework is captured nicely in Andrew Gold's chapter in this volume.[9] Though NPL rests upon external normative frameworks, it embraces law from an internal perspective. More than that, it bridges internal and external methodologies. Whereas prior "law and" movements used external frameworks to displace and perhaps squash traditional legal reasoning, NPL aims apply external norms so that they cohere and converge with the internal logic and values of the law.[10]

---

[6] Thomas W. Merrill & Henry E. Smith, *Optimal Standardization in the Law of Property: The Numerus Clausus Principle*, 110 YALE L.J. 1 (2000); Henry E. Smith, *Property as the Law of Things*, 125 HARV. L. REV. 1691 (2012).

[7] Nathan B. Oman, *The Dignity of Commerce: Markets and The Moral Foundations of Contract Law* (2017).

[8] Andrew S. Gold, *A Moral Rights Theory of Private Law*, 52 WM. & MARY L. REV. 1873 (2011); Andrew S. Gold, *A Theory of Redressive Justice*, 64 U. TORONTO L.J. 159 (2014).

[9] Andrew S. Gold, this volume.

[10] One excellent example of synthesizing internal and external approaches to private law is Andrew Gold's and Henry Smith's *Sizing Up Private Law*, U. TORONTO L.J. Advance Online, https://www.utpjournals.press/doi/abs/10.3138/utlj.2019-0038 (November 20, 2019).

B. Deference to Legal Doctrine

The second distinctive feature of NPL is often best illustrated by its contrasts. John Goldberg, soliciting a contrast with NPL, describes the rise of legal realism as an effort to reduce the law to "brass-tacks pragmatism." The sympathetic view of brass-tacks ambitions is to "push[] past the surface to get to what is 'really' at stake," to strip away the pretensions and pretenses of legal formality and to speak the blunt language of normative objectives.[11] But if NPL is a reaction to twentieth- (and twenty-first-) century realism, it is best reflected in its deference to what came before (including to what came before realism). Rather than viewing legal doctrines, processes, and terminologies as façades that obscure more honest normative or predicative forces, the language and formality of the law are accepted as a feature, not a bug, of the law's purpose.

It might be said that traditional legal scholarship identifies legal doctrines as the answer to most questions, whereas legal realism sees doctrine as, at best, a point of contrast for a more theoretically driven alternative (and at worst, a source of confusion that should be discarded). NPL treats legal doctrines as neither dispositive nor ornamental. To the contrary, because legal doctrines were typically hammered out over generations of common law decisions, the presumption is that there is wisdom in the law as it presents itself, even if that wisdom is not immediately apparent. Therefore, even while the NPL scholarly enterprise is to assess the law normatively, it cautions against subsuming the law into purely functional objectives.[12]

This is an approach that has its predecessors. Lon Fuller's seminal "Consideration and Form" would be celebrated as an exemplar of NPL scholarship because it explains a seemingly archaic legal formalism with functional language.[13] Fuller's contribution is the particular observation that the seemingly formalist consideration doctrine serves important evidentiary and channeling purposes that enhance the collective benefits of exchanges that are supported by contract law. Even more so is his agenda, stated candidly in the article's very first sentence, to uncover "the rationale of legal formalities."[14] NPL similarly identifies legal formalities and other doctrines that do not readily have functional explanations and, carefully and with deference, identifies the rationale that motivates and sustains them.

Sometimes this approach is best illustrated when it contrasts with the imperial brass-tacks inclinations of leading legal scholars. After Richard Posner's treatise, *Economic*

---

[11]   Goldberg, *supra* note 2, at 1642.

[12]   I was struck at the frequency with which participants at this *Handbook's* conference began sentences with, "There's a doctrine . . ." They meant that doctrines are, in and of themselves, important and substantive, that normative theories must take them into account and perhaps must conform to their operation. There was an active wrestling with theory and doctrine in ways that are uncommon to my law and economics conferences (in which doctrines are raised only when addressing the policy implications of normative projects) and my general faculty workshops (in which doctrines are invoked to constrain an argument).

[13]   Lon L. Fuller, *Consideration and Form*, 41 COLUM. L. REV. 799–824 (1941).

[14]   *Id.* at 799.

Analysis of the Law,[15] advanced a simple rule of wealth maximization to govern the law of waste, Tom Merrill[16] responded that, in fact, the traditional rule is better at achieving economic efficiency. Approaching the doctrine with NPL's characteristic deference, he observed that it better enables parties to achieve a mutually preferred outcome than Posner's categorical approach. Posner politely disagreed in his own response, but his assessment of Merrill's argument involved a more careful assessment of the doctrine.[17] The exchange illustrates that NPL scholars do not necessarily exhibit different normative commitments from other legal scholars. What distinguishes the NPL method is its deferential approach to the doctrines developed in the common law. The exchange also illustrates that the NPL approach might be contagious and that even those with a more imperial tendency might, after hearing NPL reasoning, become more circumspect in assessing common law doctrines.

C. The New Formalism

At the risk of over-including schools of thought that include the word "New," a central feature of NPL—connected but distinct from its deference to doctrine—is its parallels with another influential movement in legal scholarship: New Formalism.

David Charny described New Formalism as "anti-antiformalism" since it is a reaction to, and is intended as a correction to, the realist jurisprudence that wrested common law doctrines—especially contract law—from its earlier formalism.[18] Realists, led by Karl Llewellyn, sought to shape contract law in the mid-to-late twentieth century to incorporate the nascent rules embedded in the customs and practices of commercial parties.[19] According to Llewellyn, the court's job was to "look for the law in life" and then incorporate an "immanent law" to resolve disputes.[20] This meant adopting more flexible interpretive devices, including inquiring into the subjective intent of the parties, the parties' course of dealing, and the given industry's standards.[21]

New Formalism, primarily motivated to reduce the costs of contracting, squarely aims to reintroduce formalism into contract law. But unlike the formalism of the early twentieth century, in which traditional legal definitions and internal legal logic dictated

---

[15] Richard A. Posner, *Economic Analysis of Law* (8th ed. 2011).

[16] Thomas W. Merrill, *Melms v. Pabst Brewing Co. and the Doctrine of Waste in American Property Law*, 94 MARQ. L. REV. 1055 (2011).

[17] Richard A. Posner, *Comment on Merrill on the Law of Waste*, 94 MARQ. L. REV. 1095 (2011).

[18] David Charny, *The New Formalism in Contract*, 66 U. CHI. L. REV. 842 (1999).

[19] Karl N. Llewellyn, *The Common Law Tradition: Deciding Appeals* (1960).

[20] *Id.* at 122.

[21] See, e.g., Richard Danzig, *A Comment on the Jurisprudence of the Uniform Commercial Code*, 27 STAN. L. REV. 621 (1975); Zipporah B. Wiseman, *The Limits of Vision: Karl Llewellyn and the Merchant Rules*, 100 HARV. L. REV. 465 (1987).

contract law,[22] New Formalism is motivated by a desire to convey predictable outcomes to contracting parties should a dispute spill over into court. It is directed by decidedly functional motivations. Thus, the charge to invoke formalist techniques—including textualist interpretations, strict applications of parol evidence rules and statute of frauds, and eschewing limiting excuse defenses—is considered the path to achieve efficient contracts.

Among the leaders of New Formalism in contract law is perhaps the field's leading scholar, Robert Scott.[23] In contrast to the contextualism that came to dominate contract law in the latter part of the twentieth century, Scott encourages contract law to institute formal, less flexible rules to resolve disputes, especially where parties would be able to tailor those rules to their particular circumstances.[24] Similarly, Lisa Bernstein[25] has observed that even merchant communities, whose repeat dealings are infused with familiar but uncodified contexts and industry norms, institute bright-line rules to govern intercommunity disputes.[26] Scott's normative promotion of contractual formalism and Bernstein's empirical finding that merchants themselves prefer contractual formalism amount to a significant rejection of the motivations underlying, specifically, the Uniform Commercial Code and, more generally, the realists' conceptualization of contract law.

New Formalism has influenced NPL scholarship in property law as well. A leading illustration is Tom Merrill's and Henry Smith's treatment of the *numerus clausus* principle. Meaning "closed number" in Latin, *numerus clausus* stands for the notion that property law's system of estates allows for only a limited number of recognizable property interests. Though its roots lie in Roman law and its abstruseness has kept it from many mainstream property law casebooks, Merrill and Smith argue that the doctrine plays a central role in standardizing property rights.[27] Observing that "[t]he need for standardization in property law stems from an externality involving measurement costs,"[28] Merrill and Smith suggest that "[t]he *numerus clausus* principle can be seen...as a device that moves the system of property rights in the direction of the optimal level of

---

[22] For an authoritative account of the formalists, see Duncan Kennedy, *From the Will Theory to the Principle of Private Autonomy: Lon Fuller's "Consideration and Form,"* 100 COLUM. L. REV. 94, 106 (2000). For a sampling of formalism itself, see C.C. Langdell, *A Summary of the Law of Contracts* 4–5 (1880).

[23] Robert E. Scott, *The Case for Formalism in Relational Contract*, 94 NW. U. L. REV. 847 (2000); Robert E. Scott, "The Uniformity Norm in Commercial Law," in *The Jurisprudential Foundations of Contract and Commercial Law* 152 (Jody S. Kraus & Steven D. Walt eds., 2000).

[24] For a similar but more sweeping approach to contract law, see Alan Schwartz & Robert E. Scott, *Contract Theory and the Limits of Contract Law*, 113 YALE L.J. 541, 587 (2003).

[25] Lisa Bernstein, *Merchant Law in a Merchant Court: Rethinking the Code's Search for Immanent Business Norms*, 144 U. PA. L. REV. 1765 (1996); Lisa Bernstein, *Private Commercial Law in the Cotton Industry: Creating Cooperation Through Rules, Norms, and Institutions*, 99 MICH. L. REV. 1724 (2001).

[26] One critique of Professor Bernstein's seminal work is that it overstates the significance of the substance of these rigid rules in merchant communities that rely on self-enforcement. Barak D. Richman, *Norms and Law: Putting the Horse Before the Cart*, 62 DUKE L.J. 3 (2012).

[27] Merrill & Smith, *supra* note 6.

[28] *Id.* at 26.

standardization."[29] More than rescuing a doctrine (with a Latin moniker!) from obscurity, Merrill and Smith recognize the functional role played by the formality of a generations-old legal rule. Their approach does not start from first principles and then proceed to dictate what the law should be. Rather, reflecting NPL's deference to doctrine, it embraces what the law is and explains the valuable functions it serves. Perhaps more significant, they find that the very inflexibility that the formal rule supplies is central to its utility. The rigid standardization created by a seemingly outdated legal formalism serves a foundational role in supporting property markets.[30]

III. NEW INSTITUTIONAL ECONOMICS

Like NPL, NIE might not deserve its "New" moniker, as its roots extend—at least—to Ronald Coase's famous 1937 article, "The Nature of the Firm,"[31] and more likely to the writings of nineteenth- and early twentieth-century political economists. These intellectual traditions have shaped what is now known as NIE into two distinct branches.

The first branch, associated most famously with Douglass North, examines institutions as "humanly designed constraints that structure political, social, and economic interactions."[32] These constraints arise "in the form of rules and regulations; a set of procedures to detect deviation from the rules and regulations; and, finally, a set of moral, ethical behavioral norms which define the contours that constrain the way in which the rules and regulations are specified and enforcement is carried out."[33] Colloquially, this field of study focuses on the "institutional environment" or "the so-called rules of the game" that provide the framework for human interactions at an aggregate level.

The second branch of NIE, closely associated with Oliver Williamson, focuses on more micro-level behavior. Called "the governance branch" and operationalized by transaction cost economics (TCE), the foundational idea is to describe firms not in neoclassical terms as production functions but in organizational terms as governance structures. The basic insight of TCE is to recognize that we live in a world of positive transaction costs and therefore that exchange agreements must be governed; that assorted governance mechanisms are available to support exchange, but that these

[29] *Id.* at 40.

[30] It is worth noting that Merrill and Smith's approach to property law does not advocate a categorical embrace of formalism (perhaps no one advances formalism across the board, at least not any more). It is hard to defend the utility—or common sense—of some of property law's most rigid and formalistic laws. The central methodological lesson I derive from Merrill & Smith's treatment of the *numerus clausus* is their display of deference and curiosity: they seek to understand the motivation and purpose of the principle before discarding it, and they aim to explain its role rather than merely labeling it as an obsolete common law artifact.

[31] Ronald H. Coase, *The Nature of the Firm*, ECONOMICA N.S. 4:386 (1937) (reprinted in *The Nature of The Firm: Origins, Evolution, Development* 18 (Oliver E. Williamson & Sidney G. Winter eds., 1991)).

[32] Douglass North, *Institutions*, 5 J. ECON. PERSP. 97, 97 (1991).

[33] Douglass North, *The New Institutional Economics: A Symposium*, 140 J. INST. & THEOR. ECON. 7, 8 (1984).

mechanisms vary in the degree to which they can minimize transaction costs; and that, in a market economy that prizes efficiency, transaction-cost economizing governance mechanisms will arise in conjunction with particular transactions. In other words, some forms of governance are better to organize certain transactions than others, and the study of TCE focuses scholars into understanding why particular governance mechanisms succeed where others fail.

Both the *institutional* and the *governance* branches of NIE have been deeply influential inside and outside economics. And of particular significance to this volume, both have had significant effects on the study of legal institutions. The institutional branch has led economic historians and political scientists to look at how constitutions, political structures, and common law doctrines shape growth. Perhaps beginning famously with *The Calculus of Consent* by James Buchanan and Gordon Tullock, public choice scholarship has examined both written legal rules and unwritten legal conventions that affect market outcomes.[34] Political scientists, led especially by Roger Noll and his progeny (McNollgast;[35] Weingast and de Figueiredo[36]), have developed formal models of federalism, legislative procedures, and separation of powers that have reshaped how social scientists and even politicians understand the operations of government. Research by financial economists—for example, the influential series of work by Rafael LaPorta, Florencio Lopez-de-Silanes, Andrei Shleifer, and Robert Vishny (LLSV)—examined how legal origins and the structure of judicial administration continue to shape economic growth, and this scholarship led to aggressive policies instituted by the World Bank, the IMF, and several developing nations.[37] Even scholars of religion have applied institutional economics to understand how religious expressions and cultural norms have shaped economic performance over centuries (e.g., Kuran).[38] It is hard to think of anyone studying political power, political institutions, or development economics who hasn't been deeply influenced by this body of work.

The governance branch's influence on legal scholarship has been equally significant. A recent literature review revealed that "law and policy" journals had more studies relying on TCE and the governance branch than any other field except for economics.[39] Since the focus, or unit of analysis, of the governance branch of NIE is the individual transaction, contract and commercial law have been the most immediate and natural beneficiaries of the NIE framework, but the governance branch has also influenced—and been

---

[34] James M. Buchanan & Gordon Tullock, *The Calculus of Consent* (1962).

[35] McNollgast, *Administrative Procedures as Instruments of Political Control*, 3 J.L., Econ., & Org. 243–277 (1987); McNollgast, *Structure and Process, Politics and Policy: Administrative Arrangements and the Political Control of Agencies*, 75 Va. L. Rev. 431–482 (1989).

[36] Barry Weingast & Rui de Figueiredo, *Self-Reinforcing Federalism*, 21 J.L. Econ. & Org. 103 (2005).

[37] For an overview, see (LLS 2008, JEL). Despite, or perhaps because of, LLSV's influence on policymakers worldwide, its underlying conclusions and techniques have come under scrutiny. See, e.g., Holger Spamann, *The "Antidirector Rights Index" Revisited*, 23 Rev. Fin. Stud. 467 (2010).

[38] Timur Kuran, *Islam and Economic Performance: Historical and Contemporary Links*, 56 J. Econ. Lit. 1292 (2018).

[39] Jeffrey T. Macher & Barak D. Richman, *Transaction Cost Economics: An Assessment of Empirical Research in the Social Sciences*, 10 Bus. & Pol. 1 (2008).

informed by—several other areas of law, including employment law, property law, and antitrust law. NIE's influence on these four fields is discussed in depth.

A. Contract Law

At the center of governance NIE is understanding how transactional problems arise due to bounded rationality and contract incompleteness, how opportunistic behavior can exploit such transactional hazards, and how parties' anticipation of such opportunism informs the governance framework they select. The canonical governance inquiry is the question of vertical integration, also known as the make-or-buy question and embodied in the title of Oliver Williamson's seminal *Markets and Hierarchies*.[40] Following Williamson's lead, NIE predicts that hazardous transactions are more likely to be contained within a vertically integrated firm than to occur between independent transactors.[41]

More contemporary applications of NIE consider assorted legal and structural strategies that anticipate and mitigate problems that impede reliable exchange. And, ceteris paribus, more transactional hazards lead to more contractual safeguards.[42] This extension of NIE into contractual relations—contracts being a particular species of transactions—reveals the joint mission of NIE and NPL. Oliver Williamson observed this over two decades ago, remarking that "[t]here were clearly many complementarities between transaction cost economics and the new contract law. Both also shared the property that they were working out of, but deviating from, the main traditions (in economics ad law, respectively)."[43]

Theoretical parallels between NIE and the modern approach to contract law have since been substantiated empirically. Lyons[44] and Masten and Saussier[45] both offer thorough reviews of NIE and TCE-related empirical work illustrating how contracts and contracting behavior adapt to mitigate anticipated hazards. In TCE lingo, the assorted mechanisms (short of vertical integration) that govern transactions—such as complex contracts, cross-ownership, joint ventures, and other creative designs—are described as "hybrids" since they combine market with hierarchical strategies. Research surrounding hybrids could be described as institutional economists studying lawyers in action.

---

[40] Oliver E. Williamson, *Markets and Hierarchies: Analysis and Antitrust Implications* (1975).

[41] Monteverde and Teece are credited for operationalizing the first empirical test of the make-or-buy question. Kirk Monteverde & David J. Teece, *Supplier Switching Costs and Vertical Integration in the Automobile Industry*, 13 BELL J. ECON. 206 (1982).

[42] Oliver Williamson, *Comparative Economic Organization: The Analysis of Discrete Structural Alternatives*, 36 ADMIN. SCI. Q. 269 (1991).

[43] Oliver E. Williamson, *The Mechanisms of Governance* (1996), at 370.

[44] Bruce R. Lyons, *Empirical Relevance of Efficient Contract Theory: Inter-Firm Contracts*, 12 OXFORD REV. ECON. POL'Y 27 (1996).

[45] Scott E. Masten & Stéphane Saussier, *Econometrics of Contracts: An Assessment of Developments in the Empirical Literature on Contracting*, 92 REVUE D'ECONOMIE INDUSTRIELLE 215 (2000).

Conversely, as NIE and TCE direct attention at transactional hazards and illustrate how parties structure contracts to mitigate transaction costs, contract law scholars observe that contract law is also designed to mitigate the hold-up problem and related contractual hazards. This literature reflects how NIE has informed economic understandings of, and prescriptions for, contract law. Victor Goldberg is among the pioneers in this literature, employing NIE-inspired concepts to understand how contracts can be understood to manage complexity within ongoing relationships,[46] navigate relational exchange,[47] and encourage parties to make critical investments within an enduring enterprise.[48] Richard Posner, in a very famous article that targeted several doctrines in contract law, articulated how the consideration doctrine has been applied and interpreted to avoid hold-up problems.[49] Aivazian et al.[50] and Graham and Peirce[51] both employed a similar framework to understand how contract law should govern contract modifications and renegotiations, and Bar-Gill and Ben-Shahar[52] explained how the doctrine of contractual duress should be applied to mitigate contractual hold-up. Each of these works, it could be said, feature the deference quality of NPL scholarship described in the preceding section.

There is surely more work to be done to combine these two insights—that is, that institutional economics can help understand how parties structure complex contracts to avoid transaction costs and that legal scholarship can help understand how contract law mitigates transaction costs when parties confront a contingency. Unifying these approaches would be fruitful. For example, recognizing how private ordering anticipates opportunism and how contract law punishes opportunism would both inform the structure of contracts and the implementation of the law. Ben Klein astutely notes that "transactors are not always smart enough to choose the contractual arrangement that would eliminate the hold-up problem."[53] But one might say that party ignorance and other contingencies are precisely why contract law has developed as it has.

---

[46] Victor P. Goldberg, *Toward an Expanded Economic Theory of Contract*, 10 J. ECON. ISSUES 45 (1976).

[47] Victor P. Goldberg, *Relational Exchange: Economics and Complex Contracts*, 23 AM. BEHAV. SCIENTIST 337 (1980); Victor P. Goldberg, *Relational Exchange, Contract Law, and the Boomer Problem*, 141 J. INST. & THEOR. ECON. 570 (1985).

[48] Victor P. Goldberg, *The Net Profits Puzzle*, 97 COLUM. L. REV. 524 (1997).

[49] Richard A. Posner, *Gratuitous Promises in Economics and Law*, 6 J. LEGAL STUD. 411 (1977); see also Richard A. Posner, *Let Us Never Blame a Contract Breaker*, 107 MICH. L. REV. 1349 (2009).

[50] Varouj A. Aivazian, M. Penny, & Michael Trebilcock, *The Law of Contract Modifications: The Uncertain Quest for a Benchmark of Enforceability*, 22 OSGOODE HALL L.J. 173 (1984).

[51] Daniel A. Graham & Ellen R. Peirce, *Contract Modification: An Economic Analysis of the Hold-up Game*, 52 LAW & CONTEMP. PROBS. 9 (Winter 1989).

[52] Oren Bar-Gill & Omri Ben-Shahar, *The Law of Duress and the Economics of Credible Threats*, 33 J. LEGAL STUD. 391 (2004); Oren Bar-Gill & Omri Ben-Shahar, *Credible Coercion*, 83 TEX. L. REV. 717 (2005).

[53] Benjamin Klein, *Why Hold-Ups Occur: The Self-Enforcing Range of Contractual Relationships*, 34 ECON. INQUIRY 444, 445 (1996).

B. Employment Law

Just as NIE and TCE explain why some goods are purchased and others are made, it can similarly explain why some services are provided by employees inside the firm and others are serviced by contractors. Empirical studies by Nickerson and Silverman,[54] Warfield et al.,[55] Coles and Hesterly,[56] and Zinn et al.[57] all examine the make-or-buy question as it relates to employment decisions. Each study finds, in different settings, that firms use their own employees to fulfill services that involve contractual hazards, such as measurement or monitoring difficulties, complementarities with other firm functions, or opportunistic behavior from learning firm trade secrets. Cavanaugh finds similar results within bargaining problems that arise in the context of unionized labor.[58] The consistent lesson from these studies is that the employment relationship can overcome transactional hazards that arm's-length contracting cannot and that employment offers a governance framework that is economically distinct from labor contracts across firm boundaries.

Oliver Williamson has emphasized that these findings are interwoven with the law's treatment of employment. He emphasized that "each generic mode of governance (market, hybrid, hierarchy, etc.) is supported by and in significant ways is defined by a distinctive form of contract law."[59] In other words, *the governance school credits the law for enabling different forms of governance.* Invoking Ian MacNeil's[60] identification of many different "contract laws (plural)," Williamson credits the law's deference and forbearance in employment relations for empowering hierarchies to govern difficult transactions. Because the law generally refrains from intervening in employment relationships, by (for example) enforcing incomplete and indefinite employment contracts while empowering discretionary managerial control, the law—according to Williamson—becomes an important source of a firm's capacity for coordinated adaptation. Of perhaps greater interest, MacNeil's articulation of the law of relational contracts, to be

[54] Jack A. Nickerson & Brian S. Silverman, *Why Aren't All Truck Drivers Owner-Operators? Asset Ownership and the Employment Relation in Interstate For-Hire Trucking,* 12 J. ECON. & MGT. STRATEGY 91 (1999).

[55] T.D. Warfield, J.J. Wild, & K.L. Wild, *Managerial Ownership, Accounting Choices, and Informativeness of Earnings,* 20 J. ACCOUNTING & ECON. 61 (1995).

[56] J. Coles & W.S. Hesterly, *The Impact of Firm-Specific Assets and the Interaction of Uncertainty: An Examination of Make or Buy Decisions in Public and Private Hospitals,* 36 J. ECON. BEHAV. & ORG. 383 (1998).

[57] J.S. Zinn, V. Mor, O. Intrator, Z.L. Feng, J. Angelelli, & J.A. Davis, *The Impact of the Prospective Payment System for Skilled Nursing Facilities on Therapy Service Provision: A Transaction Cost Approach,* 38 HEALTH SERVS. RES. 1467 (2003).

[58] Joseph K. Cavanaugh, *Asset-Specific Investment and Unionized Labor,* 37 INDUSTRIAL RELATIONS 35 (1998).

[59] Oliver E. Williamson, *The Mechanisms of Governance* 10 (1996).

[60] Ian R. MacNeil, *The Many Futures of Contracts,* 47 S. CAL. L. REV. 691 (1974); Ian R. MacNeil, *Contracts: Adjustments of Long-Term Economic Relations Under Classical, Neoclassical, and Relational Contract Law,* 72 NW. U. L. REV. 854 (1978).

contrasted with classical contract law, allowed TCE to consider the complex contracting relationships (including those where identity, history of dealing, the benefits of reciprocity, and other contextual variables shape the contracting framework) alongside the traditional employment relationship and the labor spot market. Contract law, labor law, and employment law all create different legal rights and remedies that give the mechanisms of governance their essential attributes.

C. Property Law

Few 1L Property Law courses are taught without a thorough discussion of the Coase Theorem, which (as Daniel B. Kelly notes) "not only helped launch the modern law and economics movement but also began a revival of interest in property rights in private law."[61] More than crediting Ronald Coase's *The Problem of Social Cost*[62] with launching a wildly influential field while reinvigorating another, that same contributor lavishes Coase with even more deserved praise by crediting him with developing a framework in which the fields of law and economics can mutually inform each other: "Coase illustrated the way in which an economic approach could shed light on the law and, conversely, how attention to legal institutions could challenge conventional economic thinking."

NIE's influence on property law is not limited to Coase, of course, but much of NIE's influence—most tracking TCE's governance school—follows the Coase Theorem's insight into navigating competing uses of limited resources. And since the heart of property law is to understand how legal rules and institutions navigate conflicting interests, NIE's core methodology of identifying alternative governance mechanisms is a natural complement. More significant, NIE offers what property law lacks: a tractable way to compare the efficiencies of alternative legal and extralegal approaches. (Coase recognized this directly, describing his theorem implicitly as a way to compare governance alternatives, saying, "All solutions have costs and there is no reason to suppose that government regulation is called for simply because the problem is not well handled by the market or the firm."[63]) NIE's ability to assess how local disputes can be adjudicated most effectively is of enormous use even to traditional property law. Among the earliest and most insightful illustrations of comparative institutional analysis in property law

---

[61]   Daniel B. Kelly, this volume.

[62]   Ronald H. Coase, *The Problem of Social Cost*, 3 J.L. & ECON. 1 (1960).

[63]   *Id.* at 18. I suspect that, in a different situation, Coase very easily might have said the converse, that there is no reason to suppose that market organization is called for simply because the problem is not well handled by government regulation. Herein lies a common misunderstanding of Coase (1960): his analysis only begins in a world of zero transaction costs, and much of the paper's key insights become apparent after positive transaction costs are incorporated. The too-convenient forgetting of Coase's emphasis on a world of positive transaction costs presents what some have called a dichotomy of "Coase Versus the Coaseans." Edward Glaeser, Simon Johnson, & Andrei Shleifer, *Coase Versus the Coasians*, 116 Q.J. ECON. 853 (2001).

was Robert Ellickson's *Alternatives to Zoning: Covenants, Nuisance Rules, and Fines as Land Use Controls*,[64] which subsequently charted the architecture and logical sequencing of several Property Law casebooks.[65]

Subsequent NIE scholars have delved into common property disputes that continue to vex policymakers. One good illustration is the challenge of navigating extraction industries in which coordination among local competitors can generate collective efficiencies. Libecap and Smith[66] examine these common pool problems in the context of oil and gas operating agreements. Because property rights to crude oil and natural gas are assigned to subsurface hydrocarbons only upon extraction, firms have an incentive to competitively drill and drain a given field as rapidly as possible, even though such behavior reduces aggregate yield. Firms typically employ agreements that instruct firms to extract at a slower but collectively optimal rate, but these agreements normally require long-term commitments, involve many parties, and possess considerable uncertainty about geological and economic conditions, and thus are subject to numerous contractual hazards. Libecap and Smith use an NIE approach to explain how firms devise intertemporal incentives to relieve these contracting dilemmas, often with single and proportional cost and revenue sharing formulas. In related work, Libecap and co-authors (e.g., Libecap;[67] Libecap and Anderson;[68] Culp, Glennon, and Libecap[69]) apply a similar template to examining alternative approaches to managing water, fisheries, and climate change. The inherent difficulties in these social problems often mean that each policy strategy has its shortcomings, but these NIE scholars illustrate the need to examine different legal and policy strategies within a common template that focuses on the structure of the problems themselves. In doing so, they offer a comprehensive analysis of alternative approaches—including uses of property law, administrative regulation, and tax policy—that in traditional legal frameworks remain in individual academic silos.

NIE scholars have also contributed to other questions in property law, many employing TCE's focus on explaining specific governance arrangements around specific property. Economic historian Gillian Hamilton examines how human asset specificity shaped the drafting of prenuptial contracts in early nineteenth-century Quebec, finding that couples signing such agreements tended to choose joint ownership of property when wives are particularly important to the household enterprise.[70] And Joanne

[64] Robert C. Ellickson, *Alternatives to Zoning: Covenants, Nuisance Rules, and Fines as Land Use Controls*, 40 U. CHI. L. REV. 681 (1973).

[65] See, e.g., Thomas W. Merrill & Henry E. Smith, *Property: Principles and Policies* (3d ed. 2017).

[66] Gary D. Libecap & James L. Smith, *The Self-Enforcing Provisions of Oil and Gas Unit Operating Agreements: Theory and Evidence*, 15 J.L. ECON. & ORG. 526 (1999).

[67] Gary D. Libecap, *Contracting for Property Rights* (1989).

[68] Gary D. Libecap & Terry L. Anderson, *Environmental Markets: A Property Rights Approach* (2014).

[69] Peter W. Culp, Robert J. Glennon, & Gary D. Libecap, *Shopping for Water: How the Market Can Mitigate Water Shortages in the American West* (2014).

[70] Gillian Hamilton, *Property Rights and Transaction Costs in Marriage: Evidence from Prenuptial Contracts*, 59 J. ECON. HIST. 68 (1999).

Oxley examines how different intellectual property regimes shape interfirm alliances, finding that such alliances are structured in varying ways in accordance with the level of intellectual property protection firms expect to receive.[71] These and other studies reveal the insight at the core of the Coase Theorem, that parties will structure their private arrangements in response to the legal rules that surround them, and they articulate how TCE can enrich our understanding of legal rules (and show the folly in focusing on law alone).

NIE's "institutional environment" branch has also deeply informed our understanding of property law. Hernando de Soto's seminal works[72] focused attention on the critical role of securing property rights in facilitating economic growth. Though de Soto argued specifically that formal, state-enforced property regimes were necessary to secure property rights, Shitong Qiao,[73] focusing on China rather than Latin America, suggests that extralegal mechanisms can adequately secure property rights as well. This debate furthers NIE's embrace of comparative institutional analysis while deeply informing the connection between legal regimes and economic outcomes. More microanalytic examinations with similar themes include Victor Nee's significant work on China's hybrid economic arrangements that combine public with private instruments. Nee argues that the Chinese political environment and the nature of market reforms give Town and Village Enterprises an economizing advantage over alternative governance arrangements precisely because they rely on a combination of public and private governance, although these hybrid forms will increasingly give way to private forms of organization as the Chinese economy moves from state socialism to a market orientation.[74] Additional applications of TCE logic to economic development in lower-income nations are found in Menard and Shirley,[75] Che and Qian,[76] Husted,[77] and Bertero.[78] This line of research promises to grow in importance as developing countries continue attaining greater economic importance in the global economy.

---

[71] Joanne Oxley, *Institutional Environment and the Mechanisms of Governance: The Impact of Intellectual Property Protection on the Structure of Inter-Firm Alliances*, 28 J. ECON. BEHAV. & ORG. 283 (1999).

[72] Hernando de Soto, *The Other Path: The Invisible Revolution in the Third World* (1989); Hernando de Soto, *The Mystery of Capital: Why Capitalism Triumphs in the West and Fails Everywhere Else* (2000).

[73] Shitong Qiao, *Chinese Small Property: The Co-Evolution of Law and Social Norms* (2017).

[74] Victor Nee, *Organizational Dynamics of Market Transition: Hybrid Forms, Property Rights, and Mixed Economy in China*, 37 ADMIN. SCI. Q. 1 (1992).

[75] Claude Ménard & Mary M. Shirley, *Reforming Urban Water Systems Within Different Institutional Environment, in Economic Policy Reform: The Second Stage* (A.O. Krueger ed., 2000).

[76] Jiahua Che & Yingyi Qian, *Institutional Environment, Community Government, and Corporate Governance: Understanding China's Township-Village Enterprises*, 14 J.L. ECON. & ORG. 1 (1998).

[77] Bryan W. Husted, *Transaction Costs, Norms, and Social Networks: A Preliminary Study of Cooperation in Industrial Buyer-Seller Relationships in the United States and Mexico*, 33 BUS. & SOC'Y 30 (Apr. 1994).

[78] Elisabetta Bertero, *Restructuring Financial Systems in Transition and Developing Economies: An Approach Based on the French Financial System*, 5 ECON. OF TRANSITION 367 (1997).

D. Antitrust Law

New Institutional Economics has had a long, fairly rocky, but ultimately influential history in antitrust policy.[79] During NIE's nascent years in the 1960s and 1970s, neoclassical price theory dominated antitrust policymaking.[80] Policymakers, led by Donald Turner, then-head of the Antitrust Division of the Department of Justice, were adherents to Joe Bain's structure-conduct-performance approach to industrial organization, which suggested (among other things) that vertical restraints were evidence of market power. Ronald Coase in 1972 lamented the myopia in contemporary economic theory, saying, "if an economist finds something—a business practice of one sort or another—that he does not understand, he looks for a monopoly explanation."[81]

The emergence of NIE in the mid-1970s targeted antitrust law reform. In his release of *Markets and Hierarchies* in 1975, Oliver Williamson pressed that "[t]he policy implications of [institutional economics] that are of principal concern are those having to do with antitrust."[82] The central insight is that since vertical integration is an economic response to contractual hazards, its efficiencies should be appreciated and factored into an antitrust analysis. Far from only reflecting an expansion of monopoly power, vertical integration—and exclusive contracts and other forms of bilateral combinations—should instead be viewed less suspiciously.

Williamson's transaction cost approach soon made its way into the world of legal scholars. Robert Bork adopted a TCE approach toward understanding vertical mergers, remarking that "[w]hat antitrust law perceives as vertical merger, and therefore as a suspect and probably traumatic event, is merely an instance of replacing a market transaction with administrative direction because the latter is believed to be a more efficient method of coordination."[83] Frank Easterbrook, shortly before his appointment to the bench, similarly embraced the TCE template when he asserted that "[t]he dichotomy between cooperation inside a 'firm' and competition in a 'market' is just a convenient shorthand for a far more complicated continuum."[84] Criticism of the applied price theory approach, coupled with the success of TCE and other institutional approaches, led

[79] Parts of this section are adapted from Barak D. Richman, *The Antitrust of Reputation Mechanisms: Institutional Economics and Concerted Refusals to Deal*, 95 VA. L. REV. 325 (2009), which offers a broad attempt to integrate NIE into antitrust law and specifically to employ NIE to inform the law of concerted refusals.

[80] In reviewing an earlier version of this manuscript, Erik Hovenkamp correctly laments that neoclassical price theory remains a significant driver of current antitrust policy. He remarked that even in vertical merger cases, where one would expect NIE to have the greatest influence, the most popular efficiency justification centers on the elimination of double marginalization.

[81] Ronald H. Coase, *Industrial Organization: A Proposal for Research, in The Economic Research: Retrospect and Prospect*, Vol. 3, Policy Issues and Research Opportunities in Industrial Organization, 59, 67 (Victor R. Fuchs ed., 1972).

[82] Williamson, *supra* note 40, at 258.

[83] Robert H. Bork, *The Antitrust Paradox: A Policy at War with Itself* 227 (1978).

[84] Frank H. Easterbrook, *The Limits of Antitrust*, 63 TEX. L. REV. 1, 1 (1984).

the Department of Justice in 1982 and again in 1984 to revise its guidelines for vertical mergers substantially. The revised Guidelines expressly reflected transaction cost reasoning, with nonstandard forms of organization no longer leading to a presumption of anticompetitiveness. NIE's influence sustained in antitrust law well into the twenty-first century, with former FTC Chairman Timothy Muris describing his own approach to antitrust law as "neither Chicago School nor Post-Chicago, but rather 'New Institutional Economics.'"[85]

NIE's and TCE's direct impact on antitrust law and policy illustrates the capacity of the law to open itself to external critiques. Since antitrust law is at its core economic regulation, it might be especially amenable to guidance from economists, but collaborations among economists and antitrust scholars seems to have paved the way for fruitful dialogues in other areas of law. This is a genuine strength of the legal academy, and it is something that NPL scholars especially seem to embrace, with a receptivity to engage with scholars of multiple fields. But it is not surprising that NIE and TCE scholars were among the pioneers in informing legal policy with economic insights since NIE is both especially accessible and especially useful to legal scholars. NIE is predisposed to inserting itself into the legal academy.

IV. Common Features of NPL and NIE

The connection between NPL and NIE has long been appreciated by leaders of both fields. Intellectual pioneers of NPL, such as Robert Scott and Robert Ellickson, have credited NIE for expanding the inquiry of private law scholars. And Williamson similarly remarked, "There were clearly many complementarities between transaction cost economics and the new contract law. Both also shared the property that they were working out of, but deviating from, the main traditions (in economics and law, respectively)."[86]

But the two fields have done more than coevolve and inform each other. They share some distinct methodological and substantive similarities. These similarities might have facilitated the fields' support for each other, or they might have explained why both emerged at around the same time. My purpose here is to highlight key features that not only make these fields distinct from their predecessors but also offer lessons into what will continue to sustain both scholarly trajectories.

---

[85] Stephen Stockum, *An Economist's Margin Notes: The Antitrust Writings of Timothy Muris*, 16 Antitrust 60 (2002). Muris noted that NIE combines "theory with a study of real world institutions [and]...is heavily empirical," offering "a welcome relief for many to move away from what [he] refers to as the 'very stale' Chicago/Post-Chicago debate over economic ideology."

[86] Williamson, *supra* note 43, at 370.

A. Interdisciplinarity

A hallmark of both NPL and NIE are their emphasis on interdisciplinarity. Institutional economics developed in the first part of the twentieth century in intellectual hotbeds at Columbia and Chicago, and later at Carnegie Mellon, the University of Washington, and Washington University. One reason NIE developed in the particular places that it did was because it relied on an ongoing dialog across disciplines. The Carnegie School, for example, led by Richard Cyert, Jim March, and Herbert Simon, integrated sociology, political science, organization theory, and social psychology. It nurtured a young Oliver Williamson, who reported years later that "Cyert did not think that any of the social sciences...were self-contained."[87] For similar reasons, the Carnegie School was also an early originator of behavioral economics.

My own experience at UC Berkeley reflected these interdisciplinary values. Although NIE had largely matured by the time I arrived in the late 1990s, Oliver Williamson and Pablo Spiller designed a curriculum and inclusive workshop environment that invited regular participation from economics, finance, political science, sociology, organizational behavior, and law. Moreover, Williamson and Spiller both focused on the core intersections and tensions between the different disciplines. We were repeatedly encouraged to dissect the first principles of industrial organization, population ecology, new institutionalism in sociology, game theory, legal scholarship, and other niche fields. We were encouraged to understand how these different languages speak to each other and offered additive (not necessarily conflicting) qualities to understanding complicated human phenomena. It led to a fertile, enthusiastic, and supportive intellectual environment.

Since NPL has its home more squarely within law schools, it does not rely on multiple disciplines in the traditional sense. But one of the most promising developments in law schools has been its hiring of scholars with training from the humanities and social sciences, and this in turn has produced a variety of perspectives in which private law has been examined. This might be the field's deepest strength, as a typical law school now features instructors of a common private law subject (e.g., torts, contracts, property) with noticeably different scholarly orientations. The proximity of these different approaches ensures a continued diversity and a productive tension. A movement such as NPL, which aims to bring these voices together, serves as a platform for pluralistic inquiry into common doctrines and subjects, much as the Carnegie School bridged different social sciences.

Moreover, the current NPL provides not just the foundation for interdisciplinarity but also a coexistence of multiple normative frameworks. Unlike fields of legal study that frequently feature ideological divides (between, say, economists and historians), NPL aggressively welcomes different analytical perspectives to dissect common private law topics. (This *Handbook* is a reflection of that pluralism.) In NPL, those with orthogonal normative priors—say, deterrence versus corrective justice—can coalesce around a common scholarly enterprise and perhaps also a common set of scholarly values.

[87] *Id.* at 23.

B. A Rejection of Orthodoxy

Perhaps reflected in their use of "New," both NIE and NPL are decided reactions to an orthodoxy that preceded them. As John Goldberg eloquently noted, NPL presents itself as an alternative to "brass tacks realism."

For NIE, the "brass tacks" equivalent is economics' price theory and its too-often abstruse mathematical models. Orthodox economics treated firms as production functions and showed little curiosity as to how firms formed, functioned, and changed in response to environmental pressures. NIE scholars ridiculed this proverbial "black box" attitude toward the firm and orthodoxy's disinterest for the many ways to organize economic activity.

At the same time, NIE has been described as "different but not hostile to orthodoxy" (Williamson).[88] It is not a rejection of what came before but, rather, a distinct alternative to prevailing economics, and this moderate path reflects NIE's absorptive capacity to learn from fields with profoundly different approaches. NPL exhibits a similar capacity. As this *Handbook* illustrates, NPL scholars give heed to and appreciate a diversity of scholarship and intentionally employ these fields to understand legal doctrine. NIE recognizes the merits of orthodox economics, and NPL recognizes the merits of the pioneering realists (and of traditional case law). Neither rejects the somewhat narrow approach of its predecessors and instead seeks ways to synthesize it with complementary perspectives.

Pursuing collaborations with other fields, however, is not the same as aiming to subsume them. Neither NPL nor NIE exhibit the imperial and expansionist tendencies of both price theory and legal realism, and this is a message that I hope law schools absorb. Many subfields within economics—including those without natural overlaps—have been enriched by engaging with NIE and other scholars of organization (international trade, finance, and macroeconomics come immediately to mind), and NPL offers the same possibilities to traditional fields of law. Both NIE and NPL aim to inform adjacent fields, not conquer them or render them obsolete, and hopefully the current vanguard of "law and" scholars will continue to welcome NPL, recognizing that its growth will produce mutual benefit.

C. Inquisitiveness, Attention to Real-World Phenomena

There is something very distinctive about NPL and NIE scholarship. Part of the challenge of pursuing scholarship informed by multiple perspectives is that conclusions need to be circumspect. Oliver Williamson has credited Ken Arrow for the insight that "problems that do not fit into orthodox boxes should be addressed on their own terms."[89]

---

[88] Williamson, *supra* note 43, at 3.

[89] Williamson, *supra* note 43, at 25, citing Kenneth J. Arrow, "The Organization of Economic Activity: Issues Pertinent to the Choice of Market Versus Non-Market Allocation," in *The Analysis and Evaluation of Public Expenditure: The PPB System*, 47, 59–73 in Joint Economic Committee, The Analysis and Evaluation of Public Expenditures: the PPB System, 91st Cong., 1st Sess. (U.S.G.P.O. 1969); Kenneth J. Arrow, *The Limits of Organization* (1974).

To do so, one must "[h]ave an active mind, be disciplined, be interdisciplinary."[90] Douglass North was one who embraced Arrow's charge. By studying economic history across centuries—examining broad phenomena that are maddeningly difficult to identify and measure yet critically important to human flourishing—North exhibited the scholarly ambition and curiosity that would scare away the more tentative. It takes a certain combination of dogged curiosity with scholarly chutzpah to inquire into how both formal and informal norms shape continental economies.

The best NPL is no less ambitious. Much of NPL begins with court opinions, doctrines, or other case studies as an effort to understand real-world phenomena. It approaches not just the world as it is but also the law as it is, not aiming to reinterpret but instead to examine familiar facts with new eyes. Its frequent use of case studies—specific disputes and their surrounding events that intersect with legal proceedings—is especially revealing. It shows a doggedness to re-examine and reinterpret conventional understandings, even while it remains steadfastly deferential to the law's prevailing use. NPL aims to broaden an understanding of the law by forcing a deeper engagement with the empirical realities in which the law operates. Like NIE, NPL's potential is enormous precisely because it is born out of a realistic understanding of the world.

V. Conclusion: The Path Ahead

This chapter unabashedly shows enthusiasm for both NPL and NIE, and much of that enthusiasm grows out of features that the two fields share. At the same time, NPL does not yet deserve a status alongside NIE, which has achieved widespread recognition as a transformative field. Whereas NPL remains somewhat nascent and ill-defined, NIE is well-known, well-established, and highly decorated. For these reasons, NIE offers some valuable lessons that NPL ought to pursue.

First, NPL would benefit by following NIE's emphasis on institutions. NIE's critique of "black box" microeconomics illustrated the revolutionary value of examining structures and behavior more than market microdetails. NPL could offer a similar path by offering a grounded focus on the legal institutions that operationalize the law. The legal academy's equivalent of orthodox economics' market data—the information that is overscrutinized at the expense of appreciating real-world phenomena—are the words offered in legal opinions; and the legal academy's equivalent of orthodox economics' alluringly parsimonious micro theory is realism's emphasis on bottom-line results, ignoring the nuance and wisdom of doctrine. NPL would usefully show both the value of legal doctrines and the utility of normative approaches to those doctrines by showing the pragmatic impact of such doctrines on individuals and organizations.

Second, NPL should mimic NIE's engagement with its neighboring fields. Institutional economics raised the status and influence of psychology, sociology, history,

[90] Id.

and other fields, and it did so by persisting in a constructive engagement. This often required creating collaborations where none previously existed, but it also required a self-awareness that forced NIE scholars to remain accessible to colleagues with different orientations. Participants at the conference that launched this *Handbook* expressed an awareness that NPL's success depends on how NPL scholars interact with their colleagues in the legal academy. One conference participant warned that "we [NPL scholars] don't want to throw out doctrine—it is old and wise and deserves its place in legal scholarship." Instead, "we need to talk about doctrine in a way that fits into the law school vernacular." Another participant similarly warned that "NPL's danger lies in its isolation. NPL scholars must be relatable and accessible to other fields, as many fields fell to obsolescence or insignificance by being too technical and inaccessible." This is a strong prescription for continued vitality in law schools, and the self-awareness among NPL's leaders suggests the prescription will be followed.

Third, and more ambitiously, NPL could strive to better articulate notions of "wrongdoing," just as NIE builds itself within a parsimonious framework of efficiency and growth.[91] To be sure, NIE is better positioned for normative parsimony since economics offers one itself, whereas NPL intentionally brings together scholars with different priors (which, as I note earlier, is among its core strengths). Nonetheless, NPL would do well to identify the counterpart to "transaction costs"—something that all agree should be reduced. NPL scholars should be wary of excessive moralizing before articulating the precise morality that should be pursued (and it's not clear we've done that yet), but NPL's strong and pervasive language of philosophical morality could serve a useful purpose if it is directed at a pragmatic target that would appeal to its diverse community of scholars.

One possible normative target of NPL—one potential common identification of "wrongdoing"—could also be informed by NIE's success: the hold-up problem. A unifying normative purpose of private law is to protect transactors when they fail to preemptively protect themselves, to ask what they would have done had they been in a world of zero transaction costs. Some pioneering NPL scholarship has explicitly interpreted age-old doctrines as efforts to address the hold-up problem, even using the moralistic language of equity and good faith.[92] And in the 1987 McCorkle Lecture at Virginia Law School, Coase himself tried to use NIE, and specifically his approach in The Problem of Social Cost, to better understand both the law of blackmail and the moral outrage against blackmailers.[93] Such efforts to combine legal doctrines, moral principles, and

[91] I thank Aditi Bagchi for a comment on an earlier draft that triggered this idea.

[92] For example, see the growing body of work on "The New Equity": Samuel L. Bray, *The Supreme Court and the New Equity*, 68 VAND. L. REV. 997 (2015); Ben McFarlane, "Equity," in *Oxford Handbook of The New Private Law* (forthcoming); Henry E. Smith, "Fusing the Equitable Function in Private Law," in *Private Law in the 21st Century* 173 (Kit Barker, Karen Fairweather, & Ross Grantham eds., 2016); Henry E. Smith, "Equitable Defences as Meta-Law," in *Defences in Equity* 17 (Paul S. Davies, Simon Douglas, & James Goudkamp eds., 2018); Henry E. Smith, *Equity as Second-Order Law: The Problem of Opportunism*, Harvard Public Law Working Paper No. 15–13 (Jan. 15, 2015), https://ssrn.com/abstract=2617413.

[93] Ronald H. Coase, *Blackmail*, 74 VA. L. REV. 655 (1988).

economic misbehavior could offer a common path forward. It would also allow NIE to learn from NPL's growth, in which a better understanding of how legal actors and public institutions approach the hold-up problem (and others) would inform economic models of the law.

Even if these ambitious goals remain elusive—and to be sure, one reason they will be hard to attain is because notions of "wrongdoing" in the law alone rests on different philosophical and economic wrongs—it remains useful to remind ourselves how little we still know about public and private institutions and about the economics of private law. And thus, it remains useful to remind ourselves of the benefits of pursuing ongoing dialogs across disciplines, perhaps especially between scholars of NPL and NIE.

ACKNOWLEDGMENTS

Thanks to Henry Smith, Andrew Gold, Erik Hovenkamp, Shitong Qiao, and Scott Masten for very helpful comments on an earlier draft. I'd also like to thank the organizers of this volume and its accompanying conference, particularly since the discussions and assembled ideas inspired many of the articulations in this chapter. This New Private Law gathering reminded me of my early experiences at Berkeley's IDS 270 Seminar, the Institutional Analysis Workshop led by Oliver Williamson and Pablo Spiller, which invited an eclectic and far-reaching array of scholars to offer perspectives on organizational economics. Gatherings of this kind forge interdisciplinary scholarship without abandoning disciplinary roots.

CHAPTER 8

PSYCHOLOGY AND THE NEW PRIVATE LAW

TESS WILKINSON-RYAN

THIS chapter tries to offer a framework for understanding the most promising contributions of psychological methods and insights for private law. Psychology, the study of mind and behavior, is a natural cognate field for legal scholars, but it has only been in the last few decades that it has gained traction outside of the forensic context.[1] Private law is by definition about interactions between private citizens: their obligations, negotiations, transactions, and remonstrations. The goal in this chapter is to think systematically about psychology and law, zooming out far enough to consider the relevance of psychological research in systematic ways, to discern organizing principles for sensible applications and plausible predictions.

In order to focus attention on the psychology of private law, I am going to focus on two related domains of psychological research: cognitive and social psychology. Cognitive psychology is the study of mental processes, which we might shorthand as "thinking." Social psychology asks about the role of other people—actual, implied, or imagined—on mental states and human behavior.

This discussion is oriented around five core psychological insights, taken up in order from the most inward (calculation) to the most outward (social norms). However, as we move through these domains, the chapter assumes that readers are on board with the larger empirical project, and as such spends little time justifying the value of law and psychology as a subfield. It may be helpful at the outset, though, to lay out the general case for taking behavior and cognition seriously in the New Private Law, even for scholars who are doing positive or normative legal work, rather than descriptive or sociolegal scholarship. To oversimplify: legal scholarship by turns tries to explain legal decision-making, tries to calibrate incentives, tries to justify its values and its means. Psychology speaks to these descriptive, prescriptive, and normative models of decision-making.

---

[1] See, e.g., Krin Irvine, David Hoffman, & Tess Wilkinson-Ryan, *Law and Psychology Grows Up, Goes Online, and Replicates*, 15 J. EMP. LEGAL STUD. 320 (2018).

Experimental psychology may be descriptive/explanatory—that is, people do not breach their lending contracts because they believe breach is wrong, not just because they fear the financial consequences.[2] It may be prescriptive—that is, research suggests that imposing a weak penalty with high likelihood of detection leads to better compliance than a severe penalty with low likelihood of detection.[3] Or it may even speak more directly to the normative analysis—that is, if punitive damages are indeed not rationally linked to the severity of harm, and internal coherence is a value of the legal system, then the punitive damages system is in some important sense flawed.[4] Resting on these foundational models of decision-making, the goal here is to explore some fundamental tenets of human psychology, identify exciting work in law and psychology, and surface the next wave of research questions in the field.

This chapter also has an implicit thread worth making explicit at the outset: psychological analysis of legal decision-making challenges the work that the idea of choice and preference is doing in private law, especially in the wake of the law and economics movement. Law and economics as a subfield has found a way to talk convincingly to legal scholars about the utilitarian heart of private ordering, which is by talking about preferences—revealed preferences, idiosyncratic preferences, even inconsistent preferences—with the aim of making people better off by leveraging the gains from trade when preferences are heterogeneous. Some of the most important contributions in contract, tort, and fiduciary law have come from the insistence, since Coase, that the welfare gains from private ordering deserve serious normative attention. To perhaps state the obvious, this is the central insight of the Coase Theorem, from Kornhauser and Mnookin's bargaining in the shadow of the law,[5] from Kaplow and Shavell on fairness and welfare,[6] and the behavioral frameworks from Jolls and Sunstein.[7]

Psychologists almost never talk about preferences. We talk about decisions, choices, beliefs, and attitudes. This chapter makes the argument that, at this point, having partially integrated economic analysis into many accounts of private law, the language of choice and preference can be misleading. When we look at consumer decision-making research that shows people choosing high-fee index funds over low-fee index funds, I just do not think anyone ought to be asking the question about why people prefer high-fee index funds—they do not, at least not in any sense that survives scrutiny. It is not

[2] Zev J. Eigen, *When and Why Individuals Obey Contracts: Experimental Evidence of Consent, Compliance, Promise, and Performance*, 41 J. LEGAL STUD. 67, 88 (2012); Tess Wilkinson-Ryan & David A. Hoffman, *Breach Is for Suckers*, 63 VAND. L. REV. 1003, 1013–1018 (2010).

[3] Jonathan Baron & Ilana Ritov, *The Role of Probability of Detection in Judgments of Punishment*, 1 J. LEGAL ANALYSIS 553 (2009).

[4] Cass Sunstein, Daniel Kahneman, Ilana Ritov, & David Schkade, *Predictably Incoherent Judgments*, 54 STAN. L. REV. 1153 (2001).

[5] Robert H. Mnookin & Lewis Kornhauser, *Bargaining in the Shadow of the Law: The Case of Divorce*, 88 YALE L.J. 950 (1979).

[6] Louis Kaplow & Steven Shavell, *Fairness versus Welfare* (2002).

[7] Christine Jolls & Cass R. Sunstein, *Debiasing through Law*, 35 J. LEGAL STUD. 199 (2006); Christine Jolls, Cass R. Sunstein, & Richard H. Thaler, *A Behavioral Approach to Law and Economics*, 50 STAN. L. REV. 1471 (1998).

worth our time to go down that road, in part because even if you make the question a little deeper, it is still no good—why do people prefer high-fee index funds when fees aren't salient? It's imprecise—we mean choose here, not "prefer"—and off target.

The chapter proceeds as follows. The first half deals specifically with thinking. I begin by asking what we know about how people engage in the elemental task of calculating expected utility. How do they evaluate cost and benefit, how do they discount for time or price risk? Then I move to cognitive processes influenced by other internal states, namely, self-interest or visceral drives, respectively. The second half of the chapter deals with the social psychological self. How are we affected by our social contexts, and, finally, how do we understand our rights and obligations as participants in a society?

Put systematically, if informally, for each choice we might imagine a series of considerations: doing the math, understanding our own self-interest, reckoning with the visceral experience of being a human, internalizing social norms, and, finally, running a moral audit:

- Calculation
  - What is the value of doing this?
- Motivation
  - What do I want the value of this to be?
- Emotion
  - How important does it feel to do this?
- Social Influence
  - What do other people think I should do?
- Moral Values
  - Does doing this comport with what is right?

For each of the five levels of psychological processing, this review will offer a brief overview, a documented application from the literature, and a key open question or confusion.

I. CALCULATION: LIMITED PROCESSING CAPACITY

I would recommend that we stop debating whether a theory of substantive rationality and the assumptions of utility maximization provide a sufficient base for explaining and predicting economic behavior. The evidence is overwhelming that they do not. We already have in psychology a substantial body of empirically tested theory about the processes people actually use to make boundedly rational, or "reasonable" decisions…Economics without psychological and sociological research to determine the givens of the decision-making situation, the focus of attention, the problem of representation, and the processes used to identify alternatives, estimate consequences, and choose among possibilities—such economics is a one-bladed scissors. Let us replace it with an instrument capable of cutting through our ignorance about rational human behavior.

— Herbert Simon (1986)[8]

One of the most influential contributions of psychology for the study of legal decision-making is the straightforward observation that most people make most decisions under conditions of incomplete information, inadequate processing capacity, and limited attentional resources. The notion of bounded rationality asserted by Simon and others argues that we should stop talking about irrationality, as though decision-making is random or entirely befuddling, and start trying to understand the bounds of rationality— the constraints that operate predictably and yield reasonable but biased judgments and decisions.[9]

Private law is often concerned with private economic decision-making, and such decision-making naturally requires a high level of calculative attention to apprehend both the right facts (what is the current market value) but also to evaluate probabilities of future uncertain outcomes and to understand the subjective utility of the party whose utility matters. If I am negotiating a contract for the sale of my car, I have to figure out my own preferences. If I am a trustee choosing an investment strategy for the beneficiaries of a trust, I presumably need to understand something about their lifestyles and goals. Searching for and assimilating information, understanding risk, and accounting for change over time are high-level, resource-intensive cognitive tasks. Law and policy scholarship frequently grapples with the notion of expected value and cost-benefit analysis; these are calculations that require, basically, accuracy. This section is about how those calculations go predictably awry.

Perhaps because this area of study is closest to economics—indeed, some of its most important leaders come from economics rather than psychology—it has arguably had the most traction in legal scholarship.[10]

A. Heuristics and Biases

The enormous audience for Daniel Kahneman's popular book *Thinking, Fast and Slow* has popularized the work that he began in the early 1970s with the late Amos Tversky.[11] That work culminated in their *Science* article "Judgment under Uncertainty: Heuristics

[8] Herbert A. Simon, *Rationality in Psychology and Economics*, 59 J. Bus. S209, S223 (1986).
[9] Herbert A. Simon, "Bounded Rationality," in *The New Palgrave: Utility and Probability* 15 (John Eatwell, Murray Milgate, & Peter Newman eds., 1990).
[10] Russell B. Korobkin & Thomas S. Ulen, *Law and Behavioral Science: Removing the Rationality Assumption from Law and Economics*, 88 Cal. L. Rev. 1051 (2000).
[11] Daniel Kahneman, *Thinking, Fast and Slow* (2011).

and Biases" in which Kahneman and Tversky identified three widespread workarounds that humans employ, consciously or not, to reduce processing requirements.[12] Each of the heuristics, described briefly here, explain a pattern of biased predictions or estimates for uncertain outcomes.

The availability heuristic is an attribute substitution phenomenon. It says that when we are asked "how frequent is this event?" we substitute the question with "how easy is it to think of instances of this kind of event?"[13] This leads to biases in responses, because some kinds of event are more salient. Many people will find it easy to recall instances of death by plane crash, but very difficult to think of instances of death by pulmonary embolism, causing an overestimation of the former and underestimation of the latter. The representativeness heuristic is a similar workaround for a difficult prediction task. When the question is, "what is the likelihood that X is a Y?" we instead ask ourselves "how like the typical Y is X?" This is the famous Linda problem, in which subjects who read about an outspoken activist named Linda thought that she was very unlikely to be a bank teller—but more likely to be a feminist bank teller. Anchoring and adjustment is a process of identifying a salient number and then adjusting to approach the true value. So, for example, if I wanted to sell my car, I might look at the cost of a similar car and then adjust downward based on my private knowledge about my car's history of fender benders and hard use by messy children. The biased results that this mechanism yields are the result of predictable underadjustment from predictably unhelpful anchors. It may be useful in general to anchor my judgment of my home's worth on a comparison to another sale on my block, but it is probably not useful to anchor my judgment of the home's worth on my Social Security number, or even, for that matter, the recommendation of a developer who wants to buy my property.

A key insight about each of these proposed mechanisms is that they underlie more complex behavioral phenomena. The availability heuristic applies to a number of situations in which things feel more likely or more plausible just because they are easier to imagine. Anchoring and underadjustment affects judgments especially when people find themselves prone to particular anchors, including anchors that favor their own outcomes or preferences or ratify their own understanding.

Together, these shortcuts describe judgment under predictable constraints, with wide-ranging implications for legal decision-making. What is the likelihood of dramatic market shifts? Should the parties have foreseen a natural disaster or was it reasonably surprising? What are the odds that the jury finds for the plaintiff?

---

[12] Amos Tversky & Daniel Kahneman, *Judgment under Uncertainty: Heuristics and Basics*, 185 SCI. N.S. 1124 (1974).

[13] See, e.g., Thorsten Pachur, Ralph Hertwig, & Florian Steinmann, *How Do People Judge Risks: Availability Heuristic, Affect Heuristic, or Both?*, 18 J. EXPERIMENTAL PSYCHOL.: APPLIED 314 (2012); see also, e.g., Daniel M. Oppenheimer, *Spontaneous Discounting of Availability in Frequency Judgment Tasks*, 15 PSYCHOL. SCI. 100 (2004); João N. Braga, Mario Ferreira, & Steven Sherman, *The Effects of Construal Level on Heuristic Reasoning: The Case of Representativeness and Availability*, 2 DECISION 216 (2015); Nicholas Epley & Thomas Gilovich, *The Anchoring-and-Adjustment Heuristic: Why the Adjustments Are Insufficient*, 17 PSYCHOL. SCI. 311 (2006).

B. Prospect Theory

1. *Framing and the Decision-Making Literature*

If the previous section was about getting facts wrong, this section is about getting values wrong—or at least, getting values that systematically depart from traditional expected utility theory. Although it is tempting to shorthand Prospect Theory as loss aversion, it is in fact a specific set of predictions described by two functions: the Value Function and the Pi Function.[14] The Value Function plots the perceived value of an outcome (the subjective utility) against its objective value, typically in dollars. The Value Function is S-shaped. It shows (1) declining marginal change in utility for changes in outcomes as they move further from the reference point (diminishing sensitivity); (2) a kink in the function at the zero point (reference dependence); and (3) a steeper value curve for losses than for gains (loss aversion). The Pi function is a single curve for probability and shows perceived probability is very steep at the boundaries and much more shallow in the middle. The difference between no possibility and 1 percent possibility is much more strongly felt than the difference between 45 and 46 percent.

The centrality of reference points has been documented in extensive empirical studies.[15] In their Asian disease experiment, Tversky and Kahneman demonstrated that subjects were willing to adopt more risky policies when the outcomes of the policies were framed as losses rather than gains.[16] Terrance Odean demonstrated that investors tend to hold on too long to losing stocks, whereas they sell gaining stocks prematurely.[17] Studies have demonstrated that people are more willing to stretch their ethical boundaries when their decisions are framed as losses rather than gains.[18]

Prospect theory's insights have been applied to legal fields such as civil litigation,[19] securities law,[20] criminal behavior,[21] and plea bargaining.[22] Recently, Eyal Zamir put

[14] Daniel Kahneman & Amos Tversky, *Prospect Theory: An Analysis of Decision Under Risk*, 47 ECONOMETRICA 263 (1979).

[15] Anton Kühberger, *The Influence of Framing on Risky Decisions: A Meta Analysis*, 75 ORG. BEHAV. & HUM. DECISION PROCESSES 23 (1998).

[16] Amos Tversky & Daniel Kahneman, *The Framing of Decisions and the Psychology of Choice*, 211 SCI. 453, 453 (1981).

[17] Terrance Odean, *Are Investors Reluctant to Realize Their Losses?*, 53 J. FIN. 1775 (1998).

[18] Mary C. Kern & Dolly Chugh, *Bounded Ethicality: The Perils of Loss Framing*, 20 PSYCH. SCI. 378, 380–381 (2009); see also Jessica Schwartz Cameron, Dale Miller, & Benoit Monin, *Deservingness and Unethical Behavior in Loss and Gain Frames* (2008) (unpublished manuscript).

[19] Jeffrey J. Rachlinski, *Gains, Losses and the Psychology of Litigation*, 70 S. CAL. L. REV. 113, 121 (1996).

[20] Donald C. Langevoort, *Selling Hope, Selling Risk: Some Lessons for Law from Behavioral Economics About Stockbrokers and Sophisticated Customers*, 84 CAL. L. REV. 627, 628–629 (1996).

[21] James D. Cox, *Private Litigation and the Deterrence of Corporate Misconduct*, 60 L. & CONTEMP. PROBS. 1, 5–8 (1997); see also Alon Harel & Uzi Segal, *Criminal Law and Behavioral Law and Economics: Observations on the Neglected Role of Uncertainty in Deterring Crime*, 1 AM. L. & ECON. REV. 276, 298–299 (1999).

[22] Stephanos Bibas, *Plea Bargaining Outside the Shadow of Trial*, 117 HARV. L. REV. 2463, 2507–2512 (2004).

forward an ambitious argument according to which prospect theory explains to a large
degree the structure of law itself.[23]

In contract law, prospect theory suggests that the determination of default rules is
important.[24] If the parties view the allocation of risks created by these rules as a reference point, then contracting around them becomes an issue; the party with a right
according to the default rule will tend to view selling this right as a loss, while the opposing party will tend to view the purchase of a new right as a gain. Since losses loom more
than gains, a systematic gap in valuations is expected to emerge and the default rule is
expected to remain "sticky." Empirical evidence from insurance has corroborated the
importance of default rules as contractual reference points.[25] Eric Johnson and his colleagues compared the decisions of consumers buying insurance in Pennsylvania and
New Jersey after both states amended their laws to allow for some type of limited coverage. Importantly, while in Pennsylvania the default remained full coverage, in New
Jersey the default was set at the limited level, and consumers who wanted additional
coverage had to purchase it. The difference between the choices consumers made in the
markets was unequivocal: while only 20 percent bought additional coverage in New
Jersey, 75 percent retained full coverage in Pennsylvania.[26]

2. *Legal Reference Points*

One of the most pressing agenda items for legal scholars is to understand the role that
the law plays in establishing the reference point. Is a reference point a state of the world?
Is it a legal entitlement? This has been raised in the contracts context, and research suggests that the perceived legal rule has a strong effect on the identity of the reference
point. Oliver Hart and John Moore argue that a contract provides a reference point for
the parties' trading relationship and for their feelings of entitlement.[27] Their model
holds that a party's ex post performance depends on whether the party gets what he is
entitled to relative to the outcomes permitted by the contract. A party who is shortchanged will "shade" on performance.[28]

One way the parties can reduce this deadweight loss is for them to write an ex ante
contract that pins down future outcomes very precisely, leaving little room for disagreement and aggrievement. Hart characterizes the literature on incomplete contracts
as: typical models have buyer and seller meet and write an incomplete contract because
the future is hard to anticipate. Uncertainty is resolved over time, and the parties renegotiate their contract, in a Coasean fashion. These models assume an *ex post* efficient

[23] Eyal Zamir, *Loss Aversion and Law's Formation*, 65 VAND. L. REV. 829 (2012).
[24] Eyal Zamir, *The Inverted Hierarchy of Contract Interpretation and Supplementation*, 97 COLUM.
L. REV. 1710, 1760–1762 (1997).
[25] Cass R. Sunstein, *Switching the Default Rule*, 77 N.Y.U. L. REV. 106, 113–114 (2002); see also Russell
Korobkin, *The Status Quo Bias and Contract Default Rules*, 83 CORNELL L. REV. 608, 633–647 (1998).
[26] Eric J. Johnson, John Hershey, Jacqueline Meszaros, & Howard Kunreuther, *Framing, Probability
Distortions, and Insurance Decisions*, 7 J. RISK & UNCERTAINTY 35, 48 (1993).
[27] Oliver Hart & John Moore, *Contracts as Reference Points*, 123 Q.J. ECON. 1 (2008).
[28] *Id.* at 2.

outcome where each party shares some of the benefits of prior (noncontractible) relationship-specific investments with the other party. Recognizing this, each party underinvests *ex ante*.

Taking the moment of contract formation as the reference point, Wilkinson-Ryan and Hoffman highlight the possibility of an actor choosing the formation time to produce an advantage to herself.[29] Subjects were asked whether they would be willing to "cancel a deal" during a cooling-off period, when that period was described either as a delayed start to the contract or a free cancellation period after the contract starts. The consequences of exit were identical, but subjects reported that they would be more likely to walk away in the delayed start (no contract yet) than in the cancellation period (where that would be deviating from the status quo). In that case the framing device was essentially a legal concept alone.

II. MOTIVATION

> People are more likely to arrive at those conclusions that they want to arrive at.
>
> — Ziva Kunda (1990)[30]

Motivated reasoning describes the basic idea that goals and motives have implicit effects on perceptions, beliefs, and judgments. There are many kinds of motives, including a motive to strive for accuracy, but some motives are widely shared and systematically documented. It is highly predictable that people are motivated to think well of themselves, and I briefly review this literature in the following. It is also the case that people may be motivated to accept bad outcomes in ways that may be surprising, which I also take up in a discussion of system justification theory and law.

A. MYSIDE BIAS

One of the most intuitive and important implications of systematically flawed processing is that processing flaws favor the processor. We each approach the world with a set of beliefs and goals. The research on the broad set of phenomena understood as "myside" bias maps out a wide array of contexts in which people interpret information where

---

[29] David A. Hoffman & Tess Wilkinson-Ryan, *The Psychology of Contract Precautions*, 80 U. CHI. L. REV. 395, 399 (2013).

[30] Ziva Kunda, *The Case for Motivated Reasoning*, 108 PSYCH. BULL. 480 (1990).

plausible to support their beliefs and their goals.[31] This form of biased cognition is largely implicit and implicates availability and anchoring, among other mechanisms, to yield literally self-centered judgments.

1. *Overoptimism and Overconfidence*

Overoptimism is the canonical example of myside bias. Overoptimism encompasses a set of results that draw knowing chuckles from any audience. To wit:

- 93 percent of Americans believe they are better-than-average drivers.[32]
- Two-thirds of college professors think they are in the top quarter of teachers at their university.[33]
- 70 percent of high school students believe they are above average in leadership ability.[34]

Particularly familiar to scholars is the closely related result called the "planning fallacy," which identifies systematic and widespread overoptimism in estimating the time and resources required to complete a multistep project.[35] Overoptimism and overconfidence are one side of a coin; the flip side is motivated harsh judging of others. In evaluating whether someone took an undue risk, for example, we may see a failure of empathy because we imagine ourselves to be more cautious or responsible. The belief that *I* would have read the terms and conditions carefully,[36] or *I* would have shoveled snow from my sidewalk more quickly, can contribute to inflated expectations of reasonable behavior.

2. *Self-Serving Biases*

The role of self-interest in judgment goes beyond questions that explicitly involve the self. There are other judgments that have important implications for our own interests, because some judgments yield better or worse outcomes. To take an example close to home: imagine a faculty meeting at which professors are debating which criteria should dominate the tenure decision. On the margins, what characteristics might differentiate

---

[31] See, e.g., Raymond S. Nicherson, *Confirmation Bias: A Ubiquitous Phenomenon in Many Guises* (1998); see also, e.g., Hugo Mercier, "Confirmation Bias—Myside Bias," in *Cognitive Illusions* 99 (Rüdinger F. Pohl ed., 2016).

[32] Ola Svenson, *Are We All Less Risky and More Skillful Than Our Fellow Drivers?*, 47 ACTA PSYCHOLOGICA 143, 146 (1981).

[33] K. Patricia Cross, *Not Can, but Will College Teaching Be Improved?*, 1977 NEW DIRECTIONS IN HIGHER EDUC. 1.

[34] David Dunning, Judity Meyerowitz, & Amy Holzberg, *Ambiguity and Self-Evaluation: The Role of Idiosyncratic Trait Definitions in Self-Serving Assessments of Ability*, 57 J. PERSONALITY & SOC. PSYCHOL. 1082, 1082 (1989).

[35] Daniel Kahneman & Amos Tversky, *Intuitive Prediction: Biases and Corrective Procedure*, 17 TIMS STUD. MGMT. SCI. 313 (1979).

[36] Tess Wilkinson-Ryan, *A Psychological Account of Consent to Fine Print*, 99 IOWA L. REV. 1745 (2014).

those who care about, for example, scholarly productivity more than scholarly impact? We might suspect that people evaluate those characteristics differently based on the criterion that reflects best on themselves.

Self-serving biases have been compellingly demonstrated by Linda Babcock, George Loewenstein, and Samuel Issacharoff.[37] In their key experiment, they randomly assigned subjects to be either the plaintiff or the defendant in a simulated settlement negotiation.[38] Parties were then given the same set of documents about the underlying dispute (a car accident) and asked to negotiate an appropriate settlement. The researchers also asked the participants to report their own private view about what range of settlements would be "objectively fair." The central finding was that subjects who had the same information, and were asked to be objective and to ignore their own preferences, saw the range of fair outcomes differently. This led to a bargaining impasse, because in many cases there was no overlap, leading the parties to believe that they were being dealt with in bad faith. Self-serving biases are a phenomenon of anchoring and underadjustment—subjects anchored on the preferred outcome and then tried to adjust to accommodate the exhortation of objectivity.

3. *System Justification*

It is easy to understand the motivation to win or succeed or profit, but some otherwise predictable goals are less obvious. To start, there is an important extension of the inflated sense of self: the flip side of overoptimism about one's own skills and prospects is the overattribution of harm to others to their own poor judgment. Psychologists have described a "just world bias,"[39] the preference to believe that the world operates in basically fair ways so that bad things happen to bad people. This underlying belief system is most commonly linked to victim-blaming. Part of the appeal of blaming a victim (she should not have been walking on that dark street so late at night, etc.) is that it feels better to think harm is easily avoidable.[40]

For the last twenty-five years or so, psychologists have conceptualized this bias not just as a preference to believe in a just world but as an overarching drive to justify the status quo. System justification theory, as it is called, argues that there is a "general

---

[37] Linda Babcock & George Loewenstein, *Explaining Bargaining Impasse: The Role of Self-Serving Biases*, 11 J. ECON. PERSP. 109 (1997); Linda Babcock, George Loewenstein, Samuel Issacharoff, & Colin Camerer, *Biased Judgments of Fairness in Bargaining*, 85 AM. ECON. REV. 1337 (1995); George Loewenstein, Samuel Issacharoff, Colin Camerer, & Linda Babcock, *Self-Serving Assessments of Fairness and Pretrial Bargaining*, 22 J. LEGAL STUD. 135 (1993).

[38] Babcock & Loewenstein, *supra* note 37.

[39] See Melvin Lerner, *The Belief in the Just World: A Fundamental Delusion* (1980); Melvin Lerner & Dale T. Miller, *Just World Research and the Attribution Process: Looking Back and Ahead*, 85 PSYCHOL. BULL. 1030 (1978).

[40] See Melvin Lerner & Carolyn Simmons, *Observer's Reaction to the "Innocent Victim": Compassion or Rejection?*, 4 J. PERSONALITY & SOC. PSYCHOL. 203, 209 (1966).

ideological motive to justify the existing social order."[41] This observation explains a set of somewhat puzzling results which appear at first glance to be in conflict with the notion of overconfidence or overoptimism: in some domains, people appear to accept subordination and attribute it to their own inferiority. Why would this be? Why would swaggering drivers and self-anointed leadership prodigies be willing in some cases to relinquish their claim to an objectively fair share of resources? The argument from system justification theory is that some inequities are so embedded that to recognize them as random and unfair is literally maladaptive, insofar as the sense of futility is a mental health challenge.

Work in the psychology of contract has recently faced the question: Why are consumers so complacent and so willing to blame themselves or those similarly situated, rather than blaming the large, rich, faceless firms that draft burdensome terms? One way to think about the mounting evidence in this area is that most consumers are faced with a choice between viewing themselves as pawns or victims, or as viewing themselves as rational risk-taking agents—and that many prefer the latter. In a 2014 study, subjects were asked to determine whether a consumer's formal assent to an unread contract constituted meaningful consent to a costly term. Half of the subjects read about the hypothetical consumer's background and read the term; half saw that same information as well as a brief update that the negative eventuality came to pass. This is a classic just-world experimental paradigm, and it yielded classic results: subjects thought that the consent was more meaningful when the consumer suffered a harm. That is, when the motivation to blame the consumer was higher, because the threat to the system was more acute, the judgment came down in favor of the world (she assented!) rather than the individual.

III. EMOTIONS

> From economics, decision theory inherited, or was socialized into, the language of preferences and beliefs and the religion of utility maximization that provides a unitary perspective for understanding all behavior. From cognitive psychology, decision theory inherited its descriptive focus, concern with process, and many specific theoretical insights. Decision theory is thus the brilliant child of equally brilliant parents. With all its cleverness, however, decision theory is somewhat crippled emotionally, and thus detached from the emotional and visceral richness of life.
>
> — George Loewenstein (1996)[42]

---

[41] John T. Jost, Mahzarin Banaji, & Brian Nozek, *A Decade of System Justification Theory: Accumulated Evidence of Conscious and Unconscious Bolstering of the Status Quo*, 25 POL. PSYCHOL. 881, 881 (2004).

[42] George Loewenstein, *Out of Control: Visceral Influences on Behavior*, 65 ORGANIZATIONAL BEH. & HUMAN DECISION PROCESSES 272 (1996).

A. Emotional and Visceral Drives

"Hot cognition" describes cognitive states that are directly affected by visceral states. A more colloquial way to think about this would be to focus on the effects of emotions on thinking, but the definition of emotions, and their role in decision-making, is too unwieldy for a chapter of this length. Hot states are more precisely defined: they are visceral drives that have discernible effects on information processing.

Describing the effects of heightened emotional intensity on decision-making is almost gilding the lily; the English language includes copious idioms acknowledging our shared sense that intense feelings drive behavior. Humans may be "overwhelmed with grief," "wild with desire," and experience "paralyzing fear." And, indeed, there is a broad literature; scholars have demonstrated, inter alia, that drug cravings increase risk-seeking behavior, that fear increases risk aversion, and that anger often leads to costly aggressive behavior.

B. Hot/Cold Empathy Gap

The core challenge of hot cognition is not that it causes "irrationality" but rather that hot cognition is not intuitive or sympathetic. Psychologists have described this as the hot-cold empathy gap, and it has implications for any private law task that requires empathizing with those in visceral states. Evidence suggests that it is quite difficult to predict one's own preferences and choices under conditions of cravings, or physical discomfort, or sexual arousal, or even salient excitement.

The psychological literature on the hot-cold empathy gap offers a glimpse into this set of problems. In a "cold" state—that is, unaffected by the visceral drives that often underlie the urgency or intensity of consumption choices—decision-making is more calculated and rational. In a "hot" state, hunger, thirst, fatigue, pain, sexual arousal, drug cravings, or other physical drive states are highly salient and highly motivating. The normative status of these decisions is not inherent to the underlying drive state. If I am trying to cut down on sugar, I may prefer my cold-state decision stance and thus keep sweets out of the house even though I know I will be miserable come time for my next snack. On the other hand, my failure to bring along extra food on a long hike truly decreases my overall well-being.[43]

The "empathy gap" describes the consistent difficulty of accurately predicting the preferences and utilities of the hot state. An evocative example comes from Sayette, Loewenstein, and Griffin, who asked smokers to estimate the value of a particular smoke break to a group of people with whom they should have been quite expert at

---

[43] This section is drawn from a previous contribution of the author on fiduciaries and trust. "The Psychology of Trust and Fiduciary Obligations" in *Fiduciaries and Trust: Ethics, Politics, Economics. Oxford Library of Law* (2020).

empathizing: themselves.[44] The smokers were told that they would have to wait two hours until the next smoke break, at which point they would have the option of receiving a small payment to delay the break another ten minutes. Some smokers were allowed to precommit to accept the delay, and the payment, in advance; many of them did. Others were told of the option but not permitted to decide until the smoke break arrived. Those who had to decide whether or not to accept money for the delayed smoke break under the influence of nicotine craving (that is, hours after their last cigarette) were substantially less likely to take the payment than those who decided under conditions of satiation. One way to understand this result is that subjects choosing their smoking schedule in advance, and in a cold state, underestimated the value of satisfying an urgent nicotine craving.

The key insight of the literature on empathy gaps is not simply that people are weak-willed or easily tempted; it is that people fail to plan for their predictable failures. The failure of insight compounds the incoherent decision-making, because it interferes with an individual's ability to achieve her own goals.

IV. Social Influence

> While the fact of social influence is beyond doubt, we are only on the threshold of understanding the responsible processes. The task of inquiry in this region is to explore the ways in which group actions become forces in the psychological fields of persons, and to describe the forces within persons that cooperate with or resist those induced by the group environment.
>
> — Solomon Asch (1956)[45]

A. Conforming

Some of the most famous, and infamous, psychological studies of the twentieth century were studies of horrifying conformity. Stanley Milgram intended to show that Americans, unlike Europeans, would not be mindlessly obedient; instead he showed that merely donning a white lab coat made him sufficiently authoritative to convince some subjects to deliver apparently fatal levels of electric shock to a hapless confederate.[46] Philip Zimbardo's now-disputed Stanford Prison studies showed undergraduates playing the

---

[44] Michael A. Sayette, George Loewenstein, Kasey M. Griffin, & Jessica J. Black, *Exploring the Cold-to-Hot Empathy Gap in Smokers*, 19:9 PSYCHOL. SCI. 926–932 (2008).

[45] Solomon Asch, *Studies of Independence and Conformity*, 70 PSYCHOL. MONOGRAPHS: GENERAL AND APPLIED 1, 2 (1956).

[46] Stanley Milgram, *Behavioral Study of Obedience*, 67 J. ABNORMAL & SOC. PSYCH. 371 (1963).

parts of prison guards and prisoners, respectively, and transforming into near-caricatures of the roles—with real fights and riots putting themselves into real danger.[47]

More fine-grained work in recent decades has documented the important ways that humans change their behavior to adjust to the social expectations. Many of these changes are straightforward. Those who have to account to others for their choices are more careful and even-handed in their decision-making.[48] People being observed are less likely to cheat or steal, more likely to conform.[49] There are also less obvious effects of social context, though. The literature on the bystander effect shows that people are less likely to respond appropriately to imminent harm when they are in a group than when they are alone.[50] People appear more willing to punish others for norm violations when the punishment is observable to others.[51]

B. Social Influence Empathy Gap

In 2019, Roseanna Sommers and Vanessa Bohns published a study of social influence and privacy by asking their subjects if they'd be willing to unlock their iPhones and allow a research assistant (RA) to "look for illegal apps."[52] They randomly assigned under-graduates to one of two conditions: hypothetical and real-stakes. Those in the hypothetical condition were asked whether, if asked, they would be willing to unlock their phone and hand it over to the RA, who would take it into the next room to look it over. Those in the real-stakes condition were just asked to please hand it over so the RA could look at it. The results were striking on three levels. First: close to 100 percent of the subjects in the real-stakes condition unlocked their phones. Second, the difference between conditions was huge; less than a quarter of subjects in the hypothetical condition thought they would relinquish the phone. And third, these results held even when subjects received a disclosure explicitly reminding them that they were not obligated to give up the phone to participate in the study.

This study suggests a deep misunderstanding of the subjects on their own likely choices in the face of truly minimal social pressure.

---

[47] Craig Haney, Curtis Banks, & Philip Zimbardo, *Interpersonal Dynamics in a Simulated Prison*, 1 INTL. J. CRIMINOLOGY & PENOLOGY, 69 (1971).

[48] Jennifer Lerner & Philip Tetlock, *Accounting for the Effects of Accountability*, 125 PSYCH. BULL. 255 (1999).

[49] Robert Cialdini & Noah Goldstein, *Social Influence: Compliance and Conformity*, 55 ANNUAL REV. PSYCH. 591 (2004).

[50] Bibb Latane & John Darley, *Group Inhibition of Bystander Intervention in Emergencies*, 10 J. PERSONALITY & SOC. PSYCH. 215 (1968).

[51] Robert Kurzban, Peter DeScioli, & Erin O'Brien, *Audience Effects on Moralistic Punishment*, 28 EVOLUTION & HUM. BEH. 75 (2007).

[52] Roseanna Sommers & Vanessa K. Bohns, *The Voluntariness of Voluntary Consent: Consent Searches and the Psychology of Compliance*, 128 YALE L.J. 1792 (2019).

V. MORAL VALUES

In this section I am interested in a particular set of phenomena in which people evince preferences for other people's outcomes irrespective of whether it affects their own welfare, or indeed even if it makes themselves materially worse off.

Every society has a set of social norms, expectations of one another that are both descriptive (I think you expect this of me) and normative (I think you are right to expect this of me).[53] Some social and moral norms are widespread and predictable: reciprocity, promise-keeping, and respect for authority, for example. Reciprocity and promise-keeping are particularly important for the study of contract.

A. Norms of Fairness

The widespread norm of fair distribution is a core finding of social psychology, with implications for how private parties understand their obligations to one another even without the threat of legal intervention.[54] In many well-studied contexts, people evince strong preferences for promise-keeping, equity, and reciprocity.[55] To take four of the most famous results from experimental economics.

- Equity: The Dictator Game asks two players in a study to be a Sender and a Receiver. The Sender is allocated money, and the Receiver is passive. The modal transfer is not 0, as we might expect given that the players do not meet one another and have no obligations—it is half of the initial endowment. Subjects behave as if they have been asked to share a fair amount, and the default fair allocation is 50–50.
- Promising: In the Public Goods Game, players choose how much of their initial endowment to contribute to a group "pot." The total contributions are multiplied by 2 and redistributed evenly among the players, meaning that for any given player, the best outcome is to contribute nothing and receive a cut of everyone else's cooperative contributions. However, one of the most consistent predictors of cooperation is promising; when players promise each other to contribute, they are more likely to contribute—even when there are no sanctions for breach and all players are anonymous.
- Reciprocity: In the Trust Game, a Sender chooses how much of an initial allocation to pass to a Receiver. The passed amount triples, and the Receiver then makes the last move, choosing how much, if any, to pass back to the Sender. Most Senders

[53] Cristina Bicchieri, *Social Norms* (2005).

[54] See Ernst Fehr & Simon Gächter, *Altruistic Punishment in Humans*, 415 NATURE 137 (2002); see also Ilana Ritov & Jonathan Baron, *Reluctance to Vaccinate: Omission Bias and Ambiguity*, 3 J. BEHAV. DECISION MAKING 263 (1990).

[55] Ernst Fehr, Urs Fischbacher, & Simon Gächter, *Strong Reciprocity, Human Cooperation, and the Enforcement of Social Norms*, 13 HUMAN NATURE 1 (2004).

send some, and most Receivers make good on the investment—that is, most
Receivers pass back more than Senders sent. They reciprocate.

- Punishment: In the Ultimatum Game, two players are Sender and Receiver, as in
  the Dictator Game. But in this game, the Receiver makes the last move, deciding
  to accept or reject the Sender's allocation. Acceptance means the transfer is
  effected; rejection means both players go home with nothing. Receivers who are
  offered less than about a third of the pie are more likely to choose nothing rather
  than the inequitable distribution; they will pay to punish the Sender.

In the 1950s and 1960s, Stewart Macaulay and other colleagues working in law and
sociology interviewed businessmen in Wisconsin, to ask them about how they interact
with one another. The results of that work opened up the scholarly field of relational
contracting—a recognition that for a swath of contracting parties, repeated interactions
over time and within close-knit communities meant that the parties developed norms of
negotiation and dispute resolution outside of the courtroom.[56] Lisa Bernstein, for example, found merchants in the small diamond-trading world relied heavily on informal
norms and handshakes in order to enforce promises.[57] In effect, the evidence from these
sociological studies is about participants in real-world commerce reporting on their own
experiences—they report that their contractual commitments are moral commitments.

Finally, the most recent line of social science research to pick up on the connection
between contract and promise has come specifically from the law and psychology literature. In this literature, the moral implications of contracting have received more systematic experimental attention, especially in the context of breach.[58] Scholars including,
inter alia, Steven Shavell, Zev Eigen, Yuval Feldman, David Hoffman, and myself have
asked nonexperts to reason explicitly or implicitly through dilemmas in contract law. For
example, Shavell asked a group of law students whether it would be immoral to breach a
contract, varying the available information about the parties' preferences for risk allocation; when they lacked information to the contrary, his participants viewed breach as
immoral.[59] Other vignette-study research concludes, in tension with some descriptions
of efficient breach theory,[60] that many people view breach of contract as a moral harm

---

[56] Stewart Macaulay, *Non-Contractual Relations in Business: A Preliminary Study*, 28 AM. SOC. REV.
55 (1963) (describing interviews with businessmen in Wisconsin in the 1960s who largely viewed their
contracts as relational rather than formal).

[57] Lisa Bernstein, *Opting Out of the Legal System: Extralegal Contractual Relationships in the
Diamond Industry*, 21 J. LEGAL STUD. 115, 138 (1992) (identifying both ethical and reputational
constraints on transactors in the diamond industry).

[58] See, e.g., Tess Wilkinson-Ryan, *Legal Promise and Psychological Contract*, 47 WAKE FOREST L. REV.
843 (2012); Yuval Feldman & Doron Teichman, *Are All Contractual Obligations Created Equal*, 100 GEO.
L.J. 5 (2011); Tess Wilkinson-Ryan, *Transferring Trust: Reciprocity Norms and Assignment of Contract*, 9
J. EMP. LEGAL STUD. 511 (2012).

[59] See Steven Shavell, *Why Breach of Contract May Not Be Immoral Given the Incompleteness of
Contracts*, 107 MICH. L. REV. 1569 (2009) (acknowledging the widely held belief that breach of contract
is immoral, but arguing that may not always be the case given that contracts are incomplete and cannot
cover every contingency).

[60] See Steven Shavell, *Damage Measures for Breach of Contract*, 11 BELL J. ECON. 466 (1980) (showing
that expectation damages set incentives for breach at a level that encourages Pareto-superior transfers).

whose social and psychological costs are not worth the financial rewards.[61] Zev Eigen made the stakes of compliance very high for his subjects, foisting an extraordinarily long and onerous survey on those who agreed to take it in return for a DVD. Subjects could stop anytime, but many persisted well beyond the point of frustration; strikingly, this was especially true when they were prodded with rhetoric about the moral stakes of breaching.[62] In other studies, subjects drawn from representative samples report that they would be unwilling to breach a contract for a small profit, and indicate that only a large premium on breach would sway them from their promissory commitment.[63] Experimental studies show that willingness to breach is tied explicitly to the strength of the interpersonal commitment; the further along a deal gets on the offer-acceptance-performance continuum, the more reluctant parties are to breach, even when the costs of breach do not concomitantly increase.[64] Explicit moral values, in this case to promise-keeping and reciprocity, reliably affect legal judgment and decision-making.

B. Ambivalent Norms

The effects of norms of promise-keeping and reciprocity on contracts are intuitive, but they are not the last word on contract norms. The last substantive assertion in this chapter is that private law is a hotbed of deeply ambivalent or fragile norms, and contract is a clear example. In 2014, subjects in a small study of contract fairness were randomly assigned to be asked whether it was reasonable to expect a consumer to read (1) a fifteen-page contract or (2) a two-page contract. They overwhelmingly thought it was unreasonable to be expected to read the long contract and reasonable to be expected to read the short contract. Those same subjects were also asked whether it was the consumer's fault that he was subject to an unexpected fee buried in the fine print. Subjects in the short-contract condition thought he was clearly to blame for his misfortune—and so did the subjects in the long-contract condition.[65] Indeed, in other studies of contract, subjects have indicated that they believe that most terms are legitimate and enforceable if there is even a whiff of assent.[66] However, when they are introduced to the possibility

[61] See, e.g., Tess Wilkinson-Ryan & Jonathan Baron, *Moral Judgment & Moral Heuristics in Breach of Contract*, 6 J. EMP. LEGAL STUD. 405 (2009) (using a series of experimental questionnaire studies to show that many people view efficient breach as an affirmative wrong worthy of supracompensatory damages); see also Tess Wilkinson-Ryan, *Incentives to Breach*, 17 AM. L. ECON. REV. 290 (2015).

[62] Zev J. Eigen, *When and Why Individuals Obey Contracts: Experimental Evidence of Consent, Compliance, Promise, and Performance*, 41 J. LEGAL STUD. 67 (2012) (showing that participants in an onerous online survey were more likely to continue with the survey when they were reminded that they had agreed to finish it and were morally obligated to do so).

[63] See Wilkinson-Ryan, *supra* note 61.

[64] Tess Wilkinson-Ryan & David A. Hoffman, *The Common Sense of Contract Formation*, 67 STAN. L. REV. 1269, 1292 (2015) (finding that some subjects in an online study reported preferences to perform at the offer stage, and even more at the acceptance stage, even when it was not binding at acceptance).

[65] Wilkinson-Ryan, *supra* note 61.

[66] Tess Wilkinson-Ryan, *The Perverse Consequences of Disclosing Standard Terms*, 103 CORNELL L. REV. 117 (2017).

that others, like judges, take unfair terms seriously, their intuitions shift dramatically.[67] In contracts as in other contexts, the law itself is likely important in shaping moral and social norms. Perhaps even more complicated is the possibility that the perceived law, including misunderstandings of the law, shapes individual values with respect to important moral and legal questions. In contract, the social and moral norms are patently ambivalent: people feel strongly that we should take contracts seriously and that it is impossible to take lengthy contracts seriously. A parallel difficulty arises when norms are not so much ambivalent but fragile or inchoate. This is particularly salient in intellectual property and technology, where it is hard to think seriously about some sorts of values because most people have not thought deeply about them.

VI. Conclusion

It is fitting that this chapter ends with the ideas of ambivalent and fragile norms, because these are both some of the richest areas for future study and some of the strongest arguments for embracing a psychological approach to private law that moves past the thinner economic approach to individual preferences.

The question of how to measure preferences is a serious and deep problem for economics and for law. Psychology has no underlying assumption that preferences are stable or intransitive, and really not even a commitment to the notion of preferences at all—there are beliefs, or attitudes, or choices, and sometimes those things are most easily expressed in terms of preferences. But for legal scholars, one of the most attractive features of behavioral work has been understanding preferences for legal regimes. What is worse, theft or battery? Should specific performance be a default remedy for breach of contract? Are copyright laws too strict? And one underlying point we ought to draw from work like Sommers and Bohns on privacy, for example, is that preference elicitation has enormous consequences for preference manifestation.[68]

One of the interventions of psychology per se in the New Private Law is to reject simplistic accounts of preferences, the accounts that often creep into the "behavioral law and economics" literature. It may be *justified* in some sense to describe consumers as having preferences for bad terms or high fees, but it is more useful to conclude that these choices raise questions. The contribution of psychologists is to characterize the cognitive and emotional processes that explain or predict these choices. Indeed, we might conceive of psychological experiments as intentionally exploiting the space between the attitude and the choice, or the value and the belief.

[67] *Id.*   [68] See Sommers & Bohns, *supra* note 52.

CHAPTER 9

··

SYSTEMS THEORY

Emergent Private Law

··

HENRY E. SMITH

WE often speak of the "legal system" and even law as a "system." In what sense? Too often, "system" in law comes across as an empty slogan or as the scapegoat for the ills of our legal institutions. On this negative view, "system" is too civilian, too formalistic, and too conceptual. In reaction to the supposed excesses of "system," American private law has ironically taken too little account of a different—and more important—kind of system in the law, in which connectivity is crucial. This is the subject matter of complex systems theory, and it will shed light on how the connectivity of private law lends it much of its character.

The word "system" appears often in private law theory, usually pejoratively. But these criticisms assume too much about systems and too little about complexity. On the one hand, negative assessments rest on assumptions that the word "system," in law, can only refer to a logical or deductive system. This assumption is often coupled with a suspicion that something ideological rather than purely logical is driving the enterprise. At the same time, in situations in which issues of "complexity" come to the fore, an impoverished notion of complexity—based on the mere number of relevant variables—makes systemic considerations appear less important than they are. Theorists make the assumption that increasing complexity in the world means an increase in the number of elements or variables the law needs to track. Sometimes it is concluded that a more globally contextualized, nuanced law—maybe even some kind of public law—is required to capture this kind of complexity.[1]

---

[1] See, e.g., Thurman Arnold, *The Folklore of Capitalism* 114–116 (1937); James E. Herget, *American Jurisprudence, 1870–1970: A History* 146–147 (1990); G. Edward White, *The Evolution of Reasoned Elaboration: Jurisprudential Criticism and Social Change, in Patterns of American Legal Thought* 136, 139 (1978); see also Richard A. Posner, *Reflections on Judging* (2013) (arguing from complexity against formalism and for a new judicial realism).

Nowhere has this flattened and impoverished approach to complexity and system been more evident than in the so-called bundle-of-rights picture of property. Substantively, the bundle of rights is offered as a reductionist theory of property: property can be broken down into various rights—to exclude, to farm, to build on, to walk across, etc., etc.—all of which contribute additively to the whole bundle, which is nothing more than these parts.[2] So "property," rather than referring to anything interesting, is merely a label for a collection of rights, which can be tailored according to policy by simple addition and subtraction.

Although the strong bundle picture of property is extreme, it is emblematic of much analysis of private law and a fair amount of its practice, which implicitly assume a particular—and I will argue a wildly inapt—version of reductionism. On this version, private law can be analyzed into a set of elements and the substantive character of these elements is most of the story: the properties of each element taken in isolation can be summed up to give us the properties of the whole. Thus, properties of the law, desirable or not, such as efficiency, fairness, stability, and so on, are the sum of the contributions of individual elements such as legal rules. From marginal approaches in economics to incrementalism in common law reasoning,[3] law is treated as a heap of rules contributing to societal effects in an aggregating fashion. In economics, some of the most interesting economic models do involve collective behavior undesired by any participant. The Market for Lemons, spontaneous segregation in housing, and the Tragedy of the Commons provide dramatic examples of emergent properties.[4] I argue that such emergent properties are important feature of private law as well.

Systems theory offers notions of system and complexity that suggest more fruitful alternatives. A system is a collection of elements and—crucially—the connections between and among them; complex systems are ones in which the properties of the system as a whole are difficult to infer from the properties of the parts.[5] Complex systems include brains, social networks, economies, and ecosystems.[6] In such systems, the properties of the system are not the additive sum of the properties of its elements taken in isolation. Rather, system properties are *emergent*, meaning that they may differ from the properties of the elements that make up the system As complexity increases, emergent properties become so difficult to trace to their origins in the interplay of particular elements that reductionism of any kind is likely to fail. Emergent properties bear a

[2] See, e.g., Thomas C. Grey, "The Disintegration of Property," in *NOMOS XXII: Property* 69 (J. Roland Pennock & John W. Chapman eds., 1980).

[3] For exceptions, see Gerald Postema, *Law's System: The Necessity of System in Common Law*, [2014] NEW ZEALAND L. REV. 69.

[4] Thomas C. Schelling, *Micromotives and Macrobehavior* (1978); George A. Akerlof, *The Market for "Lemons": Quality Uncertainty and the Market Mechanism*, 84 Q.J. ECON. 488 (1970); H. Scott Gordon, *The Economic Theory of a Common Property Resource: The Fishery*, 62 J. POL. ECON. 124 (1954).

[5] Melanie Mitchell, *Complexity: A Guided Tour* (2011); Herbert A. Simon, *The Sciences of the Artificial* (2d ed. 1981).

[6] See, e.g., W. Brian Arthur, *Complexity and the Economy* (2015); John H. Miller & Scott E. Page, *Complex Adaptive Systems: An Introduction to Computational Models of Social Life* (2007).

non-straightforward relationship to the properties of the system's parts, because those parts interact in important ways. For example, biological concepts and principles cannot in practice be restated in terms of quantum physics, and social science is even further removed from such underpinnings.

Where does this leave the law? It would be nothing short of miraculous if law were not an interconnected system possessing emergent properties. And there is evidence that law does reflect a situation of organized complexity, which is neither wholly aggregative nor totally chaotic. For example, higher-order concepts in private law, such as "thing," "promise," and "causation," are far more usable in explanation than a reduction to more primitive relations (or, even more fancifully, to the atomic or subatomic level).[7]

Recognizing this reality calls for a different kind of theory about law and a more directed and experimental approach to legal reform. Because much of the action in private law comes from the connections between elements and the need for humans with finite mental resources to employ the law in dealing with the complexity of the world, many—but of course not all—of the interesting features of the private law stem from the *how* of private law rather than the *what* or *why*. It is the interplay of the purposes of private law, which might be quite various, with techniques sounding in system management, that produces the phenomenon of private law as a whole and its contribution to human flourishing in society. Without denying in the least that the system of private law has purposes, systems theory helps us understand how those purposes are—and are not—achieved. Thus, systems theory points in the direction of the New Private Law.

Section I will apply the notion of system from systems theory to the system of private law. Then section II applies the systems approach to various aspects of the law of property, including the bundle of rights, standardization, possession, title, and equity. I turn in section III to the implications of systems theory for some controversies in private law and show how they can be defused or transcended: holism versus reductionism, homogeneity versus specialization, formalism versus contextualism, and private versus public law. The systems approach is also practical, in that it provides a framework for developing rules of thumb in guiding the process of evolution in private law. The chapter ends on an even more speculative note.

I. PRIVATE LAW AS A COMPLEX SYSTEM

From the point of view of systems theory, private law is indeed a system. The system in private law is grounded in its interconnectedness, which in turn sets limits to the kind of reductionism that is appropriate for explaining and justifying private law. These

---

[7] On strong anti-reductionism, emergent system properties are not even causally traceable in principle. See, e.g., P.W. Anderson, *More Is Different: Broken Symmetry and the Nature of the Hierarchical Structure of Science*, 177 SCI. 393, 393, 395 (1972).

interconnections are as important to private law as they have been overlooked in latter day academic and judicial approaches to private law.

Systems theory abounds with definitions of "system." A typical definition that will work for our purposes is: a collection of interconnected elements. Both the elements and (especially) their connections give rise to the phenomena at the system level. A system gets its character from the connections present *and those that are not present*. If the elements are not connected at all, we don't speak of a system. If they are maximally connected (each to each), the system can be chaotic. The most interesting systems—and the ones we find in private law—involve a middle level of interconnectedness, exhibiting patterns. Following Warren Weaver, we can call this "organized complexity."[8]

Systems theory is sometimes called "complex systems theory," "complexity science," and "complex adaptive systems."[9] If anything, "complexity" is harder to define than "system," but what the popular definitions have in common is an emphasis on the interconnections among elements, as opposed to the mere elements themselves. One of the earliest systems theorists developed its methodologies to resolve the mechanism-vitalism controversy in biology that raged in the 1920s.[10]

Complex systems are closely associated with emergence. Thus, for Herbert Simon, a complex system is one in which the properties of the whole are difficult to infer from the properties of the parts, that is, they are emergent.[11] Emergence is often opposed to reductionism in general, and, as we will see, modern private law theory is riddled with excessive reductionism.

It might seem trite to call the law—or the social world of which it is a part—"complex" or "systematic." The specific notions of complexity and system in systems theory will allow a new perspective on many aspects of the legal world and may eventually lead to better predictive theories. The systems approach illuminates an aspect of the problems in private law and so helps explain the architecture of private law. I will highlight one kind of system—the system of private law itself—with side glances at the economic and social systems with which it co-evolves. Specifically relevant to the New Private Law is how private law concepts and baselines, which generally are understood as "internal" to the law, serve these "external" functions.

Seeing private law as a system has one immediate payoff, which is to cast doubt on the prevalent aggregative style of analysis. If private law were a set of rules that had only additive effects, then the effects of the whole would be the additive sum of the effects of the parts. It would further mean that improving a part automatically improves the whole system. If, however, the rules (assuming for now that the basic elements of the

---

[8] Warren Weaver, *Science and Complexity*, 36 AM. SCIENTIST 536 (1948).

[9] See Ludwig von Bertalanffy, *An Outline of General System Theory*, 1 BRIT. J. PHIL. SCI. 134 (1950); see also Mitchell, *supra* note 5.

[10] Ludwig von Bertalanffy, *Problems of Life: An Evaluation of Modern Biological Thought* (1952); see P.A. Lewis, *Systems, Structural Properties, and Levels of Organisation: The Influence of Ludwig von Bertalanffy on the Work of F.A. Hayek*, 34A *Research in the History of Economic Thought and Methodology* 125 (2016).

[11] Simon, *supra* note 5.

law are rules) interact, then we might well find that private law shows emergent properties. If we treat law as a collection of rules that contribute properties like efficiency, fairness, justice, or some kind of justice in an additive fashion, we ignore the possibility that rules or concepts might work in tandem to produce a property that is not a property of any of the parts. Private law as a whole might produce efficiency or justice even if one rule does not.

Closely related to emergence is the evolution of the system. Much of systems theory was developed to enrich evolutionary theory in biology. It has been used to capture what is evolutionary in property law as well.

To see the applicability of systems theory to property and the stakes involved, consider the intersection of two perennial topics in property theory: the bundle of rights and evolution. In classical genetics and evolution, each gene contributed additively to overall fitness, whereas in more recent models, genes can influence each other, by activation, suppression, or change.[12] That is, genes are "epistatically connected."[13] Lee Alston and Bernardo Mueller apply one such model, the famous Kauffman NK model, to the bundle of rights in property: various sticks in the bundle might be connected to other sticks. In Figure 9.1,[14] each of the N boxes represents the presence (1) or absence (0) of a stick and the curved lines stand for the K connections.

The number of such epistatic couplings has implications for the complexity of the system and how it evolves. If there are no epistatic couplings ($K = 0$), then each element (gene, legal relation) can be optimized in isolation because its contribution to the fitness of the whole is additive. At the opposite extreme, if every element is connected to every other ($K = N - 1$), the tendency is toward chaos, where any small change might produce large and wildly unpredictable effects. In the middle, where there are some epistatic couplings (K is between 0 and $N - 1$), we find Weaver's organized complexity that corresponds to a "rugged" fitness landscape (Figure 9.2), in which small changes may lead upward or downward and there may be no way to reach the global maximum by means of small changes.[15]

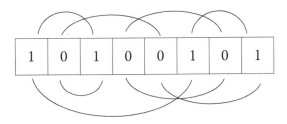

| 1 | 0 | 1 | 0 | 0 | 1 | 0 | 1 |

FIGURE 9.1. Bundle of Rights with $N = 8$ and $K = 2$

[12] Stuart Kauffman, *At Home in the Universe: The Search for the Laws of Self-organization and Complexity* (1995); Lee Alston & Bernardo Mueller, *Towards a More Evolutionary Theory of Property Rights*, 100 Iowa L. Rev. 2255 (2015).

[13] Stuart A. Kauffman, *The Origins of Order: Self-Organization and Selection in Evolution* 40–67 (1993); Alston & Mueller, *supra* note 12, at 2259, 2262–2263, 2265–2268.

[14] Alston & Mueller, *supra* note 12, at 2263.   [15] *Id.* (citing Kauffman, *supra* note 12, at 170–176).

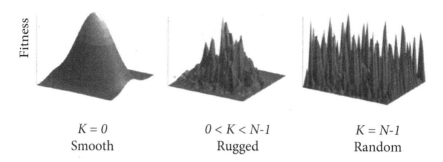

FIGURE 9.2. Change in Landscape as *K* Increases

Republished with permission of *Iowa Law Review*, from "Towards a More Evolutionary Theory of Property Rights," Lee Alston and Bernardo Mueller, Volume 100, Issue 6, © 2015; permission conveyed through Copyright Clearance Center, Inc.

The conventional bundle-of-rights picture of property assumes that each stick in the bundle contributes additively to the whole bundle (*K* = 0), which corresponds to the left-hand fitness landscape. If this were true, it would make reform easy: one simply has to maximize the contribution of each stick in order to maximize the fitness of the whole bundle. As it is said, one is ascending "Mount Fuji," that is, a single-peaked landscape with smooth sides. The (overly) pessimistic outlook would be that connections are maximal, such that any change to the bundle will produce wholly unpredictable effects and the situation would correspond to the right-hand random fitness landscape. If, instead, the sticks in the bundle are connected, but not maximally, we get the rugged landscape in the middle range.

Complexity and evolution point to the role of modularity in keeping the system manageable, which allows for an extension of evolutionary models of property rights. In the famous Demsetz Thesis, property rights emerge when spillovers are more costly than the costs of internalizing them through property rights.[16] However, evolution is a complex interplay between supply and demand factors that vary in a rugged and "dancing" landscape.[17] In situations of organized complexity, modularity permits complex behavior at lower cost.[18] Many interactions can happen locally without the cost of potential ripple effects or the cost of tracking and controlling them. The architecture of property, by employing legal things and a hybrid of exclusion and governance strategies is heavily modular.[19] Modularity promotes certain forms of evolution because variation and selection can happen on one module and the contribution of a substituted or modified module can lead to improvement toward a local optimum. Property can be regarded as law of partial separation, identifying which aspects of the world can be treated as partly (and only partly) in isolation, thus applying Simon's notion of a nearly decomposable

[16]   Harold Demsetz, *Toward a Theory of Property Rights*, 57 Am. Econ. Rev. 347 (1967).
[17]   Alston & Mueller, *supra* note 12.
[18]   Carliss Y. Baldwin & Kim B. Clark, 1 *Design Rules: The Power of Modularity* (2000); Simon, *supra* note 5.
[19]   Henry E. Smith, *Property as the Law of Things*, 125 Harv. L. Rev. 1691 (2012).

system.[20] Modularity and decomposability go far beyond property: the law of tort and the law of contract characteristically employ concepts of privity, foreseeability, and the like, along with devices to prevent decision-making by agents from being too interdependent.[21]

Another advantage of systems theory and modularity is the potential to model the law without prejudging the degree of system. Given a set of interactions between people, which might be either the existing system of legal relations or a hypothetical set of atomized relations, we can employ the kinds of algorithms developed in network theory to derive the degree of modularity that a system exhibits.[22]

In general, we should expect to find that more interconnected parts of the system (more integrated into the rest of the law) will, from a comparative point view, be the least likely to converge across legal systems, assuming that they started out in different positions.[23] And in twentieth-century American private law, systemic aspects of property have changed more slowly than more detachable aspects.[24] Moreover, we might expect that judicial modification—or even repurposing—of modules would be easier to achieve than wholesale remodularization and that within the framework of modularity, courts would be fairly good at dealing with polycentric problems (because their ripple effects can be contained).

If properties of a system and its parts are not necessarily related additively and the system is organized in modular fashion, the way is open for specialization (about which more in section III).[25] Consider as a question of possible specialization the perennial debate in law and economics about whether redistribution is better done through the tax-and-transfer system or should be done though legal rules as well.[26] Even apart from

[20] Henry E. Smith, "The Economics of Property Law," in *The Oxford Handbook of Law and Economics, Volume 2: Private and Commercial Law* 148–177 (Francesco Parisi ed., 2017). On near-decomposability, see Simon, *supra* note 5, at 209–217; see also Herbert A. Simon, *The Architecture of Complexity*, 106 PROC. AM. PHIL. SOC'Y 467, 477 (1962).

[21] Shawn J. Bayern, *The Limits of Formal Economics in Tort Law: The Puzzle of Negligence*, 75 BROOK. L. REV. 707 (2010); Nathan B. Oman, *The Failure of Economic Interpretations of the Law of Contract Damages*, 64 WASH. & LEE L. REV. 829 (2007); Henry E. Smith, *Modularity and Morality in the Law of Torts*, 4 J. TORT L. 2:5 (2011), http://www.bepress.com/jtl/vol4/iss2/art5.

[22] Ted Sichelman & Henry E. Smith, *Modeling Legal Modularity* (draft 2017); see also Matthew O. Jackson, *Social and Economic Networks* 443–457 (2008); M.E.J. Newman & M. Girvan, *Finding and Evaluating Community Structure in Networks*, 69 PHYSICAL REV. E 026113 (2004).

[23] Yun-chien Chang & Henry E. Smith, *Convergence and Divergence in Systems of Property Law: Theoretical and Empirical Analyses*, 92 S. CAL. L. REV. 785 (2019).

[24] Henry E. Smith, *The Persistence of System in Property Law*, 163 U. PA. L. REV. 2055 (2015).

[25] For an early recognition of this point, see Roscoe Pound, *Interpretations of Legal History* 154 (1923); Roscoe Pound, *The Theory of Judicial Decision III: A Theory of Judicial Decision for Today*, 36 HARV. L. REV. 940, 951 (1923). For a vehement Realist denial, see Jerome Frank, *Law and the Modern Mind* 227 (1930); see also Felix S. Cohen, *Ethical Systems and Legal Ideals* 1–40 (1933). See generally Henry E. Smith, *The Language of Property: Form, Context, and Audience*, 55 STAN. L. REV. 1105 (2003).

[26] See e.g., Ronan Avraham, David Fortus, & Kyle D. Logue, *Revisiting the Roles of Legal Rules and Tax Rules in Income Redistribution: A Response to Kaplow & Shavell*, 89 IOWA L. REV. 1125 (2004); Louis Kaplow & Steven Shavell, Should *Legal Rules Favor the Poor? Clarifying the Role of Legal Rules and the Income Tax in Redistributing Income*, 29 J. LEGAL STUD. 821 (2000).

whether doing redistribution through the private law adds a second distortion to incentives to the distortion created by taxes, we have to ask whether lawmakers have enough information to design legal rules to redistribute, especially where legal rules are part of a complex system that coevolves with the system of economic activity. It is an empirical question, once a level of redistribution is desired, which part or parts of the law are the most effective tools.

Crucial to the evolution of complex systems is feedback. As the system produces effects, those effects work directly or indirectly on the system to produce further change. Consider law and equity. Law produced injustices or inefficiencies that equity remedied, and the equitable rule sometimes became a rule of the common law, notably in the area of fraud.[27]

Feedback and evolution raise a more fundamental question about private law: Is it in an equilibrium state or not? If private law is a complex system, it may be a mistake to apply equilibrium concepts.[28] Private law, or at least parts of it, may be designed to facilitate the process of innovation, which is an out-of-equilibrium phenomenon. The system of private law and social interaction may be on the edge of chaos rather than in equilibrium on the one hand or in a state of chaos on the other.[29]

In any event, the systems approach allows us to get a better handle on what exactly is complex and what is simple about private law. The midlevel concepts of private law can be regarded as emerging out of a lower level of complexity: notions like the fee simple or assignment are midlevel concepts that are easier for users to employ. It is striking that internal accounts of private law are based on local rather than (directly) societal justice; various external accounts, from critical schools to conventional law and economics are oriented directly to macro properties rather than this lower level out of which, on the systems approach, the macro properties emerge.[30] Middle-level phenomena in private law are simpler than the complexity on which they supervene, and across the social system, they interact in a complex way that produces complex macro behavior.[31]

---

[27] In law and economics, feedback effects are located in the litigation process, which is said to produce system effects of efficiency, see George Priest & Benjamin Klein, *The Selection of Disputes for Litigation*, 13 J. LEGAL STUD. 1 (1984); Yoon-Ho Alex Lee & Daniel M. Klerman, *The Priest-Klein Hypotheses: Proofs and Generality*, 47 INT'L REV. L. & ECON. 59 (2016); see also Keith N. Hylton, *Information Costs and the Civil Justice System*, AM. L. & ECON. REV. (forthcoming), or more plaintiff-friendly law, Daniel M. Klerman & Greg Reilly, *Forum Selling*, 89 S. CAL. L. REV. 241 (2016); Todd J. Zywicki, *The Rise and Fall of Efficiency in the Common Law: A Supply-Side Analysis*, 97 Nw. U. L. REV. 1551 (2003).

[28] Lewis, *supra* note 10.

[29] César A. Hidalgo, *Why Information Grows: The Evolution of Order, from Atoms to Economies* 30–37 (2015).

[30] See, e.g., Ernest J. Weinrib, *The Idea of Private Law* 2 (1995); John C.P. Goldberg & Benjamin J. Zipursky, *Seeing Tort Law from the Internal Point of View: Holmes and Hart on Legal Duties*, 75 FORDHAM L. REV. 1563 (2006); see also David Friedman, *A Positive Account of Property Rights*, 11(2) SOC. PHIL. & POL'Y 1 (1994); Andrew S. Gold & Henry E. Smith, *Sizing up Private Law*, U. TORONTO L.J. Advance Online, https://www.utpjournals.press/doi/abs/10.3138/utlj.2019-0038 (November 20, 2019).

[31] Within law, something similar may be true of midlevel principles. Cf. Robert P. Merges, *Justifying Intellectual Property* 139–158 (2011) (discussing midlevel principles of IP law).

Finally, the nature of complex systems has implications for uncertainty and design. Some paths the law might take may not be knowable in advance. This type of mixed uncertainty and foreseeability has implications for the strategies that legal designers and more ground-level decision makers like judges should follow in tinkering with the law. Systems theory can be used to help develop rules of thumb for pushing evolution in certain directions. To begin with, change will be easier to accomplish for those aspects of the system that are less interconnected.[32] Incremental common law change can aim for local maximization, whereas a distant maximum may only be reachable through redoing the system, most often through legislation. And such major changes will be riskier the more they touch on highly connected parts of the system. Complex systems are not immune to reform, but we could be clearer about when and how much we should worry about unintended effects. Assuming additiveness of properties, as the bundle-of-rights picture of property does, is a way to make reform look easier; and yet assuming total chaos would be an overreaction.

The systems approach marks a departure in important ways from previous approaches to "system" and "complexity" in the private law. Going all the way back to the German Historical School of the nineteenth century, jurists often assumed that any system in the law had to be deductive, an assumption that came under withering criticism from Holmes and later the Realists.[33] The notion of system from systems theory need not fall into this trap, because the connections between parts of the system need not be deductive, and the system can be open instead of fully "autonomous."[34] Perhaps because theorists before the late twentieth century, with notable exceptions in Hayek and Fuller,[35] did not possess the notion of complex system, their invocations of complexity in the law, especially as a rationale for innovation or reform, were seriously incomplete and misleading. Complexity was taken to mean the number of facts, rules, and case decisions that might bear on a legal situation, rather than the interaction among them.[36] Correspondingly, the solutions were to make the law more complex in a direct fashion, and perhaps to organize it better to eliminate redundancies. Again, these solutions were embodied in rules that we meant to act in additive fashion. Much of the Restatement process and the proliferation of multifactor balancing tests in the law can be seen as a frontal assault on complexity, without the benefit of the tools of systems theory.

---

[32] See Smith, *supra* note 24; Chang & Smith, *supra* note 23.

[33] See Mathias Reimann, *Nineteenth Century German Legal Science*, 31 B.C. L. REV. 837 (1990).

[34] That systems can resolve internal contradictions features prominently in the systems theory notion of complementarity. See J.A. Scott Kelso & David A. Engstrøm, *The Complementary Nature* (2006).

[35] F.A. Hayek, "Notes on the Evolution of Systems of Rules of Conduct (1967)," in *The Collected Works of F.A. Hayek, Volume 15: The Market and Other Orders* (Bruce Caldwell ed., 2014); Lewis, *supra* note 10; Lon L. Fuller, *Principles of Social Order* (rev. ed. 2002).

[36] See Henry E. Smith, *Restating the Architecture of Property*, 10 MODERN STUDIES IN PROPERTY Law 19, 26–29 (Sinéad Agnew & Ben McFarlane eds., 2019).

In current legal theory, systems theory and complexity are making inroads,[37] and private law is no exception.[38] What is of most relevance to private law is how the structure of the law itself is a complex adaptive system and how different this type of system is from traditional notions of system in the law that have been dismissed wholesale.

II. APPLICATIONS

This section shows how, in keeping with the New Private Law, structures internal to the private law can be fruitfully analyzed with the tools of systems theory. Doing so will also allow a fresh take on the relationship between the architecture of private law and the social context with which it co-evolves. I will concentrate on the area of property.[39]

The Bundle of Rights: As we have seen, treating the bundle of rights as a complex system rather than a heap of sticks has important implications for the structure and evolution of property law and property rights.[40] The importance of complexity does not end there: fitness landscapes are a simplified picture that may sometimes need to be supplemented. First, what counts as "fitness" may change over time. Second, the fitness landscape itself is changing, in response to exogenous shocks, innovations, and even feedback from the legal system itself. Third, our knowledge of the fitness landscape is not perfect and there may be a gap between what we think it looks like and what it really is.[41] Fourth and finally, in situations of uncertainty and novelty, new possibilities may arise that were not on the original landscape at all.[42] Thus, where technological change— for example, the first use of irrigation—calls for a new branch of law, evolution may go beyond the dynamism of the picture sketched out above.

---

[37] Simon Deakin, *Legal Evolution: Integrating Economic and Systemic Approaches*, 7 REV. L. & ECON. 659 (2011); Daria Roithmayr, *Evolutionary Dynamics and Method*, Encyclopedia of Law and Economics (Gerrit De Geest ed., 2d ed. 2012); J.B. Ruhl, *Law's Complexity: A Primer*, 24 GA. ST. L. REV. 885 (2008); Adrian Vermeule, *The System of the Constitution* (2011); Joshua C. Teitelbaum, *Computational Complexity and Tort Deterrence* (Oct. 25, 2019), https://ssrn.com/abstract=3480709.

[38] David Harper, *Property Rights as a Complex Adaptive System: How Entrepreneurship Transforms Intellectual Property Structures*, 24 J. EVOL. ECON. 335 (2014); Eric Kades, *The Laws of Complexity and the Complexity of Laws: The Implications of Computational Complexity Theory for the Law*, 49 RUTGERS L. REV. 403 (1997); Jessica A. Shoemaker, *Complexity's Shadow: American Indian Property, Sovereignty, and the Future*, 115 MICH. L. REV. 487 (2017); Sichelman & Smith, *supra* note 22; Smith, *supra* note 19; Smith, *supra* note 20; Teitelbaum, *supra* note 37.

[39] For an application of complexity theory to contracts, see W. Bentley MacLeod, *Complexity and Contract*, REVUE D'ECONOMIE INDUSTRIELLE, 92, trimestre 2000, and for systems theory and torts, see Alan Calnan, *Torts as Systems*, 28 S. CAL. INTERDISC. L.J. 301(2019).

[40] This account suggests that the "Integrated" is crucial in the "Integrated Title Thesis," in J.E. Penner, this volume.

[41] Bernardo Mueller, *Beliefs, Institutions and Development on Complex Landscapes*, 7 ECON. ANALYSIS L. REV. 474 (2016).

[42] Teppo Felin et al., *Economic Opportunity and Evolution: Beyond Landscapes and Bounded Rationality*, 8 STRATEGIC ENTREPRENEURSHIP J. 269 (2014).

In any event, the strong reductionism of the bundle ultimately rests on mere assertions of the merits of reductionism and its supposed resemblance to "science." However, in science, regardless of one's ultimate views on reductionism, employing higher-level concepts is pragmatically crucial when it is not feasible to operate in fully reductionist mode.[43] Thus, it is only in academic discussions that one thinks about stating all the relations involved in owning Blackacre or in setting up a corporation in terms of all the bilateral Hohfeldian relations that make it up. Even someone thinking of buying Blackacre has no time for this.

Lest one think that the choice between a reductionist property bundle or one informed by systems theory is purely academic, the case of the right to roam is instructive. After property theorists presented the right to roam as an unalloyed Good Thing (with apparently one voice of caution), Jonathan Klick and Gideon Parchomovsky found an economically and statistically significant negative effect on land values attributable to the legislation.[44] The point here is not whether the result will hold up or whether the right to roam is a good idea (its benefits might exceed its costs, at least in some formulations and situations). Rather, when codifying a custom or inventing a new servitude, we should be clear that we are operating on the rugged landscape and proceed with some humility.

Standardization in Property: Being both in rem and in personam, property rights pose an interesting informational challenge. One aspect of the modularization of property rights is the grouping of information behind exclusion and the relative enrichment of interfaces through governance.[45] One aspect of this informational strategy is the *numerus clausus* and related standardization, which tends to project simpler, more formal messages to impersonal audiences (in rem) than to socially closer audiences (in personam).[46] In this way, property law seems to achieve the benefits of autonomy, efficiency, and stability roughly but effectively in light of the costs of providing and processing information.

A lack of systems thinking gets in the way of seeing how standardization works. If one assumes that each new purpose requires a new property form, then standardization will

---

[43] Compare Shane Nicholas Glackin, *Back to Bundles: Deflating Property Rights, Again*, 20 LEGAL THEORY 1 (2014), with James Penner, "On the Very Idea of Transmissible Rights," in *Philosophical Foundations of Property Law* 244 (James Penner & Henry Smith eds., 2013).

[44] Jonathan Klick & Gideon Parchomovsky, *The Value of the Right to Exclude: An Empirical Assessment*, 165 U. PA. L. REV. 917 (2017); *id.* at 922, 992 n.18 ("Taking a markedly more guarded approach to the issue, Henry Smith cautioned that 'giving the right-to-roam stick to a neighbor or to the public affects the value of the remaining property.'"), citing Henry E. Smith, *Property Is Not Just a Bundle of Rights*, 8 ECON. J. WATCH 279, 286 (2011); see also Smith, *supra* note 19, at 1717–1718.

[45] See Smith, *supra* note 19.

[46] Thomas W. Merrill & Henry E. Smith, *Optimal Standardization in the Law of Property: The Numerus Clausus Principle*, 110 YALE L.J. 1 (2000); Thomas W. Merrill & Henry E. Smith, *The Property/Contract Interface*, 101 COLUM. L. REV. 773 (2001); Henry E. Smith, "Standardization in Property," in *Research Handbook on the Economics of Property Law* 148 (Kenneth Ayotte & Henry E. Smith eds., 2011); Yun-chien Chang, *The Numerus Clausus Principle, Property Customs, and the Emergence of New Property Forms*, 100 IOWA L. REV. 2275 (2015).

be downplayed or missed altogether.[47] Because property forms are adaptable like building blocks, new purposes can be served (up to a point) using existing rules. Given the possibility of contracting and (if available) settling a trust, much can be accomplished without great third-party information costs.[48] Again, the interaction of simple parts can produce complex results.[49]

Possession: The concept of possession is a linchpin of property law, yet it is often seen as an empty notion. Something called "possession" is invoked in many areas of the law: acquisition, adverse possession, the property torts, and bailment, among others. The proponents of legal science, famously starting with Savigny, made possession a test case for notions of system, and by contrast Realists have proliferated as many notions of possession as there are functions it serves.[50] From a systems theory point of view, the most interesting approach to possession, initiated by Hume and extended by Sugden, sees possession as a convention originating in small-scale interactions and a perceived need to avoid damaging conflicts.[51] One could view this as a kind of evolutionary account, and indeed scholars interested in evolution are now also analyzing possession.[52]

The advantages of the systems view of possession relate both to spontaneous order and to design. From the point of view of spontaneous order, the emergence of a possession convention can be seen as the macro result of small-scale, even bilateral, interactions. On the systems approach, the benefits of a possession-based regime of acquisition and ownership (in which possessors are presumptive owners and ownership is in a sense a beefed-up right of possession) are systemic and need not be true of every instance of possessory activity. This explanation of possession captures the appeal and the limits of the bilateral morality that develops hand in hand with possessory legal norms, in a kind of co-evolution. The system itself exhibits the layering of various kinds of possession.[53] This ontogeny explains the appeal of possession to libertarians, and the limits of its attractions to others. As with other aspects of the law that systemically emerge from

[47]   Again, the Realists tended to assume that complexity of the world would be reflected directly in the law. See, e.g., the sources cited *supra*, at note 1.

[48]   See Ming Wai Lau, *The Nature of the Beneficial Interest—Historical and Economic Perspectives* (Feb. 22, 2013), https://ssrn.com/abstract=2213055; Ben McFarlane, "The Essential Nature of Trusts and Other Equitable Interests: Two and a Half Cheers for Hohfeld," in *The Legacy of Wesley Hohfeld: Edited Major Works, Select Personal Papers, and Original Commentaries* (Shyamkrishna Balganesh, Ted Sichelman, & Henry E. Smith eds., forthcoming).

[49]   For an extreme version of this argument, see Richard A. Epstein, *The Static Conception of the Common Law*, 9 J. LEGAL STUD. 253 (1980). Epstein argues that in the greater system, private law can remain not only simple but relatively static in light of its specialization in stability, with private ordering furnishing flexibility. See also Richard A. Epstein, *Simple Rules for a Complex World* (1997).

[50]   Burke Shartel, *Meanings of Possession*, 16 MINN. L. REV. 611 (1932); see also Joseph W. Bingham, *The Nature and Importance of Legal Possession*, 13 MICH. L. REV. 535 (1915).

[51]   David Hume, *A Treatise of Human Nature* (L.A. Selby-Bigge ed., 1896) (1739–1740); Robert Sugden, *The Economics of Rights, Co-operation and Welfare* (2004); see also Friedman, *supra* note 30.

[52]   See, e.g., Samuel Bowles & Jung-Kyoo Choi, *Coevolution of Farming and Private Property*, 110 PNAS 8830 (2013).

[53]   Henry E. Smith, "The Elements of Possession," in *Law and Economics of Possession* 65–102 (Yun-Chien Chang ed., 2015).

small-scale interaction, we can ask which kinds of intervention might improve on what spontaneous order has furnished so far.[54] From the point of view of the New Private Law, a systems perspective on possession also helps us get a handle on some design questions. Indeed the architecture of private law is a hybrid between the spontaneous and the designed, much like the architecture of the built environment.[55]

Title: Famously Karl Llewellyn and other Realists criticized the emphasis on title at the intersection of personal property law and sales. In older law, questions such as who bears the risk of loss could be "derived" from the notion of title. To some Realists, concepts like title were transcendental nonsense.[56] In a more moderate vein, Llewellyn believed that concepts should be no more abstract than could be justified by their usefulness. When it came to drafting the Uniform Commercial Code, Llewellyn downplayed the notion of title, questioning the value of asking "where" it was located, and yet he found title to be a useful organizing notion.[57]

The value of complex systems theory extends to institutions surrounding title. Because title conflicts involve third parties and ultimately system effects like certainty and stability, the contribution of recording and registration systems can be seen as stemming from their reshaping of the interactions of owners, purchasers, and others. Even adding up individual three-party interactions may miss the full set of interactions in title records.[58] Out of the connections between parties, including ones who do not deal directly with one another, attributes like stability and security emerge from the system.

Law and Equity: Equity cuts across the legal system, and especially in the law of property. Elsewhere I have argued that, from a functional point of view, equity, even historically, often serves as a second-order system to adjust and sometimes override the results of the system of the regular law.[59] The idea of second-order systems and control devices is familiar from systems theory.[60] Looking at equity from the systems viewpoint causes

---

[54] See Gold & Smith, *supra* note 30.

[55] Smith, *supra* note 36, see also Christopher Alexander et al., *A Pattern Language: Towns, Buildings, Construction* (1977); Christiane Herr, *Generative Architectural Design and Complexity Theory*, paper for the International Conference on Generative Art (2018), available at https://www.researchgate.net/publication/30870757.

[56] Felix S. Cohen, *Transcendental Nonsense and the Functional Approach*, 35 COLUM. L. REV. 809 (1935).

[57] Jeremy Waldron, *"Transcendental Nonsense" and System in the Law*, 100 COLUM. L. REV. 16 (2000); K.N. Llewellyn, *Through Title to Contract and a Bit Beyond*, 15 N.Y.U. L.Q. REV. 159, 169–170 (1938).

[58] Henry E. Smith, *Comment: Property as Complex Interaction*, 13 J. INST. ECON. 809 (2017). For an emphasis on different system aspects, see Benito Arruñada, *How Should We Model Property? Thinking with My Critics*, 13 J. INST. ECON. 815 (2017).

[59] Henry E. Smith, "Fusing the Equitable Function in Private Law," in *Private Law in the 21st Century* 173 (Kit Barker, Karen Fairweather, & Ross Grantham eds., 2017); Henry E. Smith, *Equity as Second-Order Law: The Problem of Opportunism* (Jan. 15, 2015), available at SSRN: http://ssrn.com/abstract=2617413 (forthcoming as "Equity as Meta-Law," 130 Yale L.J.).

[60] See, e.g., Karl Ludwig von Bertalanffy, *General System Theory* (1968); see also John H. Holland, *Hidden Order* 11–12 (1995) (discussing second-order agents and properties).

us to ask about the costs and benefits of going second order, and in particular which problems call for second-order treatment. I have argued that among such problems are problems of high uncertainty and complexity (in the systems sense), which can justify the costly effort to establish and maintain metalaw, whether jurisdictionally or doctrinally. Specifically, these uncertain and complex problems include multipolar problems, conflicting rights, and opportunism. The first category includes "polycentricity," which Fuller saw as a problem of true complexity and as calling for administration as opposed to adjudication.[61] Equity, perhaps incorporating an administrative element,[62] dealt with situations involving third parties or groups, as in the enforcement of a local property custom. The second problem, of conflicting rights, is important in areas like the property torts, where nuisance can be seen as a second-order reconciliation of neighbors' presumptive use rights. The third problem, opportunism, involves behavior that is not provably fraud but that (in some sense) unforeseeably misuses the law. Opportunism is a kind of negative feedback on the legal system, and one can see opportunistic behavior and equity as co-evolving. A familiar property example is building encroachments, which are enjoinable unless they are in good faith and enjoining them would create undue hardship, which can serve as a proxy for dangerous leverage on the part of the encroached-upon party.

The systems view of equity points to possibilities that would be difficult to see otherwise. The conventional wisdom on equity is that it involves discretion in the name of fairness or policy, and that this discretion is greatly destabilizing. Disagreement centers on whether the destabilization is worth the benefits of the tailoring and fairness it provides. However, if equity is triggered by proxies for complex problems (multipolar problems, conflicting rights, opportunism) and ranges over the law (but not vice versa), it is possible that equity may be more stabilizing than destabilizing. The open-endedness of equity is needed to meet complex problems roughly where they occur, based on the limited triggering proxies. By the "Law of Requisite Variety," a control system has to vary at least as much as what it controls.[63] At a second level, it is possible to keep a first-order system within boundaries (think thermostats).

So even though equity introduces its own uncertainty, it reduces other uncertainty. It is an empirical question which effect is greater. As a thought experiment, imagine trying to deal with all opportunism with ever more complex ex ante rules, instead of being able to intervene ex post.[64] A single-level system would be extremely complex or ineffective (or both), and we should consider whether reinforcing the dual-level structure in this aspect of the legal system would be an overall (emergent) improvement over it.

---

[61] See Fuller, *supra* note 35, at 111–121.

[62] See *Equity and Administration* (P.G. Turner ed., 2016).

[63] W. Ross Ashby, *An Introduction to Cybernetics* (1956); Y. Aulin-Ahmavaara, *The Law of Requisite Hierarchy*, 8 KYBERNETES 259 (1979).

[64] See David A. Weisbach, *Formalism in the Tax Law*, 66 U. CHI. L. REV. 860 (1999).

III. FURTHER IMPLICATIONS

Seeing law as a complex system allows us to unpack and mitigate some of the persistent dichotomies in private law theory. Let me sketch why systems theory could be brought to bear on these dichotomies, rather than attempting to resolve them here.

Perhaps most obviously, systems theory addresses the question of holism and reductionism in private law. As Herbert Simon once said, complex systems theory allows one to be an "in-principle reductionist" and a "pragmatic holist."[65] At this point, there is little that forces us to choose between in-principle reductionism and holism—and falling back on pragmatism where the in-principle approach fails. Either way, by reconciling holism and reductionism more than is conventionally thought possible, fewer substantive issues in private law should be seen as turning essentially on holism versus reductionism.

In any event, reductionism need not commit us to an additive view of law, such as the aggregative bundle-of-rights picture of property, and it does not require vagueness when dealing with the macro properties of law. Instead, much of the interesting action in private law that helps explain its contours happens at the meso level where neither additive micro models nor large statistical average-based models are appropriate. Systems theory allows for feedback by strategic actors and the co-evolution of law with economic and social systems in which it is embedded. The system in the law also reflects—and co-evolves with—the cognitive system of its participants, which is modular and makes use of principles like specific-over-general.[66] Systems theory is compatible with a range of purposes for private law—which can be seen as alternative accounts of fitness—and points to more convergence than we might expect at the level of incremental changes.

Systems theory also leads us to expect that private law need not be homogeneous, but rather that different parts of private law may be specialized. A given desideratum of private law need not be reflected in all its parts or at all levels. Every rule need not be efficient or just in order for the system to be efficient or just. Law and equity, property and contract, in rem and in personam, and the like can differ radically in their legal technology because of the different purposes they serve and because of the different audiences to which they are directed. For this reason, we should not expect all areas of private law to be equally formal or contextual, or for that matter equally closed- or open-textured. And for those specialized areas that are more open, like equity, we should not be surprised that they refer to system-level purposes and moral notions like fairness.

The idea that different levels are nontrivially related to each other puts a new gloss on the publicness of private law. Private law has macro effects that we often associate with public law. Again, that might mean that public law values are reflected in certain aspects or levels of private law but does not necessarily mean that public law values need to be

---

[65] Simon, *supra* note 5, at 195.

[66] Henry E. Smith, *On the Economy of Concepts in Property*, 160 U. PA. L. REV. 2097 (2012).

reflected in every part of the law and at every level. Thus, public law values can come into the law in various places: Should antidiscrimination law target housing markets or the law of torts and possession? Likewise, the rule of law is a system effect: it is not an additive property of the law's parts but an emergent feature of the system as a whole, as we saw with equity.[67]

Systems theory provides a framework for institutional design that gets beyond the flat, additive heap-of-rules picture assumed in much legal commentary and promoted by law reform processes like the Restatements. One of the prime lessons of the Coase theorem is that in a world of positive transaction costs, institutions matter.[68] One way of looking at complexity is as another source of transaction costs, specifically the costs of delineating and enforcing rights (or institutions generally). If so, we could bring out the role of systems theory through a similar thought experiment. Imagine that all effects relevant to the law were additive. If that looks wildly optimistic, we have reason to start caring about complexity.

Systems theory does not furnish a brief for doing nothing, nor does it point exclusively to spontaneous order. It does have implications for how we go about reforming the law, in light of the nontrivial effects on fitness that even small changes may produce. Whether it can furnish more positive predictions is less clear—as it is in systems theory more generally.

IV. CONCLUSION

Systems theory avoids the problems thought to be inherent in "system" in private law. Conventional analysis engages in sum-of-the-parts reductionism, most notably in the bundle-of-rights picture of property. By contrast, an account of private law based on "organized complexity," emphasizing significant connections between the elements of the system and corresponding to a rugged fitness landscape from evolutionary models, is far more realistic. Applying systems theory to private law leads to a better and more unified account of the bundle of rights, standardization in property, possession, title, and equity, and allows us to take seriously some of the structures of private law for functional reasons. Systems theory also promises to mitigate some of the dichotomies in private law, such as holism versus reductionism, homogeneity versus specialization, formalism versus contextualism, and the publicness of private law. In these many interrelated ways, the systems approach fits naturally in the New Private Law.

---

[67] On the rule of law and private law, see Lisa M. Austin, this volume.

[68] R.H. Coase, *The Problem of Social Cost*, 3 J.L. & ECON. 1 (1960); see generally Steven G. Medema, *The Coase Theorem at Sixty* (draft Dec. 2018). See also Barak Richman, this volume.

CHAPTER 10

··

PRIVATE LAW AND
LOCAL CUSTOM

··

NATHAN B. OMAN

I. INTRODUCTION

ONE of the striking features of private law in English-speaking countries is the extent to which it is mainly common law. To be sure, many areas of tort, contract, and property are subject to statutes, and civil law jurisdictions demonstrate that private law can be codified. Still, most Anglo-American private law is common law. This chapter explores that relationship. Both private law and the common law fit awkwardly into the dominant theoretical models of law, which emphasize regulation and social control by the state. Thus, the common law has long been criticized for failing to comply with the model of clearly articulated rules that are announced ex ante and applied ex post. The private law, for its part, contains numerous features that make it a poor candidate for a well-designed regulatory regime.

Law and economics (L&E) has dominated much of contemporary private law theory. Beginning in the 1980s, however, neoformalist[1] critics focused on features of private law that L&E can explain only awkwardly. These accounts, in turn, provide responses to many of the standard criticisms of the common law. While this movement is encouraging, theoretical challenges remain. Neoformalism, despite its ambition to take the structure of legal doctrine more seriously than L&E, has difficulty accounting for large swaths of private law. Furthermore, these theories have tended to be highly abstract, placing little or no significance on the particularity of the communities over which private law

---

[1] In this chapter, I am using the term "neoformalism" as a way of referring to the philosophically minded renaissance in private law theory that began in the 1980s with corrective justice theories of tort law and promissory or autonomy theories of contract law. See Charles Fried, *Contract as Promise: A Theory of Contractual Obligation* (1981); Ernest J. Weinrib, *The Idea of Private Law* (1995); Jules Coleman, *The Structure of Tort Law*, 97 YALE L.J. 1233 (1988).

claims authority. In contrast, the common law often evidences a parochialism that focuses on the history or practices of specific communities. A renewed focus on the classical common law theory of the seventeenth and eighteenth centuries offers one way of responding to these weaknesses in neoformalism.

In the remainder of this chapter, I will begin by situating both private law and the common law within current legal thought, showing how they are a poor fit with our most common assumptions about the law. Then I will argue that developments in private law theory suggest a convergence between private law and the common law that responds to these issues, rendering the law both intelligible and providing an answer to the common objection that the common law involves ex post facto lawmaking. Finally, I will argue that a recovery of the classical common law theory is both conceptually feasible and offers solutions to problems left currently unanswered by neoformalism.

II. Theoretical Background

Private law and common law are the problem children of contemporary legal theory. Both run afoul of the same basic assumption about law, namely, that it is primarily a mechanism through which political authorities regulate the conduct of those over whom they exercise power. This section provides an overview of this dynamic.

A. Private Law

The dominant assumption for a century or more has been that private law is simply public law by other means.[2] It is a matter of the state pursuing collective goals by regulating private behavior. Private law is thus not fundamentally different from criminal law or administrative regulations. The only difference lies in decentralized enforcement via "private" litigation. "Private" must be in scare quotes because litigants are analogous to deputy attorneys general or qui tam relators. They are de facto agents of the state in pursuit of its regulatory goals.

L&E has tended to reinforce the view that private law's "real" goal is social regulation.[3] According to L&E, all law should be thought of in terms of the incentives that it creates for legal actors and evaluated in terms of the efficiency of those incentives. The conceptual appeal of L&E lies in its simplicity and reductionism. It offers a theory that seems equally suited to analyzing crime, contract, and the Clayton Act. This flattening

---

[2] As Leon Green famously put it, tort law is merely "public law in disguise." Leon Green, *Tort Law Public Law in Disguise*, 38 Tex. L. Rev. 1 (1959). A similar assumption has motivated much of the thinking on property and contract law in the twentieth century.

[3] Guido Calabresi's argument that tort law can be thought of as trying to minimize the social cost of accidents provides an early and influential example. See Guido Calabresi, *The Costs of Accidents: A Legal and Economic Analysis* (1970).

of distinctions between doctrinal areas is reinforced by L&E's functionalism, which discounts the language and normative structure of legal doctrine as epiphenomenal.

Neoformalism runs counter to the dominant thinking. First, these theorists tend to eschew the functionalist dismissals of legal language common for much of the twentieth century. Rather, doctrinal categories and language should be seen as more or less coherent efforts to explain legal outcomes. This focus on legal doctrine contrasts sharply with the assumption, common from the Legal Realists onward, that doctrinal language is a mask of "transcendental nonsense" hiding functionalist goals.[4] Second, rather than seeing private law as serving primarily regulatory goals, neoformalist thinkers focus on the interactions between particular parties. These transactions are not mere opportunities to advance broader social goals. Rather, the purpose of private law is to empower the victims to seek individual justice against those who have victimized them. This individual justice cannot be reduced to some broader conception of policy or even social justice. Thus, a tort suit is not an awkward form of safety regulation or accident insurance. It is about a wronged plaintiff seeking redress against a tortfeasor for wrongs defined in the terms set forth by legal doctrine.[5]

B. Common Law

The term "common law" is ambiguous. Originally, it referred to the national law created by the Angevin kings in contrast to the various local laws of their Saxon subjects.[6] It was the highly centralized legislative creation of a royal bureaucracy. Later, common law came to refer to the law applied by particular English courts such as Common Pleas and King's Bench in contrast to the law applied in equity courts, prerogative courts, ecclesiastical courts, or merchant courts. Over time, the common law's legislative origins became obscured by centuries of judicial encrustations, and it came to be seen as "judge-made" law.

In the seventeenth century, jurists such as Coke, Selden, and Hale began to articulate and defend the common law as a distinctive legal form. Blackstone took up their ideas and refined them in the eighteenth century. We can refer to this synthesis as "classical common law theory," although none of these writers thought of themselves as theorists.[7] Classical common law theory made a number of interrelated claims. First, it insisted that

---

[4] See Felix S. Cohen, *Transcendental Nonsense and the Functional Approach*, 35 COLUM. L. REV. 809 (1935) (arguing that doctrinal concepts are largely vacuous).

[5] The most articulate spokespersons for this position have been civil recourse theorists, in particular John Goldberg and Benjamin Zipursky. See, e.g., Benjamin Zipursky, *Civil Recourse, Not Corrective Justice*, 91 GEO. L.J. 656 (2003), John C.P. Goldberg & Benjamin Zipursky, *The Moral of MacPherson*, 146 U. PA. L. REV. 1733 (1998). While civil recourse theorists are building on the earlier work of corrective justice scholars, methodologically they are less committed to the formalism and abstraction of writers such as Ernest Weinrib. See Benjamin C. Zipursky, *Pragmatic Conceptualism*, 6 LEGAL THEORY 457 (2000).

[6] See J.H. Baker, *An Introduction to English Legal History* 12–36 (4th ed. ed. 2002) (discussing the early history of the common law).

[7] See generally Gerald Postema, *Bentham and the Common Law Tradition* (1986) (summarizing the history of the classical common law theory and its critics).

common law was *lex non scripta* (unwritten law). As opposed to statutes, there is no authoritative linguistic formulation of common law rules. Second, the law is not made by the judges but rather is found by them in the traditions and customs of the people. Third, the common law evolves over time in response to changed circumstances and customs. Fourth, the legitimacy of the common law rests on more than simply the authority of the sovereign. Rather, it lies in the law's congruence with social norms and customs.

From at least the seventeenth century, the common law has also had its critics. Thomas Hobbes attacked Coke and his successors, insisting that law was a matter of authority rather than the "artificial reason" of judges.[8] What he meant by this was that properly speaking, law consists of rules promulgated by a sovereign to end the war of all against all that results in the absence of social control. A century later, Bentham took up Hobbes's criticisms, insisting that the common law, because of its backward-looking obscurity, could not successfully maximize utility.[9] In the twentieth century, H.L.A. Hart reformulated the positivism of Bentham and his disciples in terms that placed legislation at the center of law creation.[10] The common law's evolution via adjudication fits awkwardly at best into this model. Those working in the Hartian tradition accept, of course, that the law develops through adjudication, but, as we will see, doing so requires a distorted view of the common law. Likewise, Hart's great critic, Lon Fuller, conceptualized law as "government through rules," setting forth an "internal morality of law" that the common law seems to transgress.[11] Because it is *lex non scripta*, the demands of the common law are often unclear, making it a poor guide for behavior. Most damning, because doctrine develops through adjudication, new rules are often applied ex post facto.

III. THE CONVERGENCE OF PRIVATE LAW AND COMMON LAW

Neoformalism suggests a convergence between the structure of private law and the structure of common law. As an historical matter this convergence is unsurprising, given that it was primarily (although not exclusively) within the common law that Anglo-American private law was formed and for much of its history private law topics have garnered the lion's share of the common law's attention. There is more at work here, however, than historical accident. First, private law as an autonomous intellectual

[8] See Thomas Hobbes, *A Dialogue Between a Philosopher and a Student of the Common Laws of England* 55 (Joseph Cropsey ed., 1997) (1681) ("[T]hat the Reason which is the Life of the Law, shoud be not Natural, but Artificial I cannot conceive.").

[9] See Postema, *supra* note 7, at 286–295 (summarizing Bentham's argument for the inherent injustice and disutility of the common law).

[10] See H.L.A. Hart, *The Concept of Law* 100–10 (2d ed. 1994) (arguing that law should be understood in terms of a rule of recognition that identifies a proper lawmaking authority).

[11] See Lon L. Fuller, *The Morality of Law* 33–38 (rev. ed., 1969) (setting forth ways in which one might fail to rule through law).

discourse coheres with the common law's status as a *lex non scripta*. Second, to the extent that our theories see private law primarily as a matter of ex post recourse rather than prospective duty enforcement, they respond to functionalist objections to the ex post facto lawmaking involved in common law adjudication.

A. Lex Non Scripta and the Autonomy of Private Law

Ernest Weinrib's influential book *The Idea of Private Law* insists that private law is intelligible in its own terms and thus we need not look beyond the law to its social consequences to understand it. "If we *must* express this intelligibility in terms of purpose, the only thing to be said is that the purpose of private law is to be private law."[12] Private law pursues internal purposes that cannot be understood in terms of something else. Weinrib gives the example of love. Love cannot be understood as valuable because it serves some other purpose, like economic security, without distorting love itself. "My contention," Weinrib writes, "is that, in this respect, private law is just like love."[13]

Weinrib's claims may seem grandiose, but the common law is a discursive practice that is constantly reflecting on its own meaning. There is a vast body of case law explaining and applying private law, and it is within the categories of this case law that the intelligibility of the law is found. On reflection, however, this internal intelligibility is surprising. For example, if we follow Bentham in insisting that law must consist of rules given a fixed linguistic form, it is not clear that law contains the conceptual resources within itself for the kind of intelligibility that Weinrib assigns to private law.[14]

Consider an example drawn from the U.S. bankruptcy code. When a debtor files for bankruptcy, the code creates an "automatic stay" prohibiting any debt collection actions against the debtor outside of the bankruptcy process.[15] There are a number of exceptions to this stay, including one applying to "the exercise by a repo participant... of any contractual right... under any security agreement. . . ."[16] If we are speaking of the kind of intelligibility aimed at by Weinrib, this rule cannot be rendered intelligible. We cannot understand the normative content of the law by recourse to the statutory language itself. Rather, we must look to sources such as legislative history or judicial opinions to know that the purpose of this section is to allow large financial institutions to collect immediately on short-term loans at the expense of other

---

[12] Weinrib, *supra* note 1, at 5.   [13] *Id.* at 6.

[14] As Bentham put it:

> There is a legislator—there is a will—there is an expression of that will, a known period of its birth. Unwritten law possesses none of these qualities: its origin is unknown; it goes on continually increasing—it can never be finished; it is continually altering with observation.
>
> Postema, *supra* note 6, at 295 (quoting Bentham).

[15] See 11 U.S.C. § 362(a) (2012) (setting forth the kinds of actions prohibited by the automatic stay).

[16] 11 U.S.C. § 362(b)(17) (2012).

creditors.[17] Notice that this explanation is not "critical" in the sense of positing a "real" set of motives at work behind the ostensible reasons offered by the law.[18] The law—conceptualized à la Bentham as the statutory text—offers no explanation for itself. There is no mask to be torn away by the unmasking of the critical theorist. The code is pure Hobbesian law, authority without reason.[19]

Contrast such Hobbesian law to classic common law decisions such as *Hadley v. Baxendale*[20] or *Palsgraf v. Long Island Railroad Co.*[21] Both cases articulate rules, but neither of them provides an authoritative form for those rules. Rather, they elucidate concepts that can only be grasped through the courts' efforts to justify the outcomes in the particular cases before them. The process of reasoning is what constitutes the law itself. There is no other way for the judges in these cases to find, apply, or make it. The common law is, thus, necessarily intelligible in a way that statutory law is not. To be sure, statutory law can be rendered intelligible by extra-statutory sources. For *lex non scripta*, in contrast, the process of intelligibility *is* the primary legal material. (This is not to deny, of course, that at times judicial reasoning is muddled or incoherent.) Even the texts of judicial opinions are not controlling in the manner of statutory texts. Rather, as Blackstone put it, judicial opinions are mere evidence of the law, not the law itself.[22]

B. Ex Post Facto Law and the Nonregulatory Ambitions of Private Law

"Law has to do with the governance of human conduct by rules," wrote Lon Fuller. "To speak of governing or directing conduct today by rules enacted tomorrow is to speak blank prose."[23] Viewing law as mechanism of government and control presents a problem for the common law. Every time a common law doctrine is expanded or contracted, a new rule is announced, or a doctrine is abandoned, the law is applied retroactively in the case where it is announced. There are a number of ways of dealing with this difficulty. H.L.A. Hart, for example, suggested that "[w]here the decision of the court on

---

[17] See Bevill, Bresler & Schulman Asset Mgmt. Corp. v. Spencer Sav. & Loan Ass'n, 878 F.2d 742, 748 (3d Cir. 1989) (recounting the legislative history and policy behind exempting so-called "repo transactions" from the automatic stay).

[18] See Gary Minda, *Postmodern Legal Movements: Law and Jurisprudence at Century's End* 108 (1995) ("[T]he critical scholar tries to expose how legal analysis and legal culture mystifies outsiders and legitimates its results" (quoting Martha Minow, *Law Turning Outward*, 73 Telos 79, 85 (1986))).

[19] See Hobbes, *supra* note 8, at 69 ("For Statutes were made by Authority, not drawn from any other Principles than the care of the safety of the People. Statutes are not Philosophy as is the Common-Law, and other disputable Arts, but are Commands . . .").

[20] 156 Eng. Rep. 145 (Ex. 1854).   [21] 162 N.E. 99 (N.Y. 1928).

[22] See 1 William Blackstone, *Commentaries on the Laws of England* 69 (Wilfrid R. Prest ed., 2016) (1765) ("And indeed the judicial decisions are the principal and most authoritative evidence, that can be given, of the existence of such customs as shall form a part of the common law."). All citations to Blackstone are to the page numbers in the 1765 edition.

[23] Fuller, *supra* note 11, at 53.

such matters are regarded as precedents, their specification of the variable standard is very like the exercise of delegated rulemaking power by an administrative body . . ."[24] Fuller offered a similar explanation:

> If the court were to overrule the precedent prospectively, so that the new rule would apply only to cases arising after the overruling decision, it is difficult to see how a private litigant would ever have any incentive to secure repeal of a decision that was mistaken or that had lost its justification through a change in circumstances.[25]

For Fuller, litigants are analogous to respondents to an administrative agency's call for comments on a proposed rule, providing lawmakers with useful information.[26] Notice that Fuller's difficulties with the common law arise from his view of the law as a form of social control that makes use of rules. The law can only guide and control behavior if the rules are known in advance. So long as ex post application of rules does not happen too often, the project of legality need not fail, but common law development sits awkwardly within his framework.

Civil recourse theory, however, can simply deny that private law is a mechanism of social control. Rather, private law empowers private litigants to act against those who have wronged them.[27] It is a set of power-conferring rules rather than a set of duty-imposing rules, although obviously the language of duty is used to describe the conditions under which plaintiffs can employ the machinery of the state against those who have wronged them. This is the view of tort law taken by civil recourse theories, but it can be extended with modifications as a possible explanation for other forms of civil liability that empower plaintiffs to vindicate their private wrongs.[28] As a legal matter, we are genuinely indifferent, on the civil recourse view, as to whether a plaintiff brings suit. The purpose of the law is not to regulate behavior but to provide a mechanism for victims to act should they choose to do so. Indeed, some writers have gone so far as to suggest that tortfeasors and contract breachers have no duty to pay damages.[29] On this

---

[24] Hart, *supra* note 10, at 132.   [25] Fuller, *supra* note 11, at 57.

[26] See, e.g., United Steelworkers of Am., AFL-CIO-CLC v. Schuylkill Metals Corp., 828 F.2d 314, 324 (5th Cir. 1987), *rev'd and remanded sub nom.* United Steelworkers of Am., AFL-CIO-CLC v. St. Joe Res., 916 F.2d 294 (5th Cir. 1990) ("Two purposes of notice and comment rulemaking are to afford interested persons the opportunity to participate in the agency regulatory process and to expose the agency to the practical implications of its actions.").

[27] See generally Zipursky, *Civil Recourse, supra* note 5 (arguing that tort law should be understood primarily in terms of empowering plaintiffs to act against defendants that have wronged them); John C.P. Goldberg & Benjamin Zipursky, *Torts as Wrongs*, 88 Tex. L. Rev. 917 (2010) (same).

[28] See, e.g., Nathan B. Oman, *Consent to Retaliation: A Civil Recourse Theory of Contractual Liability*, 96 Iowa L. Rev. 529 (2011) (arguing that contract damages constitute a limited form of retaliation by promisees against wayward promisors).

[29] See Stephen A. Smith, *Duties, Liabilities, and Damages*, 125 Harv. L. Rev. 1727 (2012) (arguing that the law of remedies does not impose a duty to pay damages on defendants in private law actions); Nathan B. Oman, *Why There Is No Duty to Pay Damages: Powers, Duties, and Private Law*, 39 Fla. St. U. L. Rev. 137 (2011) (same).

view, private law simply is not about enforcing duties. If we adopt this highly plaintiff-centered view of private law, then Fuller's objections to the common law fall away.[30] This is because ultimately Fuller's concerns are ex ante concerns. It is important to recognize that Fuller does not articulate his objections in terms of what me might think of fairness or due process problems with to ex post facto law. (More on this anon.) He is concerned with whether rules are *effectively* governing. In effect, he asks, "Does the law tell people how they are supposed to act?" It cannot do this if it doesn't speak until after the action has occurred. On the other hand, if we take a very strictly ex post perspective then Fuller's concern with effective governance is simply beside the point. One can concede that ex post lawmaking is a poor form of social control but deny that social control is what the common law is doing.

In fact, few if any theorists take the extreme position that the law is completely indifferent to whether the duties specified within tort or contract are performed. Many are likely to say that there are imperfect duties to comply with the substantive rules of tort and contract, even if plaintiffs do not bring suit. The greater the emphasis that a theory places on the performance of such duties, however, the more awkward will be the ex post facto character of common law change. Even on such a mixed view, a recourse-centered vision of private law renders it more congenial to the common law than a vision that places greater emphasis on law as a mechanism of social control.

IV. Reviving the Classical Common Law Theory

While something like the civil recourse argument can respond to Fuller's objections to ex post facto laws, there remain what we could think of as due process objections to the evolution of the common law. The classical common law theory provided an answer to these objections. While appeals to Hale or Blackstone may seem anachronistic, it is possible to construct a chastened, modern version of their arguments. Such a reconstructed classical common law theory calls attention to two features of much of neoformalism: its underinclusiveness and its placelessness. A revived attention to concepts such as custom, tradition, and local practice offers potentially productive ways of considering aspects of the common law that have received insufficient emphasis in contemporary private law theory.

---

[30] See Benjamin C. Zipursky, *Torts and the Rule of Law, in Private Law and the Rule of Law* 139 (Lisa Austin & Dennis Klimchuck eds., 2015) (arguing that the ex post character of common law adjudication is less troubling for civil recourse theories); Benjamin C. Zipursky, *The Inner Morality of Private Law*, 58 Am. J. Jur. 27 (2013) (same).

A. Due Process and Ex Post Facto Law

Ex post facto laws are a species of due process failure, an arbitrary exercise of official power. Thomas Scanlon writes, "The idea of a right to due process ... involves the recognition that those subject to authority are entitled to demand justification for its use and entitled to protection against its unjustified use. . . ."[31] Legal liability is the kind of thing that requires a justification. Any person whose actions result in legal liability is entitled to ask, "Why should I suffer some negative legal consequence for this action?" From the law's internal point of view, the answer is "Because your conduct violated a legal standard." Of course, in an unjust legal system, this answer may be inadequate as a matter of political morality, but in a system of law, it will be a necessary component of any account of the legitimacy of official action. Unless there is a legal answer to the defendant's question of "Why me?" the system will involve the arbitrary and unjustified exercise of official power. This is the basic intuition behind the maxim of *nulla poena sine lege*, "there is no penalty without law."

One cannot respond to this objection by arguing that private law is a matter of ex post recourse rather than duty enforcement. Civil recourse theory provides a reply to Fuller's objection; private law need not be about "governance" in the way assumed by his argument. It is not, however, an adequate answer to the defendant who insists that it is illegitimate to impose liability on activity that was not legally objectionable at the time that it happened. This is not Fuller's objection to the functional efficacy of official action but rather a challenge to its legitimacy.

B. Reconstructing the Classical Common Law Theory

The classical theory of the common law offers a solution to this problem. There is no due process objection to imposing liability on the wrong doer because at the time she committed the wrong she violated an already existing law. When the judge announces the rule to be applied in the case, she is not creating new law but rather articulating a legal norm that already existed, at least implicitly. The common law, as Blackstone would put it, is always discovered and never simply "made up" by the judge.[32] Of course, there might be other objections at this point. The law could be iniquitous on substantive grounds, regardless of whether there is a due-process-style objection. Likewise, one might object to the coherence of the classical common law theory (more on this anon). However, provided that one accepts that theory, or a modern reconstruction of it, the due process objection has been met. There is no ex post facto lawmaking, only the discovery of preexisting law.

---

[31] T.M. Scanlon, *Due Process*, 18 Nomos 93, 97 (1977).
[32] See 1 Blackstone, *supra* note 22, at 68–70 (setting forth Blackstone's theory of adjudication and legal change).

Broadly speaking, there are three objections to the classical common law theory. The first is that it does not describe how the common law in fact works. According to the classical theory, so goes the objection, the common law is an unchanged and unchanging perfection of reason.[33] However, in reality the common law shifts over time. Accordingly, the classical theory fails as a basic descriptive matter. Second, according to the classical theory, the common law is a matter of reason rather than authority. As such, it seems to endorse a natural law position, denying that law can be discovered by recourse to social rather than moral facts. As Holmes put the point, however, "the common law is not a brooding omnipresence in the sky but the articulate voice of some sovereign or quasi-sovereign that can be identified."[34] Third, crucial to the classical common law theory is the idea of custom or tradition. Yet frequently these ideas are at best fictitious, particularly in large, pluralistic societies where it is not possible to identify *the* customs or traditions of the community.

All of these objections are less daunting than they initially appear. First, it is simply a misreading of the classical theory to impute to it the claim that the common law was unchanging. To be sure, both Coke and Blackstone tried to claim that the common law remained unchanged from the foundations of the English nation, but other thinkers were acutely aware of legal change.[35] Given that the theory was articulated in large part by legal historians such as Hale and Selden, an awareness of legal change was inevitable. Hale provided the most clear-eyed assessment, likening the common law to the ship of the Argonauts, which during the course of its voyage was repeatedly repaired so that every timber was replaced even as it remained the same ship.[36] On this reading of the classical theory, the common law is marked not by stasis but by continuity. It is a living tradition. Such a tradition is not the recapitulation of a golden past carried unchanged into the present, but rather a constant process of self-reinterpretation in light of present conditions.

The classical common law theory is also not a species of natural law. To be sure, Blackstone's writings contain natural law flourishes, but from the beginning, the classical common law theory denied that the reason of the common law was the reason of the natural lawyers. Edward Coke made the point in his famous exchange with King James I. Coke denied that the natural reason of the king could declare the common law.[37] Rather, he insisted that in the common law courts, causes "are not to be decided by

---

[33] See Edward Coke, *The Selected Writings of Sir Edward Coke: The Institutes* 701 (Steve Sheppard ed., 2003) ("For reason is the life of the Law, nay the common Law it selfe is nothing else but reason, which is to be understood of an artificiall perfection of reason, gotten by long study, observation, and experience, and not of every mans naturall reason").

[34] Southern Pacific Company v. Jensen, 244 U.S. 205, 222 (1917) (Holmes J., dissenting).

[35] See Postema, *supra* note 7, at 6 (noting Coke's extravagant claims for the antiquity of the common law).

[36] See *id.* at 6. ("[T]hey are the same English Laws now that they were six hundred years [ago].... [just] [a]s the Argonauts Ship was the same when it returned home, it was when it went out, tho' in the long Voyage it had successive Amendments, and scarce came back with any of its former Materials" (quoting Matthew Hale, *A History of the Common Law* 40 (C.M. Gray ed., 1971) (1713))).

[37] See Prohibitions del Roy, 12 Coke Rep. 63 (1607).

naturall reason but by the artificiall reason and judgment of Law, which Law is an act which requires long study and experience, before that a man can attain cognizance of it."[38] It is tempting, of course, to reject Coke's appeal to "artificiall reason" as nothing more than a bit of lawyerly obscurantism, but this would be a mistake.[39] Rather, the artificial reason of the common law should be understood as gesturing toward an appeal to social facts rather than natural law.

Gerald Postema has defended something like this position as what he calls "substantive conventionalism."[40] He argues that in order for law to provide guidance it must track to a greater or lesser degree the moral intuitions and other normative understandings of those to whom it applies. This is because in order for the law to function as a normative guide it must have some point that is understandable to those over whom it claims authority. He writes, "Cut off from ordinary daily life and social practices, law cannot hope to make its meaning accessible to norm agents."[41] The congruence of the law with social practice, however, does not require that we make heroic assumptions about the scope or homogeneity of customs and practices within the community.[42] He writes:

> What it requires, rather, are understandings on the ground, i.e. common or overlapping activities and practices that have practical meaning and force for those who participate in them.... Providing the soil into which law must sink its roots are "conversations" not creeds, practice not principles, ordinary affairs and activities, not theories or doctrines.[43]

However, when the common law is rooted in social practice and has in effect announced that it will track ordinary social conventions, it no longer claims the kind of arbitrary authority that is assumed in the formulation of the due process objection.

This approach requires, of course, that one can make non-question-begging appeals to custom and practice. There are reasons to be skeptical of appeals to custom. Even during the Middle Ages, when societies were smaller and presumably more homogenous, scholars have shown that custom was frequently invented ex post by officials to justify a

---

[38] *Id.* at 65.

[39] See, e.g., Richard A. Posner, *The Decline of Law as an Autonomous Discipline: 1962–1987*, 100 HARV. L. REV. 761, 762 (1986) ("The judges of England used it to fend off royal interference with their decisions, and lawyers from time immemorial have used it to protect their monopoly of representing people in legal matters.").

[40] See Gerald J. Postema, "Philosophy of the Common Law," in *The Oxford Handbook of Jurisprudence and Philosophy of Law* 588 (Jules Coleman & Scott Shapiro eds., 2002) (arguing that the classical common law theory can be defended in terms of substantive conventionalism).

[41] *Id.* at 614.

[42] See *id.* at 615 ("This argument does not assume that citizens must accept or endorse or commit themselves to the norms. Neither does it depend on background consensus in society on basic values or general principles, let alone what Rawls calls comprehensive moral, religious, or philosophical doctrines.").

[43] *Id.*

decision made on different grounds.[44] In modern, pluralistic societies, it seems mis-guided to speak of *the* custom of any particular community. Furthermore, to the extent that custom is identified with some unchanging essence of a particular group, like "the inherent character of the English people," it flirts with the kind of discredited essential-ism associated in the past with vicious nationalism.

That said, appeals to custom have considerably more substance than this critique suggests. First, there is often a reciprocal relationship between the law and social practice that can create considerable uniformity. Methods of holding property, assumptions about the sanctity of contracts, or the duties of care that people regard themselves as having can all be stabilized by the law itself. There is, of course, a chicken-and-egg problem with the priority of the law or of social practice. The classi-cal common law theory, however, does not require that this historical and metaphys-ical puzzle be solved. It is enough that the law accords with widely distributed social practices. Indeed, one reason that common law courts frequently give for abandon-ing a legal rule is the divergence of the law's reasoning from actual social practice.[45] Thus, barring evidence of repeated conflicts between legal doctrine and actual social practice, the law can be taken as evidence of social practice. As Blackstone put the point, "the judicial decisions are the principal and most authoritative evidence, that can be given, of the existence of such customs as shall form a part of the common law."[46] There need not be any vicious circularity here, only a recognition that the win-nowing of common law doctrine over time means uncontroversial rules are prima facie evidence of social practice.

The common law in the United States also relies heavily on the jury to resolve ques-tions regarding custom. It does this by turning questions about legal standards into factual questions to be resolved by juries. The most dramatic example of this can be seen in how the law of torts defines the scope of the duties of care. Rather than articu-lating detailed rules defining these duties, the question is left to the jury, which is told to apply their own collective understanding of how a "reasonable person" would behave.[47] To be sure, many common law jurisdictions have abandoned the jury in civil

---

[44] See generally *Custom: The Development and Use of a Legal Concept in the Middle Ages* (Per Andersen & Mia Munster-Swendsen eds., 2009) (discussing the role of custom in medieval law and arguing that it was often invented or selectively used).

[45] See, e.g., Posner v. Posner, 233 So. 2d 381, 385 (Fla. 1970) (reversing the rule that prenuptial agreements altering alimony payments are invalid based on changes in the nature of marriage); Volid v. Volid, 286 N.E.2d 42, 46–47 (Ill. App. Ct. 1972) ("Married women nowadays are increasingly developing career skills and successfully entering the employment market.... The reasons given to justify the invalidation of all antenuptial agreements which limit the obligation of support upon divorce do not warrant the condemnation of all such agreements in the name of public policy.").

[46] 1 Blackstone, *supra* note 22, at 69.

[47] See *Restatement (Second) of Torts* § 283 cmt. c (1965) ("The chief advantage of this standard of the reasonable man is that it enables the triers of fact who are to decide whether the actor's conduct is such as to subject him to liability for negligence, to look to a community standard rather than an individual one....").

cases, but in the United States it remains a mechanism by which social consensus is used to give content to the law. Similarly, in the United Kingdom, which has dispensed with the jury in civil cases, the judge is required to go through essentially the same analysis, applying ordinary social understandings of reasonableness rather than a complex doctrinal structure.[48]

C. Specificity and Locality as Challenges in Private Law Theory

A turn toward classical common law theory has implications for private law theory. One of the most striking features of neoformalism in private law over the last generation has been its abstraction and its ambition to present a universally valid theory. These theoretical drives produce approaches to private law that have two unfortunate characteristics: incompleteness and placelessness.

Consider Jules Coleman's justly influential corrective justice theory of tort law.[49] For Coleman, tort law is primarily concerned with rectifying wrongs by requiring tortfeasors to compensate those whom they have harmed. The attraction of Coleman's theory is that it illuminates and explains the bilateral structure of civil liability in tort suits. In tort actions damages are always paid from tortfeasors to tort victims. Why? For L&E theories, this bilateral structure is accidental rather than essential. Worse, it is economically perverse, because by paying even optimal fines to victims, we alter the incentives of such victims, who will alter their investment decisions in precaution based on the possibility of a judgment rather than an assessment of optimal safety expenditures in light of the risk of harm.[50]

As a theory of tort law, however, Coleman's approach is shockingly incomplete. He has virtually nothing to say about the substantive content of primary tort duties.[51] To be sure, he is at some pains to show how corrective justice can be reconciled with strict

---

[48] See Maria Lee, *The Sources and Challenges of Norm Generation in Tort Law*, 9 EUR. J. RISK REG. 34, 37 (2018) ("The English courts balance a range of factors intuitively, qualitatively, verbally, impressionistically, and on the basis of their largely tacit assessments of what is fair and socially valuable." (internal quotations and citations omitted)).

[49] See generally Jules Coleman, *Risks and Wrongs* (2002) (arguing for a corrective justice theory of tort law); Jules Coleman, *The Practice of Corrective Justice*, 37 ARIZ. L. REV. 15 (1995) (same).

[50] A similar point can be made about the law of contract damages, where it has long been recognized that requiring promisors to pay damages that create optimal incentives for breach will create suboptimal incentives to rely when paid to promisees. See generally Steven Shavell, *Damage Measures for Breach of Contract*, 11 BELL J. ECON. 466 (1980).

[51] Cf. Gregory C. Keating, *The Priority of Respect Over Repair*, 18 LEGAL THEORY 293, 319 (2012) ("The question of what rights people have is not a question of corrective justice. If anything, the question of what rights people have is a question of distributive justice. Taxonomy aside, the substantive point is this: tort law is not fundamentally about corrective justice—it is fundamentally about wrongs, and wrongs are grounded in rights.").

liability, but he has little to say about such basic questions as the scope of the duty of care or the circumstances in which strict liability is appropriate.[52] Rather, he writes:

> I reject the suggestion that an adequate account of tort practices requires that there be a general theory of the first-order duties from which we can derive them all systematically. On my view, much of the content of the first-order duties that are protected by tort law is created and formed piecemeal in the course of our manifold social and economic interactions.[53]

Of course, L&E makes precisely the claim that Coleman denies, namely, that the scope of first-order duties can be systematically derived from first principles, namely, the rational actor model and a concern for social efficiency.[54] If L&E fails as a descriptive matter, as Coleman argues, then we need some other account of why we have the particular duties that we have. The classical common law theory purports to provide an answer: we look to the prevailing beliefs and practices of the community. These are the "manifold social and economic interactions"[55] to which Coleman gestures. The problem with his theory is not that it acknowledges this fact but that the idea of corrective justice does not explain why we should look to such interactions rather than some other source.

If Coleman's theory suffers from incompleteness, autonomy theories of contract illustrate the second vice to which neoformalism is prone: a universalism that neglects the local character of much of the common law. Consider *The Choice Theory of Contracts* by Hanoch Dagan and Michael Heller.[56] Dagan and Heller have written, "[C]ontract's ultimate value must be autonomy, properly understood and refined. It cannot be welfare. Nor can foundational pluralism possibly suffice. Autonomy justifies contract."[57] Despite this uncompromising position, however, they argue that a commitment to autonomy does not imply a simple body of contract doctrine giving individuals a relatively unfettered power to legally bind themselves, a position they associate with the work of Samuel Williston.[58] Rather, drawing on the political philosophy of Joseph Raz, they argue that

---

[52]   See Jules Coleman, *The Mixed Conception of Corrective Justice*, 77 IOWA L. REV. 427 (1992) (arguing that corrective justice requires tortfeasors to correct wrongful losses even when their conduct is not blameworthy).

[53]   Jules L. Coleman, *The Practice of Principle: In Defence of a Pragmatist Approach to Legal Theory* 34 (2001).

[54]   Cf. Jody S. Kraus, *Transparency and Determinacy in Common Law Adjudication: A Philosophical Defense of Explanatory Economic Analysis*, 93 VA. L. REV. 287 (2007) (arguing that L&E can provide arguments that specify the details of contract law doctrine in a way that autonomy theories cannot); but see Scott Hershovitz, *Harry Potter and the Trouble with Tort Theory*, 63 STAN. L. REV. 67 (2010) (arguing that because an institution tort law generates costs and benefits that L&E scholars do not consider their theories are ultimately indeterminate).

[55]   Coleman, *supra* note 53, at 34.

[56]   See Hanoch Dagan & Michael Heller, *The Choice Theory of Contracts* (2017) (arguing that contract law should be thought of as existing primarily—if not exclusively—to advance autonomy).

[57]   Hanoch Dagan & Michael Heller, *Why Autonomy Must Be Contract's Ultimate Value*, 18 JERUSALEM REV. LEGAL STUD. 148, 149 (2019).

[58]   See Dagan and Heller, *supra* note 56, at 7–9 (arguing that the "Willistonian constraint" has hobbled contract law theory).

valuing autonomy creates an affirmative obligation for the state to provide citizens with a range of options from which to author their identities.[59]

The Choice Theory of Contracts is a powerful and elegant work. It reveals that the autonomy approach can contain greater doctrinal diversity than had previously been imagined. It is clearly argued, systematically building out from its core premises to the concrete structures of legal doctrine. In many ways it is a model of the philosophy of law. At the center of its argument is a vision of the freely choosing self, living amidst a society structured around the demands of that self's autonomy. This self, however, seems to be without any history or location, at least any history or location that might make normative demands on the law requiring theoretical reflection. It is contract law constructed using the view from nowhere.[60]

As a theory of law—particularly the common law—this commitment to universalism poses a jurisprudential problem. It cannot explain or illuminate the often intensely local character of the common law. Consider the case of gambling and the common law of contracts. Under the English common law inherited by the United States, wagering contracts were generally enforceable.[61] Most American jurisdictions, on the other hand, including ironically enough Nevada, refuse to enforce gambling contracts.[62] The law, however, is more complicated than this simple rule suggests. For example, many jurisdictions allow lotteries, while others make them illegal. What happens when citizens who make a contract to jointly purchase lottery tickets and share any winnings seek to have the contract enforced in a state where lotteries are illegal?

In *Meyer v. Hawkinson*,[63] the North Dakota Supreme Court faced this question. Two North Dakota couples went gambling in Winnipeg. While in Canada, they agreed to purchase tickets in the Western Canada lottery and share any monies that resulted. When one of the tickets proved a winner, the holder of the ticket refused to pay as promised, and the other couple sued in North Dakota. The case produced a sprawling decision by the North Dakota Supreme Court, with a majority, a concurrence, and a dissent.

The central dispute between the justices involved how to interpret the history of gambling in North Dakota. In the late nineteenth century, the Louisiana Lottery Company

---

[59] Compare Joseph Raz, *The Morality of Freedom* 373–377 (1988) (arguing that an autonomous life requires a sufficient range of options).

[60] Although *The Choice Theory of Contracts* seems to present itself as offering a view from nowhere, one might object that its supposedly universal vision of the autonomous self actually represents a historically and culturally contingent conception of identity, one that may have difficulty grounding the legitimacy of legal institutions in societies where it is not widely shared. See Nathan B. Oman, *Contract Law and the Liberalism of Fear*, 20 Theoretical Inquiries in Law 381 (2019) (criticizing the model of the self at the heart of *The Choice Theory of Contracts* and arguing that it cannot ground the legitimacy of contract law).

[61] See 2 E. Allen Farnsworth, *Farnsworth on Contracts* 9 n.4 (3d ed. 2004) ("Although wagering and gaming agreements were generally enforceable under the English common law, they have been condemned in most American states.").

[62] See, e.g., Sea Air Support v. Hermann, 613 P.2d 413 (Nev. 1980) (reaffirming that promises to pay gambling debts are unenforceable under Nevada contract law).

[63] 626 N.W.2d 262 (N.D. 2001).

was kicked out of Louisiana for corruption. The company went looking for a new home and hit on the idea of moving to North Dakota. Accordingly, it bribed the entire state legislature to pass a law allowing lotteries in the state, paying $500 per legislator. The state's governor hired private investigators, who unmasked the bribery. The corrupt legislators were turned out of office at the next election, and the state adopted a constitutional amendment banning all lotteries. The subsequent history of the state involved several referenda in which voters continued to express distaste for gambling in various ways. At the same time, North Dakota law was relaxed to allow small-scale lotteries as fundraisers for churches, veterans groups, and the like. The majority concluded that this history indicated that North Dakotans had an exceptionally strong policy against gambling contracts, strong enough to extend to the nonenforcement of a contract entered into in Canada regarding a perfectly legal Canadian lottery. The dissent, on the other hand, insisted that because the state allowed gambling in various situations, the public policy announced by the majority did not in fact exist.

Examples of cases involving such local histories and concerns could be multiplied across fields of private law. To be sure, there is tremendous uniformity among common law jurisdictions on many questions. However, in the eyes of the classical common law theory such uniformity is to be expected precisely because the jurisdictions share much of the same history and many of the same traditions. Not surprisingly different jurisdictions adopt similar solutions to the doctrinal puzzles created by the law. The highly abstract theories that dominate much of private law theory, on the other hand, have difficulty explaining cases such as *Meyer v. Hawkinson*, which not do turn on such first principles as autonomy, corrective justice, or the demands of human dignity. Rather, courts in such cases fit the law to the character of their particular community, with an eye to its institutions and historical development.

Any effort at rational reconstruction or interpretation of the law must take account of the local character of the common law. The virtue of a reconstructed version of the classical common law theory is that it provides an account of why the history of North Dakota should matter to the substantive content of North Dakota law. Theorists who reject this conception of the common law must grapple with how to make sense of the common law's frequent parochialism, a topic that has failed hitherto to garner sustained attention.

V. Conclusion

Private law is not a brooding omnipresence in the sky. In the common law tradition, it is a set of rules fashioned out of the practices, customs, and mores of particular communities. To be sure, abstract moral and political theories have an important role to play in elucidating the law. Much of the common law is consistent across many jurisdictions and often has close doctrinal analogs outside of the common law tradition. It is unsurprising that these structures can be explained by reference to abstract and broadly held moral principles. One of the tasks of legal theory is to articulate these principles, provide a coherent account of their relationship, and trace their implications through the law. However, it is also true that the common law is often local, idiosyncratic, and even parochial. This is a feature of the law that should be examined and explained. The highly abstract theories of neoformalism do a poor job of accounting for the local elements of the common law. At best, such elements have to be seen as historical accidents or second-best approximations of some more abstract and universal set of principles. Classical common law theory, in contrast, suggests that such parochial features are integral to the structure of the common law itself. Rather than seeing them as peripheral anomalies, they are cases lying at the conceptual core of the common law, revealing the law's intimate relationship with custom and social practice.

....

CHAPTER 11

AUTONOMY AND PLURALISM IN PRIVATE LAW

....

HANOCH DAGAN

I. INTRODUCTION

....

PRIVATE law is the law of interpersonal relationships. It structures a (subset of) the horizontal interactions of people in their personal capacity, as opposed to their capacity as subjects of the state or as co-citizens. Private law doctrines also affect, of course, public concerns, such as distributive justice, democratic equality, or aggregate welfare. But private law's distinctive role—its core responsibility—is in structuring our social, as opposed to our public, life; its doctrines address the ways in which we live and interact in the world as people, rather than as citizens. This role of private law preceded the idea of the modern state; it is clearly manifested in the transnational interactions that increasingly typify our lives; and it is no less apparent within states—in the market, the workplace, and the neighborhood (to mention just a few obvious loci).

At times, other people pose threats (actual or potential) to our natural rights, which means that part of the task of the law of interpersonal relationships is strictly defensive. But oftentimes—and this is not a particularly modern feature—private law enables us meaningfully to act and interact in the world; to make plans and pursue goals; to self-determine.

This chapter focuses on the significant subsets of private law—notably, but not only, property and contract—which contribute to people's autonomy. My core claim is that, charitably interpreted, private law is guided by an autonomy-enhancing *telos*. Private law, at its core, facilitates people's self-determination and forms the foundation of a social life premised on the maxim of reciprocal respect for self-determination.

Private law can enhance people's autonomy because its fabric is not only made of duty-imposing doctrines, as would have been the case had it contented itself with guarding people's independence. Rather, many of its rules—and, importantly, the two private law building blocks of property and contract—are essentially power-conferring. The normative powers instantiated by property law and by contract law allow people to have private authority over resources and to reliably benefit from others' promises. They thus facilitate a temporally extended horizon of action, which is conducive, perhaps crucial, to people's ability to plan. Moreover, contract and alienable property are also key for people's mobility, which is a prerequisite for self-determination; and both expand the options available to individuals to function as the authors of their own lives.

Section II discusses these happy features of private law's power-conferring doctrines. It also addresses the legitimacy challenge of these doctrines, which authorize the claims of owners and promisees and recruit the coercive power of the state to vindicate them. This challenge can be met, I argue, if, but only if, private law commits itself to ensuring that our personal relationships are premised on *reciprocal* respect for self-determination.

Such an autonomy-based private law, I then claim in section III, must be structurally pluralist. We should cultivate the heterogeneity of our existing private law, because a multiplicity of property types and contract types facilitates the rich diversity of interpersonal relationships needed for adequate self-determination. A repertoire of distinct property and contract types for any given sphere of social activity and interaction offers a cultural menu of viable alternatives, which in turn ensures meaningful choice. Law's facilitation of this autonomy-enhancing pluralism is critical because, without proactive legal support, collective action problems, bounded rationality, and cognitive failures may undermine many types of interactions, and, thus, people's ability to pursue their own conception of the good.

Structural pluralism is crucial to autonomy but still insufficient, and section IV addresses two further prescriptions, which help ensure that private law supports *only* interpersonal interactions that do not undermine autonomy. First, because self-authorship requires the ability to both write and rewrite our life stories, autonomy puts a high value on people's ability to "reinvent themselves." This is why private law typically ensures people's right to exit their existing property arrangement; this is also the reason for the limits on the range, and at times the types, of enforceable commitments people can undertake.

Alongside this prescription of regard for future self, an autonomy-based private law must be careful to support interpersonal interactions only if they comply with relational justice. Given that reciprocal respect for self-determination is the premise of private law's own legitimacy, any attempt to recruit private law in defiance of this premise must be treated as ultra vires: it is an abuse of the idea of property or of contract, that is, use of private law for a purpose that contravenes its *telos*.

II. Autonomy and Private Law

Imagine that we start from scratch (political philosophers call this the state of nature). There are people in the world, and there are resources out there, and we need to think about the rules of the interpersonal game. Rules that vindicate our natural right to bodily integrity, and thus—to some extent—to some of our physical possessions, seem easily justifiable. But can private law legitimately prescribe rules that go further than that? Should it?

These questions may seem more appropriate for a philosophical inquiry than for a private law theory. After all, private law, as we know it, surely goes far beyond its uncontroversial mission of vindicating our bodily integrity. Private law makes us owners of resources, both tangible and intangible, and recruits the coercive power of the state to vindicate our private authority, as individuals or as members of communities, over these resources. Private law is similarly receptive to certain claims of individuals to enforce others' promises even before those promises have been relied upon, so that nonperformance generates no detrimental harm.

Although these are obvious features of private law, addressing the legitimacy of the law of property and of the enforcement of wholly executory contracts must not be left to philosophical debates. A strict division of labor between justification and design is troublesome. Thus, in order critically to interrogate the legitimacy of property and contract, theorists need to appreciate the richness and possible variability that their legal underpinnings generate. By the same token, and more relevant for my current purposes, exactly because law dramatically affects the design of both property and contract, private law must resort to the normative foundation, if any, that justifies these institutions as their most fundamental—albeit by no means only—design principle.

The need to combine justification and design is not limited to property and contract. But it is particularly pertinent to these private law institutions, because they are, at their core, power-conferring. To be sure, I do not argue that property and contracts include *only* power-conferring rules. Of course, they also include duties, such as a duty not to interfere with others' rights. But these piggy-backing duty-imposing rules would be meaningless in the absence of the power-conferring institutions of property and contract because their role is to protect our ability to apply the powers enabled by these bodies of law. These duties are important—in fact, they are intelligible—because they support the legal powers that are characteristic of property and contract in the first place.[1]

The conceptual priority of powers over duties highlights the distinct legitimacy challenge of both property and contract, because these powers (unlike our right to bodily integrity) do not enjoy the uncontroversial status of preconventional rights. By constituting property, law proactively empowers owners; and by designating a subset of the promises we make contracts, it likewise enables people to do things that were impossible before. The empowering potential of both property and contact is relational; it comes from the fact that both property law and contact law vest certain people with certain normative powers over others.[2]

---

[1] This paragraph and the three following ones draw on Hanoch Dagan, *A Liberal Theory of Property* ch. 2 (2020), and Hanoch Dagan & Michael Heller, *The Choice Theory of Contracts* pt. I (2017).

[2] On normative power, see Joseph Raz, *Practical Reason and Norms* 102 (1975); Joseph Raz, *Normative Powers*, https://ssrn.com/abstract=3379368.

Indeed, it is the law which proactively renders these others—non-owners and promisors—vulnerable to such powers. Therefore, law must be answerable to the subjects of the powers it creates. It must be able to explain why non-owners should be subject to the authority it vests in owners. It should likewise account for its willingness to back up promisees' insistence on promisors' performance of promises they have not yet relied upon.[3]

Private law can offer good answers to these acute legitimacy challenges. Law justifiably confers these normative powers on owners and on promisees because such powers are crucial to their self-determination. This means that although both property and contract are conventional, they are particularly valuable conventions—indeed, they are conventions that any humanist polity must enact. Law is also justified in subjecting non-owners and promisors to these powers because *as such*—that is, as core features of autonomy-enhancing conventions—these powers deserve respect from our fellow human beings due to our preconventional right of reciprocal respect for self-determination.

Appreciating these foundational roles of private law's autonomy-enhancing *telos* and of the maxim of reciprocal respect for self-determination is critical to the design of private law. It constrains the range of possible configurations of private law, because a private law that undermines its own *telos* and justificatory premise may become illegitimate. But autonomy's status as the linchpin of the legitimacy of both property and contract implies that its role must not be limited to gatekeeping. Rather, autonomy must also play a major, albeit not an exclusive, role in assessing the performance of existing doctrine as well as guiding its future development.

With these high expectations in mind, I turn now to consider autonomy and the ways in which private law can be—and to a significant extent already is—autonomy-enhancing.

*   *   *

An autonomy-enhancing private law starts from the premise that people are entitled to act on their capacity "to have, to revise, and rationally to pursue a conception of the good."[4] They deserve to have some control over their destiny, "fashioning it through successive decisions through their lives."[5] Free individuals should be able to plot their own course through life—to have some measure of self-determination.[6]

To be sure, taken to its extreme, a conception of self-authorship (or self-determination; I use these terms interchangeably) in which one constructs a "narrative arc" for one's life in advance is a form of unfreedom. But its opposite, a conception of self-authorship in which one makes at any fork in the road freestanding decisions about which route one will choose, is also unsatisfactory. Our life story is neither a script fully written in advance

---

[3] The text roughly follows the view in which political legitimacy requires some benchmark of moral justifiability. See Allen Buchanan, *Political Legitimacy and Democracy*, 112 Ethics 689, 689–690 (2002).

[4] John Rawls, *Justice as Fairness: A Restatement* 19 (2001).

[5] Joseph Raz, *The Morality of Freedom* 369 (1986).

[6] This commitment requires that we respect each person's right to self-authorship; it does not denigrate a choice of a nondeliberative life or suggest that such respect is conditioned upon the accomplishment of a worthy life plan.

nor a set of unrelated episodes. Rather, autonomous people characteristically act piece-meal, choosing both long-term and short-term pursuits. Self-determination allows—to some extent even requires—opportunities for people to alter and even completely replace their plans.[7]

This sketch of autonomy as self-determination implies that autonomy requires appropriate mental abilities. It also necessitates a measure of independence. But autonomy is not guaranteed by a structure of negative rights.[8] Rather, a meaningful right to self-determination is dependent upon material conditions, and also requires—as Joseph Raz famously argues—an adequate range of significantly different options to make the individual's choice a genuine choice.[9] This means that a body of law which takes people's autonomy seriously must proactively support their ability to shape a life they can view as their own, and cannot be contented with merely respecting their capacity for uncoerced choice.[10]

This core responsibility of the state implies that *public law* must ensure the collective goods and the material, social, and intellectual conditions needed to enable people to become and remain self-determining individuals. These are necessary preconditions for autonomy, but they are not sufficient. *Private law*—more specifically, its power-conferring elements, on which this chapter focuses—also has an irreducible role in this fundamental state obligation. Because our practical affairs are deeply interdependent, our interpersonal interactions have freestanding significance. This means that people's self-determination cannot be fully secured by public law; private law must not abdicate its distinct responsibility to provide the variety of frameworks necessary for our ability to lead our chosen conception of life.

To see how private law is conducive to our autonomy, consider first the dramatic effect of both property and contract on our ability to plan. Because "self-determination consists in the carrying out of higher-order projects," and because each such project "can be seen as composed of a set of plans arranged in a temporal sequence," a successful exercise of self-determination is "an intertemporal achievement."[11] In other words, only by securing "a temporal horizon of action" do we become "individuals with concrete identities" and our abstract choices transform into "individual life plans."[12]

The private authority over things that property confers and the reliability of others' promises that contract ensures are best justified by reference to this understanding of self-determination as an intertemporal achievement. Thus, by allowing people to secure

---

[7] See James Griffin, *On Human Rights* 149, 151 (2008); Raz, *supra* note 5, at 384. Cf. Michael E. Bratman, *Time, Rationality, and Self-Governance*, 22 PHIL. ISSUES 73, 82 (2012).

[8] See H.L.A. Hart, *Between Utility and Rights*, 79 COLUM. L. REV. 828, 836 (1979).

[9] See Raz, *supra* note 5, at 372, 398.

[10] This view need not—and my position does not—subscribe to any form of perfectionism. Indeed, private law's commitments to structural pluralism and free exit ensure that law's neutrality is not compromised.

[11] Charles R. Beitz, *Property and Time*, 27 J. POL. PHIL. 419, 427 (2018).

[12] Lisa Austin, "The Power of the Rule of Law," in *Private Law and the Rule of Law* 270, 278–279 (Lisa Austin & Dennis Klimchuk eds., 2014).

a temporally extended control of things, property facilitates our ability to carry out meaningful projects—on our own or with the cooperation of others—and to pursue comprehensive goals and life plans, which typically require a temporal horizon of action.[13]

The same temporal function underlies contract law's vindication of promisees' expectations. By ensuring the reliability of contractual promises for future performance, rather than merely protecting against promisees' detrimental reliance, contract law enables people to extend their reach by legitimately enlisting others to their own goals, purposes, and projects—both material and social. This intertemporal dimension is prominent in relational contracts, but no less important in one-shot contracts, which are typically wholly executory. In both cases, predictability of fulfillment of expectations is key for allowing people to plan and pursue their higher-order projects and conceptions of the good.[14]

Furthermore, contract law does not anticipate only one foundational pact, in which people are bound for their lifetime; in fact, as will be discussed later, it refuses to support such agreements. And property is characteristically alienable. These are typical hallmarks, rather than fortuitous features, of our private law.[15] An autonomy-enhancing private law must be committed, as noted, to people's right to both write and *re*write their life stories. It therefore ensures their ability to withdraw or refuse to engage further; to dissociate, to cut themselves out of a relationship with other persons.

The possibility of liquidating one's holdings through the alienation of resources and entitlements makes this right to exit meaningful. The right to exit serves a protective role, because leaving is a form of self-defense, and the mere possibility of one's exit has a disciplinary function. But even if one is not worried about possible mistreatment, exit is essential to autonomy because it enables geographic, social, familial, professional, and political mobility, all of which are crucial to a self-directed life.[16]

Also implicit in these observations is private law's contribution to people's ability to choose. Contract law expands our range of meaningful choices by expanding our repertoire of secure interpersonal engagements beyond the limited realm of gift-based and similarly close-knit interactions. Property's alienability allows individuals to unbundle their estates, and—in a functioning market—"gain from the skill and knowledge of others [they] need not even know and whose aims could be wholly different from [their] own."[17] Both property and contract law further multiply the alternatives from which people can choose by constituting a variety of stable frameworks of interpersonal cooperation; different property and contract types support divergent forms of interpersonal relationships. In all these ways, private law opens up possibilities for choice that allow people to make their own judgments about what they value and how they value it, what

[13] See Beitz, *supra* note 11, at 427.
[14] See Hanoch Dagan & Michael Heller, *Autonomy for Contract, Refined*, 38 LAW & PHIL. (forthcoming).
[15] See A.M. Honoré, "Ownership," in *Oxford Essays in Jurisprudence* 107, 107, 118 (A.G. Guest ed., 1961).
[16] See Hanoch Dagan & Michael A. Heller, *The Liberal Commons*, 110 YALE L.J. 549, 569–572 (2001).
[17] 2 F.A. Hayek, *Law, Legislation, and Liberty: The Mirage of Social Justice* 109 (1982).

to own and how and with whom to own it, what to buy or sell, how hard to work, how much to save, and what to consume.[18]

Indeed, at their best, property and contract function as empowering devices for self-authorship, enabling people to act upon their own goals and values, their objectives, and their life plans. It would be wrong to conclude that either property or contract is strictly necessary for self-determination. For example, a person could choose a radically ascetic lifestyle, opting to rely on the generosity of others. But it does not seem far-fetched to conclude that by conferring on individuals the power to invoke the differing property and contract types (discussed in section III) and to employ them in the service of their life plans, private law makes a crucial contribution to people's ability to realize the right to self-authorship.

III. Private Law's Structural Pluralism

Thus far, I've defended the claim that private law's power-conferring doctrines can be justified by the critical contribution they make to people's self-determination in securing a temporal horizon of action, facilitating mobility, and ensuring choice. In this section, I argue that this undertaking requires private law to be robust and to take a structurally pluralist form.[19] In order to establish this proposition, I recruit an unsuspecting ally: Robert Nozick, whose understudied account of utopia helps to explain this pillar of private law.

Utopia, Nozick argues, must be conceptualized as "a framework for utopias, a place where people are at liberty to join together voluntarily to pursue and attempt to realize their own vision of the good life." In treating us all "with respect by respecting our rights" and in allowing us, "individually or with whom we choose, to choose our life and to realize our ends and our conception of ourselves, insofar as we can, aided by the voluntary cooperation of other individuals possessing the same dignity," this framework for utopias "best realizes the utopian aspirations of untold dreamers and visionaries."[20]

To secure these happy effects, utopia's law must reject the temptation of "planning in detail, in advance, one community in which everyone is to live." Instead, Nozick claims, it should operate as a "libertarian and laissez-faire" framework, which facilitates "a diverse range of communities," many of which will be neither libertarian nor laissez-faire, in order to enable "more persons... to come closer to how they wish to live, than if there is only one kind of community." By facilitating "voluntary utopian experimentation" and "provid[ing] it with the background in which it can flower," this utopian state invites "many persons' particular visions," enabling us "to get the best of all possible worlds."[21]

---

[18] See Debra Satz, *Why Some Things Should Not Be for Sale: The Moral Limits of Markets* 8 (2010).
[19] This section draws on Dagan, *supra* note 1, at ch. 4, and Dagan & Heller, *supra* note 1, at pt. III.
[20] Robert Nozick, *Anarchy, State, and Utopia* 312, 332–333 (1974).   [21] *Id.* at 309, 320, 332–333.

Nozick's account of a framework for utopias as the proper vision for a state that takes seriously people's right to self-determination is captivating. But here our paths diverge. Nozick believes, as noted, that only the minimal state can bring it about; and private law in the minimal state is neither robust nor structurally pluralist. Quite the contrary, the private law of the minimal state espouses the monist and thin conceptions of property as sole and despotic dominion, and of contract as merely a means for effectuating people's consent.[22] Nozick concedes that this system does not require innovation, but is not troubled by that as long as individuals can freely use these fundamental building blocks and can thus tailor their interpersonal arrangements so that they best serve their own purposes.[23]

On this front, Nozick is wrong: a genuine framework for utopias cannot plausibly be supported by the thin and reactive private law he espouses. In a genuine utopia—one that leaves people the choice of how to live, rather than imposing on them the state's preferred formula—people must have a sufficiently diverse set of viable options for a whole range of decisions. They should be able to choose, for example, whether to live in a fee simple absolute or a common-interest community; to work as an employee or an independent contractor; to do business in a partnership, a close corporation, or a publicly held corporation; and to form an intimate bond of marriage, or to cohabitate. But, as I presently explain, many of these choices cannot be properly accomplished through a hands-off or passive approach by private law.[24]

Therefore, a commitment to personal autonomy requires the law of our interpersonal relationships (namely: private law) to be *proactive*, rather than merely *reactive*. This is what explains and justifies the significant facilitative role of modern contract law, whose extensive gap-filling apparatus sharply departs from the traditional common law reluctance to enforce incomplete agreements.[25] The very same reason underlies private law's structural pluralism: its provision of a set of viable frameworks—property types and contract types—from which people can choose.

*   *   *

To see why a rich diversity of property and contract types will not spontaneously emerge without the active support of viable legal institutions (or law-like social conventions), we need to appreciate the insights of both lawyer-economists and critical scholars.

Economic analysis of private law investigates its incentive effects, and forcefully demonstrates how many of our existing practices rely on legal devices that serve to overcome numerous types of transaction costs—information costs (symmetric and asymmetric),

---

[22] See Gregory S. Alexander & Hanoch Dagan, *Properties of Property* ch. 3 (2012); Randy E. Barnett, *A Consent Theory of Contract*, 86 COLUM. L. REV. 269, 270, 302 (1986).

[23] Nozick, *supra* note 20, at 329; see also Thomas W. Merrill, *Property as Modularity*, 125 HARV. L. REV. F. 151, 157–158 (2012).

[24] Cf. Raz, *supra* note 5, at 133, 162, 265.

[25] See Hanoch Dagan, *Types of Contracts and Law's Autonomy-Enhancing Role*, 5 EUR. CONT. L. & THEORY (forthcoming).

bilateral monopolies, cognitive biases, and heightened risks of opportunistic behavior that generate participants' endemic vulnerabilities in most cooperative interpersonal interactions.[26]

Merely enforcing the parties' expressed intentions would not be sufficient to overcome the inherent risks of such endeavors. If many (most?) of these property and contract types are to become or remain viable alternatives, private law must provide background reassurances tailored to the specific category of interaction at hand, which will serve to ensure the trust so crucial for success. (Consider how many rules of both the doctrines governing commons property types and those dealing with the performance of contracts and the consequences of their breach are best understood as anti-opportunistic devices.[27]) Even where parties are guided by their own social norms, law often plays an important role in providing them background safeguards, a safety net for a rainy day that can help establish trust in their routine, happier interactions.[28]

Moreover, private law does not only help to overcome various bargaining obstacles. The practices it establishes affect our lives in an even more profound, albeit subtler, fashion. Because private law tends quietly to blend into our natural environment, its categories play a crucial role in structuring our daily interactions.[29] Thus, alongside these material effects, many of our conventions—including many social practices we take for granted as the options we currently have (think: bailment, suretyship, or fiduciary relationships)—become available to us only due to cultural conventions that often, especially in modern times, are legally constructed.[30]

Hence, if these notions were not legally coined, people would not only have to consider the transaction costs of constructing these arrangements from scratch; they would also face "obstacles of the imagination" just coming up with the options in the first place. Indeed, the property and contract types law establishes play an important cultural role. Like other social conventions, they serve a crucial function in consolidating people's expectations and in expressing the animating principles of the categories of interpersonal relationships they participate in constructing.[31]

Both the material and the cultural functions of private law imply that freedom of contract, though significant, cannot possibly replace active legal facilitation if the state's obligation to enhance autonomy by fostering diversity and multiplicity is taken seriously. Lack of active legal support is often tantamount to undermining—maybe even

[26] See, e.g., Russell B. Korobkin & Thomas S. Ulen, *Law and Behavioral Science: Removing the Rationality Assumption from Law and Economics*, 88 CAL. L. REV. 1051 (2000).

[27] See, respectively, Hanoch Dagan & Michael Heller, *Conflicts in Property*, 6 THEORETICAL INQUIRIES L. 197 (2005); Hanoch Dagan & Avihay Dorfman, *Justice for Contracts* pt. IV, https://ssrn.com/abstract=3435781.

[28] See Dagan & Heller, *supra* note 16, at 578–579; Ronald J. Gilson et al., *Braiding: The Interaction of Formal and Informal Contracting in Theory, Practice, and Doctrine*, 110 COLUM. L. REV. 1137 (2010).

[29] See, e.g., Robert W. Gordon, *Unfreezing Legal Reality: Critical Approaches to Law*, 15 FLA. ST. U. L. REV. 195, 212–214 (1987).

[30] See, e.g., Ian Ayres, *Menus Matter*, 73 U. CHI. L. REV. 3, 8 (2006).

[31] See also Charles Fried, *Contract as Promise: Lessons Learned*, 20 THEORETICAL INQUIRIES L. 367, 376–379 (2019).

obliterating—many cooperative forms of interpersonal relationships and thus people's ability to seek their own conception of the good.

This inability of a monist and reactive conception of private law to deliver private law's autonomy-enhancing promise admittedly derives from people's fallibility, notably their cognitive failures and the way they tend to prefer their self-interest to the interests of others. But these imperfections cannot be dismissed as contingent features to which private law can be indifferent. While their significance may vary from one empirical context to another, these human features are sufficiently ingrained to render irrelevant if not self-defeating bodies of law that ignore them.

To be sure, in some contexts—notably in the commercial sphere—there are powerful economic forces catalyzing demand for innovative options, so the task of private law can and should be mostly reactive. But in the other spheres of interpersonal interaction— think work, intimacy, or home—where collective action problems or other (say, cognitive or distributive) difficulties inhibit the development of new interpersonal frameworks, market demand must not delimit the state's obligation.

Put differently, our right to self-determination, which is both the *telos* of private law and the foundation of its legitimacy, may be threatened not only by having too much law. Rather, our right to self-determination can just as easily be undermined by the absence of law, the failure of private law to proactively support a sufficiently diverse range of types within a given sphere of interpersonal activity.[32] A legal system that follows Nozick's vision of utopia and properly appreciates its dependence on law instantiates a varied inventory of property types and contract types for each sphere of social life. Nothing short of the robust legal edifice of structural pluralism will do if private law is to be guided by this autonomy-enhancing *telos*.

*   *   *

Consider first the sphere in which current law nicely demonstrates the autonomy-enhancing function of private law's structural pluralism, namely, commerce. Private law offers a wide range of stable frameworks for long-term business arrangements, so as to facilitate multiple types of interpersonal interaction in this sphere. These range from agency contracts, through partnerships (notably LLCs and LLPs), to forms of corporate organizations (from closely held to public corporations).[33] Each of these private law types is characterized by its own governance structure and set of solutions to the typical difficulties (notably agency costs) that would probably have inhibited such business activities but for their legal facilitation.[34]

---

[32] Cf. Robin West, *Normative Jurisprudence: An Introduction* 201–203 (2011).

[33] See generally, e.g., William T. Allen et al., *Commentaries and Cases on the Law of Business Organization* (3d ed. 2009); Larry E. Ribstein, *The Rise of Unincorporation* (2010).

[34] See, e.g., Frank H. Easterbrook & Daniel R. Fischel, *The Economic Structure of Corporate Law* 34–35 (1991).

Private law's structural pluralism also manifests itself, albeit not in such a robust way, in other, less market-driven spheres as well. It offers a relatively rich menu of possessory rights in residential property. In addition to traditional forms, such as the fee simple, leasehold, and commons property, we now have an increasing array of shared-interest residential developments including condominiums and cooperatives. Private law likewise supports more than one alternative framework for the spheres of work (where one can be an employee or an independent contractor) and of intimacy (consider conventional marriage, cohabitation, and covenant marriage).

Securing such multiplicity is not just an add-on feature of private law. Rather, a private law system which takes its *telos* and legitimacy challenge seriously must understand this multiplicity as an essential feature. Therefore, it should treat structural pluralism as its most fundamental design principle. For each major category of human action and interaction, private law should instantiate and support a sufficiently diverse repertoire of property types and contract types, each governed by a distinct animating principle, meaning a different value or a different balance of values. These circumstances must prevail in all major spheres of human activity or interaction—freedom is not enhanced if one's choice is, for example, either to get married or enter an agency contract.

Existing law does not perfectly comply with this happy liberal picture; it would be quite surprising if it did. The notion of an autonomy-enhancing structural pluralism is not descriptive. Rather, structural pluralism is an interpretation of one of private law's characteristic features, and as such a blueprint for its *internal* critique. Making private law more compliant with structural pluralism, in other words, should not be understood as revolutionary, but rather as a constructive reform, which would simply push private law to live up to its (implicit) autonomy-enhancing promise.

Implementing this prescription is not a straightforward matter for at least two reasons.[35] One reason is that—although, all other things being equal, multiplicity of types *is* conducive to autonomy—other things are not always equal and at times more choice may be autonomy-reducing, which means of course that an unqualified call for multiplicity should be rejected. There are, more specifically, four main concerns that may require limiting multiplicity: (1) people's cognitive constraints imply that if there are too many distinct types, multiplicity might curtail their effective choice; (2) multiplicity may trigger boundary disputes arising from ex post opportunistic maneuvering; (3) in some market structures—notably, markets for unskilled workers in times of non-negligible unemployment—multiplicity might undermine the autonomy of weak parties rather than augmenting it; and (4) certain types may be particularly vulnerable to the risk of interest group rent seeking, which might yield autonomy-reducing consequences.

---

[35] The remainder of this section draws on Dagan & Heller, *supra* note 1, at 97–99, 106–107, 116–124, 128–130; and Dagan, *supra* note 1, at ch. 4. A third important reason relates to the institutional allocation of labor regarding the creation of property and contract types. See Dagan, *supra* note 1, at ch. 6; Dagan & Heller, *supra* note 1, at 130–134; Hanoch Dagan & Michael Heller, *Freedom, Choice, and Contract*, 20 THEORETICAL INQUIRIES L. 595, 615–619 (2019).

There is no reason to suspect that these concerns are all-encompassing in a way that would overwhelm the normative significance of structural pluralism. But they are certainly important—pluralism must remain a means to the law's autonomy-enhancing end. Therefore, the multiplicity injunction must be refined to accommodate them.

There is another important design challenge that structural pluralism must face. Private law should support choice within each familiar category of human activity, such that within each sphere law provides enough and sufficiently distinctive property and contract types. Defining what constitutes an "adequate range of options" within any given contracting sphere—namely: what is the right number of types and should be the variance among them—is admittedly a complex task, which should rely, at least to an extent, on empirical facts regarding people's choice mechanisms.

Incorporating such facts into the analysis is not a trivial task, and it is beyond the scope of this chapter. But the core guideline is normative: for private law types to be autonomy-enhancing, they need to be *partial functional substitutes* for each other. They need to be substitutes because choice is not enhanced with alternatives that are orthogonal to each other; but their substitutability should not be too complete because types that are too similar also do not offer meaningful choice. This means that although the distinction between different rules and different types is imprecise, changes in rules create a new type only if they generate a significant alternative category of interpersonal interaction structured around a distinct (and robust) animating principle.

Finally, a particularly attractive strategy for enriching the repertoire of existing property and contract types within a given sphere is proactively to look out for innovations—such as those based on minority views and utopian theories—that have some traction but would fail if left to people's own devices. A private law system which is genuinely committed to autonomy responds favorably to such innovations because they add valuable options of human flourishing that significantly broaden people's choices, even if the initial market demand for them is low.

One important example comes from the sphere of employment. Existing law offers a binary choice between employee and independent contractor status. But emerging new forms on the ground—such as workers seeking the creation of specifically designated worker co-ops[36]—may call for additional categories, and thus additional choice. There are also other possibilities that diverge even further from the existing employment landscape. For example, law can be instrumental in facilitating job-sharing arrangements that stabilize defaults regarding responsibility, attribution, decision-making mechanisms, time division, sharing space and equipment, and availability on "off days." By the same token, an autonomy-based approach to employment would suggest that instead of choosing between the "at will" and the "for cause" regimes as

---

[36] Other new forms of work—most notably in the platform economy—raise more complicated challenges, because they require law to adapt the means by which it secures relational justice (think, for example, about occupational health and safety, antidiscrimination, or fair pay and working time regulations). See OECD, OECD Employment Outlook 2019: The Future of Work ch. 4 (2019), https://doi.org/10.1787/9ee00155-en. But with such—far from trivial—adjustments in place, these additional forms may open up new opportunities, most notably in emerging economies. See *id.* at 56.

universal defaults, lawmakers would be advised to promulgate two parallel employment types, so that employers would need to opt in to one or the other.

IV. Autonomy beyond Pluralism in Private Law

An autonomy-enhancing private law must ensure that the boundaries between the distinct types it instantiates and supports are open, enabling people freely to choose their
own ends, principles, forms of life, and associations. This freedom curbs the coercion of
law by allowing its subjects, when navigating their courses, to bypass certain legal prescriptions and thus the power of those who issued them. More importantly for my purposes, such open boundaries are crucial to people's self-determination, because, as
noted, self-determination puts a high value on people's ability to reinvent themselves.

It is thus perfectly appropriate for private law to quite vigilantly secure people's right
to exit their existing arrangements. Thus, property law is generally suspicious of
restraints on alienation, even consensual restraints that limit mobility respecting any
particular resource. Often, statutes prohibit and courts invalidate outright restraints on
alienability; when faced with more moderate restraints, courts may impose time limits
or otherwise protect an individual's right to exit. These restrictions on alienability are
not unwarranted intrusions upon freedom. Rather, they protect against arrangements
that undermine a key purpose of freedom, that is, securing individual autonomy.[37]

Similar analysis explains—and indeed justifies—why contract law ensures that facilitating people's ability legitimately to enlist one another in pursuing private goals and
purposes must not overwhelm their right of exit from these relationships.[38] In keeping
with its autonomy-enhancing *telos*, contract law is alert to the possible detrimental
implications of its operations for the autonomy of the parties' future selves. It safeguards
our ability to start afresh by limiting the range, and at times the types, of enforceable
commitments we can undertake. In other words, the same law that confers on people
the power to commit themselves through contracts in the name of enhancing their self-
determination cannot ignore the impact of the resulting contracts on their future selves.
Because this tension is inherent in contract's raison d'être—*any* act of self-authorship
constrains the future self—contract law must be, and by and large is, careful in defining
the scope of the obligations it enforces and in circumscribing their implications.[39]

---

[37] Dagan & Heller, *supra* note 28, at 569; see also *id.* 596–601.

[38] Other, efficiency-based reasons for restricting alienability are tentative and contingent, subject to
possible technologies or legal techniques that would ameliorate impeding rationality deficiencies or
overcome pertinent market failures. See Hanoch Dagan & Michael Heller, *Why Autonomy Must Be
Contract's Ultimate Value*, 20 Jerusalem Rev. Legal Stud. 149, 150–152 (2019).

[39] This and the following two paragraphs draw on Dagan & Heller, *supra* note 14; Hanoch Dagan &
Ohad Somech, When Contract's Basic Assumptions Fail: From Rose 2d to COVID-19, https://ssrn.
com/abstract=3605411; Hanoch Dagan & Michael Heller, Specific Performance, https://ssrn.com/
abstract=3647336.

This seemingly simple statement encapsulates one of the most difficult challenges to an autonomy-enhancing contract law: identifying categories of excessive limitations on contractual parties' exit—that is, on promisors' freedom to change their minds—that undermine party autonomy to such a degree that they should not be enforceable. There is no formula for resolving this difficulty in a systemic fashion. But acknowledging the value of being able to revise or even discard one's plans as an entailment of, rather than a threat to, the normative underpinnings of contract at least provides a strong, principled justification for a number of doctrines which otherwise may seem rather puzzling. This value helps explain the *unilateral* right of termination of long-term contracts, which is semi-inalienable at least regarding certain contract types (such as agency contracts). It similarly justifies some restrictions on enforceability of employee noncompete agreements and some limits on the advance sale of future wages. Finally, the value of being able to change plans may also help justify rules that ensure that contractual commitments are not overly dogmatic, such as the doctrines governing excuse and the blanket refusal to specifically enforce contracts to render personal service.

Consider specific performance in a bit more detail. The importance of being able to change plans seems to provide a firm foundation for the common law position, in which specific performance is unavailable whenever damages are "adequate to protect the expectation interest of the injured party."[40] Other things being equal (for the promisee), contract in the common law tradition rightly opts for not compelling the promisor to act in accordance with the contractual script, allowing her to choose between doing so and covering the promisee's expectation.[41] Civil law jurisdictions reject that position and make specific performance widely available. But even these jurisdictions take people's right to change course seriously when it comes to awarding specific performance against service providers. On that front, there is no difference between the common law and the civil law: both rigidly resist specifically forcing a person to work.[42] This entrenched and widespread rule is *not* an external imposition to the logic of contract. Rather, it follows contract's *internal* logic of self-empowerment, which proscribes such excessive impositions on the self-determination of the future self.

*   *   *

The autonomy-based DNA of private law's structural pluralism and of its protection of future selves is also the premise of what I take to be the third pillar of private law: its commitment to *relational* justice. Recall that the legitimacy of both property and contract relies on their contribution to people's self-determination, which others are obligated to respect. Both owners and promisees justifiably recruit the coercive power of the

---

[40] *Restatement (Second) of Contracts* § 359(1) (Am. Law Inst. 1981).

[41] Contra Seana Valentine Shiffrin, *The Divergence of Contract and Promise*, 120 HARV. L. REV. 708 (2007). As an empirical matter, a recent study shows that most people do not perceive as immoral breach of contract followed by compensation to the promisee. See Sergio Mittlaender, *Morality, Compensation, and the Contractual Obligation*, 16 J. EMP. LEGAL ANALYSIS 119 (2019).

[42] See *Restatement (Second) of Contracts* § 367(1) (Am. Law Inst. 1981); Charles Szladits, *The Concept of Specific Performance in Civil Law*, 4. AM. J. COMP. L. 208, 226 (1955).

state to vindicate their rights because these rights rely on people's preconventional obligation of reciprocal respect for self-determination. This means that private law's legitimacy is premised upon its compliance with this maxim of just relationships. Reciprocal respect for self-determination is thus not only a possible external constraint on our private law rights; rather, it is part and parcel of their raison d'être.

This notion of relational justice, which I have developed with Avihay Dorfman in recent years,[43] is not limited to a negative duty of non-interference that is the correlative of others' right to independence. Respect for others' self-determination is hollow without *some* attention to their predicaments. By the same token, reciprocal respect for self-determination cannot be contented with a formal conception of equality that abstracts away the particular features distinguishing one person from another. Respecting another's right of self-determination necessarily requires viewing the other as he or she actually is.[44]

Relational justice must be, and to a significant degree already is, a key feature of property law because, as I've argued earlier, non-owners' deference to owners' private authority is best premised on the right to reciprocal respect for self-determination. Property law can thus legitimately sanction owners' private authority if, but only if, it ensures that owners' rights do not excessively limit (let alone undermine) non-owners' autonomy. Drawing the line of the necessary implications of this maxim involves careful attention to H.L.A. Hart's insistence that we must recognize the significance of the "unexciting but indispensable chore" of distinguishing "between the gravity of the different restrictions on different specific liberties and their importance for the conduct of a meaningful life."[45]

Elsewhere, I have attempted to translate this lesson into property law by developing and applying principled guidelines derived from the ideal of reciprocal respect for self-determination and substantive equality, the nature of legal prescriptions, and rule-of-law concerns.[46] For our purposes it is enough to invoke the first guideline, which prescribes that property's relational justice should not overwhelm the ability of *owners* to self-determine (this would have been self-defeating).[47] Accordingly, property's relational justice does not undermine the private authority property instantiates. Homeowners, for example, are rightly shielded from legal scrutiny of whom they choose to invite into their homes (at least until such invitations run afoul of criminal-law

---

[43] See, e.g., Hanoch Dagan & Avihay Dorfman, *Just Relationships*, 116 COLUM. L. REV. 1395 (2016); Hanoch Dagan & Avihay Dorfman, *Justice in Private: Beyond the Rawlsian Framework*, 36 LAW & PHIL. 171 (2018); Hanoch Dagan & Avihay Dorfman, *Interpersonal Human Rights*, 51 CORNELL INT'L L.J. 361 (2018). The following paragraphs draw on these sources.

[44] Admittedly, at times, formal equality is the all-things-considered best proxy for substantive equality. But elsewhere, the relationships aren't usually substantively equal, which means that an autonomy-enhancing law can no longer legitimately use this proxy.

[45] Hart, *supra* note 8, at 834–835.   [46] See Dagan, *supra* note 1, at ch. 5.

[47] The other two guidelines are that (1) law should not impinge upon practices (such as love or friendship) if its intervention might destroy their inherent value; and (2) law's rules need to be relatively clear, so as to provide effective guidance to its addressees and constrain officials' ability to exercise power.

proscriptions against harboring fugitives and the like). But because property's private authority is properly limited to its autonomy-enhancing function, owners' power to refuse to sell or lease, or to prevent non-owners from entering their land or using their resources is suitably restrained. Thus, common-interest-communities law, landlord-tenant law, and the law of public accommodations recognize non-owners' claims to access and, more broadly, to respect. Similarly, property law's commitment to relational justice also explains some responsibilities of property rights holders, such as the burdens they incur to reduce some accidental mistakes made by non-owners with respect to the property in question.

Contract law (charitably interpreted) likewise resorts to relational justice as an indigenous premise for delimiting the kinds of agreements that are enforceable. Agreements that fall below this threshold are not eligible for law's support because they defy contract law's raison d'être. There is again a long set of rules that secure contract law's integrity by guaranteeing its compliance with this prescription of relational justice. Some of these rules regulate the parties' bargaining process in a way that goes beyond the traditional laissez-faire mode of proscribing *active* interference by one party with the other's free will. Others—centered around the duty of good faith and fair dealing—solidify a cooperative conception of contract performance by instantiating moderate duties to assist in promoting each other's self-determination reciprocally. Yet another set of doctrines ensures that employers, landlords, or owners of public accommodations that offer services to the public do not engage in discriminatory practices that contravene the requirement of reciprocal respect for self-determination which justifies contract law. Further, they mandate the minimum level of interpersonal decency that contract law is willing to accept regarding contract types, such as employment contracts, that significantly affect the personhood of one of the parties.[48]

The freestanding significance of people's interpersonal interactions for their self-determination implies that—just like its broader responsibility to people's autonomy—private law has a distinct and irreducible role here, one that cannot be delegated to public law. But this private-law task of ensuring the justness of our horizontal relationships—in the market, the workplace, the neighborhood, and the like—need not necessarily be performed by judges; at times, regulatory agencies are better equipped for the task. The main focus of *these* agencies is accordingly relational, rather than aggregative. Indeed, many aspects of both the substance and form of agencies like the Occupational Safety and Health Administration, the Consumer Financial Protection Bureau, the National Labor Relations Board, the Office of Fair Housing and Equal Opportunity, and the Equal Employment Opportunity Commission, which may seem off track from an aggregative

---

[48] See Dagan & Dorfman, *supra* note 27. For a preliminary account, see Dagan & Heller, *supra* note 35, at 606, 611, 626, 633–635. The reliance of these rules on contract law's source of legitimacy implies that they are not tainted with paternalism. However, their normalizing effect should nonetheless be a source of concern. This concern can be ameliorated by following structural pluralism and by utilizing multiple floors. See Hanoch Dagan, *The Value of Choice and the Justice of Contract*, 10 JURISPRUDENCE 422, 431–433 (2019).

(public law) perspective,[49] become straightforward once conceptualized as responses to the horizontal, private-law challenges of participating in the creation of the infrastructure for just interpersonal relations in these core social settings.[50]

V. Concluding Remarks

Much of our private law goes beyond protecting our preconventional rights to bodily integrity. Private law confers normative powers on people and is thus the source of others' vulnerabilities. These vulnerabilities imply that private law theory must address the challenge of its own legitimacy. But they do not condemn this universe of property types, contract types, and other private law types (e.g., fiduciary types) as long as they are carefully designed so that they indeed serve people's ultimate right to self-determination.

This chapter outlines three important prescriptions that respond to this challenge: structural pluralism, regard for future selves, and relational justice. Compliance with these prescriptions goes a long way toward securing private law's legitimacy. Moreover, appreciating private law's autonomy-enhancing *telos* as a central, if not exclusive, design principle is key to enabling private law to achieve its promise.

ACKNOWLEDGMENTS

Thanks to John Goldberg, Ori Herstein, Greg Klass, Dennis Klimchuk, Paul Miller, Emily Sherwin, David Waddilove, Ben Zipursky, and participants at the Harvard Law School Conference on the Landscape of Private Law for their helpful comments.

[49] See, e.g., Cass R. Sunstein, *Is OSHA Unconstitutional?*, 94 VA. L. REV. 1407, 1410 (2008).
[50] See Hanoch Dagan & Roy Kreitner, *The Other Half of Regulatory Theory*, 52 CONN. L. REV. (605 2020).

CHAPTER 12

··

A FEMINIST
PERSPECTIVE

Private Law as Unjust Enrichment

··

ANITA BERNSTEIN

To profit from private law—a phrase understood in this chapter as the law of contracts, torts, property, and a little equity—one must act to favor oneself. Private law redresses wrongs only after listening to assertions that individuals make about their rights or interests. Because it rests on demands and denials that litigants articulate, this jurisprudence necessarily shortchanges persons who lack prerogative to say what they want and do not want, or who are punished when they appear to rank gains to themselves above the needs and wishes of others. Women exemplify the shortchanged cohort that occupies this chapter, but the contention that I explore can be extended mutatis mutandis to other subordinated classes.

Under a banner of "The Players," the first section following sketches two protagonists of private law—the individual who complains and the individual who resists another's demand—with reference to the self-regard that each needs to defeat the other in a private law action. The next section applies gender to the famed maxim *volenti non fit injuria*, a mainstay of private law, by noting that private law understands an injury to exist only when it is denounced: the section headed "Girls and Women" reviews documented barriers to the expression of protest that reduce what private-law litigation will deliver.[1] In a concluding part, I make a claim about gendered unjust enrichment.

---

[1] With the term "protest" I include expressions of resistance necessary to defend a civil action.

I. The Players

Contract, tort, and property actions reach the courts at the initiative of an aggrieved individual and invite response from persons who were served with a complaint. Self-described injury or deprivation as experienced by one who takes the role of plaintiff is a necessary constituent of every claim that private law will recognize. The equally necessary role of defendant follows.

Even very heinous wrongs find no remedy in private law until they are denounced as personal affronts. The aggrieved person, a kind of owner, holds power that he may deploy as he likes. When he chooses to let a good claim go, off it goes. If he settles it for a price unsuited to good social ends, or if a judge or jury neglects its social cost, too bad for society. If his personal characteristics or his behaviors as a plaintiff distract a factfinder from the merits of his claim and warp the result he receives, too bad for him and us. Defendants also have an ownership-ish stake in private litigation. Their postures and identities shape the price of settlement and influence the reception of their disputes in court.

Foundational characteristics like these make the dramatis personae of private law significant. Here are some traits of litigants as protagonists. This catalog of roles emphasizes the plaintiff, someone whose contention about an entitlement cranks the engine of private law.

Claimant on public attention. A plaintiff in a private law action has a grievance that he characterizes as important. The remedy he seeks typically reaches himself, but he wants the rest of us to notice his complaint. In his mind, the wrong he suffered implicates not just a personal interest of his but the law itself. He expects onlookers to care about what he will receive in court.

Claimant on the loyalty of an advocate. American litigants are only rarely entitled to paid-for counsel in the private law realm, but disputes that reach the courts that involve significant money usually also involve attorneys. Clients are entitled to loyalty from their attorneys regardless of whether these lawyers receive fee income from them.[2] An adjective that frequently modifies this advocacy is "zealous," meaning that the claimant on public attention is also entitled to professionally expended energy.[3]

Boundary defender. The rights that private law protects do not deliver reallocation overtly to follow a scheme of distributive justice.[4] Instead they conserve what had been there. Private law looks backward rather than forward, policing lines drawn in the past. Litigants assert claims about agreements they once made, injuries personal to themselves that derive from historically recognized wrongs, and possessions they might have

---

[2] See Model Rules of Professional Conduct 1.9 (ABA 1983) (recognizing duties owed to former clients); *id.*, Rule 1.8(f)(2) (finding a duty of loyalty owed to the client rather than the one paying the lawyer to represent that client).

[3] Anita Bernstein, *The Zeal Shortage*, 34 Hofstra L. Rev. 1165, 1169 (2006).

[4] I attribute this absence to the common law in Anita Bernstein, *The Common Law Inside the Female Body* 33 (2019).

gained by gift or inheritance rather than effort. As both plaintiffs and defendants, they understand themselves as standing up against boundary crossings.

Asserter of rights and interests personal to himself. Plaintiffs in private law actions must be persons who complain about infringements of their own interests.[5] No harm to themselves, no foul. Legal scholarship about standing focuses mostly on public law, but the contemporary public-law notion that litigants need a private right to get to court derives from and amounts to "a private-law model of standing."[6]

The contract category of third-party beneficiary, the tort category of bystander, and the (intellectual) property label of patent licensee are examples of private-law doctrinal rubrics found outside the plaintiff-defendant binary at the center of this jurisprudence. Persons so classified might hold rights that contract or tort or property will honor, but the derivative nature of their role is in their name as designation. My impressionistic understanding of case law suggests that the large majority of people whom judges call bystanders in tort cases are denied standing to claim and a (smaller) majority of those who want recognition as a third-party beneficiary fail to win this prize. Stinginess about the right of licensees to sue for patent infringement dates back to an opinion written by Chief Justice Taft;[7] it persists.[8] Private law, in short, offers redress mostly to persons who have unmediated, personal-to-themselves entitlements.

Writing about what he has called substantive standing, Benjamin Zipursky has gathered examples from tort law of this personal stake that plaintiffs need to survive.[9] Standing is "substantive" for these persons rather than, or in addition to, the type associated with procedure because the elements of their claim demand an impact on them. Fraud plaintiffs, for example, need more than a false statement—they must have relied on what the defendant said—and a wife harmed by scurrilous falsity spoken about her husband cannot win a defamation action because the offending remark flunks an "of and concerning" requirement.[10]

Substantive standing is powerful enough, Zipursky argues, to explain the elusive *Palsgraf*, a tale of "a wrong [that] was not a wrong in its relation to the plaintiff, standing far away. Relatively to her it was not negligence at all."[11] The law of standing more generally, along with the so-called case or controversy requirement, insists that plaintiffs and petitioners be in a position that will change after they receive the judgment they seek. These doctrines extend beyond private law: but private law exemplifies them because it always features a litigant complaining about a personal interest.

---

[5] Ehul Guttel et al., *Torts for Nonvictims: The Case for Third-Party Litigation*, 2018 U. ILL. L. REV. 1049.

[6] Cass Sunstein, *Standing and the Privatization of Public Law*, 88 COLUM. L. REV. 1432, 1433 (1988).

[7] Crown Die & Tool Co. v. Nye Tools & Machine Works, 261 U.S. 24, 39 (1923).

[8] Ortho Pharm. Corp. v. Genetics Inst., Inc., 52 F.3d 1026, 1030 (Fed. Cir. 1995); K-W2, LLC v. Asus Computer Int'l, 170 F. Supp. 3d 1340, 1348 (D. Colo. 2016).

[9] See Benjamin C. Zipursky, *Rights, Wrongs, and Recourse in the Law of Torts*, 51 VAND. L. REV. 1, 6 (1998); John C.P. Goldberg & Benjamin C. Zipursky, *Torts as Wrongs*, 88 TEX. L. REV. 917, 957 (2010).

[10] Benjamin C. Zipursky, *Substantive Standing, Civil Recourse, and Corrective Justice*, 39 FLA. ST. U. L. REV. 299, 301–303 (2011).

[11] Palsgraf v. Long Island R. Co., 162 N.E. 99, 99 (N.Y. 1928); Zipursky, *supra* note 10, at 303.

Claimant on the time and money of others. In addition to expecting a modicum of energy and devotion from their attorneys, litigants demand pricey participation from their adversaries and the public. Most of American private law comes with a right to jury trial, an assurance that sends taxpayer-funded cash to judges, judicial clerks, bailiffs, and security guards. Even jurors get paid a little. What are called the costs of litigation—for expenses like filing fees, transcripts, interpreters, expert witnesses—burden litigants who might not have wanted to incur these costs. Plaintiffs turn the other-people's-money spigot on first, but defendants also spend money not theirs when they make counter-claims and implead third parties, take the initiative in pretrial proceedings, and delay litigation to put financial pressure on vulnerable plaintiffs or increase attorneys' fees.

Refuser to cooperate and negotiate. This refusal digs into private law's preoccupation with boundaries. It complements the last role in that it fits the defendant aptly but also applies to a plaintiff. Litigants who hear what their adversaries have to say can respond with No: and although No is the default stance of a defendant, becoming a plaintiff says the same thing. Persons who filed private-law actions had other options that (if lawful) were more conciliatory. What "alternative dispute resolution" is an anti-adversarial alternative to is for the most part good old private law,[12] its doctrines as well as its procedures.[13]

The longer a private law claim lingers unsettled, the more noncooperation has per-sisted. Private law rewards the vanishingly tiny minority of obdurate litigants who stick with their dispute through trial and appeal by giving them voice in precedents, an influ-ence that settling forgoes. These people prosecuted and defended their claims because they did not, or could not, find common ground. They valued their interests more than accommodation.

II. Girls and Women

A. The Problem

Because it is committed to individual self-determination,[14] private law permits an indi-vidual to abjure everything in it that is optional. Robert Stevens makes this point by say-ing that waiver or nonassertion of any right "means that there is no right to violate, and consequently no wrong."[15] His examples of "no wrong" come from torts—Stevens finds illustrations in trespass, defamation, false imprisonment, and battery—but the general-ization applies beyond his field to every common law claim that individuals can make:[16]

---

[12] See Harry T. Edwards, *Alternative Dispute Resolution: Panacea or Anathema?*, 99 HARV. L. REV. 668, 676–680 (1986) (expressing concern about the extension of ADR to constitutional or public law).

[13] See Ray D. Madoff, *Lurking in the Shadow: The Unseen Hand of Doctrine in Dispute Resolution*, 76 S. CAL. L. REV. 161, 165–161, 166 (2002).

[14] Hanoch Dagan & Roy Kreitner, *The Other Half of Regulatory Theory* (manuscript, Nov. 2018).

[15] Robert Stevens, *Torts and Rights* 17 (2007).   [16] *Id.*

that is, to all of private law, where "to the willing there is no injury." *Volenti non fit injuria* as a judicial assertion turns up most often in tort, but contracts and property decisions also quote it approvingly.[17]

Traits of the dramatis personae we just explored are alike in that they all feature what I, here and elsewhere, have called self-regard.[18] Initiators, boundary defenders, asserters and so on ask themselves *What do I want; what don't I want?* They make action items out of their desires and aversions. Attuned especially to negative liberty—deprivations, personal injuries, and breaches of entitlements—private law is especially good at articulating the Don't Want half of this self-interrogation. Its expressions of desire say No. *I will not tolerate this tort or breach of contract or violation of my property rights; I hereby file* is one option it offers. *No thanks, I will not claim my cause of action or defense* is also available.

In telling us to choose either assertion or waiver as we please, and thereby siting self-determination at an individual level, private law shows it lacks the capacity to correct— or even to notice—aggregation-patterns that emerge in manifested preferences. When some cohorts happen to like being boundary defenders, claimants on public attention, refusers to cooperate, and so on, while others find those roles uncongenial, and both groups behave consistently with these tastes,[19] whatever distributions that private law occasions or leaves alone are not only far from unjust enrichment but good as ends in themselves. One group gets the material advantage, the other the material disadvantage, that its members wish. The first asserts, and the second waives. No harm, no foul.

What I gather by way of response to "no harm, no foul" are experiences of a modal female person from infancy to adulthood, the point where an individual can participate in private law as a litigant. She is a generalization, #notallwomen. First in infancy, then later in school, then continuing in her paid employment and the family she forms, this person is rewarded for (apparent) submission and punished for manifestations of aggression and self-regard. Compounding the effects of gender role socialization, from childhood to death she can expect to have less money to control than her male counterpart—a deprivation that trammels expressions of her will—and at no point of her life is she able to move around as freely as he.

Female-specific orders and constraints and discouragements start to pin her down before she is conscious of herself as a person, accreting before she can push back against them. The metaphor of a lobster slowly boiled in water that started out cool might, if credited, explain the apparent waiver of her private law rights. By the time she can be a plaintiff or defendant, she has learned not to strike postures that the two roles require.

---

[17] See, e.g., Tyler v. Dowell, Inc., 274 F.2d 890, 898 (10th Cir. 1960) (property; applying Utah and New Mexico law); Mitchell v. Skinner, 796 F. Supp. 1464, 1471 (N.D. Ala. 1992) (contract; court adds that Fifth Circuit precedent extends the *volenti* maxim to § 1983 civil rights actions); Munroe v. Pritchett, 16 Ala. 785, 790 (1849) (contract).

[18] Bernstein, *supra* note 4, passim.

[19] Consider, for example, the datum that all over the world, women greatly outnumber men as donors of organs like kidneys and liver tissue, while being no more physiologically suited than men to make this gift. Sohini Chattopadhyay, *My Father Needed a Liver. Did It Have to Be from Me?*, N.Y. Times, Dec. 15, 2018. This donor-gender gap is narrower in the United States but still exists. *Id.*

In claiming that the social condition of gender encourages men to assert, and women to refrain from asserting, the protests that formed the private law we now live under and constitute its doctrines, I intend no comment on the authenticity of desire, whether No can mean Yes, or the Marxian chestnut called false consciousness. A person who appears to have an entitlement honored by tort or contract or property and who has not complained might be among the willing to whom there really was no injury: I cannot know. I do, however, know about a pattern that I think is central to private law, even though readers might receive my description of it as external or peripheral.

There is in private law unjust enrichment writ large. It comes from the lifelong steeping of large numbers of human beings, more than half the population, in an ideology that they do not share in various desiderata, including the wealth of condoned self-regard that pervades private law. Half the persons living under this regime grew up to believe that they cannot have, and should not even want, recourse from those who cross their boundaries. Should they defy this teaching, they can expect to suffer in consequence.

The version of compelled self-abnegation in place today worsens the oppressions of an older and more formal exclusion. Contract, tort, property, and equity doctrines derive from assertions that men of the past wrote into writs and complaints and judgments and treatises. Women of that era could not participate as litigants, judges, and scholars. Contemporary access to these necessary roles ameliorates this exclusion but has not undone the withholding of full negative liberty from women. A flame under the lobster pot turns on before babyhood. Our heroine has a life expectancy of eighty-one,[20] of which longish span the first third or so will suffice to review common experiences that support a contention about unjust enrichment.[21]

B. Psychosocial Instructions to Hold Oneself Down

1. *Babyhood, Childhood, Adolescence*

Immediately after emerging from their mothers' bodies, if not sooner, the overwhelming majority of persons are sorted into one of two genders. Independent of the physical or biological truth it may hold, the label of girl or boy has an instant impact on environment. At this swaddled stage, babies are not yet constrained by psychosocial instructions to hold themselves down, but they have been designated as either male or female, and they interact with the world so labeled.

In one study now two generations old, researchers interviewed thirty pairs of brand-new parents, half of them parents of daughters and half of sons. The babies scored no differently on standard measures (height, weight, Apgar scores), but in day

---

[20] U.S. Centers for Disease Control, National Vital Statistic Reports, United States Life Tables, 2014 (Aug. 14, 2017).

[21] Support for what I say about contemporary American gender inequity comes from varied sources. At one end of a rigor continuum here are peer-reviewed studies; at the other, journalists' "think pieces" and writings about social trends.

one of their lives they looked different to their parents: fathers in particular, but also mothers, described these neonates in gender-stereotypical terms.[22] Decades later, a follow-up study concluded that although "parents' gender-stereotyped perceptions of newborns [had] recently declined, especially among fathers," these perceptions had "not disappeared."[23]

The newborn boy or girl becomes a toddler aware of gender. While vendors sell items with human beings younger than that age in mind (e.g., infant formula, diapers, baby-monitoring technology), the onset of toddlerhood marks the first individual consciousness that is of interest to commerce. One place to start: "Teletubbies" and "Barney & Friends," created for television viewers aged two to five. A 2002 study of these programs found female creatures portrayed as helpmeets and supporters while male creatures were cast as decision makers.[24] The authors noted that female on both shows means physically smaller than male and with fewer occupational roles; "the pattern being set is female following male."[25] Praising both programs as more gender-progressive than what had prevailed in earlier eras (think "Sesame Street"), the study nevertheless concluded that this shift has "mostly open[ed] up accepted behavior for boys, while sex-roles are primarily being reinforced for girls."[26]

Onward to school, where being classed as a boy or girl continues to affect environment. Because elementary education is a locus of government spending, a profession pursued and studied in higher education, a battleground of policy debates, and a biographical experience shared by almost all persons in the United States, it looms large in many literatures; opportunities to study gender in it have abounded. Teachers, these studies report, treat girls and boys differently.

Education scholarship has found patterns in this instruction that relate to the future for private law. Litigants make claims for themselves in the public realm, and they first learned how in school. In their 1994 book *Failing at Fairness*, Myra and David Sadker documented lesser treatments of girls in grade school.[27] David Sadker went back to this thesis in 2009 with *Still Failing at Fairness*, a different work in several respects but unchanged on the bottom line of who enjoys encouragement to speak:

> Male students frequently control classroom conversations. They ask and answer more questions. They receive more praise for the intellectual quality of their ideas. They get criticized more publicly and harshly when they break a rule. They get help when they are confused. They are the heart and center of attention.[28]

[22] J.Z. Rubin et al., *The Eye of the Beholder: Parents' Views on Sex of Newborns*, 44 Am. J. Orthopsychiatry 512 (1974).

[23] Katherine Hildebrandt Karraker et al., *Parents' Gender-Stereotyped Perceptions of Newborns: The Eye of the Beholder Revisited*, 33 Sex Roles 687, 687 (1995).

[24] Kimberly A. Powell & Lori Abels, *Sex-Role Stereotypes in TV Programs Aimed at the Preschool Audience: An Analysis of* Teletubbies *and* Barney & Friends, 25 Women & Language 14 (2002).

[25] *Id.* at 19.   [26] *Id.* at 21.

[27] Myra & David Sadker, *Failing at Fairness: How Our Schools Cheat Girls* (1994).

[28] David & Myra Sadker & Karen R. Zittleman, *Still Failing at Fairness: How Gender Bias Cheats Girls and Boys and What We Can Do About It* 65 (2009).

Even the downside of this gender allotment—the harsher and more public criticism for rule-breaking that boys receive—strengthens the connection between male gender and entitlement to the gains distributed by private law. Making a spectacle of a boy's misbehavior tells the class that what boys do is of general interest. Wrong though it is, his conduct should not be effaced or ignored. A textbook, reviewing research, confirms the public nature of what schoolboys say: "Teachers have a tendency to talk to boys from a greater physical distance than when they talk to girls," the authors conclude. "Whatever the reason, the effect is to give interactions with boys more 'publicity.' "[29] All the other allocations in the Sadker review of school unambiguously privilege and honor boys over girls as speakers and asserters of what they need.

Corresponding to school as the public realm for children, the private realm of home teaches girls that they have no refuge from self-abnegation as ideology.[30] "If children see that sex difference is the occasion for obviously differential treatment," as the political theorist Susan Moller Okin put the point, "they are surely likely to be affected in their personal moral development. They are likely to learn injustice, by absorbing the message, if male, that they have some kind of 'natural' enhanced entitlement and, if female, that they are *not* equals, and had better get used to being subordinated if not actually abused."[31]

American parents pay daughters less than half what they pay sons for household chores,[32] a transfer that steers boys more than girls into the pleasant exercise of thinking about the entertainments and comforts they want to buy or save for. Less cash teaches a girl that she is entitled to less freedom than her male counterpart and not to be surprised in her future when she receives less money from payors, about which more anon. Gendered relative poverty for her is normal.

So too are the constraints that parents around the world, including in the United States, put on daughters for being female: stay indoors, obey orders, do your chores, remember you're too vulnerable to face the world the way a boy can, remember that boys and men are predators for whose predations girls will be held responsible.[33] Oppressions like these come with no rational explanation. They ought to generate no resentment, goes the lesson. Resentment is, of course, necessary for a private-law complaint.

Bolstering the gender subordination message that parents deliver, preteen girls learn from peers that they need at least the appearance, and perhaps also the reality, of

[29] Kelvin Seifert & Rosemary Sutton, *Educational Psychology* 74 (2d ed. 2009).

[30] Cf. Catharine A. MacKinnon, *Feminism Unmodified: Discourses on Life and Law* 100 (1988) (observing that "a right to privacy looks like an injury got up as a gift").

[31] Susan Moller Okin, *Gender Inequality and Cultural Differences*, 22 POL. THEORY 1, 12 (1994).

[32] Vikki Ortiz, *Parents Pay Boys Twice as Much Allowance as Girls, Company Finds. Here's Why*, CHI. TRIB., Aug. 8, 2018 (reporting an average weekly gap of $13.80 versus $6.71). Some of the difference could be explained by the strenuousness of the boys' outdoor tasks in contrast to the interior scrubbing and dishwasher-loading that girls do, but researchers also found that parents pay boys and not girls for showering and brushing their teeth. *Id.*

[33] Kristin Mmari et al., *"Yeah, I've Grown; I Can't Go Out Anymore": Differences in Perceived Risks Between Girls and Boys Entering Adolescence*, 20 CULTURE, HEALTH & SEXUALITY 787 (2018).

submission and compliance to be sexually desirable. Skirts, heels, and tight clothes that are regarded as attractive hamper her movement and get in the way of recreation; they also thwart her travel to school on a bicycle or running from an assailant.[34] Susan Brownmiller's decades-old insight about what makes footwear not hot has stayed constant through shifts of fashion, and girls know it: "Sensible shoes aren't fun. They hold no promise of exotic mysteries, they neither hint at incapacitation nor whisper of ineffectual weaponry."[35]

"Adolescent women," writes psychologist Laina Bey-Cheng by way of summary beyond shoes, "are in the precarious position of needing to present themselves as desirable to men, though not desiring (which can be interpreted as aggressive and morally loose); sexually responsive to male desire (thus proving they are 'normal,' neither homosexual nor prudish) as well as sexually responsible."[36]

2. *At Work*

Because women have significantly less money than men at the level of both wealth and income, they will do worse than men in any locus of struggle where money strengthens the hand of a combatant. Private law is among these venues; a poorer person has less power in litigation. As a plaintiff, this poorer party is vulnerable to being pressed into a cheap or premature settlement of a good claim because she needs the money. As a defendant, she has more to lose from the risk of a costly judgment. On either side of the caption, she cannot afford counsel with too high a price tag, and regardless of whether higher-paid lawyers deliver better advocacy than lower-paid ones, they look more impressive (read intimidating) to adversaries and even judges.

Most people in the United States receive money from participation in the labor market. The large majority turn up here at some stage of their lives,[37] arriving at the workplace influenced by the gender socialization they experienced when they were younger. Employment has consequences for workers that are not only material: women not only receive less income and power than men but also systemic noncash punishments for behaviors and postures that advantage a person in the role of private law litigant.

Ideology about the labor market declaims that wage income is set at an intersection of supply and demand curves, refined further by bargaining between employees and employers. Men in this market are paid more than women for the same work and have more access to higher-paying jobs. Decades after the enactment of equal-pay legislation

---

[34] Hannah Norrish et al., *The Effect of School Uniform on Incidental Physical Activity among 10-Year-Old Children*, 3 ASIA-PACIFIC J. HEALTH, SPORT & PHYSICAL EDUC. 51, 53–54 (2012) (reporting on international studies).

[35] Susan Brownmiller, *Femininity* 186 (1984).

[36] Laina Y. Bey-Cheng, *The Trouble of Teen Sex: The Construction of Adolescent Sexuality Through School-Based Sexuality Education*, 3 SEX EDUC. 61, 69 (2003).

[37] Almost all persons in the United States not currently working are either retirees, persons likely to work in the future (i.e., children under sixteen and full-time students), the active duty military, and incarcerated persons. Mentally ill persons, a cohort commonly thought of as precluded from employment, frequently hold jobs. Sheldon Danzinger et al., *Mental Illness, Work, and Income Support Programs*, 166 AM. J. PSYCHIATRY 398, 404 (2009).

by federal and state legislatures, American women continue to earn significantly less than men; this wage gap exists controlling for seniority, experience, and full-time versus part-time employment.[38]

Women hold a minuscule share of the jobs that pay extraordinarily well—think Fortune 500 CEO, investment banker, principal of a hedge fund or successful start-up, big-ticket professional athlete, Hollywood star capable of opening a movie—while at the drabber level of cubicles or skilled trades, they simply collect less wage income than men day after day, year after year. Moving downward on the earnings ladder, we find women overrepresented among the so-called working poor in both their total number and the percentage of persons that fall in this category. Rich, poor, or somewhere in the wide middle, then, an American woman receives less income from the labor market than her male counterpart, and from there becomes worse off in the realm of private law.

Women share responsibility for this gap, goes the variant on *volenti* found here, because they failed to push for what they were worth as men do at the bargaining stage of wage-setting. Recall the role that I've labeled asserter of rights and interests personal to himself. Asserters are understood to make bank at work; from there rationales expressed as "women don't ask" or "nice girls don't ask" supposedly explain bad results for women, their lesser income in particular.[39] One might question the pinning of this blame on a person who grew up dinned to think she is not entitled to the privileges that her male peers enjoy. A female worker would have to travel back to before her babyhood to believe she should receive as much pay as a man. As the employment law scholar Charles Craver reports in his review of a book called *Women Don't Ask*,[40] lifelong social-ization has taught women workers that they are not in control of their own lives, that they will offend other people if they appear to be advocating for themselves, and that "they do not deserve very much."[41]

But let's say a woman defies this tutelage and asks. What then will happen? Women are not misperceiving the reality around them, Craver continues. Supervisors and co-workers find good results by a man attributable to "intrinsic factors such as intelligence and hard work," while attributing similarly good results by a woman to "extrinsic factors such as easier circumstances or the assistance of others. This means that male success is overvalued, while female success is undervalued."[42] Against this background, choosing Ask rather than Don't Ask with respect to gain for oneself risks appearing arrogant or delusional.[43] "Women who don't negotiate may not be refraining because they are shy," a *New Yorker* article concluded. "They may, instead, be anticipating very real attitudes and

[38] Gowri Ramachandran, *Pay Transparency*, 116 PENN. ST. L. REV. 1043, 1050–1051 (2012) (collecting data).

[39] *Id.* at 1059–1062.

[40] Charles B. Craver, *Women Don't Ask: Negotiation and the Gender Divide*, 102 MICH. L. REV. 1104 (2004).

[41] *Id.* at 1107–1109 (quoting Babcock).   [42] *Id.* at 1123.

[43] See Hannah Riley Bowles et al., *Social Incentives for Gender Differences in the Propensity to Initiate Negotiations: Sometimes It Does Hurt to Ask*, 103 ORG. BEHAV. & HUM. DECISION PROCESSES 84, 87 (2007) (reporting evidence for this conclusion from studies in which participants punished women for "perceived lack of niceness" and "[p]erceived demandingness").

very real reactions that are borne out, time and again, in the lab and in the office. Often, leaning in has an even worse effect than saying nothing."[44]

Women Don't Ask author Linda Babcock, joined by her frequent collaborator Hannah Riley Bowles, set out to investigate strategies to avoid gendered penalty for the affront of having negotiated.[45] Babcock and Bowles concluded that women workers fare best when they frame their requests "in relational terms," distancing themselves from the money they ask for and emphasizing benefits to a community.[46] "[I]t's unfortunate that women can't just ask for a raise simply because they deserve it," went one paraphrase of their findings in a how-to magazine piece. "Given that strategy is off the table, researchers have also found that there could be some advantage to blaming someone else for your request. In other words, you're suggesting, I wouldn't normally ask for this extra money, but this other person, organization, book or website suggested it was a good idea."[47] *In other words, you proceed as asserter of your own rights and interests at your peril.*

Baneful workplace consequences for women that weaken their participation in private law go beyond lower pay. A female employee will displease her supervisors and co-workers more than her male counterpart when she presses for anything, not just her salary. One investigation of this hypothesis hired actors to simulate workplace meetings recorded on video. These performers, a man and a woman, were rated as equally attractive by a separate panel and coached to deliver a nearly equal performance. More than 4,500 survey respondents were asked to rate the competency and salary-worth of the actors. They punished the female actor for scripted forcefulness and aggression significantly more severely than the male actor (who was also punished for these traits) reciting the identical lines.[48]

Closely related to gendered punishment—and equally pertinent to private law as unjust enrichment—is gendered reward. In one set of studies that looked at how women evaluated their contributions to a successful team result at work,[49] researchers gave participants positive feedback and then asked them to allot credit for this result. Unless they received "irrefutably clear" information to the contrary, women undervalued their contributions when they had a male teammate. These outcomes aligned with earlier evidence that "in the absence of performance feedback on a male sex-typed task, women working individually rated their task ability as poorly as if they had received negative feedback."[50] Private law rewards self-confidence, even self-admiration, from plaintiffs and defendants. Litigants "eat" what they "kill," and the task of killing is aided by a belief that they deserve to eat at another's expense.

---

[44] Maria Konnikova, *Lean Out: The Dangers for Women Who Negotiate*, NEW YORKER, June 10, 2014.

[45] Hannah Riley Bowles & Linda Babcock, *How Can Women Escape the Compensation Negotiation Dilemma? Relational Accounts Are One Answer*, 38 PSYCH. WOMEN Q. 80 (2013).

[46] *Id.* at 93.

[47] Kim Elsesser, *4 Key Strategies Women Need to Negotiate a Higher Salary*, FORBES, Apr. 24, 2018.

[48] David Maxfield et al., *Emotional Inequality: Solutions for Women in the Workplace* 3 (2006).

[49] Michelle C. Haynes & Madeline E. Heilman, *It Had to Be You (Not Me)!: Women's Attributional Rationalization of Their Contribution to Successful Joint Work Outcomes*, 39 *Personality & Soc. Psych.* 956 (2007).

[50] *Id.* at 957 (citation omitted).

Sexual harassment in the workplace, a problem that I have examined elsewhere in a private-law context,[51] is another source of gendered unjust enrichment. The private-law wrong here is not that sexual harassment harms women more than men (which it does): private law never harassed anyone. Unjust enrichment instead derives from the *volenti* notion that a wrong exists only when someone protests. Because complaining about sexual harassment harms workers,[52] a person who suffers this wrong will go on to suffer again should she complain: workplaces worsen the injury because they discourage protesting more than harassment itself.[53] Most victims of sexual harassment accordingly do not report their experience,[54] and when they do report, they may have good reason to regret having done so.[55] Female boundary defenders and asserters of interests get punished. Like unjustly low pay, workplace sexual harassment is typically safer for a woman to endure than denounce.

3. *Within the Family She Forms*

Most women give birth to at least one child before they die,[56] and wifehood as well as motherhood is a likely fate for a woman. Even in 2015, by which time marriage rates had been in decline for years, only a small minority of adults aged seventy-five had never been married;[57] if we omit insistence on a formal ceremony and define wifehood as a status held by the female member of a cohabiting heterosexual pair, this status becomes overwhelmingly probable for women to experience.

Negation of adult autonomy pervades pregnancy, the condition that precedes motherhood almost all the time.[58] The *New York Times* dramatized this immolation of women as agents and subjects through an extended interactive story—interviews, expository prose, videos, graphs, and still photographs—grouped under the rubric "How states are extending liberties to the unborn—by taking them from women."[59] The pregnant person in this feature is the opposite of a boundary defender or asserter of her own rights and interests. A caption of pregnant women's crimes in the story tolls like a dark bell:

[51] Anita Bernstein, *Treating Sexual Harassment with Respect*, 111 HARV. L. REV. 445 (1997); Anita Bernstein, *An Old Jurisprudence: Respect in Retrospect*, 83 CORNELL L. REV. 1231, 1242–1243 (1998) (defending redress for this wrong with reference to private law).

[52] See Anne Lawton, *Operating in an Empirical Vacuum: The* Ellerth *and* Faragher *Affirmative Defense*, 13 COLUM. J. GENDER & L. 197, 258 (2004) (summarizing studies of harms to workers who report this wrong); Nicole Buonocoro Porter, *Ending Harassment by Starting with Retaliation*, 71 STAN. L. REV. ONLINE 49, 50 (2018) (observing that retaliation for complaints can take the form of ostracism).

[53] See generally Deborah L. Brake, *Retaliation*, 90 MINN. L. REV. 18 (2005) (extending this assessment to all forms of workplace discrimination).

[54] Porter, *supra* note 52.

[55] Anne Lawton, *Between Scylla and Charybdis: The Perils of Reporting Sexual Harassment*, 9 U. PA. J. LAB. & EMP. L. 603 (2007).

[56] See Bernstein, *supra* note 4, at 146–147 (gathering data).

[57] Nathan Yau, *Percentage of People Who Married, Given Your Age*, Nov. 2017, https://flowingdata .com/2017/11/01/who-is-married-by-now.

[58] Motherhood without pregnancy is rare all over the world. Even the United States, where parenthood by adoption occurs relatively often, only 2.3% of children under eighteen living with their parents were adopted, https://travel.state.gov/content/travel/en/Intercountry-Adoption/adopt_ref/ adoption-statistics.html.

[59] Editorial Board, *A Woman's Rights*, N.Y. TIMES, Dec. 28, 2018.

Fetal assault. Depraved heart murder. Delivery of a controlled substance. Chemical endangerment of a fetus. Manslaughter. Second-degree murder. Feticide. Child abuse. Reckless injury to a child. Concealing a birth. Concealing a death. Abuse of a corpse. Neglect of a minor. Attempted procurement of a miscarriage. Reckless homicide. One segment of the feature spoke about the origin of these crimes: in past decades television and newspapers, the *Times* included, falsely portrayed black women as crack addicts "giving birth to a generation of neurologically damaged children who were less than fully human and who would bankrupt the schools and social service agencies once they came of age."[60] Deprivations of women's freedom that ensued have remained in place. Many have expanded since the crack-babies era.

In connecting this criminalization to private law, I hope not to be misunderstood. Criminalizing events and experiences associated with pregnancy does much worse harm to women than hobbling them in civil litigation. This mild and remote-looking consequence nevertheless deserves attention in a study of private law as jurisprudence. Doctrinal fields that expect litigants to possess distinct consciousness of themselves as separate persons, and that count on individuals to police the boundaries of their bodies, need to recognize the salience of gender. And of race and wealth. Women of color and poor women suffer much more at the intersection of misfortune and pregnancy than do affluent white women.

Privileged cohorts feel the impact of pregnancy-related crimes as influence rather than a direct threat to their liberty. They suffer (only) lesser infringements of themselves as boundary defenders and asserters of their own interests. Interferences with their consumption of alcohol, for example, while being or appearing pregnant.[61] Or, when their pregnancies are about to end with hospital delivery, routine episiotomies that are sometimes followed by a so-called husband stitch. Obstetricians impose these painful procedures on women not to give them medical benefit but to make their vaginas more pleasurable for someone else to penetrate.[62] Pregnancy teaches even privileged women that they are instruments rather than full persons.

One pregnancy-oppression that wealth eases but does not eliminate is workplace discrimination. Lower-paid pregnant women whose jobs demand physical labor find themselves needing what gets labeled an accommodation,[63] a favor/excuse hybrid that employers say they find burdensome.[64] An individual seeking what she needs to work effectively must assert a claim on another's time and money.

---

[60] *Can a Corpse Give Birth?*, series cited at *id.*

[61] See Laws against Serving Alcohol to Pregnant Women, American Addiction Centers, Oct. 19, 2018, https://www.alcohol.org/laws/serving-alcohol-to-pregnant-women/ (surveying laws).

[62] Virginia Braun & Celia Kitzinger, *The Perfectible Vagina: Size Matters*, 3 CULTURE, HEALTH & SEXUALITY 263 (2001).

[63] Bradley A. Areheart, *Accommodating Pregnancy*, 67 ALA. L. REV. 1125, 1128, 1159–1160 (2016).

[64] See, e.g., Young v. United Parcel Service, 135 S. Ct. 1338, 1346 (2015) (noting that the plaintiff's manager had told her that as long as she remained pregnant she was "too much of a liability"); Geduldig v. Aiello, 417 U.S. 484, 503–504 (1974) ("The essence of the State's justification for excluding [work-related] disabilities caused by a normal pregnancy from its disability compensation scheme is that covering such disabilities would be too costly.").

Testifying in 1977 at a congressional hearing on the Pregnancy Discrimination Act, *Ms.* magazine founding editor Letty Cottin Pogrebin denounced a "false choice" between a woman's "brain and uterus; between making money and making babies; between being productive and being reproductive."[65] False though the choice may be, pregnancy discrimination maintains it. A woman starts out uncompensated for the socially valuable contribution of making a baby. Employment discrimination augments this deprivation by paying her less than a man for her work and, as we just saw with respect to salary, punishing her for asserting her interests. Becoming pregnant reinforces the relative powerlessness she brings to the realm of private law.

New human life now in the offing, we bid our protagonist adieu with quick remarks about motherhood and wifehood as sources of weakness related to her participation in private law. Becoming a mother is associated with a big drop in wage income. Mothers do more housework and (the tedious constituents of) childcare than their male partners. Spare time, which plaintiffs and defendants apply to pondering what next to demand in litigation, gets hoovered up by wifehood and motherhood.

About these objectively detrimental new developments, *volenti non fit injuria* once again: if a woman likes the gendered circumstances of her life, she's fine. But some women don't—I don't—and any unjust social conditions that a woman finds objectionable oppress her. She might win a few rounds in her struggle against them, but through their prevalence they teach her that her resentment is wrong and deviant. Their prevalence also encourages her partner and children to expect sacrifice from her and pushes out of view role-model alternatives that might inspire her to seek more for herself, perhaps at the expense of other people. Moving into the life stage of wifehood and motherhood thus will diminish what a woman can extract from, and add to, the law of contracts, torts, and property.

III. Unjust Enrichment

Non fit injuria as a constituent of the *volenti* maxim implies that no loss has ensued whenever a prospective litigant has waived or accepted a violation of her private law rights. In the aggregate, gendered silence has kept complaints and defenses and imaginative extensions out of judicial decisions. Here private law gives force to its own lessening. *It's all right, don't mind me, I'm not present, I'll sit in the dark.*[66]

---

[65] Quoted in Mary Ziegler, *Choice at Work:* Young v. United Parcel Service, *Pregnancy Discrimination, and Reproductive Liberty*, 93 Den. U. L. Rev. 219, 246 (2015).

[66] Private law had been conservative enough without gender because of, among other conditions, its backward orientation. Making a generalization that extends to contracts and property too, Tsachi Keren-Paz writes that tort "is regressive by nature. One reason for this is the basic compensation principle: full compensation or *restitutio ad integrum*." Tsachi Keren-Paz, *Torts, Egalitarianism and Distributive Justice* 67 (2007). Return to an original condition entrenches distributive injustice of the past, and (the rare windfall of punitive damages or an injunction to one side) private law gives winners nothing better than *restitutio*.

Because women lack parity in the dramatis personae opportunities of private law that opened this chapter, judicial decisions in turn lack parity in their representations of individuals' life experiences. Men and what they once complained about flourish beyond their number in contract, tort, and property precedent-teachings that govern the whole population. Women receive no discount as taxpayers who finance an apparatus that systematically shortchanges them as both plaintiffs and defendants.[67] Private law correlatively makes men richer, more powerful, and better endowed in their possession of unmerited good things.

Because I do not claim that judges can remedy the wrong of private law that occupies this chapter, my contention about injustice needs an extradoctrinal understanding of the phrase unjust enrichment. Useful here is a famed series of 1950 lectures on the subject that led with two quotations. The first came from the *Restatement of Restitution*, "A person who has been unjustly enriched at the expense of another is required to make restitution to that other." The second, by the Roman jurist Pomponius: "For this by nature is equitable, that no one be made richer through another's loss."[68]

Of the two, the Pomponius maxim is better, wrote Jack Dawson, because it "combines elegance with exactness" as it "expresses both an aspiration and a standard for judgment;" it's not a legal rule.[69] Unjust enrichment declares that no one ought to be made richer through another's loss. In this view—Dawson's and mine—unjust enrichment covers more than occasions that litigation can repair. Redress is not necessarily available for every instance of it. Instead, the action lies under an umbrella of "broad issues of social justice."[70]

As stated in one recitation provisioned in judicial decisions, unjust enrichment as an action has five elements.

First, an enrichment.
Second, an impoverishment.
Third, a connection between the enrichment and the impoverishment.
Fourth, the absence of a justification for the enrichment and the impoverishment.
Fifth, an absence of a remedy provided by law[71]—"law" here meaning in contrast to equity.[72]

Enrichment? Yes. Persons brought up to assert their interests, and who are rewarded when they do so in public, enjoy a big share of private law's gains. In contrast to

---

[67] I have more to say about this problem in Anita Bernstein, *Gender in Asbestos Law: Cui Bono? Cui Pacat?*, 88 TULANE L. REV. 1211, 1254–1256 (2014).

[68] John P. Dawson, *Unjust Enrichment: A Comparative Analysis* 1 (1951).   [69] *Id.* at 1, 4–5.

[70] *Id.* at 6. See also *id.* at 5 (analogizing unjust enrichment to the Marxian labor theory of value).

[71] Arizona and Louisiana use these criteria. Telesaurus VPC, LLC v. Power, 623 F.3d 998, 1009 (9th Cir. 2010) (applying Arizona law); Andretti Sports Marketing Louisiana, LLC v. Nola Motorsports Host Committee, Inc., 147 F. Supp. 3d 537, 573 (E.D. La. 2015).

[72] Decisional law in Delaware that cites this five-part test comes from Chancery. See Jackson National Life Insurance Co. v. Kennedy, 741 A.2d 377, 394 (Del. Ch. 1999); Cantor Fitzgerald, LP v. Cantor, 724 A.2d 571, 585 (Del. Ch. 1998).

public-law distributions, which land on recipients who may have only filled out a form, contract and tort and property deliver benefits to those who stand up to pursue what these fields deliver. A complementary impoverishment follows for persons brought up to submerge their interests and defer to what others want and say they need. Gender as a social condition links the enrichment with the impoverishment. The first three elements of unjust enrichment are thus present: enrichment, impoverishment, and a connection between the two.

Absence of justification for the enrichment and impoverishment, the fourth element, is a bit more complicated because rationales for the enrichment-and-impoverishment status quo do exist. These rationales fall under the labels of, inter alia, evolutionary psychology, economic specialization within the family, female masochism, female choice, male hormones, and a design from above like "complementarity" or a curse on women that God decreed. But at least in liberal political theory, supports for patriarchy like these differ from justification. Justification comes from public reason;[73] to qualify as public reason, an assertion needs plausibility to persons other than those who will benefit if the assertion is credited.[74]

The fifth element, absence of a remedy provided by law, is starkly present. All law, not just private law, lacks a remedy for the problem of unjust enrichment and impoverishment that occupies this chapter. And that's an understatement: private law enlarges the injustice.

---

[73] Samuel Freeman, *Public Reason and Political Justifications*, 72 FORDHAM L. REV. 2021 (2014).

[74] Otherwise known as "overlapping consensus." John Rawls, *The Domain of the Political and Overlapping Consensus*, 64 N.Y.U. L. REV. 233 (1989). For a feminist perspective on this famed idea, see Seyla Benhabib, *Situating the Self: Gender, Community and Postmodernism in Contemporary Ethics* 42 (1992).

CHAPTER 13

···

HISTORICAL
PERSPECTIVES

···

JOSHUA GETZLER

IN 1345 a spirited exchange burst forth in the English Court of Common Pleas, at the tail end of a debate as to whether a vested estate in remainder could be proven by deed alone, without any further act establishing ultimate freehold.[1] A single precedent was produced by counsel suggesting the need for a final concord recording admittance to the estate by fine, in the absence of a physical entry. Such a requirement would have shut out the remainderman. The difficult, perhaps unresolvable, theoretical issue underlying this controversy was whether an estate in land should be conceptualized as a set of horizontal relationships, radiating from a proprietary asset holder with protected possession at one end, and potential trespassers and assignees on the other; or rather as a vertical relationship between lord and tenant standing in a protected personal association, with the tenant swearing fealty and service to the lord, and the lord admitting the tenant to the fee, warranting the subordinate title against outsiders, and controlling assignment of the tenancy by attornment. One of the judges wished to deny the force of the prior case requiring a fine and final accord with the higher lord, which precedent rested on the "vertical" theory; and this led to the following courtroom exchange:

Shareshull (Justice of the Common Pleas or Chief Baron of the Exchequer):
Nevertheless, no precedent is of such force as that which is reasonable.
R. Thorp (Serjeant, senior counsel):
I think you will do as others have done in a similar case, or else we do not know what the law is.
Hillary (Justice of Common Pleas):
Law is at the will of the Justices.
Stonore (Chief Justice of Common Pleas):
Certainly not; law is reason.

---

[1] Y.B. Hil. 19 Edw. 3, pl.3 (1345); Luke O. Pike, *Year Books of the Reign of King Edward the Third: Years XVIII and XIX*, at 374–379 (Rolls Series 31.B.12, 1905); Seipp No. 1345.003rs.

A twenty-first-century New Private Lawyer transported back to the mid-fourteenth century might wish to applaud all the positions evoked in this debate. Precedent must be given weight to create some fixity in the law, a conventionalist position; but the doctrinal content or rule-making extent of any precedent may be remolded by the court in the light of reason, a natural-law position; or a precedent may even be shaped according to some willed policy, a realist position. Truly, we do not need to favor one of these theories over the other. The concurrent application of precedent, reason, and policy is implicit in all casuistic judgment. In every new case counsel and judges will argue carefully over the correct interpretation and application of preceding authority, and this supposedly encourages the development of durable rules well suited to influence the next run of cases. Lord Mansfield memorably captured the ideal of a "common law, *that works itself pure*," whereby the reach of precedent is tested empirically through iterative application to cases that tend to be randomly selected by the vagaries of litigation, such that weak or unsuitable ideas will be weeded out.[2]

There is something missing from this evolutionary model. Even with the best use of reason and finest appreciation of the policies of the law, how are lawyers to extract and adapt useful rules from past cases when faced with new problems? The factual precedents do not announce a guiding rule in abstract or general terms for forward cases, but solve the instant case before the court, tailoring a solution to the facts. A case must be interpreted anew every time it is used as a relevant precedential authority (or distinguished as not binding); and fallible lawyers can misunderstand or distort the weight of the principles announced or assumed by prior decision makers. Mistakes and mutations can creep in to the evolving interpretative chain of doctrine, like damaged DNA, especially where analogies are used from adjacent legal orders.[3] Even if the precedents are perfectly understood, it is not the case that rules arising from cases at any level of specification can be mapped onto fresh cases automatically; each new case is "slightly different,"[4] and so precedents must be fitted to new cases by analogy, involving some external cast of judgment as to why the facts of one unique situation can be aligned with the facts of another. Invoking some external standard favored by the judge risks exactly what Serjeant Thorp identified in his rejoinder to Justice Shareshull: that if judges could freely manipulate the precedents then no one could be sure from moment to moment what the law is.

The solution lay not simply in lawyerly respect for historical precedents but also knowledge of how lawyers came to think about precedents. Historically, the juristic enterprise involved much more than knowledge of past decisions; it also demanded the carving out of interpretative classifications to order the precedents and guide the process of rule application and analogization. Such heuristic ordering is at the core of classical jurisprudence or legal science. New Private Law announces itself as a revival of self-consciously doctrinal tradition, thereby stepping away from the dominant realist or

---

[2] Omychund v. Barker (1744) 1 Atk. 21, 33, 26 E.R. 15, 23 per William Murray S.-G. (in arg.).

[3] Cf. Alan Watson, *Legal Transplants: An Approach to Comparative Law* (2d ed. 1993). For a case study, see Joshua Getzler, *Transplantation and Mutation in Anglo-American Trust Law*, 10 THEORETICAL INQUIRIES IN LAW 355 (2009).

[4] Cf. David Daube, *Slightly Different*, 12 IURA 81 (1961).

post-realist mindset of American law, and aligning more closely with English and Continental jurisprudence. But what could it mean to join these older traditions of doctrinal learning? What are the essential qualities of these traditions?

This chapter argues that the history of classical jurisprudence (of both common law and Civilian varieties) can offer a useful stimulus or lead—even a precedent!—in the development of the New Private Law as it explores the potential of doctrinal reasoning. Two general observations pertain here. The first is that lawyers in both continental and common-law traditions have built on traditional legal heuristics developed in second- and third-century Rome, endlessly adapting and applying these categories in the centuries since. It is possible to think about doctrine without knowledge of this deep intellectual history. Similarly, one can speak a language well without knowing anything about its grammar, just as one can play music without knowledge of theories of harmony and rhythm. But understanding the origins and structure of any language can add to the mastery and freedom enjoyed by the user. Much of this chapter will be spent uncovering the Roman institutionalist heuristics and suggesting that knowledge of these remains desirable for any lawyer seeking to wield legal doctrine as a technique of social decision and ordering. The second major point is that classicism—the deployment of precedent using organizing typologies established by legal tradition—was not always or only a conservative praxis aiming to limit (or alternatively, conceal) the political authority of the judge. The opposite could be true. Classical legal tradition could be highly adventurous, granting jurists the confidence and legitimacy to launch grand experimentation in the ordering and reform of society. Historical jurisprudence was often joined with legal rationalization projects taking the form of treatises, restatements, and codifications aiming to summarize and make available the fruits of past law for modern users. Such literatures commonly went with a strategy of extension of jurisdiction, as states and empires enlarged and consolidated their rule. Bringing all residents under a single well-understood system of private law was a potent means of state formation, knitting together subjects within a common polity by use of soft juridical power.[5] Historical jurisprudence was used in this fashion in the Roman, Napoleonic, Bismarckian, and British empires. Perhaps an exemplar of this trend was the proliferation of texts examining possession and title in nineteenth-century Germany, seeking to resolve the tensions between feudal property forms and industrial and agrarian commodification of land in the long journey to national legal unification.[6]

Historical jurisprudence also underpinned the rise of a scientific treatise tradition in nineteenth-century America and the turn to codificatory restatements in the early to mid-twentieth century, as America became a vast integrated internal market.[7] Precedential law could also be used in the reverse direction, to create subsidiarities or

[5] Cf. Lionel Smith, this volume.

[6] The two prime texts are Friedrich von Savigny, *Das Recht des Besitzes* [The Law of Possession] (1803), and Rudolf von Jhering, *Der Besitzwille* [The Will to Possess] (1889).

[7] See generally David Rabban, *Law's History: American Legal Thought and the Transatlantic Turn to History* (2013). Joseph Story and James Kent are the preeminent nineteenth-century figures; a fascinating example of a later historicizing and modernizing treatise is provided by Grant Gilmore, *Security Interests in Personal Property* (1965).

autonomous local jurisdictions carved out from within a dominant or hegemonic legal system, as where local lawyers created their own subsystem varying the law emanating from a higher political order.[8]

The New Private Law movement of this century has rather different drivers to the classical legal tradition outlined here. New Private Law has revived doctrinal thinking in order to provide a counterweight to an exaggerated dependence on social science, utilitarian and deontic ethics, and indeed raw politics in the life of private law. Awareness of the historical origins and functions of doctrinal reasoning can only strengthen this revival of Western legal tradition for modern use. In the search for origins it makes sense to seek the earliest beginnings.

I. ROMAN ROOTS

Unlike the early legal systems of the Mediterranean and Near East, including Greek, Egyptian, Akkadian, and Hebrew laws, the Romans innovated by developing a jurisprudence largely severed from religious or mythical roots,[9] perhaps reflecting the demographic basis of earliest Rome as a merger of ethnically distinct villages which needed a neutral, inclusivist civic mythology.[10] Another distinctive aspect of Roman legal culture was the early emergence of a professional caste of jurists, who saw exposition and development of the civil law as a vocation permitting a more reflective and intellectual career than senatorial politics, the magistracy, or military command. By the first century, new men making a vocation out of the law, such as Marcus Sabinus in the reign of Augustus and Tiberius, were writing detailed commentaries on the old *ius civile* being the basic civil claims embodied in the early Twelve Tables. The early jurists also advised the praetorian magistrates in charge of civil justice how to adapt and extend the flow of new formulae, or commissions instructing the lay judges deciding cases. The Praetorian Edict, or amassed collection of formulae, became the second great source of law in Rome, a set of abstract precedents of the type of actions available to all litigants, and like the old *ius civile* this historical text, especially once stabilized by the jurist Julian, attracted dense professional commentary. Sabinus and his contemporary Proculus were avid teachers as well as legal advisers, and each founded schools of professional jurists who vied to have their interpretations of the civil law and the edictal gloss prevail. Sabinus in his edictal commentaries early identified an expository split between property, obligations, and succession claims. Attempts to show philosophical or methodological differences between the schools have been inconclusive, but Peter Stein has suggested that Sabinians tended toward freer interpretation of old texts, while refusing to add to those texts by

---

[8] See, e.g., William A. Wynes, *Legislative, Executive and Judicial Powers in Australia* (1st ed. 1936, 5th ed. 1976).

[9] See James Q. Whitman, *Long Live the Hatred of Roman Law!*, 2 RECHTSGESCHICHTE 40 (2003).

[10] See Mary Beard, *S.P.Q.R.: A History of Ancient Rome* 53–89 (2015).

analogy and equity. Proculians reversed this approach, preferring to stick to literal meanings for old law and then legislate new norms by analogy.[11]

The professionalism and abstract conceptualism of the jurists reached an early peak in the career of Gaius (c. 130–180 CE), a follower of Sabinus. He took legal history seriously in establishing the meaning and application of the laws, perhaps on the Sabinian view that a genetic understanding of meaning gave the reader a heightened freedom to reconstruct the text. Gaius' historicism was announced in his commentaries on the procedural rules of the early *ius civile*:

> Since I am aiming to give an interpretation of the ancient laws, I have concluded that I must trace the law of the Roman people from the very beginnings of their city. This is not because I like making extremely wordy commentaries but because I can see that in every subject a perfect job is one whose parts hang together properly. And to be sure the most important part of anything is its beginning.[12]

Gaius constantly invoked older rules that had been superseded but that had left traces in later jurisprudence. He showed how the issuance of fresh formulae or instructions to judges on a case-by-case basis could serve to adapt existing actions to cover new causes. The mechanisms of change could be divided into three: there could be adaptations by fictions such as assumed or feigned factual pleading or normatively driven reinterpretations of semantic forms; jurists could pile exceptional rules or equities onto existing rule structures; and magistrates might leap over existing forms altogether, creating fresh actions via legislation passed in superior judicatures or assemblies, and so using political authority to drive larger-scale reforms.[13] Much of Gaius' work can be characterized as legal archaeology, concerned to excavate and understand the historic foundations of the law as a prelude to stating the contemporary rules.

Gaius accordingly used copious historical illustrations in his highly systematized introduction to classical law, known as his *Institutes*, a text developed from lectures at his *studium* in Rome.[14] Here he may have drawn from the classificatory schemes of the natural sciences as well as from the prevalent Stoic philosophy and *ars rhetorica* of his day. Gaius distinguished persons, things, and actions as the master classification, partitioning the subjects, objects, and adjectival processes of the law. Lucid subcategories were then carved out from the three main divisions. Persons were divided between freemen and slaves; one then had to investigate the powers and responsibilities of a *dominus* or *pater familias* over subordinates within the household, including women, children of different maturities, and free servants as well as slaves. Political statuses were described

[11] See Peter G. Stein, *The Two Schools of Jurists in the Early Roman Principate*, 31 CAMBRIDGE L.J. 8 (1972); Tessa Leesen, *Gaius Meets Cicero: Law and Rhetoric in the School Controversies* (2010).

[12] Dig. 1.2.1 (Gaius) (Alan Watson ed., G.E.M. de Ste Croix trans., 1985).

[13] This adumbrates Maine's famous trilogy of the engines of legal change—fiction, equity, and legislation—derived from Roman legal history and then universalized: Henry Sumner Maine, *Ancient Law* (1st ed. 1861). See further Peter G. Stein, *Legal Evolution: The Story of an Idea* 23–50 (1980).

[14] See A.M. Honoré, Gaius, *A Biography* 1–45 (1962).

as well as the rights and capacities of foreigners. Things encompassed all valuable assets, whether claimed against persons, over physical objects, or uses thereof. Things or *res* might be classified by the means of acquisition, or by the means of claiming them or enforcing their value. Delictual, contractual, and enrichment claims when viewed as rights to a debt payment or a performance hovered uneasily between assets or things in themselves, and remedies or actions to assert some prior claim or mother right.[15] Succession claims stood outside the categories of persons, things, and actions, or else could be seen as a hybrid combining all three. The sophistication of the Gaian scheme is demonstrated in his discussion of the third, properly adjectival, category of actions or legal methods by which things are claimed:

> **4.1** It remains to speak of actions. If we ask how many classes of actions there are, the better view is that there are two, real and personal (*in rem* and *in personam*). Those who say that there are four, by including those actions based on wagers (*per sponsiones*) have failed to observe the distinction between species and genus. **4.2** A personal action is one which we maintain when we sue someone who is under an obligation to us from contract or delict—that is, when our assertion is that he ought to give, do, or fulfil (*dare, facere, praestare*). **4.3** A real action is one in which we assert that a corporeal thing is ours or that a right belongs to us, as for instance a right of use or usufruct, a right of way for man or beast, of aqueduct, or a right to build higher or a right to see out. Conversely, a real action can deny that our opponent has such a right. **4.4** Actions being distinguished in this way, it is certain that we cannot claim from another something that belongs to us using the words 'if it appears he ought to give'. For something which is ours cannot be given to us. You will understand that giving something to us is defined to mean giving in such a way as to make it ours and that a thing which is already ours cannot be made more ours. It is clearly from hatred of thieves, to make them liable to more actions, that it has been accepted that, in addition to their liability to fourfold or twofold penal damages, they can also be sued using this form of claim, 'if it appears that they ought to give'. This is in addition to the availability against them of the action in which we assert that a thing is ours. **4.5** Real actions are called 'vindications'. Personal actions in which we assert that something ought to be given to, or done for us are called condictions.[16]

The power of the Gaian taxonomy lay in its fertile heuristics; the categories of subject, object, and action guided the jurists in setting the substantive content of claims, burden of proof, order of pleading, defenses, relevant evidentiary burdens, and the levels of remedy and enforcement appropriate for the claim in question. This sophistication was all the more remarkable considering that this was in large measure a non-state system with strong elements of lay arbitration. The praetors in charge of city justice were guided

---

[15] See Peter Birks, "Definition and Division: A Meditation on Institutes 3.13," in *The Classification of Obligations* 1–35 (Peter Birks ed., 1997); George Gretton, *Ownership and Its Objects*, 71 RABEL J. OF COMP. AND INT'L PRIV. L. 802 (2007).

[16] G. Inst. 4.1–5, at 232–233 (Francis de Zulueta ed. & trans., 1946); cf. J. Inst. 4.6, at 128–135 (Peter Birks & Grant McLeod eds. & trans., 1987).

by the jurists in issuing formulae and commissioning lay judges to hear cases, but the crafting of the formula ended the public element of the process. Ultimately the system was based on licensed self-help and voluntary obedience to the order of the judge. The final penalty for noncompliance was *infamia*, a removal of civic capacity involving total loss of access to the legal system and its protections that rendered the miscreant close to the status of a nonperson.[17] It is this weak or negative form of coercivity (denial of capacity) that helps to explain the paramount importance of the upstream process of formulaic justice; the jurists did not hear cases and make orders, but carefully set up the process to make sure that lay persons could run the litigations effectively as a system of "civil recourse."[18]

The Gaian taxonomy, known mainly through later jurists' redactions, proved to be of supreme importance in Western private law, offering a stable genetic code that guided jurisprudence for the next two millennia. With the recovery of Gaius' classical urtext in the early nineteenth century, it became apparent how Gaius himself placed a high regard for legal history alongside his taxonomical work. If the classificatory scheme provided a static model amenable to analytical elaboration, then the historical work showed a dynamic system evolving pragmatically, even chaotically in reaction to external events and especially to accommodate politically driven legislation. Both sides, the static and the dynamic, had to be mastered.

An important example of chaotic evolution was to be found in the *Lex Aquilia* of circa 286 BCE, an early (perhaps the earliest) plebiscitary statute that codified property damage actions, in the wake of a civil war where armies had destroyed the homesteads and farm capital of opposing populations. Terse rules to improve or replace a failing ancient system of compensation were introduced by the legislation, serving to classify and streamline causal inquiry and to ensure adequate damages awards for destruction or marring of capital by direct means, with careful setting of *quanta* to reflect the changing seasonal values and inventory cost of animate agrarian capital such as slaves and livestock.[19] An annex created a special supercompensatory regime with restitutionary or fiduciary elements to repress wrongful compromise of causes by corrupted legal intermediaries. It is notable that this first great popular plebiscite in Roman legal history concerned itself with a jurisprudence to protect the working capital of peasants in a *latifundia* economy as an emergency measure. These statutory rules were then gradually expanded by juristic interpretation to form a complete system of compensation for direct, indirect, and even pure economic harms, connected however distantly to

[17] See Thomas Rüfner, "Imperial Cognitio Process," in *The Oxford Handbook of Roman Law and Society* 257–269 (Clifford Ando et al. eds., 2016).

[18] This is to borrow with joyous anachronism the nomenclature of Benjamin C. Zipursky & John C.P. Goldberg, *Torts as Wrongs*, 88 TEX. L. REV. 917 (2010). See also John C.P. Goldberg & Benjamin C. Zipursky, *Recognizing Wrongs* (forthcoming 2020). Other methods can be used to describe the nature of "upstream" lawyers' reasoning as setting the conditions for successful dispute settlement in the forensic arena. See, e.g., Andrew S. Gold, this volume; Henry E. Smith, this volume.

[19] For recent work on the *Lex Aquilia*, see Wolfgang Ernst, *Justinian's Digest 9.2.51 in the Western Legal Canon* (2019); Joe Sampson, "lex Aquilia on wrongful damage to property," *Oxford Classical Dictionary* (2018) DOI: 10.1093/acrefore/9780199381135.013.8261.

destruction or marring of physical things. The jurists had to adduce reasons for each extension of liability, and this required theorization of what a tort system was supposed to do, namely, to distribute due responsibility for the causing of harm. The resulting delictual system outstripped its functions as a measure for repairing war damage, yet its origins in an ancient statute lent it durability as the hallowed laws of the older republican *polis*. Modern delictual or tort doctrine in Western legal tradition still draws its basic conceptual framework of direct and indirect cause and proximate and remote damage from this body of early law.[20] Gaius also gave historical accounts of the emergence of actions against theft and the actions to protect the person from assault and insult. The categories of property damage, theft, and insult could overlap, but their separation permitted fine-toothed doctrine to displace the older systems of impeachment before a large popular jury.

Gaius also showed how the contract principles of his time had arisen from three early forms: ceremonial stipulations based on promise, sales based on cash-based exchange, and conditioned transfers of possession. From these rudimentary origins the jurists elaborated fresh categories of contractual liability, first by transforming ritualistic formalities through pragmatic fictions and presumptions, and then by creating an interlocking hierarchy of actions using mixtures of fault and strict liability to uphold promissory expectations, police the quality of performances, and devise defenses. The old contractual practices of the intimate Roman community based on face-to-face transactions were thereby stretched to provide a depersonalized mercantile law for a vast trading empire.[21] Even in the developed late Imperial law, eyes could be cast back to older precedents to decide the limits of doctrinal expansion. For example, it took legislation (the 472 CE Constitutions of Leo) finally to liberalize the form and vernacular of verbal contracts and permit written notes to substitute for oral declarations, as the old stipulations were tied too securely to Latin ritual invocations to be freed up by juristic interpretation. The law of sale applying a package of rights and duties to buyer and seller had to be maintained as a cash transaction rather than barter at a nominal price, in order to fix who would be buyer and who seller, as the obligations were asymmetric.[22]

Roman property doctrine was perhaps the best example of an ancient doctrinal discourse extended by practical lawyers to conquer new terrain. The Roman jurists derived from the early formulaic actions a set of interlocking principles governing the acquisition, transfer, sharing, and extinction of property rights in land, and the various methods of asserting and remedying such rights. At the core lay a conventional *numerus clausus* (closed list) of interests, enumerating *detentio* (bare physical control), *possessio*

---

[20] See Reinhard Zimmermann, *The Law of Obligations: Roman Foundations of the Civilian Tradition* 902–921, 953–1049 (1996). We must note a separate Roman pedigree for personal damages, involving repression of public expressions of contempt, outlined in Peter Birks, *The Roman Law of Obligations* 221–246 (Eric Descheemaeker ed., 2016); Peter Birks, *The Early History of Iniuria*, 37 LEGAL HIST. REV. 163 (1969).

[21] See generally Gyorgy Diósdi, *Contract in Roman Law from the Twelve Tables to the Glossators* (1981); Laurent Waelkens, *Amne Adverso: Roman Legal Heritage in European Culture* 323–356 (2015).

[22] Cf. G. Inst. 3.141, *supra* note 16, at 196–199.

(legally protected control), *dominium* (ultimate title and right to control), *usufructus* (life- or term-limited income and usage), *emphyteusis* (contractually limited physical control), *hypothec* (secured rights to convey but not possess), and *servitutes* (incorporeal right of one owner to do actions on another's property or to restrict use of that other property). There was a parallel list of public and collective goods pertaining to land outside private interests, enumerated as *res nullius, res religiosae, res communes, res publicae,* and *res universitatis,* each with different stinting mechanisms for the relevant membership of the class granted access. Plural private interests were less easily accommodated: ostensible joint holdings found in partnership forms (possibly sole ownerships subject to strong obligational and asset partitioning claims); there could be fiduciary management suggestive of split ownership through the inter vivos *peculium* and the testamentary *fideicommissum*; and there could be plural ownerships of funds or collections of assets, the *res universitatis,* There was, however, nothing resembling the independent entity with assets and capacities separate from the natural persons who participated in it. One surmise is that Romans preferred the model of the sole trader as patrimonial owner, harnessing the energies of contractors, slaves, and family to constitute groups that acted corporately.[23] Turning to creation, transfer, and destruction of proprietary assets, interests could be dealt with under the original and derivative modes of acquisition, enumerated as *occupatio* (physical appropriation), its inverse of *derelicto* (abandonment), *traditio* (informal private transfer), *acceptio, confusio,* and *commixtio* (types of annexation and merger), *mancipatio* (formal public transfer), *in iure cessio* (release in court), *usucapio* (acquisition by tolerated use), and *praescriptio* (acquisition by nontolerated use). Settled interests were defended by variants of vindicatory, possessory, injunctive, and damages actions. Once the categories had been established by rationalization of the historical materials, the jurists could hybridize the forms to order assets in the most imaginative ways, while still tying their concepts back to simple anchoring elements. Much of this experimentation happened after Gaius' time, and his descriptions of property are relatively rudimentary but contain the germ of what followed.

Property forms might be stable at the conceptual level, but the content and function of property rights could shift rapidly in new conditions. With the continuous expansion of the Roman empire after the defeat of Carthage, imperial exploitation of conquered land and reduction of non-Romans to the status of peregrine outsiders, inferior subjects, or even tradable slave capital, risked explosive rebellion of the periphery against the metropolitan core. Here lawyers adapting historical jurisprudence provided essential techniques for maintaining civil peace and the legitimacy of Roman rule. Perhaps the most significant reform was the decision evoked in the *Constitutio Antoniniana* of

---

[23] See further Henry Hansmann, Reinier Kraakman, & Richard Squire, *Law and the Rise of the Firm,* 119 HARV. L. REV. 1333 (2006); Henry Hansmann, Reinier Kraakman, & Richard Squire, "Incomplete Organizations: Legal Entities and Asset Partitioning in Roman Commerce," ch. 8, and Andreas Martin Fleckner, "Roman Business Associations," ch. 9 in *Roman Law and Economics Volume I: Institutions and Organizations* (Giuseppe Dari-Mattiaci & Dennis P. Kehoe eds., 2020); Joshua Getzler, "Personality and Capacity: Lessons from Legal History," in *Finn's Law: An Australian Justice* 147–178 (Tim Bonyhady ed., 2016).

212 CE to grant full citizenship and legal rights and capacities on the standard Roman pattern to all territorial subjects of the Roman emperor, whatever their ethnic, religious, or political status, extending beyond the traditional kinship alliance of the Italic tribes.[24] This status expansion included full ability to own land as a *dominus* anywhere in the empire, rather than as a mere tenant of the Roman state. The extended availability of *dominium* brought with it liability to pay imperial land taxes that in turn sustained the public order guaranteeing universal property rights, as well as an expanded franchise for military service.[25] The great system of classical Severan jurisprudence established by Ulpian and his colleagues in the third century, building on centuries of prior legal development, may be seen as a vast reimagining of legal tradition as a scientific and dialectical discourse available to all, to match the universalization of Roman subjecthood made by the emperor Caracalla in that year of 212. Ulpian's universalism included a remarkable hostility to the institution of slavery, which he saw as an affront to the natural law and principles of Stoic conscience underpinning the civil law.[26]

Ulpianic jurisprudence in turn provided the foundation of the Justinianic codification of 533 CE known as the *Corpus Iuris Civilis*.[27] Justinian commissioned the leading jurists of the Eastern empire to review the entire body of historical legal doctrine and reduce it to a coherent, internally consistent whole that could be given legislative force. Justinian stated in the promulgating statute, the *Constitutio Tanta*, that a key purpose of the legislation was to knit together the newly unified empire under a common rule of law after generations of decline and conflict. Lucid, rationalized, and freely accessible private law was projected as a type of soft power contributing to a single market and military-fiscal state. Justinian appended to his codification a fresh edition of Gaius' *Institutes*, brought up to date to match the newly minted Digest of the law and to make that codification accessible to new students. The reality after Justinian was rather different in that the provinces persisted in using their own laws, combining local customs with Romanic jurisprudence in an ad hoc mix sometimes known as "vulgar law," and only resorting to the universal Justinianic *ius commune* to fill gaps or deal with cross-jurisdictional problems. Stubborn local loyalties and entrenched professional habits thus resisted the alignment of the parts of the empire under a single legal code, however excellent the imperial laws might have been.

The destiny of the Justinianic codification was not directly to provide a governing science for the late empire, but rather to preserve classical Severan jurisprudence as a resource for fresh building of laws in Europe, with a great flowering of interest in the twelfth-century renaissance. With the Glossators and Commentators, a new era begins, known as the Reception, where the prestige of the old Roman sources was harnessed by new generations of brilliant jurists keen to reanimate legal science. It was discovered

---

[24] See Dig. 1.5.17 (Ulpianus), in Digest, *supra* note 12.

[25] See Cassius Dio, *Roman History* vol. IX, bk. 78 ch. 9, at 296–298 (Earnest Cary ed. & trans., 1927).

[26] See A.M. Honoré, *Ulpian: Pioneer of Human Rights* 76–93 (2002); cf. James Q. Whitman, *Western Legal Imperialism: Thinking About the Deep Historical Roots*, 10 THEORETICAL INQUIRIES IN LAW 635 (2009).

[27] See A.M. Honoré, *Justinian's Digest: Character and Compilation* (2010).

that Justinian's Digest of classical law, supplemented by the Gaian typology, provided a host of ready-made solutions that could be combined with feudal, communal, and ecclesiastical laws to articulate a new *ius commune*. These were known also as the "Learned Laws" because they were cultivated and disseminated as much by university professors (or learned canonists) as by advocates or attorneys.[28]

II. THE PANDECTIST SUMMATION

National monarchies displaced local, imperial, and church jurisdiction in the modern period—a transition largely driven by the fiscal imperatives of warfare. Nation-states needed enhanced tax bases and unified markets, and this militated against the loose international system of Learned Laws holding together a complex of interlocking jurisdictions. In the eighteenth century the trend was to use historical jurisprudence amalgamated with a blend of Thomist and secular natural law to create national codes under the authority of a territorial monarch. So we see the formulation of the Prussian (1794), French (1804), and Austrian (1811) codes in the transition from Enlightenment despotism to Romantic nationalism.[29] The French code, heavily derived from the Roman-based commentaries and treatises of Robert Pothier (1699–1772), was notably concise and elegant, and was exported across Europe as Napoleon's empire expanded. With his defeat, an alternative codal tradition grew to prominence in Germany, based on an intense study of Roman classical doctrine known as Pandectism. This Pandectism reacted against the imposition of a foreign legal system by the Napoleonic invader, but it also wanted to escape from the scattered jurisdictions of a divided German territory. These legal nationalists therefore sought a solid juristic basis for a new German law, and they found it in a highly scientific Gaian classicism. Their project was so successful that Pandectists ended up providing the most important commentaries on the French code, annexing the prior French civil law to the German intellectual empire.[30]

The Pandectist movement was launched by luminaries such as Thibaut, Savigny, and Puchta in the early 1800s, and came to be associated with the romantic nationalism and liberalism that culminated in the 1840s. The Pandectist revival of classicism was erudite, detailed, and highly systematic—Gaianism to the nth degree. Pandectism also generated a proud new breed of university jurists, exemplified by Friedrich von Savigny, who with his friend Goethe had refounded the modern German university system with a special mission to study historical law. The Pandectists came to view Roman law as an individualistic system promoting freedom as autonomy within a participatory civil society. Only with the defeat of the liberals after 1848 and rise to domination of Prussia and the Bismarckian state did the lawyers of the movement turn their full energies to

[28] See generally Peter G. Stein, *Roman Law in European History* (1999).
[29] See further Stein, *id.* at 71–132; James Gordley, *The Jurists: A Critical History* 195–274 (2013); Franz Wieacker, *A History of Private Law in Europe* 257–275 (Tony Weir ed., 1995).
[30] Karl Salomo Zachariä, *Handbuch des französischen Zivilrechts* (1827).

codification as a national unification project, with the earlier social and historical con-sciousness of the romantic jurists overlaid and replaced by a commitment to arm's-length market relations governed by harmonized rules. This latter national phase of the movement was led in the later nineteenth century by Planck, Windscheid, and Jhering. This talented group deployed the prestige of classical Roman tradition to create a single private law and single market for the whole of Germany while respecting the fiscal and political separatism of the component states of the German federation.

The doyen of the later German-Roman Pandectist tradition was Theodor Mommsen (1817–1903). Mommsen received the Nobel Prize in Literature the year before he died, with the Nobel Committee citing him as "the greatest living master of the art of histori-cal writing, with special reference to his monumental work, *A History of Rome*." Mommsen also wrote massive tomes on Roman constitutional law and criminal law, and with Paul Krueger edited the great modern edition of the *Corpus Iuris Civilis*,[31] which, together with the palingenetic work of his younger colleague Otto Lenel on ear-lier classical law,[32] forms the bedrock of modern Roman law scholarship. Mommsen's career exemplified the world view of Pandectist historical analysis, involving intense scrutiny of Roman sources in order to isolate the key themes of private law when recast-ing the extant German *ius commune* into modern statutory form.

Pandectism amounted to a second Reception of Roman law; and in turn it sparked a counter-reaction from more conservative nationalists of the rival German historical school, led by Brunner, Gierke, Sohm, and Gneist, who focused attention on the family, corporate, guild, and governmental law of non-Roman north European tradition. Thus, legal history of many stripes ultimately contributed to the modern national codi-fication of German civil law, a movement that was completed with the promulgation of the *Bürgerliches Gesetzbuch* (*BGB*) in 1900.[33] The *BGB* went on to serve as a source and framework for civil law across the globe, exceeding even the influence of the French Code Civil. Pandectism also animated English jurists such as John Austin and Nathaniel Lindley in the late nineteenth century, and the commercial lawyers of twentieth-century America, many of whom had family connections to Germany and roots in the German universities; Friedrich Kessler and Karl Llewellyn were the exem-plars. The *BGB* was adopted by Meiji Japan, and spread thence to China and East Asia. This global influence has been the ultimate victory of the German historical schools of law, unforeseen by its own practitioners; and behind their victory lies the foundation of Gaius, Ulpian, and Justinian.[34]

Arguably the powerful continental legal-historical tradition just described has now itself slipped into historical memory, canceled by its own victories. It may have been fore-seen, even intended, that in a postcodification world, jurists should begin their work with

[31] 1872–1877.
[32] Otto Lenel, *Palingenesia Iuris Civilis* (1889); Otto Lenel, *Das Edictum Perpetuum* (1927).
[33] See James Q. Whitman, *The Legacy of Roman Law in the German Romantic Era* (1990); Michael John, *Politics and the Law in Late Nineteenth-Century Germany: The Origins of the Civil Code* (1989); Matthias Reimann, *Nineteenth Century German Legal Science*, 31 B.C. L. REV. 837 (1990).
[34] See Helmut Coing, *Europäisches Privatrecht* (1985).

contemporary interpretations of the relevant national civil code in their search for current answers. Historical study of the formation of the code and the pre-codal legal world therefore tends to be relegated to a domain of specialist scholarship. Some of the leading doctrinalists bring historical tools to bear in the interpretation of modern codified law.[35] But classical historical tradition no longer lies at the core of Civilian legal scholarship. With the formulation of the codes, the juristic mission was transformed; building up legal norms through adept use of historical material was no longer the dominant method.

III. Common Law Theory

Peter Birks suggested that in its manner of rule-making the common law more closely resembled Severan Roman jurisprudence than the codified continental systems that built on Justinian's *Corpus Juris*.[36] The royal chancery and the judges of England ran a pragmatic yet formulaic writ system harnessing local forensic and enforcement procedures. This separate development may explain why English law did not follow the European continent and take up a full Reception of Justinianic law, but rather preserved its native writ system. It was true that around 1100 there had been a direct infusion of Romanism in the language and content of the petty assizes whereby the royal courts of common law took over supervision of feudal estates by repressing illegal dispossessions. There were other entry points of Romanist ideas in the common law of covenant, of trespass, of servitudes, and nuisance. Henry de Bracton's extensive treatise on the common law, collated in the early thirteenth century, bears witness to the impact of glossatorial Roman law on the imagination of the elite lawyers of that time.[37] But there was a limit to influence; all these Civilian injections turned out to be a kind of inoculation, giving some structure and vocabulary to the developing English writ system without completely falling under the sway of Roman concepts and procedures. English lawyers were not interested in codification *tout court*, which was associated with overbearing centralized royal power. They could, however, admit legal change via court deliberations, which included interventions by the Court of Chancery and the High Court of Parliament, where many judges and lawyers sat and took a hand in drafting legislation. In a testy exchange in an early common-law court a judge cut off counsel who was offering an adventurous interpretation of a statute using these telling terms: "Do not gloss the statute for we know better than you; we made it."[38] Statutes were thus used to clear up uncertainties and controversies, to extend existing claims, or repress urgent mischiefs.

---

[35] See, e.g., Zimmermann, *supra* note 20; *Commentaries on European Contract Laws* (Nils Jansen & Reinhard Zimmermann eds., 2008).

[36] Peter Birks, *English Beginnings and Roman Parallels: Development of Common Law Relating to Early Roman Law*, 6 Irish Jurist 147 (1971).

[37] Henry de Bracton, *On the Laws and Customs of England* (Samuel E. Thorne ed. & trans., 1977).

[38] Aumeye v. Anon., Y.B. Mich. 33 Edw. 1, pl. 82 (1305) (Hengham, J.); Seipp No. 1305.118rs (referring to Statute of Westminster II, c. 2).

The common law mind was exhibited in the career of judge and jurist Matthew Hale (1609–1676), whose work provided a bridge from medieval to modern legal technique. Hale's contribution came in two seminal works of historical jurisprudence, *A History and Analysis of the Common Law of England* and the *Historia Placitorum Coronæ*, or *The History of the Pleas of the Crown*. The first history, originating probably in lectures at the Inns of Court in London, sets out the evolution of the common law almost entirely in terms of interlocking jurisdictions. Hale observes that the law of persons and things is distributed across a very wide range of writs in different court systems, including courts of Admiralty and church and prerogative courts. He argues that a unified system of substantive rights and wrongs and adjectival remedies emerges very late, with actions on the case for trespass proving a universal action in King's Bench, gathering business into that court. Hale's later work on criminal law is more abstract and rational in method. He innovated by isolating capacity as a subject matter and then expounding the distinct heads of crime as causes of action with structured elements, which could then be compared and general principles extracted. This drive to systematization distinguished Hale's work from the listings of historical writs of actions and detailed exposition of their operation, which had been the bedrock of juristic work by the great lawyers of the earlier eras such as Thomas Littleton and Edward Coke. By acknowledging that families of rules dealing with distinct subject matters could be identified independently of their procedural packaging, Hale quietly transformed English legal discourse.

In Hale's lengthy preface to Rolle's *Abridgment* in 1668, addressed squarely to students, practitioners, and we may surmise, fellow judges, he elevated the common lawyer's respect for settled precedents as the bedrock of the system. Hale acknowledged that reason, logic, and systemization had its place in legal exposition, but warned that explicit pursuit of policy or moralistic reform in curial decision-making should be resisted, since these modes of decision risked individual partiality and self-interest on the part of the judge. Common law doctrine expressed in historical precedent was "settled and known" as the collective thoughts of a dedicated legal community:

> The Common-Laws of *England* are not the product of the wisdom of some one man, or Society of men in any one Age; but of the Wisdom, Counsell, Experience and Observation of many ages of wise and observing men. . . . [T]he mutations have not been so much in the law as in the subject matter of it.[39]

Hale was reprising ideas promoted earlier by Sir Edward Coke, who stated that "Reason is the life of the law; nay, the common law itself is nothing else but reason."[40] But when Coke referred to "The law, which is perfection of reason," he clearly meant the collective

---

[39] Sir Matthew Hale, *Preface to Henry Rolle, Abridgment des Plusiers Cases et Resolutions del Common Ley*, iii–iv (1668). The abridgments showed the interlocking system of causes of action and suits by listing the *rationes* of judgments across centuries of English law-making. Rolle introduced more subject organization at the expense of detail, laying the basis for more conceptual modern treatise literatures a century later.

[40] Edward Coke, *The First Part of the Institutes of the Laws of England, or, A Commentary on Littleton* 97b, 80, 138 (1628).

wisdom of the common lawyers working within a normal science, not some natural analytical reason attained by solo ratiocination.[41] He said as much in his reported speech to King James denying the king any personal role as a judge, since the monarch

> was not learned in the Lawes of his Realm of England, and causes which concerne the life, or inheritance, or goods, or fortunes of his Subjects; they are not to be decided by naturall reason, but by the artificiall reason and judgment of Law, which Law is an art which requires long study and experience, before that a man can attain to the cognizance of it.[42]

Coke and Hale's defense of the common law mind was restated in Blackstone's *Commentaries on the Laws of England* (1765–1769), originating as lectures for genteel students at Oxford seeking a taste of the law outside the hard grind of practical lawyering at the Inns of Court. Blackstone added two new elements to Hale's method. One was an overtly Institutionalist ordering of the law, with copious references to the Justinianic system and to later Civilian literatures. The other was to apply the graceful tropes of Enlightenment natural philosophy to justify the moral norms of the law and so make the law more appealing to lay audiences. The impact of the work, especially in America, was incalculable.[43]

Blackstone's method was less influential in England itself. Practitioners continued to rely on vast digests of cases with cross-cutting headings based on the old registers of writs, organized more or less alphabetically.[44] Institutionalist treatises offering scientific organization of a specific legal subject matter were rare, with William Jones's *Essay on the Law of Bailments* (1781) being a stand-out exception. Most treatises resembled short abridgments, being collections of *rationes* loosely organized around the heads of writ and remedy. Interestingly, a new model of scientific treatise emerged in early nineteenth-century America, where classicism including Roman law was briefly prized as embodying a republican spirit to oppose to English feudalism and status hierarchy. The exemplar was Justice Joseph Story, whose treatises were polished, organized, argumentative, and rational. His work was brought out in English editions and made an enormous difference to expectations of legal literature. However, it was not until the later nineteenth century that a comparably polished English treatise literature appears, with great jurists including Anson, Dicey, Maitland, Pollock, and Salmond writing with an eye on transmission of common law doctrine to the empire in a lucid and commanding form.[45] Such jurists now

---

[41] A.W.B. Simpson, "The Common Law and Legal Theory," in *Oxford Essays in Jurisprudence: Second Series* 77–99 (A.W.B. Simpson ed., 1973); John H. Baker, *The Law's Two Bodies: Some Evidential Problems in English Legal History* (2001).

[42] Prohibitions del Roy (1607) 12 Co. Rep. 63, 65; 77 E.R. 1342, 1343.

[43] See Albert Alschuler, *Sir William Blackstone and the Shaping of American Law*, 144 NEW L.J. 896 (1994).

[44] Cf. Mike Macnair, "Institutional Taxonomy, Roman Forms and English Lawyers in the 17th and 18th Centuries," in *Pensiero Giuridico Occidentale e Giuristi Romani* 191–208 (2019).

[45] Cf. A.W.B. Simpson, *The Rise and Fall of the Legal Treatise: Legal Principles and the Forms of Legal Literature*, 48 U. CHI. L. REV. 632 (1981).

tended to be university professors rather than practitioners and were well versed in legal history and relevant branches of philosophy; yet their work basically tracked the thinking of the appellate judiciary, and for all their elegance they eschewed particular heuristics and mostly cleaved to a pragmatic functionalism.

Interestingly this was also the period when analytical jurisprudence began in earnest, as a subdiscipline remote from the textbook tradition, almost as if the heuristic and scientific tradition had been hived off as a specialism. John Austin was the pivotal figure in England, and Wesley Hohfeld a little later in the United States. The legal historians Frederic William Maitland and Oliver Wendell Holmes Jr. were also interested in legal analytics, but both looked to Germanist law and philosophy for ideas and were not much interested in Pandectism. In the past thirty years there has been a quiet Gaian revival in many of the English law schools, led by the charismatic Oxford jurist Peter Birks with his remodeling of the taxonomy of English obligations to include unjust enrichment and also to recharacterize equitable claims on a more scientific pattern.

Yet so far, American jurists have hardly been tempted by the classical traditions of historical doctrine. American legal thinking remains wedded to its pragmatic, realist, and functionalist schools, and while there is much legal history, it is not generally the history of juristic thought, but rather a demonstration of the ideological suppositions, the policy implications and real-world effects of legal decision-making.[46] This refusal of system arguably places too great a burden on the good sense and good will of lawyers every time they face a fresh decision, and courts the further risk that quickly calculated changes to reach instant solutions will set up fresh problems in adjacent or connected areas of law.[47] The New Private Law movement has suggested that practical legal reasoning may better be guided by an injection of doctrinal rigor, setting up the issues for decision by harnessing the analytical resources of precedential law. A deeper historical knowledge of the sources of our law can only strengthen this jurisprudential enterprise.

---

[46] Cf. G. Edward White, *Tort Law in America: An Intellectual History* (2d ed. 2003).
[47] Cf. Henry E. Smith, *The Persistence of System in Property Law*, 163 U. PA. L. REV. 2055 (2015).

CHAPTER 14

···

CIVIL AND COMMON LAW

···

LIONEL SMITH

I. INTRODUCTION

···

THIS chapter aims to answer the question, "what can the civil law tradition tell us about the New Private Law?" It seeks to do this by offering one civilian's perspective on private law, on U.S. private law, and on the New Private Law.[1]

In order to answer that question, it is necessary to say a little bit about what is a civilian perspective, or in other words, what makes a jurist a civilian. This is a question to which many different answers could be given. Having outlined my perspective on that question in section II, I will go on to say something (in section III) about the different perspective that a civilian may have on what is the domain of private law. In section IV, I will ask what insights the civilian's understanding of the discipline of law may offer to common lawyers. Section V is the conclusion.

II. WHAT MAKES A CIVILIAN PERSPECTIVE?

···

This is not an easy question. Many people will think immediately of the civil code, which is characteristic of the modern civilian tradition. The civil code is a very special document. In constitutional terms, it is only a statute. But it is much more than that. One distinguished civilian argued that it is, itself, a kind of constitution of civil society.[2] It is

---

[1] The author's first legal training was in the common law. In 2001, after joining the McGill Faculty of Law, he enrolled as a part-time undergraduate at the *Université de Montréal*, completing a second, civilian LLB studying exclusively private law subjects. He has taught common law and civil law at McGill and other institutions, and his private law scholarship is informed by both traditions.

[2] In a famous text, Jean Carbonnier noted that while France has had more than ten political constitutions since the Revolution, her real constitution is the Civil Code, largely unchanged since 1804: Jean Carbonnier, "Le Code civil," in *Les lieux de mémoire* 1331, 1345 (Pierre Nora ed., 1997); English translation, *Realms of Memory: Rethinking the French Past* (Pierre Nora ed., 1996).

the general juridical regulation of all interactions of citizens with one another. It is not the only regulation; civilian jurisdictions have consumer protection laws and laws about electronic payment systems just like everyone else. But it is the *general* law. It stands in relation to those special laws rather as the common law stands in relation to a statute in the common law tradition.[3] It is the starting point, to which exceptions may be made. If a codified civilian jurisdiction decides to create a trust and puts it in a special law, the message is that this is a particular thing that may be used in particular situations. If it decides to put it in the civil code, the message is that this is something for everyone. For a civilian, the civil code is freighted with symbolism.[4]

The centrality of the civil code, however, is more a consequence of the civilian mindset than the cause of it. One can be a civilian without a civil code. The Romans never had anything like one, and all civilian systems trace their origins to Roman law.[5] Nor were there any civil codes in Europe when Roman law took on its second life, as the *ius commune*. Civil codes are relative newcomers. The Republic of San Marino is said to be the oldest republic in the world, and also to be a "pure" civil law jurisdiction without a civil code.[6] South African private lawyers consider themselves to be civilians, and so usually do Scots private lawyers, and there is no civil code in either place. Conversely, the state of California has a Civil Code, and I do not understand Californian jurists to consider themselves to be civilians.[7]

---

[3] The Civil Code of Québec has a Preliminary Provision, which can be thought of as Article 0 since it comes before Article 1. In English, it reads:

"The Civil Code of Québec, in harmony with the *Charter of human rights and freedoms* and the general principles of law, governs persons, relations between persons, and property.

The Civil Code comprises a body of rules which, in all matters within the letter, spirit or object of its provisions, lays down the *jus commune*, expressly or by implication. In these matters, the Code is the foundation of all other laws, although other laws may complement the Code or make exceptions to it."

The Canadian constitution obliges the National Assembly of Quebec to legislate bilingually in English and French (Constitution Act, 1867, s. 133), but the legislator can perhaps be forgiven for resorting to Latin to render the phrase that in the French text is *droit commun*.

[4] In discussing the law of contracts, for example, civilians will characteristically distinguish the position as it is in civil law from the position in consumer law (see, e.g., Didier Lluelles & Benoît Moore, *Droit des obligations* § 2535 (3d ed. 2018)); the former is the generality, the latter is the special case.

[5] Not, however, all principles or rules of civilian systems are of Roman origin. Of course much of Roman law has long been abandoned, and conversely, many parts of modern civilian orders have other derivations. In French and Quebec law, the system of intestate succession derives mainly from French customary law; the Quebec principle of almost complete freedom of testation is of English origin.

[6] See Peter Stein, "Civil Law Reports and the Case of San Marino," in *The Character and Influence of the Roman Civil Law: Historical Essays* 115, 126 (Peter Stein ed., 1988), and the San Marino Declaration of the Rights of Citizens and of the Fundamental Principles of San Marino Law (Law of 8 July 1974, no. 59, as amended by art. 4 of the Constitutional Law of 26 February 2002, no. 36), whose art. 3 *bis*, 7th paragraph, provides (my translation): "In the absence of legislation, custom and the *ius commune* constitute supplementary sources of law."

[7] The California Civil Code derives from the codification projects of David Dudley Field, which were more successful in relation to civil procedure, although some other states enacted his civil code. Curiously, and unlike any civilian civil code I know, this Code enacted as law a series of "maxims of jurisprudence," some of which can be traced to the final title of Justinian's *Digest*, 50.17 (see also Peter Stein, *Civil Law Maxims in Moral Philosophy*, 48 TULANE L. REV. 1075 (1974)). These are a mix of aids to interpretation and rebuttable presumptions. Thus it is apparently the law of California that "One must

How else then may we try to understand what is a civilian? F.H. Lawson was a distinguished English jurist who understood both traditions as well as anyone. A Romanist and the first holder of Oxford's Chair of Comparative Law, he was learned in the civil law in its origins and in its modern manifestations; learned, too, in the common law, taking his second first-class degree in Jurisprudence at Oxford, being called to the English Bar, and eventually writing on the common law of property, that most idiosyncratic aspect of the genius of the common law.[8] In the 1950s he gave the Cooley Lectures at the University of Michigan, in the published version of which he said:

> The civilian likes to be able to see clearly the shape and limits of the abstract concepts and doctrines with which he has to work before he starts to work with them. Moreover, the law resembles the game of chess: the concepts must move according to clear and definite rules; and indeed very often they are like the pieces in chess, which are defined only in terms of the moves they can make. The common lawyer is much more inclined to use a concept of half-known outline as soon as he knows it is capable of performing the actual limited task he wants it to perform, leaving for further consideration what its other possibilities may be. Common law concepts are much more like human beings whose personalities become known only by experience and may easily change in course of time.[9]

Lawson, of course, is not the only one who has articulated a distinction that is based on the difference between conceptualism on the one hand, and pragmatism and casuistic reasoning on the other.[10] One of the most perfect examples of this kind of common law reasoning comes, appropriately, from the law reports. In a dispute resolved by the English Court of Appeal in 1975, a landlord—the lord of the manor and a member of the

---

not change his purpose to the injury of another" (art. 3512), "He who takes the benefit must bear the burden" (art. 3521), "For every wrong there is a remedy" (art. 3523), and "Superfluity does not vitiate" (art. 3537). Article 3509 clarifies that "The maxims of jurisprudence hereinafter set forth are intended not to qualify any of the foregoing provisions of this code, but to aid in their just application." For an argument that the corresponding maxims have been misused in Montana, see Scott J. Burnham, *Let's Repeal the Field Code!*, 67 MONT. L. REV. 31, 32, 52 (2006).

[8] In 1958 Lawson published the first volume in the Clarendon Law Series, *Introduction to the Law of Property*. In its current form (Frederick H. Lawson & Bernard Rudden, *The Law of Property* (3d ed. 2002)), it remains unique for its combination of accessibility and breadth of vision. Bernard Rudden, Lawson's successor as Professor of Comparative Law, joined for the second edition, published in 1982 just before Lawson's death in 1983. You know that a book is conceptual when twenty years and more can rightly be allowed to elapse between editions.

[9] Frederick H. Lawson, *A Common Lawyer Looks at the Civil Law* 66 (1953).

[10] In this chapter, when I use the ideas of "casuistry" and "casuistic" reasoning, it is not in any pejorative sense, even though most dictionary definitions of these words are negative and assimilate casuistry to quibbling and sophistry. What I mean by "casuistry" is reasoning by concrete examples and through drawing distinctions between cases. See Paul du Plessis, *Borkowski's Textbook on Roman Law* 46 (5th ed. 2015): "The character of classical legal writing [i.e., in the first two and a half centuries CE in the Roman Empire] was primarily casuistic, i.e. involving extensive discussion of cases, both actual and hypothetical. There was little abstract reasoning, philosophical inquiry, or historical content." See also François X. Testu, "Casuistique," in *Dictionnaire de la culture juridique* 169 (2003), linking this mode of reasoning to the emergence of the case law method of teaching in the United States.

House of Lords—had delivered a notice to one of the tenant farmers, aimed at terminating the farmer's lease so that the farmer would have to vacate the farmhouse and the land.[11] Required to give a year's notice, he came to the house (with a witness) and finding that it had no mailbox or mail slot, he slid the envelope containing the notice under the door. The evidence of the farmer and his wife was that five months later, they found the envelope underneath the linoleum floor covering when they were replacing it. They said that the notice must have gone under the linoleum when it was pushed under the door. Since the notice had to be given a year in advance of the date of termination, they argued that it had not been validly served. The trial judge did not believe their story and ordered them to leave. In the Court of Appeal, the parties asked the Court to resolve the point of law that would arise on the assumption that their account was accurate. Was the notice validly served through the landlord's doing an objectively reasonable act aimed at delivering it to the tenant? Or did valid service depend on the tenant's actually acquiring subjective awareness of the notice?

This question would typically be resolved by a civilian through the use of juristic concepts and categories. She might ask: is service of a notice to quit a *juridical act*—an act of a party that has legal effects through the intention of that party to bring about those effects?[12] Or is it rather a *juridical fact*—a fact that brings about effects in law, without regard to anyone's intentions in that respect?[13] If it were a juridical act, it would be subject to a set of general rules; for example, it could probably be annulled if it were delivered by mistake. Classifying it as a juridical act would raise further questions: is it a unilateral juridical act (like the making of a will or the forgiveness of a debt) or a bilateral one (like the making of a contract)? If it were unilateral, then one party alone could bring about the legal effect, but if bilateral, then the consent of both parties would be required. Such is the conceptual approach.

The traditional approach of the common law is, in my view, wonderfully illustrated by a question asked during oral argument. Counsel for the tenant argued that there was no valid service unless the notice was served in such a way that it was observable by the tenant. The recorded reaction of one member of the panel was the following:

STAMP L.J.: Suppose the dog eats it?[14]

Of course it would be overly simplistic to contrast the conceptualist civilian with the casuistic common lawyer. The classical Roman lawyers were quite casuistic, as the *Digest*

---

[11] Lord Newborough v. Jones, [1975] Ch. 90.

[12] France Allard et al., *Private Law Dictionary and Bilingual Lexicons—Obligations* (Les Éditions Yvon Blais 2003), online: https://nimbus.mcgill.ca/pld-ddp/dictionary/search, s.v. "juridical act": "Manifestation of intention of one or more persons in a manner and form designed to produce effects in law."

[13] *Id.*, s.v. "juridical fact²": "Occurrence to which the law attaches legal effects independently of the will of the persons concerned." The superscripted figure in my reference indicates that I am quoting the second (of two) defined senses of the expression.

[14] Lord Newborough v. Jones, *supra* note 11, at 93. The tenant lost. In the terms of the civilian categories set out previously, the court can be understood to have concluded that the service was a unilateral juridical act which the landlord had validly performed in due time.

of Justinian shows.[15] But the civilian way of thinking evolved. We can perhaps attribute the conceptualism of the civilian tradition to the rise of the modern university, almost a thousand years ago, bringing with it the birth of law as a university discipline. Since that time, for civilians the study of law begins with a text of law. For the first university civilians, that text was the *Corpus Iuris Civilis*, the "body" of the civil law. Now it is usually a civil code. It was the increasing conceptualism of the civil law that led to the systematization of the chaotically organized material in the *Digest*.[16] This in turn—along, of course, with nineteenth-century nationalism—led to the rise of civil codes.[17] Conceptualism may demand a code, since a code takes many positions on concepts and disputed points, even if it cannot always resolve them or exhaust the universe of juristic concepts.[18]

Of course, the common law has always had concepts. Littleton's *Tenures*, first published in the late fifteenth century, is at least as conceptually sophisticated as anything appearing contemporaneously on the Continent of Europe. Many property law courses are taught in the twenty-first century in the law faculties of the common law world in roughly the same way that they were taught a hundred years ago, stressing the distinctions between vested and contingent interests, and within the former, between those that are vested in interest and those that are vested in possession, and between those that are defeasible and those that are determinable. These are hard-edged, conceptual distinctions and mastering them requires conceptual legal reasoning. To say that an interest is vested not contingent, even though it is only vested in interest and not vested in possession, and even though it is defeasible, is a highly conceptual conclusion that has very practical consequences; for example, that interest is not subject to the rule against perpetuities.

The common law is now a university discipline, but this is a recent development. Roughly contemporaneous with the founding of the first universities was the birth of English law as a new start, a separate body of law.[19] It was not a university discipline but

---

[15] This, of course, is another generalization. Gaius, whose *Institutes* were the foundation of Justinian's *Institutes*, aimed to adopt a conceptual approach and the result was a kind of juridical immortality. See Peter Birks & Grant McLeod, "Introduction," in *Justinian's Institutes* 7, 16–18 (Peter Birks & Grant McLeod trans., 1987), and Joshua Getzler, "Historical Perspectives," in this volume.

[16] Stein observes that only in the sixteenth century were jurists willing to suggest that the disorderly presentation of the *Digest* could be improved upon: Peter Stein, *The Quest for a Systematic Civil Law*, 90 PROCEEDINGS OF THE BRITISH ACADEMY 147, 154 (1995): "For the first time the content of Justinian's law was separated from its form, for the humanist systematisers combined enormous respect for the substance of Roman law, with complete disregard for the way it was presented."

[17] René David & John E. C. Brierley, *Major Legal Systems in the World Today* 63–65 (3d ed. 1985); Franz Wieacker, *A History of Private Law in Europe* 363–366 (Tony Weir trans., 1995); Peter Stein, *Roman Law in European History* 110–111 (1999).

[18] A good example is the development in French law of the concept of the "patrimony," which took place with very little codal support: Nicholas Kasirer, *Translating Part of France's Legal Heritage: Aubry and Rau on the* Patrimoine, 38 R.G.D. 453 (2008); Alexandra Popovici, "Trusting Patrimonies," in *Trusts and Patrimonies* 199 (R. Valsan ed., 2015). Perhaps paradoxically for my suggestion that conceptualism is more central in the civilian tradition than the presence of a civil code, Michele Graziadei rightly points out that in the years following the enactment of a civil code, there may be less room for conceptualism as scholarship is dominated by exegesis of the new text: see, e.g., Stein, *supra* note 17, at 123.

[19] Or more than one: John H. Baker, *The Law's Two Bodies* (2001).

the pragmatic resolution of disputes according to custom and precedent.[20] The common law *could* not become a university discipline until after the day of Blackstone, who was the first professor of the common law in the late eighteenth century.[21] It *did* not become a university discipline until about a hundred years later.[22] It is no wonder that common law reasoning remains casuistic. But nineteenth-century academic jurists of the common law were happy to work with juristic concepts (even if many of them were, tellingly, borrowed from the civil law).[23]

Thus I do not say that the common law tradition lacks concepts or is anti-conceptual. Such a position would be crude and indefensible. I only suggest (as Lawson did) that in the civil law, concepts tend to come first. In the tradition of the common law, more likely to come first is casuistry: reasoning by cases and examples, and seeking the crucial distinctions between them, which generates intuitions or conclusions about the correct outcomes. More likely to come afterward is the use of inductive conceptual reasoning to make sense of those outcomes. Nor is it any wonder that while a civilian is used to treating a text of law, whether Digest, code, or statute, as a natural starting point, a common lawyer tends to think of statute law as an intrusion on the seamless web of the law.

These contrasts may shed some light on the evolution of academic discourse in the common law, an evolution that now includes the New Private Law. Some years ago, Lawson himself discussed the ways in which the academic branch of the common law was becoming more civilian.[24] More recently Peter Birks, like Lawson a Romanist and a common lawyer, inspired a whole generation of scholars to be more conceptual. Anyone

---

[20] Those who say that stare decisis is a relatively recent phenomenon must be speaking of its formalized manifestation. The Year Books, which date from the reign of Edward I (1272–1307), are indicative of the common law's respect for precedent; they are not official records but the notes of observers. Nor are these the earliest reports of cases; it is now possible to read meticulously edited and translated reports from late in the reign of Henry III (1216–1272): *The Earliest English Law Reports*, vol. I (Paul Brand ed., 1996); *The Earliest English Law Reports*, vol. III (Paul Brand ed., 2005). Privately made reports of pleading in cases were created, it seems, for learning the law: John H. Baker, *An Introduction to English Legal History* 178–179 (4th ed. 2002); but you can only learn the law from the cases if the cases make the law. See also Joshua Getzler, "Historical Perspectives," this volume.

Again, it is important not to be dogmatic; in different ways at different times and places, civilians may see case law as a source of law (to use the civilian term), and to that extent law reports are needed. See Stein, *supra* note 6; Mathieu Devinat, *La règle prétorienne en droit civil français et dans la common law canadienne : étude de méthodologie juridique comparée* (2005); Stefan Vogenaur, "Sources of Law and Legal Method in Comparative Law," in *The Oxford Handbook of Comparative Law* 877, especially 898–899 (Mathias Reimann & Reinhard Zimmermann eds., 2d ed. 2019).

[21] Until then, the only law taught in England's universities was Civil law and Canon law (Baker, *supra* note 20, at 170); unless we count the Inns of Court and Chancery as a university: John H. Baker, *The Third University of England* (1990).

[22] Baker, *supra* note 20, at 171–172.

[23] The borrowing of civil law concepts in the elaboration of textbooks on contract and tort, following the abolition of the forms of action in the mid-nineteenth century, is discussed in Lionel Smith, *Common Law and Equity in R3RUE*, 68 Wash. & Lee L. Rev. 1185, 1189–1191 (2011). For the borrowing of a civilian idea of unjust enrichment later in the century, see Andrew Kull, *James Barr Ames and the Early Modern History of Unjust Enrichment*, 25 Oxford J. Legal Stud. 297 (2005).

[24] Frederick H. Lawson, "Doctrinal Writing: A Foreign Element in English Law?," in *Ius Privatum Gentium: Festschrift für Max Rheinstein* 191 (Ernst von Caemmerer et al. eds., 1969).

who thinks that Birks did not bring a new way of thinking to the legal academy was not there at the time.[25] In his own subject matter, the law of restitution, his scholarship was a counterpoint to *Goff and Jones on the Law of Restitution*, which was at the time not particularly conceptual but rather casuistic and deferential to authority.[26] The long tradition of the common law may be changing, but it has not gone away. Birks's project of systematizing private law in the common law along civilian lines provoked some strong reactions.[27] His approach to legal scholarship has been characterized by some judges of the High Court of Australia as illegitimate "top-down" legal reasoning.[28]

Another sign that the long casuistic tradition of the common law will not disappear overnight is the degree of deference shown by some common law scholars toward the courts. Lord Goff of Chieveley told an anecdote that a young German student once said to him that "In Germany, the professor is God; in England, the judge is God."[29] Of course, in the common law judges make the law, which is not true, or not true in the same way, in the civil law, and since university jurists are theorizing the law it may be natural for them to treat those who make it with deference. And yet, it does not follow that a scholar should set their research agenda on the basis of what the courts did or said last week; and no scholar is bound by any judgment of any court. In 1999, there was a big reform of the rules of civil procedure for England and Wales, which involved some efforts to update terminology. For example, what used to be called a "Mareva injunction," named for a case,[30] thenceforth was to be called a "freezing injunction."[31] For no obvious reason, although the rules retain the word "defendant" for defendants, they use the word "claimant" for plaintiffs.[32] I have never ceased to be astonished by the fact that since then, every English law journal and legal publisher has stopped using the word "plaintiff" and

---

[25] For a view from Germany, see Martin Flohr, *Rechtsdogmatik in England* (2017), reviewed in English by Michele Graziadei, *Not on the Other Side of the Channel!*, 27 RECHTSGESCHICHTE—LEGAL HISTORY 362 (2019) online http://rg.rg.mpg.de/en/.

[26] See now the retitled Charles Mitchell et al., *Goff & Jones: The Law of Unjust Enrichment* (9th ed. 2016).

[27] Paul Matthews, *Review: English Private Law*, 6 JERSEY L. REV. 115 (2002). For a reaction to Birks's final book, which suggested a civilian orientation for the law of unjust enrichment, see Steve Hedley, *The Empire Strikes Back? A Restatement of the Law of Unjust Enrichment*, 28 MELB. U. L. REV. 759 (2004). For a more sympathetic review of *English Private Law* from a bijural scholar, see Nicholas Kasirer, *English Private Law, Outside-In*, 3 OXFORD U. COMMONWEALTH L.J. 249 (2003).

[28] Carmine Conte, *From Only the "Bottom-up"? Legitimate Forms of Judicial Reasoning in Private Law*, 35 OXFORD J. LEGAL STUD. 1 (2015).

[29] Robert Goff, *The Search for Principle*, 69 PROCEEDINGS OF THE BRITISH ACADEMY 169, 185 (1983); republished as Robert Goff, "The Search for Principle," in *The Search for Principle: Essays in Honour of Lord Goff of Chieveley* 313, 327 (William Swadling & Gareth Jones eds., 1999). Conversely, in one of his most brilliant texts, Peter Birks said of academic legal literature's being taken seriously by English practitioners and judges, "[t]he situation which we take for granted is a situation which is no older than the Second World War." Peter Birks, *The Academic and the Practitioner*, 18 LEGAL STUD. 397, 398 (1998).

[30] Mareva Compania Naviera SA v. Int'l Bulkcarriers SA, [1975] 2 Lloyd's Rep. 509, [1980] 1 All E.R. 213.

[31] Civil Procedure Rules, Practice Direction 25A.

[32] *Id.*, Part 2, 2.3(1): "'claimant' means a person who makes a claim; . . . 'defendant' means a person against whom a claim is made."

instead used the word "claimant." Why should the rules of court change the English language? Why should they change the language of a discipline? The *Oxford English Dictionary* finds the earliest known use of "plaintiff" in 1325, and that in a statute.[33] When university jurists treat judges and practitioners as holding ultimate authority, they risk confusing law as a community of practice and law as an academic discipline. But that tendency is itself a legacy of the history of the common law.

III. WHAT IS THE DOMAIN OF PRIVATE LAW?

This brief section asks, what exactly is the domain or scope of private law? The civilian may also have a different answer to this question.

Near the beginning of Justinian's *Institutes* we read:

> There are two aspects of the subject: public and private. Public law is concerned with the organization of the Roman state, while private law is about the well-being of individuals. Our business is private law. . . . All our law is about persons, things or actions.[34]

The division into persons, things, and actions has evolved over the centuries, but the foundational division between public law and private law remains central to civilian thought. The centrality of the civil code, where it exists, has already been mentioned. In civilian discourse, one is far more likely to encounter the expression "civil law" than the expression "private law." The Romans called their private law *ius civilis*, which means "the law for citizens," because it governed Romans and not others.[35] This is the expression that gives us the label "civil code."[36]

Although Roman law did not have a civil code in the modern sense, the civil code of today embodies the civilian idea of private law.[37] It is interesting, however, to note that its scope may be much wider than the understanding of "private law" that is held by many of those working in the common law world on what is now often called "private law

---

[33] *Oxford English Dictionary* online: https://www.oed.com, s.v. "plaintiff." The evolution noted there shows that the word existed in Middle English, meaning that it is older than the modern English language.

[34] Justinian, *Institutes*, *supra* note 15, at I.1.4; I.2.12.

[35] For more discussion of the meanings of "civil," see Peter Birks & Grant McLeod, "Introduction," *id.* at 8–9.

[36] The German *Bürgerliches Gesetzbuch* is translated into English as "civil code" for the same reasons, the elements referring to a legal code for citizens.

[37] For this reason, one scholar criticized the Civil Code of Québec on the basis, among others, that it contained provisions that belonged in special laws or even in administrative regulations: Pierre Legrand, *Bureaucrats at Play: The New Quebec Civil Code*, 10 BRIT. J. CANADIAN STUD. 52 (1995). For the story of how he could not get the article published in Quebec, see Pierre Legrand, *Comparative Contraventions*, 50 McGILL L.J. 669 (2005).

theory." Every civil code has provisions on the law of persons, a field that is hard to find in the common law. This includes the legal persons that are creatures of the law, but also extensive rules about natural persons: rules on names, and decision-making for and on behalf of children and others who lack full legal capacity, and on the steps by which a child typically becomes fully autonomous in law. The code probably regulates the problems that arise when a person goes missing. It also has extensive provisions on what a common lawyer would call family law. These govern filiation, which is the identification of a juridical parent-child relationship, and the obligations that ensue. The code regulates who can marry, the obligational and property effects of marriage, the effects of divorce, and the "marital regimes" that govern the property of the parties during the marriage and on its end, by death or otherwise. The code contains a full regulation of the law of succession, both testate and intestate.

In other words, for the civilian private law is not demarcated as the implementation of a particular kind of justice but as a field of justice, that between citizens. Much of a civil code can be understood as implementing norms of corrective or commutative justice. But think about the rules that tell you who shall benefit when a person dies intestate. Shall everything go to the surviving spouse? What if it is a de facto spouse? Or should some go to the children, and if so, how much? The public interest in the contract of marriage is evident in many ways, not least of them being that the parties must generally go to court to dissolve this particular contract. And yet family law and succession are, for the civilian, clearly part of civil (or private) law; indeed they are at the core of it.

One reading of the evolution of private law theory in the common law world in recent decades is that it is concerned with a much narrower field. Many scholars pay very little attention, for example, to family law and the law of inheritance. This may simply reflect differences of opinion as to what is foundational, although I suspect that it may reflect a deeper divergence of views as to what is definitional about private law. If the unity of private law is thought to lie in a principle, like corrective justice, it will have a different scope than that which civilians assign to it.[38] The civilian conception is that civil law, being all the law that applies between citizens, may call on a range of principles.[39]

The evolution of the New Private Law in respect of its scope and ambition will certainly be watched by civilians.[40]

---

[38] The hugely (and justly) influential Ernest J. Weinrib, *The Idea of Private Law* (1995), which argues that private law instantiates corrective justice, does not address succession or family law. Nicholas J. McBride, *The Humanity of Private Law* (2019), argues that private law aims to promote human flourishing; it makes reference to marriage and succession.

[39] Cf. Hanoch Dagan, *The Limited Autonomy of Private Law*, 56 Am. J. Comp. L. 809 (2008), who invokes family property law in support of an argument that private law in some situations aims to promote social values beyond the bilateral right-duty relationship between the parties.

[40] The present volume reflects a wide vision of private law, including Margaret F. Brinig, "New Private Law and the Family," this volume.

IV. What Does the Civil Law Have to Teach Private Law, Old or New?

The common law of trusts is a field driven by practice. In recent decades it has begun to attract substantial theoretical debate. But some examples will show how the field has been affected by an absence of conceptualism, and this may carry wider lessons for other parts of private law.[41]

One of the most important cases in the Commonwealth in recent decades is *McPhail v. Doulton*.[42] The trustees of a trust were obliged (not merely empowered) to distribute property among a class of beneficiaries who were not named but described; they included the relatives and dependants of anyone who worked for, or who had worked for, a particular company. Was this valid? The House of Lords said, by a bare majority, that it was; such a loosely defined class of trust beneficiaries was acceptable.[43] The leading speech of Lord Wilberforce, still read by law students all over the world, is wholly pragmatic in its reasoning. The decision was one of several that have engendered a situation in which trust drafters feel free to create trusts in which the obligations of trustees are almost completely undefined. The property goes to whomever they choose.[44]

What would a civilian say? A trustee owes a range of obligations to the beneficiaries of the trust, including the core of the trust itself which is traditionally defined as an obligation relating to the benefit of the trust assets. In the civil law there is a general theory of obligations. Within that theory, a legal obligation needs a debtor and creditor.[45] Of course, it is possible to have joint debtors or joint creditors; there can be more than one person on either or both ends of the obligation. But the idea that a person—a trustee—can owe an obligation relating to the benefit of property to a class that includes the "relatives and dependants" of everyone who ever worked for a company would be seen as

---

[41] I mentioned earlier (text *supra* after note 18) that the common law has a long history of its own conceptual apparatus in relation to estates in land, and also (*supra* note 23) that common law jurists borrowed civilian concepts in relation to the law of obligations. For the law of trusts, as they are understood in the common law, there was nothing to borrow.

[42] McPhail v. Doulton, [1971] A.C. 424.

[43] It is important to underline that this was not a case in which the trustees were only empowered to distribute the funds among the class; a wide class of objects is acceptable in such a case. In fact, whether the trustees were obliged or only empowered was an issue of interpretation in the case, but it was held unanimously that they were obliged to distribute the property. The implication is that the members of the class did not have merely a hope of receiving something; as a class, they had an entitlement. Traditionally, at least, this means that as individuals, they had the rights of trust beneficiaries to enforce the trust, which encompasses rights to demand information about the trust and its holdings, and about trustee investment and other decisions, and rights to enforce the fiduciary and other duties of the trustees.

[44] Lionel Smith, *Massively Discretionary Trusts*, 70 C.L.P. 17 (2017).

[45] The words "debtor" and "creditor" are not used only for money claims but as labels that apply to all obligations.

impossible, just as it would be impossible to owe an obligation to pay $100 to such an undefined group. That is not what an obligation means in civil law.[46]

The common law traditionally refuses to permit non-charitable purpose trusts. You cannot, for example, create a trust whose purpose is to improve the alphabet of the English language.[47] The decision in *McPhail* can be seen as a watering down of that refusal.[48] The rule against such trusts is explained in different ways, sometimes by saying that there is no one to enforce the trust, or that such trusts create obligations of uncertain scope. Conceptually, the explanation is that a trust is an obligation relating to property, and an obligation needs a creditor. The civilian might object to the alphabet-improvement trust at a higher level as well, based on the theory of the patrimony which, among other things, says that one is responsible for one's actions and that such responsibility is exigible against one's assets.[49] At a general level, this way of thinking forbids the possibility that a person could at one and the same time alienate property (making it unavailable to his creditors) while remaining the ongoing author of the purposes for which that property can be used. *Donner et retenir ne vaut.*[50]

A similar story is visible in U.S. trust law. If the New Private Law has recently emerged in U.S. legal scholarship, what is the Old Private Law? My understanding is that the New Private Law is new in being a reaction to the dominant voice of U.S. legal scholarship in the twentieth century, which was characterized by a particular kind of interaction between law and a certain understanding of economics. That dominant voice denied that there was any interesting distinction between public and private law; both are just forms of regulation with similar justifications.[51] If that be the Old Private Law, then we might describe as the Really Old Private Law the U.S. legal scholarship of the nineteenth century, which is more recognizable in its methodology and epistemology to civilians and to common law jurists from other jurisdictions.[52]

---

[46] The common law "duty of care" is often owed to an undefined class. In the civil law, liability for careless harm is understood to arise from fault, usually without the analysis of a preexisting duty of care, although paradoxically it appears that the common law on this point was developed under the influence of civilians of the natural law school: David Ibbetson, *How the Romans Did for Us: Ancient Roots of the Tort of Negligence*, 26 U.N.S.W. L.J. 475 (2003). A civilian, however, is likely to use "duty" as a wider word than "obligation" (Allard et al., *supra* note 12, s.v. "obligation²," contrasted with "obligation¹," a wider sense that corresponds to "duty"). An obligation in this narrow sense, like the obligation of a trustee or an obligation to pay damages, is enforceable in court and is part of the creditor's patrimony. It complies with the general theory of obligations. A duty to take care is not directly enforceable, the benefit of it is not a patrimonial asset, and it is not subject to the general theory of obligations.

[47] Re Shaw, [1957] 1 W.L.R. 729.

[48] That is, if such trusts were permitted there could have been no problem with the trust in *McPhail*; the decision was an expansion of which trusts could be validly created without infringing the prohibition.

[49] See the citations *supra* note 18.

[50] A maxim of old French customary law, which means, loosely, "you can't have your cake and eat it too."

[51] See John C.P. Goldberg, *Introduction: Pragmatism and Private Law*, 125 HARV. L REV. 1640, 1641 (2012).

[52] In the traditions of France and Quebec, the *ancien droit* is the expression for the uncodified law (whether customary or Roman in origin) that was in place before codification. It may be treated as a source of wisdom even if it is no longer formally a source of law.

The founders of American Legal Realism, which led to the Old Private Law, attacked what they called the formalism of the Really Old Private Law.

> For the last few dark and stormy decades, ever since it irreversibly dismantled its formalist home, legal scholarship has been traipsing from door to door, looking for a methodological refuge. The doors at which it has knocked have included literature, philosophy, economics, political science, and sociology. Most of the residents have turned legal scholarship away with a meager handout and an explanation that they had problems enough of their own. Economics, which suffers few such doubts, invited it in and tried to gobble it up.[53]

It is unlikely that people of the intelligence of O.W. Holmes Jr. and Karl Llewellyn intended to attack the conceptualism of law, but it is arguable that this was exactly the result.[54]

Andrew Kull has told the story of how the legal realist Thurman Arnold mocked the conceptualism of Austin Scott when Scott released tentative drafts of the first *Restatement of Trusts*.[55] The outcome, Kull suggests, was Scott's decision that constructive trusts would be left out and placed instead in the *Restatement of Restitution*—even though a constructive trust is, conceptually, a trust, and even though many constructive trusts have nothing to do with unjust enrichment.[56]

Another example comes from the use of trusts as will substitutes. On one account that has been highly influential, people should be allowed to avoid the rules on formalities for wills by creating instead revocable inter vivos trusts, but the law should not accept the seemingly inevitable consequence that the beneficiaries of an existing trust have a present interest and therefore rights of due administration, even if their interest be defeasible.[57] This seems to defy the conceptual logic of both wills and trusts. Surely you

---

[53] Edward L. Rubin, *Law and and the Methodology of Law*, 1997 WIS. L. REV. 521, 521.

[54] For a longer argument about how the pragmatism of legal realism evolved into skepticism about the concepts internal to private law, see Goldberg, *supra* note 51, at 1645–1648. Hanoch Dagan aims to rehabilitate American Legal Realism in Hanoch Dagan, *Reconstructing American Legal Realism & Rethinking Private Law Theory* (2013). I make no claim here about what it was, or is, or should be, but I do make a historical claim about one of its effects. Chaim Saiman argues that when American Legal Realism removed conceptual analysis from private law, other fields—public, procedural, and statutory law—took over the role of "general law" and became loci for conceptual analysis: Chaim N. Saiman, *The Domain of Private Law: Conceptual Thought in Anglo American Law* (2019), online at https://ssrn.com/abstract=3324016.

[55] Andrew Kull, *Restitution and Reform*, 32 S. ILL. U. L.J. 83, 90–92 (2007).

[56] The current *Restatement (Third) of Restitution and Unjust Enrichment* maintains (§ 55, cmts. *a*, *b*, and *c*) that all constructive trusts are creatures of unjust enrichment, and yet itself gives examples of those that are not (§ 55, illus. 21 and 22 and cmt. *j*: constructive trusts that enforce agreements). For a fuller discussion, see Lionel Smith, *Legal Epistemology in the* Restatement (Third) of Restitution and Unjust Enrichment, 92 B.U. L. REV. 899 (2012).

[57] John H. Langbein, *The Nonprobate Revolution and the Future of the Law of Succession*, 97 HARV. L REV. 1108, 1126–1129 (1984); see also Robert H. Sitkoff & Jesse Dukeminier, *Wills, Trusts, and Estates*

either tried to give an asset, or an interest, with effect only on your death—in which case you tried to make a will and must use the mandatory form—or, if you have avoided that, it must be because you gave it (or some right to it) away while you were still alive.[58] The only alternative seems to be that you have done neither, and legally or at least beneficially, the property is still yours; *donner et retenir ne vaut*.[59] To put it another way: if your revocable inter vivos trust did not create a present interest in another person in the relevant property, then when you die, that property is entirely yours and will fall into your estate, which is exactly what the trust was supposed to avoid.[60]

Whether or not the outcome can be attributed to American Legal Realists, the civilian (and even the common law jurist from outside the United States) cannot avoid being struck by the pragmatism of some aspects of U.S. law. Pragmatism can be helpful, practical, and liberating, but when it starts to disregard concepts, the results can be unpredictable.[61]

444–453 (10th ed. 2017), agreeing with Langbein's argument and showing how it has persuaded some courts and is reflected in § 603 of the Uniform Trust Code (2000, as amended 2004), enacted in many states. The matter is also discussed in John D. Morley & Robert H. Sitkoff, "Trust Law," this volume.

[58] The U.S. law in this area is described as a "theoretical mish-mash" in the leading treatise, Austin W. Scott, William F. Fratcher, & Mark L. Ascher, *Scott and Ascher on Trusts*, vol. 2, § 10.8 (4th ed. 2006).

[59] If a person purports to constitute themself the trustee of a trust, but retains full and beneficial control over the trust property through the holding of non-fiduciary powers over that property, then even according to the terms of the documentation there may be no effective creation of a trust (a point left open in *Clayton v. Clayton*, [2016] NZSC 29). In other words, nothing at all happened in law when the trust was supposedly created. This is because conceptually a trust is an obligation relating to the benefit of property, and if the trustee can do whatever he or she wishes with the trust property, there is no genuine obligation and therefore no trust. The majority U.S. position (*supra* note 57) is that the settlor/trustee owes no duties while alive; it is unclear what definition of "trust" makes this possible.

Conceptually different, but having a similar effect, is the idea of the "sham" trust that is increasingly important in the common law world. This is a situation in which a person creates the form of a trust but without any intention that the formal terms of the trust be complied with (see Antle v. R., 2010 FCA 280; JSC Mezhdunarodniy Promyshlenniy Bank v. Pugachev, [2017] EWHC 2426). If the documentation is a sham, the formal terms of the trust will not be treated as effective. But, of course, if the trust were a sham, it would not be effective as a will substitute.

Under either theory, the settlor remains the full beneficial owner. The property would pass to his or her estate on death and the trust, since it did not create any interests in others while the "settlor" was alive, would be ineffective as a will substitute.

[60] The U.S. position creates the result that a person can opt out of testamentary formalities so long as they call their document a revocable trust rather than a will, even though the legal effects are identical (Langbein, *supra* note 57, at 1129–1130). The position elsewhere in the common law world is that since testamentary formalities are mandatory, it is the law that must decide which dispositions are testamentary and therefore attract those mandatory rules. What makes a disposition testamentary is not the name of the document but the substantive legal characteristic that it operates to transfer a testator's property upon death: Baird v. Baird, [1990] 2 A.C. 548. If it seems paradoxical that the U.S. law looks to form and not substance, this is in a context in which courts and scholars apparently aim to assist people to avoid an inefficient and expensive probate system.

[61] No legal tradition or jurisdiction is immune from questionable legislation, but it is arguable that the pragmatism of U.S. trust law is encouraging the client-driven enactment of state legislation that is objectionable from the point of view of the coherence of the legal system: Lionel Smith, *Give the People What They Want? The Onshoring of the Offshore*, 103 Iowa L. Rev. 2155 (2018).

v. CONCLUSION

From a civilian perspective, the future of the New Private Law will be interesting indeed. Will it avoid the deference to practitioners that characterized the Really Old Private Law and still characterizes private law in some parts of the common law world?[62] Will it fall into the habit of the Old Private Law, that seems to equate conceptualism with legal fiction? Finally, will it approach other disciplines on the basis that the law can engage with them as an equal partner, rather than being treated as a conceptually empty shell that has everything to learn and nothing to teach?[63] If it can meet these challenges, there is every reason to think that the New Private Law will be the most interesting private law we have seen yet.

ACKNOWLEDGMENTS

I thank Andrew Gold, Michele Graziadei, and Alexandra Popovici for insightful comments.

---

[62] For suggestions that the New Private Law aims to combine respect for private law's self-understanding with external perspectives and criteria, see Goldberg, *supra* note 51, and Andrew S. Gold, "Internal and External Perspectives," this volume.

[63] For a rare attempt to turn the tables, see Bruce Chapman, *Legal Analysis of Economics: Solving the Problem of Rational Commitment*, 79 CHI.-KENT L. REV. 471 (2004).

PART II

CORE FIELDS OF
PRIVATE LAW

CHAPTER 15

....

FUNCTION AND FORM IN CONTRACT LAW

....

ALAN SCHWARTZ AND DANIEL MARKOVITS

I. INTRODUCTION

WE sketch a functionalist account of contract law and then sketch another account, which we call—loosely—formalist. Our goal is to exhibit the two most basic approaches to this body of law and to observe the relations between them.

Functionalism and formalism proceed from distinct (roughly speaking, teleological and deontological) theories of value, and they take different phenomena (roughly speaking, outcomes and doctrines) as their explananda. But functionalist and formalist accounts of *contract law* more nearly complement than compete with each other. Often, the two accounts reach congruent conclusions from distinctive directions—they agree, one might say, but for different reasons. Another way to put this result is that functionalist and formalist accounts are *theoretically dissimilar* but *operationally similar*.[1]

We address contract particularly rather than legal theory generally, in the hope that placing functionalism and formalism into conversation concerning contract—a concrete, specific, department of law—will deepen the levels on which arguments about contract law are conducted. We do not propose that the two approaches can be reconciled in general (and do not seek to settle any irreconcilable differences between them). But we do believe that certain features of contract, both in practice and in doctrine,

---

[1] Two theoretically different contract law rules are operationally similar if the same court would reach the same outcome on the same facts more often then not when applying either rule. And two contract law theories are operationally similar if a majority of their theoretically derived rules are operationally similar. Commentators apply an intuitive version of this test when they claim that efficiency and autonomy theories of contract are similar "on the ground," and we make the more novel claim that functionalist and formalist theories are similar in the same sense. A comparison of cases from different jurisdictions—the California and New York interpretive rules, for example—could illuminate operational similarity, but the better test would be in the laboratory. Subjects chosen for their relevant similarities could be given the same case and told to use theoretically dissimilar rules to reach a decision.

bring function and form into rough alignment in this department of law. We return to these features at the end of this chapter—although necessarily only briefly and tentatively—to reflect on them and what they reveal about contract law and practice.

A functionalist approach is teleological: it specifies the goal(s) the law should attempt to achieve and specifies the means the law deploys to achieve those goals and, normatively, evaluates the means/ends fit. As an example, many law and economics scholars believe that contract law should maximize welfare. Protecting the expectation interest is welfare maximizing; making penalty clauses unenforceable may not be. In these cases, as generally, law is a means to ends that might be fully specified without making any essential reference to the fact that the ends are promoted through law. Functionalists therefore treat legal outcomes as fundamental and treat doctrine as having merely instrumental interest, and indeed as epiphenomenal.[2]

A formalist approach elaborates an interpretation of the norms and relations that are immanent in the law. The focus on immanence reflects the formalist's belief that the values law instantiates cannot be specified without making essential reference to the fact that they are instantiated in *law*—that is, in a system of rules claiming distinctively legal authority. To stay with the same examples, the formalist asks whether preferring expectation damages over specific performance embodies the normative structure of exchange agreements and, relatedly, whether penalizing (rather than merely extracting compensation from) breachers betrays this structure. Formalists therefore ask whether specific doctrines fit the generic norms that the departments of law to which they belong instantiate. This makes doctrine, rather than outcomes, the central focus of formalist legal analysis.[3]

A functionalist believes that formalist approaches are arid. Whether contract doctrine fits, or can creatively be made to fit, a theory should not matter. What matters is whether doctrine achieves some useful social purpose, or can be made useful. A formalist believes that functionalist approaches cannot explain law, which has an autonomous existence that other ends must accommodate, and which the regulator can override but not alter. Formalists especially resist the idea that law is merely a means to independent ends.

II. THE FUNCTIONALIST APPROACH

A. Basic Functions

Goals imply tasks. Hence, we begin with the two goals that a functionalist approach could pursue: welfare and autonomy (with both understood, roughly, in terms of preference-satisfaction). The tasks that these goals imply are subject to an institutional

---

[2] See Jody Kraus, "Philosophy of Contract Law," in *The Oxford Handbook of Jurisprudence and Philosophy of Law* 692 (Jules L. Coleman & Scott Shapiro eds., 2002).

[3] See *id.* In another variety of this approach, "The theorist delves into existing rules and doctrines and evaluates them, aiming to unmask the moral principles that serve as their foundation, whether or not officials or judges have explicitly articulated or endorsed them." George Letsas & Prince Saprai, "Foundationalism About Contract Law: A Sceptical View," Manuscript (2019), at 2.

constraint: contract law is largely a judicial creation. Hence, the tasks that functional goals imply must be consistent with the strengths and limitations of courts as lawmakers. The most important implication of the law's court-centeredness is the *delegation* of primary responsibility for implementing goals to private agents.

Starting with welfare, a made contract is ex ante efficient: the buyer expects to prefer the goods or services to his money and the seller expects to prefer the money to delivering the goods or rendering the services. A court that wants to maximize welfare cannot itself order agents to trade whenever agents hold these preferences for two reasons. First, in a large economy, firms and persons make millions of contracts each year. A court cannot know who any of these agents are or with whom they should trade. Second, a court cannot recover the preferences of even the private agents whom it can identify. These preferences either are in individual agents' heads or must be derived from contexts to which a court has no independent access. A court-centered contract law therefore best implements the exchange efficiency branch of the welfare goal by delegating to private agents the task of making efficient trades.[4]

A made contract also advances the autonomy of the parties to it. The power to make credible commitments allows agents to enlist others in plans that extend over time, and in which first-movers render themselves vulnerable to exploitation. Again, a court cannot know who any of these agents are, so as to order them to make autonomy-promoting trades, nor could it have independent access to the possible projects that motivate even agents of whom it is aware in making those trades. The court thus must again delegate the task of autonomous trading to private agents.

The two epistemological limitations on the judicial function—not knowing who potential trading agents are and not knowing their preferences—have three significant implications for any functional approach. First, as said, a functionalist court must rely on private agents to achieve the external goals that the court believes society should pursue. At the same time, courts have two residual roles to perform. Initially, courts best enable the private agents to make credible commitments by *enforcing* the promises they make to each other. Further, the delegation to the private agents that both the efficiency and autonomy goals require presupposes that the agents trade under a set of "ideal initial conditions": that the agents are informed, sophisticated (enough to understand what they are doing), rational, and free from coercion. As any of these conditions becomes attenuated, the inference that a made trade was ex ante maximizing for the agent or advanced her autonomy becomes less plausible. A court *can* learn whether the ideal conditions were satisfied or not. The legal question presents to the court as an agent attempting to avoid a made trade on the ground that one or more of the ideal conditions did not hold when the agent agreed to trade: that she was uninformed, misled, and so forth. Here, the court knows who the agents are and the fact-finding task is within judicial competence.

In sum, a functional approach to contract law that pursues welfare or autonomy requires courts to perform at least two tasks: enforcing made trades and ensuring that

---

[4] Exchange efficiency holds that assets should be owned by their highest valuing users. On a functional account, contract law implements exchange efficiency when it enforces trades made under ideal initial conditions. Such trades do transfer assets to the agents who value them the most.

the initial conditions—the context—in which the agents agreed to trade were such as to give a court confidence that the trade was utility maximizing or autonomy enhancing. Contract law, however, in actual practice performs more tasks than enforcing and policing. We next ask how many, if any, of these tasks a welfare maximizing or autonomy enhancing contract law requires.

B. Interpretation

A third essential task for a functionalist, court-centered contract law is interpretation. A welfare approach to interpretation seeks to create efficient incentives for agents to invest in maximizing value; uncovering "intent" is a means.[5]

To see how, let two merchant agents agree to trade cotton, which comes in types from superfine—grade 1—to very coarse—grade 7. The seller delivers grade 4 cotton, which the buyer rejects. The welfare maximizing court must locate the agents in a "type space." If the agent constitutes the type that would trade grade 4 cotton, the court should find that the seller performed and order the buyer to pay.

The agents can send three costly "signals" of their type to the court: the contract; the performance; and trial evidence. The contract may not individuate the agents perfectly—narrow them to a single type—because contract writing is costly. The court must therefore update its estimate of the parties' type by observing the seller's performance. The seller's investment in performance therefore has two functions: to increase the probability that the seller delivers a compliant performance; *and*, because what the seller tenders is evidence of what the agents intended the seller to tender, to communicate the agents' type to the court. Notice that the contract and the performance are complements: the more evidence of the contracting dyad's type the contract contains—the agents' industry, their goals—the more able the court is to infer type from the seller's physical performance.

The seller's incentive to invest in rendering a compliant performance is increasing in her belief that she will be rewarded for a compliant performance. The welfare maximizing court thus orders the buyer to pay when the court is confident that the performance the seller tendered is the performance that agents of the type before the court would tender. Importantly, the court could hold this belief on the basis of the contract and the performance signals alone. In such a case, the court would order the buyer to pay without having a trial because trials are the most costly type signal. But if, say, the court is unsure that the agents intended to trade grade 4 cotton or a different grade, the court then admits trial evidence: industry custom; course of dealing; precontract memoranda. Notice now that the contract and the trial are substitutes because the agents can include evidence of type in the contract. Hence, the more informative the contract is the less informative the trial has to be.

---

[5] The interpretation literature is too large to cite in a short chapter. A recent exposition of the incentive approach is Alan Schwartz & Joel Watson, *Conceptualizing Contract Interpretation*, 42 J. LEGAL STUD. 1 (2015).

This welfare maximizing view of interpretation is concerned not so much with mean-ing as with incentives. The interpretive rules should induce the agents to make cost justi-fied investments along the three signaling margins: the contract, the performance and, if the court permits, the trial. The court, in turn, should order the buyer to pay only when the court has formed a well-grounded belief, on the basis of the signals it observes, that the dyad before it is the type that intended to trade the performance the court sees.

We make four remarks. First, this view of interpretation is consistent with the objec-tive theory of contract, under which a party means what her contract partner could reasonably believe she meant. The theory creates an incentive for an agent to invest in communicating his actual intention. But because the theory is enforced by a court, the agent's incentive is actually to communicate its intention—that is, its type—to the judge. Words, however, are both costly to utter and, as seen, are only one of the three signaling media the court will use to identify type. A commitment to the objective theory of contract thus is a commitment to a view of interpretation that takes communication costs into account. By contrast, much of the positive law, including in the *Restatements*, purports to commit to the objective theory *but also* to commit to the view that courts should always consider trial evidence: evidence of type. This is *not* to take costs into account.

Second, the central debate in the interpretation literature is between contextualists—who want to base interpretations on every relevant datum—and textualists—who want to focus on the contract (and unavoidably the performance). The functionalist approach sketched here elides this debate. Contextualist evidence is trial evidence, and a court should admit it when the court is uncertain about the parties' type on the basis of the contract and the performance signals. Uncertainty here is itself functionalist: the ques-tion is whether the probability that the court will order the buyer to pay for, *but only for*, a compliant performance is high enough to give the seller an incentive to invest effi-ciently in performance.

Third, welfare views of interpretation are distinct from accuracy views, whose goal is for the court to be as sure as a court can be of what the parties intended before it orders or releases a party. The accuracy view yields too many trials, as measured by the gain in accuracy against the cost, and surprisingly yields contracts that are too long. Though contracts and trials are substitutes, when every dispute will be tried, parties have an incentive to write long, detailed contracts, in order to channel and shorten the inevitable and costly trials.

Finally, although autonomy is often thought to favor the accuracy view—because free agents should be ordered to do only what they actually promised to do—this is error. An autonomy-pursuing contract law delegates to private agents the task of pursuing, and enlisting others to pursue, their projects. Rational agents pursue projects subject to cost constraints. Hence, even the autonomy view implies an interpretive theory that takes contract writing, performance, and trial costs into account. The welfare view provides a sophisticated account of how to find intention—here, type—subject to cost constraints. Thus a functionalist contract law that pursues either the welfare goal or the autonomy goal will adopt a similar interpretive theory.

C. Defaults

A contract law that enforces agreements, interprets agreements, and polices the circum-stances under which agreements are made needs few rules: a functional contract law can be small. But the positive law, apparently, includes many rules. Article 2 of the UCC, regulating the sale of goods, contains approximately 106 sections; The *Restatement (Second) of Contracts* contains approximately 350 sections.[6] Private agents can vary every UCC and *Restatement* section except those that impose duties of good faith and fair dealing and the interpretive rules.[7] The UCC and *Restatement* sections thus func-tion as implied terms in agreements unless parties displace them. Contract law is a set of default rules, and the set seems large.

Functionally, however, the law probably is small. To see why, a contract contains t_1, t_2, $t_3, \ldots$, T terms. The price and quantify terms are always present, but the neither the UCC nor the *Restatement* set prices or quantities. Define a substantive term—a remedy, a quality obligation—as t_{1s}, t_{2s}, $t_{3s}, \ldots T_s$. The total substantive UCC or *Restatement* terms in a contract is denoted T_{sr}, so that contract law would supply many terms if the ratio of legally supplied substantive terms to total substantive terms, T_{sr}/T_s, in actual contracts is large. The ratio should vary with subject matter. An acquisition or franchise agreement contains many terms so the ratio likely is small, but a simple sales contract contains few terms so the ratio of state supplied terms to total terms could be larger. While the actual ratio is generally unknown, analysis suggests that actual ratios are very small.

So far, we have elided the question why the state should supply any substantive contract law rules at all. The case for public defaults is that contract terms can be public goods. Suppose then that a contract term—a term regulating excuse, say—would create a benefit of b_i that would be shared between two contracting agents. The cost of drafting the term includes the cost of understanding what an excuse term should do and then writing one. Let that cost be c_i. Then the argument is that private agents will supply too few rules. Our illustrative dyad would not create an excuse term if $c_i > b_i$: that is, if the cost exceeded the benefit. An efficient excuse term may benefit other contracting parties, however. Define the total social benefit from a good excuse term across all contracting parties who would use it as B. Because our originating dyad could not capture the benefits to third parties unless it could prevent copying, and because copying is hard to stop, there will be no excuse term: the cost to each contracting dyad of creating the term exceeds the gain. But if the total social benefit from creating the term would exceed the cost—$B > c_i$—there appar-ently is a constructive role for the state: to create an excuse term, at cost c_i, and then to sup-ply the term to the market thereby permitting agents, at low cost, to realize the benefit B.

Contract law is largely a judicial creation, so it is apparently a court that should be the state rule creator. Courts, however, cannot easily play this role. Courts decide cases; they do not create rules independently of adjudications. Also, courts have a limited and

---

[6] Uncertainty exists because some sections are definitions. The text attempts to count substantive sections.

[7] Even here, agents can create the standards that channel court findings regarding good faith.

narrow fact-finding apparatus. A court thus could not measure the total social benefit from the illustrative excuse rule. There then are two questions: How did the common law of contract come to be? And what does the best creation story tell about the case for state supplied contract law rules?[8]

Beginning with the first question, define a "context" as a set of agents in similar or related areas of commerce. Thus, a trade would be a context, as would a set of retail clothing stores and their suppliers or a set of coal mining companies and public utilities. Consider a case in which a retailer sues a clothing manufacturer for nondelivery and the seller defends on the ground that the clothes were to be made from foreign fabrics and major weather disruptions caused the seller's foreign fabric supplier to default. The agents' contract does not contain a term regulating this possibility. The court will have to supply a term to resolve the dispute, but because cases are precedents the term will look forward: that is, the court will ask whether the term it creates would reflect an acceptable solution for agents who function in the clothing context. Let the term excuse the supplier.

Suppose next that the court sees a case in which a public utility is suing its mining company supplier for nondelivery and the supplier defends on the ground that a major weather disruption prevented it from mining for several months. The contract does not contain a term regulating this possibility. The court likely would follow the earlier case as a precedent: that is, the court would excuse the mining company.

Notice two things about this illustration. First, the court's excuse term conditions on *verifiable information.* The supplier could prove (or the buyer disprove) the occurrence of severe performance affecting weather conditions. Second, the later contracting parties— the public utility and the mining company—*did not write an excuse term.* Rather, these agents accepted the prior case's rule should there be a dispute: that rule thus functioned for them as a default. And this must be because the default solved a contracting problem for agents that function in their context as well as in the original context.

Successful common law contract rules—those that survive as precedents—thus satisfy two constraints: the rules condition on verifiable information and the rules apply "transcontextually." A transcontextual rule constitutes an acceptable solution to a frequently occurring contracting problem—regulating when to excuse a seller's performance—for agents in many contexts. The set of rules that satisfy both constraints is small. Market damages are another illustration. A disappointed promisee can recover the difference between the contract and market prices, both of which are verifiable; and market damages protect the promisee's expectation, which is exchange efficient and so the damage rule is acceptable to agents that function in many contexts. There are not many more illustrations.

Completing the functional argument, there are few (none?) unsuccessful *common law contract rules.* If a rule would not be acceptable in the context in which it arose, or acceptable only in that context, agents that function in other contexts will contract out. And then the original rule *could not* be a precedent because courts would lack later opportunities to apply it. Consider, for example, the rule that a seller makes an implied

---

[8] Much of what follows is based on Alan Schwartz & Robert E. Scott, *The Common Law of Contract and the Default Rule Project,* 102 Va. L. Rev. 1523 (2016).

warranty of quality. This rule hangs around because it is in a statute—the UCC—but the rule is largely unsuccessful because parties in contexts in which warranty damages could be large routinely disclaim the implied warranties. In their place, parties make express warranties and then regulate the damages applicable for breach.

Return now to the public goods case for defaults. This case posits a rule creator who could sum the benefits and costs to private agents of creating acceptable contracting solutions in many contexts. Such a rule creator would need "context expertise"—what could disrupt a mining contract—and a fact-finding apparatus. The drafters of UCC Article Two and the *Contracts Restatement* lack these qualifications. And private agents contract out of many of their solutions, such as the warranty rules, the consequential damage rule, and the excuse rule.

Good contract law rules are public goods, but they arise organically, as a product of private contracting and judicial enforcement. A contract law that arises in this way must satisfy the constraints of verifiability and transcontextuality. And because these are challenging constraints, a functional contract law is small. In spite of initial appearances, the true numerator in the earlier analysis—T_{sr}—is small while the denominator remains T_s.

We make two further remarks. First, the state rule creators—the UCC and *Restatement* drafters—implicitly recognize their limitations. The two contract law sources contain many standards. Agents are instructed to behave "reasonably," "conscionably," "seasonably," and the like. Standards are transcontextual—reasonable behavior is always good—but standards may condition on unverifiable behavior. For example, an agent may claim that her contract partner behaved unreasonably according to trade custom. Custom evidence is costly to introduce, usually contested, and may not be completely accessible to the court. As a consequence, standards can create moral hazard and agents contract out of them when contracting out is permitted.[9] Relatedly, "fair" contract rules are bad defaults. A fair rule actually is a standard, that permits (or directs) courts to evaluate whether the private agents' behavior, or their contract, satisfied an exogenous usually abstract moral criterion. Fair rules thus also create moral hazard. And to sum up, much that is taught as contract law—the UCC and *Restatement* sections—would be dysfunctional if it actually affected behavior.

D. Individual Persons

Contract law largely applies to deals between firms. These agents make agreements that extend through time, and the agents have enough at stake to write things down. Contract law seldom applies to contracts between individual persons.[10] The question whether it is contract law or something else when a firm contracts with a person is open. Is it labor

---

[9] There is moral hazard because an agent for whom a deal has turned out badly will sometimes claim the existence of a custom that would permit the agent to escape. The cost and ambiguity of litigating custom issues facilitates such strategic behavior.

[10] Family law and property law involve contracts between persons, but these bodies of law rather than contract itself regulate the transactions.

law or contract law when the person sells her services to the firm? Is it consumer law or contract law when the firm sells goods to the person? To the extent that a contract is jointly determined through bargaining, the mass consumer transaction is not a contract. And the cases in most modern contracts casebooks do not involve these transactions. On the other hand, the consumer consents to some aspects of every such deal: price, quantity, the product itself; delivery time; down payment. There are contractual aspects to the mass consumer case. Perhaps as a consequence, there is a *Restatement of "Consumer Contracts"* in progress. It thus is useful to ask what a functional view of consumer contract law would look like.

Such a law would modify what it means for a person to consent to a contract. On the traditional view, a promisee learns about her deal *only* from reading the contract. Hence, when persons do not read—the common case—they cannot consent. A different view of consent would hold that a person consents to a deal when she knows what a term does and buys anyway. On this view, a consumer consents to the aspect of the automobile warranty that requires her to get warranty service at an authorized dealer. The data show that consumers learn about such requirements through a variety of sources, of which only one is the written contract.[11] Hence, the claim that consumers do not consent to the substance of the documents they sign is overstated. And this reasoning suggests that consumer contract law could perform a version of the four functions sketched previously: enforcing terms of which the consumer probably was aware and so consented to; policing the originating circumstances to ensure that the consumer had, or could have had, sufficient knowledge and sophistication; interpreting the contract both to identify what the consumer could reasonably take it to say and to create incentives for the consumer to learn and for the firm to be clear; and supplying rules that would function efficiently in a variety of consumer contexts.

The policing function here has an institutional implication, however. Traditionally, when a court finds that one or more of the ideal conditions that ensure actual consent are absent, the court does not enforce the contract. This is useful because agents often cause the absence of the condition. For example, an agent coerces another or conceals or misrepresents a material term. Not enforcing the contract creates an incentive for the misbehaving agent to change. In the consumer area, the absence of conditions often is systemic. Agents seldom read terms because they lack the skill to interpret documents whose addressees are primarily judges. Solving systemic problems is not a judicial function. Thus, an agency or legislature should respond to the failure to read with effective disclosures, such as creating formats that much reduce the cost of reading only the important terms that consumers commonly misunderstand.

There is a very different functional view of the consumer case that accepts the definition of a contract as a jointly determined agreement. On this view, the consumer contract is not so much a contract as it is a product. Just as an actual product has several features—color, weight, a safety guard—a consumer contract/product has several terms—a price, a warranty, a payment schedule. The absence of codetermination is not a

---

[11] See Ian Ayres & Alan Schwartz, *The No-Reading Problem in Consumer Contract Law*, 66 STAN. L. REV. 545 (2014).

problem in product markets. That products come in standard sizes, or stoves have one or two ovens but not three, is not a policy concern. The welfare maximizing state's goal is to ensure competitive markets, which supply as much variety as consumers in the aggregate are willing to pay for, and to have price approximate cost. The typical consumer thus wants one or two ovens, depending on her circumstances, but few consumers want three. That stoves do not contain three ovens is normatively acceptable.

On this view of the individual person case, the relevant functional question thus is whether the "market for contracts" is performing competitively. The policy issues are whether consumers search sufficiently, whether contracts fail to contain terms that studies show consumers prefer, and whether terms are priced noncompetitively. Consumer contract law thus is more a branch of antitrust than a branch of contract law generally.

We do not adjudicate between the two views of consumer contract law here, partly because they have similar institutional implications: creating the conditions under which consumer consent is actual also is creating the conditions under which effective competition can occur.

III. THE FORMALIST APPROACH

A. Basic Form

A formalist need not expressly embrace Ernest Weinrib's cryptic aphorism that "the sole purpose of private law is to be private law"[12] in order to proceed in its spirit, insisting that private law does not instrumentally promote extralegal values so much as instantiate distinctively legal ones. For the case of contract—the law of agreements—these distinctive values concern the possibility that parties that possess private (and often competing) motives might nevertheless achieve, and share, a fully first-personal perspective on the joint activity that their contracts specify. Contract, that is, establishes relationships in which contracting parties might pursue their competing interests, including by using each other, while still treating each other with the respect that their status as free and equal persons requires.[13]

Formalists elaborate the value of this shared yet first-personal perspective in different ways. Some (for example, Seana Shiffrin) emphasize that contract law provides public, political recognition of the equal moral status of contracting parties, especially in the face of the (often unequal) bargaining power and contractual competencies that they confront and exhibit when contracting.[14] Others (for example, Arthur Ripstein and

---

[12] Ernest J. Weinrib, *The Idea of Private Law* 8 (1995).

[13] Again, we assume here, and partly show, that formalist and functionalist theories yield similar results when applied to cases.

[14] See, e.g., Seana Valentine Shiffrin, *The Divergence of Contract and Promise*, 120 HARV. L. REV. 708, 749–753 (2007).

Charles Fried) emphasize that contract extends freedom, understood in the Kantian sense of pursuing chosen rather than externally imposed ends,[15] to the sphere of private right, concerning both things and other persons.[16] Still others (for example, Peter Benson and Daniel Markovits) emphasize that contracts create a thin form of community, characterized by a particular normative orientation (perhaps justice in transactions or respectful recognition) among the parties to them.[17]

As did their functionalist counterparts, all these formalist approaches again delegate the power to create contracts and to fix their contents to private agents. Regardless of whether contract is understood to allow agents to interact as equals, to secure their ends consistent with their freedom, or to recognize each other (at arm's length), it is the contracting parties who must determine the terms on which they contract. Where functionalists emphasize deference to contracting parties because courts cannot know what the parties' ends are or how best to promote them, formalists emphasize deference because only the parties, and not the state, can vindicate their equality, enact their liberty, or recognize one another.

The formalist thus gives an ontological cast to the constraints on courts and deference to parties that functionalists regard as epistemological. For the formalist, a contract just is a relation generated by the parties to it, and the contract's value inheres in its being that. This reframing carries through, moreover, to the functionalist's two central tasks. Formalists must also enforce made agreements (so that the law can vindicate contracting parties' engagements) and ensure that the parties act in circumstances such that the agreements that they make are genuinely theirs. Finally, the formalist reframing also carries through to the three other features that our rehearsal of functionalist contract law has identified as essential.

B. Interpretation

Formalists accept that contract law deploys so-called objective rather than subjective standards of intention. Offer and acceptance are both understood as outward manifestations of intent "so made as to justify another person in understanding" that bargains are invited or assented to.[18] Moreover, interpretation—under both textualist and contextualist approaches—is understood to fix contractual meaning by reference to shared, public understandings among communities of interpreters rather than by reference to the subjective, private beliefs of those who created a particular contractual text.

---

[15] This is not the same as the idea of freedom deployed by functionalists, who understand contract as a technology for promoting autonomy.

[16] See, e.g., Arthur Ripstein, *Force and Freedom: Kant's Legal and Political Philosophy* 107–144 (2009); Charles Fried, *Contract as Promise* 1–27 (1981).

[17] See Peter Benson, *Justice in Transactions: A Theory of Contract Law* (2019); Daniel Markovits, *Contract and Collaboration*, 113 YALE L.J. 1417 (2004).

[18] *Restatement (Second) of Contracts* § 24. See also *id.* § 50.

Functionalists, we have already observed, can straightforwardly explain these generic doctrines in terms of the epistemic limitations of courts. Formalists have a harder time accounting for contract law's objective turn. But the formalist position is not hopeless; and an analogy to the functionalist's epistemic point, which sounds in the ontology of agreement, is available to formalist contract theory.

Contracting parties can gain a shared, first-personal perspective on their joint conduct only interpersonally—that is, only through public norms that abide in the open, outside of the necessarily private spaces of each contracting agent's mind. Equality, mutual freedom, and recognition—the three faces of formalist contract law—can be successfully achieved only *intersubjectively*, in a perspective that both parties to contracts can access but that (for this very reason) cannot be reduced to either party's point of view. Courts, moreover, give a contract's intersubjective existence an authoritative positive expression and thereby create the perspective that the parties can jointly but first-personally endorse; and contracting agents, when they recognize the court's authority, endorse this perspective.[19] Where the functionalist turns to objective standards out of epistemic deference in the service of promoting the contracting parties' private interests, the formalist embraces objective standards because they constitute mutual intelligibility. Contract law's objective accounts of offer, acceptance, and interpretation are necessary for realizing (literally, making real) the values that formalist theories of contract celebrate.

C. Defaults

Like functionalists, formalists also focus on the background rules of contract law because these are (in the nature of things) the rules that all of contract law shares. But formalists frame these background rules very differently from functionalists, and this difference opens a window onto the divergent concerns of formalist and functionalist legal thought.

Functionalists conceive of background rules as defaults that complete the agents' contracts and, once implied into contracts, operate structurally in parallel to the expressly agreed terms.[20] Formalists do not deny that some background rules have this supplementary character, but they focus their attention elsewhere, on background rules that function not as gap-fillers but as presuppositions—as rules without which the party-made aspects of a contract would be unintelligible.

These background rules, formalists add, are not like the mandatory rules that functionalists sometime contrast with defaults. The lawmaker chooses mandatory rules to promote (in a functionalist way) ends that she thinks she can achieve more effectively than the private agents can achieve for themselves. Such rules are, therefore, expressions

---

[19] This is a private law analog to the role some accounts give to positive law in the public sphere. See, e.g., Jeremy Waldron, *Kant's Legal Positivism*, 109 HARV. L. REV. 1535 (1996).

[20] See, e.g., Ian Ayres & Robert Gertner, *Filling Gaps in Incomplete Contracts: An Economic Theory of Default Rules*, 99 YALE L.J. 87 (1989).

of the lawmaker's epistemic confidence. The formalist's presuppositions, by contrast, are not chosen, at the discretion of the lawmaker, to serve independent ends. Rather, they articulate necessary preconditions for contracts—comprised of express terms, default terms, and mandatory terms in the functionalist sense—to arise at all.

Remedies give this idea its most straightforward illustration. Contracting parties cannot create the foundations of remedy law because they cannot solve the infinite regress that arises when one of them fails to honor whatever remedy rule they have agreed to. At bottom, remedies must appear as background rules. The rule, memorialized in UCC § 2-719(2)'s provision that where an "exclusive or limited remedy" "fail[s] of its essential purpose," the general remedies provided by the UCC become available, makes this point express.[21] As the comments to the section observe, "it is of the very essense of a sales contract that at least minimum adequate remedies be available."[22] The formalist takes this observation about essences seriously, noting that contract's nature—the features that make it a distinctive form of legal obligation—requires that the law at least minimally protect contractual entitlements. It is not that the law chooses to do so in the (functionalist) service of some other policy aims. Rather, the law must do so if it is to be contract law properly so-called at all—and to sustain the distinctive relations of equality, freedom, and recognition that contracts generate.

Other doctrines may also be understood as creating necessary presuppositions: a careful analysis puts offer, acceptance, and interpretation into this category, especially in light of the otherwise curious fact that whereas the law will impute efficient or otherwise rational gap-filling terms once a contract has been made, it will not impute an offer and acceptance simply on the ground that the parties would have been rational to contract. Similar accounts might also be offered of the bargain theory of consideration, which ensures that contracts are exchanges. At the same time, the class of doctrines that has this character is narrowly cabined; and formalists therefore agree with functionalists that the set of background rules of contract law is, in the end, small.

Whereas the functionalist theory of contract interpretation can make many concrete doctrinal recommendations that the formalist cannot match, the formalist theory of background rules has real advantages over its functionalist alternative. In particular, the formalist need not explain why the state should exercise its discretion to provide precisely the background rules (and in their precise form) that the formalist casts as presuppositions. Contract's inner logic answers this question on its own; and contract law's necessary presuppositions constitute the answer.

D. Individual Persons

Formalists and functionalists display nearly opposite sensibilities—and strengths and weaknesses—with respect to the types of parties whose contracts they most successfully explain.

---

[21] See Unif. Commerical Code § 2–719(2).   [22] See *id.* § 2–719(2) cmt[1].

Functionalists naturally focus on commercial contracts involving firms. Because firms are constructed to seek profits and are managed by experienced professionals, they overwhelmingly adopt the ends and display the forms of means-ends rationality that underwrite the epistemic and other assumptions that drive functionalist contract theory. Functionalists can say useful things about noncommercial contracts among natural persons, but they must tread carefully here, trimming their analytic sails and ceding substantial ground to other departments of law.

Formalists, by contrast, naturally emphasize noncommercial contracts among natural persons. These are the parties that most obviously and securely invoke the values—equality, liberty, community—that formalist contract theory emphasizes; and these are the parties that most confidently possess the intentional capacities out of which contracts, on the formalist picture, are built. If formalists nevertheless wish to address commercial contracts between firms—or indeed contracts involving organizations more generally—then they must display just as much care and even caution as functionalists do on the formalists' natural ground.

The safest route, therefore, is for formalists to cede the field—at least of commercial law—to functionalists and to focus elsewhere. Many formalists do just this, at least implicitly, as the examples through which they develop their theories disproportionately involve contracts for the personal provision of personal services—between a plumber and a homeowner, perhaps[23]—or even agreements between friends. But other formalists aspire to occupy a larger share of contract law as it is practiced, and they therefore address cases that are more difficult for them, including sometimes even commercial contracts among firms.

Formalists might most modestly pursue this aim along two straightforward paths. The first seeks to impute organizational contracts to natural persons who stand, speaking a little loosely, as principals behind the organization-agents who contract. Organizations that pursue a higher purpose that is largely shared by most of their members—for example, mission-driven clubs, charities, and universities—are most immediately amenable to this treatment. It intuitively seems apt to attribute at least some of the Sierra Club's contracts to its members, or some of a university's contracts to its professors. Even contracts among commercial firms might, in this way, be attributed to their natural-person owners. A second straightforward path seeks to identify circumstances in which organizations might meaningfully be treated as if they themselves possess intentions and, moreover, invoke analogs of equality, liberty, and community, perhaps based on philosophical accounts of collective intention.[24] Both efforts are entirely familiar, even if neither is completely successful.

A bolder approach flips the script. Where familiar efforts to attribute organizational contracts to natural persons treat the organizations as agents and look for principals to

[23] This example comes from Seana Shiffrin, *Could Breach of Contract be Immoral?*, 107 MICH. L. REV. 1551, 1564 (2009).

[24] See, e.g., Philip Pettit, "Collective Intentions," in Intention in Law and Philosophy 241–254 (N. Naffine, R.J. Owens, & J. Williams eds., 2001), and Philip Pettit, *Responsibility Incorporated*, 117 ETHICS 171 (2007).

whom the agents' contracts might be attributed, this formalist approach treats organizations as principals and seeks to attribute organizational contracts to the natural persons who, acting as agents, negotiate and execute them. To take a concrete example: where familiar approaches seek to attribute a firm's contracts to its owners, this approach seeks to attribute the firm's contracts to the employees who (acting as the firm's agents) make and perform them. The bold approach has the benefit of tracking lived experience: owners, who hold diversified portfolios, rarely focus on the performance of portfolio firms and even more rarely on any such firm's contracts. By contrast, agents and especially employees have their professional projects and ambitions wrapped up with the firms whose work they do. A person whose investments include shares in a mutual fund that holds shares in GE likely does not even know that she belongs among GE's owners. But GE's employees come, in carrying out the firms' projects, to take the projects for their own, as their life's work.

Organizations, including commercial firms, enable the natural persons who act as their agents to enter into the types of relationships that formalist contract theory describes, even though they do not themselves contract as principals. Indeed, natural persons can enter into agreements as agents that they could not prudently or even possibly make as principals, because they could not afford the risk of legal liability or marshal the resources that these agreements involve. (Just imagine an agreement made by engineers at GM and GE, on behalf of their respective firms, to exchange intellectual property and expertise in the service of multimillion dollar research projects.) Law, as it happens, underwrites such practices, by shielding natural persons who make contracts as agents from the liabilities that they cannot afford to bear as principals. An example is the rule that when an agent acting within the scope of her authority contracts on behalf of a disclosed principal, the agent is not personally liable under the contract unless she (now acting on her own behalf) and the contractual counterparty agree to make her so.[25] This rule protects the firm's agents in much the same way in which the limited liability associated with the corporate form protects the firm's owners. It therefore supports agential contracting and the formalist values that such contracting might involve.

It thus is open to the formalist to argue that a combination of institutional structures and legal rules extends the reach of her theory across much of commercial life, if only she can reformulate her account of the contract relation to encompass persons who make contracts as agents rather than as principals. Formalists have not so far pursued this approach to organizational contracts; but functionalists have (until recently) had relatively little to say about contracts among unsophisticated, noncommercially motivated natural persons. The two approaches might thus expand their scopes together, to converge on a more fully shared subject.

---

[25] See, e.g., *Restatement Third of Agency* § 6.01. See also Daniel Markovits, A New Theory of the Firm (lecture given at the International Society for the New Institutional Economics, Florence, Italy, 2013) (unpublished manuscript on file with author). See also Gabriel Rauterberg, Agency Law as Asset Partitioning (unpublished manuscript on file with author).

IV. TWO VIEWS OF A SINGLE SUBJECT

These examples suggest a striking convergence of function and form in contract law. Functionalist and formalist approaches to this body of doctrine may pursue different preoccupations and display different strengths and weaknesses, but they do not fundamentally oppose each other. Indeed, they function more nearly as complements than as competitors.[26] We have not canvassed all of contract law, of course.[27] But we have addressed enough of the law to establish a stark contrast between contract and other departments of private law. In tort, for example, functionalist accounts emphasize reducing the costs of accidents and often embrace strict liability and even no-fault insurance. Formalists, by contrast, emphasize rights and wrongs, characterized in terms of corrective justice or civil recourse, and can even be heard to say that understanding tort law as an instrument for reducing the costs of accidents is like understanding the "Apollo space programme" as a "way of developing non-stick pans."[28]

This makes it natural to ask why function and form fit so peculiarly well in contract law. The most immediate answer, we think, is that functionalists and formalists share a basic understanding of what a contract is—namely, a legal relation that creates and shares surplus produced through mutually beneficial, free exchange. Contract-parties coordinate their conduct to pursue the functional purposes that they bring to their contracts so that, as Kant might have said, they might have the benefit of using each other as means without treating each other *merely* as means, because (through their agreements) they recognize each other as ends in themselves.[29] In addition, functionalists and formalists share a basic understanding of the mode of contractual sharing—namely, that it is what one of us has called sharing ex ante, on terms fixed in advance of creating the

---

[26] Indeed, in some areas of doctrine, functionalist and formalist analyses can be almost perfectly complementary. Our earlier work on the expectation remedy illustrates this possibility in considerable detail. See Daniel Markovits & Alan Schwartz, *The Expectation Remedy Revisited*, 98 VA. L. REV. 1093 (2012); Daniel Markovits & Alan Schwartz, *The Expectation Remedy and the Promissory Basis of Contract*, 45 SUFFOLK L. REV. 799 (2012) (symposium in honor of the thirtieth anniversary of the publication of *Contract as Promise*); and Daniel Markovits & Alan Schwartz, *The Myth of Efficient Breach: New Defenses of the Expectation Interest*, 97 VA. L. REV. 1939 (2011).

[27] We suspect that other contract doctrines are also amenable to our approach. For example, contract law treats formation and mistake in ways that are more inclined to impute rationalizing terms to incomplete or imperfect contracts where there is a clear intent to trade than to impute such an intent where none exists, simply because it would be rational for the parties to have traded. (For just one example of this, compare the law's treatment of unilateral mistakes and misunderstandings, as in *Restatement Second of Contracts* §§ 20, 153, 154.) Functionalists might explain this difference by reference to the distinctive costs of identifying and curing mistakes within and without the umbrella of an intent to trade, while formalists might emphasize the constitutive role that a shared intent to trade plays in bringing the parties into a contract relation to begin with. These are suggestive rather than comprehensive observations, of course. But they suggest that the main lesson of our argument—that, *in contract*, functionalists and formalists reach similar conclusions for different reasons—applies outside of the doctrines through which we develop it.

[28] Cf. Robert Stevens, *Torts and Rights* 326 (2007).

[29] See Immanuel Kant, *Groundwork of the Metaphysic of Morals* 427–430 (H.J. Paton trans., 1964) (1785).

surplus, rather than sharing ex post, on terms that adjust to the interests of the parties as they evolve over the course of performance.[30] Functionalist and formalist accounts of contract complement each other because the two camps, in spite of their differences, address the same basic legal relation. Functionalists and formalists reach aligned conclusions for divergent reasons.

This alignment has deep roots. The economic markets that contract law (literally) makes establish a distinctive life-world. Functionalists emphasize the allocative properties of this life-world—the relations between persons and things, and in particular the relations of production and consumption, that it sustains. Formalists, by contrast, emphasize the solidaristic properties of market exchange—the relations among persons that markets sustain. Market societies merge these two perspectives, giving priority to neither. The architectural maxim—coined by Louis Sullivan and made famous by the Bauhaus—that form follows function certainly applies. But in contract law its converse applies equally—as function also follows form.

ACKNOWLEDGMENTS

We are grateful to the participants at the Private Law Conference, Harvard Law School (2019) and to Gregory Keating, Hanoch Dagan, and Henry Smith for helpful comments.

---

[30] See Daniel Markovits, "Sharing Ex Ante and Sharing Ex Post: The Non-contractual Basis of Fiduciary Relations," in *The Philosophical Foundations of Fiduciary Law* (Andrew S. Gold & Paul B. Miller eds., 2014).

CHAPTER 16

....

TORTS

....

JOHN C.P. GOLDBERG

THIS chapter begins with a deliberately unambitious description of Anglo-American tort law. Though straightforward, it will strike some readers, including many from the U.S. legal academy, as off the mark. This is because it makes no mention of the Hand Formula, cheapest cost avoiders, and other concepts that at least two generations of law students have been taught to regard as central to the subject.

These omissions are deliberate. While not wholly ungrounded in doctrine, economic interpretations of tort law introduce serious and needless interpretive difficulties. My point is not that economic analysis has nothing to offer when it comes to adjudicating tort cases or evaluating tort law. Rather, it is that tort law's central concepts—such as negligence law's notion of fault—are *not themselves* economic. Efforts to characterize tort as a scheme of efficient deterrence should thus be abandoned. Instead—and in keeping with the emphasis of the New Private Law on analysis that is down-to-earth without being reductionist—tort is better understood as law that defines injurious wrongs and provides victims of such wrongs with an avenue through which to redress them.

I. WHAT IS TORT LAW?

....

Lawyers and law professors seem to agree on what they are talking about when they talk about tort law. Defamation and fraud, medical malpractice and products liability, trespass and conversion—all of these topics fall within its ambit, as do others.

This apparent agreement notwithstanding, various familiar questions are often asked about the subject. Is tort law remedial or substantive? Does tort liability hinge on misconduct and the aspiration to deter it, or on injuries and the aspiration to compensate them? Are torts genuine or merely nominal wrongs?[1]

---

[1] "Nominal" here conveys the thought that torts are wrongs only in that the law labels them as such, irrespective of whether they carry hallmarks of wrongdoing in other domains, particularly morality.

Consideration of the core features of Anglo-American tort law reveals that each of these questions is badly framed. Tort law is substantive *and* remedial. It hinges liability on misconduct *and* injury. Torts are genuine wrongs *and* legally recognized wrongs. To say all of these things at once: tort law identifies and enjoins the commission of certain injurious wrongs[2] and empowers victims of such wrongs to obtain redress through the courts.

The common law of torts has roots that are in one important respect remedial. It has been the availability of courts over the centuries to hear complaints and provide remedies that has driven its development, and that of private law generally. Yet this development has consisted in large part of the adoption, refinement, and revision of substantive rules and standards. As it did in 1500 and 1700, tort law today contains a collection of conduct-guiding directives or norms, though the composition of the collection has changed over time. For example, judicial decisions defining and applying the tort of libel have long directed individuals to refrain from publishing a defamatory writing about another. Likewise, the modern law of products liability directs commercial sellers to refrain from injuring members of the public by placing defective products into commerce. Tort law's substance is also bound up with its remedial dimension in a second way. In specifying the content of the different torts, courts are identifying a species of wrongdoing that is distinct from others (such as crimes), in part because these are wrongs for which wrongdoers are subject to liability to their victims.

Relatedly, the commission of a tort, and hence tort liability, involves both misconduct and injury. There are two sides to each tort: an actor side and a victim side. These two sides are *integrated* rather than haphazardly conjoined, as is particularly evident in torts such as battery and trespass to land.[3] The implicit directive built into the definition of battery—"Don't touch another in an inappropriate or harmful manner, that is, Don't hit another, kick another, fondle another, spit on another, etc."—quite obviously fuses misconduct and injury.[4]

Torts are also genuine wrongs. For a tort to be committed, a person or entity must injure another by acting or failing to act in a manner that falls below a standard of

[2] As explained in this chapter an "injurious" (or "injury-inclusive") wrong is one defined such that it cannot be committed without an actor violating a standard of conduct so as to generate a setback for another. Consider negligence: unless an actor's careless conduct proximately causes bodily harm (or some other setback) to another, the tort has not been committed. I leave aside for the moment precisely the sorts of setback courts have deemed or could deem an injury.

[3] Ernest J. Weinrib, *The Idea of Private Law* 64–65 (1995); Martin Stone, "The Significance of Doing and Suffering," in *Philosophy and the Law of Torts* 135 (Gerald J. Postema ed., 2001).

[4] Other torts, including negligence, do not wear their integrated nature on their sleeves. In some instances, one can more cleanly separate the misconduct side of the tort (e.g., defendant's inattentive driving) from the setback side (e.g., plaintiff's bodily injury). Yet, as noted earlier, the tort of negligence is no less an injurious wrong than battery. Specifically, it is the breach of duty owed to another to avoid proximately causing injury to her through conduct that is careless as to her. A truck driver who foreseeably causes a local business to lose revenue by carelessly crashing into and damaging a bridge that the business's customers use to reach it does not commit the tort of negligence because courts have declined to recognize a duty to avoid causing "pure economic loss" through careless conduct. See, e.g., Aikens v. Debow, 541 S.E.2d 576 (W.Va. 2000).

conduct set by an applicable legal directive.[5] The different torts mark off things that persons must not do to another (or must do for another) and thus earn opprobrium when done (or not done). This is why tort liability is not properly characterized as a tax or price on permitted conduct. The commercial seller of a defective product that, in the ordinary course, injures a consumer, acts less well than it was required to act, even though it is not necessarily at fault or blameworthy for doing so, and hence is subject to liability to the consumer. By contrast, a consumer who purchases a product in the ordinary course has done nothing wrong, but may nonetheless be required to pay a tax on the purchase. The standards against which wrongfulness is measured in tort are legal, not moral, though the former tend to mimic, shadow, or incorporate the latter, as well as to help shape them. A homeowner who operates a kennel from a suburban home populated by constantly barking dogs that disturb her neighbor's sleep may well face liability. If so, it is because her conduct and its effects fit the definition of the legally recognized wrong of private nuisance.

The collection of torts that have been identified by Anglo-American courts and legislatures is neither haphazard nor the expression of a single substantive principle. Instead, it reflects the conferral on courts of jurisdiction to hear claims of "trespass" (to use the terminology of the old writ system)—claims of mistreatment that, when validated, entitled the claimant to a court-ordered remedy.[6] Unsurprisingly, tort complaints have centered on setbacks implicating aspects of individual well-being, including harm to reputation, loss of privacy, violations of bodily integrity, as well as interferences with freedom of movement, property rights, and decisional autonomy. In turn, courts have decided when to validate complaints, and when and how to provide redress. Appropriately for officials fashioning "common law," judges have usually kept tort law's substance close to prevailing moral norms. A person without legal training will not be surprised to learn that courts have deemed assault, battery, conversion, defamation, and most of the other torts to be injurious wrongs.

In identifying various wrongfully inflicted injuries, tort law specifies obligations that run between and among members of a polity. It is in this sense conduct-guiding—a point that will be obvious to any lawyer who has given advice to a client about the conduct that tort law forbids or requires. At the same time, tort law reflects a political obligation that runs between government and citizen—the obligation of a government whose law recognizes certain injurious wrongs to make its courts available to putative victims of such wrongs, such that they can, upon proof of claim, obtain a remedy from those who have, in the eyes of the law, wrongfully injured them. Tort law thus not only defines and proscribes injurious wrongs, it confers on victims the ability, in principle, to hold to account those who have wrongfully injured them. When a tort is committed, it

---

[5] Torts sometimes consist of failing to rescue or protect another from injury. For example, a business that does not take reasonable measures to aid a customer stricken while on its premises is subject to liability for injuries that would have been prevented had it provided aid.

[6] I do not mean to suggest that Anglo-American private law's litigation-centered, bottom-up form of law generation is necessary for the existence of tort law. It may be that civilian legal systems contain, or could contain, tort law as herein defined.

generates in the victim a claim for redress, usually in the form of money damages. It is the victim's prerogative whether to assert this claim. If she does assert it, she does so as a matter of right. Prevailing in a tort suit often is not easy—plaintiffs must overcome various procedural and evidentiary hurdles that aim to ensure that allegations are validated before a defendant is adjudged a tortfeasor. Yet those who do prevail are *entitled* to a court-ordered remedy that will usually consist of a monetary payment in an amount that stands to compensate the victim for her tort-related losses. Thus, our imagined sleep-deprived kennel neighbor can, if her suit is successful, obtain damages compensating her for the inconveniences she has suffered.

Compensation for a victim's tort-related losses is the default rule of tort redress. Victims of certain egregious wrongs may also obtain punitive damages. And some tort plaintiffs (including many nuisance plaintiffs) obtain injunctive relief. This is one reason why it is misleading to assert that the animating principle of tort law is restoration of the status quo ante, or making victims whole. While tort law is administered by governmental institutions, it is not a governmental program that aims to deliver end-states such as these. As noted, it defines forms of injurious misconduct and empowers victims of such misconduct to obtain redress through civil litigation. How victims choose to exercise those powers is mainly their business, and if some victims make a knowing and voluntary choice not to sue, or to settle for less than full compensation, the system is working as it should.

II. The Not-So-Puzzling Persistence of Interpretive Economic Theories

A knowledgeable late nineteenth-century scholar would readily recognize the foregoing description of tort law.[7] Yet many contemporary law professors will find it alien. After all, it makes no mention of cheapest cost avoiders, liability rules, transaction costs, or the Hand Formula.

Readers inclined to *understand* tort law through the lens of these economic concepts will be tempted to conclude that the preceding summary is a bit of sectarianism disguised as description—that it surreptitiously takes a side in yet another familiar dichotomous debate, this one between deontic (rights-based) and welfarist accounts of tort law. One aspiration of the New Private Law movement, however, is to demonstrate that this dichotomy is no more helpful than those critiqued earlier. Rights, fairness, justice, responsibility, and welfare all figure in, or bear a significant relation to, tort law.[8] And

---

[7] See John C.P. Goldberg & Benjamin C. Zipursky, "Thomas M Cooley (1824–1898) & Oliver W Holmes (1841–1935): The Arc of American Tort Theory," in *Scholars of Tort Law* (James Goudkamp & Donal Nolan eds., 2019).

[8] For example, while it is not the aim of tort law to see to it that justice is done as between tortfeasor and victim, tort law in fact often allows for such justice to be achieved. Moreover, by discouraging wrongs and empowering victims, tort can help constitute a just polity. See generally John C.P. Goldberg & Benjamin C. Zipursky, Recognizing Wrongs 350–358 (2020).

economic analysis, no less than philosophical analysis, can and has illuminated particular issues and tort law generally.[9] Still, particular torts such as negligence are not accurately expressed through economic concepts, nor does tort law as a whole boil down to Kaldor-Hicks efficiency. Tort law has been shaped by considerations of welfare and justice, and can always be assessed by reference to such considerations. Moreover, its operation in principle stands to contribute to the justness of the legal systems of which it is a part. But on the question of what tort law *is*, the answer is clear—it is a law of wrongs and redress.

If the content and character of Anglo-American tort law is not adequately captured in economic terms, why do so many U.S. legal academics suppose that it is? The explanation is multifaceted. There are the powerful figures of Judges Calabresi and Posner. Economic analysis also plays well to academics enthralled with the thought that legal analysis might attain a rigor associated with mathematics and natural science. Insofar as economists have at times blurred problematic interpretive claims with less problematic conceptual or prescriptive claims, they may have succeeded in papering over the deficiencies of the former.[10] Finally, interpretive economic analysis has engaged legal academics in the United States because, even though it gets too many things wrong, it gets some important things right. The remainder of this chapter aims to expose the kernels of truth embedded in interpretive economic accounts and to explain why they do not in the end lend credence to those accounts but instead support the wrongs-and-redress view.

A. Legal Directives, Legal Wrongs: The Hand Formula

Law professors in the United States today almost reflexively associate negligence law, if not all of tort law, with the "B < P x L" formula invoked by Learned Hand in the *Carroll Towing* case.[11] That they do so is a tribute to the influence of Judge Posner, who famously argued that *Carroll Towing* teaches us that the failure to use reasonable care just is the failure to take cost-justified precautions against causing losses to others.[12]

The problems with Posner's rendering of the Hand Formula are legion.[13] For one thing, it does not actually capture Hand's thinking. In *Carroll Towing*, the district court had ruled that the issue of the complainant/barge-owner's fault could be resolved under a bright-line rule, according to which it is not careless to leave one's barge without a bargee absent an emergency. In reversing, Hand offered B < P x L not as a formula for determining fault but to emphasize that the fault inquiry is too indeterminate to be governed by

---

[9] In addition to the works discussed later in the text, see, e.g., Mark A. Geistfeld, *A Roadmap for Autonomous Vehicles: State Tort Liability, Automobile Insurance, and Federal Safety Regulation*, 105 CAL. L. REV. 1611 (2017); Henry E. Smith, *Modularity and Morality in the Law of Torts*, 4 J. TORT L. (2011); Robert Cooter, *Prices and Sanctions*, 84 COLUM. L. REV. 1523 (1984).

[10] John C.P. Goldberg, *Twentieth-Century Tort Theory*, 91 GEO. L.J. 513, 515, 544–553 (2003) (discussing interpretive and prescriptive economic theories of tort).

[11] U.S. v. Carroll Towing Co., 159 F.2d 169 (2d Cir. 1947).

[12] Richard A. Posner, *A Theory of Negligence*, 1 J. LEGAL STUD. 29, 32 (1972).

[13] Subsequent references to "the Hand Formula" are to Posner's rendering of it.

any such simple rule.[14] Not only are determinations of fault dependent on a variety of fact-specific assessments, they necessarily involve a balancing of subjective values that does not lend itself to rational determination.[15] The idea that legal fault involves an objective assessment of precaution costs and expected losses is completely at odds with Hand's approach.[16]

That the putative poster child for the economic account of negligence law is nothing of the sort is not the biggest problem facing that account. State courts define fault as a "lack of ordinary care," and "the failure to use that degree of care that a reasonably prudent person would under the circumstances."[17] The Hand Formula fails to map on to these descriptions in several ways:

- It depicts fault as turning on an actor's decision about what precautions to take. In many instances legal fault is executory or fault-in-the-doing: for example, distracted driving, or walking with one's head buried in one's phone. B < P x L sheds no light on this archetypical form of careless conduct.[18]

---

[14] Benjamin C. Zipursky, *Sleight of Hand*, 48 WM. & MARY. L. REV. 1999, 2007–2010 (2007).

One can better understand *Carroll Towing* by comparing it to another famous decision concerning claimant fault. In *Pokora v. Wabash Ry.*, 292 U.S. 98 (1934), Justice Cardozo, like Judge Hand in *Carroll Towing*, criticized a prior decision—Justice Holmes's opinion for the Court in a case called *Goodman*—for having suggested that there was, or could be, a hard-and-fast rule of comparative fault. And, like Hand, Cardozo in *Pokora* insisted that the issue of fault is not amenable to resolution under a rule. To propose (as Holmes had in *Goodman*) a simple rule that drivers with an obstructed view of a railroad crossing must exit their vehicles to look for oncoming trains would demand of them an "uncommon" precaution. (B!) *Id.* at 104. Moreover, such a precaution, even if efficacious in some settings, was likely to be "futile, and sometimes even dangerous" in others. (P x L!) *Id.* Because the burdens and benefits of different precautions would vary in different grade-crossing scenarios, Cardozo called for "caution in framing standards of behavior that amount to rules of law." *Id.* at 105. No one thinks of *Pokora* as providing a definition of fault. Rather, it is understood to caution against overly precise specifications of that concept. This is exactly how *Carroll Towing* should be understood.

[15] Gregory C. Keating, *Reasonableness and Rationality in Negligence Theory*, 48 STAN. L. REV. 311, 332 (1996). Economists often assert that individuals' subjective preferences must be taken as given when making policy choices. Hand, by contrast, insisted that supposedly objective values—such as cost-minimization or Kaldor-Hicks efficiency—are themselves not rationally defensible. See, e.g., Learned Hand, *Mr. Justice Holmes*, 43 HARV. L. REV. 857, 860 (1930). On his view, the justification of liberal democracy and the rule of law resides not in their ability to promote welfare or respect rights, but in their provision of a regime to which most citizens will acquiesce, thus providing a stable environment in which individuals can attempt to satisfy their personal preferences. *The Spirit of Liberty: Papers and Addresses of Learned Hand* 15, 71, 229, 307 (Irving Dilliard ed., 3d ed. 1960). Posner has noted these aspects of Hand's thought, though without acknowledging that they render his interpretation of *Carroll Towing* problematic. Richard A. Posner, *The Problems of Jurisprudence* 129 n.10 (1990).

[16] Hand's non-Posnerian understanding of negligence is also on display in his explanation of why the question of due care ordinarily is for jurors. As he put it in a later opinion, "their decision is thought most likely to accord with commonly accepted standards, real or fancied." Conway v. O'Brien, 111 F.2d 611, 612 (2d Cir. 1940), *rev'd*, 312 U.S. 492 (1941). In other words, for Hand, a jury finding of negligence is a convergence among jurors' opinions as to the undesirability of the defendant's behavior. A judge charged with reviewing such a verdict cannot scrutinize it for its soundness: it is neither sound nor unsound. Rather, the judge's function is to ensure that the jurors' collective opinion is mainstream ("commonly accepted"), thereby contributing to popular acceptance of court decisions and the law.

[17] Patrick J. Kelley & Laurel A. Wendt, *What Judges Tell Juries About Negligence: A Review of Pattern Jury Instructions*, 77 CHI.-KENT L. REV. 587 (2002).

[18] Zipursky, *supra* note 14, at 2017–18.

- It offers an optimizing conception of fault: to act prudently is to take all but only cost-efficient precautions. By contrast, jury instructions' references to *ordinary* care, and the care that a *reasonably prudent* person would take, convey a notion of *moderate* care.[19]
- It has trouble accounting for the relation of legal fault to custom. Another of Hand's aphorisms holds that "in most cases reasonable prudence is in fact common prudence."[20] There is little reason to suppose that custom consistently calls for the taking of cost-efficient precautions.[21]
- It is morally obtuse. The ordinary care standard links to custom in part to connect it to norms of positive morality. By contrast, the Hand Formula does not allow for certain "Bs" and "Ls" to be filtered out on moral grounds.[22]
- It frames the question of fault by reference to whether an actor failed to take a precaution that "society" would want the actor to take. Fault in negligence law does not concern whether the defendant was careless tout court, but whether she was careless in regard to aspects of the well-being of persons such as the plaintiff.[23]

Given these difficulties, one might fairly wonder how the Hand Formula has captured the hearts and minds of legal academics. A standard explanation is that, if only by isolating considerations relevant to the breach issue, it beats the alternatives, particularly the nebulous reasonably prudent person standard. This explanation is unsatisfying for three reasons. First, as just explained, it often does not succeed in capturing the relevant considerations. Second, if its value resides merely in inviting us to consider the burdens along with the benefits of taking certain precautions, it stands alongside many other alternative formulations that can also deliver that (modest) value.[24] Third, there is little reason to suppose that the Hand Formula lives up to its name by actually rendering the breach inquiry more determinate than it is under the reasonably prudent person standard. Mathematical symbols certainly project rigor. Yet assignations of values to them in particular cases by judges (or juries) will typically be less transparent and trustworthy than invocations of custom and positive morality called for by the ordinary care standard.

---

[19] *Id.* at 2021.

[20] The T.J. Hooper, 60 F.2d 737 (2d Cir.) (Hand, J.), *cert. denied*, 287 U.S. 662 (U.S. 1932).

[21] William M. Landes & Richard A. Posner, *The Economic Structure of Tort Law* 132–133 (1987) (arguing that customary care will tend to be optimal when transaction costs are low but acknowledging that negligence law's treatment of custom does not distinguish between low-transaction-cost and high-transaction-cost scenarios).

[22] For example, the mild inconvenience to a beachgoer who refrains from speeding in order to obtain a good tanning spot has no claim to being counted as a "B" to be balanced against the "Ls" of bodily injuries that might result from his dangerous driving. Keating, *supra* note 15, at 324–335. Likewise, the Hand Formula seems to entitle drivers to exercise less care when they drive in poorer neighborhoods, given that expected losses in these circumstances will be lower. Arthur Ripstein, *Equality, Responsibility, and the Law* 59 (1998).

[23] John C.P. Goldberg & Benjamin C. Zipursky, *The* Restatement (Third) *and the Place of Duty in Negligence Law*, 54 VAND. L. REV. 657, 685 (2001).

[24] See, e.g., Weinrib, *supra* note 3, at 149–150 (arguing that Lord Reid's opinion in *Bolton v. Stone*, [1951] App. Ca. 850 (H.L.), articulates a moral conception of fault by which the failure to take costly precautions to prevent a far-fetched risk of injury does not constitute carelessness).

So what's to like here? In fact, the Hand Formula and the picture of negligence of law built around it give expression to three important features of negligence law, and tort law more generally.

First, it conveys clearly that tort law contains *conduct-guiding rules*. In the early and mid-twentieth century, some scholars were inclined to think of modern tort law primarily as a means of enabling certain accident victims to secure compensation for their losses. Hence their embrace of notions of strict "enterprise" liability that divorce liability from wrongdoing. Partly because of his Reaganite conservatism, but also because of his appreciation of doctrine, Posner turned to the Hand Formula as a way of expressing his recognition that tort law is not a distributive mechanism or a compensation system. Rather, it is law that requires us to adjust our conduct in light of the potential consequences of our actions for others. The idea that tort law sets norms and contains directives is indeed basic. The mistake was to move from this general idea to the problematic claim that negligence law is built around a *particular directive*—namely, one that requires actors to take cost-justified precautions.

Second, the Hand Formula conveys that the guidance provided by negligence law comes from *positive law*, and hence may not mimic morality. Judges have crafted tort law with an eye toward the particular demands and needs of the legal system. In doing so, they have rendered it "objective" in ways that arguably depart from moral standards. Most notably, tort law, including negligence law, leaves little room for excuses of a sort that would tend to mitigate or undermine judgments of wrongdoing in other domains of life (for example, that one acted under duress).[25] An approach such as Posner's, which allows for the existence of gaps between legal and moral notions of fault, thus compares favorably to others that deny or downplay such gaps. For example, at least by the time of *Law's Empire*, Ronald Dworkin's Hercules, in the name of making negligence law the best it can be, was probably prepared to expand negligence liability beyond anything the courts have recognized.[26]

Third, the Hand Formula reflects, though again in a somewhat stilted way, the idea that negligence, like all torts, is a legal *wrong*. In this respect, it links to an account of tort law that is superior to assiduously amoral views of the sort articulated by Holmes. Seeking to banish moral notions from common law, Holmes cast legal negligence as the failure of a person to take advantage of a safe-harbor granted by government that enables members of the polity to avoid having to bear losses suffered by another. The Hand Formula, by contrast, presents legal fault as a variant on moral fault in the following important sense. Legally faulty conduct provides a legitimate ground for criticism and complaint:

> . . . [A] judgment of negligence has inescapable overtones of moral disapproval, for it implies that there was a cheaper alternative to the accident. Conversely, there is no moral indignation in the case in which the cost of prevention would have exceeded the cost of the accident. . . .[27]

[25] Posner, *supra* note 12, at 31–32; John C.P. Goldberg & Benjamin C. Zipursky, *The Fault in Strict Liability and the Strict Liability in Fault*, 85 FORDHAM L. REV. 743, 747 (2016).

[26] Ronald Dworkin, *Law's Empire* 238–247 (1986) (suggesting that Judge Hercules would find in English tort law a general rule of liability for all foreseeably and carelessly caused emotional distress).

[27] Posner, *supra* note 12, at 33.

While the Hand Formula does not accurately capture the content of the judgment at issue, it does correctly convey that such a judgment is being rendered.[28]

To sum up: the Hand Formula conception succeeds in emphasizing that negligence law, like tort law more generally: (1) consists in part of conduct-guiding rules; (2) sets distinctively legal standards of conduct; and (3) grounds liability in wrongdoing. The attractiveness of the Formula resides in its indirect invocations of these characteristics, rather than succeeding on its own terms as an interpretation of negligence law's notion of fault.

B. Responsibility and Redress: The Cheapest Cost Avoider and Liability Rules

Guido Calabresi's "cheapest cost avoider"—the person or entity best positioned to identify precautions against a certain kind of loss and to implement them in a cost-effective manner—is no less a fixture of economic accounts of tort law than is the Hand Formula. Although more naturally wielded as a prescription for reform,[29] it is sometimes invoked to explain and shape doctrine. For example, in *Taber v. Maine*, Judge Calabresi applied an expansive conception of *respondeat superior* liability partly on the ground that such a conception tracks when employers are in the best position to take steps to prevent employee torts.[30]

Tort law does not recognize a general rule according to which an actor is entitled to avoid liability by establishing that another was in a better position to avoid causing the type of loss suffered by the plaintiff. Far from it. Under modern common law principles, a retailer of a defective product who has no basis for assessing or controlling the product's dangers can be held strictly liable for injuries it causes to consumers: the fact that the manufacturer is much more likely to be a better cost avoider is irrelevant.[31] Likewise, causation requirements often protect cheapest cost avoiders from liability.[32] The list goes on: parents are spared from vicarious liability for the torts of their young children; possessors generally avoid liability for injuries caused by their dangerous premises to adult trespassers; and (as Calabresi himself emphasized) the fault requirement of negligence sits badly with cheapest cost avoidance.[33] Moreover, a great deal of tort law has nothing to do with

---

[28] Goldberg, *supra* note 10, at 553 ("One imagines a person who hears a tale of medical malpractice shaking his head and proclaiming, 'It is so awful when doctors fritter away our resources like that. If only they would stop squandering social wealth.'").

[29] Guido Calabresi, *The Costs of Accidents: A Legal and Economic Analysis* 136 (1970) (acknowledging that actors who play no role in bringing about certain kinds of losses, and hence face no tort liability for such losses, might well be cheapest cost avoiders).

[30] 67 F.3d 1029, 1037 (2d Cir. 1995).

[31] *Restatement (Third) of Torts: Products Liability* § 1 (1998).

[32] Guido Calabresi, *Concerning Cause and the Law of Torts: An Essay for Harry Kalven, Jr.*, 43 U. CHI. L. REV. 69, 85 (1975) (arguing that but-for causation is merely one "useful way of totting up some of the costs the cheapest cost avoider should face in deciding whether avoidance is worthwhile").

[33] Guido Calabresi & Jon T. Hirschoff, *Toward a Test for Strict Liability in Torts*, 81 YALE L.J. 1055, 1059 (1972).

accident-avoidance. It is only by unjustifiably equating tort law with accident law that one can even begin to think of tort law as organized around this principle.[34]

As was the case with the Hand Formula, we are left to puzzle over the appeal of interpreting tort law to instantiate an economic concept. And again, the answer cannot simply be that it invites us to think generally about who is well-positioned to fend off an accident, since pretty much any account of tort law and tort duties will take this consideration into account in some manner.

A better answer is that the concept of the cheapest cost avoider conveys indirectly that tort law is about interpersonal *responsibility* (among other things). The concept of responsibility has many referents.[35] One of particular relevance to tort law is responsibility as answerability. Tort law's rules generate responsibilities to refrain from injuring others, the violation of which leave violators vulnerable to being made to answer to those others. Torts are response-able wrongs; they define circumstances in which a person can be made to respond to a court order issued at the demand of her victim(s).

It follows that, when courts are fashioning the rules of tort liability, they are in part making judgments about when, in light of precedent and principle, it is appropriate for the law to render an actor answerable to another for having wrongfully injured him. For cases that raise the issue of answerability in the particular context of accidents, an actor's relative ability to foresee and avoid such injuries is highly relevant, as it is in ordinary morality. The fact that a person or entity is in a relatively good position to anticipate, and to take steps to avoid causing, a certain kind of injury marks the beginning of an argument for their being answerable if they end up causing such an injury. But it is only a beginning. In tort, answerability hinges on actually doing something to another (or failing to do something for another) and is limited by various other considerations. This is why notions of causation, fault, and the like are central to much of tort law as it applies to accidents, and why the relatively spare notion of the cheapest cost avoider cannot hope to convey the terms on which tort law actually imposes liability.

A familiar and important expression of the moral idea from which cheapest-cost-avoider-thinking draws unwarranted plausibility is the courts' long-standing emphasis on foreseeability as a necessary (but not sufficient) condition for negligence liability. Consider this passage from Lord Esher's influential early articulation of how modern negligence law incorporates a notion of foreseeability drawn from the "rules of right and wrong" (i.e., ordinary morality). A legal duty to take care to avoid injuring another is owed, he reasoned,

> whenever one person is by circumstances placed in such a position with regard to another that every one of ordinary sense who did think would *at once* recognise that if he did not use ordinary care and skill in his own conduct with regard to those circumstances he would cause danger of injury to the person or property of the other, a duty arises to use ordinary care and skill to avoid such danger . . .[36]

---

[34] John C.P. Goldberg & Benjamin C. Zipursky, *Torts as Wrongs*, 88 TEX. L. REV. 917, 920–924 (2010).

[35] John C.P. Goldberg & Benjamin C. Zipursky, "Tort Law and Responsibility," in *Philosophical Foundations of the Law of Torts* 17, 19 n.9 (John Oberdiek ed., 2014).

[36] *Heaven v. Pender*, [1883], 11 Q.B.D. 503 (C.A.) (emphasis added).

As conveyed by Esher's use of the phrase "at once," the fact that an actor is in a particularly good position to appreciate that his conduct may result in injury to certain others is a reason to deem her under a legal duty to take care to avoid causing injury to those others and to hold her answerable to them if she does carelessly injure them.[37]

The relevance of one's being in a good position to appreciate and manage a danger to one's obligations is equally present in modern landmark cases. *Tarasoff v. Regents* and *Kline v. 1500 Mass. Ave. Apt. Corp.* are obvious examples.[38] Another—authored by Judge Posner— is *Beul v. ASSE, Inc.*[39] There, a student exchange service was held liable for negligently failing to monitor a placement so as to prevent the host father from sexually and emotionally abusing a teenage student. It is possible that ASSE was the cheapest cost avoider of the plaintiff's ordeal. But, as Posner's opinion acknowledges (albeit inadequately), the plaintiff's school was also a plausible contender for that title. In any event, *Beul* does not turn on a judgment about efficient deterrence, but about what sort of protections a placement agency owes to the vulnerable exchange students, such that its failure to provide those protections will render the agency negligent and hence answerable when a student is victimized.[40]

Calabresi (with Douglas Melamed) is also famously credited for distinguishing between "liability" and "property" rules.[41] Others have plumbed the complexities of this distinction. For now it suffices to note that, insofar as the idea of a liability rule partakes of the Holmesian divorce of liability from wrongdoing, it fails to capture the nature of tort liability.[42] Tort damages are not the price to paid for the privilege of injuring another. There is no such privilege. Indeed, one who adopts the view that tort damages are prices will find themselves at risk of having to pay punitive damages for willful or wanton misconduct. Tort damages are redress for a wrong that has been done, payable in the first instance by wrongdoer to victim.

---

[37] Much the same sentiment is expressed in Cardozo's landmark *MacPherson* opinion. MacPherson v. Buick, 111 N.E. 1050, 1053 (N.Y. 1916) ("If to the element of danger there is added knowledge that the thing will be used by persons other than the purchaser, and used without new tests, then . . . the manufacturer of this thing of danger is under a duty to make it carefully.").

[38] Tarasoff v. Regents of Univ. of Cal., 551 P.2d 334 (Cal. 1976) (in bank) (a therapist whose patient professes violent intentions toward a third party that the therapist has reason to take seriously owes the third party a duty to take reasonable steps to warn her of the danger); Kline v. 1500 Mass. Ave. Apt. Corp., 439 F.2d 477 (D.C. Cir. 1970) (the possessor of an apartment building in a high-crime neighborhood owes residents a duty to take reasonable steps to protect them from being attacked in common areas); Benjamin C. Zipursky, *Foreseeability in Breach, Duty, and Proximate Cause*, 44 WAKE FOREST L. REV. 1247, 1263–1264 (2009). Inconveniently for Calabresi, even when liability attaches to background actors (such as the therapist who treated Tarasoff's assailant), it also attaches to immediate wrongdoers (such as the assailant himself).

[39] 233 F.3d 441 (7th Cir. 2000).

[40] John C.P. Goldberg & Benjamin C. Zipursky, *Civil Recourse Defended: A Reply to Posner, Calabresi, Rustad, Chamallas and Robinette*, 88 IND. L.J. 569, 584–588 (2013).

[41] Guido Calabresi & Douglas A. Melamed, *Property Rules, Liability Rules and Inalienability: One View of the Cathedral*, 85 HARV. L. REV. 1089 (1972).

[42] See *id.* at 1092 (stating that, when the law protects entitlements with liability rules, "transfer or destruction is *allowed* on the basis of a value determined by some organ of the state . . .") (emphasis added); *id.* at 1106–1108 (suggesting that a government's exercise of the eminent domain power exemplifies the idea of a liability rule).

This said, there are important distinctions to be drawn between different kinds of legal wrongdoing and legal responsibility, and the idea of a liability rule can thus be grasped as an understandable if unsatisfactory attempt to isolate the particular kind of wrongdoing and responsibility that is at work in this area of the law. In tort litigation, there is no prosecutor, and the defendant is not threatened or met with hard treatment, loss of liberty, or punitive fines. Yet tort liability is still a response to wrongdoing. One who defrauds or defames another has, in a very straightforward sense, wrongfully injured the other. Reactive attitudes such as resentment are in play, and rightly so. The victim has grounds to complain of having been mistreated and to redress for the mistreatment. But standard tort redress is its own kind of response.

Talk of victim redress seems inevitably to invite the worry that, if torts are conceived of as wrongs, tort remedies must be understood as embodying barbaric notions of revenge. The worry is unwarranted. Even supposing that vengeance is sometimes a justified response to certain kinds of wrongs, torts usually are not wrongs of this sort. No one is entitled to vengeance for a carelessly caused slip-and-fall. In most cases, redress consists of fair compensation for the plaintiff's losses, though additional damages are available for certain egregious forms of mistreatment.[43] The idea of liability rules has enjoyed buoyancy by suggesting that tort liability is not a matter of state condemnation, and in that sense stands apart from core criminal law. But the latter notion is better captured by recognizing the distinctively noncriminal form of accountability for wrongdoing that is provided through tort law. Again, tort damages are not fees. They are court-ordered redress, issued upon the demand of the plaintiff and upon proof of wrongful injury.

C. Injury-Inclusive and Strictly Defined Wrongs: The Coase Theorem

It is no accident that Ronald Coase's famous "theorem" was born in part of nuisance law.[44] Among torts, nuisance more readily lends itself to analysis in terms of "reciprocal" causation than others. After all, it almost always involves a conflict of uses between or among nearby plots of land. Moreover, a nuisance plaintiff can prevail without proving that the defendant intended to interfere, or that she failed to exercise due care in preventing interference. It suffices (prima facie) to prove that she interfered unreasonably with the plaintiff's use and enjoyment of his land, where unreasonableness is gauged primarily by reference to the nature of the locality and the legitimate expectations of those who inhabit it. Hence the strictness of nuisance liability in chestnuts such as *Sturges v. Bridgman*—the case of the unfortunate confectioner whose mortars were located so as to deprive the plaintiff doctor of quiet to which he was entitled, given the character of the neighborhood.[45]

---

[43] Benjamin C. Zipursky, Palsgraf, *Punitive Damages, and Preemption*, 125 HARV. L. REV. 1757, 1777–1779 (2012).

[44] Ronald H. Coase, *The Problem of Social Cost*, 3 J.L. & ECON. 1 (1960).

[45] (1879) 11 Ch D 852 (Eng.).

Still, there is little reason to think that nuisance law calls for judges in particular cases to decide, on welfarist grounds, which of two conflicting activities the law ought to permit, or to devise rules that will remove impediments to transactions so as to enable higher-value users to engage in those uses.[46] In the standard case, nuisance liability rests on a judgment that one person has put her land to use in a way that unduly burdens her neighbor(s) by subjecting them to excessive noise, vibrations, or nauseating odors, or by requiring them to take steps to shield themselves from encountering activities that they ought not to have to encounter in or around their premises.[47] In other words, liability for nuisance really is wrongs-based, even though the conception of wrongdoing involved is far from the sort of specific-intent wrongfulness that characterizes *mala in se* crimes, and also somewhat removed from notions of negligence.

So if the Coase Theorem, too, does not capture nuisance law (much less tort law), wherein lies its surface interpretive plausibility? Two features of the Coasean approach stand out. The first is its recognition that torts such as nuisance are injury-inclusive wrongs. As noted earlier, each tort has two sides. Other wrongs (for example, the crime of narcotics possession) can be defined without reference to an interaction between or among two or more persons. Torts cannot. All torts are reciprocal in the sense of involving an interaction between two or more persons, not in the peculiarly agnostic sense conveyed by the Coase Theorem.

The second feature of tort law that is alluded to by the Coase Theorem is the relatively unforgiving standards that it sometimes adopts when defining what counts as wrongdoing.[48] For purposes of establishing liability for compensatory damages, tort law on the whole is famously indifferent to an actor's having been well-meaning, having undertaken her best efforts, or having had a plausible excuse. Nuisance law partakes of this kind of strictness by being largely indifferent to the extent to which a defendant has made efforts to avoid interfering with his neighbors. That the confectioner in *Sturges* took great pains to prevent his operation from bothering his neighbor (assuming he did) is beside the point. Yet it is a fallacy to move from tort law's unwillingness to give wrongdoers a break to the thought that tort law has nothing to do with right and wrong and hence requires welfarist analysis to fill the void. Given the character of the relevant neighborhood, the doctor in *Sturges* enjoyed a legal entitlement to a certain degree of quiet—a right that the confectioner's operations infringed. No less than the suburban kennel owner mentioned earlier, the confectioner was doing something with his

---

[46] Christopher Essert, *Nuisance and the Normative Boundaries of Ownership*, 52 TULSA L. REV. 85, 93–94 (2016); Donal Nolan, "'A Tort Against Land': Private Nuisance as a Property Tort," in *Rights and Private Law* 459 (Donal Nolan & Andrew Robertson eds., 2011); Henry Smith, *Exclusion and Property Rules in the Law of Nuisance*, 90 VA. L. REV. 966 (2004).

[47] See, e.g., Mark v. State Dep't of Fish & Wildlife, 84 P.3d 155 (Or. App. 2004) (affirming injunctive relief for nuisance where the defendant permitted persons to use its land to engage in sexual activity in plain view of plaintiffs' residence). Although *Mark* is sometimes described as a case of "moral nuisance," the basis for liability was not the immorality per se of public sex acts (assuming they are immoral), but rather their being performed in circumstances such that the plaintiffs were required to take unusual steps to avoid being confronted by them.

[48] Goldberg & Zipursky, *supra* note 26, at 752–754.

property that he was not permitted to do: he acted wrongfully by generating noises and vibrations in a manner that exceeded the bound of the "live and let live" principle embedded in nuisance law. By contrast, were the confectioner to have held a noisy New Year's Eve party that, once each year, kept the doctor from a good night's sleep, the doctor would not have had a valid nuisance claim. Absent some special circumstance, it is entirely acceptable, not wrongful, for the owner of a property in a residential area to hold the occasional noisy party, particularly on a recognized holiday.

III. Conclusion

An understanding of tort law is available that is pragmatist rather than Platonic, yet does not partake of the backflips required of standard-issue interpretive economic analysis. In the spirit of the general approach to law that goes under the heading of "the New Private Law," this chapter offers a sketch of that account.

The torts recognized by courts and legislatures identify ways of interacting with others that are injurious and not to be done. These conduct-guiding norms are plural in substance: they do not boil down to a single rule, such as a rule requiring that cost-efficient precautions be taken against causing losses to others. The particular tort of negligence requires (when a duty is owed) an actor to avoid injuring another by conduct that lacks the care that would be taken by a reasonably prudent person. For other torts, the measure of conduct has little or nothing to do with precaution-taking. It does not follow that tort law is a hodgepodge—as suggested earlier, it can be loosely organized around mistreatments involving interferences with aspects of individual well-being. Battery, defamation, and fraud are not the same wrong, but it is hardly surprising that each is a recognized legal wrong for which victim redress is available through the courts.

Tort law's standards of conduct are legally defined and thus may stand somewhat apart from moral standards. Still, it would be a mistake to leap to the conclusion that tort standards are completely detached from ordinary morality. If tort law is to help guide conduct, if it is not going to catch us completely off guard, and if it is to maintain some legitimacy as an institution that claims to render us answerable to each other, its wrongs must resemble notions of wrongdoing found in everyday life. It is one thing for courts to define negligence law's reasonably prudent person standard in a way that subjects to liability actors who, outside of the law, would be regarded as having a good excuse for their carelessness.[49] It is another for them to impose "tort" liability with indifference to whether the conduct at issue was marked by the sorts of deficiencies that generally make conduct eligible to be deemed wrongful and injurious.

Because torts are wrongs, their commission generates criticism, disapproval, resentment, and related reactions that attend other forms of wrongdoing. Liability is likewise understood as negative rather than neutral: as something in the same family as blame

---

[49] John C.P. Goldberg, *Inexcusable Wrongs*, 103 CAL. L. REV. 467, 487–490 (2015).

and punishment. Yet responsibility in tort is of a distinctive sort—it takes the form of accountability or answerability to one's fellow citizens for having wrongfully injured them. Unsurprisingly, in this domain, an actor's ability to anticipate and take steps to prevent the occurrence of such an injury is often crucial to a finding of wrongdoing in the requisite sense, and hence of answerability.

Scholars who attempt to reduce tort law to economic concepts cannot but fail. And yet economic analyses of the subject have been onto something. Some arguably fit tort law better than certain alternatives, including those that would treat it as a system for allocating losses irrespective of wrongdoing. All told, however, there is a better path. To see it, one must abandon the reductionist instincts that drive so much of modern legal scholarship. Once these are put aside, one can readily grasp tort law for what it is.

ACKNOWLEDGMENTS

Thanks for helpful comments to Jacob Gersen, Andrew Gold, Daniel Hemel, Dan Kelly, Barack Richman, Henry Smith, and Ben Zipursky. This chapter reflects two decades of collaborative work with Professor Benjamin Zipursky. For a synthetic statement of our view, see John C.P. Goldberg & Benjamin C. Zipursky, *Recognizing Wrongs* (2020).

CHAPTER 17

....

PROPERTY

....

J.E. PENNER

I. INTRODUCTION: THE BUNDLE
OF RIGHTS CHALLENGE

WHEN I began thinking about property many moons ago, the central landmark was the idea that property had a "nominalist" ontology and was in danger of "disintegration" as a working legal category for that very reason. Singer explained nominalism as an idea opposed to what he called "conceptualism":

> Conceptualism is the belief that concepts at a high level of generality and abstractness are operative, in the sense that they correspond to elements of the real world and are the basis of numerous and concrete subrules that can be deduced from them.... Nominalism is the belief that concepts at only a very low level of generality and abstractness are operative. Thus general concepts, such as "law" or "property" or "rights," are seen merely as convenient categorizations of experience. We put into those categories the rules and meaning we choose to put into them. They do not of themselves determine their scope or consequences....
>
> Nominalists as well as conceptualists claim that at some level, words and concepts correspond to objects or experience in the real world. The difference is the level of generality at which concepts are thought to be "real." Whether one is a nominalist or conceptualist depends on a comparative judgment of the level of generality of operativeness of concepts.[1]

The themes of this chapter are explored in much greater detail in J.E. Penner, *Property Rights: A Re-Examination* (2020).

[1] Joseph William Singer, *The Legal Rights Debate in Analytical Jurisprudence from Bentham to Hohfeld*, 1982 WIS. L. REV. 975, 1016–1017.

Thomas Grey makes a similar claim in his influential "The Disintegration of Property":

> [D]iscourse about property [among property "specialists", that is, lawyers or econo-mists] has fragmented into a set of discontinuous usages. The more fruitful and useful of these usages are stipulated by theorists; but these depart drastically from each other and common speech. Conversely, meanings of "property" in law that cling to their origin in thing-ownership are integrated least successfully into the general doctrinal framework of law, legal theory, and economics. It seems fair to conclude from a glance at the range of current usages that the specialists who design and manipulate the legal structures of the advanced capitalist economies could eas-ily do without the term "property" at all.[2]

It seems to me that a good case might be made that "nominalism" about property has had a significant impact in U.S. case law.[3] Our concern here, however, is whether it is a helpful stance to take as a theorist of property. I shall argue it is not. I shall contend that there are indeed "high" level abstractions about property which we cannot plausibly do without if we are to understand property rights and property law doctrine, and further-more, that the "bundle of rights" challenge, hereafter "BOR," does not assist us in mak-ing sense of these abstractions.

II. THE CONCEPTUAL FAILURE OF BOR AND THE "NEW PRIVATE LAW" AS IT RELATES TO PROPERTY

BOR may be stated thus:

> Any legal configuration understood to be a property right, say a fee simple in Blackacre, is in fact an aggregate of norms, such as the liberty to enter Blackacre, the power to license others to enter, the liberty to build upon Blackacre, the power to grant an easement over Blackacre, and so on. There is no necessary and sufficient set of these constituting norms which make up the "property right" to Blackacre. Different aggregates will occur in different circumstances, and so the legal labeling of some such aggregate as a "property" right cannot properly be done on the basis of some central constituting norms, such as the right that oth-ers exclude themselves from Blackacre, or the right to deal with the title to

---

[2] Thomas C. Grey, "The Disintegration of Property," in *Nomos XXII: Property* 69, 72–73 (J. Roland Pennock & John W. Chapman eds., 1980).

[3] See, e.g., the majority decisions in Moore v. Regents of the Univ. of Cal., 793 P.2d 479 (Cal. 1990), United States v. Craft, 535 U.S. 274 (2002), and State v. Shack 277 A.2d 369, 372–375 (N.J. 1971); see also Henry E. Smith, *The Persistence of System in Property Law*, 163 U. PA. L. REV. 2055, 2074–2083 (2015).

Blackacre.[4] Therefore determining whether, for example, rights in respect of excised human cells[5] count as property rights is largely a matter of policy considerations, not a matter of "legal analysis." There is no "internal" organizing principle which makes sense of the fact that certain property norms seem to go together.

BOR is generally regarded as being underpinned by what might be called the Hohfeld-Honoré synthesis.[6] The synthesis rests upon a fairly serious mistake,[7] which is that while the Hohfeldian examination of jural norms is *analytic* if it is anything, Honoré's elaboration of the incidents making up ownership is anything but—it is *functional*. By functional I mean that Honoré describes the situation of the owner, not principally in terms of his Hohfeldian powers, duties, and rights vis-à-vis others, but in terms of the social or economic advantages that an owner has by virtue of his position, and the terms and limitations of those advantages.

That Hohfeldian jural relations are analytic is evident. Hohfeld[8] aimed to produce an exhaustive analysis of the fundamental relations out of which the legal position of any one person vis-à-vis any other can be comprehensively formulated. That Honoré's list of incidents[9] is functional is also plain. Here is the list:

1. "The right to possess, *viz.* to have exclusive physical control of a thing"[10]
2. "The right to use ... use refers to the owner's personal enjoyment and use of the thing"[11]
3. "The right to manage ... the right to decide how and by whom a thing shall be used. This right depends, legally, on a cluster of powers, chiefly powers of licensing acts which would otherwise be unlawful and powers of contracting"[12]

---

[4] As Dennis Klimchuk has reminded me, following or extending Grey's "disintegration of property thesis," one might contend that a more thorough-going nominalism could treat the person at the "advantage" end of any Hohfeldian jural relation, viz. any right holder, power holder, liberty holder, or immunity holder, as having a property right. On this version of nominalism, a property right is just any legal advantage. Of course at this point, "property" no longer is a distinguishing feature of any jural relation.

[5] E.g., *Moore*, 793 P.2d at 479; Yearworth and others v. North Bristol NHS Trust [2009] EWCA (Civ) 37, [2010] QB 1.

[6] See, e.g., Stephen R. Munzer, *A Theory of Property* 17–27 (1990). It was also underpinned specifically in the United States by various attitudes of the Legal Realists. For discussion, see Smith, *supra* note 3.

[7] Not adequately addressed, I now think, in J.E. Penner, *The "Bundle of Rights" Picture of Property*, 43 UCLA L. REV. 711, 754–767 (1996) [hereinafter Penner, *Bundle*]. There I focused on the fact that Honoré's list of incidents depended upon the existence of a "thing," some res, whereas Hohfeld's notion of rights in rem sought to displace things as an organizing feature of property rights; I still think that is right, but I proffer here a different difficulty, which I think has more traction in illuminating the tripartite structure of title or ownership. See also J.E. Penner, *Hohfeldian Use-Rights in Property*, in *Property Problems: From Genes to Pension Funds* (J.W. Harris ed., 1997).

[8] Wesley Newcomb Hohfeld, *Some Fundamental Legal Conceptions as Applied in Judicial Reasoning*, 23 YALE L.J. 16 (1913); Wesley Newcomb Hohfeld, *Fundamental Legal Conceptions as Applied in Judicial Reasoning*, 26 YALE L.J. 710 (1917).

[9] A.M. Honoré, "Ownership," in *Oxford Essays in Jurisprudence* 107 (A.G. Guest ed., 1961).

[10] *Id.* at 113.   [11] *Id.* at 116.   [12] *Id.* at 116.

4. "The right to the income"[13]
5. "The right to capital...the power to alienate the thing and the liberty to consume, waste, or destroy the whole or part of it"[14]
6. "The right to security...Legally, this is in effect an immunity from expropriation"[15]
7. "The incident of transmissibility"[16]
8. "The incident of absence of term"[17]
9. "The prohibition of harmful use"[18]
10. "Liability to execution"[19]
11. "Residuary character"[20]

Honoré's list of incidents is a "functional" analysis of property, not a legal-analytic one. We can affirm this by noting, first, that rather than framing the right to possess in terms of a right to the immediate, exclusive possession of a thing that correlates with a duty imposed upon all others not to interfere with that thing, Honoré speaks of the owner's "exclusive physical control." This is functional or empirical, concerning physical engagement and the possibilities that that affords. It is worth noting that in some respects the description is not even really apt. I am not sure what it means to be "in physical control" of Blackacre, for instance. And my ownership of Black Beauty is not diminished in the least even if I am a terrible rider and cannot control him at all. Clearly the idea is something like the owner alone has the liberty to engage in various ways with the thing he owns. But even so, the notion of control is not easily framed in terms of jural relations, as Holmes long ago pointed out.[21]

As to the second incident, the right to use, I think it is now fairly clear that there is, at common law, prima facie, no such thing.[22] I say "prima facie" because while it is generally the case that one's property rights cannot be framed in terms of any list of legally defined particular use rights, nor is there a legally defined general, single, use right, it has been argued that the general duty not to interfere with the property of others is sometimes framed in terms of interference with use, in particular in the tort of nuisance to land. We shall consider nuisance.[23] The general point is that the right to immediate, exclusive possession protects an owner's *interest* in using the things he owns, and thus this interest may justify the right;[24] indeed, one might say this exclusive liberty is the whole point of owning some things—clothing, bottles of wine, and so on. Nevertheless the idea of use does not prima facie inform any particular jural relations between the owner and others.

---

[13] *Id.* at 117.   [14] *Id.* at 118.   [15] *Id.* at 119.   [16] *Id.* at 120.
[17] *Id.* at 121.   [18] *Id.* at 123.   [19] *Id.* at 123.   [20] *Id.* at 126.

[21] Oliver Wendell Homes Jr., *The Common Law* 174 (Mark DeWolfe Howe ed., 1963) (1881) ("The law does not enable me to use or abuse this book which lies before me. That is a physical power which I have without the aid of the law. What the law does is simply to prevent other men to a greater or less extent from interfering with my use or abuse.").

[22] See J.E. Penner, "The Right to Property: The Exclusion Thesis," in *The Idea of Property in Law* 68–104 (1997); Arthur Ripstein, "Possession and Use," in *Philosophical Foundations of Property Law* (James Penner & Henry E. Smith eds., 2013).

[23] Section IV.B.   [24] For a contrary view see Ripstein, *supra* note 22.

We can go on. I take it that the third, fourth, and fifth incidents speak for themselves as "economic" incidents of ownership, not juridical ones. There is, in law, no right "to manage," to "income,"[25] or to "capital," per se,[26] and Honoré seems fully to appreciate this when he says, "[The right to manage] depends, *legally*, on a cluster of powers, chiefly powers of licensing acts which would otherwise be unlawful and powers of contracting."[27]

We could continue,[28] but I take it the point is made. One cannot simply regard Honoré's incidents as substantial juridical norms which fill in the battery of multital jural relations to generate a complete bundle of rights which an owner is supposed to have.

It is worth emphasizing that the Hohfeldian cannot reconfigure Honoré's incidents so that most of them can be represented as Hohfeldian jural relations, for two reasons. The first has to do with the nature of a function and its contrast with jural relations. A jural relation is not a function, at least in the sense with which Honoré is concerned. Von Wright's distinction between results and consequences[29] is illuminating here. The exercise of a power bears an "intrinsic" relation[30] to the *result* of its exercise, but not to whatever other *consequences* flow from its exercise. For example, when X exercises a power of sale over her laptop to sell it to Y, the result of that exercise is that title passes to Y. If Y does not acquire title, then there has been no sale. It may be the case, in consequence of this, that Y must pay sales tax. That is certainly a consequence of the sale, but not its result. The power of sale would be the same if sales taxes were abolished tomorrow. So it is a mistake to think that when X sells her laptop to Y she exercises a power to impose a sales tax on Y. So though it might, *might*, be a consequence of one's having various rights and powers in respect of one's property that one may manage it, this is a consequence of the exercise of those powers in a particular context, and depends on what one means by "manage." But such a functional "power" to manage is not a jural relation of any kind with respect to anyone.[31] The second reason is that certain of the incidents, such as income and transmissibility, concern cases where title arises or passes by operation of law, for example on the birth of a calf or by inheritance, and Hohfeld never clearly analyzed rights, duties, powers, and so on that arise or are transmitted by operation of law.

Leaving the Hohfeld-Honoré synthesis behind, another thought which seems to underscore the BOR point of view is that it best explains the way in which there are a number of possible, but differently juridically configured, interests in land. One immediately thinks of

---

[25] Unless income is restricted to "natural" income, like the apples on one's apple tree, or the calf born of one's cow.

[26] Of course, under a trust, income and capital rights are regularly created. But trusts are not merely proprietary devices but also a matter of the obligations that a trustee owes the beneficiaries.

[27] Honoré, *supra* note 9, at 116 (emphasis added).

[28] Some of the incidents, such as the absence of term, or the right's "residuary" character, could not really be counted as part of the BOR in any case, since they are meant to be important defining features of certain of the rights in the bundle.

[29] Georg Henrik von Wright, *Norm and Action: A Logical Inquiry* 39–41 (1963).

[30] Joseph Raz, *Practical Reason and Norms* 103 (1990); cf. Carl Wellman, *A Theory of Rights: Persons Under Laws, Institutions, and Morals* 45 (1985).

[31] I am not casting doubt on the possibility that in other areas of legal doctrine, say that of company law, a legally defined office of manager can be part of the law, in the same way that the law of trusts creates the office of a trustee.

such interests as are found in the *numerus clausus*: possessory rights, powers of transfer, security interests, easements, and so on. But this thought leads to a second proposition about BOR: BOR essentially weds the idea of title to property with the power to undertake contractual (or similar) obligations. Let me explain.

Besides the right to immediate, exclusive possession, the power to license others to enter into or take possession while retaining title,[32] and the power to dispose of one's title, by grant of a lesser title or outright transfer, the other elements of the *numerus clausus* originated in contract.[33] A mortgage, a title-transfer security, was originally simply a conditional contractual transfer. The same was true of leases. And contract remains a basis for creating nonproprietary interests of similar kinds to the property interests one can create. I can contractually license you to use a right of way over Blackacre for a period of ten years or for so long as I remain owner of the property, whichever is less. And I can contractually grant you a conditional power to take possession of Blackacre, and thereupon grant you a power to sell it, the condition for which is that I have defaulted upon repayment of a loan from you, which conditional power is to last as long as my debt to you remains outstanding, or for so long as I remain owner of Blackacre, whichever comes first. This may not be a particularly good form of security, but the law perfectly allows the creation of such a thing.

The point to grasp is that the powers of title to grant mortgages, leases, restrictive covenants, and so on arose because the law determined in its wisdom to allow certain *originally purely contractual* obligations of the owner to "run with the land,"[34] that is, to bind successors in title to the obligor and, in cases such as easements, to pass to successors in title of the obligee. The same is true of the trust, although the obligations were recognized in equity, not in the common law.

I am not in the least disputing that this was a good thing, but allowing this development of the law is quite clearly a matter of policy: we do not extend all the same sorts of powers to owners of chattels, and civil law jurisdictions do not extend all of them to land and they do not (as a matter of applying civil law concepts, at least) recognize trusts at all.

By failing to realize the different *origin or source* of different property interests, the BOR theorist fails to see the different *nature* of these interests.[35] These are not simply different configurations of Hohfeldian jural relations which any system of property might adopt. Rather, they reflect clear policy preferences having to do not just with the scope of property rights but also with the power to voluntarily undertake obligations. In a sense BOR deracinates these interests, taking them all as being "property interests" with a similar sort of standing, when they are clearly distinctive. For example, they typically[36]

[32] Under which I mean to include the power to put property in custody or "representative possession" of the owner, and cases of bailment. See Michael Bridge, *Personal Property Law* 39–40 (4th ed. 2015); *id.* at 59–68.

[33] Broadly speaking, to include the ability to impose binding obligations by way of covenant and, in equity, to cover the case of the trust.

[34] Or with property rights more generally, real and personal, in the case of trust assets.

[35] A point made in Penner, *Bundle, supra* note 7, at 727–728.

[36] The exception is the easement, which binds in both ways: the successor to the servient tenement owner is bound by the covenant creating the easement, and all third parties are liable in an action (in English law) for nuisance if they interfere with the easement-holder's right, for example, blocking the entrance to a right of way.

partake of a quite different "in rem" nature.[37] A mortgagee's interest is "in rem" in the sense that it binds successors in title to the mortgagor and, in that sense, could in principle bind anyone because anyone in principle might be a successor to the mortgagor. But it doesn't bind in rem in the same way that my right to immediate, exclusive possession of my wristwatch does. That right binds in rem in the sense that everyone, right now, is under a duty not to interfere with my watch. The creation of a mortgage does not impose any sort of in rem obligation on everyone, right now. It is just this sort of important distinction, about as important a distinction as one could find in the law of property given the special importance of rights in rem to the nature of property in tangibles, that BOR does not merely fail to accommodate and explain but positively obscures.

If, therefore, we look carefully at these "obligational" members of the *numerus clausus*, we can analytically reduce the "closed number" to three: the possessory right, namely, the right to immediate, exclusive possession, and the two powers that go with title, namely, the power to license others to enter into or take possession while retaining title, and the power to dispose of one's title, by grant of a lesser title or outright transfer.[38] In certain cases, the exercise of these powers will give rise to obligations that will "run" with the owner's title to her property,[39] or in others with both her and her counterparty's titles to the property.[40]

In these "running with the land cases," the members of the list can then be understood to reflect various ways in which an owner may come under an obligation, for various purposes and with various conditions, now usually legally regulated and circumscribed, to exercise either or both of his two powers of title: (1) the power to grant possessory licenses, for example, to license another to enter upon land for a limited purpose (an easement or profit) or to take possession of the thing whilst he retains title (e.g., a bailment, to give vacant possession to a mortgagee prior to the latter's exercise of a power of sale); and (2) the power to deal with title, either by granting, where possible, a lesser title, such as a lease or a life estate, or by transferring title outright. Both of these powers can sometimes be exercised by others (by agents, pledgees, mortgagees, and so on).

Following this reduction to three, we do have a sort of "bundle" of jural entities, one right and two powers, which characterize ownership. Ownership, or title to property, is "complex" to that extent. Ownership, then, comprises an underlying right, the right to immediate, exclusive possession, plus powers to deal with that right. The case of intangible property, such as choses in action, is even simpler, since the underlying right confers no right to genuine *possession* of any tangible thing at all;[41] all we have are an underlying right, for example, to be paid $10, say, which is *inherently* "exclusive" in the

[37] J.E. Penner, "Duty and Liability in Respect of Funds," in *Commercial Law: Perspectives and Practice* (John P. Lowry & Loukas A. Mistelis eds., 2006).

[38] For an application of this sort of analysis to the trust, see J.E. Penner, *The (True) Nature of a Beneficiary's Equitable Proprietary Interest Under a Trust*, 27 CAN. J.L. & JURISPRUDENCE 473 (2014).

[39] An example is a profit a prendre, which can be held "in gross."

[40] An example is an easement, where there must be both a dominant and servient tenement.

[41] The case of documentary intangibles is a complication, not an exception. Certain intangible rights may be represented via the possession of certain tangibles, typically documents, whose exchange, for example, can result in the exchange of the intangible underlying rights.

sense that nothing any third party does can extinguish this right in normal circum-stances, and a power to deal with it, by assignment, and so on.[42] On this perspective, a property right is a right which has the character of "alienable exclusivity."

The tripartite structure of title set out here obviously relates property both to the law of tort and to the law of voluntarily undertaken obligations or contract, understood broadly to include the law of covenants and voluntary obligations undertaken in equity. Regarding the former, the right to immediate exclusive possession of tangible property is the counterpart formulation of the duty not to trespass on the property of others, or, via application rules of strict liability and negligence, to cause that property damage. I shall call this norm "BPrN," for the Basic Property Norm—the exclusionary norm for tangible property. Regarding the property/contract interface and the *numerus clausus*, ignoring the contractual side is perhaps the worst facet of treating these relationships as just "sticks" in a property bundle that can be handed out by an owner.[43]

Singer eventually retreated from a pure or purist nominalism.[44] In view of the work of Merrill and Smith, he is willing to acknowledge standard packages which make up the property interests the law recognizes. He now joins a particular U.S. tradition of legal schol-arship, in which figures like Alexander, Penalver, Radin, Dagan, and Dorfman are represen-tative, which aims to understand these various packages in terms of a richer moral-political perspective in which different political values such as autonomy, liberty, solidarity, commu-nity, and so forth contour property law, and in particular to examine what justifiable limita-tions upon the basic right of exclusion and two powers of·title can exist. It is beyond the scope of this chapter to investigate this literature, but whatever its merits, it underscores the defeat of BOR. The high-level or abstract concepts I have identified in the tripartite struc-ture of title *do* structure our understanding of property rights and property law doctrine, and do so splendidly. They organize our ideas about property rights from "first principles," so to speak, and illuminate (with the help of the law of obligations) the *numerus clausus*.

Higher order or abstract legal concepts, which on BOR are merely provisional legal "complexes" like the fee simple, or the trust, or the contract, regularly feature in laws which are followed all the time. To just consider some U.K. legislation, Section 1 of the Law of Property Act 1925, the Trustee Act 2000, and the Contracts (Rights of Third Parties) Act 1999 frame genuine legal rules which feature the concepts of the fee simple absolute in possession, the trust, and the contract, respectively. The examples can, of course, easily be multiplied. The concept of damages for breach of contract, with vari-ants such as expectation damages and reliance damages, is very general and abstract, but

---

[42] I therefore do not think one needs to show that the exchange value of intangible rights like choses in action is protected by exclusionary rules. See Thomas W. Merrill, *Property and the Right to Exclude*, 77 NEB. L. REV. 730, 751 (1998). No exclusionary rules are necessary when something is inherently intangible—there can be no crossing of a boundary where no boundary exists. That is, in the case of an intangible there is nothing to exclude anybody from.

[43] Penner, *Bundle, supra* note 7, at 739–742; Penner, *supra* note 22, at 74, 93–96. I thank Lisa Austin for making me emphasize these points.

[44] Joseph William Singer, *Democratic Estates: Property Law in a Free and Democratic Society*, 94 CORNELL L. REV. 1009 (2009).

it does essential work nonetheless. So also does the concept of trespass, which applies to many different sorts of particular fact situations.

These sorts of considerations prompt the point that Hohfeld's analysis was in terms of fundamental jural relations each of which explicated a different notion of "right." Moreover, the idea was that a complete legal picture of the way that each individual stood, as a matter of law, vis-à-vis all others could be framed in terms only of these jural relations, seeing the individual in a web of jural relations, as it were. Assuming that this analysis is to be understood as a comprehensive analysis of existing law and how it applies to individuals, then it seems to suggest that the notion of a legal rule qua high-level abstraction (of which a legal definition is a kind) is somehow not part of legal reality. But since it is obvious that the *source* of the individual jural relations in which one person stands to others is the application of abstract legal rules, both duty-imposing rules and power-conferring rules, it seems clear that the law does operate with abstractions of this kind. Doing away with these "abstractions" and treating only the resultant configuration of jural relations as legally real would give rise to a *loss* of legal understanding, because we would be blinded to the reasons why any particular jural relation arose in the first place. This thought is particularly vivid in the case of contracts. There could be no contracts if individuals had no power to enter into them; but this power is obviously abstract in the sense that (barring illegal contracts) one can in principle enter into a contract about anything—that is, create any set of jural relations obtaining between the counterparties bounded only by their wills and their imaginations. But the resulting set of jural relations are still a legally significant abstract thing—a contract—whatever that set contains.

The New Private Law takes doctrine seriously. In the case of property law that means taking its higher level rules and concepts (call this "conceptualism" if you like) seriously, and trying to make sense of them. Pursuing that path in a preliminary way is what I have set out to do so far in this chapter, by focusing on the tripartite notion of title as the elemental feature which helps to organize our basic notions of property. In the remainder I hope to point out some of the different approaches, and tensions, in the New Private Law scholarship.

III. Two "Instrumentalisms" and Kantianism

In identifying Henry Smith and me as "instrumentalists" about the law of property, Christopher Essert puts the point in this way:[45]

> [For instrumentalists] property rights are a tool or instrument to be used to serve some interest that exists independently of it, or some general advantage that is conceivable in non-property terms.

[45] Christopher Essert, *Nuisance and the Normative Boundaries of Ownership*, 52 Tulsa L. Rev. 85, 100–101 & n.81 (2016).

For a non-instrumentalist—and I shall only consider here the Kantian non-instrumentalist, if only for the reason that recent work by Ripstein has developed this view in a way that demands attention—questions of interest or advantage are conceptually posterior to the way in which rights establish how we stand in relation to one another. To put this in terms of a kind of slogan, private law rights establish the kinds of interests we can have, thus establishing the kinds of interests which the law protects. In other words, we do not first consider what interests we might have in, say, the use of things, and then use the law as an instrument to protect them. Rather, property rights, as a manifestation of right more generally, make it plain that the only "interest" that the law protects is the "interest"—it is rather the duty we owe to ourselves—not to be subordinated to others.

As is well known, Ripstein's version of private right turns on the idea that no one is in charge of anyone else.[46] More specifically, Kant's private right ensures the independence from the interferences of others of our choices concerning the "means" that we have, our bodies, and our property. Another way of putting this idea is that private right entitles us to a realm of agency: the ability to pursue purposes, the ends we set ourselves, in so far as we do that by using our means in various ways. For Kant, your private rights are relational and negative; they concern the actions of others, prohibiting their acting so as to interfere with your means by damaging or usurping them. You do not have any "positive" rights in your property: no one else is under a duty to assist you in the use of your means, or to provide a favorable environment for their use. Finally, the function of property rights is essentially allocative. In order to have a regime of right which makes necessary reference to the concept of a person's own means, we have to know which means are yours and which are mine. That problem needs no solution in the case of the right to our bodies, which for Kant is "innate," but it does require a solution as regards "acquired" rights. For example, we need to have a power to create contractual rights and a power to appropriate unowned things.

This is a powerful and prima facie attractive account of private law. As Ripstein says,[47]

> The idea of independence carries the justificatory burden of the entire argument, from the prohibition of personal injury, through the minutiae of property and contract law, on to the details of the constitutional separation of powers. Kant argues that these norms and institutions do more than enhance the prospects for independence: they provide the only possible way in which a plurality of persons can interact on terms of equal freedom. Kant's concern is not with how people should interact, as a matter of ethics, but with how they can be forced to interact, as a matter of right.

Turning to our two "instrumentalisms," Merrill and Smith begin with the idea that the law of property is an instrument for allocating and defining the use of "external

---

[46] Arthur Ripstein, *Private Wrongs* (2016) (especially chapters 2 and 3); see also Arthur Ripstein, this volume.

[47] Arthur Ripstein, *Force and Freedom: Kant's Legal and Political Philosophy* 14 (2009).

resources," and it is to be judged on the basis of how well it does that.[48] As Smith succinctly puts it:[49]

> Property law coordinates activities and resolves conflict between members of society over external resources.

One of their central ideas is that legal doctrine reflects a "property" or "exclusion" strategy which contrasts with a governance strategy in respect of the rules governing resources.[50] The moving idea here is that a system which instantiates use rights in resources can, under the "property" or "exclusion" strategy, "delegate" to the owner the right to determine, among the range of uses to which a resource can be put, which uses will be made of that asset, by giving him the right to exclude all others from making use of it (or interfering with his uses of it). Alternatively, where the costs of achieving a particular social goal warrant it, a "governance" strategy can be adopted. Under this strategy, either by allowing the owner to contract with others or by instituting public regulations, a more fine-grained "rights to specific, enumerated uses" regime for the property can be realized.

One of the benefits of being a New Private Law instrumentalist is that one can benefit from the insights of other instrumentalists, without thinking that their views cover the whole instrumentalist terrain—that is, they do not identify all of the considerations which figure in a comprehensive assessment of whether the law is doing its job well. So I am happy to commend Merrill and Smith's work as a leading source of instrumentalist insight.

Briefly, my own instrumental approach is somewhat different, drawing upon the works of Joseph Raz, fundamentally, and more recently on the works of John Gardner. This tradition might be called "reasons fundamentalist" instrumentalism (RFI). Only a very brief sketch is warranted here.

The basic ideas underlying RFI are two. First, we have the moral duties we have because as the sorts of rational creatures we are, we can respond to reasons; and we have the moral rights we have because we can rightly hold others to respect those reasons when the reasons reflect important interests that we have. Gardner develops the

---

[48] Thomas W. Merrill & Henry E Smith, *The Property/Contract Interface*, 101 Colum. L. Rev. 773 (2001) [hereinafter Merrill & Smith, *Property/Contract*]; Thomas W. Merrill & Henry E. Smith, *What Happened to Property in Law and Economics?*, 111 Yale L.J. 357 (2001); Thomas W. Merrill & Henry E. Smith, *The Morality of Property*, 48 Wm. & Mary L. Rev. 1849 (2007).

[49] Smith, *supra* note 3, at 2057.

[50] Although Merrill and Smith are clear that these represent poles of a spectrum, and intermediate strategies will also be adopted where the information/transaction costs analysis warrants them. See, e.g., Thomas W. Merrill & Henry E Smith, *Optimal Standardization in the Law of Property: The Numerus Clausus Principle*, 110 Yale L.J. 1, 38 (2000); Merrill & Smith, *Property/Contract*, *supra* note 48, at 809–851; Henry E. Smith, *Exclusion Versus Governance: Two Strategies for Delineating Property Rights*, 31 J. Legal Stud. S543 (2002); Henry E Smith, *Mind the Gap: The Indirect Relation Between Ends and Means in American Property Law*, 94 Cornell L. Rev. 959 (2009) [hereinafter Smith, *Mind the Gap*]; Bernard Rudden, "Economic Theory v. Property Theory: The *Numerus Clausus* Problem," in *Oxford Essays in Jurisprudence, Third Series* 239 (John Eekelaar & John Bell eds., 1987) is rightly credited with bringing the concept of the *numerus clausus* to the attention of the current generation of property scholars.

idea in terms of "basic responsibility"[51] and the inescapability of morality.[52] As to the former, Gardner writes:[53]

> Basic responsibility is what it sounds like. It is an ability. More fully, it is the ability and propensity to have and to give self-explanations in the currency of reasons. The ability and the propensity are but two sides of the same coin. As beings who are able to respond to reasons we cannot avoid being disposed to respond to them. There is nowhere to hide from them. . . .

Thus morality is, as Gardner puts it, "inescapable" for creatures like us: engagement with moral norms is an inescapable part of rational, and hence human, nature.[54]

The second aspect of RFI concerns the instrumentality of law. There are circumstances where our compliance with our duties to observe reasons can be assisted by a public authority with the power rightfully to guide, and ultimately, on occasion, to coerce our behavior. The law is instrumental in the sense that it gives assistance to its subjects in making this compliance actual without causing too much collateral damage along the way. In what circumstances does morality require us to follow the law—or to put it another way, in what circumstances does morality "incorporate" legal norms, such that the legal norms are also inescapable moral norms? The simple answer is whenever we would better comply with the moral norms that otherwise apply to us apart from the law when we follow the law rather than our own appraisal of the norms in question. This is nothing more than Raz's dependence thesis in relation to his service conception of practical authority.[55] But there are many considerations, not the least of which are the law's expense, clumsiness, and liability to inflict collateral damage which go to show that this simple principle is often difficult to apply in practice.

With these two instrumentalisms and Kantian theory in hand, I now want to show a couple of ways in which their applications play out in property law.

IV. THE NEW PRIVATE LAW OF PROPERTY: TWO APPLICATIONS

A. The Numerus Clausus

I have already argued that the *numerus clausus* rights that were contractual in origin arose for what I called issues of policy. That is, of course, very sketchy, but all I meant to indicate was that different legal systems determine by their own lights the merits of

[51] John Gardner, *The Negligence Standard: Political Not Metaphysical*, 80 MOD. L. REV. 1 (2017).
[52] John Gardner, *Nearly Natural Law*, 52 AM. J. JURIS. 1 (2007).
[53] Gardner, *supra* note 51, at 11.   [54] Gardner, *supra* note 52, at 2.
[55] Joseph Raz, *The Morality of Freedom* 43–53 (1986).

extending in personam rights so as to give them certain in rem effects. Much more sophisticated work on this score has been done by Merrill and Smith.

In a series of papers,[56] Merrill and Smith illuminate the *numerus clausus* from the perspective of information costs/transaction costs economic reasoning. The basic idea is that if one restricts property interests to a closed list of well-known interests, this standardization is efficient in terms of information costs/transaction costs because property interests concern third parties: property interests are in rem in either of the two ways I described earlier. If any sort of obligation could be attached to the title to a property, then this would impose costs not only upon the parties to the arrangement but on others; in particular, third parties seeking to deal with owners of the kind of asset in question would be required to investigate whether such an obligation "ran" with the land, and the greater the range of such possibilities, the greater the information costs that would fall on would-be transactors. From this perspective, the story I have told about those members of the *numerus clausus* that originated in contract (or in equitable obligations, in the case of trust), and now "run" with the property, are the product of a "mixed" strategy, permitting important but limited powers to create particular property interests via a use-by-use governance strategy. It is perhaps worthwhile to note here that the original English feudal system of tenures allowed the creation of a wide variety of positive obligations which "ran" with the land; the inflexibilities and inefficiencies of the system became apparent almost immediately following the conquest, and they were all eventually commuted into money rents or abolished.[57] I expect Merrill and Smith would have an easy time of tracking this steady move away from an excessive governance strategy to a simpler exclusion strategy.

As to the Kantian approach, it is not clear to me that it has the resources to say much of substance about the *numerus clausus*. The Kantian can, I think, explain the particular rights as rights to means, which have the same negative relational structure as other private rights. And Ripstein[58] is clear that Kantian right is necessarily determined or made precise only by legislation or judicial rule-making. My worry here is that Kantian right, or rather whatever strictures it imposes on this lawmaking, does not seem to account for any *creativity* in the law, whereas it is easy for the instrumentalist to so account. If a particular idea for dealing with things, say a security interest, that is, an interest *sourced* in contract but given in rem effect *by the making of law*, seems to be a good innovation with practical benefits, then ceteris paribus, the law can institutionalize it. But I do not see how this "in remification" of a voluntarily undertaken obligation, its "propertization," can be seen as merely the determination or outworking of the basic Kantian idea of private right, including its distinctions between acquired rights, that is, between contract rights and property rights.

---

[56] Merrill & Smith, *supra* note 50; Merrill & Smith, *Property/Contract, supra* note 48; Smith, *Mind the Gap, supra* note 50.

[57] J.H. Baker, *An Introduction to English Legal History* 223–229 (2002).

[58] Arthur Ripstein, this volume, Part III.

B. The Puzzle of Nuisance

A very orthodox statement of the tort of nuisance is this:

> A private nuisance is an unreasonable interference with the use and enjoyment of land.[59]

For the BOR theorist, the law of nuisance amounts to the law's undertaking to balance the costs and benefits of conflicting uses on a case-by-case basis, one "property" stick at a time. As many scholars have exhaustively detailed, this characterization of nuisance law is hopeless, for it fails to treat nuisance as a tort, a wrong.[60] But given what I said earlier about the nature of BPrN not turning on any specific use-rights, a tort conventionally framed in terms of an interference with use pokes a hole, perhaps a significant hole, in the theory of property rights I have presented. As Nolan puts the point,[61]

> [P]rivate nuisance demonstrates that it cannot be right to conceive of property rights solely in terms of a right to exclude others.

I should only note here all the scholarly work that has been done to associate nuisance with the right to exclude, in particular the relation between nuisance and trespass.[62] But picking up a couple of points from Ripstein, Nolan, and Weinrib, I am going to suggest a possible way forward which preserves the structure of BPrN while fitting the tort of nuisance within it.

Ripstein helpfully categorizes wrongs as falling under two kinds or types: using and damaging.[63] When I use your property, I treat it as if it were mine, not yours. Elsewhere Ripstein frames this idea as my *usurping* your property.[64] By using or usurping your property, whether intentionally or not,[65] I make a sort of claim—the act expresses my regarding your property to be at my disposal. Damage-causing wrongs need express no such claim; I can, for example, damage your property by acting negligently without at the same time using it as my own. While both kinds of wrong violate BPrN, by violating your exclusive right to your property, they do so in different ways.[66] My suggestion is

---

[59] *Winfield & Jolowicz on Tort* (Edwin Peel & James Goudkamp eds., 19th ed. 2014), [15–008], quoted in Donal Nolan, "The Essence of Private Nuisance," in *Modern Studies in Property Law, Vol. 10*, at 72 (Ben McFarlane ed., 2019). See also the other formulations cited there: all refer to use and enjoyment.

[60] See, e.g., Henry E. Smith, *Exclusion and Property Rules in the Law of Nuisance*, 90 VA. L. REV. 965 (2004); see also Essert, *supra* note 45; Nolan, *supra* note 59; J.E. Penner, *Nuisance and the Character of the Neighborhood*, 5 J. ENVTL. L. 1 (1993).

[61] Nolan, *supra* note 59, at 86.

[62] Smith, *supra* note 60; Essert, *supra* note 45; Nolan, *supra* note 59; Thomas W. Merrill, *Trespass, Nuisance, and the Costs of Determining Property Rights*, 14 J. LEGAL STUD. 13 (1985); Simon Douglas & Ben McFarlane, "Defining Property Rights," in *Philosophical Foundations of Property Law* (James Penner & Henry E Smith eds., 2013).

[63] Ripstein, *supra* note 46, at 43–51.   [64] *Id.* at 234–235.

[65] As for example when I take your umbrella thinking it is my own.

[66] One act can, of course, constitute both wrongs, as for example when I throw a rock through one of your windows just because I like the way that glass smashes.

that scholars have unwittingly failed to notice a property tort that does not fall into either of these categories, and that responds to a right not to be excluded, which might be called a "deprivation tort."

Consider unlawful distraint or distress, the action for detinue, and false imprisonment.

A landlord wrongs his tenant when he unlawfully distrains, that is, takes possession of, his tenant's goods as a kind of security, typically for the payment of rent.[67] No proof is required that the wrongful distrainor of goods used them (if he did, then he would also be liable for conversion) or that he damaged them. The gravamen of the wrong is that he unjustly deprived the plaintiff of his rightful possession. Detinue, the action against someone for "wrongful" detention of goods, applies in any number of situations. Again, no proof of use or damage is required.[68] Although I cannot go into details here, I should also say the personal tort of false imprisonment has this form. Liability does not turn on damage to the victim, nor on any using of him (as would be typical of a sexual assault). It turns on a deprivation of liberty.

Here is a clearly similar case under the English law of nuisance. When I dump a load of bricks on the public highway preventing you from accessing your easement of way, I have neither damaged anything of yours nor used anything of yours. I have merely deprived you of your right. As Nolan puts it,[69]

> rights of this kind...clearly rest not a right to exclude but on (something like) a right not to be excluded.

Analyzing nuisance more generally, consider two perspectives on the tort. Nuisance can be seen as the tort of depriving the landowner not of any particular use she may wish to make of the land but of the "usability" of the land.[70] On this view the landowner is substantially deprived of her liberty to use the land. A slightly different view is that a nuisance substantially deprives the landowner of *access* to her land, not by physically removing her but indirectly, say by smoking her out of her house or garden. It is not my purpose here to weigh these competing perspectives, but to suggest that both turn on the idea of deprivation, not any actual use by the tortfeasor or damage to the landowner's property. On either view the tort is properly encompassed by BPrN: it is not to be understood as protecting the right of an owner to use her property in any particular way.

Very roughly, Weinrib contends that from the Kantian perspective no rightful private law could be such as to render the usable resources of the world "res nullius," say norms that imposed duties on everyone never to make use of things.[71] It seems to me, similarly, that neither should private law allow individuals unilaterally to make another person's property "res nullius," or substantially so, for example, by depriving the owner of access

---

[67] F.W. Maitland, *Equity, Also the Forms of Action at Common Law: Two Courses of Lectures* 355 (1909, reprinted 1929). The action of replevin allowed the tenant to recover the goods until such time as the lawfulness of the distraint could be determined.

[68] Bridge, *supra* note 32, at 91–93.

[69] Nolan, *supra* note 59, at 86.   [70] Nolan's view, see *id.*

[71] Ernest J. Weinrib, *Ownership, Use and Exclusivity: The Kantian Approach*, 31 Ratio Juris 123 (2018).

to it or the liberty to use it. I therefore draw upon Weinrib's discussion to bolster the claim made here that besides use- and damage-based torts, there is a third kind—a "deprivation" tort. This illuminates not just the law of nuisance but our understanding of BPrN more generally.

V. Conclusion

I hope I have convinced the reader that, as regards property law, the New Private Law is not *that* new. But its strength has definitely grown in the last decade, as the citations in this chapter will attest. That is indeed something to celebrate.

Acknowledgments

I am grateful for comments by Dennis Klimchuk, Ben McFarlane, Tom Merrill, Paul Miller, Henry Smith, and Ben Zipursky. I am also grateful for discussions with Chris Essert, Donal Nolan, and Arthur Ripstein regarding section IV.B.

CHAPTER 18

··

UNJUST ENRICHMENT
AND RESTITUTION

··

ANDREW BURROWS

NEW Private Law adopts a methodology that takes seriously both doctrinal and deeply theoretical analyses of private law. In this sense it adopts both "internal" and "external" perspectives.[1] Rather than dismissing "black letter law," it regards a full understanding of the rules and concepts used in private law as essential in developing theoretically accurate normative and functional analyses of private law. From an English lawyer's perspective, New Private Law is to be particularly welcomed as reinforcing the importance of legal doctrine which appeared, from our side of the Atlantic, to be in danger of becoming a lost science in the U.S. legal academy. This is not to deny that, for decades, the problem of striking the right balance between doctrine and deeper theory has been the subject of debate among academic private lawyers throughout the common law world.

With that general perspective on New Private Law in mind, this chapter first examines, at a high level of generality, the apparent contrast between the English and U.S. approaches to the law of unjust enrichment (otherwise known as the law of restitution) over the last forty years. It then focuses on a very specific legal question that has recently troubled the English courts (the meaning of "at the expense of") to illustrate the English doctrinal approach epitomized in the writings of Peter Birks (and the most prominent recent challenge to it).

---

[1] See Andrew S. Gold, this volume.

I. English and United States Approaches to the Law of Unjust Enrichment since 1980

A. English Fervor Not Matched in the United States

In England and Wales, no area of private law has been subjected to greater academic scrutiny in the last forty years than the law of unjust enrichment. The subject has spawned hundreds of law journal articles, scores of monographs and textbooks, and even the creation of a dedicated law review (the *Restitution Law Review*, first published in 1993).

It is not easy to pinpoint precisely why the area has so caught the attention of U.K. academia. The following are some possible explanations. First, the late recognition and development of the subject in English law has enabled academics, in the modern era, to have particular influence in shaping case law in this area. So it is that courts at all levels have cited, and relied on, academic work in deciding cases in this "novel" area. Secondly, the historical judicial acceptance of plainly fictional reasoning (in particular, the "implied contract" explanation for the restitution of money paid, for example, by mistake or for a consideration that has failed) has rendered modern judges particularly receptive to new, more convincing reasoning based on unjust enrichment, advocated by academics. Thirdly, there is the relative paucity of statute law in this area, which enhances the prominence of case law, study of which many academics find more interesting and exciting than the dry words of statutes. Fourthly, the recognition that the subject comprises case law within both common law and equity raises interesting issues of coherence across that notorious historical divide. Finally, there is the intense complexity and challenge posed by many of the questions raised, which academics are ideally placed to tackle.

One might add to those suggestions, the role of particular individuals. Foremost is the inspirational brilliance of the pioneering work of Robert Goff (who later became senior Law Lord in the House of Lords, the equivalent of today's President of the U.K. Supreme Court) and Gareth Jones (Professor at Cambridge). Together, they wrote the first full English law text on the subject in 1966, *The Law of Restitution*,[2] which argued that there is, and long has been, an English law of restitution concerned with the reversal of unjust enrichment (while also maintaining that this body of law was traditionally obscured by fictions, such as that restitution rests on an implied contract, in turn prompting unhelpful descriptions of the common law part of the subject as "quasi-contract"). By organizing the case law pertaining to awards of restitution for unjust enrichment across English common law and equity, Goff and Jones are commonly credited with having "created" this "new" subject in England and Wales. Even more important

---

[2] Now in its ninth edition, with a different title, *The Law of Unjust Enrichment* (Charles Mitchell, Paul Mitchell, & Stephen Watterson eds., 2016).

in academia was the role played by Peter Birks, a charismatic genius who, coming to the subject through Roman Law, pushed forward its conceptual design in *An Introduction to the Law of Restitution*, published in 1985,[3] and subsequently in a torrent of articles and books. His characteristic style was to apply tight analytical reasoning, alongside the articulation of new precise terminology, to explore and fill out his interpretation of what constituted the modern English law of unjust enrichment. He made this enterprise of conceptual reasoning both exciting and challenging. Far from being seen as old-fashioned, it caught the imagination of scholars.

Although courses on the law of unjust enrichment remain rare in British law schools—the feeling persists that the subject lies outside the main core and is, in any event, too difficult for undergraduates—some of the most influential postgraduate taught courses—the LLM at Cambridge and at University College London, and especially the BCL at Oxford—have included optional courses on Restitution which have been attended by many who have gone on to become academic lawyers or barristers. Some of these barristers have subsequently been appointed judges. Those courses have in this way had a significant impact, albeit over the long term, on the shape of English law.

Since the 1970s, we have witnessed in the courts in England and Wales the gradual acceptance of the Goff and Jones "unjust enrichment" thesis. This culminated in the authoritative acceptance in 1991 by the House of Lords, in the seminal case of *Lipkin Gorman v. Karpnale Ltd.*[4] (with the leading judgment, in a rather neat full turn of the circle, being given by Lord Goff), that there is an English law of unjust enrichment (or restitution). Throughout, there has been a close relationship between academics and judges in working out the ingredients of this "new" subject. Unjust enrichment has therefore been one of the "hottest" of topics not only for academic private lawyers but also in the courts.

For those looking in from other jurisdictions, it may be puzzling to understand why there have been so many recent landmark cases on the English law of unjust enrichment. This has been largely a matter of luck. There just happen to have been two major rafts of important litigation that have required the courts to apply, and hence to work out the details of, the law of unjust enrichment. The first, in the 1990s, was litigation about interest rate swap transactions. These were contracts between local authorities and banks, used by the former as a means of raising money, whereby the parties were speculating about interest rates. When those contracts were ultimately held to be void, as being outside the powers of the local authorities, there were numerous cases, several going to the appellate courts, dealing with claims for the restitution of money paid under those void contracts.[5] More recently, and ongoing and involving restitutionary claims for staggeringly large sums of money (running into tens of billions of pounds), have been actions against the Revenue (HMRC) for overpaid tax, especially where the tax charged was invalid under European Union law.[6]

---

[3] Revised edition in 1989.   [4] [1991] 2 A.C. 548.

[5] See *Lessons of the Swaps Litigation* (Peter Birks & Francis Rose eds., 2000).

[6] See *Restitution of Overpaid Tax* (Steven Elliott, Birke Häcker, & Charles Mitchell eds., 2013) and the cases discussed in the second part of this chapter.

It should be added that in a nonfederal jurisdiction, such as England and Wales, with a system of precedent, single decisions of the appellate courts are binding and constitute the present state of the law. They are not only scrutinized by lower courts who are required to apply them but also by the many mainstream academics who are interested in describing, interpreting, and critically analyzing the case law.

The explosion of interest in unjust enrichment in England and Wales may also be said to have had some effect in sparking an increased academic interest in this area of the law in civilian countries (such as Germany) and mixed jurisdictions (such as Scotland and South Africa), which have long had a law of unjust (or "unjustified") enrichment. In particular, this has led to fruitful work being carried out by comparative lawyers as well as academic projects to harmonize and codify the law of unjust enrichment across Europe.[7]

In contrast, and until the New Private Law movement that has inspired this book, there appears to have been a decline of interest over the same period in the law of unjust enrichment/restitution in the United States. At first sight this is very odd because, within common law jurisdictions, American academics writing at the end of the nineteenth century (such as Ames[8] and Keener),[9] and certainly the American Law Institute's first *Restatement of Restitution* in 1937, led the way in rejecting the implied contract fiction and in advocating unjust enrichment as underpinning restitution at common law and in equity. With Seavey and Scott as the reporters, the first *Restatement of Restitution* was a monumental work, which had a major impact across the common law world. In particular, it was an inspiration for the writings of Goff and Jones (Jones had sat at the feet of both Scott and Seavey at Harvard Law School).[10] In the United States, the work of great scholars, such as Dawson and Palmer,[11] complemented and built on that first *Restatement*. Yet, since the 1980s, there appears to have been a decline of interest in, and understanding of, the subject. As Saiman has observed in a penetrating article, the United States refused to join the "global restitution party."[12]

Why has that been so? There are several possible explanations. First, there has been a decline of interest in private law in U.S. academia, where scholarly enthusiasm centers around constitutional and administrative law. Secondly, the doctrinal approach to scholarship that is epitomized by the work of Birks—namely, the articulation of rules

---

[7] See, e.g., *Principles, Definitions and Model Rules of European Private Law* (Christian von Bar, Eric Clive, & Hans Schulte-Nölke eds., 2009).

[8] Andrew Kull, *James Barr Ames and the Early Modern History of Unjust Enrichment*, 25 O.J.L.S. 297 (2005).

[9] William A. Keener, *A Treatise on the Law of Quasi-Contracts* (1893). See also Frederic C. Woodward, *The Law of Quasi Contracts* (1913).

[10] Gareth Jones, *The Law of Restitution: The Past and the Future, in Essays on the Law of Restitution* 1 (Andrew Burrows ed., 1991).

[11] E.g., John P. Dawson, *Unjust Enrichment, A Comparative Analysis* (1951); John P. Dawson & George E. Palmer, *Cases on Restitution* (2d ed., 1969); George E. Palmer, *The Law of Restitution* (1978) (with supplements); John P. Dawson, *Erasable Enrichment in German Law*, 61 B.U. L. REV. 271 (1981); John P. Dawson, *Restitution without Enrichment*, 61 B.U. L. REV. 563 (1981).

[12] Chaim Saiman, *Restitution in America: Why the US Refuses to Join the Global Restitution Party*, 28 O.J.L.S. 99 (2008).

that are largely justified by internal logic, and the law being seen as an autonomous discipline—is out of favor in the United States, where it tends to be dismissed as formalist, old-fashioned, and dull. Thirdly, at a deeper level, the U.S. legal system diverged from English law in becoming immersed in legal realism, with its skepticism towards the coherence of legal rules. As Saiman writes:

> Since outcomes could no longer be legitimated via the technical and conceptual analysis of legal rules, realists began to look towards extra-doctrinal sources for justification. Post-realist American thought is an ongoing search for a compelling replacement to traditional doctrinal analysis.[13]

Fourthly, economic analysis of law has dominated private law scholarship in the United States over the last forty years. By definition, it represents a multidisciplinary approach to the law whereby, if examined at all, unjust enrichment is explored only at a high level of generality and filtered through metrics of economic efficiency. In contrast, economic analysis has not taken hold in English legal academia. Finally, U.S. courts' refusal to develop a federal common law,[14] and the diffuse treatment of private law across the states, has had a dampening effect on the interests of judges and academics in the subject.

While the contrast between the United Kingdom and the United States in relation to unjust enrichment is intriguing, it should not be exaggerated. There are at least two reasons for thinking that the contrast is not as sharp as has so far been depicted.

First, since the turn of the century there has been a revival of American interest in private law, especially tort law. This volume—and the label New Private Law—reflects this. Moreover, as regards unjust enrichment, a new *Restatement (Third) of Restitution and Unjust Enrichment* was published in 2011 by the American Law Institute (the second having been started but abandoned in draft form in the early 1980s). This new *Restatement* was primarily the work of Andrew Kull and took some thirteen years of work to complete. It is a superb piece of traditional legal scholarship and has revived some interest in the subject in the United States.[15]

Secondly, even within the legal academy in the United Kingdom, there has been skepticism, at the fringes, about the Birksian approach to legal scholarship and about the whole modern unjust enrichment movement. One fierce and consistent critic has been Steve Hedley. Since the mid-1980s, he has written articles and books arguing that to recognize unjust enrichment is misguided and leads to undesirable results.[16] Recently, there has been a new wave of skepticism with a particular focus on the idea that the scheme for unjust enrichment advocated by Birks is problematic because it cannot be

---

[13] *Id.* at 107.   [14] Erie Railroad Co. v. Tompkins, 304 U.S. 64 (1938).

[15] See, e.g., *Restitution Rollout: The Restatement (Third) of Restitution and Unjust Enrichment*, 68 WASH. & LEE L. REV. (2011); *Symposium: A Conference on Restitution and Unjust Enrichment*, 92 B.U. L. REV. (2012); Ward Farnsworth, *Restitution* (2014).

[16] See, e.g., Steve Hedley, *Unjust Enrichment as the Basis of Restitution—An Overworked Concept*, 5 Legal Stud. 56 (1985); *A Critical Introduction to Restitution* (2001).

justified normatively (i.e., by moral reasoning).[17] It is thought to have been misleading to treat the subject as if coherently based on a number of simple propositions that can be justified by internal logic and by a general appeal to justice. Moreover, it is strongly arguable that U.K. academia in general has moved to being less interested in private law than public law. Indeed, the sort of doctrinal scholarship exhibited by Birksian "restitution scholars" has tended to be criticized for the same sort of reasons that led to its falling out of favor in the United States.[18]

Nevertheless, while for those two reasons great care should be taken in making the contrast, it continues to be true as a general proposition that academic interest in the law of unjust enrichment remains much greater in the United Kingdom than in the United States. It also appears to be true that knowledge of, and understanding of, the law of unjust enrichment among judges and practicing lawyers is more embedded in the United Kingdom than in the United States.[19] And the highest courts in the United Kingdom are more likely to be asked to decide difficult questions on the law of unjust enrichment—or at least questions that are explicitly framed as involving the law of unjust enrichment—than are those in the United States.[20]

B. The English Law of Unjust Enrichment, the U.S. Restatement (Third) of Restitution and Unjust Enrichment, and Methodology

In thinking about the scope and structure of the subject, it has become conventional in English law, applying the work of Birks, first to distinguish between restitution for unjust enrichment and restitution for wrongs. This turns on the cause of action. A civil wrong, such as a breach of contract or tort or an equitable wrong, may trigger restitution, stripping the defendant of wrongfully acquired gains, rather than the usual compensatory damages. But even if restitution is given, the cause of action is still the wrong. All that the courts are doing is giving the claimant a different remedy (restitution not compensation)

[17] See especially Robert Stevens, *The Unjust Enrichment Disaster*, 134 L.Q.R. 574 (2018). See also Nils Jansen, *Farewell to Unjustified Enrichment*, 20 EDIN. L.R. 123 (2016); Peter Watts, *Unjust Enrichment—The Potion that Induces Well-Meaning Sloppiness of Thought*, 69 C.L.P. 289 (2016).
[18] See Andrew Burrows, "Challenges for Private Law in the 21st Century," in *Private Law in the 21st Century* 29, 32–40 (Kit Barker, Karen Fairweather, & Ross Grantham eds., 2017).
[19] See, e.g., the exasperation expressed by Kull in Andrew Kull, *Common-Law Restitution and the Madoff Liquidation*, 92 B.U. L. REV. 939, 940 (2012) ("A wave of Madoff litigation has begun to flow through the courts. But…it appears that no one involved in these lawsuits—on either side of the bench—has thought to ask how the central issues would be analysed and decided as a matter of common law. The significance of the law of restitution has been almost entirely overlooked.").
[20] It may be that in the United States the questions are being raised but are framed as involving, e.g., constitutional law or procedural law or the law on good faith reliance rather than been seen as questions on unjust enrichment: see Chaim Saiman, *The Domain of Private Law: Conceptual Thought in Anglo-American Law* (forthcoming).

for that cause of action. For example, in *Attorney General v. Blake*,[21] it was accepted that an account of profits could be awarded against the notorious spy, George Blake, to strip him of profits made by his breach of contract with the government in publishing a book about his life as a secret agent for the Russians. The cause of action was breach of contract so that, for example, the limitation period ran from the date of the breach of contract and not from when he made profits. That is to be contrasted with where the cause of action is unjust enrichment—not a civil wrong—so that the cause of action cannot accrue until, at the earliest, the defendant has been enriched.

The essential underlying point is that restitution is a remedy not a cause of action; and we normally classify our subjects according to causes of action (events) not remedies (responses). So we have the subjects of contract and tort, not compensation. It follows that, in English law, the subject now tends to be referred to as the law of unjust enrichment (not the law of restitution) and excludes restitution for wrongs. Restitution for torts falls within the law of torts, restitution for breach of contract falls within the law of contract, and so on.

Confining ourselves, therefore, to restitution for unjust enrichment, the structure of such a claim can be usefully broken down into four linked but distinct questions. Has the defendant been enriched? Was that enrichment at the claimant's expense? Was that enrichment at the claimant's expense unjust? Are there any defenses? Birks emphasized that this was a structure that helped to rationalize and render readily comprehensible the decisions laid down in the cases, but that the details of the law—the specific answers to these four questions—were contained in what the cases had laid down: the scheme was therefore looking down at the cases and not up at some general moral or other "nonlegal" answer to the four questions.[22] In the same vein, the U.K. Supreme Court has recently stressed that the four stages do not themselves provide legal answers; rather, the answers to what the law is requires one to look at what has been laid down in past cases.[23]

Of the four questions, the one that requires most analysis is the third, the so-called "unjust question". The approach that has been traditionally taken in English law is that it is for the claimant to establish that there is an "unjust factor". Unjust factors include that the claimant's intention in conferring a benefit on the defendant was impaired because of, for example, mistake, duress, undue influence, or incapacity; or that the claimant's conferral of the benefit was conditional on an event or state of affairs that has not eventuated (this has traditionally been termed "failure of consideration", although one might more simply call it "failure of condition"). There are other unjust factors (Birks described them as "policy-motivated restitution")[24] that have nothing to do with problems affecting the claimant's consent. These include state unlawfulness (i.e., the ultra vires exaction of taxes) or necessity (as where necessitous services are rendered by the claimant to the defendant). This "unjust factors" approach to the "unjust question" contrasts with the

---

[21] [2001] 1 A.C. 268 (HL).
[22] Peter Birks, *An Introduction to the Law of Restitution* 19 (rev. ed. 1989).
[23] Investment Trust Companies v. HMRC [2017] UKSC 29, [2018] A.C. 275, at [41]–[42].
[24] Peter Birks, *An Introduction to the Law of Restitution* ch. 9 (rev. ed. 1989).

traditional civilian approach where the courts are concerned with whether there is a juristic basis for the enrichment. Juristic bases include, for example, contracts, gifts, statutes, and judgments. In his final book, Birks abandoned the unjust factors scheme that he had spent most of his life perfecting, and dramatically swung over to a more civilian approach with his central new argument being that the unjust question is best answered by requiring an "absence of basis".[25]

It can be seen immediately from this outline of the structure of a claim for unjust enrichment in English law, that the approach taken is highly conceptual. The case law is to be approached by a logical scheme that can be stated at a high level of generality even if one can agree that it is the answer given to those questions in the cases that is the law. The ALI's *Restatement (Third) of Restitution and Unjust Enrichment*, by contrast, takes a more contextual and less conceptual approach than did Birks. In Chapter 1 on "General Principles" there are only four black letter propositions—none of which deal with what is meant by "enrichment", "at the expense of", or the approach to the "unjust question".[26] Moreover, no fundamental distinction is drawn in these general principles between restitution for unjust enrichment and restitution for wrongs. Nor is there any place for the four-step analysis.

As one would expect, therefore, even though the *Restatement Third* may be described, like the predominant academic analysis in English law, as taking a doctrinal (or "black letter law") approach, there are significant differences between the two. While both may be said to be attempting to set out the best interpretation of the law, the predominant English approach does so in a more conceptually tight way than does the *Restatement*. This leads to a question that English doctrinal scholars have only recently addressed and which Birks barely, if ever, directly addressed. What is the precise methodology being adopted by Birksian "restitution scholars"?

Accepting that one is aiming to produce the best interpretation of the law, one may say that the criteria that are being applied in determining whether one interpretation is better than another include fit, coherence, accessibility, practical workability, and normative validity. One's model should fit the vast bulk of the rules and principles (one cannot simply say that most of the rules and principles cannot be explained and must be ignored); it should do so in a way that is coherent or rational by treating like cases alike and unlike cases differently; the interpretation should be as simple to understand—as accessible—as possible; the account of the law must be one that works in practice because law is preeminently a practical discipline; and the interpretation should be one that can be morally justified even if that moral justification goes no deeper than relying on what are perceived to be widely shared moral values. It should be added that a useful technique for testing some of these criteria is to look not only at the legal rules and principles established in case law (and statute) but also at hypothetical examples that have not yet come before the courts.

---

[25] Peter Birks, *The Law of Unjust Enrichment* (2d ed. 2005).

[26] *Restatement (Third) of Restitution and Unjust Enrichment* § 1 cmt. *b* (Am. Law Inst. 2011) briefly looks at the "unjust question." Oddly, while the Restatement appears to adopt an unjust factors approach, that comment purports to favor an approach focusing on "no adequate legal basis."

It can be seen that, on this version of the methodology—and this seems to be in line with the pluralism favored by New Private Law—there is no suggestion that there is a sole all-embracing justification of private law or the law of unjust enrichment.[27] Rather, even applying his "absence of basis" approach to the "unjust question", Birks saw the law as a complex mix of principle and policy. Certainly, the idea that has been so influential in the United States—that the law is best understood as effecting economic efficiency—has not found favor in the United Kingdom and is barely discussed in any detail by U.K. academics.

What has become increasingly influential in English academia, as a contrast to Birks's mix of principle and policy, has been work on corrective justice.[28] Weinrib has argued that private law (and while he primarily focused on tort law, his theory is intended to cover unjust enrichment) is concerned to restore the parties to the position they were in before—to correct an injustice—and is not concerned to redistribute rights afresh.[29] In Aristotle's terminology, one is concerned with corrective, not distributive, justice. Weinrib's detailed "correlativity" elaboration of his distinctive approach to corrective justice is particularly problematic. For example, it contradicts much of the law of unjust enrichment (and private law generally) in so far as it indicates that policy goals, such as deterrence or punishment or minimizing waste or avoiding the floodgates of litigation or encouraging insurance—because they do not concern merely the parties—are irrelevant. Nevertheless, a similar approach (of policy minimalism) has been taken by, for example, Stevens who, through an important recent article,[30] has become the most influential critic of the Birksian approach to unjust enrichment.

II. What Is Meant by "At the Expense of the Claimant" in the Law of Unjust Enrichment?

For the remainder of this chapter, I aim to illustrate the approach of Birksian doctrinal scholarship—the sort of scholarship that has dominated the U.K. restitution movement and, in taking doctrine seriously, may be said to be supported by New Private Law scholarship—by considering in detail a central topic within the law of unjust

[27] Cf. as regards tort, James Goudkamp & John Murphy, *The Failure of Universal Theories of Tort Law*, 21 Legal Theory 47 (2015) (arguing that Posner's economic analysis, Weinrib's corrective justice approach, and Stevens's "torts and rights" thesis fail on their own terms because they purport to be "universal theories of tort law" and yet they cannot explain several central aspects of tort in the common law world).

[28] See Gregory C. Keating, this volume.

[29] Ernest J. Weinrib, *Corrective Justice in a Nutshell*, 52 U. Toronto L.J. 349 (2002). An earlier full version of the theory, albeit modified since, was set out in *The Idea of Private Law* (1995).

[30] See *supra* note 17.

enrichment that has recently been the focus of attention by the U.K. Supreme Court in two leading overpaid tax cases: *Investment Trust Companies v. HMRC*[31] and *Prudential Assurance Co. Ltd. v. HMRC*.[32] What is meant by enrichment being "at the expense of the claimant"?

There are at least three facets to this question. They can be illustrated by three hypothetical examples.

(a) C pays $1,000 to X by mistake. X, as a result, pays D $750 as a gift. Is C entitled to restitution of $750 from D? This raises what may be described as "the third-party issue."

(b) C mistakenly cuts down trees on her land, which enhances the view that her neighbor, D, has from his land thereby increasing the market value of D's land by $5,000. Is C entitled to restitution of $5,000, or, at least, the market value of the work in cutting down the trees, from D? This raises what may be described as "the incidental benefit issue."

(c) C pays $10,000 to D by mistake. D uses that $10,000 to make a profit of $6,000. Is C entitled to restitution of $16,000 from D? This raises what may be described as "the consequential benefit issue."

A. The Third-Party Issue

In *Investment Trust Companies v. HMRC (ITC)* the claimants had paid value-added tax (VAT) on contracts with "managers" for investment management services provided to them. The managers had in turn paid VAT to HMRC in respect of those contracts. It transpired that, on a correct understanding of EU law, VAT should not have been charged for those services. Section 80 of the VAT Act 1994 allowed the managers to claim back from HMRC VAT that had been paid but was not due within a limitation period of three years. The managers had successfully done so and, in line with the regulatory scheme, had paid across the VAT recovered to the claimants. However, the claimants were out of pocket in respect of VAT paid outside the three-year limitation period (referred to as the payments in the "dead period"). What the claimants therefore sought in this case, inter alia, was to "leapfrog" over the managers by bringing a common law mistake-of-law claim for restitution of unjust enrichment against HMRC in respect of the VAT payments in the dead period.

The Supreme Court held that the claim should fail. For our purposes, it is the reasoning that the claimant clients could not here satisfy the "at the expense of" requirement—because the enrichment of HMRC was at the expense of the managers only and not at the expense of the claimant clients—that is of predominant importance. The single judgment of the Supreme Court was given by Lord Reed. There are three points to make in understanding his judgment on "at the expense of."

---

[31] [2017] UKSC 29, [2018] A.C. 275.   [32] [2018] UKSC 39, [2018] 3 W.L.R. 652.

(1) The essential answer to the question posed was that, in general, a claimant is entitled to restitution only if that claimant has made a direct transfer of value to the defendant. This may be described as the "direct providers only" general rule.[33] In particular, Lord Reed firmly rejected the view that the crucial question was whether there was a "but for" causal connection between the claimant's loss and the defendant's gain. He said: "A 'but for' causal connection between the claimant's being worse off and the defendant's being better off is not . . . sufficient in itself to constitute a transfer of value."[34] This cutting back of "but for" causation in favor of a direct transfer of value is of huge importance in limiting the scope of the law of unjust enrichment.

(2) Lord Reed accepted that there are exceptions to the "direct providers only" rule. But in his view most of those exceptions, for example, agency, tracing and, what he termed, "co-ordinated transactions" or a "single scheme,"[35] can be analyzed as situations where there is the equivalent of a direct transfer.[36]

(3) On the facts, HMRC's enrichment was not at the expense of the claimants because there was no direct transfer of value by the claimants to HMRC. There was a transfer of value from the claimants to the managers and a subsequent transfer of value from the managers to HMRC. But one could not collapse the two into a transfer by the claimants to HMRC because none of the exceptions to the "direct providers only" rule was in play (e.g., there was no agency, no tracing, and no single scheme).[37]

It follows that, in English law, the answer to hypothetical example (a) given earlier is that C cannot claim restitution from D because the direct transfer of value was made to D by X not by C. This is to apply the general "direct providers only" rule, and in that hypothetical example there is, on the face of it, no exception in play.

Assuming that that is the law, can it be justified?

Applying a Birksian doctrinal approach, which looks at reasons of both principle and policy, one strategy toward the "at the expense of" issue is to start off by asking whether there is a "but for" causal connection between the claimant's loss and the defendant's gain. If there is, then one may move on to examine whether there are particular policy concerns that override that starting point. For example, an important policy concern might be that, if more than one claimant is entitled to restitution from the defendant, there is a risk of the defendant being exposed to double liability. Another concern might be that, once one allows leapfrogging, the law may be rendered excessively complex with lots of potential claimants and difficulties in deciding priority between them. A further policy concern might be that one is disrupting the transaction between X and D. In the hypothetical example, the transaction between X and D is a gift. Had D been a bona fide

---

[33] Andrew Burrows, *The Law of Restitution* 69–85 (3d ed. 2011).
[34] Investment Trust Companies [2018] A.C. 275, [52].   [35] *Id.*, [61].   [36] *Id.*, [48].
[37] Indeed, as made clear at [71]–[72], there was not even "but for" causation between HMRC's gain and the payments by the claimants because the managers' liability to pay VAT to HMRC arose irrespective of whether the claimants paid or were charged VAT.

purchaser for value without notice, D might have had a defense. But the same concern to uphold the security of D's receipt may apply in relation to gifts or other transactions where no value is given by D.

An alternative strategy—and the one favored by the Supreme Court—is that one should state the rule narrowly, in terms of a "direct providers only" rule, while allowing exceptions and possible gradual incremental development outward as cases come before the courts. This may be said to rest on the fear that, if one starts off with a wide "but for" causal test, with the onus on the defendant to satisfy the court that there are policy reasons to override that starting point, the law of unjust enrichment may be too wide and intrusive, thereby excessively undermining the stability of benefits received. English lawyers are particularly conscious of the dangers of starting with a wide principle and relying on grounds of policy to cut that back, because that was the discredited strategy—which led to the law being regarded as out of control—for ascertaining the duty of care in the tort of negligence, adopted in *Anns v. Merton London BC*.[38]

On the facts of *ITC*, it might further be argued that there was a particular policy reason for denying the claim. This was the serious disruption of public finances that restitution would cause. If the claims were permitted, HMRC would face a mass of tax restitution claims. While there may be other ways of properly protecting the public purse, such as the development of a tailored defense of disruption to public finances or through the standard defense of change of position, the former defense does not at present exist in English law and, while the latter exists, it is very difficult for a governmental defendant to demonstrate factually that it has changed its position. It should also be noted that in English law there is a particular problem with relying on limitation periods to protect HMRC because, where the cause of action in unjust enrichment rests on the claimant's mistake, Section 32(1)(c) of the Limitation Act 1980 means that time does not begin to run until the claimant could reasonably have known of the mistake;[39] and that may not be until decades after the payments.

Applying a doctrinal analysis, one might also suggest that an analogy can be drawn between the "at the expense of" enquiry and the law on causation of loss in tort and contract. That law requires more than a "but for" causal link and instead insists that there is no break in the chain of causation, for example, by a third party's intervention. That approach can be justified, on policy grounds, as ensuring that the burden of liability for loss is fairly placed on the defendant rather than on someone else. Analogously, in the context of unjust enrichment, one might say that X's intervention constitutes a break in the chain of causation from C to D and that D's liability, if any, should therefore be to X only and not to C.

Although I suspect that many New Private Law scholars would place more emphasis on fully articulating the policy concerns that I have just set out, it is important to appreciate that, for those who reject the relevance of policy concerns, a different explanation for the "direct providers only" rule must be found. One example of this is the recently

---

[38] [1978] A.C. 728.
[39] C.f. Charles Mitchell, "Unjust Enrichment," in *Principles of the English Law of Obligations* 302–303 (Andrew Burrows ed., 2015).

formulated "normative" approach of Stevens.[40] He warmly welcomes the decision in *ITC* but criticizes the reasoning of the Supreme Court for being unable to articulate *why* its limitation on recovery is justifiable. His approach, which he grounds in corrective justice, sees "at the expense of" and the enrichment of the defendant as fundamentally linked because the claimant must render a performance to the defendant, which must be accepted by the defendant, in order for the defendant to be liable to make restitution. This is highly controversial. Why, normatively, should an accepted "performance" be seen as having such force? If the defendant has clearly been benefited, why should it matter that the defendant has not "accepted" in any meaningful sense? Can it be correct that performance has to be "for D," as Stevens insists? But while it may be argued that Stevens's theory raises more questions than it answers, it does neatly tie in with a narrow approach to "at the expense of." So in *ITC*, there was a performance by the managers to HMRC by paying the tax and there was a performance by the customers to the managers in paying the price for the services, including the tax, but there was no performance by the claimant clients to HMRC: therefore, on Stevens's view, restitution was correctly denied.

B. The Incidental Benefit Issue

In *ITC*, it was also decided that, in general, there can be no restitution for "incidental benefits."[41] These are benefits that are conferred as a secondary consequence from (i.e., incidentally to) C's actions.[42] Incidental benefits were held to be not "at the expense of" the claimant in the required sense. A tree-clearing hypothetical example—as in our hypothetical (b) —was referred to, as was the well-known pedagogical example of C mistakenly heating her own flat and thereby also heating the upstairs flat of D. It was denied that there should be restitution in either example.

Assuming that the law now is that, in general, there can be no restitution for "incidental benefits," because not at the expense of the claimant in the required sense, how might that be justified?

A possible justification in terms of policy is that stretching the law of unjust enrichment to cover incidental benefits constitutes an unacceptable legal interference with the freedom of defendants who, in relation to the incidental fallout of the claimants' actions, are entitled to retain, without payment, windfall benefits.[43] Put another way, at the point

---

[40] *Supra* note 17.

[41] Importantly, this led to the overruling of the decision in TFL Management Services Ltd. v. Lloyds TSB Bank plc [2013] EWCA Civ 1415, [2014] 1 W.L.R. 2006.

[42] See Andrew Burrows, *A Restatement of the English Law of Unjust Enrichment* 54–55 (2012).

[43] *Restatement of Restitution (First)* § 106 (Am. Law Inst. 1937) ("A person who, incidentally to the performance of his own duty or to the protection of the improvement of his own things, has conferred a benefit upon another, is not thereby entitled to contribution"). The second illustration given is based on *Ulmer v. Farnsworth*, 15 A. 65 (1888), in which the claimant drained his own land and thereby enhanced the value of a neighbor's land. Cf. *Restatement (Third) of Restitution and Unjust Enrichment* § 30 cmt. *b* (Am. Law Inst. 2011) (arguing that to call the benefits "incidental" is a conclusion not a reason and going on to indicate that the true reason for denying restitution is a concern for the defendant's autonomy).

where benefits are incidentally rather than directly conferred the law should not seek to reverse a person's good luck. A possible counterargument to this is that security of receipt is already adequately catered for either by the insistence that the defendant can subjectively devalue the benefit or by the operation of the standard change of position defense. As an alternative justification, one might be tempted to say that, as a matter of legal causation, the benefiting of C is essentially coincidental to what C is doing and there should be no liability for coincidental benefits just as there is no liability for coincidental losses in tort (as where C is hit by a falling tree on the way to hospital, having been injured by D).[44] Yet another analogy may be drawn with collateral benefits in tort: they are generally ignored in calculating the claimant's loss on the grounds that they are too indirectly connected to be taken into account in reducing the claimant's loss, even though the "but for" causal test may be satisfied.[45]

Applying Stevens's normative thesis, incidental benefits do not count because there is no performance, accepted by the defendant, in these situations. Indeed for him the Supreme Court's reliance on a notion of "incidental benefits" was misconceived. This was to invoke a "policy exception," without providing an explanation as to why it should matter that the benefit was incidental, and was simply an ad hoc addition "introduced to explain away examples that do not fit the theory."[46]

C. The Consequential Benefit Issue

We turn, finally, to our third hypothetical example and to the second of the recent leading tax cases. In *Prudential v. HMRC*, the Supreme Court, controversially overruling an earlier decision in *Sempra Metals Ltd. v. IRC*,[47] held that there can generally be no (non-statutory) claim in unjust enrichment for interest (whether simple or compound). The relevant claims in issue were for overpaid advanced corporation tax, including compound interest. The claimants had been charged advanced corporation tax contrary to EU law. The Supreme Court's decision was that the claimants' entitlement to restitution did not extend to interest on the taxes mistakenly paid and nor could there be an award of interest where the tax had been set off later against mainstream corporation tax (which was the equivalent of repayment of the tax). This means that, if C pays $1,000 to D by mistake, and D has the use of the $1,000 for five years, and C then seeks restitution, C is entitled to restitution of $1,000 but is not entitled to any interest in the law of unjust enrichment (although, where proceedings have been brought, there can be a statutory award of simple interest under Section 35A of the Senior Courts Act 1981). It also follows that, in the hypothetical example (c) given earlier, the claimant is entitled to restitution of $10,000 not $16,000.

---

[44] Andrew Burrows, *Remedies for Torts, Breach of Contract and Equitable Wrongs* 107 (4th ed. 2019).
[45] *Id.*, ch. 8. Eli Ball argues that there should be no restitution of incidental benefits by drawing an analogy with proprietary "abandonment": *Abandonment and the Problem of Incidental Gains in the Law of Restitution of Unjust Enrichment*, R.L.R. 49 (2011).
[46] Stevens, *supra* note 17, at 579.   [47] [2007] UKHL 34, [2008] 1 A.C. 561.

This is controversial because in *Sempra Metals* the House of Lords had earlier decided that compound interest could be awarded as restitution for unjust enrichment in over-paid tax (and other) cases. This was on the reasoning that such cases concerned two immediate transfers of value: the transfer of the payment and the transfer of the use value of the payment.[48] The Supreme Court rejected that analysis, apparently on the view that there was only one transfer of value. Although a defendant may have causally gained, by reason of the consequential benefit, that was by reason of the defendant's fail-ure to pay back the money. It was in essence no different from where a claimant mistak-enly delayed in failing to enforce a debt owed to the claimant by the defendant; and restitution would not be given in that situation for the gain the defendant had made because of that mistake.

If that is the law, can it be justified? Again one can say that the courts are concerned to limit the scope of unjust enrichment so as to minimize the law's intervention in revers-ing benefits, thereby protecting security of receipt and the autonomy of defendants. The law's intervention should be confined to the immediate benefit only and not consequen-tial benefits. One might perhaps draw an analogy with the law on damages for torts and breach of contract where remote consequential losses are irrecoverable so as to ensure that only a fair and reasonable burden of liability is placed on the defendant. However, the difficulty is in drawing the line between immediate and consequential benefits. The reasoning in *Sempra Metals*, that there were two immediate benefits transferred—the payment and its use value—is a powerful one. In contrast, no such argument could be made as regards the hypothetical example (c) set out earlier, so that unjust enrichment would certainly not reach the $6,000 profit. The Supreme Court appeared to rely on Stevens's view to the effect that there was only one performance by the taxpayer to, and accepted by, HMRC, and that was the payment. There was no additional performance comprising the use value.

D. Conclusion on "At the Expense of" and Concluding Thoughts

What has clearly emerged from the two recent decisions on "at the expense of" is that the U.K. Supreme Court is anxious to ensure that the law of unjust enrichment is nar-rowly confined. Although the two cases concerned claims against HMRC, where there were particular policy reasons to restrict the ambit of unjust enrichment, the reasoning is designed to apply to all claims, whoever the defendant may be. In gen-eral terms, the cases establish that the benefit has to be directly conferred by the claimant on the defendant, so that a party earlier in a chain of transactions cannot claim against the final recipient, and incidental and consequential benefits do not count. Using the language of causation, direct causation is required. Applying the methodology of Birksian doctrinal scholarship (while noting Stevens's critique of it),

---

[48] *Id.* at [102] (Lord Nicholls).

I have explored some possible justifications for that narrow approach. Ultimately one might say that the courts are concerned about the potential width and disruption caused by an excessively wide law of unjust enrichment and regard the best strategy as being to establish a general narrow starting point from which, over the course of time, exceptions can be confidently recognized by a careful process of incremental development.

I have suggested that the mix of principle and policy adopted by Birks's doctrinal approach is in line with New Private Law. Having said that, I anticipate that New Private Law scholars would tend to reject as over-rigid aspects of his approach and would push the balance more toward a deeper analysis than Birks thought necessary of the policy concerns and the normative underpinnings of the law. It may be that New Private Law could also embrace aspects of the critique of Stevens while tending to reject his Weinribian premise that there is one fixed normative structure for private law.

CHAPTER 19

··

FIDUCIARY LAW

··

W. BRADLEY WENDEL

MANY discussions of the law of fiduciary relationships and duties begin by lamenting its confused state. In the first chapter of his great treatise, Professor (and later Judge on the Federal Court of Australia) Paul Finn writes that the legacy of scholarly inattention to fiduciary law has been doubt and confusion, and "the term 'fiduciary' is itself one of the most ill-defined, if not altogether misleading terms in our law."[1] The problem may stem from the wide range of institutional roles to which the label "fiduciary" has been ascribed. Trustees, corporate directors, partners, court-appointed receivers, lawyers, investment advisers, physicians, public officials, and the state with respect to indigenous peoples have all been deemed fiduciaries. There is also a wide range of duties described in the characteristic terminology of fiduciary law as duties of loyalty, care, trust, confidence, good faith, and fair dealing. Some scholars accordingly criticize fiduciary law for its absence of organization, rigor, and a system.[2] These critics contend that a term that is too open-ended lacks explanatory power.[3] Others perceive the flexibility, adaptability, and context-specificity of fiduciary duties and remedies as one of fiduciary law's chief virtues, and their diversity as a resource from which courts can draw to tailor the law to serve its ends.[4] A satisfying theory of an area of private law need not necessarily be monistic, with one principle of value (such as efficiency) serving to organize the doctrine in a field.[5]

This chapter considers fiduciary law within the framework of private law theory more generally. Private law theory aims to take law seriously without assuming it is a "brooding

---

[1] Paul D. Finn, *Fiduciary Obligations* 1 (1977).
[2] Peter Birks, *Equity in the Modern Law: An Exercise in Taxonomy*, 26 U. W. AUSTL. L. REV. 1, 5 (1996); Frank H. Easterbrook & Daniel R. Fischel, *Contract and Fiduciary Duty*, 36 J.L. & ECON. 425 (1993).
[3] James J. Edelman, *When Do Fiduciary Duties Arise?*, 126 L.Q. REV. 302 (2010).
[4] Julian Velasco, *How Many Fiduciary Duties Are There in Corporate Law?*, 83 S. CAL. L. REV. 1231, 1234 (2010).
[5] Hanoch Dagan & Sharon Hannes, "Managing Our Money: The Law of Financial Fiduciaries as a Private Law Institution," in *Philosophical Foundations of Fiduciary Law* 91, 93 (Andrew S. Gold & Paul B. Miller eds., 2014); Henry E. Smith, "Why Fiduciary Law Is Equitable," in *id.*, at 272–273 [hereinafter Smith, "Fiduciary Law Is Equitable"].

omniscience in the sky."[6] It adopts the perspective of one who seeks to give an account of the law from a participant's point of view—that is, that of a lawyer or judge using legal doctrine to argue in favor of a result, as opposed to that of an external observer evaluating the law with respect to policies the law might promote. Yet private law theory does not proceed in a vacuum, isolated from background normative considerations. It seeks to render law intelligible with reference to human ends and values. For example, a distinctive feature of law is that it provides individuals with the power to demand accountability from others. It does so not only with reference to its own highly developed doctrine but also under the constraint of practices and norms that make up professional craft and ethics. Law is therefore distinct from politics and morality, but it is not an artificial system with no normative significance.[7]

Fiduciary law and private law theory seem made for one another. Fiduciary law is centrally focused on the morally attractive end of maintaining relationships of trust and confidence among individuals. But it does so by bracketing highly abstract normative theory in favor of well-developed legal constructs such as duties of loyalty and care. It is comfortable with pluralism, complexity, and context-specificity. And it represents a rational structure that is not wholly dependent on external criteria yet does not aspire to strict independence from empirical considerations and normative values.

Fiduciary law nevertheless poses some challenges for private law theory. As an evolving field, it may grow in unanticipated directions and risk the loss of its former coherence. The possibility of this loss of a coherent organizing structure has motivated considerable recent work in the theory of fiduciary law, and also in legal theory more generally, as scholars seek to understand how normative pluralism can coexist with stable, rational legal doctrine.

I. Methodology

The goal of a theoretical account of any field of law is to make it intelligible, "to show how the characteristic modes of reasoning, the questions asked, and the inferences permitted or refused fit into an integrated pattern."[8] We look to a theory of fiduciary law to furnish an explanation of its observable features, including its scope (what roles, offices, or legal relationships will be subject to fiduciary duties), the requirements of fiduciary duties such as loyalty, and the remedies that are available when these duties are breached. Fiduciary law is an interesting subject for a theoretical account only if it is distinctive.[9]

---

[6] Southern Pacific Co. v. Jensen, 244 U.S. 205, 222 (1917) (Holmes, J., dissenting).

[7] John C.P. Goldberg, *Pragmatism and Private Law*, 125 HARV. L. REV. 1640 (2012).

[8] Arthur Ripstein, *Private Wrongs* xi (2016).

[9] Leonard I. Rotman, *Understanding Fiduciary Duties and Relationship Fiduciarity*, 62 McGILL L.J. 975, 986 (2017) [hereinafter Rotman, *Relationship Fiduciarity*]; Leonard I. Rotman, *Fiduciary Law's "Holy Grail": Reconciling Theory and Practice in Fiduciary Jurisprudence*, 91 B.U. L. REV. 921, 932 (2011) [hereinafter Rotman, *Holy Grail*].

If what are called fiduciary duties are, in fact, nothing more than the voluntarily assumed obligations of the parties, or what parties to a hypothetical bargain would have agreed to, there would be no call for a theory of fiduciary relationships apart from what is already part of a theory of contracts. Some scholars worry that fiduciary relationships are no longer a distinctive legal category, and therefore that the characteristic terminology of fiduciary law, such as loyalty and good faith, merely obscures the application of legal principles that have been developed elsewhere, in the law of contracts, tort, and restitution.[10] Others respond by seeking the essence of fiduciary law in goals and doctrinal machinery that cannot be reduced to other legal concepts without distortion. For example, many scholars argue that discretionary power over the property or interests of another is the sine qua non of a relationship properly described as fiduciary.[11] A feature such as discretionary power offers a parsimonious theoretical explanation of fiduciary duties in terms of the distinctive feature of relationships to which they attach.

On the other hand, some degree of pluralism in a theoretical explanation of fiduciary law may be inevitable given its origins in equitable notions such as trust and conscience.[12] Equity by nature is context-specific and flexible, as it must be if its aim is to deter opportunism by sophisticated actors who know how to exploit loopholes in the law.[13] It is therefore not surprising that fiduciary concepts have been applied differently to such actors as trustees, corporate directors, lawyers, and investment advisers. A concept such as loyalty may mean something different in each of these varying contexts; the loyalty required of a trustee may be different from that required of a participant in a joint venture.[14] A theoretical explanation of fiduciary law would be inadequate if it failed to account for all of its observed features, including its context-sensitivity and adaptability.[15]

The trouble with analytical pluralism is that it may undercut the explanatory significance of the categories it employs. It is well and good to say that the content of fiduciary duties varies according to circumstances—trustees have more stringent obligations than corporate directors, for example. If there is too much contextual variation, however, there seems to be little point in treating a diverse set of relationships and obligations as instantiations of a common concept. This is not only a theoretical problem; it may raise difficulties for judges who are called upon to apply fiduciary doctrine to new categories beyond those actors and activities traditionally subject to fiduciary duties.

For example, must a closely held corporation disclose to one of its shareholders, who is already contractually obligated to sell his shares to the corporation upon terminating employment, that the corporation is in negotiations with a third party over a

---

[10] Peter Birks, *The Content of Fiduciary Obligation*, 34 Isr. L. Rev. 3, 5 (2000).

[11] Paul B. Miller, "The Identification of Fiduciary Relationships," in *The Oxford Handbook of Fiduciary Law* (Evan J. Criddle, Paul B. Miller, & Robert H. Sitkoff eds., 2019); D. Gordon Smith & Jordan C. Lee, *Fiduciary Discretion*, 75 Ohio St. L.J. 609 (2014); D. Gordon Smith, *The Critical Resource Theory of Fiduciary Duty*, 55 Vand. L. Rev. 1399, 1403 (2002) [hereinafter Smith, *Critical Resource*].

[12] Rotman, *Relationship Fiduciarity*, *supra* note 9, at 980.

[13] See Smith, "Fiduciary Law Is Equitable," *supra* note 5, at 265.

[14] Andrew S. Gold, "The Loyalties of Fiduciary Law," in *Philosophical Foundations of Fiduciary Law*, *supra* note 5, at 176.

[15] Benjamin Zipursky, *Pragmatic Conceptualism*, 6 Legal Theory 457 (2000).

possible merger?[16] Setting aside for now the problem that "[t]he notion that a corporation owes a fiduciary obligation to its own shareholders poses analytic challenges of heroic dimensions,"[17] the question is how one would know whether the relationship of closely held corporation to shareholder is one to which fiduciary duties should apply. If most fiduciary relationships bear the hallmark of difficult-to-observe discretion and the power of the agent to affect the principal's welfare,[18] then a closely held corporation might not owe fiduciary duties to its shareholder. On the other hand, courts sometimes say that fiduciary duties may arise whenever one has reposed trust and confidence in another, regardless of whether the relationship in general would count as fiduciary.[19] The shareholder in the closely held corporation may have trusted that the corporation would not make employment decisions with an eye toward the value of the stock, and so may have been vulnerable to opportunistic behavior by the corporation on this basis alone.[20] However, as the dissenting judge pointed out, parties to contracts are always vulnerable to abuse, and can protect themselves through the express terms of a contract—no need for heightened fiduciary duties in this case.[21] If the law wishes to impose a heightened standard of conduct upon one of the parties, there had better be a principled reason for regarding that party as a fiduciary, not merely an ad hoc determination that the party's conduct was wrongful and deserved to be punished.

II. Fiduciary Law

Fiduciary duties originated in equitable relief granted in favor of a party who reposed confidence in another party. This confidence could be in respect of property entrusted to another, or it could result from a grant of power to act in a way that could affect the interests of the enstrustor. Reposing trust could also take the form of relying upon the advice of another. A pattern of equitable relief granted in these cases gave rise to the principle "that if a confidence is reposed, and that confidence is abused, a court of equity shall give relief."[22] Equity thus channels the activities of the fiduciary to ensure that his or her actions are always for the other's benefit. This is a demanding obligation, so it is important to know in advance which relationships will be burdened with fiduciary status.

[16]   Jordan v. Duff & Phelps, Inc., 815 F.2d 429 (7th Cir. 1987).
[17]   Deborah A. DeMott, *Beyond Metaphor: An Analysis of Fiduciary Obligation*, 37 DUKE L.J. 879, 884 (1988).
[18]   Robert H. Sitkoff, "An Economic Theory of Fiduciary Law," in *Philosophical Foundations of Fiduciary Law, supra* note 5, at 197, 200.
[19]   See, e.g., Burdett v. Miller, 957 F.2d 1375 (7th Cir. 1992).
[20]   See Smith, "Fiduciary Law Is Equitable," *supra* note 5 (arguing that the best functional explanation for fiduciary law is the prevention of opportunism).
[21]   *Jordan*, 815 F.2d at 448 (Posner, J., dissenting).
[22]   L.S. Sealy, *Fiduciary Relationships*, 20 CAMBRIDGE L.J. 69, 70 (1962).

A. The Essence of a Fiduciary Relationship

Frequently cited characteristics of fiduciary relationships include discretion,[23] control over the property of another, imbalance of power, inequality, dependence or vulnerability of one of the parties,[24] and placement of trust and confidence in another.[25] One feature common to most fiduciary relationships is that the relationship exists for the benefit of one of the parties.[26] Trustees, personal representatives, corporate directors, lawyers, agents, investment advisers, and receivers all have an obligation to act to advance the interests of another person. In addition to the requirement of benefiting the entrustor, another characteristic of fiduciary relationships is that the entrustee has considerable autonomy to determine how to serve the other's interests. Generally the entrusting party is not in a position to supervise, control, or monitor the activities of the other. This may be because the power of the entrustee involves specialized knowledge, as with professionals such as lawyers and physicians. Lacking the entrustee's knowledge and expertise, the entrustor cannot specify in advance all of the things the agent is supposed to do.[27] Equity therefore intervenes in fiduciary relationships to enforce the requirement that the entrustee act for the benefit of the entrustor.

A further characteristic of relationships in which one party is subject to fiduciary duties to another is the commitment to exercise discretion on behalf of another.[28] There is considerable debate over whether discretion is a necessary or a sufficient condition for characterizing a relationship as involving fiduciary duties. Paul Miller has argued that discretionary power is a necessary condition for the imposition of fiduciary duties and that the power of a fiduciary is a form of authority, derived from the legal personality of the entrustor.[29] If discretion is not a necessary condition, then some other fact about the course of dealing between the parties—such as one's reposing trust and confidence in the other—may be sufficient for a fiduciary relationship.[30] Entrusting some aspect of one's interests to another, in circumstances in which control or monitoring of the other is costly or impossible, may give rise to fiduciary obligations. If entrustment is the test

[23] See, e.g., Galambos v. Perez, [2009] 3 S.C.R. 247 (Can.) (fiduciary relationships arise where one party has the "discretionary power to affect the legal or vital practical interests of the other.").

[24] See, e.g., Hodgkinson v. Simms, [1994] 3 S.C.R. 377, 405 (Can.) (vulnerability is an important indicator of the existence of a fiduciary relationship, but by itself neither necessary nor sufficient).

[25] See, e.g., Hosp. Prods Ltd. v. US Surgical Corp. (1984) 156 CLR 41 (Austl.) (Gibbs, CJ) (relationship of confidence not conclusive of fiduciary obligations); see also Sealy, *supra* note 22, at 74–79; Paul B. Miller, *Justifying Fiduciary Duties*, 58 McGILL L.J. 969, 1011 (2013).

[26] Finn, *supra* note 1, at 9–10. Some relationships that are clearly fiduciary in nature, such as those among partners, involve parties who can protect their own interests in various ways, such as by bargaining for contractual protection and monitoring the performance of the other party, There may be other fiduciary relationships that are not aimed at serving the interests of a beneficiary, but instead are best understood as furthering some abstract purpose. See Paul B. Miller & Andrew S. Gold, *Fiduciary Governance*, 57 WM. & MARY L. REV. 513 (2015).

[27] Easterbrook & Fischel, *supra* note 2, at 426–427.   [28] DeMott, *supra* note 17, at 908.

[29] Miller, *supra* note 25, at 1011–1013. For a critique of the view that discretion is a necessary condition, see Arthur B. Laby, *Book Review*, 35 LAW & PHIL. 123 (2016).

[30] See, e.g., Bristol & West Building Soc'y v. Mothew [1988] Ch. 1 at 18.

for a fiduciary relationship, however, one may still question whether the interest of the entrusting party must be some tangible or intangible property interest, or whether it is enough that it be a significant legal or practical interest.[31]

Proponents of a narrow scope for fiduciary relationships (i.e., a more demanding test, perhaps regarding some characteristic as a necessary condition) may worry that a more open-ended standard will result in the inefficient imposition of excessively demanding duties on parties who would prefer to negotiate for less stringent terms of dealing.[32] That is an instrumental argument against fiduciary duties, based on the extralegal value of economic efficiency. One may also make a non-instrumental or jurisprudential argument that, whatever the scope of fiduciary relationships, it should be clear ex ante both to courts and to parties who might find themselves subject to fiduciary duties.[33] The ideal of the rule of law demands that duties be established with precision, for the benefit of parties to whom they apply.[34] Fiduciary concepts should not be used by judges to punish conduct that they happen to regard as inappropriate.[35]

Consider these instrumental and non-instrumental reasons for a broad or narrow definition of fiduciary relationships in the context of an example involving the obligations of lawyers.

The act of reposing trust and confidence, in the absence of a grant of full discretionary power to the entrustee, is an important characteristic of the attorney–client relationship. A federal court of appeals discussed the prerequisites for the formation of a fiduciary relationship in one of the most important cases in the development of attorney conflict-of-interest doctrine in the United States, *Westinghouse Electric Corp. v. Kerr-McGee Corp.*[36] The case arose out of the representation of opposing parties by the law firm of Kirkland & Ellis. The firm's Chicago office was representing Westinghouse, a manufacturer of nuclear reactors, in litigation over its uranium supply contracts with numerous energy companies. One aspect of that litigation was an antitrust claim asserted by Westinghouse against the energy companies, claiming anticompetitive behavior in the uranium market by companies including Kerr-McGee, Gulf, and Getty. At the same time, the Washington, D.C., office of the law firm was representing the American Petroleum Institute (API), lobbying Congress in opposition to a proposal to, among

---

[31] Robert Cooter & Bradley J. Freedman, *The Fiduciary Relationship: Its Economic Character and Legal Consequences*, 66 N.Y.U. L. Rev. 1045 (1991); Miller, *supra* note 11; Smith, *Critical Resource, supra* note 11.

[32] Larry E. Ribstein, *Fencing Fiduciary Duties*, 91 B.U. L. Rev. 899, 903–904 (2011).

[33] Katharina Pistor & Chenggang Xu, "Fiduciary Duty in Transitional Civil Law Jurisdictions: Lessons from the Incomplete Law Theory," in *Global Markets, Domestic Institutions: Corporate Law and Governance in a New Era of Cross-Border Deals* 77 (Curtis J. Milhaupt ed., 2003); Smith, "Fiduciary Law Is Equitable," *supra* note 5, at 278.

[34] Birks, *supra* note 10, at 5.

[35] See, e.g., Desimone v. Barrows, 924 A.2d 908, 932 (Del. Ch. 2007) (noting that courts express a "justified concern that concepts of fiduciary duty not be used in an unprincipled and wholly-elastic way to reach any and all behavior that, upon first blush, strikes judges as inappropriate."). Peter Birks likewise cautioned against "[t]he habit of throwing fiduciary language at any moral outrage." Birks, *supra* note 10, at 5 n.5.

[36] Westinghouse Elec. Corp. v. Kerr-McGee Corp., 580 F.2d 1311 (7th Cir. 1978).

other things, require oil and gas companies to divest themselves of alternative energy holdings, such as uranium. Lawyers in the Washington office of Kirkland sent written questionnaires and conducted in-person interviews with officers of API member companies, seeking information about the companies' alternative energy assets. The lawyers assured the member companies that the information would be kept strictly confidential. The firm used the information to bolster the API's submission to Congress, contending that the uranium market was sufficiently competitive.

Kerr-McGee, Gulf, and Getty were members of the API and also plaintiffs in the uranium supply contract litigation against Westinghouse. They were dismayed to discover that the law firm representing the API was also representing Westinghouse, and in the latter representation was seeking to establish an illegal conspiracy in restraint of trade in the uranium industry. The formal client of the firm was the trade association, the API, which had an engagement agreement with the firm and paid the firm's bills. Did the firm also have fiduciary relationships with the member companies? There was no express agreement from the firm to the member companies to provide legal representation. The district court concluded that the firm owed no fiduciary duties to the member companies, because the traditional indicia of an agency relationship, including the right of the principal to control the conduct of the agent, were absent. The Seventh Circuit Court of Appeals, however, said this test was too narrow. "A fiduciary relationship may result because of the nature of the work performed and the circumstances under which confidential information is divulged."[37] The member companies divulged confidential information to the law firm, with the expectation that it be held confidential, and were justifiably worried that "their disclosures [would] return to haunt them" in the uranium antitrust litigation. Confidential market-share data revealing, for example, close coordination by the member companies in setting uranium prices, could be used by Westinghouse to show an illegal restraint of trade. Because the law firm received this information under circumstances in which it would be reasonable for the member companies to expect it to be held confidential and not used against them on behalf of another client of the firm, the firm had a fiduciary relationship with the member companies as well as to its formal client, the API. Enforcing the fiduciary duty of loyalty to the member companies required the equitable remedy of disqualifying the law firm from representing Westinghouse in the uranium antitrust litigation.

It is not exactly right to describe the law firm as exercising discretionary power over the interests of the API member companies. In fact, its power over the interests of any client would be limited to carrying out the lawful instructions of the client with respect to the objectives of the representation, as defined by the client. In *Westinghouse*, the member companies and the law firm had not expressly agreed to form a professional relationship. However, the firm was in a position to exploit its access to the companies' confidential information, not for its own self-interested reasons but for the benefit of another firm client, Westinghouse. This raises the central doctrinal and theoretical issue: Is it appropriate to hold that the law firm had a fiduciary relationship with the

---

[37] *Id.* at 1320.

member companies, arising from the companies' entrustment of confidential information to the firm as part of its representation of the API? In terms of ex ante predictability, would a reasonable lawyer at the firm know that by promising officers of the member companies that the information would be held in confidence, the law firm would thereby acquire a fiduciary relationship with each company whose information it acquired?

The relationship between lawyer and client is paradigmatically a fiduciary one, yet it is awkwardly characterized as involving discretionary power by the lawyer over the interests of the client.[38] A case like *Westinghouse* shows that entrusting some aspect of one's legal interests—here, highly confidential market data—to a lawyer may give rise to a fiduciary duty of loyalty. The firm's resulting duty is to avoid using confidential information to the detriment of the entrusting party. The trial court's remedy of disqualifying the law firm enforced the firm's duty of loyalty to the member companies, which the court believed was breached by the firm's ongoing representation of the companies' adversary in the antitrust litigation.

Other courts have concluded, on the contrary, that reposing trust and confidence in another is not conclusive of a fiduciary relationship. (I place trust in my auto mechanic, for example, but no one would contend that mechanics are fiduciaries.) As a matter of giving a theoretical explanation, therefore, one may take different approaches: *Westinghouse* may be seen as an outlier—either a mistake by the court, or an ad hoc category of fiduciary relationships. It may show that no one single characteristic of fiduciary relationships may be regarded as necessary or sufficient. Or, one may seek to bring the case within an existing theoretical position, for example, by contending that the law firm really did have discretionary power in some sense over the interests of the member companies.

The issues here are not for theorists alone. Lawyers and judges also look to fit new cases within existing legal doctrine, so that the novel instance "go[es] with the grain rather than across or against it."[39] Lawyers and judges may proceed by analogy—for example, contending that the member companies are sufficiently like clients of the law firm to be regarded as the beneficiaries of the law firm's fiduciary duties—without being unduly concerned about the coherence of the field as a whole.

B. The Content of Fiduciary Duties and Remedies

Fiduciary obligations express the overarching concern that, whatever the fiduciary does, it should be primarily or exclusively in the service of the beneficiary.[40] Importantly, they do not seek to specify in advance all of the things the fiduciary must do, or what is in the beneficiary's interests. A fundamental premise of fiduciary law is that the fiduciary must

---

[38] Alice Woolley, *The Lawyer as Fiduciary: Defining Private Law Duties in Public Law Relations*, 65 U. Toronto L.J. 285 (2015).

[39] Hanoch Dagan, *Doctrinal Categories, Legal Realism, and the Rule of Law*, 163 U. Pa. L. Rev. 1889, 1898 (2015).

[40] Finn, *supra* note 1, at 15–17.

have autonomy to determine *how* to act in the beneficiary's interests. While doing so, however, a fiduciary must be "seen in the garb Equity imposes on him, that is, as one who in the exercise of his powers is bound to act in what he believes to be his beneficiaries' interests."[41]

The core fiduciary duties, at least in the United States, are loyalty and care. (Fiduciary law scholars outside the United States sometimes express skepticism that care is a *fiduciary* duty.) The duty of loyalty is perhaps the most distinctive feature of the fiduciary relationship. It developed from the law of trusts, which in turn grew out of the relief granted in equity where one party reposed confidence in another. A natural extension of the duty of loyalty of trustees was the "trust-like" duty owed by corporate directors. At least in corporate law, a fiduciary must go beyond honesty and fairness and act to further the best interests of the beneficiary.[42] This may mean, for example, refraining from entering into transactions that put the fiduciary's interests into conflict with those of the beneficiary, or acting on the basis of the fiduciary's self-interest. Fiduciaries may not benefit themselves, or a third party, at the expense of their beneficiary if there is some nexus between the fiduciary relationship and the benefit.[43] The content of these general obligations may vary by field.

In American corporate law, for example, the duty of loyalty purports to prohibit "all possibility of profit flowing from a breach of the confidence imposed by the fiduciary relation."[44] However, self-interested transactions by corporate directors may be permissible if they are fair and approved by disinterested directors.[45] The duty of loyalty amounts to a requirement that a corporate fiduciary act with an objectively reasonable good-faith belief that the actions are in the best interests of the corporation and its shareholders.[46] The duty of loyalty can therefore be understood as not limited to the negative duty to avoid self-interested transactions, but including the positive duty to act in furtherance of the corporation's best interests.[47]

In the American law governing lawyers, the fiduciary duty of loyalty plays an important role in regulating conflicts of interest. The possibility that an attorney could use the confidential information of one client—or even a nonclient, as in the *Westinghouse* case—to the advantage of another client is a sufficient basis for disqualifying the attorney, and indeed the entire law firm, from representing the client who might be benefited by the disclosure

---

[41] *Id.* at 39.
[42] DeMott, *supra* note 17, at 882. The traditional position in trust law is that the trustee must act in the *sole* interests of the beneficiary, not merely in the beneficiary's best interests. This rule has its critics. See, e.g., John H. Langbein, *Questioning the Trust Law Duty of Loyalty: Sole Interest or Best Interest?*, 114 YALE L.J. 929 (2005). It remains the dominant view, however. See *Restatement (Third) of Trusts* § 78, cmt. *b.*
[43] Rotman, *Relationship Fiduciarity*, *supra* note 9, at 984.
[44] Guth v. Loft, Inc., 5 A.2d 503 (Del. 1939).
[45] See, e.g., Solomon v. Armstrong, 747 A.2d 1098, 1115–1116 (Del. Ch. 1999); In re Walt Disney Co. Derivative Litig., 731 A.2d 342, 368 (Del. Ch. 1998).
[46] Stone v. Ritter, 911 A.2d 362 (Del. 2006).
[47] Leo E. Strine Jr. et al., *Loyalty's Core Demand: The Defining Role of Good Faith in Corporation Law*, 98 GEO. L.J. 629 (2010).

or adverse use of the confidential information. Numerous provisions of state rules of professional conduct, and hundreds of decided cases have created an intricate structure of rules and exceptions, but the underlying idea remains a strict, but in some cases waivable, duty of loyalty owed to anyone who reposes trust and confidence in a lawyer.

The duty of care requires fiduciaries to do a good job in pursuing the beneficiary's interests. In this respect fiduciary law is close to the requirement imposed on certain professionals by tort law to use reasonable competence and diligence in the service of another's objectives.[48] In the United States, the fiduciary law duty of care is frequently discussed in the context of the duties of corporate directors, albeit as viewed through the lens of the more permissive business judgment rule. (The duty of care is less well developed outside the United States, and in some legal systems may not be regarded as a fiduciary duty at all.) The American corporate-law duty of care requires directors to make careful, informed decisions about matters calling for their decision, to acquire adequate information, and to devote sufficient time to reviewing relevant information and making a decision. However, under the business judgment rule, reviewing courts will presume that directors made a decision on an informed basis, in good faith, and with an honest belief that it was in the best interests of the corporation.[49] Some scholars contend that the duty still has some bite as a rule specifying the conduct required of directors,[50] but the signal sent by the highly deferential business judgment rule interferes with the intended message that corporate directors as fiduciaries owe stringent duties of competence and diligence. Here is a situation in which Meir Dan-Cohen's famous metaphor of acoustic separation between conduct rules and decision rules would be useful.[51] In other fiduciary settings, however, liability for failure to use sufficient care is not as unusual and thus the deterrent signal is stronger. At least in the United States, an active and sophisticated plaintiffs'-side legal malpractice bar ensures that lawyers fulfill their duty of competent representation owed to clients.

It is easy to state duties of loyalty and care at a high level of generality. Specifying those duties in particular contexts, however, is frequently the occasion for litigation. A theoretical question that may be raised in this connection is whether fiduciary duties—as distinct from those arising from contract—may be understood only, or at least more clearly, with reference to considerations from background morality. For example, knowing what it means to be a loyal trustee, corporate director, or lawyer may require first grasping the qualities of a loyal person, outside the institutional context of the role. Court decisions respecting fiduciary relationships are often characterized by moralistic language. In the United States, citations are legion to a famous passage from a decision of Judge Benjamin Cardozo, involving an allegation of breach of duty by a one party in a joint venture to the other. Salmon had failed to disclose to Meinhard that he had obtained an opportunity to lease the building to a third party. Judge Cardozo wrote the

---

[48] See, e.g., *Restatement (Third) of the Law Governing Lawyers* § 16(2) (Am. Law Inst. 2000).

[49] See, e.g., Aronson v. Lewis, 473 A.2d 805, 812 (Del. 1984).

[50] Julian Velasco, *A Defense of the Corporate Law Duty of Care*, 40 J. CORP. L. 647 (2015).

[51] Meir Dan-Cohen, *Decision Rules and Conduct Rules: On Acoustic Separation in Criminal Law*, 97 HARV. L. REV. 625 (1984).

opinion for the New York Court of Appeals holding that Salmon's self-dealing was a breach of his fiduciary duty, and in doing so recognized that legal duties may be defined by background moral considerations:

> Joint adventurers, like copartners, owe to one another, while the enterprise continues, the duty of the finest loyalty. Many forms of conduct permissible in a workaday world for those acting at arm's length, are forbidden by those bound by fiduciary ties. A trustee is held to something stricter than the morals of the market place. Not honesty alone, but the punctilio of an honor the most sensitive, is then the standard of behavior. As to this there has developed a tradition that is unbending and inveterate. Uncompromising rigidity has been the attitude of courts of equity when petitioned to undermine the rule of undivided loyalty by the "disintegrating erosion" of particular exceptions. Only thus has the level of conduct for fiduciaries been kept at a level higher than that trodden by the crowd.[52]

By distinguishing fiduciary duties from the "morals of the market place," Judge Cardozo suggests that understanding the content of fiduciary duties requires going beyond the duties assumed by the parties to a contract.

The passage from *Meinhard v. Salmon* is open to different, theoretically interesting interpretations. The most obvious is that giving content to the duty of loyalty requires grasping what "the finest loyalty" or "the punctilio of an honor the most sensitive" requires in other contexts such as friendship and family relationships. (In the terminology of general jurisprudence, this understanding of *Meinhard* may be taken as support for inclusive positivism or some variety of antipositivism.)

A different interpretation equates the morals of the marketplace with efficiency-based economic rationality and imposes a higher duty on fiduciaries. On this view, fiduciary obligations are genuinely duties—not aspirations, in Fuller's sense—but they are stricter than those assumed by the parties to an actual or hypothetical contract.[53] This may mean that they refer to extralegal moral conceptions of loyalty, but it also may be possible to construct a noneconomic account of loyalty starting with the self-understanding that runs throughout fiduciary law.[54] If understanding fiduciary duties does require resort to extralegal concepts, one would expect more judicial attention to concepts like honor, explicitly mentioned by Judge Cardozo, and how honor related to other normative considerations. If not, one may be forced to conclude that the moralistic language is merely a rhetorical makeweight, unconnected with the content of fiduciary duties.

Many modern courts eschew reference to extralegal moral values and, directly contradicting Judge Cardozo's rejection of the morals of the marketplace, attempt to specify fiduciary duties with reference to what parties to a bargain would agree to in the absence of transaction costs. Judge Frank Easterbrook, who prior to taking the bench as a federal

[52] Meinhard v. Salmon, 164 N.E. 545, 546 (N.Y. 1928).
[53] Rotman, *Holy Grail, supra* note 9, at 932.
[54] Andrew S. Gold, "Interpreting Fiduciary Law," in *Research Handbook on Fiduciary Law* 37 (D. Gordon Smith & Andrew S. Gold eds., 2018).

court of appeals judge was a prominent law-and-economics scholar, wrote that the fiduciary duty of loyalty is nothing more than "a standby or off-the-rack guess about what parties would agree to if they dickered about the subject explicitly."[55] On this approach, fiduciary duties function as default rules or gap-filling terms, not mandatory duties.[56] While the hypothetical-bargain understanding of the content of fiduciary duties may have once been against the grain of most decided cases, nowadays it would not be an outlier at all within the field of fiduciary law, at least in the United States in the corporate law context.[57] However, a committed contractualist, who believes that fiduciary duties are nothing more than the product of a hypothetical agreement in the absence of transaction costs, would be hard pressed to account for the existence of mandatory or non-waivable duties.[58] The contractualist explanation encounters the further difficulty of accounting for fiduciary duties that arise by implication from the entrustment of an important interest into the care of another, as in the *Westinghouse* case discussed previously. Joint ventures, similarly, are not necessarily governed by contract. They may be implied from an understanding among the parties that they will work toward a common objective, but they are nevertheless recognized as giving rise to fiduciary duties.[59] One who attempts to reduce fiduciary duties to those assumed by the parties via contract must therefore account for duties that cannot be varied by agreement of the parties and duties that arise independently of contract.

One of the most important distinctions between fiduciary law and the related areas of tort and contract is that remedies for breaching fiduciary duties are not confined to compensatory damages designed to rectify the loss to the plaintiff. Fiduciary law provides additional remedies, most notably disgorgement of profits wrongfully obtained. The disgorgement remedy is measured by an unfaithful fiduciary's gain, not the beneficiary's loss.[60]

In an important Australian case, *Hospital Products, Ltd. v. United States Surgical Corp.*,[61] Blackman, an authorized distributor of an American company's medical devices in Australia, went into business for himself, manufacturing knock-off devices (which were unprotected by patent in Australia) in competition with the American company. There was no doubt that this conduct breached the distributorship agreement between Blackman and the American company. The agreement required Blackman to use "best efforts" to distribute the American company's products in Australia. Thus, Blackman was liable for compensatory damages for breach of the contract. The issue in the High Court of Australia was whether Blackman had also breached a fiduciary duty to the American company, subjecting him and his Australian company to a constructive trust in favor of the American company over the profits made in violation of Blackman's duty of loyalty. Contract damages were considerably less than the equitable relief sought

[55] Jordan v. Duff & Phelps, Inc., 815 F.2d 429, 436 (7th Cir. 1987).

[56] Sitkoff, *supra* note 18, at 204.   [57] Gold, *supra* note 54, at 43–45.

[58] Sitkoff, *supra* note 18, at 205; Edelman, *supra* note 3.   [59] Edelman, *supra* note 3, at 310.

[60] Miller, *supra* note 25; James Barr Ames, *Following Misappropriated Property into Its Product*, 19 HARV. L. REV. 511 (1905).

[61] Hosp. Prods Ltd. v. US Surgical Corp. (1984) 156 CLR 41 (Austl.).

by the American company—disgorgement of the wrongfully obtained profits. The American company therefore argued that Blackman was a fiduciary, not merely the counterparty in an ordinary commercial transaction. Chief Justice Gibbs, in his opinion, deemed it "artificial in the extreme" to understand the American company as having entrusted some aspect of its interests to Blackman, in the same way a person may entrust another with property to deal with on his or her behalf. The significance of this conclusion about Blackman's lack of fiduciary status came in the denial of the remedy sought by the American company, which was disgorgement of the profits Blackman made from his self-dealing.

III. The Justification of Fiduciary Duties and Fiduciary Theory

Some justifications of fiduciary obligations are instrumental; that is, they seek to promote some social end or value by structuring legal doctrine in the right way. These theories owe a great deal to American legal realism—not necessarily the skeptical, deconstructive strand of realism that sought to establish the incoherence of legal formalism but the commitment, associated with Roscoe Pound, to look to the social sciences to illuminate and guide the operation of legal institutions.[62] These realist-derived theories seek to connect legal doctrine and policy concerns fairly directly.[63] The New Private Law literature, by contrast, emphasizes that law is a distinctive form of reasoning that imposes constraints on actors within the legal system (such as lawyers and judges), and that it cannot be reduced to other forms of reasoning, including politics and policy science.[64] Private law theorists argue that the law's claim to authority depends on its capacity to articulate recognizable norms of conduct which can serve as reasons for law's subjects.[65] One issue at the intersection of fiduciary law and New Private Law theory is therefore whether fiduciary law is best understood instrumentally, as furthering some end or value, or whether this is too much of a concession to the policy-science strand of legal realism.[66] The scholars cited here agree, however, that New Private Law theory can tolerate indirect instrumentalism, in which legal decisions do not directly aim at underlying policies but instead are guided by legal doctrinal mechanisms which themselves are justified on policy grounds.

For example, the standard economic account of fiduciary duties begins with the assumption that certain relationships involve agency costs. One person, the principal, engages another, the agent, to take actions that are difficult to monitor. The agent has discretion to act on the principal's interests but might exercise that power to do things

---

[62] Gerald J. Postema, *Legal Philosophy in the Twentieth Century: The Common Law World* 127–131 (2011).

[63] Henry E. Smith, *Property as the Law of Things*, 125 Harv. L. Rev. 1691, 1693 (2012).

[64] Dagan, *supra* note 39.   [65] Goldberg, *supra* note 7, at 1656.

[66] Andrew S. Gold, this volume.

that accrue to her own benefit, rather than to the benefit of the principal. If the agent can be deterred from acting in self-interested ways, however, the costs to the principal of monitoring the agent's activities, and running the risk of harm resulting from disloyal behavior by the agent, can be reduced. Of course, the parties may specify in advance what duties the agent owes the principal. When high transaction costs make it unlikely that the parties actually will agree to a contract specifying the agent's duties with suffi-cient particularity, courts will enforce the terms of a hypothetical bargained-for agree-ment. Fiduciary duties are thus nothing more than those duties the parties themselves would have preferred in a world free of transaction costs.[67] In functional terms, these duties deter the fiduciary from engaging in disloyal or careless acts by threatening him or her with after-the-fact liability for breach.[68]

A different instrumental account might use a value other than economic efficiency to explain and justify the imposition of fiduciary duties. One might argue, for example, that fiduciary law should be understood in terms of maintaining the social value of trust and interdependency.[69] Granted, a relationship of trust may also be one in which agency costs are minimized, but trust is not itself instrumental to economic efficiency. Rather, it is a social value the law promotes because of its connection with human flourishing.[70]

The economic approach to fiduciary duties has been quite influential, particularly in the United States, but also in other Anglophone jurisdictions.[71] As a result, some inco-herence has crept into fiduciary law.[72] Historically, fiduciary law grew out of remedies applied to redress the self-interested dealings of parties in a relationship of trust and con-fidence; the duties correlated with these equitable liabilities were not thought to be the same as the duties for which the parties would have bargained. If it is descriptively true that modern court decisions reflect the economic approach to justifying fiduciary duties and specifying their content, this may affect the theoretical explanation one gives of fidu-ciary status and obligations. On Zipursky's pragmatic conceptualist approach to legal theory, an explanation of a field of law must account for how various observed features of the field hang together.[73] At one time it may have been the case that the field of fiduciary law hung together around the idea of protecting certain socially valuable relationships characterized by a high degree of trust and confidence. Now, however, other fields of law, such as contracts, challenge the aspirations of fiduciary law to distinctiveness. For this reason, many private law theorists rely on the ethical application of law (not just in the context of fiduciary duties) to ensure that law maintains its capacity to articulate norms of guidance that are intelligible to its subjects. Judicial and lawyering craft supply the neces-sarily stability and connection to the human values served by the law.[74]

[67] Easterbrook & Fischel, *supra* note 2, at 427; Sitkoff, *supra* note 18, at 199.
[68] Sitkoff, *supra* note 18, at 201.
[69] Rotman, *Relationship Fiduciarity, supra* note 9; Tamar Frankel, *Fiduciary Law* (2011).
[70] See Matthew Harding, *Trust and Fiduciary Law*, 33 OXFORD J. LEGAL STUD. 81 (2013).
[71] Edelman, *supra* note 3.   [72] Gold, *supra* note 54.
[73] Zipursky, *supra* note 15, at 471–472.
[74] W. Bradley Wendel, *The Rule of Law and Legal-Process Reasons in Attorney Advising*, 99 B.U. L. REV. 107 (2019); Dagan, *supra* note 39, at 1896.

Fiduciary law from a lawyer's or judge's point of view is best understood as proceeding via what has been variously described as casuistry,[75] reflective equilibrium, analogical reasoning, ascription and limitation,[76] or simply the common law method. In a case like *Westinghouse*, described earlier, one may ask whether a third party who has entrusted confidential information to a law firm is similar to a firm client, in relevant respects, and whether this similarity justifies imposing fiduciary duties on the firm toward the third party. Or, in the *Hospital Products* case from Australia, whether the distributor of the company's products is sufficiently like an agent, a trustee, or another party who is in a fiduciary relationship with the company. The method of casuistry does not require normative theorizing, or that the field be coherent at the level of foundational principles. Rather, it depends on analogies between the facts and principles justifying the outcomes in specific cases. Over time, proceeding by analogy may expand the range of relationships subject to fiduciary duties, as they are shown to be similar to existing categories of fiduciary relationships. More generally the field is structured by analogies beginning with the core instance of trustees. Corporate directors are naturally understood as having "trustee-like" duties with respect to the corporation. Attorneys are not like trustees in some respects, but in other ways they do have a relationship of trust and confidence with respect to important interests of their clients. And so on. These rhetorical moves are licensed by a conceptual structure, the mastery of which is equivalent to competent and ethical lawyering or judging.[77]

There is only so much overall unity that can be expected from a common law field that has grown and adapted over time as new types of commercial relationships have developed. That does not mean either that the field is an incoherent mess or that decisions are driven directly by instrumental concerns. But the weakness of purely functional explanations of fiduciary law is that they presuppose a degree of coherence that is not to be found in modern judicial decisions. Some fiduciaries exercise discretionary power with respect to their beneficiaries, but others, like lawyers and investment advisers, do not. Some fiduciary duties can be understood as the product of a hypothetical bargain, but the parties to an actual bargain may wish to vary duties that the law regards as mandatory. Insistence on too much coherence at a theoretical or normative level fails to take the law, as it is, seriously, which is a core commitment of private law theory.

---

[75] DeMott, *supra* note 17.

[76] Joshua Getzler, "Ascribing and Limiting Fiduciary Obligations: Understanding the Operation of Consent," in *Philosophical Foundations of Fiduciary Law, supra* note 5, at 39.

[77] Zipursky, *supra* note 15, at 475.

···

CHAPTER 20

TRUST LAW

Private Ordering and the Branching of American Trust Law

···

JOHN D. MORLEY AND ROBERT H. SITKOFF

I. INTRODUCTION

···

THE common law trust sits at the heart of Anglo-American private law. For centuries, the trust has enabled private parties to order their affairs in an impressive variety of ways. "The purposes for which we can create trusts," says the leading treatise, "are as unlimited as our imagination."[1] In addition to facilitating gifts down the generations, the trust has also conveyed land, managed wealth, structured secured loans, resolved bankruptcies, issued bonds, securitized assets, and organized major businesses. In the early twentieth century, Frederic Maitland, the great English legal historian, summed up the trust's significance: "If we were asked what is the greatest and most distinctive achievement performed by Englishmen in the field of jurisprudence, I cannot think that we should have any better answer to give than this, namely, the development from century to century of the trust idea."[2]

Despite the trust's immense importance, it has received little attention from social scientists. The law-and-economics movement, in particular, has only recently begun to take the trust seriously,[3] and economic scholarship on trust law remains underdeveloped in comparison to other private law fields. The thinness of economic scholarship on trust law,

---

[1] Austin Wakeman Scott & Mark L. Ascher, *Scott and Ascher on Trusts* § 1.1, at 4 (6th ed. 2019) [hereafter *Scott and Ascher on Trusts*].

[2] *The Collected Papers of Frederic William Maitland* 271–284, at 272 (H.A.L. Fisher ed., 1911).

[3] See, e.g., Henry Hansmann & Ugo Mattei, *The Functions of Trust Law: A Comparative Legal and Economic Analysis*, 73 N.Y.U. L. REV. 434 (1998); Robert H. Sitkoff, *An Agency Costs Theory of Trust Law*, 89 CORNELL L. REV. 621 (2004); Max M. Schanzenbach & Robert H. Sitkoff, *Did Reform of Prudent Trust Investment Laws Change Trust Portfolio Allocation?*, 50 J.L. & ECON. 681 (2007); Robert H. Sitkoff, "Trust Law as Fiduciary Governance Plus Asset Partitioning," in *The Worlds of the Trust* (Lionel Smith ed., 2013).

however, should not obscure the deep tradition of doctrinal, historical, and jurisprudential scholarship in the field. Even before Maitland's work in the early twentieth century, scholars on both sides of the Atlantic had long focused on the trust as a major source of inquiry.

The law of trusts thus presents an especially fruitful field in which to employ the analytical tools of the "New Private Law."[4] Centuries of legal scholarship have given us a rich institutional understanding of trust law, but we are just now beginning to combine that understanding with the insights of social science. The field has ample room for the "inclusively pragmatic" approach to private law urged by the leaders of the New Private Law movement.[5] The law of trusts is replete with categories that we can take seriously as theoretical and doctrinal constructions, even as we pragmatically explore their functions in facilitating private ordering.

To that end, this chapter proposes a legal and functional taxonomy of contemporary American trust law.[6] Our argument is not merely that trust law serves different sets of purposes. Rather, our claim is that in both doctrine and practice the law of trusts has developed into a set of distinct categories that branch outward from its central historical core. To break down trust law in this way is to approach it pragmatically, by asking about its functions, and also inclusively, by accepting that the law's conceptual categories are interesting objects of inquiry in and of themselves.

Our taxonomy divides the law of trusts into two top-level categories: *donative* and *commercial*. We further divide donative trusts into *revocable* and *irrevocable private* trusts as well as *charitable* trusts. We show how the law has divided among these different branches and offer some initial reflections, rooted in on-the-ground trust practice, about the reasons why it did so.

We also note that the top-level divide between donative and commercial trusts reflects the deep logic of private law in facilitating private ordering. The law of donative trusts reflects the policy of *freedom of disposition,* and the law of commercial trusts reflects the policy of *freedom of contract.*[7] These two policies are overlapping and not mutually exclusive, but they are nevertheless separate. Collectively they underpin the distinctiveness of the different branches of trust law in service of private ordering.

II. A TAXONOMY OF TRUST LAW

We divide contemporary American trust law in both form and function along the lines of the organizing taxonomy illustrated by Figure 20.1.

---

[4] See John C.P. Goldberg, *Introduction: Pragmatism and Private Law*, 125 HARV. L. REV. 1640, 1650–1663 (2012).

[5] *Id.*

[6] Our focus is on *American* trust law, which differs in meaningful respects from the law in the British Commonwealth. Within American law, our focus is on the *express trust.* We set to the side the *constructive trust,* which in American law is a remedy to make restitution for unjust enrichment, and the *resulting trust,* which in American law is an equitable reversionary interest. See *Scott and Ascher on Trusts, supra* note 1, § 2.1.1. We also set to the side "regulatory trusts" as per *infra* note 9.

[7] See Robert H. Sitkoff & Jesse Dukeminier, *Wills, Trusts, and Estates* 591 (10th ed. 2017).

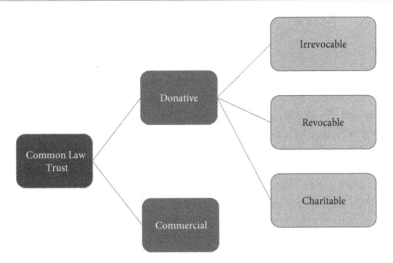

FIGURE 20.1. Taxonomy of American Trust Law

In the donative branch, the trust paradigmatically involves familiar estate planning objectives such as avoiding probate, ensuring ongoing financial support for a surviving spouse or children, and the making of charitable gifts.[8] In the commercial branch, the trust paradigmatically involves a bargained-for exchange, such as secured lending, bond issuance, or the organization of an investment company.[9]

These two major branches of contemporary American trust law reflect mirror-image principles.[10] In donative applications, the trust implements a settlor's *freedom of disposition*—the autonomy of an owner of property to dispose of her property gratuitously on the terms and conditions she desires.[11] In commercial applications, the trust implements a settlor's *freedom of contract*—the autonomy of a person to enter into a voluntary exchange with others on terms and conditions of the parties' choosing.[12]

These overlapping but conceptually distinct policies together point contemporary American trust law toward supporting individual autonomy in private ordering. However, the manner by which trust law implements this purpose varies across its different branches. The formal legal rules and the norms and customs of trust practice, including especially those relating to a trustee's fiduciary duties, have developed into distinct branches along the lines depicted in Figure 20.1. Contemporary American trust law applies different formal rules to the different branches of trust practice in a manner that reflects those branches' distinctive functional needs.

---

[8] See *id.* at 391–392.

[9] See John H. Langbein, *The Secret Life of the Trust: The Trust as an Instrument of Commerce*, 107 Yale L.J. 165, 167 (1997) (defining a commercial trust as "a trust that implements bargained-for exchange, in contrast to a donative transfer"). We set to the side trusts that arise in various regulatory contexts, such as environmental remediation trusts, what Langbein aptly called "regulatory compliance trusts." *Id.* at 174–177.

[10] See, e.g., Hanoch Dagan, this volume.

[11] See Robert H. Sitkoff, *Trusts and Estates: Implementing Freedom of Disposition*, 58 St. Louis U. L.J. 643 (2014).

[12] See Charles Fried, *Contract as Promise: A Theory of Contractual Obligation* 7–27 (2d ed. 2015).

III. Donative Trusts

The first major branch of contemporary American trust law is the *donative* branch. The essential characteristic of a trust in this branch is that it effects a gratuitous transfer of property in service of the settlor's freedom of disposition. This branch includes, for instance, a trust made by a settlor to transfer property at death outside of probate (i.e., a will substitute), a trust for the support of a surviving spouse upon the settlor's death, a trust for the education of grandchildren, a trust for a mentally or physically incapacitated sibling, or a trust to support a charitable purpose.

At its core, a donative trust implements a settlor's freedom of disposition by allowing the settlor to make a gift of property across time to one or more beneficiaries or for one or more charitable purposes subject to the terms and conditions prescribed by the settlor. Both the law governing such trusts and the norms and customs of practice applicable to them have evolved in a manner that reflects this donative rather than commercial character, and that further reflects important distinctions between private trusts that are *irrevocable* versus *revocable* or instead if the trust is *charitable*.

A. Donative Irrevocable Private Trust

The first sub-branch of donative trusts is the *irrevocable private trust*. The paradigmatic use of such a trust in contemporary practice is for wealth management within a family and down the generations—what has been aptly dubbed a *management trust*.[13] By making a transfer in trust rather than outright, a settlor ensures that the property will be managed and distributed in accordance with the settlor's wishes as expressed in the terms of the trust rather than according to the whims of the beneficiaries. A trust thus allows a settlor to postpone important decisions about the investment and distribution of the trust property, leaving those decisions to be made by the trustee in view of changing market conditions and the beneficiaries' evolving circumstances, but within the framework established by the settlor.[14] In this application, therefore, the trust is a powerful tool for implementing a settlor's freedom of disposition.

The most distinctive evolutionary development within this branch of trust law concerns the *powers* and *duties* of a trustee.[15] Today, the law of trustees' powers and duties in

---

[13] See John H. Langbein, *Rise of the Management Trust*, 143 TR. & EST. 52 (Oct. 2004). Following a colloquial meaning, a revocable trust as described *infra* section III.B could likewise be called a management trust.

[14] Such a trust can also be structured to reduce tax liabilities and to protect the trust property from creditor claims. See, e.g., Sitkoff & Dukeminier, *supra* note 7, at 696–727 (creditors), 813–815 (taxes), 929–982 (taxes).

[15] The following discussion draws on David J. Feder & Robert H. Sitkoff, *Revocable Trusts and Incapacity Planning: More than Just a Will Substitute*, 24 ELDER L.J. 1, 7–9 (2016), which relied heavily on Langbein, *supra* note 13, and John H. Langbein, *The Contractarian Basis of the Law of Trusts*, 105 YALE L.J. 625, 640–644, 666 (1995).

an irrevocable trust provides a ready-made governance regime for a settlor who wishes to create a trust for wealth management down the generations. This evolution was necessary because trust law was not always so conducive to this use of a trust.

In late medieval and early modern times, when wealth was primarily held in land and the trust was used mostly as a conveyancing device to circumvent primogeniture and feudal death taxes (note the parallel to revocable trusts used as will substitutes, which we discuss later[16]), a trustee needed few powers. The main task of the trustee was to pass ownership of the family's land to the next taker in accordance with the terms of the trust. The beneficiaries of these conveyancing trusts, who typically lived on the land, were safeguarded by the rule that the trustee had no powers other than those expressly granted by the terms of the trust. Trustee disempowerment was thus the original form of beneficiary safeguard.

Over time, as the nature of wealth holding evolved from land to interests in business entities and other financial assets, trust law and practice evolved to accommodate ongoing administration of these assets down the generations. For this use of the trust, which has to do more with management than conveyancing, the trustee would need broad powers of administration—for example, powers to invest and reinvest the trust assets, to vote securities held in the trust, to take or make loans, and so on. Accordingly, trust lawyers commonly overcame the no-powers default rule of the common law by including an expansive schedule of trustee powers in their trust instruments. Eventually, as provisions for broad powers became a normal and customary drafting practice and standard boilerplate, most states enacted statutes that presumptively gave trustees an expansive statutory list of powers.[17] Even now that these statutes have been widely adopted, many drafters continue to include an expansive schedule of trustee powers in their trust instruments.[18]

With the broadening of a trustee's powers, a new system of beneficiary safeguard was needed. Trust practice today safeguards a beneficiary by constraining the trustee with an elaborate system of fiduciary duties. All of a trustee's actions (or failures to act), even if they are within the trustee's expressly granted powers, are nonetheless subject to judicial review for consistency with the trustee's fiduciary duties of loyalty, prudence, impartiality, disclosure, and so on.[19] The *Restatement (Third) of Trusts* describes this "basic principle of trust administration" thus: "a trustee presumptively has comprehensive powers to manage the trust estate and otherwise to carry out the terms and purpose of the trust, but...all powers held in the capacity of trustee must be exercised, or not exercised, in accordance with the trustee's fiduciary obligations."[20]

---

[16] See *infra* section III.B.

[17] The Uniform Trust Code (UTC) (2000), following the lead of the Uniform Trustees' Powers Act (1964) and similar legislation, provides a trustee by default with "all powers over the trust property which an unmarried competent owner has over individually owned property," and supplements this broad statement with a nonexhaustive illustrative list of more specific powers. UTC §§ 815(a)(2)(A), 816.

[18] See, e.g., Northern Trust, Will & Trust Form 201, at 201–231 through 201–235 (2004).

[19] See, e.g., Robert H. Sitkoff, "Fiduciary Principles in Trust Law," in *The Oxford Handbook of Fiduciary Law* 41 (Evan R. Criddle, Paul B. Miller, & Robert H. Sitkoff eds., 2019).

[20] *Restatement (Third) of Trusts* § 70 cmt. a (2007); see also UTC § 815(b).

The evolution from limited powers to expansive powers subject to fiduciary duties is especially pronounced in the area of trust investment.[21] The law first prescribed legal lists of permitted investments, which tended to favor traditional investments such as government bonds and first mortgages on real property. To overcome the disempowerment of trustees by the legal lists, trust lawyers often included a provision in their trust instruments that empowered a trustee to make any investment even if not of a type or kind that was otherwise permitted by trust law. Eventually, the legal lists were replaced by the so-called "prudent man" rule, which was nominally more empowering, but which in application came to favor government bonds and to disfavor stocks, similar to the old legal lists. Boilerplate empowerment of the trustee to invest in any type or kind of investment thus persisted to overcome the courts' constrained application of the prudent man rule. Today, all states have replaced the prudent man rule with the "prudent investor" rule, which empowers a trustee to invest in any type or kind of property, subject to fiduciary risk management rules that typically require a diversified overall investment strategy with portfolio-level risk and return objectives reasonably suited to the trust.[22]

In sum, the quintessence of the donative irrevocable private trust branch of contemporary American trust law—the branch that covers a management trust for wealth management down the generations in a dynastic trust—is the rise of law and practice that broadly empowers a trustee but subjects the trustee's exercise or nonexercise of her powers to fiduciary duties. Crucially, the fiduciary duties of a trustee in an irrevocable trust are owed to the trust beneficiaries, defined as anyone who is potentially eligible ever to receive a distribution from the trust.[23] The hallmark of a modern donative irrevocable trust, in other words, is broad empowerment subject to fiduciary duties enforceable by a beneficiary. Such a management trust "is essentially a gift, projected on the plane of time and so subjected to a management regime."[24]

B. Donative Revocable Private Trust

The second sub-branch of donative trusts is the *revocable private trust*. A revocable trust is a trust that allows the settlor to take back the trust property and terminate the trust. Under traditional law, a trust was presumptively irrevocable. Today, however, this default has largely been reversed so that a trust is presumed to be revocable unless its terms provide otherwise.[25] Like an irrevocable trust, a revocable trust implements a settlor's freedom of disposition, but it does so in a narrower set of ways.

---

[21] Other specific examples of this general evolutionary trend abound, including so-called *directed trusts* and *trust decanting*. See, e.g., John D. Morley & Robert H. Sitkoff, *Making Directed Trusts Work: The Uniform Directed Trust Act*, 44 ACTEC L.J. 1 (2018); Robert H. Sitkoff, *The Rise of Trust Decanting in the United States*, 23 TR. & TR. 976 (2017).

[22] See, e.g., Max M. Schanzenbach & Robert H. Sitkoff, *The Prudent Investor Rule and Market Risk: An Empirical Analysis*, 14 J. EMP. LEGAL STUD. 129 (2017).

[23] See *Restatement (Third) of Trusts* § 94 (2012). For an application, see, e.g., Jo Ann Howard & Assoc., P.C. v. Cassity, 868 F.3d 637, 646–647 (8th Cir. 2017).

[24] Bernard Rudden, *Book Review*, 44 MOD. L. REV. 610, 610 (1981).

[25] See Sitkoff & Dukeminier, *supra* note 7, at 453–454.

1. *Revocable Trust as Will Substitute*

A revocable trust is most commonly used as a *substitute for a will*. If a settlor conveys property to a revocable trust prior to the settlor's death, then after the settlor's death, the trust property will be distributed or held in further trust in accordance with the trust's terms. By funding the trust, the settlor transfers legal title to the trustee, obviating the need to change title at the settlor's death by probate administration or otherwise. In this use of the trust, we find a modern echo to the ancient use of the trust to convey land while avoiding primogeniture and the feudal death taxes.

A revocable trust is an especially apt will substitute precisely because it is revocable. During life, a will is freely changeable ("ambulatory," in the jargon), and the testator is free to do with her property as she wishes during her life notwithstanding a contrary disposition in her will. A revocable trust is likewise freely changeable, and the settlor Can take back the property to do with it as she wishes. For both a will and a revocable trust, therefore, the donor can arrange for a gift during lifetime that does not become final and irrevocable until the donor's death.

Just as the law of trusts has adapted to accommodate the use of an irrevocable trust for family wealth management that continues down the generations, it has also evolved to accommodate the use of a revocable trust as a will substitute. This evolution is especially pronounced in two features of modern American revocable trust law.[26]

First, under modern law, a beneficiary of a revocable trust has no legally enforceable interest so long as the trust remains revocable. As we have seen, in an irrevocable trust, the duties of the trustee run to the beneficiaries. The same was true under the traditional law of revocable trusts, for which courts supposed a beneficiary to have a present enforcement right.[27] This supposed enforcement right, reflecting a present interest in the trust, was what courts said differentiated a revocable trust from a will, allowing such a trust to pass property at death without satisfying the formalities required for a will.[28]

Today, however, American law provides that the duties of the trustee of a revocable trust run exclusively to the settlor.[29] Thus, under modern law, just as a beneficiary under a will has no cognizable legal right under that will prior to the donor's death, neither does a beneficiary have a cognizable legal right under a revocable trust. Extending the analogy of a revocable trust to a will, modern law provides that the trustee of a such a trust must "comply with a direction of the settlor even [if] the direction is contrary to the terms of the trust or the trustee's normal fiduciary duties."[30] At the same time, however,

---

[26] A third and related evolutionary development in revocable trust law is the validation by statute in all states of a *pour over* from a will to an unfunded revocable trust. Under traditional law, because a trust cannot exist without property, the trustee of an unfunded trust could not be a valid will beneficiary. By reversing that rule, the statutes have enabled the rise of unfunded revocable trusts to which a donor devises her probate estate. See *id.* at 466–467.

[27] See *id.* at 445–447.   [28] *Id.*

[29] UTC § 603 (amended 2018); *Restatement (Third) of Trusts* § 74 (2003); Sitkoff & Dukeminier, *supra* note 7, at 447–453.

[30] *Restatement (Third) of Trusts* § 74(1)(a)(i) (2003).

such a trust is deemed not to be testamentary, and thus is valid to pass property at death without the formalities of a will.[31]

Second, reflecting the power of the analogy of a revocable trust to a will, courts and legislatures increasingly apply to a revocable trust many of the rules of construction for a will, such as revocation on divorce of a bequest to a spouse, and many of the substantive policy limits on freedom of disposition by a will, such as the spousal forced share.[32] The logic behind most of the rules of construction—implementing a testator's probable intent—applies with the same force to a revocable trust used as a substitute for a will. Likewise, because the substantive limits on freedom of disposition by will, such as the spousal share, reflect policy judgments about the proper extent of freedom of disposition at death, they should also apply to a revocable trust.

In this doctrinal evolution, in which the law of revocable trusts has been reworked to align with the law of wills, function has come to triumph over form. Perhaps the most arresting example concerns the rights of a settlor's creditors. Under traditional law, a creditor of a settlor had no recourse against the trust property through the settlor's power of revocation—a creditor could not compel a revocation, which was treated as a power personal to the settlor.[33] Under modern law, by contrast, the settlor's power to revoke the trust and take back the trust property is regarded as equivalent to outright ownership and, hence, the trust property is subject to the claims of the settlor's creditors during life and at death.[34]

2. *Revocable Trust in Planning for Incapacity*

In addition to its use as a will substitute, the revocable trust is also commonly employed in contemporary practice to plan for *incapacity*. If a person becomes mentally incapacitated or otherwise unable to manage her own affairs, the person can avoid the cumbersome intervention of a court-appointed conservator if the person has funded a revocable trust while the person was still competent. Even if the settlor had been serving as sole trustee, a successor trustee can take over without court involvement if the settlor becomes incapacitated and the terms of the trust prescribe a mechanism for determining the settlor's incapacity.[35] For a settlor who already plans to fund a revocable trust to avoid probate, the marginal cost of also avoiding conservatorship upon incapacity by including an appropriate further provision in the terms of the trust is trivial.

The main question for law reform around this use of a revocable trust is whether upon the settlor's incapacity the other beneficiaries of the trust should have standing to enforce

---

[31] "If a property owner intends and takes steps to create a trust by declaration or transfer during life, the trust is not 'testamentary'…and is not subject to the Wills Act." *Id.* § 25 cmt. *b*; see also Sitkoff & Dukeminier, *supra* note 7, at 447–448.

[32] *Restatement (Third) of Property: Wills and Other Donative Transfers* § 7.2 (2003).

[33] See *Restatement (Second) of Trusts* § 330 cmt. *o* (1959).

[34] See, e.g., UTC § 505(a)(3); *Restatement (Third) of Trusts* § 25 cmt. *e* (2003).

[35] A typical drafting strategy is to require agreement of the settlor's physician and certain identified persons (commonly the settlor's spouse or children). See Feder & Sitkoff, *supra* note 15, at 31–32 (discussing such clauses and quoting a formbook example).

the trust—that is, whether this use of the trust as a conservator substitute differentiates it from a pure will substitute.[36] There is a strong argument that a "rule of presumptive standing for revocable trust beneficiaries upon the settlor's incapacity...is...more likely to implement the typical settlor's actual or probable intent."[37] The cases, the *Restatement of Trusts*, and the Uniform Trust Code point in contradictory directions on this issue, though the trend in the case and statute law is against recognizing such standing.[38]

C. Donative Charitable Trust

In general, the same rules that apply to a private trust also apply to a *charitable trust*. But there are some defining differences. The most significant difference is that a charitable trust must be for a public benefit via a recognized *charitable purpose* rather than for one or more ascertainable beneficiaries. The list of permissible charitable purposes, which derives from a codification by Parliament more than four hundred years ago,[39] is "the relief of poverty, the advancement of education or religion, the promotion of health, governmental or municipal purposes, or other purposes the achievement of which is beneficial to the community."[40] A trust for one or more of these purposes is a charitable trust and therefore need not have an ascertainable beneficiary.[41]

In recognition of the public benefit conferred by a charitable trust, such a trust is exempt from the Rule Against Perpetuities and may endure forever.[42] In consequence, a charitable trust may be more freely modified than a private trust. Under the cypres doctrine, if a charitable trust's specific purpose becomes illegal, impossible, impracticable, or wasteful, a court may direct application of the property to another purpose within the settlor's general charitable intent, one that "reasonably approximates the designated purpose."[43]

---

[36] See *id.* at 3–4 (advocating a "conservator substitute model"); see also Grayson M.P. McCouch, *Revocable Trusts and Fiduciary Accountability*, 26 ELDER L.J. 1 (2018).

[37] Feder & Sitkoff, *supra* note 15, at 4.   [38] *Id.*

[39] The Statute of Charitable Uses Act 1601, 43 Eliz. I, c. 4 (Eng.). On the reception of this statute into American law, see Vidal v. Girard's Executors, 43 U.S. 127, 192–196 (1844).

[40] Uniform Trust Code § 405(a) (2000); see also *Restatement (Third) of Trusts* § 28 (2003) (similar); *Restatement of Charitable Nonprofit Organizations* § 1.01(b) (T.D. No. 1, 2016) (similar).

[41] Under traditional law, a trust that lacked one or more ascertainable beneficiaries (and therefore failed to qualify as a private trust) was valid only if it was for one or more recognized charitable purposes (and thus qualified as a charitable trust). A trust for a *noncharitable purpose* was not permitted. Today this rule has been relaxed in all states to recognize certain noncharitable purpose trusts. Qualifying noncharitable purposes include the care of a pet animal or the preservation of a grave. See Sitkoff & Dukeminier, *supra* note 7, at 422–428; Adam J. Hirsch, *Bequests for Purposes: A Unified Theory*, 56 WASH. & LEE L. REV. 33 (1999).

[42] Favorable tax treatment is also available if the trust qualifies, as would be typical, as charitable under federal or state tax law. See, e.g., Marion R. Fremont-Smith, *Governing Nonprofit Organizations: Federal and State Law and Regulation* 241–300 (2004).

[43] *Restatement (Third) of Trusts* § 67 (2003).

Finally, because a charitable trust must have a charitable purpose rather than an ascertainable beneficiary, the question arises, who will enforce the trust? American law relies on a combination of the state attorneys general, donors, and federal tax authorities, rather than beneficiaries. The consensus view is that individually and collectively these modes of enforcement are inadequate,[44] but there is not a consensus on how better to enforce charitable trusts.[45]

D. The Place of Donative Trusts in American Legal Practice

In the culture of American trust practice, donative trusts are distinct from commercial trusts. In law firms, donative trusts are the province of the estate planning lawyers, not the business or corporate lawyers. Banks and other financial institutions also commonly segregate donative trusts from other activities, often placing them in "wealth management" departments under the supervision of "fiduciary officers." In law schools, donative trusts are taught within the rubric of succession law, organized around freedom of disposition, in a course called "Trusts and Estates" or the like.[46]

IV. COMMERCIAL TRUSTS

Next to the donative trust stands another branch of trust law and practice, lesser known but still immensely important: the *commercial trust*. As John Langbein has observed, although the donative trust is the paradigm of a trust in American legal culture, in fact the great bulk of assets held in trust have been placed there for commercial purposes.[47] The essential characteristic of a commercial trust is that it implements an exchange of value in exercise of the parties' freedom of contract. A commercial trust carries out a bargained-for commercial exchange. The law governing a commercial trust and the customs of practice surrounding it tend to reflect this distinctive purpose.

The line between commercial and donative trusts is long-standing. In *Morrissey v. Commissioner*, decided in 1935, the U.S. Supreme Court pointed to "the transaction of business" as the essential characteristic of a commercial trust.[48] The Court differentiated a donative trust from a commercial trust as follows: "In what are called 'business trusts' the object is not to hold and conserve particular property, with incidental powers, as in the traditional type of trusts, but to provide a medium for the conduct of a business and sharing its gains."[49] Similarly, a 1929 article in the *Harvard Law Review* remarked that "modern

[44] See, e.g., Jonathan Klick & Robert H. Sitkoff, *Agency Costs, Charitable Trusts, and Corporate Control: Evidence from Hershey's Kiss-Off*, 108 COLUM. L. REV. 749, 780–783 (2008).

[45] See, e.g., Lloyd Hitoshi Mayer, "Fiduciary Principles in Charities and Other Nonprofits," in *The Oxford Handbook of Fiduciary Law* 121–123 (Evan R. Criddle, Paul B. Miller, & Robert H. Sitkoff eds., 2019).

[46] See Sitkoff, *supra* note 11.   [47] See Langbein, *supra* note 9.

[48] 296 U.S. 344, 356–357 (1935).   [49] *Id.*

business has become honey-combed with trusteeship. Next to contract, the universal tool, and incorporation, the standard instrument of organization, it takes its place wherever the relations to be established are too delicate or too novel for these coarser devices."[50]

A. Corporation Substitute and Other Uses

Some commercial trusts resemble corporations.[51] Instead of tradable certificates of stock, a business trust can issue tradable certificates of beneficial ownership. Instead of titling property in the name of a corporation, a commercial trust may title its property in the names of its trustees in their fiduciary capacities. Instead of bylaws and articles of incorporation, a trust may have a declaration of trust. And instead of directors, a trust may have trustees.[52]

Other commercial trusts serve to structure loans, bonds, or insolvencies. In secured lending transactions, borrowers have long used trusts to provide guarantees to lenders. A borrower conveys property to a trustee with instructions to return the property to the borrower if the borrower repays the loan and to grant the property to the lender if the borrower defaults. In bankruptcy and insolvency, debtors and courts often employ a trustee to sell the debtor's property in an orderly manner and distribute the proceeds to creditors. In corporate bond practice, a trust is often used to overcome a collective action problem among bondholders by allowing a trustee to act on behalf of all of the bondholders.[53]

Historically, the trust offered several advantages over the corporate form. The first was freer formation. Until fairly recently, trusts have been much easier to form than corporations.[54] Before the mid-nineteenth century, forming a corporation required special permission from the king, Parliament, or a state legislature, and this permission did not always come easily. A trust, by contrast, required only a private declaration or deed of trust, which needed no action from anyone other than the person forming the trust (and the trustee, if a third party).

Second, a trust avoided regulation. Until the mid-twentieth century, state corporation statutes imposed burdensome regulations on the corporate form. State corporate law commonly prohibited a corporation from growing beyond a certain size, owning real estate, or investing in the shares of other corporations. These rules did not appear in trust law, so they could be avoided by organizing a business in trust. The trust became especially popular in Massachusetts in the early twentieth century partly as a way to avoid Massachusetts' famously restrictive corporate law. To this day, a trust for corporation-like purposes is commonly known throughout the country as a "Massachusetts trust."[55]

[50] Nathan Isaacs, *Note, Trusteeship in Modern Business*, 42 HARV. L. REV. 1048, 1060–1061 (1929).

[51] See John Morley, *The Common Law Corporation: The Power of the Trust in Anglo-American Business History*, 116 COLUM. L. REV. 2145 (2016).

[52] The Court noted these analogies in *Morrissey*, 296 U.S. at 359.

[53] Federal law requires use of a trust in certain bond offerings. See Trust Indenture Act of 1939, 15 U.S.C. §§ 77aaa–77bbbb (2019).

[54] See Morley, *supra* note 51.

[55] See *Comment, Massachusetts Trusts*, 37 YALE L.J. 1103 (1928); Sitkoff & Dukeminier, *supra* note 7, at 399.

The trust has largely disappeared from the organization of conventional business companies. But the trust remains common among asset securitization vehicles and mutual funds, which early in their history were known as "investment trusts."[56] Mutual funds continue to be formed as trusts rather than as corporations to avoid the corporate law requirements concerning shareholder voting and related matters of governance and to take advantage of special features of business trust law, such as the ability to issue shares in different series with distinct liabilities to creditors.[57]

B. Distinctive Law for Commercial Trusts

The popularity of the trust in commerce has pushed courts and state legislatures to develop a distinct body of law for these kinds of trusts. Some courts have held that because a business trust is distinct in function and purpose from a donative trust, rules developed for a donative trust should not reflexively be applied to a business trust.[58] In consequence, "a specialized case law has arisen applicable to a common-law trust with a business purpose."[59] This case law is especially deep in Massachusetts, where the state's Supreme Judicial Court has said that "[i]t is appropriate to treat business trusts on a somewhat different basis from private trusts."[60] Thus, we find in the case law differentiation between business trusts and donative trusts, at least in certain areas.[61]

---

[56] See Morley, *supra* note 51.

[57] See John Morley & Quinn Curtis, *Taking Exit Rights Seriously: Why Governance and Fee Litigation Don't Work in Mutual Funds*, 120 YALE L.J. 84 (2010) (explaining why redemption rights diminish a mutual fund shareholder's interest in voting); Langbein, *supra* note 9, at 183–185; iShares Trust, Registration Statement (Form N-1A), 2–3, Aug. 16, 2017, https://www.sec.gov/Archives/edgar/data/1100663/000119312517258768/d426583d485bpos.htm (listing seventy-six exchange-traded funds as series of the iShares Trust, a Delaware statutory trust).

[58] See, e.g., Bank of New Jersey v. Abbott, 503 A.2d 893, 897–898 (N.J. App. Div. 1986) (acknowledging "the differences between business and liquidation trusts and ordinary testamentary trusts" in applying nonetheless a probate code rule on fiduciary compensation to a business trust); In re Carriage House, Inc., 120 B.R. 754, 763 (Bankr. D. Vt. 1990) (stating that "each business trust, as any contract at common law, must be treated *sui generis*" and noting "features of a business trust that distinguish it from a private trust").

[59] Uniform Statutory Trust Entity Act (USTEA) pref. note (2009, last amended 2013).

[60] Swartz v. Sher, 184 N.E.2d 51, 54 (Mass. 1962); see also First Eastern Bank, N.A. v. Jones, 602 N.E.2d 211, 212 (Mass. 1992) (holding that a statutory reform to trustee liability was applicable only to "a trust...of the donative type associated with probate practice" and not to a "business trust"); Town of Hull v. Tong, 442 N.E.2d 427 (Mass. App. 1982) (differentiating between business trusts and donative trusts in applying limitations statutes governing creditor claims); Northstar Financial Advisors, Inc. v. Schwab Investments, 807 F. Supp. 2d 871, 876–879 (N.D. Cal. 2011) (reviewing authority treating fiduciary litigation involving a mutual fund organized as a Massachusetts business trust differently from a donative trust).

[61] See In re Trust Known as Great N. Iron Ore Properties, 263 N.W.2d 610, 620 (Minn. 1978) ("But we need not finally decide the proper characterization of the trust to resolve the extent of the trustees' duties because it has been recognized that even a common-law or Massachusetts business trust, although governed by special corporate-like rules in certain respects, is subject to the underlying equitable and fiduciary duties toward trust beneficiaries imposed by the common law of trusts.").

By way of illustration, there is a deep disagreement among courts applying New York law about whether an indenture trustee is subject only to those duties provided for by the terms of the indenture agreement, or also to the additional fiduciary duties arising under the common law that would be applicable to a trustee of a donative trust. Tracing back to *Hazzard v. Chase National Bank of City of New York*,[62] decided in 1936, one line of cases holds that "[t]he corporate trustee has very little in common with the ordinary trustee, as we generally understand the fiduciary relationship.... The trustee under a corporate indenture...has his rights and duties defined, not by the fiduciary relationship, but exclusively by the terms of agreement. His status is more that of a stakeholder than one of a trustee."[63] Another line of cases rejects *Hazzard*, however, and holds that an indenture trustee is subject not only to those duties provided for by the terms of the indenture agreement but also to the additional fiduciary duties arising under the common law as would be applicable to a trustee of a donative trust. This line traces back to *Dabney v. Chase National Bank*, decided in 1952, in which the court applied the "fundamental duty" under trust law of "undivided loyalty" to an indenture trustee.[64]

Some of the adaptation of the law of trusts to commercial purposes occurred remarkably early on. Case reports from English and American courts in the late eighteenth, nineteenth, and early twentieth centuries show extensive disputes about whether a trust used for commerce should be able to litigate without the joinder of its many beneficiaries.[65] Similar disputes took place about whether a commercial trust should be able to offer those beneficiaries a form of limited liability akin to that of a modern corporation.[66] Neither of these issues arose with regard to donative trusts.

C. Recognition in Canonical Authority

Reflecting the tendency in the cases toward differentiation of a commercial trust from a donative trust, the canonical secondary authorities applicable to a donative trust—most prominently the *Restatements of Trusts*, the Uniform Trust Code, and the leading Scott treatise[67]—tend to disclaim or at least caution against their application to a commercial trust.[68] Let us begin with the Scott treatise:

> The obvious difficulty with attempting to integrate any significant coverage of trusts used commercially into a generalized study of trust law is that commercial trusts

[62] 287 N.Y.S. 541 (N.Y. Sup. Ct. 1936), *aff'd*, 257 A.D. 950 (1939).

[63] 287 N.Y.S. at 570; see also AG Capital Funding Partners, L.P. v. State Street Bank & Trust Co., 896 N.E.2d 61, 66–67 (N.Y. 2008); Meckel v. Continental Resources Co., 758 F.2d 811, 816 (2d Cir. 1985).

[64] 196 F.2d 668, 670–671 (2d Cir. 1952) (internal quotations omitted); see also Beck v. Manufacturers Hanover Trust Co., 632 N.Y.S.2d 520, 526–527 (N.Y. App. Div. 1995); U.S. Trust Co. of New York v. First Na. City Bank, 394 N.Y.S.2d 653, 660–661 (N.Y. App. Div. 1977).

[65] Morley, *supra* note 51, at 2167–2197 (describing debates over limited liability and personhood in litigation).

[66] *Id.*   [67] See Sitkoff & Dukeminier, *supra* note 7, at 387–391 (describing sources of trust law).

[68] The Bogert treatise does deal with commercial trusts, but it does so by treating them as a distinct body of trust law. See George Gleason Bogert et al., *The Law of Trusts and Trustees* §§ 1161–1165 (2019).

have, as their central purposes, objectives that are completely alien from those effecting gratuitous transfers. Yet it is the latter around which the law of trusts developed. Moreover, the terms of commercial trusts typically do indicate departures, and often quite substantial departures, from one or more of the familiar standards of trust law.... Commercial trusts thus ... [are] sufficiently different, in both purpose and operation, to justify separate treatment.[69]

Accordingly, the treatise "deals primarily with the more traditional use of the trust, in which the purpose generally is to confer, gratuitously, upon one or more persons, the beneficial ownership of property."[70]

The Uniform Trust Code keeps a similar distance from commercial trusts. It states that it "is directed primarily at trusts that arise in an estate planning or other donative context," in contrast to "commercial trusts" that "are often subject to special-purpose legislation and case law, which in some respects displace the usual rules stated in this Code."[71] The *Restatement (Third) of Trusts* likewise cautions against application to a business or commercial trust. It excludes business trusts from its scope, reasoning that "[a]lthough many rules of trust law may also apply to business and investment trusts, many of these rules do not; instead other rules are drawn from other bodies of law that are specially applicable to those activities even when conducted in trust form."[72]

D. Statutory Business Trusts

The adaptation of the trust to commercial purposes, and its branching off from donative trust law, has reached its apogee in the enactment of statutory business trust acts by a majority of states.[73] The modern versions of these statutes—in particular the Delaware Statutory Trust Act (DSTA), which is the leading business trust statute and which served as the model for the Uniform Statutory Trust Entity Act (USTEA)—provide for a statutory trust entity with many of the attributes of a corporation, but with fewer regulations on governance and with novel features, such as the "series" concept noted earlier,[74] that are especially useful to certain types of enterprises.[75]

USTEA offers many innovations, including the recognition of a statutory business trust as a separate entity distinct from its trustees. Most strikingly, under USTEA a statutory business trust may sue and be sued and hold property in its own name, rather than in the names of its trustees.[76] USTEA also provides wide latitude for modifying the otherwise applicable fiduciary principles of trusteeship.[77] Because these statutes validate

---

[69] 1 *Scott and Ascher on Trusts*, *supra* note 1, § 2.1.2, at 38 n.7 (internal quotations and citations omitted).

[70] *Id.* § 2.1.2, at 39.

[71] UTC § 102 cmt.   [72] *Restatement (Third) of Trusts* § 1 cmt. *b* (2003).

[73] See Robert H. Sitkoff, *Trust as "Uncorporation": A Research Agenda*, 2005 U. ILL. L. REV. 31, 35–36.

[74] See *supra* note 57 and text accompanying.

[75] See USTEA pref. note (2009, last amended 2013).

[76] See USTEA §§ 307–308; see also Del. Code tit. 12, § 3804(a).

[77] See USTEA §§ 104(7), 505; see also Del. Code tit. 12, § 3806(c).

the trust form as a permissible mode of business organization and bring statutory clarity to business trust practice, statutory business trusts have become increasingly preferred over common law trusts for commercial applications.[78]

At the same time, USTEA confines its sphere of application to trusts that do not have a "predominantly donative purpose."[79] This limit "addresses the concern that a statutory trust might be used in an estate planning or other donative context to evade public policy limitations on donative transfers."[80] USTEA also addresses the reverse problem of application of donative trust principles that are inapt for commercial contexts, such as inalienable beneficial shares by way of a spendthrift clause,[81] with provisions that reverse those rules.[82] These provisions reflect a recognition by the drafters of USTEA that "a business trust is a creature of freedom of contract," whereas a donative trust "implement[s] the donor's right to freedom of disposition."[83]

E. The Place of Commercial Trusts in American Legal Practice

Unlike the donative trust, which in the American tradition has been subsumed within the practice of estate planning, the commercial trust has not developed a unified field of practice with ownership over it. The commercial trust has generated no discernible culture of practice and no regular class in law schools. One likely explanation is that commercial trusts are too varied and disparate. Commercial trusts are used to structure commercial deals, but such deals vary so widely that the day-to-day practice of commercial trusts tends to be the province of the different groups of lawyers who specialize in each of those various types of deals. Bankruptcy trusts tend to be handled by bankruptcy lawyers and mutual fund trusts tend to be handled by mutual fund lawyers. Likewise, in day-to-day banking and financial institution practice, commercial trusts are normally handled by something like the "corporate and institutional services" department rather than the "wealth management" department.

V. CONCLUSION

The core claim of this chapter is that the American law of trusts has branched into two distinct categories, *donative* and *commercial*, with the donative category separating into three further sub-branches, *revocable* and *irrevocable private trusts* and *charitable trusts*.

---

[78] See USTEA pref. note (2009, last amended 2013) (Filing data show that the DSTA "dominates the field, both in new statutory trust formations and in the aggregate number of statutory trusts.").

[79] See *id.* § 303(b).   [80] *Id.* cmt.

[81] See Sitkoff & Dukeminier, *supra* note 7, at 703–712.   [82] See USTEA § 602.

[83] See *id.* § 602 cmt.

This branching, which is evident in both formal law and the norms and customs of practice, reflects underlying differences in facilitating private ordering in service of either *freedom of disposition* or *freedom of contract*.

The taxonomy of contemporary American trust law that we propose is consistent with the vision of the New Private Law. Rather than seeking an essential function of trust law by trying to reduce the whole field to an artificially parsimonious set of "brass tacks,"[84] we propose a multiplicitous and therefore more nuanced structure. Trusts are used for many purposes and the law has evolved the complexity necessary to accommodate all of them.

Like the rest of the New Private Law movement, however, our approach does not content itself with merely cataloging doctrinal complexity. We seek also to uncover the functional logic of this complexity. The different branches of trust law each have a different policy logic. We try to make sense of them by identifying their distinctive functional purposes rooted in freedom of disposition for donative trusts and freedom of contract for commercial trusts. The categorization we propose is thus "inclusively pragmatic."[85] It takes both the doctrine and theory of trust law seriously and gives each its proper place. We hope this categorization will be a first step toward opening the law of trusts to a deeper understanding made possible by the New Private Law.

ACKNOWLEDGMENTS

The authors thank Derek Ho, Dan Kelly, John Langbein, Paul Miller, James Penner, Henry Smith, and participants in the Landscape of Private Law Conference at Harvard for helpful comments and suggestions, and Catherine Wiener for excellent research assistance.

In accordance with Harvard Law School policy on conflicts of interest, Sitkoff discloses certain outside activities, one or more of which may relate to the subject matter of this chapter, at https://tinyurl.com/ycuut88c.

Portions of this chapter derive without further attribution or acknowledgment from Robert H. Sitkoff & Jesse Dukeminier, Wills, Trusts, and Estates (10th ed. 2017) and from the authors' consulting engagements in In re Bank of New York Mellon Corp. Forex Transactions Litigation, 12-ms-2335 (LAK) (S.D.N.Y), and The People of the State of New York, by Eric T. Schneiderman, Attorney General et al., Plaintiffs v. The Bank of New York Mellon Corporation and The Bank of New York Mellon, Defendants, Index No. 114735/09, Supreme Court, New York County, New York.

---

[84] Goldberg, *supra* note 4, at 1641–1645.   [85] *Id.* at 1651, 1663.

CHAPTER 21

....

CORPORATIONS

....

PAUL B. MILLER

I. INTRODUCTION

THE New Private Law movement (NPL) has reinvigorated theoretical interest in private law, especially in the United States where legal realism has cast its longest shadow. Most of those allied to the NPL share two commitments. The first is to the value of work of interpretive theory, aimed at explaining private law from an internal point of view. Much of this work is conceptual rather than normative, or prioritizes plausible conceptual interpretation over robust normative interpretation. The second is to the value of methodological diversity. Where theorists of old may have been minded to find disagreement with those working from different methodologies, the new wave sees the merit and potential complementarity of interpretive theory that prioritizes explanation, whether it employs methods of philosophy, economics, psychology, history, or another discipline.

Interpretive theories that are focused on elucidating legal concepts aim at explanation of those concepts. But that is not to say that they are merely descriptive. More is involved than restatement of doctrine or discussion of its evolution. Most interpretive theories—including those developed under the aegis of the NPL—offer a simplified rendering of legal concepts, aimed at illuminating something core or essential to them and at making them more amenable to understanding. Often, interpretive simplification is quite radical.[1] This is especially true of interpretive theories of fundamental private law (property, contract, tort, and fiduciary law). Consider, for example, theories of contracts as enforceable promises,[2] torts as a law of civil recourse for wrongs,[3] private ownership as a sphere of exclusive authority over property,[4] and fiduciary law as a set of principles

---

[1] By which I mean radically simple or neat, not unorthodox.
[2] Charles Fried, *Contract as Promise* (2d ed. 2015).
[3] John C.P. Goldberg & Benjamin C. Zipursky, *Torts as Wrongs*, 88 TEX. L. REV. 917 (2010).
[4] Thomas W. Merrill, *Property and the Right to Exclude*, 77 NEB. L. REV. 730 (1998).

governing mandates of representation.[5] Each offers an interpretation of a complex body of law that simplifies it greatly in order to illuminate it and render it more amenable to understanding.

Theorists typical of the NPL are mindful of the challenge of balancing interpretive fidelity[6] and parsimony. We worry about oversimplification and try to avoid materially incomplete or false renderings, being unwilling to purchase parsimony at such cost to fidelity. It is difficult to say how successful we have been thus far. However, there is reason to think that the balance is more readily struck in interpretive theories of fundamental private law—that is, bodies of law that generally[7] supply legal forms of interaction that are basic, in the sense of being irreducible. *Irreducible forms of interaction* are singular, even if the bodies of law in which they are expressed may not be.[8] Thus, we have less reason in general to be concerned about interpretive oversimplification in these fields than in others, supposing the focus of interpretation is a particular form of interaction.

There is greater reason for concern when one ventures beyond fundamental private law and considers *compound forms of interaction*. A compound form of interaction is one that is constituted in part by the combination of two or more irreducible forms of interaction. Compound forms draw upon the simpler structures provided by contract, property, tort, and fiduciary law; as the compound is developed, it might reshape these structures for improved functionality. Depending on the compound form and its extension within a given legal system, the sound functioning of interfaces between it and other forms of interaction may also entail modification of rules associated with the ordinary operation of those forms of interaction.

Compound forms are products of mature legal systems, and most have them in abundance. Organizations and other devices for fiduciary administration are prominent exemplars. Consider, for example, the trust, the partnership, the corporation, and comparatively newer structures, like LLCs and benefit corporations.

Fellow travelers in the NPL have largely hewed to fundamental private law. Most of us are tort, property, contract, or fiduciary theorists. Fiduciary theory offers entrée to theoretical interpretation of compound forms, because they generally entail fiduciary administration. But NPL theorists—fiduciary theorists included—have still to devote significant attention to these forms of interaction and the methodological challenges that they present.[9]

---

[5] Paul B. Miller, "Fiduciary Representation," in *Fiduciary Government* (Evan J. Criddle, Evan Fox-Decent, Andrew S. Gold, Paul B. Miller, & Sung Hui Kim eds., 2018).

[6] Fidelity being a function of the accuracy of the representation of a concept.

[7] Which is not to say that all of fundamental private law consists exclusively in irreducible forms of interaction. Property, for example, includes compound forms of interaction. I am grateful to Lisa Austin for emphasizing this point.

[8] For example, because the body of law generates more than one form of interaction, and the multiple forms are conceptually independent.

[9] For a notable exception, see Andrew S. Gold & Henry E. Smith, *Scaling Up Legal Relations, The Legacy of Wesley Hohfeld* (Shyam Balganesh, Ted Sichelman, & Henry E. Smith eds., 2020).

In addressing these challenges, one could choose any compound structure. However, the corporation[10] is arguably the most prominent compound form in modern common law systems. Of equal importance, it has attracted extensive interpretive analysis, most predating the NPL, and so a focus on the corporation might help to illustrate the comparative advantages of an interpretive approach that reflects the commitments of the NPL. Of the corporation, more readily than the alternatives, one can ask: How should NPL theorists approach compound forms of interaction? What pitfalls ought we to try to avoid?

This chapter addresses both questions. Briefly, I claim that leading theories of the corporation share a telling flaw: each is *disintegrative*, promoting a reductionist and thus oversimplified representation of the corporation. By way of alternative, I describe and recommend an *integrative* approach. In broad terms, integrative interpretation involves elucidation of the contributions that fundamental private law and organizational law[11] make to the constitution and functioning of compound forms of interaction.

The chapter will unfold as follows. Section II canvasses leading theories of the corporation, explaining the sense in which each is disintegrative and lacking in interpretive fidelity. Section III explains integrative interpretation and its importance in the analysis of compound forms of interaction. Section IV sketches an agenda for an integrative theory of the corporation, while section V anticipates some of its implications for debates over corporate personality, agency, purpose, and fiduciary duties. Section VI concludes.

II. Disintegrative Theories of the Corporation

The last fifty years have witnessed a proliferation of theories of the corporation. Some may be purely positive but most are also normative, whether they promote free market or regulatory ideologies.[12] Thus, for example, contractarian theories invite one to view the corporation as an extension of private ordering by contract, implying that those who incorporate are entitled as a matter of natural right to support by a liberal facilitative state.[13] In turn, concession theories suggest that the corporation is a subordinate body

---

[10] A note of clarification: I will refer throughout to the *corporation* in the singular. There are, of course, different kinds of corporations—or, rather, uses made of the corporate form—in contemporary law. As section II will reveal, interpretive analysis is easily led astray by a narrow focus on business corporations. In addressing the corporate form in the singular, I mean to attend to general features of the corporate form.

[11] That is, rules peculiar to the law of a particular kind of organization. Often, said rules supplement, extend, or reform those derived from fundamental private law.

[12] See William W. Bratton, *The "Nexus of Contracts" Corporation: A Critical Appraisal*, 74 Cornell L. Rev. 407, 407 (1989) on the elusiveness of theories "simultaneously possessing the virtues of accuracy and political neutrality."

[13] Frank H. Easterbrook & Daniel R. Fischel, *The Corporate Contract*, 89 Colum. L. Rev. 1416, 1434–1444 (1989); Bratton, *supra* note 12, at 432: "The nexus of contracts assertion has a political aspect . . . The assertion . . . suggests limits on the state's legitimate role in the corporate firm's life."

politic, implying that incorporation should be viewed as a privilege subject to implied social license and extensive regulatory oversight.[14]

Setting to one side their divergent positive and normative claims, leading theories of the corporation share an embrace of radical interpretive simplification. As noted earlier, the impulse to simplify radically may cause little mischief where directed at an irreducible form of interaction. However, it causes real mischief where indulged in relation to compound forms. Here, it tends to result in *disintegrated*—partial and fragmentary—representations.

The theorist who interprets a compound form of interaction in a radically simple way will choose one of two paths. Both involve simplification by reduction: an argument that the "essence" of the compound is of a piece with a more primitive or basic concept or category. Those who take the first path recognize the structure as contributing to private ordering and represent it as an implication or type of irreducible form of interaction supplied by fundamental private law (for example, a kind of contract, form of property, or type of fiduciary relation). Those who take the second path treat the structure as a product of public law, addressed to conventional public law concerns. Both pathways are well worn and few are explicit about their reasons for choosing one or another. In what follows, I note some examples of work by scholars who have taken the first—and now most popular—of the two.

A. The Corporation as Nexus of Contracts

We may begin with the dominant theory of the corporation: that which represents it as a nexus of contracts.[15] This theory asserts that the corporation is an inherently contractual form of organization that serves as a "nexus" for coordinated transactional activity—that is, contracting—between factors of production and consumption (e.g., management, providers of equity and debt financing, employees, consumers, and so on) that enable business corporations to produce and sell goods or provide services for profit.[16] The theory suggests that corporate law is enabling of contracting in this sense, providing terms that save on transaction, information, and other costs.[17]

The nexus of contracts account is popular partly because it supplies a compelling positive economic theory of the economic logic of corporate organization for private enterprise. Those who inspired the theory aimed to address a puzzle in economic theory: Why do firms emerge and displace bilateral exchange relationships? Why organize

---

[14] Stefan Padfield, *Rehabilitating Concession Theory*, 66 OKLA. L. REV. 327 (2017).

[15] Michael Klausner, *The Contractarian Theory of Corporate Law: A Generation Later*, 31 J. CORP. L. 779 (2006).

[16] Easterbrook & Fischel, *supra* note 13, at 1418: "The corporation is a complex set of explicit and implicit contracts."

[17] *Id.* at 1444: "One natural question after all this business of corporation-as-contract is: why law? Why not just abolish corporate law and let people negotiate whatever contracts they please? The short but not entirely satisfactory answer is that corporate law is a set of terms available off-the-rack so that participants in corporate ventures can save the cost of contracting."

rather than transact?[18] Early contractarians identified some plausible economic reasons, including: (1) hierarchical organization enables effective and efficient coordination on a large scale; (2) law contributes cost savings by providing terms of organization; and (3) agency costs endemic in organization can be kept within economically reasonable limits.[19]

Of course, a theory can provide a good account of the economic logic implicit in the revealed preference for a particular form of organization without providing a good account of how that form should be understood as a matter of *law*. The lawyers behind the nexus of contracts theory seem not to have grasped that.[20] The theory provides important interpretive insight on one point of law: the corporate form does enable the coordination of contractual relations in service of corporate purposes. Thus, the corporation functions in law partly as a "nexus" for coordinated contracting. The problem from the perspective of interpretive fidelity is that the nebulous reference to "nexus" at once reduces the corporation to one—but only one—of its several legal capacities and either elides or understates the roles served by legal concepts of personality, agency, and fiduciary administration in facilitating the phenomena described (the coordination of contracting). There are other problems, too, including ignorance of the wider impact of the corporate form on civil liability. These issues have been covered extensively elsewhere.[21] The important point is to notice that they are a predictable result of disintegrative or reductive interpretation.

B. The Corporation as Commons

Consider now Simon Deakin's theory of the corporation as commons.[22] Deakin highlights characteristics of the corporation that the contractarians ignored. But his work is normatively motivated, too. Deakin accuses contractarians of complicity in the 2008 financial crisis, linking the nexus of contracts theory with a destructive obsession with short-term shareholder return. Deakin claims that his alternative "better describes the legal structure" of the corporation and supports socially conscientious corporate behavior.[23]

---

[18] Ronald Coase, *The Nature of the Firm*, 4 ECONOMICA 386 (1937).

[19] Michael Jensen & William Meckling, *Theory of the Firm: Managerial Behavior, Agency Costs and Ownership Structure*, 3 J. FIN. ECON. 305 (1976).

[20] Indeed, many appear to have confused the challenge of explaining the economic motivation for incorporation of a business with that of explaining the corporation, as such. See Easterbrook & Fischel, *supra* note 13, at 1418–1419: "The view one takes of corporations and corporate law is apt to depend on one's assumptions about how investors, employees, and other players come to be associated in a venture."

[21] Bratton, *supra* note 12. See also Melvin A. Eisenberg, *The Conception that the Corporation Is a Nexus of Contracts, and the Dual Nature of the Firm*, 24 J. CORP. L. 819 (1998).

[22] Simon Deakin, *The Corporation as Commons: Rethinking Property Rights, Governance and Sustainability in the Business Enterprise*, 37 QUEEN'S L.J. 339 (2012).

[23] *Id.* at 339.

Deakin's key interpretive argument is that the corporation should be understood as a "common resource." This is said to follow from analysis of property entitlements in, and contributions to, corporations by various stakeholders. Each contributes to the corporation something that they "own" in support of its practical capacity to realize its ends. Thus, shareholders supply capital, lenders extend credit, employees provide labor, managers supply managerial expertise, and so on. These contributions are often provided on the footing of contract. But, according to Deakin, it is more important to view them as investments in a common pool of corporate resources premised on an expectation of sharing in sustainable returns.[24] Thus, he argues, the corporation should be viewed as a mechanism for creating and administering a common resource, with corporate law protecting stakeholder investments through property entitlements characteristic of those held in relation to common resources.[25]

Deakin's theory offers interpretive insight. It highlights that corporations can own (and thus pool) assets, and that corporate governance in business corporations partly involves strategic coordination in pursuit of opportunities for growth in the deployment of assets. It also emphasizes that corporate law includes rules that protect the interests of those who have property at stake in a corporation. However, Deakin's theory also illustrates the downsides of reductive interpretation. The corporation is not a nexus, but nor is it a commons. Partly, that is because the corporation is not in law a thing, or a mere asset-pooling device. It is a personified entity. As an artificial person, the corporation can be made to acquire and hold property and to make use of its property for specified purposes. Those who contribute resources to the corporation trade property rights in those resources for other rights (e.g., shareholders exchange capital for property in shares; employees supply labor in exchange for wages, etc.). Deakin's theory thus gives a skewed representation of property in corporations. And it downplays other facets of the corporation, including fiduciary administration and the plural legal capacities of the corporation. Here, too, then, we find deficits that are a predictable result of representing compound forms as singular or irreducible ones.

C. The Corporation as Site for Fiduciary Administration

We have considered theories that reduce the corporation to forms of interaction found in contract and property. We may round out our discussion by considering those that treat it as a form of fiduciary administration. These theories tend to collapse the distinction between general characteristics of the corporate form and related, but ultimately

---

[24] According to Deakin, corporate law "has a dual function: specifying the conditions under which various contributors of inputs (or as they are sometimes called, corporate 'constituencies' or 'stakeholders') can draw on the resources of the firm while at the same time, preserving and sustaining the firm's asset pool as a source of productive value." *Id.* at 368.

[25] *Id.* at 373–376, drawing on Edella Schlager & Elinor Ostrom, *Property Rights Regimes and Natural Resources: A Conceptual Analysis*, 68 LAND ECON. 249 (1992).

contingent, matters of corporate governance.[26] The corporation is represented as a site for enactment of fiduciary administration, and answers to problems of determining the ends and means of corporate governance—that is, for whom managers are fiduciaries, and how they are to act as good fiduciaries—are framed as broad interpretative statements about the nature and social purpose(s) of corporations.

We have been considering relatively recent theories of the corporation, and I will note a recent example here, too. But it is important to recognize that this line of argument has older, powerful roots in Adolf Berle and Gardiner Means' classic *The Modern Corporation and Private Property*.[27] Grappling with the rapidly increasing social and economic influence of business corporations, Berle and Means provided a lasting representation of the corporation in attempting to explain the impact of ever-more-pervasive investment in corporate stock on the extant system of private property.

According to Berle and Means, the most significant feature of the corporation is that it provides for fiduciary administration of private property on a massive scale. Corporations, they famously observed, enable the separation of ownership and control of property in business. Shareholders contribute property (equity) to the corporation but cede control to managers (directors and officers) who need not (and often do not) contribute property of their own. With this in mind, Berle and Means represented the corporation as the site of an agency relationship: one that they, and many others since, frame as implicating shareholders as principals and managers as fiduciaries. In turn, corporate law is understood as primarily responsive to problems generated by this relationship (i.e., agency problems or costs).

Scholars—including Berle—would subsequently refine this picture. For example, it was fashionable for a time to frame corporate fiduciary administration in terms of the trust, rather than agency, and Berle and Merrick Dodd instigated an unending debate whether managers should be considered fiduciaries of shareholders (in the manner of a private trust) or of a broader set of stakeholders (in the manner of a public trust).[28] But the basic picture stuck: the corporation came to be understood primarily as a site for fiduciary administration, and corporate law as shaped by the imperative of responding to associated exigencies.

I promised a recent example, and it is hard to do better than the team production theory of Margaret Blair and the late Lynn Stout.[29] Like their contemporaries, Blair and Stout write with normative purpose. With Deakin, they believe that contractarians

[26] It should be noted that some scholars who have provided influential models of corporate governance are careful to limit their claims to the interpretation of rules relating to governance. So, for example, Stephen Bainbridge's influential director primacy theory is explicitly framed as a theory of governance, rather than of the corporation as an entity as such. See generally Stephen Bainbridge, *Director Primacy: The Means and Ends of Corporate Governance*, 97 Nw. U. L. Rev. 547 (2003).

[27] Adolf A. Berle & Gardiner C. Means, *The Modern Corporation and Private Property* (1932).

[28] Adolf A. Berle, *Corporate Powers as Powers in Trust*, 44 Harv. L. Rev. 1049 (1931); E. Merrick Dodd Jr., *For Whom Are Corporate Managers Trustees?*, 45 Harv. L. Rev. 1145 (1932); Adolf A. Berle, *For Whom Corporate Managers Are Trustees*, 45 Harv. L. Rev. 1465 (1932).

[29] Margaret M. Blair & Lynn A. Stout, *A Team Production Theory of Corporate Law*, 85 Va. L. Rev. 248 (1999).

share blame for ills wrought by single-minded pursuit of short-term shareholder return. They, too, believe that contractarians slight stakeholder contributions. And they, too, wish to theorize the corporation in a way that pays due recognition to property in the corporation in situ and in its productive activity (i.e., in resource contributions that enable production). It is only that, rather than focus on underlying property relationships, Blair and Stout emphasize fiduciary administration of corporate property.

Brian Cheffins has, I think fairly, characterized the team production theory as a modern refinement of Dodd's managerialism.[30] After all, its centerpiece is the claim that the corporate form enables and calls for the fiduciary administration of property for the benefit of multiple stakeholders. More specifically, their rendering emphasizes the central role of fiduciary administration in the *business* of business corporations (i.e., production). The theory notes that fiduciaries ensure coordination between stakeholder groups ("team members") who contribute to the common enterprise (again, production, for profit) of the corporation. Corporate fiduciaries arrange for stakeholder contributions, plan for production, ensure efficient coordination in the execution of these plans, and make decisions about the disposition of corporate profits.

Here again we find interpretive insight. The team production theory corrects for a significant deficiency of leading contractarian theories: a tendency to mischaracterize or understate the significance of fiduciary administration to the corporation. The theory shows how fiduciary administration, supported by fiduciary duties, enables corporations to function as intended. But it does not go much further than that. Blair and Stout claim that their model is "consistent" with the significance to the corporation of personality, limited liability, and perpetual existence. But to say that a theory is consistent with the salience of a set of concepts is not to say that it offers a good interpretation of a construct in which they figure. Ultimately, the team production model does not even offer a good *legal* interpretation of fiduciary administration. That is, it does not explain precisely how and why fiduciary administration is central to the corporation as a legal form, the uses for which extend beyond business, and so beyond production. Again, we find that reductive interpretation leaves us wanting for the bigger picture.

III. The Case for an Integrative Theory of the Corporation

We have seen that disintegrative theories are prevalent and that they threaten to distort as much as they promise to enlighten. The lesson is that one should resist the urge to simplify radically in interpreting the compound forms like the corporation. Consistent with the spirit of the NPL, interpretation should instead be premised on recognition

---

[30] Brian R. Cheffins, *The Team Production Model as a Paradigm*, 38 SEATTLE U. L. REV. 397, 415–416 (2015).

that: (1) private law includes compound as well as irreducible forms of interaction; (2) compound forms are constituted, in part, by the combination of irreducible forms; and (3) analysis of compound forms should elucidate the craft of compounding and its key effects as a matter of *law*. This work—work of *integrative* theory—will involve identifying: central "bonding"[31] concepts within the compound; contributions—whether central or peripheral—of fundamental private law; and the sui generis modification or supplementation of concepts and rules derived from fundamental private law in the constitution of the compound or in its accommodation within private law more broadly.

Integrative interpretation has a downside: the representations it provides are more intricate, and so less parsimonious. But this is an inevitable concession to the complexity of the construct interpreted, and it is offset by the upside of interpretive fidelity: notably, an improved understanding of the compound form of interaction and the ingenuity it manifests.

IV. Developing an Integrative Theory of the Corporation

A. Overview

I have suggested that compound forms like the corporation cannot be properly interpreted in reductive terms. Interpretive theories that reduce a compound to a singular form of interaction misrepresent part of the form as the whole. They also tend to under- or overstate the significance of state provision for incorporation on distinctive terms (i.e., on terms otherwise unavailable at private law).

An integrative approach avoids these problems. It can allow for the essential role of the state. And it can do so without diminishing the contributions of fundamental private law. My aim here is to provide a blueprint for development of an integrative theory of the corporation. In section V, I will draw out some interpretive implications of the blueprint for debates over what are here identified as central "bonding" concepts in the corporate form—corporate personality, agency, purpose, and fiduciary duty.

B. The Role of the State

Most interpretive theories reduce the corporation to an irreducible form of interaction supplied by fundamental private law. But an alternative is to treat it as a pure product of public law. Concession theories are the obvious example. According to concession theorists, though corporations act within the ambit of private law, we mustn't be misled: they are

---

[31] That is, concepts that contribute most centrally to the legal meaning of the compound.

whole-cloth creations of the state, made in its image. The corporation is a subordinate body politic, a Leviathan in miniature, made to serve public purposes specified by the state.

Here, too, one finds interpretive insight. Concession theorists note, rightly, that for a long period, incorporation was not made generally available through enabling legislation. Instead, it was provided for by ad hoc exercise of prerogative power (legislative or executive action) for prescribed public purposes. Concession theorists also emphasize, again correctly, that even with the advent of enabling legislation, some of the central features of the corporate form must be provided for legislatively (e.g., personality and limited liability).

These observations are well noted. But conclusions drawn from them do not follow. It is important to recognize that some features of the corporate form are available only through state provision. They represent important contributions of organizational law. But this does not imply that the corporation is a *mere* concession of the state, much less a modality of public ordering. Dependence on state provision does not distinguish corporate from other private law. After all, forms of interaction rooted in contract, property, tort, and fiduciary law are also ultimately a matter of state provision. The state must decide whether to enforce private bargains and if so, which ones, and on what terms. The state must decide whether and how to define forms of private property. The state must determine which interests to protect via recognized torts of interference or injury. The state must decide whether to facilitate representation on fiduciary terms. And so on. Is it helpful to view *all* forms of interaction in private law as products of state "concession"? Not if one is making the point merely to attach to it an assertion that the state has retained a capacious discretionary privilege to override lawful private purposes in the use of these forms. One can only safely attach to the fact of state provision those constraints that may fairly be deduced from constating acts (e.g., enabling orders or legislation).

If concession theory overstates the contribution of the state to the corporate form (taking it to be everything), contractarian theory understates it (taking it to be nothing). The challenge for work of integrative theory will be to strike the right balance. Meeting that challenge will involve recognition of: (1) the initiative of the state in enabling incorporation; (2) the role of the state in providing, through constating acts, for rules that supplement or amend those derived from fundamental private law, making the corporation suitable for intended uses and less prone to unintended uses; and (3) the role of the state in adapting rules of fundamental private law in order to accommodate (recognize as legally consequential) acts and interactions undertaken corporately.

C. Concepts Central to the Corporate Form

As just noted, some of key features of the corporate form are the product of specific endowment by the state. Others are supplied by fundamental private law. I shall mention four concepts presently, noting reasons for considering them "central" to the corporate form and briefly explaining how an integrative theory might address them. They are: corporate personality, agency, purpose, and fiduciary duty.

For decades it has been en vogue to deny the importance of *personality* to the corporate form. Corporate personality has been dismissed as mere "artifice" or "fiction,"[32] as if that resolved anything about its significance in law and in practice. Others view personality as just one option among many for reducing the cost and complexity of coordinating behavior through organizations.[33] Still others demur on the basis that one cannot get a handle on corporate personality without becoming forever caught up in ontological and moral questions about group agency and the moral status of persons.[34] None of these reasons has much force, taken as excuses for ignoring corporate personality. And, in acting on them, we've been slighting the most central "bonding" concept in the corporate form.

An integrative theory should start with personality. As common lawyers of old recognized, the concept is foundational to the legal idea of a corporation.[35] Other concepts central to the corporate form—agency and fiduciary duty—are premised on it. The corporation is in need of agency by dint of its personality; likewise, it is by virtue of enjoying personality that it can personally claim the benefit of fiduciary duties. Conceptual dependency is also found in rules governing relationships between corporate constituents and those defining terms of corporate civil and criminal liability. These rules prevent constituents and others from mistaking or misrepresenting their own actions and endowments for those held corporately, and they likewise give effect to the idea that an organization, personified, is a legally responsible actor. Adopting a wide-angle view, it does not take much to appreciate that personification is not just one option among many to facilitate effective coordination; it has made it infinitely easier for individuals to coordinate because personification enables a group to be treated in law—and hence in spheres of life shaped by law—as a single, purposive being.

Most forms of organization implicate legal agency. The corporate form is no exception, save that *corporate agency* is (1) an inevitability, given the artificial nature of corporate personality, and (2) unusual, for the related reason of the inherent incapacity of the corporation as principal. The corporation is treated in law as a person, but it is incapable of acting for itself. If the attribution of personality is to be legally and practically effective, the corporation must have agents, for it can only act purposively through them. Inasmuch as corporate agency involves representation of a corporate person, the corporation itself is the principal to which its agents are presumptively accountable. But unlike the paradigmatic principal, the corporation cannot monitor or control its agents, nor

---

[32] John Dewey, *The Historic Background of Corporate Personality*, 35 YALE L.J. 655 (1926); Easterbrook & Fischel, *supra* note 13, at 1426: "The 'personhood' of a corporation is a matter of convenience rather than reality."

[33] See the discussion in John Armour & Michael J. Whincop, *The Proprietary Foundations of Corporate Law*, 27 OXFORD J. LEGAL STUD. 429 (2007).

[34] Questions of the sort addressed in Philip Pettit, *Responsibility Incorporated*, 117 ETHICS 171 (2007). For critique of the underlying assumption, see Richard Schragger & Micah Schwartzman, "Some Realism About Corporate Rights," in *The Rise of Corporate Religious Liberty* (Micah Schwartzman, Chad Flanders, & Zoe Robinson eds., 2016).

[35] William Blackstone, "Of Corporations," in *Commentaries on the Laws of England* (1979); F.W. Maitland, *Moral Personality and Legal Personality*, 6 J. SOC'Y COMP. LEGIS. 192 (1905).

define the scope or ends of their agency. It is, of course, the nature of corporate personality that generates the unique properties of corporate agency. Nevertheless, agency is as central to the corporate form as is personality. After all, if the law did not enable corporate persons to act through agents, corporate personality would be a useless fiction indeed. Thus, corporate agency also deserves priority consideration in an integrative theory of the corporation.

Just as it has been fashionable to dismiss personality as a quaint preoccupation of formalistic analysis, so, too, little attention has been paid to *corporate purpose*. Many write about it in the context of debate over the *social* purpose(s) of corporations. But few analyze corporate purpose as a *legal* concept.[36] And that is unfortunate because it, too, is central. Lest I be misunderstood, I am not claiming that in practice corporate purpose(s) are routinely specified with precision for *all* kinds of corporation, much less so as to limit significantly corporate capacity or agency. The point is structural: whatever the kind of corporation, constating acts will either specify corporate purpose(s) *or* grant incorporators the freedom to do so. The salience of corporate purpose in *law* is a function the nature of corporate personality. The artificial nature of corporate personality means that it can be construed broadly or narrowly. Corporations are personified ultimately to enable effective pursuit of the purposes of original incorporators and those who succeed them in control over the entity. They—and the state—therefore have a legitimate interest in the power to define and limit the capacity of the corporation and/or the authority of its agents. Corporate purpose clauses are a device through which this power may be exercised. To the extent that purpose clauses enable modulation of corporate personality and agency, they also warrant priority consideration in an integrative theory of the corporation.

Whatever its purposes, a corporation would be powerless to pursue them were it not for corporate agency and would, in turn, be without apt legal recourse against its agents absent *fiduciary duties*. As is by now a running theme, corporate fiduciary duties have been a bugbear for theorists. Early contractarians were inclined to explain them away.[37] Others accepted their importance but were led to implausibly narrow interpretations of their content and function.[38] The way forward is to recognize the centrality of fiduciary duties while avoiding interpretive excess. Corporate agents are accountable as fiduciaries for faithful and prudent pursuit of corporate purposes, however those purposes are specified. The plasticity of corporate purpose implies recognition that the content of corporate fiduciary duties—that is, what/whose interests an agent must have in mind—will depend on how the purposes of the entity were stipulated.

---

[36]   On the historical relationship between legal and social/political conceptions of corporate purpose, see Christopher M. Bruner, *Power and Purpose in the "Anglo-American" Corporation*, 50 VA. J. INT'L L. 579 (2010).

[37]   Frank H. Easterbrook & Daniel R. Fischel, *Contract and Fiduciary Duty*, 36 J.L. & ECON. 425 (1993).

[38]   See generally Lionel D. Smith, "Contract, Consent, and Fiduciary Relationships," in *Contract, Status, and Fiduciary Law* (Paul B. Miller & Andrew S. Gold eds., 2016).

D. Internal Governance

Corporate personality, agency, purpose, and fiduciary duties are central to corporate form. But they do not exhaust it. Organizational and fundamental private law make other key contributions, including establishment of terms on which corporations are to be governed and its members are to interact, that is, rules of corporate governance.

The concepts central to the corporate form shape its other, more peripheral and adaptable, elements, and that holds for rules of corporate governance. So, for example, rules providing for division of powers and permissible delegation of power within corporations vary by kind of corporation but are premised on underlying concepts of agency and fiduciary duty.

Bearing this in mind, an integrative theory should account for the fact that organizational law supplies much of the basic structure—rules relating to the when, how, and by whom—of decision-making within corporations. For instance, it mandates governance by boards, divides powers between constituents, establishes procedures for meetings and decision-making within and outside of meetings, and establishes disclosure and reporting requirements. None of this is derived from fundamental private law. Instead, contributions of fundamental private law to corporate governance—apart, critically, from those of fiduciary law—are relatively modest. In canvassing them, an integrative theory might address the extent to which governance arrangements are amenable to ex ante specification by incorporators. It should recognize that in business corporations, shareholders can agree contractually to terms governing the exercise of rights and powers incidental to their shares. It should note that corporate agents work subject to contracts that will usually contain terms defining the scope of their agency and performance-related expectations. It should also allow that the discretion of agents is constrained by their obligation to respect property interests and contractual rights security holders have in corporate securities.

Terms of interaction for constituents are concerned with interpersonal causes of action rather than corporate decision-making as such. Again, an integrative approach should notice the contributions of organizational and fundamental private law. It might take note, for example, of curiosities relating to recourse for breach of fiduciary duty. Where a manager is in breach, the right of action is conventionally enjoyed by the corporation as principal as a matter of fundamental private law. But organizational law enables the assertion of claims through derivative actions, in recognition that agents who have wronged the corporation will not be inclined to enforce its rights. An integrative theory might also examine the contributions that equity, property, and organizational law make to the protection of security holders in business corporations (e.g., via disclosure rules and equitable remedies such as the wind-up remedy and oppression remedy). There is no inevitability in the way that terms of interaction for constituents are defined precisely because different kinds of corporation have different constituencies. But an integrative theory can recognize this contingency while framing the roles respectively for organizational and fundamental private law in supplying apt terms.

E. Implications of the Corporate Form for Fundamental Private Law

For corporate personality to be legally and practically meaningful, it must be possible for corporations to act purposively. This implies recognition, in law, of the legal agency of the corporation. To be recognized in law as an agent, in turn, implies that one's acts and their ordinary legal significance are attributed to you, and no one else, including, as appropriate, acts involving the acquisition and exercise of legal rights, the performance of legal duties, the satisfaction of liabilities, and the exercise of powers. It also encompasses, negatively, personal answerability for wrongs as well as dereliction in the exercise of rights or discharge of liabilities.

The legal agency of a corporation is realized through the representative acts of its agents. These acts are taken on the footing of the corporation's capacity: to contract and to exercise associated rights and powers, perform associated duties, and satisfy associated liabilities; to acquire, use, enjoy, license, alienate, and otherwise act on property rights; to sue and be sued in tort law in relation to the commission of civil wrongs; and to undertake and discharge fiduciary mandates or be sued for fiduciary breach or wrongful procurement of same. The key takeaway is that for the corporate form of organization to be effective—and for corporate personality to be meaningfully *real* for the purposes of the law, and so not merely a *fiction*—it must have outward implications through legal recognition of the legal agency of corporations.

But what might the integrative theorist examine? First and foremost: examples of accommodations that fundamental private law has made in order to recognize the legal agency of corporations. In contract law, for example, one might consider the allowance made for corporate ratification of pre-incorporation contracts, which has required the relaxation of privity rules and suspension of the conventional logic of the law of agency. In tort law, one thinks of accommodations made for limited liability, including, notably, deviation from the presumption of personal liability for tortious acts. And this is but a sampling.

V. Wider Interpretive Implications

We have identified explananda of an integrative theory of the corporation. The primary task of interpretive theory is to illuminate legal concepts. But success on this score can yield other benefits, including clarification of issues in debate that turn on sound interpretation of concepts. Because this chapter is a mere blueprint for the development of a theory, it is not possible to draw strong wider implications from it. However, I will speculate about some that are pertinent to debates that engage concepts of personality, agency, purpose, and fiduciary duty.

A. Corporate Personality

Given that corporate personality has been all but ignored recently,[39] one might think that excavation of this concept would hold little wider interest. But that is not so. Reflecting on section II, an integrative theory might permit reframing what are ostensibly competing comprehensive theories of the corporation as complementary partial perspectives. The complementarity can be appreciated by noting that the theories highlight different facets of the corporate form, facets that have the significance attributed to them by dint of corporate personality. Thus, for example, the elusive "nexus" of contracts that enables the coordination of contractual relations is a function of the corporation's capacity to contract coupled with agency. Similarly, to the extent that the corporation serves as an asset-aggregating device, whether or not as a "commons," it achieves these functions by virtue of its capacity to acquire, own, and alienate property. Similar observations may be made in relation to other interpretive claims, from those bearing on the asset partitioning function of the corporation to others focusing on the indeterminacy of corporate interests.

Interpretive analysis of corporate personality could pay other dividends. Some might result from analysis of the artifice involved in attributing personality to groups. Recognition that corporate personality is artificial—that is, that there is nothing in the nature of a corporation as such, that compels legal *recognition* of personality—implies that corporate personality may be conditioned. It is sometimes said—even as a matter of positive law— that corporations enjoy all of the capacities of natural persons, but strictly speaking this is not true, not least because taken literally it would support nonsensical conclusions (e.g., that a corporation has the capacity to enjoy and assert a right against wrongful imprisonment). Being artificial, the actual extent of corporate personality is the product of contingent choices. Lawmakers decide for what purposes a corporation may be treated as a person in law; that is, what capacities, in particular, are to be allowed it, and whether and when these capacities may be suspended or their ordinarily legal implications overlooked. The value of these inquiries will be in revealing the legal significance of personification and its limits. This, in turn, might permit dissipation of persistent worries that the attribution of personality to corporations implies an ill-thought anthropomorphization of groups.[40]

This line of inquiry opens another. Recognition that corporate personality is artificial brings to mind the question why we ascribe personality to corporations in the first place. Addressing this question well requires that one attend to the general social purposes of personifying associations. The interpretive theorist cannot, qua interpretation, offer complete answers. But, ranging over different kinds of corporation, she can show how, by virtue of its manifold legal implications, personification enables more effective and efficient organization, and so makes it more likely that groups will coordinate effectively in pursuit of common ends.

---

[39] Save for the spate of writing about whether corporations ought to be considered persons under the U.S. Constitution following the decisions in *Citizens United v. FEC*, 558 U.S. 310 (2010), and *Burwell v. Hobby Lobby Stores, Inc.*, 134 S. Ct. 2751 (2014).

[40] See, e.g., Jeffrey D. Clements, *Corporations Are Not People* (2012).

B. Corporate Agency

An integrative theory promises to vindicate the emphasis on agency in economic theories of the corporation. But as work of interpretive *legal* theory, it would focus on legal agency rather than the broader conception of agency found in economic theory. The point of legal agency is not, directly, to allow corporations to pursue specific economic purpose(s). Most abstractly, its point is to enable corporations to function *as such*; that is, to act purposively through law.

Analysis of corporate agency might focus on wider ramifications of the fact that corporate principals have no purposes of their own, being incapable of setting them for themselves. Economic theorists have often been preoccupied with generic agency costs in corporations. But costs and other risks of corporate agency are exacerbated by the artificial personality of the corporation. The corporation is not able to issue directions to agents, nor is it able to monitor their performance. The unusual breadth of corporate agency, coupled with the incapacity of the principal to exercise control, creates unique problems. And it bears emphasis that these problems are universal, arising in all kinds of corporation incorporated for all manner of purposes.

An integrative theory might highlight ways in which corporate law has adapted to meet these concerns. One strategy is that of mandating or permitting stipulation of corporate purposes. Another is found in provisions for corporate governance. Member corporations (e.g., business corporations) are subject to checks-and-balances facilitated by allocation of supervisory powers to nonagents (members, such as shareholders); other corporations are subject to different supervisory structures. Fundamental private law plays a role too, supplying more generic controls over agents, including fiduciary and contractual constraints.

Bearing in mind that governance structures vary by kind of corporation, an integrative theory could also dispel the notion that corporate governance assumes a natural hierarchy among constituents. Considerations of corporate form do not provide any support for shareholder, managerial, or director primacy. How power ought to be allocated between constituents will depend on contingent factors including the nature of the corporation, its purposes, financing, and usual activities. Thus, the observed variation in provisions for division of power across kinds of corporation: all or most feature boards with some authorization to delegate; some feature enfranchised members; some enable outright displacement of boards by members; and some—for example, government corporations—provide for supervisory control by a person, official, or institution independent of the corporation. This suggests that debates over the relative power of constituents are not *about* the corporate form as such. Rather, they bear on the adaptation of corporations to their purposes.

C. Corporate Purpose

Corporate purpose—where provided for—helps to partly close a gap generated by the lack of intentionality of corporate persons. Artificial persons are inherently incapable of setting their own ends and forming associated intentions. Specification of corporate purposes has the effect of making intentions of the incorporator or the state those of the entity. The stipulation of particular corporate purposes allows us to view the corporation as capable of purposive action—that is, as willingly pursuing *specific*, *intended* ends, and as authoring those ends and the actions taken to achieve them. Specification of purposes can also have a negative, jurisdictional function; the state or incorporators can rule some purposes out of bounds, limiting the capacity of the corporation and/or the authority of its agents, even if this does not imply, remedially, that acts taken beyond authorized purposes can be struck or disowned.

An integrative theory of the corporation could helpfully show how purpose clauses affect the scope and execution of corporate agency relationships and orient the operation of corporate fiduciary duties. But perhaps the most important implication would be to unsettle the widespread view that the corporate form is marked by singularity of purpose.

As noted earlier, few address corporate purpose in a general, structural sense. But many have offered competing views on "the" purpose of the business corporation, supposing an inherent singularity of corporate purpose.[41] Thus, many argue that the purpose of a corporation is to maximize firm profits for the benefit of shareholders. Others argue that it is to support general social and economic development or to provide stable employment. Still others claim that it is pursuit of sustainable profit for the joint benefit of stakeholders. Unsurprisingly, proponents of these positions have not taken notice of other kinds of corporation. But considerations of corporate purpose take on a different hue when one is considering a government-owned corporation, nonprofit corporation, or a benefit corporation. The integrative theorist, having taken in this landscape in full, can usefully interject by pointing out that the underlying supposition of singularity of purpose is false. Corporations have whatever purpose(s) the law mandates or permits to be attributed to them. Corporations of a given type may tend—as a matter of policy or practice—to have a certain kind of purpose. But even here, generalizations run one into difficulty. Multiple purposes can be posited for a corporation, and corporations of a single type may have purposes specified differently in different jurisdictions. In critical terms, an integrative theory gives us reason to reject essentialist accounts of corporate purpose, but in constructive terms it allows us to better appreciate the adaptability of the corporate form.

D. Corporate Fiduciary Duties

Of all concepts central to the corporate form, corporate fiduciary duties have attracted the most extensive treatment.[42] Consider the vast tracts on the content of duties of care

---

[41] See, e.g., David G. Yosifon, *The Law of Corporate Purpose*, 10 BERKELEY BUS. L.J. 181 (2013); contrast Lyman Johnson, *Unsettledness in Delaware Corporate Law: Business Judgment Rule, Corporate Purpose*, 38 DEL. J. CORP. L. 405 (2013).

[42] See generally Julian Velasco, "Fiduciary Principles in Corporate Law," in *The Oxford Handbook of Fiduciary Law* (Evan J. Criddle, Paul B. Miller, & Robert H. Sitkoff eds., 2019).

and loyalty. Consider, too, the rich literature on good faith. An integrative theory can shed little further light here. However, it might profitably explore points of variation across different kinds of corporation. How are duties of loyalty and care variably defined for governmental, nonprofit, or benefit corporations, for example? What might explain the variation?

Consistent with the themes of variegation and the hazards of oversimplification, an integrative theory might also usefully reorient debate over the proper beneficiaries of corporate fiduciary duties. For whom are corporate agents fiduciaries?[43] One is often encouraged to disregard the formalities of corporate personality and agency in this context. Formally, directors and officers are representatives of the personified corporation, meaning the corporation is the beneficiary of corporate fiduciary duties. But, it is stressed, corporations have no interests of their own, and surely agents must act as fiduciaries for *some* person or group if fiduciary constraints are to be meaningful at law and successful in focusing agents in practice. And so debate falls prey to essentialism again, with disputants picking different constituencies—shareholders, several constituencies jointly, or "society"—as proper beneficiaries.[44]

An integrative approach can show the error in essentialism here, too. It is the corollary of that found in essentialist accounts of corporate purpose. Fiduciary loyalty, understood most abstractly, compels the fiduciary's fidelity to the purposes that define the fiduciary's mandate.[45] Translated to the present context, this implies that corporate fiduciary duties require corporate agents to faithfully pursue the corporation's purposes. What this requires more specifically will depend on how the purposes of the corporation are defined. And, as intimated earlier, one should only expect this to vary. In some cases, corporate purpose might contemplate the development and pursuit of a specific course of business for the benefit of shareholders, and corporate fiduciary duties will be so oriented. In another, a corporation may have multiple purposes and in that case fiduciary duties will be adapted accordingly. All of which is simply to say that there is no one right answer to the problem of specifying "proper" beneficiaries of corporate fiduciary duties, because specification depends not on resolving conflicts between constituents but instead on clarifying the purposes of a given corporation.

VI. Conclusion

In this chapter, I have considered how one might—consistent with the New Private Law—approach the interpretation of compound forms of interaction, taking the corporation as an example. I noted the tendency of existing theory to promote radically simple

---

[43] *Supra* note 28.

[44] See, e.g., Jonathan R. Macey, *Fiduciary Duties as Residual Claims: Obligations to Nonshareholder Constituencies from a Theory of the Firm Perspective*, 84 CORNELL L. REV. 1266 (1999).

[45] Paul B. Miller, "Dimensions of Fiduciary Loyalty," in *Research Handbook on Fiduciary Law* (D. Gordon Smith & Andrew S. Gold eds., 2018).

representations of the corporation. While radically simple interpretation has its place in the analysis of irreducible forms of interaction such as those found in contract, property, and fiduciary law, it is inadequate to the analysis of the corporation and other compound forms. It overlooks the integration of elements supplied by fundamental private law, as well as the compounding process (combination, alteration, and admixture) accomplished by organizational law. I have argued for an integrative approach to the interpretation of compound forms of interaction, explaining what integrative interpretation involves, what it might look like as applied to the corporation, and what implications it might hold for debates over concepts central to the corporate form.

ACKNOWLEDGMENTS

I am grateful for detailed comments from Lisa Austin, Rick Brooks, Mark Gergen, Andrew Gold, Dan Kelly, Ben McFarlane, and Arthur Ripstein and for additional comments from participants in the conference on the Landscape of Private Law at Harvard Law School.

CHAPTER 22

....

THE EMPLOYMENT RELATIONSHIP AS AN OBJECT OF EMPLOYMENT LAW

....

ADITI BAGCHI

EMPLOYMENT law is voluminous and uncoordinated. Many specialized bodies of doctrine are common law.[1] The Department of Labor also administers about 180 statutes with 20 different enforcement procedures.[2] There are still more federal statutes outside its jurisdiction, not least of which is the National Labor Relations Act with its own dedicated agency, the National Labor Relations Board. Each state has its own set of employment laws with important variation among the states. Remedies also vary, from compensatory and punitive damages to only back pay and reinstatement.[3]

It is difficult, then, to make a true and encompassing statement about the purposes of employment law. No doubt it serves many purposes, but it is worth distinguishing between at least two types of purpose, of public and private flavor, respectively. First, employment law is a kind of economic policy that aims to regulate wage and employment levels, and to ensure public safety. On this public side of employment law, we constrain what employees can agree to in significant part to advance the interests of others,

---

[1] Matthew W. Finkin, *Law Reform American Style: Thoughts on a Restatement of the Law of Employment*, 18 LAB. LAW. 405, 409 (2003) (describing the common law of employment to encompass primarily the doctrine of respondeat superior, employee privacy, the law of covenants not to compete, and rules in connection with employee handbooks).

[2] Craig Becker, *Thoughts on the Unification of U.S. Labor and Employment Law: Is the Whole Greater than the Sum of Its Parts?*, 35 YALE L. & POL'Y REV. 161, 165 (2016).

[3] *Id.* at 166.

usually other employees.[4] At stake is public justice, or the justice of our basic structure.[5] Second, and perhaps of less immediate concern to many scholars of employment law,[6] employment law governs a bilateral relationship between employer and employee.[7] It aims to promote the justice of that relationship in ways that are familiar from our private law regimes of contract and tort.

Within the second broad set of purposes—which I refer to here as "private" or "private law purposes"—we can make a further distinction. On the one hand, there are some rights and restrictions that speak to realizing or preserving free choice for each employee and employer. These parts embody the first-order commitment to private ordering that underpins our employment law regime. In principle, employees and employers deal with each other because they choose to do so, and on terms on which they mutually agree. Another set of doctrines places boundaries on private choice. We can understand many (albeit not all) of these restrictions as ruling out or disfavoring certain interpersonal relationships because they are essentially disrespectful and incompatible with a collective understanding of human flourishing. To be sure, these boundaries reflect a communal (or socially imposed) understanding of the limits of reasonable behavior. But we should not mistake this collective understanding or even social commitment for an essentially public purpose. The target of the social norm and its legal counterpart alike is private tyranny, very much in the spirit of any number of tort doctrines that regard certain excesses of private power as wrongful.[8] While some of employment law concerns primarily public justice, just as significant an animating purpose is the justice of private relations.

Employment consumes most of the waking hours of most people. Its fingerprints color the remaining hours of the day. Our relationship with our employer is, for better and for worse, one of the most formative and consequential private relationships in our lives. Employment law can be understood to avoid oppression and total control of one person by another, or to articulate and defend the justice of private relations in its particular sphere. Because the object of even straight-up public employment regulation is

---

[4] Aditi Bagchi, *The Political Morality of Convergence in Contract*, 24 Eur. L.J. 36, 49–52 (2018) (discussing policy motivations behind restrictions on impermissible work and minimum compensation rules).

[5] See John Rawls, *A Theory of Justice* 257 (1993) (describing basic structure of society as first subject of justice). See also William E. Forbath, *The Distributive Constitution and Workers' Rights*, 72 Ohio St. L.J. 1115 (2011) (arguing for constitutional implications for labor rights).

[6] Many scholars emphasize the public law dimensions of employment law in part because of continuous underinvestment of public resources in this area, which arguably leads to excessive reliance on modes of enforcement associated with private law. See Cynthia Estlund, *Rebuilding the Law of the Workplace in an Era of Self-Regulation*, 105 Colum. L. Rev. 319, 322 (2005) (citing literature that argues that "civil litigation is a costly, slow and often inaccessible mechanism for securing workplace rights"). This is not universally true, however; for example, whistle-blower statutes and most OSHA regulations offer no private rights of action. *Id.* at 394.

[7] Cf. David J. Doorey, *A Model of Responsive Workplace Law*, 50 Osgoode Hall L.J. 47, 56 (2012) (distinguishing self-regulation and deregulation in that only the latter is designed to pursue public policy objectives).

[8] Similarly, tort doctrines like battery embody social norms against unlawful touching, but the aim is to prevent wrongful imposition by one person on another. See Gregory C. Keating, *Nuisance as a Strict Liability Wrong*, 4 J. Tort L. 1, 58 (2012) ("Battery . . . protects our authority over our persons.").

to manage that private relationship, and not just to manage its broader economic repercussions, even the most regulatory parts of employment law have a private law cast. The result is that private and public purposes mingle interestingly in this domain.[9]

My focus here will be on the dimensions of private law that can be understood in some substantial part as constituting "right" relations between employers and employees based on principles derivative from contract and, less directly, from tort. I will not offer a comprehensive overview of employment doctrines but an interpretive scheme that identifies and sorts out the ways in which employment law promotes justice between employees and employers, even as it advances political justice writ large.

I. Promoting Private Ordering

The bedrock principle of employment in the United States sets us apart from the rest of the democratic postindustrialized world: the at-will employment doctrine. That doctrine creates a default of at-will employment. A bare majority of employment contracts in the United States specifically contract for at-will status, and another one third are silent and thus at-will by default.[10] The at-will doctrine that thus governs the vast majority of American workers is justified on public policy grounds.[11] But it can also be understood as promoting free contract for employers over time. Were employers limited to terminating employees for just cause, or even for articulated cause, they would be substantially constrained in their ability to move on—whether on to a new business practice or simply on to another employee. The at-will default gives them continuous choice on the market. Of course, they are free to opt out and commit themselves more robustly to those employees with the labor market power to command job security. Most employees lack that market power and remain at-will. They can be terminated "for good reason, bad reason or no reason," and until then, they are subject to daily employment contracts that the employer can modify at any time.

The doctrine is arguably so at odds with what Americans think is decent and fair that they do not realize that they are subject to it. Workers consistently overestimate the scope of their employment-related rights, especially constraints on dismissal.[12]

---

[9] See, e.g., the Fair Labor Standards Act (FLSA), 29 U.S.C. § 201 et al. The FLSA had the dual purpose of compensating "those who labored in excess of the statutory maximum number of hours for the wear and tear of extra work and to spread employment through inducing employers to shorten hours." Bay Ridge Operating Co. v. Aaron, 334 U.S. 446, 460 (1948).

[10] Kenneth Dau-Schmidt & Timothy Haley, *Governance of the Workplace: The Contemporary Regime of Individual Contract*, 28 COMP. LAB. L. & POL'Y J. 313, 337 (2007).

[11] See Richard A. Epstein, *In Defense of the Contract at Will*, 51 U. CHI. L. REV. 947 (1984).

[12] See Richard B. Freeman & Joel Rogers, *What Workers Want* 145–150 (2006). See also Ian Eliasoph, *Know Your (Lack of) Rights: Reexamining the Causes and Effects of Phantom Employment Rights*, 12 EMP. RTS. & EMP. POL'Y J. 197, 199 (2008) ("To bridge the gulf between knowledge that employment is obviously regulated and ignorance as to the detail of such regulation, employees rely on immediately accessible cues, such as observed workplace norms and intuitive concepts of fairness, which in other circumstances might loosely approximate the contours of law.").

They perceive "[p]hantom rights" which undermine their demand for unions and legal reform.[13]

The benefits of at-will employment to employers (and perhaps, consumers) come at enormous cost to the employees subject to an at-will regime. This is especially true given changes in actual practices, which may be responsive to competitive pressures; increasingly, sudden dismissal is not merely legally permissible, it is a real likelihood.[14] And it is not merely subjectively oppressive to employees; because persons require some modicum of independence to function as a party to contract, the radical imbalance it creates between employers and most employees is in tension with the general aspiration to private ordering. Employee consent to particular terms of at-will employment reveals little information about their preferences except that they strongly prefer employment over unemployment. At-will employment is the foundation of American employment law, but much of what comes after aims to curb its excesses.

Given that at-will employment compounds the market leverage that employers already enjoy, in no way does the remainder of employment law, which is largely oriented to granting employees' rights, offset the principle of at-will employment in magnitude. Nevertheless, we can understand many clusters of doctrine as promoting counterpart contractual freedom for employees in two respects. One set of doctrines helps to ensure that employment contracts reflect the actual understanding of their parties, and are not subject to problems of opportunism or simple breach. These are familiar objectives from general contract law, and they help employees realize the promise of free choice—the great promise inherent in the acclaimed move from status to contract.[15] Another set of doctrines helps to preserve freedom of contract for employees over time, or to preserve freedom of choice given the dynamics of employment that tend otherwise to undermine freedom over time.

A. Realizing Free Choice

One might wonder why employment law should undertake to protect employees from opportunism in contract, or straightforward breach of contract. After all, much of the apparatus of contract law is designed to protect contracting parties from opportunism, as well as more simple cases of breach. Why should a specialized body of law be necessary to advance this quite general aim in the context of exchange?

The realm of employment poses several challenges to contract. Contract law takes the baselines that people bring to the market as given and largely assumes that parties will usually enter into agreements that will make them better off. To some extent, this is true

---

[13] *Id.* at 199.

[14] *See* Dau-Schmidt & Haley, *supra* note 10, at 313–314 ("The paradigmatic employment relationship in the United States and other developed countries has moved away from a long-term relationship governed by internal labor market rules within a centralized managerial structure, toward a short-term relationship governed by international labor markets in a decentralized managerial structure.").

[15] Henry Maine, *Ancient Law* 169–170 (1876).

of our legal paradigm with respect to employment. Employment law does not question the legitimacy of the market mechanism for dictating most of the terms of employment. Fundamentally, those who come to the market with specialized, highly valuable skills are richly rewarded; those who do not bring significant endowments to the labor market fare poorly in it. But most employment decisions by employees are driven by material need; they are not properly characterized as choices made in order to improve welfare.[16] For many employees, contract decisions are not a matter of maximization but of crude necessity. They are not *choosing* among employment packages; they are seizing whatever rope might be flung their way.

The result is that the choice of an employee to accept the terms of a particular employment offer does not reveal much about her preferences. It might very well be that she would prefer more compensation for worse health care, or less compensation for more parental leave. Because terms of employment are not tailored to individual employees, and because individual employees are not shopping around for optimal fit, there is reason to think that terms are not welfare-maximizing at the level of the individual employment contract. In particular, employees tend to agree to almost total discretion by employers even where it is likely that, absent transaction costs, they might settle on terms that are mutually preferable.

If employers had truly unfettered discretion over employment, there would be no contract. That is, if employers failed to undertake any meaningful commitment to employees—to compensate them some minimal amount—they would not offer consideration and their agreements would not be legally binding. If their promise to compensate were subject to conditions entirely under the employers' control, then too employers' promises would be illusory, and the contract would fail for mutuality under ordinary contract principles. As it is, we understand that employers do assume some obligations to employees that they cannot escape at will, even in an at-will regime. Employees are often not in a position to demand that their entitlements, or the obligations of employers, are expressly memorialized. Some parts of employment law can be understood as, in part, ensuring that the contract law recognizes the bargain that was struck between employers and employees, even where that bargain does not include procedures or a balance of power that would render the bargain self-enforcing—as most commercial contracts would aspire to do.

Although employers do not have to agree to term contracts or any restriction on their right of dismissal, they often do. Perhaps the human dynamic that arises in a workplace leads employers to cede some power in the interests of a more hospitable work environment. In any event, employers and employees sometimes mutually understand that dismissal will only be permissible under particular conditions. Still, their mutual understanding is regularly at odds with legal treatment of their relationship.[17] Only in exceptional cases is evidence of those mutual understandings sufficient to satisfy the

---

[16] For a lengthier discussion of material need and contract, see Aditi Bagchi, *Voluntary Obligation and Contract*, 20 THEORETICAL INQUIRIES L. 433 (2019).

[17] See Ian Macneil, *The Relational Theory of Contract* 301 (2001).

doctrine of implied contract.[18] Similarly, common law has developed to treat employee handbooks as contractual, and any language specifying procedures prior to discipline or dismissal are binding unless they are expressly disavowed.[19] However, by now employers' commitments in handbooks are usually subject to legal disclaimers that render them unenforceable. The duty of good faith in employment contracts operates to prohibit opportunistic dismissal that is intended to avoid a promised payout, as in a year-end bonus, but it too is narrowly cabined.[20] These doctrines only aim to enforce mutual agreement between the parties; but in the grossly asymmetrical context of at-will employment, employees need special doctrinal support to "defend" their share of the employment bargain that they made.[21] Although these doctrines do not succeed in realizing employee free choice, they at least appear to acknowledge and advance that purpose.

Along similar lines, employment law interprets the employment contract to prohibit dismissal on certain grounds. For example, common law and statutory developments "prohibit[] discharge for performing public duties or engaging in lawful off-duty activities," such as refusing to perjure oneself, reporting illegality, performing jury service, or filing for workers' compensation.[22] While these restrictions can be understood on public policy grounds, they also contain the power of the employer in ways that are probably consistent with the expectations of most employees.

Finally, at-will employment renders employees so wholly dependent they are unusually vulnerable to opportunistic behavior by employers, as in the context of their pensions. Thus, the Employee Retirement Income Security Act restricts employers' access to funds that should be set aside for payment of promised pensions.[23] In principle, ordinary contract law should suffice to protect employees' interests in deferred compensation. In reality, absent statutory constraints, employers are able to exercise their power over pension funds to the detriment of employees' contractual interest. The imbalance of power between employers and employees requires more active legal intervention in their contractual relation, if only to realize the bargain as it was made.

B. Preserving Free Choice

The doctrine of at-will employment compounds the inequality of power that arises in the first instance from markets with more labor supply than demand and with capital that is more mobile than labor. Under these bargaining conditions, employees are

---

[18] *Restatement of Emp't Law*, § 7.08.

[19] See Shah v. Am. Synthetic Rubber Corp., 655 S.W.2d 489 (Ky. 1983); Toussaint v. Blue Cross & Blue Shield of Mich., 292 N.W.2d 880, 884 (Mich. 1980); Pine River State Bank v. Mettille, 333 N.W.2d 622 (Minn. 1983); Weiner v. McGraw-Hill, Inc., 443 N.E.2d 441, 442 (N.Y. 1982).

[20] See Rachel Arnow-Richman, *Modifying at-Will Employment Contracts*, 57 B.C. L. Rev. 427, 470 (2016).

[21] See Dau-Schmidt & Haley, *supra* note 10, at 315 ("[T]here has been a modest erosion of the traditional common law doctrine of employment at will. . . . These common law and statutory exceptions have circumscribed an outline of basic common law protection against the worst abuses of employer power in the system of individual contract.").

[22] *Id.* at 337, 339–340.   [23] 29 U.S.C. § 1001.

not well positioned to preserve their long-term interests at the expense of their immediate needs.

Of course, we allow contracting parties to trade off their short-term interests against long-term interests all the time. Indeed, the capacity to bind oneself over time is arguably an important moral capacity that contract law helps us to socially construct. But this capacity comes at a cost, and the legal regime of contract balances the interests of parties at a moment in time with their interests at later times.[24] It appropriately declines to defer absolutely to a party at any given moment with respect to her later interests. This imperative is especially acute in the context of contracting decisions that a party does not even experience as choices, ones where the trade-offs across time are not deliberate, if they are even knowing.

Employment law can be understood, again in part, to preserve the possibility of choice *in employment* at later points in time. In this way, it might be thought to preserve the legitimacy of the contractual model we apply to employment. For example, employees agree to terms of employment that undermine their mobility, such as overbroad covenants not to compete. And courts refuse to enforce such covenants when they unduly restrict employee mobility.[25] Although this line of cases is now rooted primarily in public policy, it originally appealed equally to unconscionability, which concerns equity between the parties to contract.

Employees' economic dependency on employers may be immobilizing in itself, in that many employees cannot afford any rupture in the employment relationship that might come with a search for alternative employment. Employees who actually quit their jobs are not entitled to unemployment benefits. But employees who choose to "pull back" or effectively trigger termination in subtle ways can usually successfully claim benefits, and this makes it marginally more feasible to resist and move on. Here, too, the doctrine of employment law at issue does not dramatically alter the landscape, but adjusts entitlements in a fashion that preserves some margin of long-term freedom of contract for employees.[26]

The single most important workplace regime that promotes long-term private ordering that is responsive to employee preference is the highly imperfect collective bargaining regime of the National Labor Relations Act (NLRA). Of course, it has important regulatory aims.[27] After all, it was adopted shortly after the Great Depression with a

---

[24] For a more far-ranging discussion of the morality of long-term commitment, see generally Aditi Bagchi, *Contract and the Problem of Fickle People*, 53 WAKE FOREST L. REV. 1 (2018).

[25] See generally Viva R. Moffat, *Making Non-Competes Unenforceable*, 54 ARIZ. L. REV. 939 (2012).

[26] Other employment policies like workers' compensation and rules concerning worker safety also may enforce the employment contract, but workers do not bring claims again employers directly. Their administrative enforcement mechanisms are inconsistent with traditional models of private law. See Richard A. Bales, *The Discord Between Collective Bargaining and Individual Employment Rights: Theoretical Origins and a Proposed Reconciliation*, 77 B.U. L. REV. 687, 701 (1997) (administrative agencies exclusively enforce OSHA workplace safety standardsand state workers' compensation statutes). Nevertheless, those bodies of employment law can be understood to advance some of the traditional purposes of private law alongside their more apparent public law objects.

[27] Cf. Cynthia Estlund, *Labor Law Reform Again? Reframing Labor Law as a Regulatory Project*, 16 N.Y.U. J. LEGIS. & PUB. POL'Y 383 (2013) (favoring a regulatory perspective on labor law).

clear eye toward macroeconomic benefits. But the drafters of the NLRA rejected the neo-corporatist model with which the National Economy Recovery Act experimented until struck down by the Supreme Court. The NLRA regime was designed instead as a voluntarist system of self-governance by contract.[28]

Among its stated purposes in Section 1 is leveling the imbalance of bargaining power between employers and employees.[29] Its provisions granting employees rights of self-organization are expressly oriented to facilitating employee choice, starting with elaborate procedures by which employees may elect representatives to negotiate their interests at arm's- length with employers. Employers are not required to agree to anything in particular.[30] But employees by force of collective mobilization can extract concessions on the terms and conditions of employment. Collective bargaining agreements also usually secure procedures that govern discipline and dismissal. Within the model of free contract—albeit by way of a unique regime of rights and duties[31]—collective bargaining enables employees to give life to preferences that are effectively irrelevant to the individual employment contracts of many employees.

Over time, the NLRA has come to play an increasingly small role in the private sector. It has now been largely displaced by the law governing individual employment contracts, which is the focus of this chapter.[32] Employment law has overtaken labor law in salience both at work and in the courts.[33] Its rise appears predicated on the fall of labor law, but it does not function comparably or show the same priorities.[34] Where collective bargaining agreements reined in employer discretion on promotion, discipline, and dismissal and

[28] See Cynthia L. Estlund, *The Ossification of American Labor Law*, 102 COLUM. L. REV. 1527, 1529 (2002) (observing that collective bargaining was intended to correct the failings of individual contract at a time when mandatory regulation of contract remained suspect); Archibald Cox, *The Legal Nature of Collective Bargaining Agreements*, 57 MICH. L. REV. 1, 2, 6 (1958) (describing collective bargaining as a mode of self-governance). See also Cynthia Estlund, *Something Old, Something New: Governing the Workplace by Contract Again*, 28 COMP. LAB. L. & POL'Y J. 351 (2007) (describing neutrality agreements as worker efforts to privately contract for protections that government failed to deliver, reminiscent of initial turn of labor movement toward voluntarism and a focus on collective bargaining).
[29] National Labor Relations Act § 1, 29 U.S.C. § 151.
[30] NLRB v. Am. Nat'l Ins., 343 U.S. 395, 402 (1952).
[31] Cynthia Estlund, *Are Unions a Constitutional Anomaly?*, 114 MICH. L. REV. 169 (2015) (noting that unions are subject to a unique regime of rights, powers, restrictions, and duties).
[32] Dau-Schmidt & Haley, *supra* note 10, at 314 ("More and more American workers find themselves in a system of workplace governance based on individual contract within a context of common law rules and state and federal legislation rather than collective bargaining.").
[33] See Comm'n on the Future of Worker-Management Relations, U.S. Departments of Labor & Commerce, Fact Finding Report 105 (1994).
[34] See Alexander MacDonald, *Permanent Replacements: Organized Labor's Fall, Employment Law's (Incomplete) Rise, and the Way Forward*, 50 IDAHO L. REV. 19 (2013) (observing that though employment law is more universal than labor law, it is also shallower, offering little to no protection against falling wages and arbitrary discharge). See also William Corbett, *Waiting for the Labor Law of the Twenty-First Century: Everything Old Is New Again*, 23 BERKELEY J. EMP. & LAB. L. 259 (2002) (describing fall of collective bargaining law and rise of a patchwork employment law in its place); Katherine Van Wezel Stone, *The Legacy of Industrial Pluralism: The Tension Between Individual Employment Rights and the New Deal Collective Bargaining System*, 59 U. CHI. L. REV. 575, 576 (1992) (noting that employment law emerged to replace a fading system of collective bargaining).

aimed for higher wages, longer leave, and more generous health and pension benefits, individual employment law focuses on nondiscrimination, privacy, and nonretaliation. Only the FLSA's overtime provisions speak to the basic question of wages.

Many scholars have offered autopsies of labor law in the United States, attempting to explain its collapse here, while collective bargaining remains an accepted feature of economic life in many other developed countries.[35] Some would fault inadequate state support.[36] Others point to the doctrine of preemption, which exempted union workers from many employment statutes and thus left them with fewer protections than non-union workers.[37] Others point to broader shifts in intellectual currents that rendered unions suspect.[38] Legal doctrines that limited union utility may also have undermined their social status and mobilizing capacity.[39]

Other scholars are less worried by the death of collective bargaining and see possibilities for collective action and empowerment in employment law proper, or the body of law addressed primarily to individual contract.[40] Ironically, to the extent the labor movement seeks refuge in individual employment statutes like the FLSA, it must abandon the voluntarist approach that is characteristic of collective bargaining under the NLRA. Regulation of the individual employment contract entails the imposition of mandatory terms; it crowds out voluntary agreement. Some would go further and avoid courts by moving adjudication of workplace rights broadly to a specialized tribunal.[41] Some are skeptical about any lighted path absent new national direction.[42]

For my purposes here, I have named the NLRA regime as just one—albeit especially notable—body of employment law (or broadly conceived, workplace law) that aims to

---

[35] John Godard, *The Exceptional Decline of the American Labor Movement*, 63 INDUS. & LAB. REL. REV. 82 (2009) (describing various facets of American exceptionalism in regard to labor law); Estlund, *Ossification, supra* note 28, at 1531 (observing the unique stagnancy of American labor law).

[36] Kenneth G. Dau-Schmidt, *A Bargaining Analysis of American Labor Law and the Search for Bargaining Equity and Industrial Peace*, 91 MICH. L. REV. 419, 513 (1992) (observing that since both parties to collective bargaining have incentives to engage in inefficient behavior, government regulation is needed to prohibit waste and "promote industrial peace").

[37] Van Wezel Stone, *supra* note 34, at 578.

[38] Reuel E. Schiller, *From Group Rights to Individual Liberties: Post-War Labor Law, Liberalism, and the Waning of Union Strength*, 20 BERKELEY J. EMP. & LAB. L. 1 (1999) (arguing that the intellectual shift that disfavored interest groups as democratically suspect led to changes in labor law that ultimately weakened labor movement).

[39] Catherine L. Fisk, *Union Lawyers and Employment Law*, 23 EMP. & LAB. L.J. 57 (2002) (arguing against prohibitions-against-unions provision of legal assistance to nonmember employees).

[40] See Benjamin I. Sachs, *Employment Law as Labor Law*, 29 CARDOZO L. REV. 2685, 2689 (2008) (noting that "employment law can in fact function as a substitute form of labor law" by insulating workers' organizational activity from employer interference); Kate Andrias, *The New Labor Law*, 126 YALE L.J. 5 (2016) (observing that political unionism may be replacing voluntarism, or collective bargaining within a system of private ordering).

[41] See John N. Raudabaugh, *Labored Law: Bilateralism or Pluralism, Ossification or Reformation?*, 87 INDIANA L.J. 105, 117 (2012) (raising the possibility of replacing the National Labor Relations Board with an "Article III workplace law court").

[42] Paul C. Weiler, *Governing the Workplace: The Future of Labor and Employment Law* (1990) (critiquing both the "blunt instrument" of workplace regulation and the limited and costly avenue of litigation).

protect employee choice and promote private ordering of employment relations over time. Although its decline may have plateaued, unions still represent only about 11 percent of the U.S. workforce.[43] We should therefore look for other steps we could take within the framework of employment law as we know it—that is, without upsetting at-will doctrine as such—that could ameliorate the problem of grossly imbalanced power and the attendant spiral away from employment relationships recognizable as free.[44]

Myriad legislative proposals would correct for particular abuses by employers. Most prominent are draft bills that completely ban covenants not to compete,arbitration clauses, or terms that prohibit any collective adjudication of claims. It is hard to tell what will come of these proposals. But even absent legislative activity, there are some general steps that courts could take to support employment law's function as an enabler of freedom of contract in the realm of employment. For example, courts could interpret the individual employment contract and what it requires of employers and employees, by reference to social context, including market practice. This does not require that courts incorporate any public agenda directly. Rather, they should interpret what it means for an employer to treat employees reasonably given the express terms of contract, such as those relating to wages and termination. A contract that expressly limits employer obligation along various dimensions should imply few employee obligations that are not similarly express. Employers' obligations should be read in a manner that renders the exchange a rational bargain from which each side can expect to profit. Again, this interpretive move would merely extend protection of free contract in the realm of employment, properly understood to encompass not only robust choice for employers but also real and persistent choice for employees. While other realms of exchange might not require active promotion of basic contract principles, the headwinds against free exchange of labor require that employment law adopt a protective stance.

II. Mandatory Relational Boundaries

Not all legal treatment of the employment contract can be understood as deferential to private ordering. Some restrictions on employer conduct operate against oppression in a more general way. They are not calculated either to realize the parties' mutual understanding or to preserve the employee's ability to exit the relationship. They seem to deem certain ways of relating to one another unsavory, inconsistent with collective values, or simply unjust. They embody a kind of "anti-domination" principle located in private

---

[43] Union Membership and Coverage Database from the CPS, Unionstats.com, http://unionstats.gsu .edu/.

[44] Cf. Noah D. Zatz & Eileen Boris, *Seeing Work, Envisioning Citizenship*, 18 Emp. Rts. & Emp. Pol'y J. 95, 100 (2014) ("Work often is associated with effort elicited by obligation and constraint. It is hard; it is structured; it is mandatory; it is not leisure. It is involuntary, not necessarily at the moment of entry into employment . . . but in the substance of a relationship defined by subject to another's control and direction").

rather than constitutional law.[45] Three primary areas in which employment law curbs private domination are discussed here: nondiscrimination, wage and safety minimums, and privacy (understood here as freedom of private conduct).

There are good policy reasons for making it possible for employers to lord over employees. Many but not all kinds of employer discretion promote labor productivity because the employer can deploy labor resources optimally and redirect them quickly as circumstances change. Many employees willingly accept the sweeping authority of employers in the workplace in exchange for compensation; if the labor market functions at all, we can expect employers who offer more job protections and employee voice to offer lower compensation too, based on the trade-offs employees are prepared to make.

But even theorists of the firm like Ronald Coase seem to expect that the employment contract will be more bounded than it is.[46] For while some authority by employers over employees supports the efficiency of internalizing production within a firm—rather than dealing with suppliers and independent contractors—some of the authority that the courts recognize as a default is more sweeping, such as employer authority over the personal lives of employees. While courts do not expressly grant that authority, it derives from the right of employers to dismiss on *any* grounds that is not expressly protected.[47]

Even if it turns out that radical autocracy in the workplace is economically fruitful and would obtain at least initial consent from employees, it is not a morally and socially acceptable way for people in a liberal democracy to interact with one another. "Bowing and scraping" before other persons, Immanuel Kant observed, is "unworthy of a human being."[48] As Elizabeth Anderson wrote more recently, "[e]quals are not dominated by others; they do not live at the mercy of others' wills."[49] Citing Joseph Raz and his account of the limits of consent as a basis for authority, John Gardner argues that "[i]t is simply unbelievable that anyone, paying wages or otherwise, could enjoy legitimate authority over such an extensive swathe of another's life irrespective of how the use of that commandeered time contributes constitutively to the life of the person who is subject to the authority."[50] Even if the material needs of an employee lead her to accept autocratic conditions at work, deferring to her choice privileges her contractual freedom over other freedoms that citizens in a liberal democracy should enjoy.[51] Similarly, Hugh Collins concludes that "the contract of employment embraces an authoritarian structure that appears to be at odds with the commitment of liberal societies to values such as liberty,

---

[45] The antidomination principle is commonly associated with the equal protection clause. See Owen M. Fiss, *Groups and the Equal Protection Clause*, 5 PHIL. & PUB. AFF. 107 (1976); Reva B. Siegel, *Equality Talk: Antisubordination and Anticlassification Values in Constitutional Struggles over Brown*, 117 HARV. L. REV. 1470 (2004).

[46] Ronald H. Coase, *The Nature of the Firm*, 4 ECONOMICA 386, 391 (1937).

[47] Elizabeth S. Anderson, *Private Government* 52–53 (2017).

[48] Immanuel Kant, *The Metaphysics of Morals* 188 (Mary Gregor ed. & trans., 1996).

[49] Elisabeth S. Anderson, *What Is the Point of Equality?*, 109 ETHICS 287, 315 (1999).

[50] John Gardner, "The Contractualisation of Labour Law," in *Philosophical Foundations of Labour Law* 23 (Hugh Collins, Gillian Lester, & Virginia Mantouvalou eds., 2019).

[51] *Id.* at 12 (2019) (describing "how easily freedom of contract can become an enemy of all other freedom").

equal respect, and respect for privacy."[52] Neither freedom of discretion in one's movements nor economic security is guaranteed by the Constitution, but a modicum of each is essential to a liberal and egalitarian way of life, and therefore supported broadly by our tort regime. Social equality is threatened "when employer practices needlessly lead to hierarchies within or outside the workplace."[53] Recognizing moral and social limits to how people can treat each other, particular doctrines limit the power that employers exercise over employees. These include rules prohibiting discrimination on protected grounds, rules imposing minimum wage and safety standards, and rules protecting privacy.

The one dimension on which employer control of employees is subject to a vigorous statutory scheme is nondiscrimination. Although employers are entitled to distinguish among employees for an infinite list of arbitrary reasons, in practice, "employers must be careful about whom they fire, why they fire, and how they fire" and must document their decisions in anticipation of litigation.[54] This is because Title VII prohibits discrimination in employment on grounds of sex, race, religion, and other similar categories.[55]

Beyond protecting vulnerable groups identified on these particular grounds, state legislatures and federal agencies have attempted to prevent blanket refusal to consider candidates based on other criteria such as criminal history, poor credit, or unemployment.[56] Joseph Fishkin argues that these restrictions are an attempt to remove bottlenecks that limit opportunity.[57] Such an explanation is grounded in public law and is plausible. But we can also understand these nondiscrimination principles as attempts to rein in total employer discretion with its devastating moral effect on relationships between employers and employees, which are among the most embracing relationships in the lives of the latter. "Unconstrained, subjective selection systems" foster discrimination, including sexual harassment.[58] Private tyranny is ultimately incompatible with the rule of law in a society where people have rights against each other as well as obligations to each other.[59]

The second most important category of employment litigation arises under the Fair Labor Standards Act, which establishes minimum wage and overtime rights, and the

---

[52] Hugh Collins, "Is the Contract of Employment Illiberal?," in *Philosophical Foundations of Labour Law* 48 (Hugh Collins, Gillian Lester, & Virginia Mantouvalou eds., 2019).

[53] Samuel R. Bagenstos, *Employment Law and Social Equality*, 112 MICH. L. REV. 225, 227 (2013).

[54] Corbett, *supra* note 34, at 262.   [55] 42 U.S.C. § 2000e.

[56] Joseph Fishkin, *The Anti-Bottleneck Principle in Employment Discrimination Law*, 91 WASH. U. L. REV. 1429, 1431–1432. (2014). See also Danieli Evans Peterman, *Socioeconomic Status Discrimination*, 104 VA. L. REV. 1283 (2018) (arguing for extending nondiscrimination principle to socioeconomic status).

[57] *Id.*

[58] Vicki Schultz, *Reconceptualizing Sexual Harassment, Again*, 128 YALE L.J. FORUM 22, 51–52 (2018).

[59] In her chapter, Lisa M. Austin discusses several relationships between private law and the rule of law. See Lisa M. Austin, this volume. Austin argues that private law can be conceived as serving the rule of law inasmuch as it constrains arbitrary exercise of power by nonstate actors. See also Gerald Postema, "Fidelity in Law's Commonwealth," in *Private Law and the Rule of Law* 17–19 (Lisa M. Austin & Dennis Klimchuck eds., 2014) (describing the rule of law as constraint of arbitrary exercise of power).

Occupational Safety and Health Act of 1970 (OSHA).[60] The FLSA relies primarily on private enforcement, while the OSHA has a dedicated federal agency.

On their face, wage regulations might seem starkly different from safety regulations. But these two statutes both posit minimum terms—not just mandatory terms, in the way that much of employment law does. Even when workers would be willing to work for less than minimum wage, without "time and a half" for overtime hours, or under dangerous conditions, the federal government effectively rules out the sale of labor on such terms. To be sure, these laws are intended to regulate a market for the benefit of all workers, even at the expense of some whose welfare is probably diminished by them, at least in their own estimation.[61] But the public discourse around these statutes seems to contemplate that paying workers too little or subjecting them to avoidable physical danger is also wrongful to those workers themselves, irrespective of the terms to which they might have consented. Again, employment on some terms is considered inconsistent with interpersonal respect. Employing workers on terms that do not make it possible for them to afford what we collectively regard as necessary, or subjecting them to dangers that most Americans would regard as intolerable, is fundamentally disrespectful in much the same way as behavior actually recognized as tortious.

None of this is to suggest that American employment law succeeds in establishing respectful relations. Moreover, it may be in the course of receding from this basic purpose of employment law. Because workers' rights are disproportionately dependent on private enforcement, recent cases that curtail the ability of workers to sue employers effectively wind back substantive employment protection.[62]

The final category of employment laws that aims to curb employer discretion and thereby preserve the conditions for mutual civil respect in the workplace limits the kinds of private conduct by employees that employers can control. The Privacy Act of 1974 limits how federal agencies and their contractors use data about individuals, including employees; access to such data casts a shadow over the private lives that the data describes.[63] The Electronic Communications Privacy Act restricts eavesdropping by employers where employees can reasonably expect privacy, but does not apply where employers have employee consent or where surveillance is by and of use of the employer's server.[64] Some states have passed statutes limiting the collection of biometric data, and others have passed statutes granting a measure of privacy on social media.[65]

None of this amounts to robust protection of private conduct or private information. Indeed, U.S. protection of employee privacy is comparatively weak.[66] The German

---

[60] FLSA, 29 U.S.C. § 201 et al.; OSHA, 29 U.S.C. § 15.   [61] See Bagchi, *supra* note 4.

[62] J. Maria Glover, *All Balls and No Strikes: The Roberts Court's Anti-Worker Activism*, 2019 J. Disp. Resol. 129 (2019).

[63] 5 U.S.C. § 552(a).   [64] 18 U.S.C. §§ 2510–2511.

[65] State Social Media Privacy Laws, Nat'l Conf. St. Legislatures (Jan. 2, 2018), http://www.ncsl.org/research/telecommunications-and-information-technology/state-laws-prohibiting-access-to-social-media-usernames-and-passwords.aspx.

[66] Matthew W. Finkin, *Menschenbild: The Conception of the Employee as a Person in Western Law*, 23 Comp. Lab. L. & Pol'y J. 577, 587 (2002).

Federal Labor Court has recognized that employees have a right to private life outside the domain of employers' control except inasmuch as their private behavior affects the workplace.[67] By contrast, outside of whistle-blowing and concerted activity, private sector employees in the United States have little right to free speech at work.[68]

A sphere for private conduct—for private judgment and morally significant private choice—is essential to the citizen to whom a liberal polity caters. A liberal state, after all, aims more than others to enable private life, which is meaningful precisely because it is replete with significant choices about how to live. Employees who have little room to maneuver outside the control of their employers are effectively deprived of the private life that a liberal state aims to protect.

Together, nondiscrimination, minimum term regulations, and privacy rules limit how radically an employer can dominate her employees. This is a critical function of employment law, albeit one that our current regime performs inadequately.

III. Conflict between Public and Private Purposes of Employment Law

Most doctrines governing employment simultaneously advance public purposes while promoting just private relations. The primary work of this chapter has been to tease out the latter effect, which is sometimes dwarfed by the more salient public dimensions of employment law. It is not clear what is to be gained by pronouncing one set of its objectives dominant over the other, but the dual purposes of employment law are not always harmonious. They intersect at some challenging points. To illustrate conflict, and the ways in which a sprawling "body" of law inconsistently chooses between public and private values, I briefly study nondisclosure agreements, which press the public interest in transparency against private choice.

At least some kinds of nondisclosure agreements in the workplace are harmful to third parties.[69] It is tempting to argue that these agreements are bad for those who enter them as well, and that because their choice is compromised in some way, ordinary contract principles do not favor enforcement.[70] It is almost certainly true that some

---

[67] Judgment of June 6, 1994, BAG (Bundesarbeitsgericht) reported in SAE 1995, at 103, 106.

[68] See Nicholas Bernberg, *The Legal Standard for Determining Employee Disloyalty under Section 7 of the NLRA*, 9 WAKE FOREST J.L. & POL'Y 117 (2018); Staughton Lynd, *Employee Speech in the Private and Public Workplace: Two Doctrines or One*, 1 BERKELEY J. EMP. & LAB. L. 711 (1977).

[69] See Andrew F. Daughety & Jennifer F. Reinganum, *Informational Externalities in Settlement Bargaining: Confidentiality & Correlated Culpability*, 33 RAND J. ECON. 587 (2002) (criticizing agreements for secrecy); Alison Lothes, *Quality, not Quantity: An Analysis of Confidential Settlements and Litigants' Economic Incentives*, 154 U. PA. L. REV. 433 (2005) (arguing that whether confidentiality is socially beneficial depends on whether the information deters wrongdoers and facilitates compensation for victims, or whether it encourages nuisance suits).

[70] See e.g., Brittany Scott, *Waiving Goodbye to First Amendment Protections: First Amendment Waiver by Contract*, 46 HASTINGS CONST. L.Q. 451 (2019) (arguing that free speech rights should be waivable only when waiver is "knowing, voluntary, and intelligent").

employees need the "hush money" associated with nondisclosure agreements badly, or fear the repercussions of angering an employer who has the power to cut them off from future work. But in many cases, it is also plausible that employees who agree to nondisclosure agreements stand to gain more from those agreements than they will lose; their choice to enter those contracts is meaningful and rational for them.[71]

One might also argue that nondisclosure agreements do not matter that much because other kinds of terms, such as arbitration terms, can be used to secure much of the same secrecy.[72] But in a number of cases—and given the volume of nondisclosure agreements, the subset is not small—the enforceability of a nondisclosure agreement makes it more likely that other employees and government enforcement agencies will not learn of improper conduct by an employer.

The recent #MeToo movement has highlighted the social ills wrought by nondisclosure agreements. But it has also brought to light how hard it already is for female employees to avoid having their employment revolve around their sex, and how hard it is for victims of sexual harassment to move on from abusive employment relationships. If a nondisclosure agreement increases the compensation that victims are paid, and if secrecy is a low price to pay for those who do not want to talk about it anyway, we should be careful about banning such an agreement. The private right of an employee to decide what is best for her and act on that judgment is directly at odds with a public interest in using her experience to improve employment conditions for her peers.

Ultimately, we may be justified in curtailing private choice in this sphere, at least if we do more to ensure that victims are compensated for their injuries without having to promise secrecy *and* if we can lower the enduring costs of workplace abuse over the course of a victim's career. The regulatory challenge in this domain highlights that the applicable legal regime must be responsive to more than one animating purpose. The purposes of private law roughly capture one side of the dilemma.

Of course, one might frame the debate about nondisclosure agreements differently. Maybe the relevant private law interest lies in deterring sexual harassment. And maybe the public law interest lies in the sanctity of settlement agreements and limiting litigation. My aim here has been to highlight the ways in which employment law gives life to principles of choice and respect in private relations that are familiar to us from private law. These principles largely reinforce the more public dimensions of employment law, which aim to make the social institution of labor more just. Sometimes, as in the case of nondisclosure agreements, they appear to come apart. There is no more consensus on what choice and respect require of the employment relationship than there is general agreement on what justice requires of the labor market. Normative uncertainty about the demands of public and private purpose alike enables their spectral coexistence throughout employment law.

---

[71] See Burt Neuborne, *Limiting the Right to Buy Silence: A Hearer-Centered Approach*, 90 U. Colo. L. Rev. 411 (2019) (arguing that rights of the listener rather than rights of the speaker are a better basis for limiting the enforceability of nondisclosure agreements).

[72] Christopher R. Drahozal & Laura J. Hines, *Secret Settlement Restrictions and Unintended Consequences*, 54 U. Kan. L. Rev. 1457, 1459 (2006).

One of the lessons of New Private Law has been that legal concepts can serve to manage such complexity.[73] We could attempt, with respect to each of the myriad questions presented in connection with the employment relation, to dive down and work out an answer to the first order, all-encompassing questions of what is fair and efficient—simultaneously considering the effects of a rule on choice and tyranny, and the welfare of all the world. Employment law as we know it makes the questions more manageable: it borrows from principles and concepts familiar to us from contract and tort and attempts to operationalize them within its particular domain of human life. The framework it ultimately imposes does not evenly reflect the principles we find in contract and tort. Even setting aside conflicts with public law, the balance that employment law strikes between choice and antidomination, falls short. Viewing employment in part through the lenses of its ambitions derived from private law delivers one compelling mandate for reform.

---

[73] See John C.P. Goldberg, *Introduction: Pragmatism and Private Law*, 125 HARV. L. REV. 1640, 1653–1654 (2012).

CHAPTER 23

....

NEW PRIVATE LAW
AND THE FAMILY

....

MARGARET F. BRINIG

To the extent that legal academics have tried to capture family law systematically, they have typically used the framework, and sometimes specifically the language, of contract. This chapter will make the case that a more apt analogy, and one that can help explain the public/private division that is inherent in family law, is covenant. Covenant, in fact, may be one of the structural strands of private law along with the more discussed contract, tort, and property. As a concept, it is of the same vintage, appearing early in the Book of Genesis, itself compiled from oral tradition.

I. WHAT IS A COVENANT?
....

While lawyers may think of covenants as especially serious contracts ("contract under seal" or "covenants that run with the land"), historically in the family context covenant has meant more than that. Appropriate to the involvement of religion with families, religions following the Torah or Qu'ran or Bible are full of covenants.[1] The whole idea of covenant depends upon support from outside: extended family, religious community, and the state or God.[2] Practically speaking, the state is always involved in the restrictions on entering marriage (and sometimes the procedures involved), as well as conditions and procedures for leaving marriage. While the rules are for the most part the same throughout the English-speaking world, a Massachusetts case makes the

---

[1] See Scott Hahn, *A Father Who Keeps His Promises: God's Covenant Love in Scripture* 26 (2011).

[2] See, e.g., Margaret F. Brinig, *Family, Law and Community: Supporting the Covenant* (2010); Margaret F. Brinig, *From Contract to Covenant* (2000); and Margaret F. Brinig, *Status, Contract and Covenant*, 79 CORNELL L. REV. 1597, 1598–1599 (1993).

point well, distinguishing the roles of the marrying couple and the state. *French v. McAnarney* notes that:

> While only the parties can mutually assent to marriage, the terms of the marriage—who may marry and what obligations, benefits, and liabilities attach to civil marriage—are set by the Commonwealth. Conversely, while only the parties can agree to end the marriage (absent the death of one of them or a marriage void ab initio), the Commonwealth defines the exit terms.[3]

Thus marriage begins with a contract made between spouses, as all covenants begin with promises. While it may be more difficult to see a parent-child contract, especially at childbirth, even unplanned pregnancies to unmarried mothers can involve a kind of promise.[4] Some public rituals undertaken by new parents can also be thought of in terms of promises to the community (at a baptism, for example, or at a bris (literally covenant), where an infant male is joined to the Abrahamic covenant between God and the Jewish people). But unlike a contract, an exchange of goods and services, a covenant is a gift[5] of one's whole self.[6] It thus is perhaps the most private of legal relationships and the most relational.

Covenant involves the giving of oneself, an exchange of persons, rather than goods, to another. It supplies our needs for human flourishing—permanence, unconditional love, and community (religious or secular) support—because it gives "space for the meaningful exercise of individuality and liberty."[7] In the overflowing of love between persons that constitutes sexual relations, the marital covenant typically also involves procreation and the nurture of children in the faith.[8] Because of the involvement of God and/or the state, it necessarily has public as well as private aspects.

---

[3] 290 Mass. 544, 546 (1935).

[4] Kathryn Edin & Maria Kefalos, *Promises I Can Keep: Why Poor Women Put Motherhood before Marriage* (2005).

[5] See, e.g., Emily J. Stolzenberg, *The New Family Freedom*, 59 B.C. L. REV. 1983, 2041 (2018); and Ira M. Ellman, *Contract Thinking Was Marvin's Fatal Flaw*, 76 NOTRE DAME L. REV. 1365, 1375 (2001); Daniel Markovits, "Promise as an Arm's Length Relation," in *Promises and Agreements: Philosophical Essays* 295, 295–296 (Hanoch Sheinman ed., 2011); and Margaret Radin, *Market-Inalienability*, 100 HARV. L. REV. 1949, 1855 n.24, 1860 (1987).

[6] See, e.g., Pope Francis, *Amoris Laeticia* (2016). In ¶ 121, he wrote: "Infused by the Holy Spirit, this powerful love is a reflection of the unbroken covenant between Christ and humanity that culminated in his self-sacrifice on the cross." And in ¶ 319: "Marriage is also the experience of belonging completely to another person. Spouses accept the challenge and aspiration of supporting one another, growing old together, and in this way reflecting God's own faithfulness."

[7] Janet Moore, *Covenant and Feminist Reconstructions of Subjectivity Within Theories of Justice*, 55 CONTEMP. PROBS. 159, 167–180, 183 (1992); Geoffrey P. Miller, *Contracts of Genesis*, 22 J. LEGAL STUD. 15, 24 (1993); William J. Everett, *Contract and Covenant in Human Community*, 36 EMORY L.J. 557, 559 (1987).

[8] John Witte Jr. & Joel A. Nichols, *More than a Mere Contract: Marriage as Contract and Covenant in Law and Theology*, 5 U. ST. THOMAS L.J. 595, 605 (2009). As Scott Hahn notes, the marriage sacrament is the only one that results in a gift. *The First Society: The Sacrament of Matrimony and the Restoration of the Social Order* (2018). While procreation cannot be a part of same-sex marriages, as opponents have argued, childrearing can be (and frequently is).

II. One System or More?

While some fields seem to be for the most part dominated by private law, with enforcement by the sovereign the only necessary public involvement, scholars have conceived of two distinct systems governing families at least since the publication of Jacobus ten-Broek's series of articles in the *Stanford Law Review* more than fifty years ago.[9] TenBroek described one, largely public, California system that governed the poor, while another, largely private, determined legal matters for the relatively wealthy. While to some extent this distinction holds true today,[10] the expansion of privacy doctrines in constitutional law[11] as well as increased federal incursions through additions to the Social Security Act,[12] have narrowed applicability of private family law for everyone. To some extent, increasing legal recognition of marital and premarital contracts since the early 1970s has enhanced the ability of individual couples to customize many effects of marriage.[13] Only a tiny number of couples actually seek premarital agreements, however.[14] Meanwhile, the contemporary no-fault divorce system,[15] with the corollary expansions of divorce mediation,[16] collaborative divorce,[17] and shared parenting governed by individualized

---

[9] Jacobus tenBroek, *California's Dual System of Family Law: Its Origin, Development and Present Status*, 16 STAN. L. REV. 257, 900 (1964) and 17 STAN. L. REV. 614 (1965).

[10] See, e.g., Dorothy E. Roberts. *Shattered Bonds: The Color of Child Welfare* (2001; paperback, 2002); Dorothy Roberts, *Welfare Reform and Economic Freedom: Low-Income Mothers' Decisions about Work at Home and in the Market*, 44 SANTA CLARA L. REV. 1029–1963 (2004); Jill Hasday, *The Canon of Family Law*, 57 STAN. L. REV. 825, 832 (2004). Cf. June Carbone & Naomi Cahn, *The Triple System of Family Law*, 2013 MICH. ST. L. REV. 1185 (2013).

[11] David D. Meyer, *The Constitutionalization of Family Law*, 42 FAM. L.Q. 529 (2008).

[12] Child custody jurisdiction and child support enforcement are increasingly governed on the federal level. See, e.g., 42 U.S.C. § 659 (mandating garnishment for child support enforcement), and the PKPA, Parental Kidnapping Prevention Act (Pub. L. 96-611, 94 Stat. 3573, enacted Dec. 28, 1980; 28 U.S.C. § 1738A, as well as interstate compacts (UIFSA and UCCJEA) regulating the "home state" for matters of custody jurisdiction and interstate enforcement of custody. See the summary of these acts at http://www .uniformlaws.org/shared/docs/interstate%20family%20support/UIFSA_2008_Final_Amended%202015_ Revised%20Prefatory%20Note%20and%20Comments.pdf; and http://www.uniformlaws.org/ ActSummary.aspx?title=Child%20Custody%20Jurisdiction%20and%20Enforcement%20Act, respectively.

[13] See, e.g., Barbara A. Atwood, *A New Uniform Law for Premarital and Marital Agreements*, 46 FAM. L.Q. 313 (2012).

[14] See, e.g., Margaret F. Brinig, *Result Inequality in Family Law*, 46 AKRON L. REV. 471, 493 (2016) (symposium issue). For reasons why this may be so, see Heather Mahar, *Why Are There So Few Premarital Agreements?*, Harvard Law and Economics Discussion Paper No. 436 (2003) (to propose one indicates distrust of the partner or overoptimism about the success of the future marriage).

[15] While damages for breach of marital contracts of permanence, fidelity, and love might have made sense under a fault system, it does not for a system in which either party may leave for any reason at any time. June Carbone & Margaret Brinig, *Rethinking Marriage: Feminist Ideology, Economic Change, and Divorce Reform*, 65 TULANE L. REV. 953, 957–961 (1992).

[16] See, e.g., Michael J. Trebilcock & Rosamin Keshvani, *The Role of Private Ordering in Family Law*, 41 U. TORONTO L.J. 533, 549 (1991); Robert H. Mnookin & Lewis Kornhauser, *Bargaining in the Shadow of the Law: The Case of Divorce*, 88 YALE L.J. 950 (1979).

[17] See, e.g., J. Herbie DiFonzo, *A Vision for Collaborative Practice: The Final Report of the Hofstra Collaborative Law Conference*, 38 HOFSTRA L. REV. 669 (2009).

parenting plans[18] has pushed both the poor (those with minor children, anyway) and the wealthy into private, though sometimes default,[19] systems.

A hundred and fifty years ago, there were clear theories of family law. For marriage, these were largely based upon Christian ideas of indissolubility, monogamy, and the importance of procreation.[20] However, marriage and even parent-child relations also had the flavor of hierarchical relationships (like master-servant) based upon patriarchy and thus gender.[21] Since the historic ideas have been discarded, much private family law as contemporarily viewed sounds in contract.[22] This is true across the Atlantic as well: Oxford Professor John Eekelaar argues that family law should not encourage a model of "proper" family life in the interests of stability, but should allow people to make their own decisions.[23] In a very recent paper, Columbia Professor Emily Stolzenberg argues that the "incoherence" of U.S. family law, and concomitant harmful results for women and children, come from the neoliberal state's adoption of autonomy as a property right and its simultaneous decision to maintain a system privatizing dependency.[24]

III. A New Private Law for Families

With these caveats, there should still be room to discuss a New Private Law of the family. Mary Ann Glendon argued about the dangers of thinking in terms of "rights talk" rather than more communitarian goals. However, Glendon recognized that the concept of family was changing in the Western world in her important *The New Family and the New*

[18] See, e.g., Marsha Kline Pruett & J. Herbie DiFonzo, *Closing the Gap: Research, Policy, Practice, and Shared Parenting*, 52 FAM. CT. REV. 152 (2014).
[19] For example, Arizona's custody statute specifies "maximum parenting time" with each parent unless there is proof of unfitness or abuse to a parent that directly affects the child. Ariz. Rev. Stat. § 25-403.07.
[20] Nicholas C. Bala, *The History and Future of Marriage in Canada*, 4 U. TORONTO J.L. & EQUALITY 20 (2007).
[21] See, e.g., Chester G. Vernier & John B. Hurlbut, *The Historical Background of Alimony Law and Its Present Statutory Structure*, 6 LAW & CONTEMP. PROBS. 197 (1939); W. Blackstone, *Commentaries on the Laws of England* (1765), Book 1, ch. 15, at 430. On gender, see Sarah Fensternaker Burk, *The Gender Factory: The Apportionment of Work in American Households* (1985), and Steven L. Nock, *Marriage in Men's Lives* (Press 1998).
[22] See, e.g., Marjorie McGuire Shultz, *Contractual Ordering of Marriage: A New Model for State Policy*, 70 CAL. L. REV. 204 (1982); Brian Bix, *Private Ordering and Family Law*, 23 J. AM. ACAD. MATRIMONIAL L. 249 (2019). For concerns, see Robert E. Rowthorn, *Marriage and Trust: Some Lessons from Economics*, 23 CAMBRIDGE J. ECON. 661 (1999). For a Canadian law and economics view, see Trebilcock & Keshvani, *supra* note 16. Perhaps the most ambitious piece of this type is Elizabeth S. Scott & Robert E. Scott, *Marriage as Relational Contract*, 84 VA. L. REV. 1225 (1998); see also Lloyd Cohen, *Marriage, Divorce, and Quasi Rents; Or, "I Gave Him the Best Years of My Life,"* 16 J. LEGAL STUD. 267, 300 (1987).
[23] John Eekelaar, *Family Law and Personal Life* 64 (2017). For children, Eekelaar shows how the traditional powers given to parents have been shaken by the values of the rights of the child. He would instead base family law on respect for personal intimacy. A cogent review is Maebh Harding, Family Law and Personal Life – By John Eekelaar, 27 LEGAL STUD. 743 (2007).
[24] See Stolzenberg, *supra* note 5, at 1985–1987, 2039 (2018).

Property.[25] As the concept of family as contract was beginning to take hold, Georgetown Professor Milton Regan, currently best known for his work in professional ethics and national security, suggested that thinking primarily in these terms was misplaced: a more appropriate way of thinking about families was in terms of a re-envisioned status.[26] My own addition to the discussion likewise suggested, this time based on the Judeo-Christian idea of covenant, that the goals of contracting (or the law and economics ideas of Gary Becker, maximizing household wealth in a broad sense) both missed the point.[27] Families are not simply units for producing goods, even broadly defined so as to include children; but are primarily useful as sites of human flourishing.[28] I argued that the family currency is thus not reciprocity, whether of money or services or sex, but unconditional love.[29] Thus much of the way I have taught about ongoing, as opposed to dissolving, families, while recognizing a role for government "at the margins" where protection of dependence is warranted, sees family units as something like greenhouses in colder climates, permeable by sunlight but largely immune from predations of climate, pests, or predators.[30] Some of the services "publicly" provided to families and children arguably mimic, more efficiently, choices most parents would make.[31] Of course, the privacy this implies can of course be criticized because of the "hidden" abuses that it makes possible.[32]

[25] See, e.g., Mary Ann Glendon, *The New Family and the New Property* (1981); Mary Ann Glendon, *Family Law Reform in the 1980s*, 44 LA. L. REV. 1553 (1984); and Alice Rossi, *A Communitarian Position on the Family*, 82 NAT'L CIVIC REV. 25 (1993).

[26] Milton C. Regan Jr., *Family Law and the Pursuit of Intimacy* (1993).

[27] Brinig, *supra* note 2 (Status, Contract, and Covenant).

[28] See, e.g., Stolzenberg, *supra* note 5, at 2051; Gregory S. Alexander & Eduardo M. Peñalver, *An Introduction to Property Theory* 80–101 (2012); Milton C. Regan, *Law, Marriage, and Intimate Commitment*, 9 VA. J. SOC. POL'Y & L. 116, 123, 143 (2001).

[29] Catharine Beecher wrote in the nineteenth century, "Now the family state is instituted to educate our race to the Christian character . . . to train the young to be followers of Christ, Woman is its chief minister, and the work to be done is the most difficult of all. . . ." Catharine Beecher, *Woman's Profession as Mother and Educator with Views in Opposition to Woman Suffrage* 175 (1872). Compare Stolzenberg, *supra* note 5, at 2038–2039 ("Not only do they leave untouched the current system of privatizing dependency, under which many individuals lack the material resources necessary to life, but they also fail to challenge choice logic, which can corrode affective ties.").

[30] See also Elizabeth S. Scott & Robert E. Scott, *Parents as Fiduciaries*, 81 VA. L. REV. 2401 (1995). For marriage, the governance the Scotts envision is largely through social norms. See Scott & Scott, *Marriage as Relational Contract*, *supra* note 22. Stolzenberg, *supra* note 5, at 1991 claims that rather than freedom to pursue chosen relationships, autonomy "increasingly grounds claims that individuals should also be free to choose their family obligations—and, by extension, to avoid family obligations that they did not 'choose' ex ante." Marriage, as opposed to cohabitation, as well as formal contract demonstrate such a choice. *Id.* at 2002.

[31] Gary S. Becker & Kevin M. Murphy, *The Family and the State*, 31 J.L. & ECON. 1 (1988) (public education and Social Security).

[32] See, e.g., Jana C. Singer, *The Privatization of Family Law*, 1992 WIS. L. REV. 1443, 1445. Both the "me too" movement and the abuses by those in religious authority justifiably strike against any claims either that this is so unlikely to occur that "piercing the veil" isn't worth the harm, see, e.g., State v. Rhodes, 61 N.C. 253 (1868), or that the abusers have a privilege created either by a duty to discipline (Prov. 21:21) or by contract ("[T]he husband cannot be guilty of a rape committed by himself upon his lawful wife for by their mutual matrimonial consent and contract the wife hath given up herself in this kind unto her husband which she cannot retract." Sir Matthew Hale, *Pleas of the Crown* 629 (1847)).

While marriage is "intimate to the degree of being sacred,"[33] leaving family relations at the mercy of laissez-faire simply does not work despite contemporary urgings to the contrary.[34] As more than one writer has noted, modern marriage, for example, does not have a unifying theory; it "lacks any convincing narrative about what marriage is."[35] While of course legislatures are free to, for example, enact more- or less-restrictive divorce laws or vary the age at which couples can validly enter marriage, recognize the contracting rights of married women, or even decide whether premarital contracts may regulate the default "terms" of the marital status, the core of what law recognizes as marriage has remained the same for hundreds, if not thousands, of years.[36]

Martha Fineman, now of Emory Law School, has written for years about dependency, claiming that there is both inevitable dependency, for the very young and very old, and derivative dependency, for those who care for those inevitably vulnerable.[37] Unlike marriage, these caregiving functions are permanent. She believes that adult relationships, including marriage, are inherently transitory as well as being hierarchical, and so she would entirely scrap the privileging of marriage, replacing it with community support for both types of dependent people (the "caregiving dyad"). She would also do away with traditional custody rules, resting decisions about parenting after separation upon the parent (who could be either mother or father) who has played the nurturing role (that is, who is the caregiver). While this program obviously solves some of the problems seen by Stolzenberg with the privatization of support, it is both politically unfeasible[38] and neglects the children's best interests, which are generally best served by meaningful relationships with both parents.[39]

---

[33]   Griswold v. Connecticut, 381 U.S. 479, 486 (1965).

[34]   Jennifer Roback Morse, *Love and Economics: Why the Laissez-Faire Family Doesn't Work* (1998). See also Jean Bethke Eshtain, *Public Man, Private Woman: Women in Social and Political Thought* 123, 326–327 (1981).

[35]   Patrick Parkinson, *Can Marriage Survive Secularization?*, 2016 ILL. L. REV. 1749, 1749 (Professor at University of Sydney). In Australia, the Supreme Court recognized that "the status of marriage, the social institution which that status reflects, and the rights and obligations which attach to that status never have been, and are not now, immutable." Commonwealth v. Australian Capital Territory, (2013) 250 CLR 441, 456. In her new *Obligation and Commitment in Family Law* (2018), British Professor Gillian Douglas works out the problems of enforcing obligations between people linked together by love in terms of commitment.

[36]   This sounds a great deal like the pragmatic and contingent laws discussed by John Goldberg in his introduction to the New Private Law Symposium, John C.P. Goldberg, *Introduction: Pragmatism and Private Law*, 125 HARV. L. REV. 1640 (2012).

[37]   Martha Albertson Fineman, *The Neutered Mother, The Sexual Family and Other Twentieth Century Tragedies* (1995). See also Martha Albertson Fineman, *Masking Dependency: The Political Role of Family Rhetoric*, 81 VA. L. REV. 2181 (1995). She, in *The Autonomy Myth: A Theory of Dependency* 33 (2004), as well as many other feminist writers, is critical of the "insufficient recognition of a public responsibility to support families' efforts." Linda C. McClain, *The Place of Families: Fostering Capacity, Equality, and Responsibility* at 5 (2006). See also Deborah Dinner, *The Divorce Bargain: The Fathers' Rights Movement and Family Inequalities*, 102 VA. L REV. 7, 84; Maxine Eichner, *The Privatized American Family*, 93 NOTRE DAME L. REV. 213, 215–216 (2017); Stolzenberg, *supra* note 5, at 2019.

[38]   See, e.g., Lloyd R. Cohen, *Rhetoric, the Unnatural Family, and Women's Work*, 81 VA. L. REV. 2275, 2288–2289 (1995).

[39]   See, e.g., Eleanor Willemsen & Michael Willemsen, *Symposium, A Review of Martha Fineman's the Neutered Mother, the Sexual Family, and Other Twentieth Century Tragedies: She Threw Out the Baby with the Old Feminism*, 36 SANTA CLARA L. REV. 477, 480 (1996).

Stolzenberg maintains that while courts recognize dependency in the context of children, they ignore it in the case of dependent adults, vindicating only autonomy claims. To secure rights to property acquired during relationships, cohabitants must either ceremonially marry or contract with some degree of specificity.[40] Stolzenberg rejects equitable remedies championed by other scholars as a "middle-of-the-road approach" because equity fails either to satisfy calls for greater family freedom or to effectively provide for the poorer partner.[41] Even though divorce severs most marital obligations, many states require spouses divorcing insane partners to continue their support obligations.[42]

Strangely, perhaps, some of the most powerful language about the family's connection to community can be found in same-sex marriage cases. For example, in *Goodridge v. Massachusetts Dep't of Public Health*, the court noted:

> Without the right to marry—or more properly, the right to choose to marry—one is excluded from the full range of human experience and denied full protection of the laws for one's "avowed commitment to an intimate and lasting human relationship." Because civil marriage is central to the lives of individuals and the welfare of the community, our laws assiduously protect the individual's right to marry against undue government incursion. Laws may not "interfere directly and substantially with the right to marry."[43]

Similarly, in *Obergefell v. Hodges*, the U.S Supreme Court noted not only the benefits accorded by the states to married couples but also the stability and increased status a legal relationship confers.

> There is no difference between same- and opposite-sex couples with respect to this principle. Yet by virtue of their exclusion from that institution, same-sex couples are denied the constellation of benefits that the states have linked to marriage. This harm results in more than just material burdens. Same-sex couples are consigned to an instability many opposite-sex couples would deem intolerable in their own lives. As the state itself makes marriage all the more precious by the significance it attaches to it, exclusion from that status has the effect of teaching that gays and lesbians are unequal in important respects. It demeans gays and lesbians for the state to lock them out of a central institution of the nation's society. Same-sex couples, too, may aspire to the transcendent purposes of marriage and seek fulfillment in its highest meaning.[44]

---

[40] *Id.* at 2019–20.

[41] *Id.* at 2029 (discussing, inter alia, Hanoch Dagan, *The Law and Ethics of Restitution* 165–167; Henry E. Smith, "Property, Equity, and the Rule of Law," in *Private Law and the Rule of Law* 224, 225 (Lisa M. Austin & Dennis Klimchuck eds., 2014)).

[42] See, e.g., Ark. Code Ann. § 9-12-301 (B)(i)(2017); Cal. Fam. Code 2313; Kan. Stat. Ann. 60-1601 (b); Nev. Rev. Stat. § 125.010 (1).

[43] 798 N.E.2d 941, 957 (Mass. 2003) (citations omitted).

[44] 576 U.S. ___ (2015); Slip opinion at 17.

IV. IS THE FAMILY LAW OF THE UNITED STATES DISTINCTIVE?

There are several anomalies to the prevailing position on family in the United States compared to the rest of the modern world. One is that while human rights (of children) stand at the centerpiece of much of the world's ideas about family law,[45] the United States alone has not ratified the U.N. Convention on the Rights of the Child. Instead, the law of parent and child is based on parents' rights.[46] The second, also related to parental duties, is that compared to most other Western countries, the United States provides little public support for maintenance, childcare, and parental leaves.[47] These all continue to be largely privatized, though the federal government requires through Social Security legislation that child support amounts be set through statewide guide-lines and provides for federal help with child support enforcement. While all law relating to children is supposed to be in their best interests, wide latitude is given to parents in providing for them.[48]

In some parts of Western Europe, Australia, and Canada, mere "living together" can generate duties and obligations as well as privileges that equate, or nearly equate, to those associated with marriage.[49] However, in the United States, with the exception of Washington State (on dissolution),[50] cohabiting unmarried couples never enjoy precisely the same privileges and protections as do married couples. Despite the typical U.S. penchant for individuality, independence, and autonomy, one must at least enter into a state-licensed "domestic partnership" or what remains of "civil union" postmarriage equality to claim the more than a thousand benefits available to married under federal law[51] and still more under the various state laws.[52] This remains true in Britain as well.[53]

[45] See, e.g., Parkinson, *supra* note 35, at 1751.
[46] Troxel v. Granville, 530 U.S. 57, 66 (2000).
[47] See Barbara Bennett Woodhouse, *A World Fit for Children Is a World Fit for Everyone: Ecogenerism, Feminism, and Vulnerability*, 46 HOUSTON L. REV. 817, 833–838 (2009).
[48] See Elizabeth S. Scott & Robert E. Scott, *Parents as Fiduciaries*, 81 VA. L. REV. 2401 (1995) (arguing that except when the parents grossly violate these duties, they are allowed to choose how to exercise them as a reward for the many and varied costs of their care).
[49] See Bala, *supra* note 20, at 27: "Except for in Quebec, for many, but not all legal purposes, those who live together without marrying will, after a period of cohabitation, acquire the rights and obligations of those who choose to marry." In the Victoria and Queensland provinces of Australia, couples can merely register their relationship. Registered Relationships Act 2008 (Victoria) or Registered Relationships Act (2001) (Queensland). But for purposes of federal benefits, they will be treated as de facto married after two years. Parkinson, *supra* note 35, nn.76–78.
[50] Connell v. Francisco, 898 P.2d 831, 835–836 (Wash. 1995).
[51] See United States v. Windsor, 133 S. Ct. 2690–2691.
[52] See, e.g., Goodridge v. Massachusetts Dept. Pub. Health, 400 Mass. 309, 321, 798 N.E.2d 941 (2003).
[53] Ruth Deech, *Getting Married*, 4 INT'L J. JURIS. FAM. 1 (2013).

While in many ways the tendency toward a "clean break"[54] upon dissolution of marriage has made relationships less permanent,[55] and cohabitation is still less stable than marriage,[56] the opposite has been true for parent-child relationships. Single mothers who did not place their children for adoption historically were expected to raise them on their own.[57] Most parents on divorce would leave custody with primary caretaker mothers, with noncustodial fathers "visiting" children only every other weekend and paying support. In many cases, contact with fathers (and sometimes the support as well) vanished over time,[58] especially if either parent remarried. The trend

[54] See, e.g., Pelech v. Pelech, (1987) 7 RFL (3d) 225, 268, 272 (Supreme Ct. Canada). For commentators, see Anne L. Alstott, *Neoliberalism in U.S. Family Law: Negative Liberty and Laissez-Faire Markets in the Minimal State*, 77 LAW & CONTEMP. PROBS. 25, 35; Elizabeth S. Scott, *Rehabilitating Liberalism in Modern Divorce Law*, 1994 UTAH L. REV. 687, 704; Dinner, *supra* note 37, at 139–140.

[55] The institution of marriage, according to Trebilcock and Keshvani, *supra* note 16, at 537–538, no longer has its basis in a "partnership for life" model, but instead "focuses upon a union favoring equality of the partners and individual responsibility, 'allowing men and women to define their own roles within marriage' and to determine the consequences of marriage breakdown." In Canada, for example, only 10.2 percent of the cases resulted in an award of spousal support. See L.D. Bertrand et al., Phase 2 of the Survey of Child Support Awards: Final Report, Department of Justice Canada, Mar. 2005, available at http://www.crilf.ca/Documents/Survey%20of%20Child%20Support%20Awards%20-%20Final%20Report%20-%20Jan%202005.pdf (at 13 sec. 3). See also Lyudmila Woman, *Alimony Demographics*, 20 J. CONTEMP. LEGAL ISS. 109 (2001–2012) (15 percent in 1985, citing U.S. Bureau of the Census, Current Population Reports, Series O-23, No. 54, Child Support and Alimony: 1985 (Supplemental Report), at 14 (issued Mar. 1989)).

[56] See Marriage and Cohabitation in the United States: A Statistical Portrait Based on Cycle 6 (2002) of the National Survey of Family Growth. Series 23, Number 28 (PHS) 2010–1980, Feb. 2010. This is also true in other OECD countries. K.E. Kiernan, "Cohabitation and Divorce across Nations and Generations," in *The Potential for Change across Lives and Generations: Multidisciplinary Perspectives* (P. Lindsay Chase-Lansdale, Kathleen E. Kiernan, & Ruth J. Friedman eds., 2004). Also available as CASEpaper (65), http://sticerd.lse.ac.uk/Case/. In the United States, while the gross divorce rate peaked in 1981 and has declined since to predivorce reform levels, the number of marriages has decreased. See Betsey Stevenson & Justin Wolfers, *Marriage and Divorce: Changes and their Driving Forces*, NBER Working Paper No. 12944 (2007). Marriage has become increasingly rare for the lowest third in socioeconomic terms, divorce very common in the middle third, and quite uncommon in the highest third. Carbone and Cahn, *Triple System*, *supra* note 10. A high (and sometimes still increasing) divorce rate is common internationally. For Canada, see Statistics Canada, Divorces 2001–2002 (Ottawa, 2004). See OECD Family Database, http://www.oecd.org/els/family/database.htm & Chart SF3.1.CC (updated July 25, 2018). (Crude divorce rate, 1970, 1995, and 2016 or latest available year) (showing increases for 12/33 OECD countries, while falling in 18, including the United States).

[57] While the current Indiana Code allows all fathers visitation under parenting guidelines, custody, both physical and legal, is always awarded to fit unmarried mothers unless there is an agreement to the contrary. See IND. CODE § 31-14-13-1(1) (LexisNexis 2010). See generally Marcia J. Carlson, Sara S. McLanahan, & Jeanne Brooks-Gunn, *Coparenting and Nonresident Fathers' Involvement with Young Children After a Nonmarital Birth*, 45 DEMOGRAPHY 461 (2008). For an historical analysis, see Bala, *supra* note 20, at 22.

[58] See, e.g., Judith A. Seltzer, *Relationships Between Fathers and Children Who Live Apart: The Father's Role After Separation*, 53 J. MARRIAGE & FAM. 79 (1991); E. Mavis Hetherington, Martha Cox, & Roger Cox, *Divorced Fathers*, 25 THE FAMILY COORDINATOR 417 (1976). This was still more true of unmarried fathers.

today is for fathers to be more involved with children while the parents live together and to have a much greater role after a split—frequently equal decision-making and in a substantial number of cases shared parenting.[59] The co-parenting relationship therefore continues, at least aspirationally, even though the marital bond does not. Property acquired during the marriage is almost always shared equally at divorce, reflecting an equality between the spouses, whether or not their market earnings are equal.[60] And biological fathers are almost always responsible for child support, even if parenthood is involuntary.[61]

[59] See, e.g., Brinig, *Result Inequality, supra* note 14, at 487 & n.68 for some examples of U.S. state practices. While Australia has sported a fairly typical no-fault divorce system for many years, it has made waves with its unique procedures: a national system of family centers, as well as a mediation culture derived from indigenous traditions in which children's voices are clearly heard. Fam. Law Act (Australia) 1975 §§ 69cc(3)9a) and 69CD(2), http://www.familytransitions.com.au/Family_Transitions/Family_Transitions_files/Post%20Separation%20parenting%20arrangements%20and%20developmental%20outcomes%20for%20children%20 percent26 percent2oinfants%202010.pdf. However, when these contradict the views of litigating parents, the courts may outweigh their preferences. Bondelmonte v. Bondelmonte, [2017] HCA 8, (2016) 259 CLR 662 (involving children who wished to live in New York with relocating father).

Further, infant overnights and shared parenting has been strongly criticized by some psychologists. Jennifer McIntosh et al., Post Separation Parenting Arrangements: Outcomes for Infants and Children, Sydney, Australia: Australian Government, 2010, available at http://www.familytransitions.com.au/Family_Transitions/Family_Transitions_files/Post%20Separation%20parenting%20arrangements%20and%20developmental%20outcomes%20for%20children%20 percent26 percent2oinfants%202010.pdf; R. Emery, *Renegotiating Family Relationships*, at 118–119 (2012); Samantha Tornello et al., *Overnight Custody Arrangements, Attachment, and Adjustment Among Very Young Children*, 75 J. MARRIAGE & FAM. 871 (2013). See generally Marcia Kline Pruett, Jennifer E. McIntosh, & Joan B. Kelly, *Parental Separation and Overnight Care of Young Children, Part I: Consensus Through Theoretical and Empirical Integration*, 52 FAM. CT. REV. 240 (2014).

[60] See, e.g., Margaret F. Brinig, *Marital Property: An American Perspective, International Survey of Family Law* 509 (Bill Atkin ed., 2016). See also Martha Albertson Fineman, *The Illusion of Equality: The Rhetoric and Reality of Divorce Reform* (1991); for Britain and more generally about gender inequality, see Kat Banyard, *Equality Illusion: The Truth about Women and Men Today* (2010). For a defense of rule equality, see Herma Hill Kay, *Equality and Difference: A Perspective on No-Fault Divorce and Its Aftermath*, 565 U. CINN. L. REV. 1 (1987); Herma Hill Kay, *An Appraisal of California's No-Fault Divorce Law*, 75 CAL. L. REV. 291, 313 (1987). For a (twenty-year-old) summary of the debate, see Joan Williams, *Do Women Need Special Treatment?: Do Feminists Need Equality?*, 9 CONT. LEGAL ISS. 279 (1998). Outside law, political scientist Jean Bethke Eshtain worried about the more androgynous forms of equality and the overdependence on public support. *Antigone's Daughters: Reflections on Female Identity, and the State*, 2 DEMOCRACY 46 (1982).

[61] Stolzenberg, *supra* note 5, at 2008. In this way paternity logic becomes rather like an assumption of the risk doctrine, for, in her terminology, "partners [are] declared to have assumed the risk of procreation." While parental intent (autonomy) is critical in the context of assisted reproduction, surrogacy, same-sex and step-parenting, it is a one-way ratchet that needs to dovetail with privatizing dependency. Stolzenberg, *supra* note 5, at 2014. That is, once assumed, it cannot be repudiated.

V. The Complexities of Family Law

Besides always having a public, statutory side, family law is uniquely interdisciplinary. This is most obvious in custody evaluations[62] and child welfare proceedings where testimony from mental health or social work professionals helps answer what is in the best interest of the child.[63] Interdisciplinarity has increasingly become commonplace in U.S. Supreme Court opinions ranging from the same-sex marriage case of *Obergefell v. Hodges*[64] to the Amish parents' clash with compulsory public education of teenagers of *Wisconsin v. Yoder*.[65]

Family law also integrates materials from a number of the broad areas considered in the New Private Law: contracts, torts, property, corporate, and fiduciary law. In addition, criminal law, civil procedure, administrative law, dispute resolution, and constitutional law are all part of a typical family law course. It therefore stands at the intersection of public and private, interdisciplinarity and legal doctrine, and various substantive fields. Finally, as has already been mentioned, it has at minimum roots in natural law and religion[66] more than any other field with the possible exception of equity.[67] And that is where most discussions of covenant begin.

As I have written, families can be thought of in three stages, which manifest covenant in three discrete ways. The first, or creation change involves courtship or the choice to bear or adopt a child (though this may be a negative decision where the pregnancy is unintended) or when couples drift into a cohabiting relationship.[68] In this stage, some, or even primary, analogies can properly be made to contract.

In the second stage, while a family (covenant) relationship exists, whether between spouses or between parent and child, I have argued that the law should discard any language of exchange[69] and use that of covenant, that is, the language of love and gift.

---

[62] See, e.g., Forrest S. Mosten & Lara Traum, *Interdisciplinary Teamwork in Family Law Practice*, 56 Fam. Ct. Rev. 437 (2018). For a more critical discussion, see Sarah H. Ramsey and Robert F. Kelly, *Social Science Knowledge in Family Law Cases: Judicial Gate-keeping in The Daubert Era*, 59 U. Miami L. Rev. 1 (2004).

[63] See also Judy Cashmore & Patrick Parkinson, *The Use and Abuse of Social Science Research Evidence in Children's Cases*, 20 Psych., Pub. Pol'y & L. 239 (2014) (Australia).

[64] Obergefell v. Hodges, 576 U.S. ___ (2015). The opinion featured psychological evidence about same-sex parenting and poll evidence of growing acceptance of the concept of same-sex marriage.

[65] Wisconsin v. Jonas Yoder, 406 U.S. 205 (1972) (including sociological evidence on the Amish vocational education of teenagers and on their way of life).

[66] For a discussion, see Witte & Nichols, *supra* note 8, at 603–606, discussing the common "goods" of marriage of the three religions of the Book and how covenant and contract parts of marriage are reflected in each.

[67] Both family law cases and other equitable matters were originally heard in ecclesiastical courts.

[68] Brinig, *From Contract to Covenant, supra* note 2.

[69] Gary L. Hansen, *Moral Reasoning and the Marital Exchange Relationship*, 131 J. Soc. Psych. 71 (1991).

Thus, unlike some feminists,[70] I see little harm from courts' reluctance to enforce marital homemaking contracts.[71] Further, I endorse supporting marriage over cohabitation because I see the former as a covenant-like relationship, unlike the latter.[72] I support extending paternal leave and other family support policies that will encourage fathers to feel free to be as involved as desired with their children, thus supporting their permanent and unconditional relationships with them.[73]

In the third stage, when the covenant relationship is legally severed by dissolution of a marriage or emancipation of a child, I believe that enough of the relationship remains to speak in terms of franchise.[74] This language, which implies continuing regard, may provide a more satisfactory way of thinking about the relationships of separated or divorced co-parents or of parents and their grown children. While clearly there are divorced couples who seem to be able to make completely "clean breaks" (though not many of these share children)[75] as well as a small percentage that will continue to litigate even to the point of financial ruin (and certainly of harm to their children), there is still enough tying most together for law to encourage and foster healthy relationships. A punitive child support enforcement regime will not do this, particularly for indigent parents.[76] Nor will a custody system that has become so politicized that it encourages the lack of agreement on common values.[77] Reported grandparent visitation cases are

[70] Katharine Silbaugh, *Marriage Contracts and the Family Economy*, 93 Nw. L. Rev. 65 (1998); and Katharine Silbaugh, *Turning Labor into Love: Housework and the Law*, 91 Nw. U. L. Rev. 1 (1996); Lenore J. Weitzman, *Legal Regulation of Marriage: Tradition and Change: A Proposal for Individual Contracts and Contracts in Lieu of Marriage*, 62 Cal. L. Rev. 1169 (1974).

[71] See Margaret F. Brinig & Steven L. Nock, "Weak Men and Disorderly Women: Divorce and the Division of Labor," in *The Law and Economics of Marriage and Divorce* (Antony Dnes and Robert Rowthorn eds., 2002).

[72] Brinig, *From Contract to Covenant*, supra note 2; Brinig, *Family, Law and Community*, supra note 2; and Brinig, *Marry Me Bill: Should Cohabitation Be the (Legal) Default Option?*, 64 La. L. Rev. 403 (2004).

[73] These may require special incentives, as paternal leaves have in Scandinavian countries that have tried them. See, e.g., Linda Haas & Tina Rostgaard, *Fathers' Rights to Paid Parental Leave in the Nordic Countries: Consequences for the Gendered Division of Leave*, 14 Community, Work & Fam. 177 (2011).

[74] See also Regan, *Pursuit of Intimacy*, supra note 26, at 96, writing that status "proclaims that some obligations may remain even when a partner has decided to leave." The self is not defined in terms of choice, but in terms of relationship to others. *Id.* at 102.

[75] For example, legally speaking, there was at least one postdivorce motion in 35 percent of the 463 Arizona divorce cases begun in 2008 in which fathers paid child support. For more about these cases, see Brinig, *Result Inequality*, supra note 14.

[76] Margaret F. Brinig & Marsha Garrison, *Getting Blood from Stones: Results and Policy Implications of an Empirical Investigation of Child Support Practice in St. Joseph County, Indiana Paternity Actions*, 56 Fam. Ct. Rev. (Oct. 2018).

[77] See Pruett, McIntosh, & Kelly, supra note 61; Elizabeth S. Scott & Robert E. Emery, *Gender Politics and Child Custody: The Puzzling Persistence of the Best Interest Standard*, 77 Law & Contemp. Probs. 69 (2014).

also legion,[78] suggesting that it would be far preferable to work out these disputes privately rather than in court. The legal problem is well voiced by Emily Buss:

> In application, however, the middle ground is standardless, offering no clear, principled basis on which to distinguish appropriate from inappropriate state interference. As a result, courts are left to make family law policy absent the constraints of either meaningful standards or the democratic process, and children can be expected to suffer a triple loss: they lose the individualized expertise of their parents and the community-wide expertise of democratic lawmaking, and in their place they gain the additional harm associated with this ongoing constitutional litigation.[79]

Taken together, the New Private Law theorists have successfully set forth unifying theories that account for, better explain, and systematize many fields of law. This chapter, with its new strand of covenant, adds to the body of work. Family law presents a field where, although (and in some ways because) the field deals with some of the most private aspects of life, concepts completely appropriate with transactions of various kinds fall short. Explaining trust, intimacy, and flourishing requires a new vocabulary of love and gift and a way of thinking often persisting over more than one generation.

---

[78] While states all have statutes permitting visitation at least on some occasions (most often upon divorce or the death of the grandparents' child), the Supreme Court case of *Troxel v. Granville*, 530 U.S. 57 (2000), seems to have popularized litigation on both grandparents' and parents' part.

[79] Emily Buss, *Adrift in the Middle: Parental Rights after* Troxel v. Granville, 2000 SUP. CT. REV. 279, 302.

CHAPTER 24

···

FALSE ADVERTISING
LAW

···

GREGORY KLASS

ONE might reasonably wonder why a chapter on false advertising law appears in a volume on private law theory. In the United States false advertising law lives in statutes and regulations; it is enforced by federal agencies and state attorneys general; and its rules can seem designed more to promote consumer welfare and market efficiency than to enforce interpersonal obligations or compensate for wrongful losses. If one views the divide between public and private law as a fixed border between independent regions, false advertising law appears to fall in the domain of public law.

This chapter's working hypothesis is that that picture is a false one. Although it can be helpful to distinguish private from public law, the line between them is not so sharp. Laws that fall on the private side of the divide can be designed in light of purposes and principles commonly associated with public law, and vice versa. U.S. false advertising law provides an example. Despite the fact that it is commonly classified as public law, one can find in it structures, functions, and values commonly associated with private law. The structural features include horizontal duties, transfer remedies, private enforcement, and judge-made rules. These features are partly remnants of earlier private law causes of action. But as legislators and courts adapted those old actions to the new phenomenon of mass consumer marketing, they imposed on advertisers new types of obligations. Those obligations suggest, to use Henry Smith's term, an emergent ethics of false advertising.[1] Although it differs from its common law ancestors, false advertising law can be understood within the private law framework.[2]

False advertising law is unusual in that it imposes on advertisers one duty owed to two distinct categories of persons.[3] The duty not to engage in deceptive advertising is owed

---

[1] Henry E. Smith, this volume.

[2] For comparable analysis of a neighboring field, see Mark P. McKenna, *The Normative Foundations of Trademark Law*, 82 NOTRE DAME L. REV. 1839 (2007).

[3] Or depending on how one individuates duties, two duties with the same content owed to different persons.

both to consumers, who might be deceived by an advertisement, and to honest competitors, who might lose sales as a result of consumer deception.

The content of the duty differs from false advertising law's common law ancestors. With respect to consumers, common law duties not to lie or negligently make false statements are replaced by the responsibility not to cause consumers to hold false beliefs. Inquiries into meaning and truth thus give way to questions about cause and effect. With respect to competitors, common law duties not to defame are replaced by a duty to adhere to commonly recognized rules of the marketplace. The wrong of calumny is supplanted by the wrong of cheating. Like other areas of private law, there are ethical aspects to these legal obligations. But they differ from those of false advertising law's common law ancestors.

This chapter argues also that although an advertiser's duties can be understood in private law terms, advertising's one-to-many structure poses practical challenges to traditional private law mechanisms and the values sometimes associated with them. Despite the fact that U.S. false advertising law includes backward-looking consumer remedies, the small sums at stake, the difficulty of proving causation and individual loss, and the costs of distributing awards make it difficult to fully compensate consumer victims. For some of the same reasons, consumers often do not exercise their power to sue false advertisers. Finally, although the relevant statutes are drafted to invite judges to develop something like a common law of false advertising, courts of general jurisdiction are ill-equipped to make many of the factual determinations false advertising law requires.

Section I provides a brief introduction to U.S. false advertising law and identifies several structural features associated with the private law. Section II analyzes false advertising law's consumer-oriented duties. Section III discusses an advertiser's duties to its competitors. Section IV examines practical impediments to consumer lawsuits, consumer-oriented remedies, and adjudicative resolution of false advertising claims. These impediments suggest often unnoticed factual predicates of the traditional private law framework.

I. Background

A. False Advertising Law in the United States

False advertising law in the United States is an assemblage. Its primary components are Section 5 of the Federal Trade Commission Act, Section 43(a) of the Lanham Act, and state consumer protection and false advertising statutes. This section provides an overview of each.

When enacted in 1914, Section 5 the Federal Trade Commission (FTC) Act focused not on consumer protection but on "unfair methods of competition in commerce."[4] Early judicial decisions on the scope of Section 5 were mixed. Some courts read it as

---

[4] Act to Create the Federal Trade Commission, Pub. L. No. 203, ch. 311, § 5, 38 Stat. 717, 719 (1914).

limited to already recognized forms of unfair competition, or to require evidence of harm to competitors.[5] Others suggested that practices that were deceptive or unfair to consumers fell within Section 5's ambit because they could be assumed to harm honest and upstanding competitors.[6] In 1938, Congress codified and extended the broader readings by amending Section 5 to additionally prohibit "unfair or deceptive acts or practices."[7] The House Report explained that the purpose of the new language was to "prevent such acts or practices which injuriously affect the general public as well as those which are unfair to competitors."[8] The 1938 amendment also added a new Section 12 expressly providing that false advertising qualifies as an unfair and deceptive practice.[9]

The FTC Act does not create a private right of action but vests sole enforcement authority in the Federal Trade Commission. In its present form, the Act provides a variety of remedies. The FTC can issue cease-and-desist orders, seek injunctive relief via the courts, and ask for civil penalties.[10] The Act also provides for "such relief as the court finds necessary to redress injury to consumers or other persons . . . resulting from [a] rule violation."[11] That relief can include "rescission or reformation of contracts, the refund of money or return of property, the payment of damages, and public notification respecting the rule violation or the unfair or deceptive act or practice."[12]

The other major federal false advertising statute is the Lanham Act, first enacted in 1946. The Lanham Act is primarily a federal trademark law, protecting both registered and unregistered marks. Like the FTC Act, the Lanham Act originally focused on unfair competition, not consumer protection. As enacted, however, Section 43(a) prohibited the use of any "false designation of origin, or any false description or representation" of goods or services.[13] As with Section 5 of the original FTC Act, courts disagreed on the scope of Section 43(a). Some circuits adopted narrow readings, emphasizing the connection to the common law tort of passing off one's own products as those of another.[14] Others read "any false description or representation" in Section 43(a) to capture other forms of false advertising.[15] In 1988 Congress amended

---

[5] See, e.g., FTC v. Gratz, 253 U.S. 421, 427–429 (1920), *overruled by* FTC v. Brown Shoe Co., 384 U.S. 316 (1966); FTC v. Raladam Co., 283 U.S. 643, 651 (1931).

[6] See, e.g., FTC v. Winsted Co., 258 U.S. 483, 493 (1922); FTC v. R.F. Keppel & Bro., 291 U.S. 304, 312–313 (1934).

[7] Act to Amend the Act Creating the Federal Trade Commission, Pub. L. No. 75-447, ch. 49, § 3, 52 Stat. 111, 111 (1938) (codified as amended at 15 U.S.C. § 45).

[8] H.R. Rep. No. 1613, 75th Cong., 1st Sess., 3 (1937); see also FTC v. Sperry & Hutchinson Co., 405 U.S. 233, 244 (1972) (discussing legislative history of the FTC Act).

[9] *Supra* note 7, at § 4, 52 Stat. at 114–115 (codified as amended at 15 U.S.C. § 52).

[10] 15 U.S.C. §§ 45(b), 45(m)(1)(A), 54(a).   [11] 15 U.S.C. § 57b(b).   [12] *Id.*

[13] Act of July 5, 1946 (Lanham Act), Pub. L. 79-489, ch. 540, § 43(a), 60 Stat. 427, 441 (codified as amended at 15 U.S.C. §§ 1051–1127).

[14] E.g., Clamp-All Corp. v. Cast Iron Soil Pipe Inst., 851 F.2d 478, 491 (1st Cir. 1988); Fur Info. & Fashion Council, Inc. v. E.F. Timme & Son, Inc., 501 F.2d 1048, 1051 (2d Cir. 1974).

[15] E.g., U-Haul International, Inc. v. Jartran, Inc., 681 F.2d 1159, 1161–1162 (9th Cir. 1982); L'Aiglon Apparel v. Lana Lobell, Inc., 214 F.2d 649, 651 (3d Cir. 1954).

the Lanham Act to conform to the broader readings by adding Section 43(a)(1)(B), which prohibits

> any word, term, name, symbol, or device, or any combination thereof, or any false designation of origin, false or misleading description of fact, or false or misleading representation of fact, which . . . in commercial advertising or promotion, misrepresents the nature, characteristics, qualities, or geographic origin of his or her or another person's goods, services, or commercial activities.[16]

Courts have uniformly read this language to prohibit any advertising that actually deceives or has the tendency to deceive a substantial portion of the audience as to a material fact.[17]

Keeping with its origins in unfair competition law, courts have continued to hold that the Lanham Act grants standing only to competitors.[18] Consumers do not have a federal right of action against false advertisers. The Lanham Act offers competitor-plaintiffs a range of remedies, including damages in the amount of lost sales or the defendant's profits, negative injunctions against the deceptive behavior, and occasionally an order that the defendant engage in corrective advertising.[19]

If consumers wish to sue a false advertiser, they must turn to state consumer protection laws. Many of these laws were enacted in the late 1960s and early 70s, and all were designed to protect consumers. Because the statutes commonly adopt the "unfair and deceptive acts and practices" language of the FTC Act, they are often referred to as "UDAP" statutes. In addition to UDAP statutes, some states also have laws that specifically address false advertising.[20] State statutes commonly provide for enforcement both by state attorneys general and consumer lawsuits.[21] Remedies to consumers generally include compensatory damages, rescission, and restitution. Many statutes also provide for minimum per-violation awards, damage multipliers, punitive damages, and attorney's fees.[22]

B. Private Law Elements in False Advertising Law

With this basic description of U.S. false advertising law, I now turn to its private-law aspects. The best definition of "private law" depends on a theorist's interests. Like Thomas Merrill, I employ a catholic, multifactor conception.[23] Laws traditionally

---

[16] Trademark Law Revision Act of 1988, Pub. L. No. 100-667, § 132, 102 Stat. 3946 (codified as amended at 15 U.S.C. § 1125(a)(1)(B)).

[17] See, e.g., Scotts Co. v. United Indus. Corp., 315 F.3d 264, 272 (4th Cir. 2002) (citing cases).

[18] See, e.g., Lexmark International, Inc. v. Static Control Components, Inc., 572 U.S. 118, 129 (2014). This despite the fact that the Lanham Act grants standing to "any person who believes that he or she is or is likely to be damaged by such act." 15 U.S.C. § 1125(a)(1).

[19] 15 U.S.C. §§ 1116(a), 1117(a).

[20] See, e.g., Cal. Bus. & Prof. Code § 17500 (2019); N.Y. Gen. Bus. L. § 350-a (2019).

[21] See Dee Pridgen & Richard M. Alderman, *Consumer Protection and the Law* §§ 6.2 & 7.1 (West 2018).

[22] *Id.* at § 6.1.   [23] Thomas W. Merrill, this volume.

understood as belonging to private law are characterized by four structural features: horizontal duties, private transfer remedies, private enforcement, and common law origins. Each appears in U.S. false advertising law. That fact does not in itself entail that false advertising law should be classified as part of the private law in any theoretically interesting sense—that it serves functions or embodies values characteristic of private law. But identifying relevant structural features is a start.

Laws categorized as private law establish horizontal duties: obligations persons owe to one another.[24] A duty is horizontal if its violation wrongs someone—a person to whom the duty was owed.[25] The private law does not include duties owed to the state,[26] such as the duty to pay taxes, or to no one, such as victimless crimes. Under U.S. false advertising law, the legal duty not to engage in deceptive advertising appears to be owed to two categories of persons: consumers and competitors.

A second characteristic of private law is that the legal response to a violation includes a transfer from the wrongdoer to the victim. That transfer might take the form of the payment of money, an injunction enforceable by the victim, or the transfer of a legal entitlement. U.S. false advertising law includes transfer remedies of these types. The Lanham Act provides competitors both injunctive and monetary relief. And the remedial measures found in the FTC Act and state UDAP statutes include transfers to consumer victims, often in the form of money damages. Both the FTC Act and UDAP statutes, however, include remedies not traditionally associated with the private law, such as fines, administrative orders, and injunctions granted state enforcement bodies.

The third design element is perhaps most familiar: private law puts the victim in charge of pursuing the remedy. The private law is a sphere of private enforcement. Here, too, U.S. false advertising law is partly private and partly public in structure. Both the Lanham Act and state UDAP statutes empower putative victims of false advertising—competitors and consumers respectively—to sue. The FTC Act and state UDAP statutes, however, also provide for public enforcement.

Finally, private law is often viewed as belonging to the common law. Legislation at most makes changes around the edges, or codifies judge-made rules. Here false advertising law might appear to differ, as it is a creature of statutes and, to some extent, regulations issued by the FTC or state attorneys general. That said, like many other laws that address fraud and deception,[27] those statutes draw on common law concepts and are worded in ways that invite courts to fill in the details. This is especially true of the

---

[24] Private laws establish jural relations other than duties—powers, privileges, immunities, and so forth. When thinking about false advertising law, it is simpler to focus on duties.

[25] Or more precisely, the violation of a horizontal duty "involves an interference with one of a set of individual interests that are significant enough aspects of a person's well-being to warrant the imposition of a duty on others not to interfere with the interest in certain ways, notwithstanding the liberty restriction inherent in such a duty imposition." John C.P. Goldberg & Benjamin C. Zipursky, *Torts as Wrongs*, 88 TEX. L. REV. 917, 937 (2010). This fairly minimalist definition skips over several interesting nuances, such as whether a wrong should always be conceived as the violation of a right.

[26] Except insofar as the state acts in a private capacity, as when it enters into a contract.

[27] For example, the federal mail and wire fraud statutes, which prohibit "any scheme or artifice to defraud." 18 U.S.C. §§ 1341, 1343 (2019).

Lanham Act, which is enforced solely through private suits. Courts play an essential role in the elaboration of false advertising law.

The fact that U.S. false advertising law exhibits these structural features does not entail that false advertising law qualifies as private law in anything but the thinnest sense. If private law is an interesting theoretical category, it is because its structural features reflect distinctive functions or social values. To say that false advertising law displays features of the private law in a more interesting sense requires a theory of private law that ascribes to it distinctive purposes or principles.

That is not the project of this chapter. Instead, I approach the question from below. Sections II and III compare advertisers' horizontal duties to analogous or ancestral common law torts. Despite differences, the duties false advertising law imposes can be understood in ethical, nonconsequentialist terms familiar to the private law. Section IV then discusses challenges mass consumer advertising poses to the realization of values associated with transfer remedies, private enforcement, and the role of courts.

II. An Advertiser's Duties to Consumers

False advertising law imposes a duty on advertisers not to deceive consumers.[28] Insofar as the duty is owed consumers, the most similar torts are deceit and negligent misrepresentation, which also address harms deception causes the deceived—as distinguished, say, from defamation, which addresses harms to persons about whom false statements are made. The duty that false advertising law imposes on advertisers, however, is very different from those torts. This section advances two claims: that the differences are partly explained by the fact that our everyday interpretive practices and moral intuitions are not well-suited to the communications one finds in mass advertising; and that the duty false advertising law imposes on advertisers can nonetheless be understood as an ethical obligation.

There are three salient differences between an advertiser's legal duties and the duties imposed on a speaker by the torts of deceit and negligent misrepresentation. First, whereas the common law torts require proof that the defendant made a false statement of fact on which the plaintiff relied, false advertising law asks whether the advertisement caused in consumers a false belief. The first element of both deceit and negligent misrepresentation is that the defendant made a false statement of fact.[29] The falsehood might be express—a literal falsehood—or implied—as in the familiar doctrine of half-truths. In either case, truth is a defense to the tort. Truth is not always a defense in false advertising actions. Both the FTC Act and most state UDAP statutes prohibit not false statements but "deceptive acts and practices." And most courts have read the Lanham Act to sometimes

---

[28] There are shades of difference here between the FTC Act, the Lanham Act, and relevant state laws. But all are similar enough in approach to be treated together.

[29] See *Restatement (Second) of Torts* §§ 525, 552 (1977).

impose liability when consumers draw false inferences from an advertiser's true statements.[30] The ultimate question in most false advertising cases is not whether the advertisement was true or false but whether it deceived or was likely to deceive consumers.[31]

Second, whereas the torts of deceit or negligent misrepresentation require a showing that the plaintiff's reliance was justifiable or reasonable,[32] most false advertising laws have no justified-reliance requirement.[33] All that is required is that the advertisement caused or had a tendency to cause false beliefs in a substantial portion of the audience. Third, whereas the torts require a showing of fault, liability for false advertising is generally strict. Actual or probable deceptive effect is enough, whether or not the advertiser was or should have been aware of that effect. Taking the second and third points together, we might say that false advertising law expects less of consumers and more of advertisers than do the correlate torts.

What explains these differences?[34] The torts of deceit and negligent misrepresentation deploy our everyday interpretive abilities and moral sensibilities to draw a clear, if not always crisp, line between the permissible and the impermissible. A person commits one or the other tort when she intentionally, recklessly, or negligently says something false with the intent to cause a hearer to rely, the hearer does reasonably rely, and the hearer suffers a loss as a result. Our everyday interpretive abilities and moral sensibilities are less well-suited to the interpretation and evaluation of advertisements.[35] Ordinary

[30] See, e.g., Williams v. Gerber Products Co., 552 F.3d 934, 938–939 (9th Cir. 2008) (holding that the packaging words "Fruit Juice" juxtaposed alongside images of fruits like oranges, peaches, strawberries, and cherries could potentially suggest that those fruits or their juices are contained in the product, in violation of California's UDAP statute, which prohibited "not just advertisement that is false, but also advertisement which, although true . . . has a capacity . . . to deceive or confuse the public."); Am. Home Prod. Corp. v. Johnson & Johnson, 654 F. Supp. 568, 591 (S.D.N.Y. 1987) (holding that the literally true statement "hospitals recommend acetaminophen, the aspirin-free pain reliever in Anacin-3, more than any other pain reliever" violated the Lanham Act based on evidence that consumers mistakenly inferred that most hospitals recommended Anacin-3). A well-known outlier is Judge Easterbrook's opinion in Mead Johnson & Co. v. Abbott Laboratories, 201 F.3d 883 (7th Cir. 2000) (suggesting that the literal meaning of "1st Choice of Doctors" insulated advertiser from liability, even if evidence suggested that most consumers took away the message that the product was the choice of most doctors).
[31] This oversimplifies a bit. Courts have held that a literally false statement might violate false advertising laws without separate evidence of consumer deception, on the theory that a literal falsehood can be presumed deceptive.
[32] For more on how this element of the torts has shifted over time, see Mark P. Gergen, A Wrong Turn in the Law of Deceit, 106 GEO. L.J. 555 (2018).
[33] Some courts have read false advertising statutes to prohibit only advertisements likely to deceive a reasonable consumer. The requirement is not, however, uniform, and judicial understandings of reasonableness are often highly forgiving. See Seana Valentine Shiffrin, "Deceptive Advertising and Taking Responsibility for Others," in The Oxford Handbook of Food Ethics 470, 476–479 (Anne Barnhill et al. eds., 2018).
[34] I discuss the themes in this paragraph and the next in greater detail in Gregory Klass, Meaning, Purpose and Cause in the Law of Deception, 100 GEO. L.J. 449 (2012). See also Shiffrin, supra note 33, at 474 n.12.
[35] Rebecca Tushnet has pushed back against such claims and argued that courts and juries are more capable of recognizing implicit and deceptive messages than current Lanham Act jurisprudence recognizes. Rebecca Tushnet, Running the Gamut from A to B: Federal Trademark and False Advertising Law, 159 U. PA. L. REV. 1305, 1318–1327, 1337–1344 (2011).

rules of linguistic interpretation presuppose conversation, shared context, and a degree of cooperation. Advertisements are not conversations, but messages broadcast to a large, heterogeneous audience; they seek not only to communicate, but also to influence; and they use text, sound, and images in ways very different from ordinary conversation.[36] All this can make it difficult to parse what an advertisement says—which implications it is reasonable to draw from it. Nor is it obvious how to apply cooperative conversational ethics to advertisers. Because our society values economic activity, businesses are permitted to promote, push, and even puff their products.[37] And because our culture places a high value on individual autonomy, state attempts to regulate speech based on its persuasive power are treated with suspicion.[38] We presume individuals are competent to decide for themselves. As a result, it is not always obvious where to draw the line between, on the one hand, advertisers' permissible attempts to affect consumers' beliefs, preferences, and choices and, on the other, wrongful deception or other forms of manipulation.

The inability of everyday conversational norms to identify what advertisements mean, advertisers' obligations to consumers, and how much to expect of consumers themselves partly explains the law's turn toward a more consequentialist and welfarist framework.[39] That turn also enables false advertising law to address aspects of advertising that have no analog in the common law torts.[40] Whereas truthfulness is a binary quality, an advertisement might inform one portion of the audience and deceive another, or one element in it might both contain useful information and mislead.

---

[36] For a discussion of the role of images in advertising and judicial attempts to take account of them, see Rebecca Tushnet, *Looking at the Lanham Act: Images in Trademark and Advertising Law*, 48 Hous. L. Rev. 861, 895–916 (2011).

Advertisements are in this respect comparable to statements by issuers of securities, although the communicative contents are of course very different. Thus Donald Langevoort has argued that ordinary rules of conversational implicature—such as the half-truth doctrine—should not always apply in securities fraud cases. Donald C. Langevoort, *Half-Truths: Protecting Mistaken Inferences by Investors and Others*, 52 Stan. L. Rev. 87 (1999).

[37] For example: "Opinions are not only the lifestyle of democracy, they are the brag in advertising that has made for the wide dissemination of products that otherwise would never have reached the households of our citizens." Presidio Enterprises, Inc. v. Warner Bros. Distributing Corp., 784 F.2d 674, 685 (5th Cir. 1986).

[38] For more on this point, see David A. Strauss, *Persuasion, Autonomy, and Freedom of Expression*, 91 Colum. L. Rev. 334, 353–360 (1991).

[39] See, e.g., Richard A. Posner, *Regulation of Advertising by the FTC* (American Enterprise Institute for Public Policy Research, 1973); Howard Beales, Richard Craswell, & Steven C. Salop, *The Efficient Regulation of Consumer Information*, 24 J.L. & Econ. 491 (1981); Richard Craswell, *"Compared to What?" The Use of Control Ads in Deceptive Advertising Litigation*, 65 Antitrust L.J. 757 (1997); Richard Craswell, *The Efficient Regulation of Consumer Information*, 24 J.L. & Econ. 491 (1981); Richard Craswell, *Regulating Deceptive Advertising: The Role of Cost-Benefit Analysis*, 64 S. Cal. L. Rev. 549 (1991).

[40] Richard Craswell has explored these aspects in detail. See, e.g., Richard Craswell, *Interpreting Deceptive Advertising*, 65 B.U. L. Rev. 657 (1985); Richard Craswell, *Taking Information Seriously: Misrepresentation and Nondisclosure in Contract Law and Elsewhere*, 92 Va. L. Rev. 565 (2006); Richard Craswell, *Static Versus Dynamic Disclosures, and How Not to Judge Their Success or Failure*, 88 Wash. L. Rev. 333 (2013).

A purely consequentialist approach can balance the welfare gains from information some consumers receive against the welfare losses from the false messages received by those or other consumers. Having replaced the inquiry into truth with one into deceptive effect, the law can also look beyond an advertisement's communicative content to its potentially deceptive form, such as its use of images or placement of text. The same goes for assessing disclosures or disclaimers. Although disclosures and disclaimers can render an impliedly false advertisement truthful, they do not always prevent its deceptive effects. And like the advertisement itself, a disclosure or disclaimer is likely to affect different audience members differently and might contain multiple messages. In short, if it is difficult to say when an advertiser crosses the line from permissible persuasion to impermissible manipulation, with the right tools it is possible to determine when an advertisement's deceptive effects are likely to cause a net reduction in consumer welfare.

Such consequentialist and welfarist inquiries are sometimes associated with attempts to erase the distinction between private and public law.[41] By the same token, false advertising law's imposition of strict liability on advertisers and inattention to the reasonableness of consumer reliance might be taken to mean that we have left the realm of moral or ethical obligations commonly associated with the private law.

But if advertisers' legal duties to consumers differ from the common law obligation to tell the truth and questions of relative fault, that does not mean that they have no ethical content.[42] Edward Balleisen describes how the nineteenth-century emergence of new technologies of production, distribution, and promotion generated novel ways for sellers to interact with buyers.

> Opportunities for fraud . . . were particularly salient in the nineteenth-century United States, where technological breakthroughs, transformations in finance and business organization, and the rapid creation of an integrated national economy sparked a series of economic booms, and where migration and the shifting boundaries of social class loosened traditional forms of communal authority. These conditions encouraged the flowering of a booster ethos suffused with thoroughgoing optimism and celebration of the rapid accumulation of wealth; they also fostered the emergence of pervasive information asymmetries. Optimism bred credulousness and willingness to take on risk. Profound differences in access to market intelligence limited the ability of investors and consumers to assess the claims of the parties with whom they contemplated doing business. This combination increased the payoffs and lowered the costs associated with fraud.[43]

This was the milieu in which modern mass advertising was born, a form of communication that challenged both existing understandings of sellers' moral obligations to

---

[41] See, e.g., John Goldberg's arguments in this volume that economic accounts of tort law fail to capture core aspects of it. John C.P. Goldberg, this volume.

[42] The argument in this and the next paragraph might be compared with John Goldberg and Benjamin Zipursky's account of strict liability in *The Strict Liability in Fault and the Fault in Strict Liability*, 85 FORDHAM L. REV. 743 (2016).

[43] Edward J. Balleisen, *Fraud: An American History from Barnum to Madoff* 75 (2017).

buyers and existing private law actions. The law evolved in response to those challenges by assigning advertisers new types of legal obligations. These legal obligations, in turn, can be understood to reflect ethical obligations that come with these new forms of communication and persuasion.

Seana Shiffrin has recently argued that false advertising law tracks moral obligations that appear in relationships in which one side's autonomy is enhanced by giving a degree of responsibility to the other, including responsibility for the first side's own mistakes. Suppose a father sees on a bottle of baby formula, "1st Choice of Doctors."[44] If he thought about it, he might recognize that "1st" is not a cardinal, but an ordinal number. If he thought a bit more, he might realize that "1st Choice of Doctors," could mean only first choice of doctors who express a preference, and that if most doctors do not have a preference, the phrase might not mean that a majority, or even a plurality, of doctors recommend the product. Although the ideally reasonable consumer might do all this, it is not obvious that it would be a productive use of his mental energy. On any given day, a consumer is likely to encounter many advertisements and make many small purchasing decisions. Because consumers are not gods, a rule that expects them to stop and think about every claim is not likely to increase consumer autonomy but reduce it.

The point is not simply that advertisers are the least-cost avoiders, but that mass consumer markets generate new types of moral relationships between producers and consumers. Shiffrin argues that by choosing to participate in and benefit from mass consumer markets, advertisers acquire a responsibility not to cause false beliefs in consumers.

> Conceiving producers as having quasi-fiduciary responsibilities to consumers is a way of underscoring that, if it is to be justified, our property and production system must be regarded as a decentralized yet cooperative project for mutual gain; thus, its design should follow that conception. Then, the assignment of greater responsibility for consumers follows as a natural complement to affording producers greater control and access to the modes of production. The producer has these property rights as a decentralized agent of the public cooperative project and heightened communicative responsibilities figure among the complimentary components of that role as an agent.[45]

Such moral responsibilities recommend imposing on advertisers strict liability for deceptive advertising without inquiring into the reasonableness of consumer reliance. The new obligations that the law imposes on advertisers reflect new ethical relationships generated by mass consumer markets.

---

[44] The example comes from *Mead Johnson v. Abbott Laboratories, supra* note 30.

[45] Shiffrin, *supra* note 33, at 489. Elsewhere Shiffrin contrasts the duty not to deceive with the duty not to lie:

> The wrong of lying, by contrast, is not essentially that it risks implanting or leaving false beliefs in the recipient's mind. Rather, the wrong of lying is that it operates on a maxim that, if it were universalized and constituted a public rule of permissible action, would deprive us of reliable access to a crucial set of truths and a reliable way to sort the true from the false. Deception is wrong because it unduly hazards the false for the deceiver's own purposes, whereas lying is wrong because it places the certainty of truth out of reach for the liar's own purposes.

Seana Valentine Shiffrin, *Speech Matters: On Lying, Morality and the Law* 23 (2014).

III. An Advertiser's Duties
to Competitors

Although an advertiser's duty not to deceive consumers differs from correlate tort obligations, the idea that those duties are owed to consumers is fairly straightforward. That a duty is owed to someone entails that that person is likely to be harmed by its violation.[46] Because false advertising clearly harms consumers, it is easy to understand why advertisers might owe them a duty not to deceive. Less obvious is that an advertiser might owe the very same duty—the duty not to deceive consumers—also to its competitors. This section explores that aspect of false advertising law.[47]

A deceptive advertisement might harm competitors in any of several ways. The two most obvious are when an advertiser makes a false and disparaging claim about a competitor or its products and when an advertiser seeks to pass off its own products as those of a competitor. Call the injuries that result from such acts "nominative harms," as they derive from statements, express or implied, about the competitor or its products. Alternatively, or in addition, a false advertisement might harm a competitor by luring customers away from it. An honest business might find it difficult to compete with the apparent deals offered by a dishonest one. Call these "lost-volume harms." Finally, false advertisements can cause generic harms to all competitors. Left unchecked, they reduce the credibility of commercial advertising in general, causing consumers to be skeptical of truthful claims businesses make and the quality of goods or services in a market.

The principal torts giving competitors standing to sue for deceptive acts, including false advertisements, target nominative harms.[48] Slander of title and trade libel both involve derogatory falsehoods about the plaintiff's goods, services, or business.[49] In trademark infringement and passing off, the defendant misrepresents its own products as those of the plaintiff.[50] And in each the legal wrong corresponds to a familiar ethical wrong. Trade libel and slander of title are examples of calumny. Passing off is a type of free riding and, when the defendant's products are of lower quality, akin to disparagement.

As mentioned in section II, early judicial construction of the FTC Act and the Lanham Act tended to read them in light of the torts identified in the previous paragraph, restricting their scope to nominative and closely related harms. The 1938 amendments to the FTC

---

[46] To be clear, the converse is not necessarily true. The fact that B is or is likely to be harmed by A's action does not entail that A has an obligation to B not to do it.

[47] For an instructive discussion of many of the issues in this section, albeit with a somewhat different focus, see Nicolas Cornell, *Competition Wrongs*, 129 Yale L.J. 2030 (2020).

[48] Torts designed to protect competitors that address nondeceptive behavior, such as intentional interference with contractual relations and wrongful exercise of market power, lie at a greater distance from false advertising law.

[49] See *Restatement of Torts* §§ 624, 626 (1938) (rules for slander of title and trade libel); *Restatement (Second) of Torts* § 623A cmt. *a* (1977) (injurious falsehood torts apply "chiefly in cases of the disparagement of property in land, chattels or intangible things or of their quality.").

[50] See *Restatement of Torts* §§ 717, 741 (1938) (rules for trademark infringement and passing off).

Act and the 1988 amendments to the Lanham Act expanded the scope of each.[51] The new "unfair or deceptive acts and practices" language in the FTC Act added harms to consumers, establishing the FTC's role as a consumer protection agency. The amendments to the Lanham Act extended it beyond passing off to reach any advertiser representation about "his or her or another person's goods, services, or commercial activities."[52] The false representation no longer needed to relate to the competitor's product.

This shift from nominative to lost-volume harms might be read to mean that the Lanham and FTC Acts have evolved from laws designed to protect competitors to laws designed to protect consumers. It is the nature of competition for sellers to lose business to one another—to experience lost volume—without being wronged. Ronald Dworkin calls these "bare competition harms."

> No one could begin to lead a life if bare competition harm were forbidden. We live our lives mostly like swimmers in separate demarcated lanes. . . . [E]ach person may concentrate on swimming his own race without concern for the fact that if he wins, another person must therefore lose.[53]

The obvious victim of a false advertisement is the deceived consumer. Any resulting lost-volume harms to competitors are by comparison incidental and diffuse—incidental because the duty not to deceive is owed the consumer audience; diffuse because it is impossible to know which, if any competitor, might have lost a sale. On this view, competitors are given standing to sue not to vindicate their own losses but to serve as private attorneys general, with the real goal being to protect consumers. As one court has opined, "[w]hile the Act is not directly available to consumers, it is nevertheless designed to protect consumers, by giving the cause of action to competitors who are prepared to vindicate the injury caused to consumers."[54]

There is something to this reading. When deciding Lanham Act cases, courts regularly emphasize the need to protect consumers from false advertising, and the focus in litigation is on consumer harms. Consider the rule for determining whether an advertisement has deceived a substantial portion of the audience. Courts generally agree that what counts as a substantial portion depends on the magnitude of the harm to individual consumers. A smaller number of deceived audience members might qualify as

---

[51] The history of trademark law exhibits a similar trajectory from nominative harms to less direct harms, which there fall under the headings of consumer confusion. See McKenna, *supra* note 2.

[52] Trademark Law Revision Act of 1988, Pub. L. No. 100-667, § 132, 102 Stat. 3946 (codified as amended at 15 U.S.C. § 1125(a)).

[53] Ronald Dworkin, *Justice for Hedgehogs* 287–288 (2011).

[54] Alpo Petfoods, Inc. v. Ralston Purina Co., 720 F. Supp. 194, 212 (D.D.C. 1989), *aff'd in part, rev'd in part*, 913 F.2d 958 (D.C. Cir. 1990); see also Coca-Cola Co. v. Procter & Gamble Co., 822 F.2d 28, 31 (6th Cir. 1987) ("[C]ompetitors have the greatest interest in stopping misleading advertising, and . . . section 43(a) allows those parties with the greatest interest in enforcement, and in many situations with the greatest resources to devote to a lawsuit, to enforce the statute rigorously."); Jean Wegman Burns, *Confused Jurisprudence: False Advertising under the Lanham Act*, 79 B.U. L. Rev. 807, 874–877 (1999) (arguing that the purpose of the Lanham Act is to protect consumers).

"substantial" if the falsehood is likely to cause them more severe harms.[55] The rule has nothing to do with the nature of the harm, actual or probable, to the competitor-plaintiff. All that matters is harm to consumers. More generally, to establish Lanham Act standing a competitor "need not plead actual harm; the likelihood of harm is the statutory criterion."[56] Whether the competitor-plaintiff was actually harmed enters into litigation, if at all, only at the case's conclusion and only should a successful plaintiff seek damages in addition to or instead of injunctive relief.

There is no doubt that consumers benefit from competitor suits under the Lanham Act and that this is a good thing. But the fact that the contemporary Lanham Act is designed to protect consumers does not entail that consumer protection is its sole purpose.

As originally enacted, both the FTC Act and the Lanham Act targeted unfair competition, not consumer deception. During these periods, some courts and commentators sought to extend the statutes' reach by identifying ways in which a false advertisement that did not mention a competitor's product—that did not cause it a nominative harm—might nonetheless wrong the competitor.[57] An example is Justice Brandeis's 1922 majority opinion in *FTC v. Winsted Hosiery Co.* At issue was a challenge to an FTC finding that the defendant's false labeling of its underwear as woolen constituted unfair competition, despite the absence of trade libel or passing off—in other words, despite the absence of a nominative harm.

> [The facts show] that the practice constitutes an unfair method of competition as against manufacturers of all wool knit underwear and as against those manufacturers of mixed wool and cotton underwear who brand their product truthfully. For when misbranded goods attract customers by means of the fraud which they perpetrate, trade is diverted from the producer of truthfully marked goods. That these, honest manufacturers might protect their trade by also resorting to deceptive labels is no defense to this proceeding brought against the Winsted Company in the public interest.[58]

---

[55] See, e.g., Firestone Tire & Rubber Co., 81 F.T.C. 429 (1972), *aff'd*, 481 F.2d 246 (6th Cir. 1973); Am. Home Prods. Corp. v. Johnson & Johnson, 654 F. Supp. 568 (S.D.N.Y. 1987). As the *Restatement of Unfair Competition* explains, "when the potential injury to the deceived consumers is relatively great, a more modest likelihood of harm to competitors may be sufficient to subject the actor to liability." *Restatement (Third) of Unfair Competition* § 3 cmt. *e* (1995).

[56] Hall v. Bed Bath & Beyond, Inc., 705 F.3d 1357, 1367 (Fed. Cir. 2013) (quoting 15 U.S.C. § 43(a)(1)'s provision that a false advertiser "shall be liable in a civil action by any person who believes that he or she is or is likely to be damaged by such act.").

[57] In addition to the sources discussed in this paragraph, see, e.g., Ely-Norris Safe Co. v. Mosler Safe Co., 7 F.2d 603, 604 (2d Cir. 1925), *rev'd on other grounds*, 273 U.S. 132 (1927) (suggesting a single-source exception to the requirement of a nominative harm); *Restatement of Torts* § 761 (1939) (suggesting that any competitor whose goods had ingredients or qualities falsely claimed by another had standing to sue); Milton Handler, *False and Misleading Advertising*, 39 YALE L.J. 22, 34–42 (1929) (arguing that lost-volume harms should suffice for competitor standing).

[58] FTC v. Winsted Hosiery Co., 258 U.S. 483, 493 (1922). The Court adopted similar reasoning twelve years later, in a case involving candy packaging designed to manipulate children by offering them a chance at prizes:
> A method of competition which casts upon one's competitors the burden of the loss of business unless they will descend to a practice which they are under a powerful moral compulsion not to adopt, even though it is not criminal, was thought to involve the kind of unfairness at which the [FTC Act] was aimed.

FTC v. R.F. Keppel & Bro., 291 U.S. 304, 313 (1934).

Writing in 1948, Rudolph Callmann, drawing on the civil law, argued along the same lines that "the action for unfair competition is not founded upon a violation of property rights but upon the failure to respect an affirmative code of ethics that stems from the competitive relationship."[59] The 1938 and 1988 amendments to the FTC and Lanham Acts, which expressly authorized the FTC and competitors to go after false advertisers, rendered such arguments unnecessary. But their logic still holds. A false advertiser wrongs its competitors by not adhering to the ethics of the marketplace. The wrong is the wrong of gaining an unfair advantage through cheating.[60]

Which acts qualify as cheating depends on the rules of the marketplace. Steven Gelber has argued, for example, that in the nineteenth-century United States it was generally expected that a horse trader would try to put one over on the buyer.[61] In such a market the buyer who has been taken in might consider himself wronged. Common wisdom held that professional horse traders were scoundrels. But the seller who lost a sale to a competitor's deceptive practices would have no cause for complaint. "The morality—or more precisely, immorality—of horse trading derived from the way it operated as a game.... Horse traders expected to be judged by the ethics of the game."[62] In such a market, although a seller's deceptive acts might wrong the buyer, they would not wrong other sellers. The commonly understood rules of the market permitted such behavior.

Gelber's account of horse trading illustrates what Balleisen describes as "the historically contingent nature of what constituted fraud and who qualified as an authoritative interpreter of commercial culture, especially in domains of economic life characterized by a great deal of entrepreneurial innovation."[63] The past century and a half have seen a seismic shift away from caveat emptor, both in the law and in the broader culture. With respect to advertising, the origin of the change lay not in a new understanding of what businesses owed one another. The duty to play by the rules of the game does not specify what those rules are. It came, rather, from new understandings of businesses' obligations to consumers—as exemplified by the changes to the FTC and Lanham Acts and enactment of state UDAP statutes. Today the commonly recognized norms of the consumer marketplace prohibit deceptive advertising. Violating those rules harms consumers—as deceptive advertising always has. But with the emergence of the rules of the consumer market, we can now say it also wrongs honest competitors. This is the ethical component of competitor suits under the Lanham Act.

---

[59] Rudolph Callmann, *False Advertising as a Competitive Tort*, 48 COLUM. L. REV. 876, 877 (1948).

[60] Cornell, *supra* note 47, identifies another example of competitor standing for violations of rules designed to protect neither competitors nor competition: competitor suits for violations of employment laws. See, e.g., Commercial Cleaning Servs. v. Colin Serv. Sys., 271 F.3d 374, 378 (2d Cir. 2001) (competitor standing under Racketeer Influenced and Corrupt Organizations Act, 18 U.S.C. § 1961 et seq., for alleged hiring of undocumented aliens); Diva Limousine, Ltd. v. Uber Techs., Inc., No. 18-CV-05546-EMC, 2019 WL 2548459 (N.D. Cal. June 20, 2019) (competitor standing under California's Unfair Competition Law, Cal. Bus. & Prof. Code § 17200, for alleged misclassification of ride-share drivers as independent contractors).

[61] Steven M. Gelber, *Horse Trading in the Age of Cars: Men in the Marketplace* 8–10 (2008). Although one suspects that Gelber is sometimes given to hyperbole, his description of the horse market is highly engaging. "Nobody—not your neighbor, your best friend, your church brethren, not even the minister himself—could be trusted in a horse trade." *Id.* at 9.

[62] *Id.* at 15.   [63] *Supra* note 43, at 99–100. For more on the shift, see *id.* at 50–54, 97–99.

IV. Transfer Remedies, Private Enforcement, and Courts

Section II identified four structural features commonly associated with the private law, each of which appears in U.S. false advertising law: horizontal duties, transfer remedies, private enforcement, and the role of courts. I have so far focused on the horizontal duties advertisers owe consumers and competitors. Although not equivalent to ancestral torts, those duties are comprehensible in terms familiar to the private law. Advertisers are responsible for not deceiving consumers, even when the deception is in a sense the consumer's own fault. And they have an obligation to competitors to play by commonly understood rules of the market, or a duty not to cheat. I now consider the other structural features false advertising law shares with the private law.

Competitor suits under the Lanham Act look very much like other private lawsuits and might advance the same values. Although lost-volume injury can be difficult to prove, competitors regularly receive injunctive relief and sometimes monetary damages. Competitor-victims of false advertising have the resources to go to court to vindicate their rights, and they regularly do. With respect to competitors, then, private enforcement and transfer remedies might serve the same purposes or advance the same values in false advertising law they do elsewhere in the private law.[64]

The nature of mass advertising, however, creates significant hurdles to both consumer-oriented transfer remedies and consumer enforcement.

Some challenges to providing consumer transfer remedies are of a piece with providing compensation to consumers generally. It is expensive to deliver small monetary awards to a large, diffuse, often heterogeneous group of victims.[65] Others are specific to false advertising. Because advertisements are broadcast to a large, passive audience, it can be especially difficult to determine who received the message and was harmed as a result. Nor is it always obvious how to quantify harms to consumer victims. Papa John's false advertisements about the quality of its pizza ingredients might cause Domino's to lose business,[66] but how should we value the harm to the consumer who chose to eat one

---

[64] A more substantive theory of the purposes and principles of private enforcement and transfer remedies would have more to say on this matter. Benjamin C. Zipursky, for example, argues in this volume that private enforcement addresses the worry that public enforcement will "render individual protection extraordinarily vulnerable to the influence of the rich, powerful, and well connected, as against the poor, powerless, and unconnected." Benjamin C. Zipursky, this volume. It is not obvious that the same worry applies to the typical Lanham Act plaintiff, which is a large, well-resourced corporation.

[65] Although this sentence might seem obvious, there is surprisingly little empirical evidence for it. Based on a 2015 review of the literature, Brian Fitzpatrick and Robert Gilbert conclude that the "existing data on consumer class actions is far from sufficient to make any conclusions about whether they can serve a compensatory function." Brian T. Fitzpatrick & Robert C. Gilbert, *An Empirical Look at Compensation in Consumer Class Actions*, 11 N.Y.U. J.L. & Bus. 767, 778 (2015).

[66] See Pizza Hut Inc. v. Papa John's Int'l, 80 F. Supp. 2d 600 (N.D. Tex. 2000) (granting successful Lanham Act plaintiff injunctive relief and costs of running corrective advertisements), *rev'd on other grounds*, 227 F.3d 489 (5th Cir. 2000).

company's pizza rather than the other's? Finally, whereas injunctive relief might provide a direct benefit to a competitor that has suffered a lost-volume harm and protect consumers going forward, it is not obvious how such relief benefits the consumer victim of an earlier false advertisement. Although it is reasonable to think that the producer of a deceptive advertisement owes something to consumers deceived by it, it is not always obvious what that is or how to get it to them.

Consumer enforcement also faces challenges. Because compensatory measures are low, consumer suits often take the form of class actions. Here the structure of U.S. false advertising law poses doctrinal hurdles. Although advertisements often reach a national audience, consumers have standing to sue only under state laws that vary across jurisdictions, making it difficult or impossible to bring nationwide class actions. More generally, one might wonder whether aggregating claims serves values commonly associated with private enforcement. By distributing enforcement powers to the private sphere, class actions might serve a democratizing or equalizing function. But because the decision makers in a class action are the attorneys who organize and litigate the suit, it is not obvious that class actions significantly advance the autonomy interests of class members in the ways individual enforcement actions can.[67]

A third challenge to a private law approach to false advertising cases applies to both competitor and consumer suits. Courts of general jurisdiction do not have the institutional competence to answer all the factual questions a false advertising case typically poses. Judges and juries are well equipped to address the factual questions that appear in a typical deceit or negligent misrepresentation case: What did the defendant say? Was it true or false? Was the defendant at fault for the falsehood? Was the plaintiff at fault for relying? They have less competence with respect to the central factual question in false advertising litigation: Did the defendant's advertisement cause or was it likely to cause a false belief in a substantial portion of its audience? Answering that question commonly requires the use of empirical studies such as copy tests and surveys, together with the expertise of social psychologists and others. Judges and juries are unlikely to have the background needed to evaluate evidence of this type.[68] The FTC and some state attorneys general, in distinction, are repeat players with their own economists, psychologists, and other experts. And when a public enforcement body designs an empirical study or hires an expert, it does not have a financial stake in the results. False advertising law's shift away from an inquiry into truth and fault and toward questions of cause and effect

---

[67] For the tensions between the management of class actions and the values of private enforcement, see Howard M. Erichson & Benjamin C. Zipursky, *Consent vs. Closure*, 96 CORNELL L. REV. 265, 311–320 (2011).

[68] See Burns, *supra* note 54 at 864–867 (listing reasons why courts are ill-equipped to determine whether an advertisement is false or misleading); Richard J. Leighton, *Literal Falsity by Necessary Implication: Presuming Deception without Evidence in Lanham Act Cases*, 97 TRADEMARK REP. 1286 (2007) ("Many federal judges appear to have reservations about the need for, and reliability of, perception surveys and other extrinsic evidence offered to show how a challenged claim is interpreted by its intended audience."); Rebecca Tushnet, *It Depends on What the Meaning of "False" Is: Falsity and Misleadingness in Commercial Speech Doctrine*, 41 LOY. L.A. L. REV. 227, 253 (2007) (expresses the "suspicion . . . that juries may not be better at [deciding whose meaning to endorse], and may systematically be worse than agencies with experience evaluating a variety of advertising claims over time.").

has not robbed it of its ethical content. But that shift has perhaps rendered traditional forms of adjudication less suited to its enforcement.

The remedies and adjudicative mechanisms one finds in contract, tort, property, and other more traditional areas of private law were not handed down from on high. They were designed to address practical problems generated by specific types of interactions in particular social contexts. Horizontal duties built on the basis of commonly understood moral obligations, backward-looking transfer remedies, and private enforcement in courts of general jurisdiction function well when applied to breaches of exchange agreements, accidents, trespass, and the like. Those mechanisms are not equally suited to the one-many relationships generated by mass consumer markets, including the relationship between advertiser and its audience.

V. CONCLUSION

In the past century and a half, mass consumer markets have created the conditions for new forms of interpersonal wrongs. These include not only deceptive advertising but also defective products and unfair adhesive contract terms. In the United States, the legal response has largely been piecemeal, transmutative, and generative. Early legislation addressing false advertising drew on design elements from the common law, and U.S. false advertising law continues to exhibit those genetic markers. But they do not express themselves in the same form. As false advertising law has evolved, it has imposed on advertisers new types of obligations, and it has turned to new mechanisms of enforcement and remedial rules better suited to the one-many structure of consumer transactions.

Notwithstanding the law's adoption of a consequentialist and welfarist framework, however, advertisers' obligations to consumers and to competitors can be understood in ethical terms familiar to the private law. Rather than a duty not to lie or utter falsehoods, advertisers have a responsibility to consumers not to cause them false beliefs. Rather than a duty not to disparage another business or its products, advertisers have a duty to competitors to play by the rules of the marketplace. In this respect, U.S. false advertising law shows its private law roots, even if its branches extend well beyond them.

CHAPTER 25

THE NEW PRIVATE LAW AND INTELLECTUAL PROPERTY

Calibrating Copyright on the Common Law Continuum

MOLLY SHAFFER VAN HOUWELING

I. INTRODUCTION

A hallmark of the New Private Law (NPL) is attentiveness to and appreciation of legal concepts and categories, including the traditional categories of the common law.[1] These categories can sometimes usefully be deployed outside of the traditional common law, to characterize, conceptualize, and critique other bodies of law. For scholars interested in intellectual property (IP), for example, common law categories can be used to describe patent, copyright, trademark, and other fields of IP as more or less "property-like" or "tort-like."

---

[1] See generally Henry E. Smith, *Intellectual Property and the New Private Law*, 30 HARV. J.L. & TECH. 1, 6 (2017) ("New Private Law ('NPL') is a family of approaches united by the commitment to take the structure of private law seriously. . . . Furthermore, we can transcend the compartmentalization of private law if we ask how its various parts might work in tandem to achieve social objectives."); John C.P. Goldberg, Introduction: Pragmatism and Private Law, 125 HARV. L. REV. 1640, 1652 (2012) ("[A] hallmark of the New Private Law is its appreciation of nuances in the conceptual structure of the law."); *id.* at 1653 ("Our laws work through an abundance of categories and concepts. There is public law and there is private law. Within private law, there are the categories of tort, contract, and unjust enrichment, among others.").

In my own work I have focused on analyzing IP through the lens of property, observing how some characteristic attributes (and potential pathologies) of tangible property law manifest themselves in IP, copyright in particular.[2] In this chapter I take a different tack inspired by the insights of NPL: investigating both the property- and tort-like features of IP to understand the circumstances under which one set of features tends to dominate and why. I pursue this investigation primarily by surveying several doctrines within the law of copyright that demonstrate how courts move along the property/tort continuum depending on the nature of the copyrighted work at issue—including, in particular, how well the work's protected contours are defined. This conceptual navigation is familiar, echoing how common law courts have moved along the property/tort continuum to address disputes over distinctive types of tangible resources.

Before proceeding, let me offer a preliminary comment on this property/tort distinction. In one sense it is incoherent. Property rights are enforced through tort causes of action. Indeed, an entire body of tort law is devoted to property torts, including trespass to land and nuisance. Nonetheless, "property" and "tort" often serve as useful shorthand for a collection of characteristics that we associate with distinct types of common law claims.[3] Because I understand the New Private Law to be careful but not dogmatic about categories, I deploy this shorthand here.

---

[2] See, e.g., Molly Shaffer Van Houweling, "Intellectual Property as Property," in *Research Handbook on the Law and Economics of Intellectual Property, Volume 1: Theory* (Ben Depoorter & Peter S. Menell eds., 2019); Molly Shaffer Van Houweling, *Tempting Trespass or Suggesting Sociability? Augmented Reality and the Right to Include*, 51 U.C. DAVIS L. REV. 731 (2017); Molly S. Van Houweling, Disciplining the Dead Hand of Copyright: Durational Limits on Remote Control Property, 30 HARV. J.L. & TECH. 53 (2017); Molly Shaffer Van Houweling, "Exhaustion and Personal Property Servitudes," in Research Handbook on Intellectual Property Exhaustion and Parallel Imports (Irene Calboli & Edward Lee eds., 2016); Molly Shaffer Van Houweling, *Exhaustion and the Limits of Remote-Control Property*, 93 DENV. L. REV. 951 (2016); Molly Shaffer Van Houweling, "Technology and Tracing Costs: Lessons from Real Property," in *Intellectual Property and the Common Law* 385 (Shyamkrishna Balganesh ed., 2013); Molly Shaffer Van Houweling, *Land Recording and Copyright Reform*, 28 BERKELEY TECH. L.J. 1497 (2013); Molly Shaffer Van Houweling, *Atomism and Automation*, 27 BERKELEY TECH. L.J. 1471 (2012); Molly Shaffer Van Houweling, Touching and Concerning Copyright, Real Property Reasoning in MDY Industries, Inc. v. Blizzard Entertainment, Inc., 51 SANTA CLARA L. REV. 1063 (2011); Molly Shaffer Van Houweling, *Author Autonomy and Atomism in Copyright Law*, 96 VA. L. REV. 549 (2010); Molly Shaffer Van Houweling, The New Servitudes, 96 GEO. L.J. 885 (2008); Molly Shaffer Van Houweling, Cultural Environmentalism and the Constructed Commons, 70 LAW & CONTEMP. PROBS. 23 (2007); Molly Shaffer Van Houweling, *Cultivating Open Information Platforms: A Land Trust Model*, 1 J. TELECOMM. & HIGH TECH L. 309 (2002).

[3] See, e.g., Stewart E. Sterk, *Strict Liability and Negligence in Property Theory*, 160 U. PA. L. REV. 2129, 2129–2130 (2012) ("Property theorists typically conceptualize property as a strict liability regime. . . . Tort law, by contrast, combines principles of strict liability with those of negligence.").

II. Property Things and Tort Things

What are the supposed hallmarks of "property"?[4] One is that property governs human relationships that are mediated by things,[5] with rights that are "in rem" or "good against the world."[6] Another is that property regimes give owners the right to exclude others from the things to which the regimes apply.[7] As Henry Smith has described, this "exclusion" mechanism, which gives property owners discretion to decide how the resources they own will be used, contrasts with a "governance" mechanism, by which legal rules determine in a more fine-grained way what behavior is permissible.[8] Smith describes exclusion as "property-like" and governance as "tort-like."[9] He roughly associates exclusion with "property rule" remedies like injunctions or sanctions and governance with "liability rule" compensation or prices.[10]

The distinction between exclusion and governance (and between the property and tort regimes with which these mechanisms are associated) is more of a continuum than a dichotomy.[11] Even with regard to rights that attach to things, the nature of the thing at issue can have implications for where on the exclusion/governance continuum the legal

---

[4] On the scholarly effort to define property as a distinct legal category, not merely a bundle of rights, see generally Katrina M. Wyman, *The New Essentialism in Property*, 9 J. LEGAL ANALYSIS 183 (2017).

[5] See generally, e.g., Henry E. Smith, *Property as the Law of Things*, 125 HARV. L. REV. 1691 (2012); Thomas W. Merrill & Henry E. Smith, *What Happened to Property in Law and Economics*, 111 YALE L.J. 357, 359 (2001); J.E. Penner, *The "Bundle of Rights" Picture of Property*, 43 UCLA L. REV. 711, 799–818 (1998); Michael J. Madison, *Law as Design: Objects, Concepts, and Digital Things*, 56 CASE W. RES. L. REV. 381 (2005); Clarisa Long, *Information Costs in Patent and Copyright*, 90 VA. L. REV. 465, 471–474 (2004); Emily Sherwin, *Two- and Three-Dimensional Property Rights*, 29 ARIZ. ST. L.J. 1075, 1086 (1997).

[6] See generally Thomas W. Merrill & Henry E. Smith, *The Property/Contract Interface*, 101 COLUM. L. REV. 773, 780 & n.14 (2001).

[7] See, e.g., Thomas W. Merrill, *Property and the Right to Exclude*, 77 NEB. L. REV. 734 (1998).

[8] See Henry E. Smith, "Governing Intellectual Property," in *Research Handbook on the Economics of Intellectual Property Law, Volume 1: Theory* (Ben Depoorter & Peter S. Menell eds., 2019); Henry E. Smith, *Exclusion Versus Governance: Two Strategies for Delineating Property Rights*, 31 J. LEGAL STUD. 433 (2002).

[9] E.g., Henry E. Smith, *Exclusion and Property Rules in the Law of Nuisance*, 90 VA. L. REV. 965, 1023–1024 (2004); Henry E. Smith, *Intellectual Property as Property: Delineating Entitlements in Information*, 116 YALE L.J. 1742, 1757 (2007).

[10] See, e.g., Henry E. Smith, *Property and Property Rules*, 79 N.Y.U. L. REV. 1797 (2004); Henry E. Smith, *Exclusion and Property Rules in the Law of Nuisance*, 90 VA. L. REV. 965, 980 (2004). On the history of courts' "general predisposition towards granting injunctive relief in relation to property rights," see Shyamkrishna Balganesh, *Demystifying the Right to Exclude: Of Property, Inviolability, and Automatic Injunctions*, 31 HARV. J.L. & PUB. POL'Y 593, 639–646 (2008). But cf. Samuel L. Bray, *The Supreme Court and the New Equity*, 68 VAND. L. REV. 997, 1016 ("It was once said . . . that equity could never enjoin a trespass. Now it is widely (though inaccurately) thought that the very meaning of a property right is that a court *will* enjoin a trespass.").

[11] Smith, *Intellectual Property as Property*, *supra* note 9, at 1746 (describing "the spectrum from exclusion to governance").

regime settles. In other words, the nature of the thing at issue can have implications for the strength of the right to exclude.

For example, courts faced with property claims attached to resources with boundaries that are difficult to define or provenance that is difficult to trace sometimes resist granting the types of strong rights to exclude and supracompensatory remedies that are associated with paradigmatic property rights.[12] In such cases, courts move along the common law continuum toward approaches more often associated with tort law (in particular the law of accidents), including fault- and harm-based rules about behavior. For example, courts have refused to apply a strict trespass paradigm to air rights in cases involving airplane overflights, instead giving owners of surface rights only a more contingent and contextual right to object to unreasonably harmful uses of the airspace above their land.[13] Similarly, in a classic case at the property/tort interface, the court in *Keeble v. Hickeringill* did not enjoin any interference with ducks in flight over a decoy pond, instead condemning only malicious interference with the pond owner's lawful and productive activity.[14] In *Moore v. Regents of the University of California*, the California Supreme Court rejected a claim of conversion for unauthorized use of excised human cells, while recognizing fault- and harm-based theories against the doctors who treated the patient whose cells were removed.[15] Moving into the realm of intangibles, the court in *International News Service v. Associated Press* did not grant AP a property right good against the world to its uncopyrighted news stories, but only a right to object to the unfairly harmful behavior of a direct competitor.[16]

Although in cases like these courts are arguably (and sometimes expressly) finding "no property," that does not necessarily result in a finding of no liability for the defendant. Instead, the courts shift from a strong right to exclude to more fine-grained consideration of the defendant's behavior—including whether it has in fact harmed the plaintiff.[17] This move is a sensible one if the problem with recognizing property rights in these situations is the risk that people will be unfairly (and inefficiently) surprised by property rights that are difficult to notice and/or navigate. By relaxing the strict liability approach that applies to interferences with clearly demarcated property rights, courts can differentiate these fault-less defendants from others who knowingly or unreasonably caused harm.[18]

---

[12] See generally Henry E. Smith, *Semicommons in Fluid Resources*, 20 MARQ. INTELL. PROP. L. REV. 195 (2016) (Eighteenth Annual Honorable Helen Wilson Nies Memorial Lecture); Sterk, *supra* note 3, at 2133.

[13] See, e.g., Hinman v. Pac. Air Transp., 84 F.2d 755, 758–759 (9th Cir. 1936) ("In the instant case, traversing the airspace above appellants' land is not, of itself, a trespass at all, but it is a lawful act unless it is done under circumstances which will cause injury to appellants' possession."); see also United States v. Causby, 328 U.S. 256, 267 (1946) ("Flights over private land are not a taking, unless they are so low and so frequent as to be a direct and immediate interference with the enjoyment and use of the land.").

[14] 103 Eng. Rep. 1127 (Q.B. 1707).   [15] 793 P.2d 479 (Cal. 1990).

[16] 248 U.S. 215, 235–236 (1918).

[17] See generally Shyamkrishna Balganesh, *Quasi-Property: Like, But Not Quite Property*, 160 U. PA. L. REV. 1889, 1893 (2012).

[18] See generally Stewart E. Sterk, *Property Rules, Liability Rules, and Uncertainty About Property Rights*, 106 MICH. L. REV. 1285 (2008); Sterk, *supra* note 3.

III. IP Subject Matter and the Property/ Tort Continuum

As the moniker "intellectual property" suggests, the body of law that gives specified people the right to control uses of intellectual works is often (but controversially) described as a type of property law.[19] A frequent normative move within IP scholarship is to argue that the property-like character of IP is undesirable and that the law should be more attentive to concepts of harm, fault, and foreseeability drawn from non-property torts.[20] A common observation underlying these arguments is that IP presents special problems associated with notice that make strong rights to exclude particularly problematic—compared, in particular, to property rights in land.[21]

The various bodies of law grouped under the heading Intellectual Property differ with regard to the subject matter to which they apply. Different subject matter presents different risks of confusion about boundaries. And, consistent with the common law's variable treatment of rights attached to different sorts of tangible things, these bodies of law also vary in their placement along the property/tort continuum. For example, patent law—with its express articulation of boundaries in the form of patent claims and its dearth of exceptions—is relatively property-like; copyright law—with its lack of ex ante claiming and its equitable fair use defense—tends to drift toward the fault- and harm-based notions associated with tort.[22]

---

[19] See generally Oskar Liivak & Eduardo M. Peñalver, The Right Not to Use in Property and Patent Law, 98 Cornell L. Rev. 1437, 1440–1441 & nn.18–20 (2013) (citing commentary critiquing and embracing the idea of IP as property).

On the history of the term "intellectual property," see Justin Hughes, A Short History of "Intellectual Property" in Relation to Copyright, 33 Cardozo L. Rev. 1293 (2012); Mark A. Lemley, Property, Intellectual Property, and Free Riding, 83 Tex. L. Rev. 1031, 1033–1034 (2005).

[20] E.g., Sterk, supra note 3, at 2150–2151; Oren Bracha & Patrick Goold, Copyright Accidents, 96 B.U. L. Rev. 1025 (2016); Avihay Dorfman & Assaf Jacob, Copyright as Tort, 12 Theoretical Inquiries L. 59, 93–94 (2011); Wendy J. Gordon, Harmless Use: Gleaning from Fields of Copyrighted Works, 77 Fordham L. Rev. 2411 (2009); Christina Bohannan, Copyright Harm, Foreseeability, and Fair Use, 85 Wash. U. L. Rev. 969 (2007); Shyamkrishna Balganesh, Foreseeability and Copyright Incentives, 122 Harv. L. Rev. 1569 (2009). But cf. Mark Lemley, Property, Intellectual Property, and Free Riding, 83 Tex. L. Rev. 1031, 1072 (2005) (urging caution about adopting a tort alternative to the property paradigm).

[21] See, e.g., James Bessen & Michael J. Meurer, Patent Failure: How Judges, Bureaucrats, and Lawyers Put Innovators at Risk 46–72 (2008); William M. Landes & Richard A. Posner, The Economic Structure of Intellectual Property Law 16 (2003); David Fagundes, Crystals in the Public Domain, 50 B.C. L. Rev. 139, 158 (2009); Jeanne C. Fromer, Claiming Intellectual Property, 76 U. Chi. L. Rev. 719, 725–726 (2009); Long, supra note 5, at 482–489; Smith, Intellectual Property as Property, supra note 9, at 1799–1819; Christopher Sprigman, Reform(aliz)ing Copyright Law, 57 Stan. L. Rev. 485, 500–501 (2004); Sterk, Property Rules, supra note 18, at 1296–1299; Peter S. Menell & Michael J. Meurer, Notice Failure and Notice Externalities, 5 J. Legal Analysis 1, 2 (2013). Cf. Sterk, Property Rules, supra note 18, at 1296 (noting how unclear property rights can be even in the real property context, which is "often treated as a refuge for clear legal rights").

[22] See Smith, Intellectual Property as Property, supra note 9, at 1799–1814; Henry E. Smith, Intellectual Property as Property: Delineating Rights in Information, 117 Yale L.J. Pocket Part 87, 91 (2007); Shyamkrishna Balganesh, Tiered Originality and the Dualism of Copyright Incentives, 95 Va. L. Rev. in Brief 67, 68–69.

Although each of the various fields of IP applies to specific categories of subject matter, with characteristics that help to explain the law's rough placement on the property/tort continuum, no field of IP is monolithic in terms of the subject matter it protects. Each field applies to a wide range of intangible things. How, then, might the doctrinal characteristics that correspond to the nature of protectable subject matter vary within a given field of IP? If patent is more property-like (dominated by "exclusion" in Smith's taxonomy) and copyright is more tort-like (with more rules about "governance") in part because of the subject matter to which they apply,[23] then we might expect some differences within these fields as well as between them, based on the specific subject matter at issue.

With few exceptions, patent and copyright grant nominally uniform sets of rights to all of the categories of subject matter to which they apply.[24] When subject matter questions arise in IP cases, they are typically couched as on/off questions—is the subject matter at issue protectable or excluded from protection? So, for example, when a court considering a patent infringement claim finds that the patent claims merely a product of nature or abstract idea, the patent is invalidated and the defendant is not liable. It is less common for a copyright to be invalidated for lack of copyrightable subject matter. But copyright's denial of protection to "any idea, procedure, process, system, method of operation, concept, principle, or discovery"[25] means that a defendant is not liable if what she copied from the plaintiff's work falls into one of those categories.

In practice, however, courts considering both copyright and patent cases seem sometimes to modulate their approaches on the property/tort continuum when faced with problematic subject matter.[26] Or, in a slightly different move that accomplishes much the same result, they consider tort-like concepts of harm and fault in the process of determining whether the subject matter at issue is protectable or not. This type of analysis seems to fly in the face of the logic of the law: if the subject matter is protected, the owners get exclusive rights and can object to infringing behavior; if the subject matter is not protected, notions of harm and fault should be irrelevant. But as the behavior of common law courts considering property claims to other types of ephemeral resources demonstrates, making finer adjustments on the property/tort continuum can be a sensible way to grapple with the information cost problems associated with poorly delineated property rights without allowing defendants who intentionally cause harm to escape liability. On close inspection, every field of IP seems to adjust the strength of the right to exclude afforded to rights holders depending on the specific nature of the subject matter at issue. I will illustrate how this works in practice with examples drawn primarily from copyright.

---

[23] Smith also emphasizes the ease or difficulty of specifying permissible and nonpermissible uses—with high degree of difficulty weighing in favor of rules of exclusion that give property owners the ability to authorize (or forbid) use. See Smith, *Intellectual Property as Property, supra* note 9, at 1783–1795.

[24] See generally Michael W. Carroll, *One for All: The Problem of Uniformity Cost in Intellectual Property Law*, 55 Am. U. L. Rev. 845 (2006).

[25] 17 U.S.C. § 102(b).

[26] Cf. Carroll, *supra* note 24, at 890 (observing that patent and copyright "reduce uniformity costs by adopting standards rather than rules to define the scope and subject matter dimensions").

IV. Fair Use and the "Nature of the Work"

Copyright law's fair use doctrine is the most obvious place where the law adjusts its protection based on notions of fault and harm.[27] Use of a copyrighted work that falls within the copyright owner's exclusive rights is nonetheless not infringing if it amounts to "fair use," with fairness assessed via consideration of statutory factors that include, most importantly, the "purpose and character of the use" and "the effect of the use upon the potential market for or value of the copyrighted work."[28] As several commentators have noted, the existence of this type of defense makes copyright law generally more tort-like than patent law (which has no equivalent, apart from very rarely applied doctrines like the experimental use defense and reverse doctrine of equivalents).[29] More interesting for my purposes is the extent to which fair use is especially available for types of works that feature especially abstract or fuzzy subject matter.

The availability of fair use for works with problematic subject matter is a subset of a more general phenomenon that has garnered widespread recognition due in large part to Wendy Gordon's pioneering work on *Fair Use as Market Failure*.[30] Gordon observed how fair use is deployed to overcome a number of different obstacles to market transactions.[31] This role for fair use is most evident in the effect-on-the-market factor: if there is no functioning market (and none is likely to arise) due to market failure, then the defendant should be able to count this factor in her favor. If she otherwise behaves reasonably—for example, with a socially beneficial purpose and without taking more than necessary to achieve that purpose—then she is likely to escape liability. To put it another way: the existence of market failure (and a favorable assessment on the effect-on-the-market factor) means that a defendant will not be held strictly liable; instead, the court will determine liability based on its consideration of the defendant's state of mind (her purpose) and the harmfulness (or not) of her behavior. It will shift on the property/tort continuum to take account of the difficulty of expecting users to transact in advance. In close cases, it might find liability but award only compensatory damages.[32]

[27] See generally Bracha & Goold, *supra* note 20.   [28] 17 U.S.C. § 107.

[29] E.g., Smith, *Intellectual Property as Property*, *supra* note 9, at 1786, 1812–1814. On the absence (and desirability) of a fair use equivalent in patent law, see generally Katherine J. Strandburg, *Patent Fair Use 2.0*, 1 U.C. Irvine L. Rev. 265; Maureen A. O'Rourke, *Toward a Doctrine of Fair Use in Patent Law*, 100 Colum. L. Rev. 1177 (2002).

[30] Wendy J. Gordon, *Fair Use as Market Failure: A Structural and Economic Analysis of the* Betamax *Case and Its Predecessors*, 82 Colum. L. Rev. 1600 (1982).

[31] *Id.* at 1627–1636.

[32] See, e.g., Campbell v. Acuff-Rose Music, Inc., 510 U.S. 569, 578 n.10 (1994) ("Because the fair use enquiry often requires close questions of judgment as to the extent of permissible borrowing in cases involving parodies (or other critical works), courts may also wish to bear in mind that the goals of the copyright law . . . are not always best served by automatically granting injunctive relief when parodists are found to have gone beyond the bounds of fair use.").

There is another way in which fair use might be deployed more directly to modulate copyright in cases involving difficult subject matter boundary questions. Another statutory fair use factor directs courts to consider "the nature of the copyrighted work."[33] The factor seldom receives much attention or weight in the fair use analysis.[34] In one of the Supreme Court's handful of fair use cases considering the statutory factors, Justice Souter did not find the factor of much use in "separating the fair use sheep from the infringing goats."[35] Where courts do attend to the "nature of the copyrighted work" factor, they seldom explicitly deploy it as a lever for addressing information cost problems associated with specific types of subject matter. Their analysis more typically emphasizes either the desert/incentive of the copyright owner (greater in the case of more creative works at the "core" of copyright)[36] or the public importance of dissemination of the work (greater in the case of factual works).[37] Together, these concerns mean that the "nature of the copyrighted" work factor weighs in favor of fair use of relatively factual as opposed to creative works.[38]

Although information cost concerns are not typically an explicit part of courts' analysis, this differential treatment of types of works often does mean that fair use is more likely when the work in question includes a potentially confusing mix of protectable and non-protectable elements. This is true, for example, of literary works that are highly factual, software that contains many elements dictated by the functions the software is designed to serve,[39] musical works that combine common themes, and derivative works that largely replicate works in the public domain.[40] As I will describe more fully later, courts often

[33] 17 U.S.C. § 107.

[34] See Jennifer Urban, *How Fair Use Can Help Solve the Orphan Works Problem*, 27 BERKELEY TECH. L.J. 1379, 1393 (2012); Barton Beebe, *An Empirical Study of U.S. Copyright Fair Use Opinions: 1978–2005*, 156 U. PA. L. REV. 549, 610 (2008); Pierre N. Leval, *Toward a Fair Use Standard*, 103 HARV. L. REV. 1105, 1116 (1990); Robert Kasunic, *Is That All There Is? Reflections on the Nature of the Second Fair Use Factor*, 31 COLUM. J.L. & ARTS 529, 530 (2008).

[35] See, e.g., Campbell v. Acuff Rose, 510 U.S. 569, 586 (1994) (observing that the factor is of little use in separating fair from unfair parodies, in particular, "since parodies almost invariably copy publicly known, expressive works"); see also Authors Guild v. Google, 804 F.3d 202, 220 (2d Cir. 2015) ("The second factor has rarely played a significant role in the determination of a fair use dispute.").

[36] *Campbell*, 510 U.S., at 586 ("This factor calls for recognition that some works are closer to the core of intended copyright protection than others, with the consequence that fair use is more difficult to establish when the former works are copied."); Stewart v. Abend, 495 U.S. 207, 237–238 (1990) (contrasting fictional short story with factual works).

[37] See, e.g., Harper & Row Publishers, Inc. v. Nation Enterprises, 471 U.S. 539, 563 (1985) ("The law generally recognizes a greater need to disseminate factual works than works of fiction or fantasy.") (citing Robert A. Gorman, *Fact or Fancy? The Implications for Copyright*, 29 J. COPYRIGHT SOC. 560, 561 (1982)). Courts also consider whether a work was published or not, with publication typically weighing in favor of fair use, although it is not determinative. See Beebe, *supra* note 34, at 613; 17 U.S.C. § 107 ("The fact that a work is unpublished shall not itself bar a finding of fair use if such finding is made upon consideration of all of the above factors.").

[38] See generally 4 *Nimmer on Copyright* § 13.05[A][2][a].

[39] See, e.g., Sega v. Accolade, 977 F.2d 1510, 1524 (9th Cir. 1992).

[40] Cf. Davidson v. United States, 138 Fed. Cl. 159, 174 (2018) (considering fair use question with regard to a sculptural replica of the Statue of Liberty and finding that "its intended use as a replica mitigates in favor of defendant").

characterize copyright protection for such works as "thin," with this thinness weighing in favor of fair use.[41] As a practical matter, this characterization means that works that are at the edge of copyright's protectable subject matter do not receive protection from the same broad range of behavior as works that are more solidly within copyright's heartland. This softening of the exclusive right can help to alleviate the otherwise harsh consequences of holding defendants responsible for copying elements that they might reasonably have mistaken for material in the public domain. Borderline subject matter, in combination with socially beneficial purpose and little harm to the copyright owner, can add up to a compelling fair use case. The result is akin to common law cases like *Keeble v. Hickeringill*: interference with birds in flight (which, if owned, would be hard to distinguish from unowned birds) would not be actionable if the defendant had a valid purpose to pursue its own duck decoy operation (as opposed to merely undermining the plaintiff's operation).[42]

There are other types of problematic copyrighted works for which the "nature of the work" factor could be deployed to address information cost problems. These include, for example, works for which the copyright status was unclear to the defendant or permission was difficult to acquire because of missing information about the work or its owner. As a result of changes wrought by the Copyright Act of 1976 (and subsequent legislation), works of this type probably vastly outnumber works for whom the copyright status and owner's identity are clear. Because copyright now arises automatically as soon as an original work of authorship is fixed, copyrights are proliferating on works that need not have any copyright information associated with them, and for which there may be no ownership information on file with the Copyright Office. Such works can quickly become "orphans," for which the information necessary to acquire permission for reproduction and other copyright-regulated uses is unavailable even to diligent good-faith users.[43] Using the "nature of the work" factor to move from property-like to tort-like treatment of cases that arise from these circumstances would be consistent with the common law's treatment of similarly problematic subject matter.[44]

V. "THIN COPYRIGHT" FOR MARGINAL SUBJECT MATTER

The Copyright Act defines the subject matter of copyright as "original works of authorship fixed in any tangible medium of expression."[45] But it also recognizes that, within any given protectable work, the "scope" of copyright does not extend to certain

[41] See, e.g., Swatch Group Mgmt. Servs. v. Bloomberg LP, 756 F.3d 73, 89 (2d Cir. 2014); Faulkner Press, L.L.C. v. Class Notes, L.L.C. 756 F. Supp. 2d 1352 (N.D. Fla. 2010).
[42] 103 Eng. Rep. 1127 (Q.B. 1707).
[43] See generally U.S. Copyright Office, Report on Orphan Works (2006).
[44] See generally Urban, *supra* note 34, at 1395–1401.
[45] 17 U.S.C. § 102(a).

embedded elements, namely, "any idea, procedure, process, system, method of operation, concept, principle, or discovery."[46] Some works are composed primarily of unprotectable elements, combined in a way that evinces not much more than the modicum of creativity required to qualify for copyright protection. As mentioned earlier, copyright protection for these works is therefore "thin." One way to understand this aspect of copyright doctrine is that the copyright owner in a thin work has the same right to exclude as any other copyright owner; the res to which that right to exclude attaches is just quite small. But another way to understand this aspect of the doctrine is that the copyright owner of a thin work has a right with regard to her work that is less a right to exclude than a tort-like right to object to very specific conduct—namely, verbatim copying and not much more. So, for example, the Ninth Circuit has said that "[w]hen idea and expression coincide, there will be protection against nothing other than identical copying of the work."[47] Similarly, the Seventh Circuit has said that "where idea and expression are indistinguishable, the copyright will protect against only identical copying."[48] Thus, when determining whether the copyright in particularly thin works has been infringed, some courts penalize only egregious behavior by defendants.[49]

As Shyam Balganesh has observed: "Thickness operates as a direct measure of the copyright entitlement's exclusionary robustness. The thicker the entitlement, the greater the forms and types of copying that are likely to be actionable; conversely, the thinner the entitlement, the fewer the forms and types of copying that are considered actionable."[50] One explanation for this approach focuses on "how deserving the work is of copyright protection."[51] An additional explanation is that search and avoidance costs are unjustifiably high for works that contain a large proportion of unprotected elements. A user could easily misjudge the dividing line (or expend resources to avoid doing so that far outweigh the societal benefits).[52] Note that litigation costs may also be high in such cases, which involve not only sorting of protected and unprotected subject matter but also often difficult questions of whether the defendant in fact copied or instead coincidentally applied the same thin veneer of expression to elements found in the public domain.[53]

In describing the special standards courts apply to thin works, Balganesh laments that "copyright's extensive reliance on real-property analogies fails to capture" this aspect of

---

[46]   Id. § 102(b).

[47]   Sid & Marty Krofft Television Prods., Inc. v. McDonald's Corp., 562 F.2d 1157, 1168 (9th Cir. 1977); see also Frybarger v. IBM Corp., 812 F.2d 525, 530 (9th Cir. 1987).

[48]   672 F.2d 607, 616 (7th Cir. 1982); see also Reed-Union Corp. v. Turtle Wax, Inc., 77 F.3d 909, 914 (7th Cir. 1996); Incredible Techs. v. Virtual Techs., 400 F.3d 1007, 1014 (7th Cir. 2005).

[49]   See Shyamkrishna Balganesh, The Normativity of Copying in Copyright Law, 62 DUKE L.J. 203, 223 (2012) (discussing "super-substantial similarity" test applied to works with thin copyrights).

[50]   Id. at 207.   [51]   Id. at 225.

[52]   Cf. Sterk, supra note 3, at 2144 (describing doctrines that "have developed in response to situations in which it is reasonable for resource users to bypass formal rules because both demarcation of boundaries and compliance with legal requirements can be costly").

[53]   See, e.g., Ty, Inc. v. GMA Accessories, Inc., 132 F.3d 1167, 1179 (7th Cir. 1997) ("[T]wo works may be strikingly similar—may in fact be identical—not because one is copied from the other but because both are copies of the same thing in the public domain.").

the doctrine.[54] In fact, by applying different standards to works with especially thin copyrights—standards that hold defendants responsible only for the most egregious forms of verbatim copying—copyright courts are making a familiar move on the property/tort continuum.[55] As described earlier, tangible property law can demonstrate a similar fluidity, at least when the law encounters new and/or problematic subject matter (excised cells, birds in flight), or new circumstances that problematize existing subject matter (e.g., airspace).[56]

VI. Adjusting Remedies for Poorly Delineated Subject Matter

Another common technique that courts considering tangible property disputes apply in cases of unclear subject matter involves adjusting remedies toward the liability rule protection loosely associated with tort law as opposed to the property rule protection loosely associated with property rights.[57] Mistaken boundary cases are a familiar example, as Stewart Sterk has observed.[58] Courts in copyright and patent cases are increasingly using the same technique—sometimes in explicit acknowledgment of the problems caused by enforcing property rights attached to unclear subject matter with property rules.[59]

Probably the most well-known recent example of this type of remedial flexibility is Justice Kennedy's concurring opinion in *eBay v. MercExchange*. Justice Kennedy raised the specter of uncertain patent rights (as well as the prospect of opportunistic hold-up by patent owners) to support the majority's conclusion that courts should not automatically grant injunctions upon a finding of patent infringement.[60] Pointing specifically to business method patents, he opined that "[t]he potential vagueness and suspect validity of some of these patents may affect the calculus" under the Court's test.[61]

---

[54] Balganesh, *supra* note 49, at 209.

[55] For examples of analogous patent doctrines that can be deployed to stretch the bounds of patent enforcement in cases of knowing copying, see Sarah R. Wasserman Rajec, *Infringement, Unbound*, 32 HARV. J.L. & TECH. 117 (2018).

[56] See generally Smith, *supra* note 12.   [57] See generally Sterk, *Property Rules*, *supra* note 18.

[58] See generally *id.* at 1320–1323; Sterk, *supra* note 3, at 2146. Henry E. Smith, *Institutions and Indirectness in Intellectual Property*, 157 U. PA. L. REV. 2083, 2127–2129 (2009). Cf. Mark P. Gergen et. al., *The Supreme Court's Accidental Revolution? The Test for Permanent Injunctions*, 112 COLUM. L. REV. 203, 239 (2012) ("In building-encroachment cases, courts will enjoin bad-faith violators even if, by statute or case law, the jurisdiction provides only for damages in cases of good-faith encroachment.").

[59] See generally Sterk, *supra* note 3, at 2155.

[60] eBay Inc. v. MercExchange, L.L.C., 547 U.S. 392, 396–397 (2006) (Kennedy, J., concurring). Regarding patent hold-up, Justice Kennedy observed: "When the patented invention is but a small component of the product the companies seek to produce and the threat of an injunction is employed simply for undue leverage in negotiations, legal damages may well be sufficient to compensate for the infringement and an injunction may not serve the public interest." *Id.*

[61] *Id.* at 397 (Kennedy, J., concurring).

In copyright, courts deciding close cases often suggest that injunctive relief might not be appropriate. For example, in *New York Times Co., Inc. v. Tasini*,[62] the U.S. Supreme Court held that the *New York Times* had infringed the rights of freelance authors when it relicensed their articles to database publishers without going back to the authors for permission—a holding that turned on interpretation of an undefined term in the Copyright Act. But the Court explained that "it hardly follows from today's decision that an injunction against the inclusion of these Articles in the Databases . . . must issue."[63] Similarly, the Court observed in Campbell v. Acuff-Rose Music, Inc., that the goals of copyright are "not always best served by automatically granting injunctive relief" in light of the "close questions of judgment" between fair and unfair uses.[64]

Other proposals would make the availability of IP remedies turn more explicitly (and dramatically) on how clearly the owner has announced their subject matter. Many proposals for addressing the orphan works problem, for example, involve limiting remedies against good-faith users of works whose rights and/or owners are difficult to identify.[65] In a similar vein, Peter Menell and Michael Meuer suggest a number of reforms designed to incentivize rights holders to provide more notice about the subject matter they claim, including reforms that would calibrate the damages available to patent owners based on their payment of differential filing fees that could help to signal the importance of their inventions.[66]

VII. PROTECTION THAT CHANGES OVER TIME

In addition to subject matter, another variable that influences the ease or difficulty of noticing and negotiating over property rights is time: with the passage of time, boundaries and owners can both become more difficult to identify. The identity of owners can change many times due to voluntary transfers, death, bankruptcy, and so on. Physical signs can fade. Problems related to time often intersect with problems related to subject

---

[62] 533 U.S. 483 (2001).   [63] Id. at 505.

[64] 510 U.S. 569, 578, n.10 (1994); see also Abend v. MCA, Inc., 863 F.2d 1465, 1479 (9th Cir. 1988), *aff'd* sub nom., Stewart v. Abend, 495 U.S. 207 (1990); New Era Publications Int'l, ApS v. Henry Holt & Co., 884 F.2d 659, 661 (2d Cir. 1989); Silverstein v. Penguin Putnam, Inc., 368 F.3d 77, 84–85 (2d Cir. 2004). More recently, courts have applied *eBay* in the copyright context. See, e.g., Christopher Phelps & Assocs. v. Galloway, 492 F.3d 532, 544–545 (4th Cir. 2007) (affirming denial of permanent injunction against leasing or sale of house that infringed architectural plans). See generally 4 *Nimmer on Copyright* § 14.06.

[65] See, e.g., U.S. Copyright Office, *supra* note 43, at 95 ("[I]f the user has performed a reasonably diligent search for the copyright owner but is unable to locate that owner, then that user should enjoy a benefit of limitations on the remedies that a copyright owner could obtain against him if the owner showed up at a later date and sued for infringement."); Hansen, David R. et al., *Solving the Orphan Works Problem for the United States*, 37 COLUM. J.L. & ARTS 1, 31–35 (2013).

[66] Menell & Meurer, *supra* note 21, at 49–50; see also Herbert Hovenkamp, *Notice and Patent Remedies*, 88 TEX. L. REV. 221, 224 (2011) (advocating adoption of a remedial principle in patent law that "*remedies must be administered so as to encourage optimal and timely private disclosure as well as optimal, cost-justified private search*") (emphasis in original).

matter. Where the nature of the subject matter makes physical signaling difficult, the potential deterioration of other types of information (e.g., human memories) is especially likely to lead to foiled transactions and/or unfair and inefficient surprise.

Tangible property law includes a number of mechanisms by which protection can shift from strong exclusion toward governance in light of the passage of time. Take the doctrine of laches, for example, which can bar equitable relief in cases of unreasonable delay that has prejudiced the defendant. Compensatory damages might still be available in such a case (depending on the applicable statute of limitations), but not the strong injunctive relief typically associated with the right to exclude.[67]

Another example is the approach that both courts and some legislatures take to the problem of old servitudes. Because servitudes are nonpossessory interests that run with land to constrain and obligate parties outside of contractual privity, they present special and well-documented information cost problems.[68] These can become worse over time.[69]

On the one hand, servitudes are designed to be durable, and thus to facilitate efficient long-term land use planning that would be difficult to accomplish through bilateral contractual measures alone. And yet, this durability can undermine efficiency when land use needs change and transaction costs make the restrictions difficult to renegotiate. Servitude doctrine transparently reflects this logic: servitudes can be terminated (or modified, or enforced only with damages as opposed to injunctions) due to "changed conditions."[70] This doctrine allows courts to apply a governance approach to old servitudes, taking into account whether a restriction or obligation would in fact serve its purpose in an individual case.

Along similar lines, Abraham Bell and Gideon Parchomovsky have observed that the conditions justifying strong rights to exclude backed up with property rules can erode or emerge over time, justifying a switch from a property rule to a liability rule (or vice

[67] See Petrella v. Metro-Goldwyn-Mayer, Inc., 572 U.S. 663, 667–668 (2014) (holding that laches could not bar a claim for damages brought within the Copyright Act's three-year limitations period, but that "[a]s to equitable relief, in extraordinary circumstances, laches may bar at the very threshold the particular relief requested by the plaintiff"); see also SCA Hygiene Products Aktiebolag v. First Quality Baby Products, LLC, 137 S. Ct. 954 (2017) (following *Petrella* in patent context); Bray, *supra* note 10, at 1034–1036 (discussing *Petrella*); Samuel L. Bray, *A Little Bit of Laches Goes a Long Way: Notes on* Petrella v. Metro-Goldwyn-Mayer, Inc., 67 VAND. L. REV. EN BANC 1 (2014) (explaining, in advance of the Supreme Court's decision in *Petrella*, that "laches typically applies to claims for an injunction, specific performance, constructive trust, and accounting for profits, but not to claims for legal remedies").
[68] See generally Van Houweling, *The New Servitudes, supra* note 2; Carol M. Rose, "Servitudes," in *Research Handbook on the Economics of Property Law* 296 (Kenneth Ayotte & Henry E. Smith eds., 2011).
[69] See generally Julia D. Mahoney, *Perpetual Restrictions on Land and the Problem of the Future*, 88 VA. L. REV. 573 (2002).
[70] See generally El Di, Inc. v. Town of Bethany Beach, 477 A.2d 1066 (Del. 1984) (holding that the application of a restrictive covenant that prohibited the sale of alcohol in part of town was inequitable as a result of changed conditions); *Restatement (Third) of Property: Servitudes* § 7.10 (2000) ("Modification and Termination of a Servitude Because of Changed Conditions"); Van Houweling, *Disciplining the Dead Hand, supra* note 2, at 71–73; Susan F. French, *Toward a Modern Law of Servitudes: Reweaving the Ancient Strands*, 55 S. CAL. L. REV. 1261, 1300–1302 (1982).

versa).[71] Patents and copyrights exhibit this feature in that they both expire, shifting from property rule protection (at least in some cases) to what Bell and Parchomovsky call a "zero order" liability rule.[72]

Apart from that dramatic and across-the-board statutory acknowledgment of the importance of time to the protectability of intellectual subject matter, courts could apply time-sensitive doctrines that are less strict and more forgiving—that is, less property-like—after the passage of time. This approach would result in a softening of property rights where the subject matter in question is relatively old. Both Justin Hughes and Joseph Liu have suggested that the passage of time should be a factor weighing in favor of fair use for copyright defendants.[73] I have elsewhere suggested that copyright law should look to tangible property doctrines like changed circumstances to counter the ill-effects of excessively long copyright terms.[74]

VIII. Equitable Estoppel and Information Incentives

Sometimes the boundaries of property are unclear because the owner has failed to take reasonable measures to mark them. A variety of doctrines applicable to tangible and intangible property shift from exclusion to governance under such circumstances. Stewart Sterk gives protection for bona fide purchasers of real property as one example of this approach: where an owner has not recorded her interest, notice-based recording acts "do not protect true owners against subsequent purchasers who have acted with reasonable care."[75]

In copyright law, the consequences for failure to register copyrights (and, hence the incentives to do so) are less powerful. In general, under current law, someone who exercises an exclusive right of a copyright owner without authorization is liable for infringement even if the copyright was not registered at the time of infringement and the defendant had no notice of it.[76] However, the remedies available to copyright owners

---

[71] Abraham Bell & Gideon Parchomovsky, *Pliability Rules*, 101 MICH. L. REV. 1, 51–52 (2002); see also French, *supra* note 70, at 1301 (describing how the changed conditions doctrine "is applied primarily as a defense to the issuance of injunctions to enforce equitable servitudes," and may allow the benefitted party to seek damages).

[72] Bell & Parchomovsky, *supra* note 71, at 42.

[73] Justin Hughes, Fair Use Across Time, 50 UCLA L. REV. 775, 775 (2002); Joseph Liu, Copyright and Time: A Proposal, 101 MICH. L. REV. 409, 410 (2002).

[74] Van Houweling, *Disciplining the Dead Hand*, *supra* note 2.

[75] Sterk, *supra* note 3, at 2142; see generally Van Houweling, *Land Recording and Copyright Reform*, *supra* note 2.

[76] For a "United States work" (as defined in 17 U.S.C. § 101), registration is generally a prerequisite for instituting a civil suit for copyright infringement. 17 U.S.C. § 411(a). But registration is not a prerequisite to accrual of the infringement cause of action, and nor is any other type of notice. See generally R. Anthony Reese, *Innocent Infringement in U.S. Copyright Law: A History*, 30 COLUM. J.L. & ARTS 133, 134 (2007) (observing that "features of copyright law that made it easy for most users to determine whether their use would fall within a copyright owner's exclusive rights and whether the work they sought to use was indeed protected by copyright have mostly been eliminated").

can vary considerably depending on the registration status of the work. With few exceptions, statutory damages and attorney's fees are not available for infringement that precedes copyright registration.[77] And statutory damages can be limited in other cases of unclear boundaries, "where the infringer sustains the burden of proving, and the court finds, that such infringer was not aware and had no reason to believe that his or her acts constituted an infringement of copyright."[78]

There are other, subtler, doctrines within copyright law that can shift treatment of alleged infringers along the property/tort continuum in cases where property owners have contributed to confusion about their rights. Equitable estoppel is the clearest example.[79] Where a defendant has taken reasonable care to avoid infringing and the plaintiff has failed to use available methods to alert the defendant to her rights, some courts have applied equitable estoppel to deny liability altogether or at least to limit the available remedies.

Consider, for example, *DeCarlo v. Archie Comic Publications*.[80] There the plaintiff, DeCarlo, claimed to own copyrights in comic book characters (Josie and the Pussycats) that the defendant had been exploiting based on its understanding that it owned them as works for hire.[81] The defendant had been publishing comic books with a copyright notice asserting its ownership, whereas the plaintiff had remained silent.[82] As the court explained:

> ACP's copyright notice on the Josie periodicals read "Cover and content protected by copyright throughout the world," indicating that ACP indeed did believe that it possessed the rights not only to the composite work but also to the individual works within it. The fact that plaintiff never attempted to register or renew a copyright in any work that included any Josie character would indicate to ACP that plaintiff had no claim to the Josie characters, or at least never intended to pursue such a claim. And plaintiff did nothing to refute that assumption. In short, DeCarlo's failure ever to voice a complaint or make a competing claim in the face of numerous opportunities to do so . . . gave ACP the right to rely on his silence.[83]

Under these circumstances—where the defendant had used the means at hand to assert its claim and the plaintiff had not—the court held that silence was sufficient to trigger estoppel.

Perhaps the most striking example of this approach is *Field v. Google*, where equitable estoppel was one of the many bases on which the court rejected a copyright infringe-

---

[77] 17 U.S.C. § 412.

[78] *Id.* § 504(c)(2) (providing that, in such a case, "the court in its discretion may reduce the award of statutory damages to a sum of not less than $200"). Where, by contrast, a court finds willful infringement, "the court in its discretion may increase the award of statutory damages to a sum of not more than $150,000." *Id.* The default range for statutory damages is $750–$30,000 per work infringed. *Id.* § 504(c)(1).

[79] This discussion draws on Molly Shaffer Van Houweling, *Equitable Estoppel and Information Costs in Contemporary Copyright*, 23 LEWIS & CLARK L. REV. 553 (2019).

[80] DeCarlo v. Archie Comic Publ'ns, Inc., 127 F. Supp. 2d 497 (S.D.N.Y. 2001).   [81] *Id.* at 499.

[82] *Id.*   [83] *Id.* at 511.

ment suit brought by a website owner who objected to Google's practice of providing users with access to cached copies of websites.[84] Key to the court's analysis was the fact that Field could easily have used standard technical measures to inform Google of its objections but instead remained silent:

> Field was aware of steps he could take to ensure that his web site would not be archived and not included in Google's cache. . . . Field could have informed Google not to provide "Cached" links by using a "no archive" meta-tag or by employing certain commands in robots.txt file. Instead, Field chose to remain silent knowing that Google would automatically interpret that silence as permission to display "Cached" links.[85]

These approaches to silence by plaintiffs who could easily have nipped an infringement dispute in the bud are consistent with the *Restatement of Torts*, which provides the following as one form of estoppel:

> If one realizes that another because of his mistaken belief of fact is about to do an act that would not be tortious if the facts were as the other believes them to be, he is not entitled to maintain an action of tort for the act if he could easily inform the other of his mistake but makes no effort to do so.[86]

The commentary explains that "[t]his principle frequently operates to prevent a person from claiming property from another who has taken it innocently."[87]

Thus, although both copyright and trespass to land are generally considered strict liability property torts, estoppel can introduce concepts of relative fault that operate to forgive "innocent" infringers where boundaries are fuzzy due in part to the property owner's misrepresentations (or misleading silence) about them.[88]

IX. Conclusion

Intellectual property critics who worry about the law overreaching and therefore compromising its very purpose of promoting progress in science and the useful arts often lament the extent to which the law is "property-like," suggesting that it would be better if the law accounted for fault and harm in ways that are more typically associated with nonproperty torts. Other observers have noticed that individual bodies of law under the IP umbrella in fact vary in how strongly they exhibit property-like characteristics. Here

---

[84] Field v. Google Inc., 412 F. Supp. 2d 1106, 1109 (D. Nev. 2006).

[85] *Id.* at 1117.   [86] *Restatement (Second) of Torts* § 894 (1979).   [87] *Id.* cmt. *e.*

[88] For a similar argument in the patent context, see, e.g., Hovenkamp, *supra* note 66, at 225 ("We could go a long way toward improving the patent notice system by focusing the inquiry not on whether the pantee complied with the law, but rather on whether the patentee gave adequate and timely notice under the circumstances.").

I have tried to demonstrate, with examples drawn primarily from copyright law, how courts use a variety of doctrinal tools to move along the property/tort continuum within a body of IP law. They take fault and harm into account more readily when the subject matter at issue in the particular case is problematic—difficult to distinguish from the public domain, difficult to match with its owner after the passage of time, and/or difficult to understand because of the owner's failure to send clear signals about its status. Although some of these problems are especially likely to arise in the realm of intellectual creations—with their inherently fuzzy boundaries—these techniques for navigating along the property/tort continuum are not unique to the IP field. Indeed, they are familiar to scholars of tangible property, where courts similarly tend to soften property rules and remedies when rights are claimed in connection with unclear, novel, or otherwise problematic subject matter. The New Private Law's careful attention to doctrine and categorization invites us to observe these moves, to acknowledge their inner logic, and to apply them to new problems.

ACKNOWLEDGMENTS

Thanks to the organizers of and participants in the Landscape of Private Law conference at Harvard Law School for the invitation and insights.

CHAPTER 26

TRADITIONAL KNOWLEDGE AND PRIVATE LAW

RUTH L. OKEDIJI

A recent candidate for private property rights, traditional knowledge (TK), faces uncommon skepticism both from intellectual property (IP) enthusiasts and those committed to a robust public domain. The World Intellectual Property Organization defines TK as a body of knowledge—including know-how, skills, practices, symbols, and signs—that is "developed, sustained and passed on from generation to generation within a community, often forming part of its cultural or spiritual identity."[1] TK may be employed in a variety of cultural practices, some of which might be sacred, purely ceremonial, or that relate to governance functions, or some combination of these. In this chapter, I focus on a narrow subset of TK, namely, knowledge goods created by Indigenous people[2] and communities.

Although Indigenous People live in diverse geographical, cultural, and political contexts, many are governed by a complex web of duties, customs, and values that inform the production and use of their knowledge. This includes economically valuable knowledge about medicinal or therapeutic applications of animal and plant genetic resources on their land. Strengthening the capacity of Indigenous people to engage in market

---

[1] See https://www.wipo.int/tk/en/tk/. See also WIPO, Traditional Knowledge and Intellectual Property, Background Brief, WIPO (2015), https://www.wipo.int/edocs/pubdocs/en/wipo_pub_tk_1.pdf.

[2] There is significant debate over what constitutes an Indigenous group particularly in Africa. See David Maybury-Lewis, *Indigenous Peoples, Ethnic Groups, and the State* (2d ed. 2001). There is an estimated 350 million to 500 million Indigenous people in the world. See Cultural Survival, https://www.culturalsurvival.org/. See also World Bank, Indigenous Peoples, World Bank (Apr. 2, 2019), https://www.worldbank.org/en/topic/Indigenouspeoples.

exchange is thus essential for the well-being of their communities; such capacity is the first line of defense against structural conditions that threaten their existence and disable continued production of creative goods. Accordingly, many proponents of TK seek legal protection comparable to the bundle of exclusive rights afforded creators of knowledge goods in the conventional IP system. Arguments in favor of IP rights to Protect TK are bolstered by the undisciplined global rise of IP protection and reinforced by the open-ended subject matter provisions of leading IP treaties.[3] For their part, opponents deny that TK meets traditional justifications for private property rights and argue instead that property rights in TK threaten the vitality of the public domain.[4]

The political economy of IP lawmaking, both national and global, may explain why TK has fared badly in the legislative and treaty arenas.[5] But other actors—domestic courts, government agencies, and international organizations—are also important sources of protection for knowledge goods, yielding a patchwork of private, administrative, and judge-made law that supplements IP legislation. Strong resistance to property rights in TK Suggest that other private law regimes could be important sources of redress for Indigenous communities. But, as I argue here, TK protection in the image of private law poses important risks for both IP law and for Indigenous people.

First, claims that sound in property, torts, contracts, and equity on the whole offer much stronger protection than the narrow vision of IP rights that fuels current TK debates. Private property rights for individual members, for example, may be incongruent with the institutional frameworks for knowledge governance that persist in many Indigenous communities. Further, ad hoc deployment of other private law tools is likely to undermine the predictability and security necessary to ensure the integrity of Indigenous norms and values, including participation in economic transactions with third parties. Moreover, reliance on IP reproduces dependence by Indigenous communities on the state—a relationship already fraught with distrust and conflict.

Second, the overlapping private law tools available for TK protection in national (and regional/international) laws threaten to impose significant social and transactional costs on third parties. Contracts, torts, and claims that sound in equity lack the sort of explicit public interest safeguards, such as fair use, durational limits, and other

---

[3] Berne Convention for the Protection of Literary and Artistic Works, art. 15(4), July 24, 1971, 25 U.S.T. 1341, 828 U.N.T.S. 221; TRIPS: Agreement on Trade-Related Aspects of Intellectual Property Rights, Apr. 15, 1994, Marrakesh Agreement Establishing the World Trade Organization, Annex 1C, 1869 U.N.T.S. 299, 33 I.L.M. 1197 (1994).

[4] See, e.g., Stephen R. Munzer & Kal Raustiala, *The Uneasy Case for Intellectual Property Rights in Traditional Knowledge*, 27 CARDOZO ARTS & ENT. L.J. 37 (2009).

[5] See generally *Protecting Traditional Knowledge: The WIPO Intergovernmental Committee on Intellectual Property and Genetic Resources, Traditional Knowledge and Folklore* (Daniel F. Robinson, Ahmed Abdel-Latif, & Pedro Roffe eds., 2017); Ruth L. Okediji, *A Tiered Approach to Rights in Traditional Knowledge*, 58 WASHBURN L.J. 271 (2019) (describing institutional constraints at the World Intellectual Property Organization for a TK treaty).

limitations and exceptions that make any system of proprietary rights in knowledge goods tolerable in a liberal society.

Designing a legal framework for TK requires a response to the question why the costs of legal protection are a necessary public investment. Shouldn't TK leak into the commons and enrich human well-being more broadly? The answer I offer here is simple: failure to protect TK occasions harm; it inhibits the capacity for exchange and retards economic development in Indigenous communities. Additionally, harmful use of TK presents challenges to cross-border scientific research necessary to address pressing public health and environmental challenges.[6] Harmful uses of TK disrupt the expectations of Indigenous creators and users that have evolved around specific patterns of engagement informed by the well-defined norms of the collective. Drawing from the literature on small-world networks,[7] I argue that harmful TK use violates the organizational structure of Indigenous and local communities by destabilizing institutions that enable coordination of interests both within groups and between groups and third parties.

Section I summarizes the international landscape for TK, highlighting the incorporation of private law tools. In section II, I identify three possible types of harms that flow from the misuse of TK: relational harm, communal harm, and developmental harm. For such harms, individual private property (and common property for that matter) offers limited recourse. Section III reflects on other private law mechanisms that could extend to TK, illustrating the capacious nature of protection Indigenous peoples could potentially receive. I conclude, however, that reliance on private law to redress harms to Indigenous people resulting from TK misuse may end up imposing undue costs on Indigenous peoples and on the IP system from which they seek reprieve.

---

[6] Jerome H. Reichman et al., *Governing Digitally Integrated Genetic Resources, Data, and Literature: Global Intellectual Property Strategies for a Redesigned Microbial Research Commons* (2016). See also Jerome H. Reichman, George Haringhuizen, Carolina dos Santos Ribeiro, & Paul F. Uhlir, *Sharing Genetic Sequence Data for Global Health Under the Nagoya Protocol to the Convention on Biological Diversity* (2019) (draft on file with author). By harmful use, I mean unauthorized use that is also inconsistent with the governance norms of the Indigenous community and thus inhibits private ordering.

[7] See Duncan J. Watts, *Networks, Dynamics, and the Small-World Phenomenon*, 105 AM. J. Soc. 493 (1999). Not all Indigenous groups exhibit small-world characteristics, and some scholars may argue that Indigenous groups are more akin to "clique networks" or ethnic groups. Avner Greif's influential work on private ordering and contract enforcement among Maghribi traders explicitly notes the role of social identity in forming the network. See Avner Greif, *Contract Enforceability and Economic Institutions in Early Trade: The Maghribi Traders' Coalition*, 83 AM. ECON. REV. 525, 539 (1993). Greif emphasizes the collectivist culture of the Maghribis as an important feature of the traders' coalition. See Avner Greif, *Cultural Beliefs and the Organization of Society: A Historical and Theoretical Reflection on Collectivist and Individualist Societies*, 102 J. POL. ECON. 912 (1994). See also Avner Greif, *Reputation and Coalitions in Medieval Trade: Evidence on the Maghribi Traders*, 49 J. ECON. HIST. 857, 868 (1989). Lisa Bernstein describes small, geographically concentrated, close-knit groups as "clique networks." See Lisa Bernstein, *Contract Governance in Small-World Networks: The Case of the Maghribi Traders*, 113 Nw. U. L. REV. 1009 (2019).

I. The Emerging Global Legal Landscape

A. Three Challenges of Private Property for Traditional Knowledge

A universally accepted definition of TK remains elusive, but there are minimum criteria to which most Indigenous groups and local communities adhere: TK results from inter-generational transfers of knowledge; is expressed through a diversity of objects—real and incorporeal; and is deeply connected to the land in which Indigenous people live.[8] This body of knowledge defines social relations within Indigenous communities: it is the basis for designing local institutions responsible for governance, religion, and the regulation of economic life. In Indigenous communities, and increasingly in international law, TK is understood as a system of governance that establishes rights, defines customs, and allocates duties.[9] Within this system, there are correlating rights and harms in the creation, use, and dispossession of informational goods.

Contracts and torts provide immediate opportunities for Indigenous communities to obtain redress for TK misuse because these regimes are embedded in a number of applicable international instruments. For example, the Convention on Biological Diversity[10] (CBD) and its Nagoya Protocol[11] require contractual agreements that define terms of access to, use, and sharing of economic benefits in dealings with Indigenous communities over their knowledge goods. Not only do the international agreements address substantive issues, they also prescribe equitable principles for procedural fairness. For example, the U.N. Declaration on the Rights of Indigenous People (UNDRIP) specifies that "States shall provide redress through effective mechanisms, which may include restitution," where the "cultural, intellectual, religious and spiritual property" of Indigenous people is "taken without their free, prior and informed consent or in violation of their laws, traditions and customs."[12] The quintessential features of consent, harm, duty, and redress (including equitable redress) suggest a vision of TK as a creature of private law.

Notwithstanding explicit references in the CBD and Nagoya Protocol to governance values in torts and contracts, the quest for the strongest possible form of control over

[8] The World Intellectual Property Organization (WIPO) defines traditional knowledge as "a living body of knowledge that is developed, sustained and passed on from generation to generation within a community, often forming part of its cultural or spiritual identity."

[9] James Anaya, *Indigenous Peoples in International Law* (2d ed. 2004); Ruth L. Okediji, *Traditional Knowledge and the Public Domain*, CIGI Papers No. 176 (June 2018), https://www.cigionline.org/publications/traditional-knowledge-and-public-domain.

[10] See Convention on Biological Diversity art. 1, June 5, 1992, 31 I.L.M. 822.

[11] Nagoya Protocol on Access to Genetic Resources and the Fair and Equitable Sharing of Benefits Arising from their Utilization, Oct. 29, 2010, U.N. Doc. UNEP/CBD/COP/DEC/X/1 [hereinafter Nagoya Protocol].

[12] United Nations Declaration on the Rights of Indigenous Peoples, art. 11(2), Oct. 2, 2007, A/RES/61/295 [hereinafter UNDRIP].

TK has compelled advocates and scholars to consider the mandatory minimum rights required in the WTO TRIPS Agreement as the best model for TK protection. At least three reasons complicate this effort.

First, debates over the protection of TK adhere closely to the conventional bundle-of-rights approach to private property. An emphasis on rights invariably invites the need to balance those rights with duties—duties that would be owed by Indigenous communities to the world beyond them. But there understandably is deep ambivalence in attempting such a discourse of duties with communities that are still experiencing the effects of recognized historical injustices. As a result, the balancing exercises embedded in IP discourse paradoxically make individual private property rights a less (morally) comfortable regime for TK protection.

Second, in most countries, the legal status of Indigenous people remains contested. To the extent that land rights are involved in issues of TK governance, as is often the case, the status of land historically occupied by Indigenous people is a significant barrier to effective TK protection.[13] The challenge, however, goes deeper than questions of sovereignty over land. Private law frameworks comprise rules that govern relationships between persons presumed to have equal rights (if not equal capacity) in law—people who have rights to claim things, to receive things, and to exchange things. The construction of citizenship in relation to Indigenous people remains singularly difficult because state power to regulate Indigenous communities relies on dynamic interpretations of treaties historically negotiated with explicit colonial objectives and repressive policies. Indigenous communities typically lack standing *as communities* to claim rights or to prohibit conduct otherwise encouraged by law, such as engaging in criticism or modification of Indigenous creative works under free speech principles. The constraints that flow from unsettled constitutional questions about sovereignty and citizenship thus complicate the extent to which public law values can appropriately inform the limits of a private property model for TK.

Third, most of the international treaties that address TK protection assume an indissoluble link between legal rights *for* Indigenous people and legal rights *in* TK. This approach is evident in UNDRIP, which recognizes the right of Indigenous people to practice, maintain, protect, and develop manifestations of their cultures in a variety of knowledge goods.[14] It is also evident in the Nagoya Protocol, which notes, for example, "the interrelationship between genetic resources and traditional knowledge [and] their inseparable nature for Indigenous and local communities,"[15] and states that "it is the right of Indigenous and local communities to identify the rightful holders of their traditional knowledge associated with genetic resources, within their communities."[16] These international instruments establish the corpus of norms that animate TK governance, and they have greatly influenced a growing body of national TK laws.

---

[13] Graham Dutfield, *Protecting Traditional Knowledge: Pathways to the Future* 48 (ICTSD Publication, 2006).

[14] *Supra* note 12.   [15] Nagoya Protocol, *supra* note 11.   [16] *Id.*

These three limits reveal a crucial challenge for the design of legal protection for TK. On the one hand, classic private property rights make TK transactions extremely difficult since information about ownership, cost, value, and potential use depend heavily on access to the physical lands where Indigenous people live—and Indigenous people often are not legal owners of the land. In this context, the powerful right to exclude that is property's sine qua non is merely illusory; access to TK is effectively obtained once access to physical lands is possible.[17] At the same time, the absence of any kind of legal regime for plant genetic and other information resources developed or cultivated by Indigenous groups undermines the welfare gains from new inventions. Scientists and third parties wrongly assume that the knowledge obtained from Indigenous lands is part of a global commons, or that it resides in some metaphorical public domain.[18] The resulting controversies—which are numerous—disrupt and undermine scientific research as, increasingly, Indigenous groups contest IP rights granted for TK products and have had a measure of success.[19]

B. Private Law and the Treaty Framework for Traditional Knowledge

The first half of the twenty-first century was characterized by several milestones in the protection of Indigenous interests under public international law. First, the creation in 2000 of the WIPO Intergovernmental Committee on Intellectual Property and Genetic Resources, Traditional Knowledge and Folklore (IGC)[20] facilitated negotiations for an international legal instrument to govern access to Indigenous people's knowledge, but progress has been uneven. Second, the 2007 UNDRIP[21] enshrined the principle of "free, prior and informed consent" that subsequently informed national laws governing third-party access to TK.[22] The UNDRIP also contains language recognizing the rights of Indigenous people to own and control their traditional knowledge, to be consulted about its use, and to make decisions regarding this knowledge.[23] Third, the 2010 Nagoya Protocol substantially buttressed the limited protection for genetic resources in the CBD. Whereas the CBD identified "fair and equitable" benefit sharing as a general

[17] This was the origin of the idea that plant or animal genetic resources were "the common heritage of mankind." See Reichman et al., *supra* note 6.

[18] See Okediji, *supra* note 5.

[19] See, e.g., Elisabeth Pain, *French Institute Agrees to Share Patent Benefits after Biopiracy Accusations*, SCIENCE, Feb. 10, 2016, https://www.sciencemag.org/news/2016/02/french-institute-agrees-share-patent-benefits-after-biopiracy-accusations.

[20] See generally Robinson et al., *supra* note 5.   [21] See UNDRIP, *supra* note 12.

[22] Prior informed consent (PIC) refers to permission given by a competent national authority in a provider country to access genetic resources in line with national legal and institutional frameworks. PIC is required under the Convention on Biological Diversity (Article 15.5) and the Nagoya Protocol (Article 6.1).

[23] See UNDRIP, *supra* note 12, e.g., arts. 11(2), 28, 31.

requirement,[24] the Nagoya Protocol imposed specific consent and benefit-sharing duties on the utilization of TK associated with genetic resources.[25]

Finally, this global normative framework has been strengthened by developments at the national level. In addition to the de facto customary international law framework,[26] national sui generis regimes for the protection of TK are on the rise globally.[27] For example, Canadian case law recognizes a legal duty to consult with Indigenous communities and engage them in participatory decision-making.[28] The relatively broad scope and low trigger threshold of this duty have provided significant opportunities for Indigenous relationship-building and political empowerment. In New Zealand, a similar duty, or *rangatiratanga*, has also been recognized, and legal steps have been taken to provide reparations to the Maori for land seizures under the 1840 Treaty of Waitangi through the Waitangi Tribunal.[29] In 1991, six Maori tribes, or "iwi," alleged that New Zealand's entry into and domestic implementation of international intellectual property instruments without proper consultation with Maori breached its obligations under the Treaty of Waitangi, resulting in the loss of genealogies, oral traditions, *moteatea* (laments), *haka* (war dance), philosophy, conceptions of time, spirituality, naming traditions, and medicinal and therapeutic treatments.[30]

In Australia, frustration with the slow pace of legal reform has led to the development of soft-law mechanisms, or so-called "Cultural Protocols," which provide detailed guidance to companies, government departments, and other stakeholders on productive interaction and relationship-building with Indigenous communities.[31] These Protocols are designed to facilitate engagement with Indigenous communities, and they explicitly depend on recognition of a host of common law tools including misappropriation, unfair competition, passing off, and estoppel. Private law thus fills important gaps in the legal treatment of TK by shoehorning aspects of TK into relatively malleable IP stan-

[24] Convention on Biological Diversity art. 1, June 5, 1992, 1760 U.N.T.S. 79; 31 I.L.M. 818 [hereinafter CBD].

[25] UN Environment, About the Nagoya Protocol, Convention on Biological Diversity (2019), https://www.cbd.int/abs/about/.

[26] This includes certain intellectual property instruments and treaties, especially in the copyright field. For example, see United Nations Educ., Sci., and Cultural Org. (UNESCO) & World Intellectual Prop. Org. (WIPO), Model Provisions for National Laws on the Protection of Expressions of Folklore Against Illicit Exploitation and Other Prejudicial Actions, Feb. 15, 1983, UNESCO/WIPO/FOLK/AFR/2.

[27] Margo A. Bagley, *Toward an Effective Indigenous Knowledge Protection Regime: Case Study of South Africa*, CIGI Papers No. 207, 2018, https://www.cigionline.org/publications/toward-effective-Indigenous-knowledge-protection-regime-case-study-south-africa.

[28] Haida Nation v. British Columbia (Minister of Forests) 3 S.C.R. 511 (Canadian Supreme Court, 2004); Taku River Tlingit First Nation v. British Columbia (Project Assessment Director) 3 S.C.R. 550 (Canadian Supreme Court, 2004); Beckman v. Little Salmon/Carmacks First Nation, 3 S.C.R. 103 (Canadian Supreme Court, 2010).

[29] Graeme W. Austin, *Re-Treating Intellectual Property—The Wai 262 Proceeding and the Heuristics of Intellectual Property Law*, 11:2 CARDOZO J. INT'L & COMP. L. 333 (2003).

[30] *Id.*

[31] Interview with Terri Janke of Terri Janke & Company, Feb. 28, 2019, Sydney, Australia. See also Terri Janke, *Indigenous Cultural Protocols and the Arts: A Book of Case Studies* (2016).

dards, or by weighing the Indigenous cultural landscape as a source of duties well beyond the scope of conventional IP rights.

For example, in a landmark decision, *Milpurrurru v. Indofurn*,[32] the Federal Court of Australia ruled that works based on traditional dreaming themes can contain sufficient creativity to merit copyright protection. The court held that though the "dreaming of the Wititj [mythical rainbow serpent] is often told in Aboriginal artwork, the particular depiction of the tail and the rarrk used . . . [was] original and distinctive."[33] The court recognized the cumulative nature of Indigenous creativity, thus extending copyright's originality doctrine to every generation's retelling of its spiritual and cultural narratives.

In another decision, *Bulun Bulun v. R & T Textiles*,[34] the Federal Court of Australia refused to recognize communal ownership of artwork by the Ganalbingu people, but it did recognize a fiduciary relationship between an individual artist and the community whose ritual knowledge he had sought to depict.[35] According to the court, the artist bore "obligations as a fiduciary not to exploit the artistic work in a way that is contrary to the laws and customs of the Ganalbingu people, and, in the event of infringement by a third party, to take reasonable and appropriate action to restrain and remedy infringement of the copyright in the artistic work."[36] The court reasoned that although the fiduciary relationship did not vest an equitable interest in the Ganalbingu people in the ownership of the copyright in the artwork, they held a right in personam to bring action against Mr. Bulun Bulun in the event of a breach of his fiduciary obligations.[37] In practice then, this fiduciary obligation constrains exploitation of property rights by linking the incorporeal interests of the Indigenous people to any use of the copyrighted work that incorporates TK. No IP right would accomplish this much.

II. TRADITIONAL KNOWLEDGE AND THE QUESTION OF HARM

A. Wrongs versus Harms in Relation to Traditional Knowledge

Efforts to assess the economic value of TK utilized in goods and services have focused on well-documented cases of "bio-piracy"—the unauthorized access and utilization of plant genetic resources and associated TK that may result in the grant of IP protection for nonmembers of the Indigenous community. In the paradigmatic case, scientists obtain information about plants that are medicinally beneficial, including how the plants are used and for what ailments. Relying on this data, the scientists develop useful drugs protected by IP rights usually with no compensation flowing back to the Indigenous community.

[32] Milpurrurru v. Indofurn, 130 ALR 659 (Federal Court of Australia, 1994).   [33] *Id.* at 78.
[34] Bulun Bulun v. R&T Textiles Pty Ltd., FCA 1082 (Federal Court of Australia, 1998).   [35] *Id.*
[36] *Id.*   [37] *Id.*

Variations of the classic case abound, with examples that include unmistakable acts of fraud or other wrongdoing, such as breach of conditions of prior informed consent (PIC) and mutually agreed terms (MAT)[38] that flow from obligations in the CBD and Nagoya Protocol.[39] Other examples involve socially or ethically questionable conduct in relation to TK, such as the derogatory use of a sacred song or ritual, desecration of ritual practices, or violations of other cultural norms. Wrongful acts are, however, difficult to evaluate because TK has no independent legal status. Further, significant disagreements may exist, even within groups, about what constitutes an accepted use or practice. Custodians and members of Indigenous and local communities may have no right to exclude third parties from conduct that may be harmful but that does not constitute breaches of positive law, such as failure to obtain PIC or to comply with MAT. Absent a legal baseline defining what duty is owed by third parties to Indigenous and local groups, even causes of action such as misappropriation that may apply to certain species of objectionable conduct in the market[40] are likely to be unsuccessful.

The unsettled legal status of TK partly reflects an impoverished view of property, a result both of the bundle-of-sticks approach[41] and the underdevelopment of other forms of property such as common property. The wrongs that relate to TK reflect a diversity of interests about specific *uses* of TK, specific *types* of TK, and TK as a *system* of management within a collective, reflecting norms, duties, values, and rights of members. The nature and legitimacy of TK draws heavily on spatiotemporal narratives, emphasizing intergenerational linkages and a sacred affinity to land, animal, and plant life.[42] The dominant view of property as a bundle of discrete rights conflicts with this wholistic and interdependent set of interests.

B. The Idea of Harm in Traditional Knowledge

Effective protection for TK ultimately is about legal pathways to restoring participatory engagement in society for Indigenous people. To create these pathways, the harms Indigenous people experience must find expression in law. Many informational goods exhibit classic network effects; they gain and retain value because of dense networks of

[38] Mutually agreed terms (MAT) constitute a private agreement reached between the users and providers of genetic resources on the conditions of access and use and the benefits to be shared between both parties. MAT is required by Article 15.4 of the CBD and Article 5.1 of the Nagoya Protocol.

[39] See Winston P. Nagan, Eduardo J. Mordujovich, Judit K. Otvos, & Jason Taylor, *Misappropriation of Shuar Traditional Knowledge (TK) and Trade Secrets: A Case Study on Biopiracy in the Amazon*, 15 J. TECH. L. & POL'Y 9, 64 (2010); and Winston Nagan, *Protecting the Economic Patrimony of Indigenous Nations: The Case of the Shuar*, 46 POL'Y SCI. 143 (2013).

[40] See Int'l News Serv. v. Associated Press, 248 U.S. 215 (1918).

[41] Henry Smith has been a leading critic of the bundle-of-rights approach. See, e.g., Henry E. Smith, *Property as the Law of Things*, 125 HARV. L. REV. 1691 (2012); Henry E. Smith, "Restating the Architecture of Property," in 10 *Modern Studies in Property Law* (Ben McFarlane & Sinéad Agnew eds., 2019).

[42] David Turnbull, "Narrative Traditions of Space, Time and Trust in Court: Terra Nullius, "Wandering," the Yorta Yorta Native Title Claim, and the Hindmarsh Island Bridge Controversy," in 1 *Expertise in Regulation and Law* (Gary Edmond ed., 2004).

relations that foster their use, consumption, and exchange.[43] TK and associated goods do not have this particular externality—for example, wider use by outsiders is not necessarily a source of value to the Indigenous community though the larger public may benefit from commercialized applications of TK. What TK does share with informational goods is an elemental feature of information networks: the value (including economic value) of relationships.[44]

In the classic IP discourse, incentives and rights are designed primarily for individual actors with little acknowledgment of the community and collective contexts that are a precondition for creative expression.[45] Membership in social communities (including firms) supplies and multiplies important incentives for creative activity.[46] Such membership (or citizenship) defines terms of access to economic and cultural resources that are the raw materials for creative engagement. Citizenship secures an individual's stake in the quality of the material environment and so motivates private investment in activities that are likely to resolve problems faced by the community as a whole. Citizenship also secures rights of access to public goods, including educational, health, and cultural resources, that inform the quality of human capital in a society, which in turn generates capacity for economic development.[47]

Conventional justifications for IP rights insufficiently value the role of the collective in galvanizing and sustaining creative activity. Because IP rights emphasize individual creators and minimizes inputs from the community, the rights inevitably are "supersized." However, commentators largely agree that modern IP laws increasingly reflect less about how the creative process really works, and more about the political economy of the information society, including the rise of super firms[48] Some of the default rules in IP, such as strict liability for copyright infringement or work-made-for-hire, unduly tax the kind of socially productive information exchanges that could facilitate mutually beneficial transactions across distinctive communities and markets. A key example of such information exchange is open source licensing arrangements that use copyright ownership to enforce norms of sharing. IP entitlements safeguard the network of relationships by requiring participants to share their contributions on nonexclusive terms.

A strong defense for TK, then, is that legal protection secures relationships that, in turn, facilitate coordination among interested actors by providing baseline rules around which

---

[43] James Boyle, *The Second Enclosure Movement and the Construction of the Public Domain*, 66 LAW & CONTEMP. PROBS. 33 (2003).

[44] Yochai Benkler, *The Wealth of Networks: How Social Production Transforms Markets and Freedom* (2006).

[45] For an argument that the public is a co-author of every copyrighted work which reflects a dimension of the relational claim, see Lior Zemer, *The Idea of Authorship in Copyright* (2007).

[46] For support of this claim in conventional IP see, Mark A. Lemley, *The Myth of the Sole Inventor*, 110 MICH. L. REV. 709 (2012). See also Benkler, *supra* note 44.

[47] See, e.g., Ruth L. Okediji, "Reframing International Copyright Limitations and Exceptions as Development Policy," in *Copyright Law in an Age of Exceptions and Limitations* (Ruth Okediji ed., 2017).

[48] See, e.g., Diane Zimmerman, *Copyrights as Incentives: Did We Just Imagine That?*, 12 THEORETICAL INQUIRIES IN LAW 29 (2011); Kevin J. Hickey, *Copyright Paternalism*, 19 VAND. J. ENT. & TECH. L. 415 (2016). See Julie E. Cohen, Julie E. Cohen, Configuring the Networked Self: Law, Code, and the Play of Everyday Practice (New Haven, Conn.: Yale University Press 2012).

diverse engagements can be structured. Strengthening the capacity of Indigenous and local groups to engage in market exchange is essential for the well-being of their communities and for sustaining the structural conditions that make the continued production of their knowledge goods possible. What opponents of TK sometimes really mean is that the baseline rules for exchange relations with Indigenous communities are unfamiliar and it is too costly to learn them. But there are also costs associated with *not* learning those rules.

At least three categories of harm flow from unauthorized access to, and use of, TK. Following are brief descriptions of each category. The categories are not fully developed descriptions. Rather, they are meant to highlight key features of the kinds of harm that could justify the imposition of duties on third parties.

1. *Relational Harm*

An essential feature of TK in Indigenous communities is its role in the formation of Indigenous cultural identity. As leading Australian Indigenous lawyer Terri Janke observes, TK "connects Indigenous people to each other."[49] The networks of relationships that comprise the community is explicitly recognized in the UNDRIP, which acknowledges that rights belong to both the collective and to individuals.[50]

The unauthorized use of TK may disrupt this formation process in significant ways. When Indigenous communities claim that unauthorized use of their knowledge and cultural goods distorts the integrity of the goods or debases their function, it is in regard to the incapacity of those goods, once removed and utilized without authorization, to serve as mediums of beliefs, values, and connectedness to each other and to their institutions and land. Relational harm thus consists of the loss of cohesion among individual members of the collective, and between individual members and the TK goods through which their sense of personhood is actualized.[51]

When expressed in music, inventions, or art, TK embodies the dignity and autonomy interests associated in liberal societies with self-actualization. Peggy Radin's influential analysis of the Hegelian personhood theory provides a notable example: .

> A person cannot be fully a person without a sense of continuity of self over time. To maintain that sense of continuity over time . . . one must have an ongoing relationship with the external environment, consisting of both "things" and other people. . . . One's expectations crystallize around certain "things," the loss of which causes more disruption and disorientation than does a simple decrease in aggregate wealth. For example, if someone returns home to find her sofa has disappeared, that is more disorienting than to discover that her house has decreased in market value by 5%.[52]

---

[49] Interview with Terri Janke, Apr. 2018.

[50] See UNDRIP, *supra* note 12. The Preamble notes, for example, that Indigenous peoples possess "collective rights which are indispensable for their existence, well-being and integral development as peoples." See also arts. 1, 7, and 40.

[51] See generally, Terri Janke, *Our Culture: Our Future—Report on Australian Indigenous Cultural and Intellectual Property Rights, Michael Frankel & Company* (1998), http://docs.wixstatic.com/ugd/7bf9b4_ 2740d8cff7d24320b70f8a34015f9a53.pdf.

[52] Margaret Jane Radin, *Property and Personhood*, 34 STAN. L. REV. 957, 1004 (1982).

In short, harm occurs when the "deep complementarity between individual agency and social arrangements"[53] (i.e., relationships) is disrupted, whether these are relationships between persons or between persons and things.[54] Relational harm can thus occur on two levels. Stealing from a stranger occasions a disruption in the relationship between the person and her property; stealing from a friend involves disruption of both types.

2. *Harm to the Collective*

Flowing from relational harm is a second category of harm, namely, harm to the collective network structure. Many, though not all, Indigenous groups exhibit the dominant features of small-world networks—short average path lengths between nodes (i.e., dense ties) and high "clustering coefficients."[55] These features heighten the potential for conflict in the Indigenous networked society when new norms are forcibly introduced (e.g., individual property rights or the public domain) that separate nodes in the network, or by repeated disruptions of the structure of informational flows critical for maintaining the network's equilibrium and its capacity to promote exchange and innovation among members.[56]

Collective harm thus occurs when a significant number of members of the group views conduct as transgressive of certain social expectations within the group regardless of whether any economic loss is triggered. In this kind of harm, the community or the collective's identity *as a group*, and its sense of well-being and security, is compromised by the unauthorized conduct, thus jeopardizing fundamental conditions for human flourishing. Analogies from non-Indigenous communities are helpful. Consider, for example, the sense of loss and disturbance experienced when an individual who shares the group's racial, economic, or cultural characteristics is denied basic civil rights. Those who share the attributes of victims of legal wrongdoing, or who are related to victims, can also experience harm even if they personally have not been targeted.[57]

Similarly, unauthorized access and use of TK may produce cultural and economic instability within the Indigenous group. The alienation and commodification of TK beyond the boundaries of the collective hinders continuity of cultural practice and displaces internal governance mechanisms. For example, in Australia, TK is held by Indigenous elders who belong to ancestral chains of custody.[58] The elders are responsible

---

[53] Amartya Sen, *Development as Freedom*, xii (1999).   [54] *Id.*

[55] Matthew O. Jackson & Brian W. Rogers, *The Economics of Small Worlds*, 3 J. EUR. ECON. ASS'N 617, 619 (2005) ("clustering coefficients measure the frequency with which two neighbors of a given node are themselves connected"). Indigenous groups do not exhibit small-world characteristics just because of their dense social ties and geographical concentration. However, Avner Greif's influential work on private ordering and contract enforcement among Maghribi traders explicitly notes the role of social identity in forming the network. See Greif, *Contract Enforceability*, supra note , at 525, 539. See also Bernstein, *supra* note 7.

[56] Peter Drahos, *Intellectual Property, Indigenous People and Their Knowledge* 6–11 (2014).

[57] *Restatement, Third, Torts: Liability for Physical and Emotional Harm, § 48: Negligent Infliction of Emotional Harm Resulting from Bodily Harm to a Third Person* (2010).

[58] See also Terri Janke & Peter Dawson, *New Tracks: Indigenous Knowledge and Cultural Expression and the Australian Intellectual Property System* (2012).

for overseeing the dissemination of knowledge, ensuring the development of new knowledge, and setting terms of access and use by members of the collective. Based on a number of case studies, Peter Drahos concludes that the ancestral system of knowledge governance in Australia required "stability of structure and the mechanisms to deal with environmental changes" and that these features enabled Indigenous communities to adapt to large-scale environmental changes such as droughts and ice ages.[59]

Even when there is no cultural offense, collective harm can occur when there is a breach of fundamental notions of right and wrong. An individual who allows her friend to copy her answers to an exam causes harm by contributing to the erosion of a common set of ethical values. In this vein, a key concern of Indigenous communities is that harmful use of TK produces a "dismantling" of systems of knowledge production and preservation, with significant ecological and economic consequences.[60] Harm to the collective upends obligations of mutual support and undermines compliance with internal community norms.

3. *Developmental Harm*

Neither individual nor common property regimes are applied to TK today, yet historical evidence shows that trading networks emerged across Indigenous groups in various regions.[61] Harmful use of TK depletes the range of assets that Indigenous communities might use to advance economic and cultural development through beneficial trade. In a number of leading articles, Lisa Bernstein argues that exchange transactions can occur in small-world networks with dense ties between members, as in other networks that exhibit certain features, including limited membership and the power to exclude.[62] As a system characterized by dense networks of custodial relationships, TK enables conditions for economic development because internal norms of knowledge production in the community enable the exclusion of nonmembers. The goods produced by the community, whether individually or through culturally mediated offices, provide opportunities for self-actualization and, where acceptable, trade with nonmembers. In small-world networks, both the production of knowledge and the terms of exchange often are defined by the same institutions responsible for guarding the norms that define obligations of membership. The community's growth and development are intrinsically tied to the capacity of individuals to participate in the design and enforcement of those norms.

---

[59] Drahos, *supra* note 56, at 8–9.

[60] *Id.* at 7–8. See also Robin Ayres & Gabrielle Sullivan, *Fake Art Harms: Culture Discussion Paper* (Arts Law Centre of Australia and Indigenous Art Code, 2017) (noting at least four ways in which the dismantling of Indigenous communities occurs: "It misappropriates Aboriginal and Torres Strait Islander culture and undermines the role of Aboriginal and Torres Strait Islander communities; denies Aboriginal and Torres Strait Islander artists of economic and other opportunities; deceives consumers; and disadvantages Australian businesses who take an ethical and culturally empathetic approach to their work.").

[61] Marcia Langton, Odette Mazel, & Lisa Palmer, *The "Spirit" of the Thing: The Boundaries of Aboriginal Economic Relations at Australian Common Law*, 17 AUSTRALIAN J. ANTHROPOLOGY 307 (2006).

[62] Bernstein, *supra* note 7.

By developmental harm, I mean the erosion of human capital formation occasioned by harmful TK use.[63] The unauthorized use of TK displaces the custodial system that is at the heart of Indigenous approaches to knowledge production; it also distorts the institutional values that entrench care for Indigenous knowledge systems as an integral feature of self-governance.[64] Further, developmental harm encompasses the disabling of means of exchange between Indigenous people and third parties by, for example, defining certain expressions of TK as excluded from legal protection due to countervailing interests in the broader society. Developmental harm thus is at the core of claims of "biopiracy" and misappropriation, as well as the other myriad ways (including through the IP system) that Indigenous knowledge assets are re-presented in modern markets by third parties as goods without a known source or origin (e.g., genetic resources), or goods fashioned from knowledge in the so-called public domain.[65]

These harms—relational, communal, and developmental—have (imperfect) analogues in a variety of private law regimes and in theory are redressable in equity. But given the limited emancipatory power of public international law for Indigenous communities, the granularity of private law offers the greatest potential for meaningful redress at the national level.

III. Privacy Law, Native Title, and Quasi-Property Rights

Unbridled resort to private law for TK protection comes at a price: torts, implied contracts, and equitable claims impose high information costs on third parties, impermissibly expands the group of duty bearers, and arguably compromises the public domain.[66] Standard private law lacks the balancing limits that are a quintessential feature of IP regimes, and this produces unintended consequences for all actors in the innovation ecosystem. In particular, reconfiguring TK in the image of private law highlights gaps in our current treatment of informational goods and provides justification for claims that

---

[63] See, e.g., Christiaan Grootaert, *Social Capital: The Missing Link?*, Social Capital Initiative Working Paper No. 3, The World Bank, Social Development Family, Environmentally and Socially Sustainable Development Network (1998).

[64] See, e.g., Karen Christine King, How Understanding the Aboriginal Kinship System Can Inform Better Policy and Practice: Social Work Research with the Larrakia and Warumungu Peoples of Northern Territory (Australian Catholic University: ACU Research Bank, 2011).

[65] A recent example is the rise of fake Aboriginal art in Australia, which has attracted intense scrutiny from the government, advocacy groups, and Indigenous communities. In response, nonprofit organizations launched a "Fake Art Harms Culture" campaign "to address the widespread sale of works that have the 'look and feel' of being Indigenous but that have no connection to Aboriginal and Torres Strait Islander communities." See Ayres & Sullivan, *supra* note 60.

[66] Strong property rights augmented by equitable doctrines could have the same effect in IP: Henry E. Smith, "Equitable Intellectual Property: What's Wrong with Misappropriation?," in *Intellectual Property and the Common Law* (Shyamkrishna Balganesh ed., 2013).

sound in different regimes. New applications of privacy rights, for example, could offer approaches for analyzing TK that may produce greater alignment between the economic harms associated with IP and the relational interests in TK that facilitate private ordering in relations with Indigenous groups.

A. New Prospects in Private Law

1. *Privacy*

Certain types of TK—particularly sacred knowledge—cannot be developed much less shared outside the Indigenous community. The disclosure of such knowledge may violate customary laws that define institutional roles and that delineate between categories of obligations, wrongs, and remedies. When sacred knowledge is openly accessible rather than carefully modulated, it loses its capacity for intergenerational social integration.[67] The forced disclosure of such information to government agencies not only reinscribes historical colonial power relationships,[68] but heightens the vulnerability of such information to misappropriation by third parties. For this reason, TK producers could benefit from the recognition of privacy interests so that members of an Indigenous group can engage in productive activities with a reasonable sense of security. Privacy law, extended beyond individuals to groups, can insulate sacred spaces, knowledge, and traditions from intervention or violation, whether through required disclosure or by Confirming of the right to prevent intrusion or acquisition by others.

In this expanded vision of privacy, individual and group interests in TK can be accommodated. The individual right to privacy, applied to Indigenous groups, could be used to protect TK from forced disclosure to government agencies when IP rights in the product are sought by the community. Privacy enhances the capacity of a group to enjoy collective autonomy and dignity by controlling cultural heritage, and preserving intracommunity relationships.[69] The UNDRIP specifically invokes the right of Indigenous peoples to "maintain, protect, and have access in privacy to their religious and cultural sites."[70]

In liberal societies privacy is defined principally in individual terms and suffers from a series of systemic weaknesses, including the absence of constitutional protection; the absence of a privacy tort; narrow definitions of "personal information"; and significant exemptions to federal privacy legislation.[71] For example, although the Australian Privacy Act 1988 (Cth) defines "sensitive information" to include religious and philosophical

---

[67] Kay Mathiesen, *A Defense of Native Americans' Rights over Their Traditional Cultural Expressions*, 75 THE AMERICAN ARCHIVIST 456 (2012).

[68] Joel Wainwright & Joe Bryan, Cartography, *Territory, Property: Postcolonial Reflections on Indigenous Counter-mapping in Nicaragua and Belize*, 16 CULTURAL GEOGRAPHIES 153 (2009).

[69] Mathiesen, *supra* note 67. See also Julie E. Cohen, *What Privacy Is For*, 126 HARV. L. REV. 1904 (2013).

[70] UNDRIP, *supra* note 12, art. 12(1).

[71] Monique Mann, Privacy in Australia: Brief to UN Special Rapporteur on Right to Privacy (Australian Privacy Foundation, 2018).

beliefs,[72] which could theoretically be interpreted to include Indigenous cultural beliefs, the Act is designed to "promote the protection of the privacy of individuals," not groups.[73]

State legislation in Australia has gone further to protect the privacy of Indigenous culture, at least with regard to physical objects. All sacred sites in the Northern Territory, for example, are protected by the Northern Territory Aboriginal Sacred Sites Act 1989 (NT), which contains strict secrecy provisions. It is an offense, punishable by 400 penalty units or imprisonment for two years, to "make a record of, or communicate to a person, information of a secret nature according to Aboriginal tradition."[74] Naturally, a limitation of this protection lies first in government recognition of certain land as a "sacred site," and protective legislation varies greatly by state. Nonetheless, statutory acknowledgment of secrecy and privacy interests for Indigenous people is a step in the right direction.

2. *Private Databases*

Administrative regulations governing patent law could require the maintenance of a private database of TK which, like prior art, can support the rejection of a patent application but does not form part of the public domain. Once an element of TK has been used by a patent examiner to make a determination about the patent's novelty or nonobviousness, it must remain within the private database of TK and be withheld from the public at large. The creation of a private TK database would frame privacy in positive terms—as the active construction of safe spaces for Indigenous empowerment rather than the negative act of avoiding surveillance or misappropriation.[75] The database could be designed, administered, and managed by Indigenous people and could serve as a living resource to facilitate intergenerational transfers of knowledge.[76]

B. Classic Regimes

1. *Contracts and Trade Secrets*

Trade secret law offers significant advantages to Indigenous communities over copyright and patent law due principally to the possibility of protection in perpetuity. Private contractual arrangements that impose a duty of confidentiality on recipients have successfully protected TK interests. In *Foster v. Mountford*,[77] for example, members of the Pitjantjara Council obtained injunctive relief to restrain the publication of a book containing information, which, if revealed to the women, children, and uninitiated men of their community, might undermine the community's social stability.[78] The court found

---

[72] Privacy Act 1988 (Cth), § 6.   [73] Privacy Act 1988 (Cth), § 2A(a).

[74] Northern Territory Aboriginal Sacred Sites Act 1989 (NT), § 38.

[75] Jason Young & Michael Gilmore, *Subaltern Empowerment in the Geoweb: Tensions between Publicity and Privacy*, 46 ANTIPODE 574 (2014).

[76] Janke & Dawson, *supra* note 58; Commonwealth of Australia, IP Australia—Innovate Reconciliation Action Plan: 2015–2018 (2015).

[77] Foster v. Mountford, 14 ALR 71 (High Court of Australia, 1977).

[78] Valentina Vadi, *Intangible Heritage: Traditional Medicine and Knowledge Governance*, 2 J. INT. PROP. L. & PRAC. 682 (2007).

that the information was of deep religious and cultural significance and that its publication amounted to a breach of confidence. The duty of confidentiality, however, only binds the parties to the agreement, not third parties who may obtain access to the knowledge through unauthorized means. Moreover, an equitable action for breach of confidence can prevent the disclosure of private information, but is of little value *after* information has been disclosed.[79]

2. *Sui Generis Regimes in Perpetuity—Native Title*

Finally, there is the prospect that states might develop successive sui generis regimes each time there is a plausible claim to harm not addressed by other means. In Australia, the sui generis native title regime recognizes preexisting Indigenous rights and interests under customary law. As early as 1993, the explicit statutory inclusion of "hunting, gathering and fishing" rights within the scope of native title demonstrated the robustness of native title.[80] Indeed, some scholars believe that a right to protect traditional knowledge within native title can be inferred from the body of case law which recognizes not just land rights but land *use* rights, as well as the extensive class of activities (including "gathering") protected under the Native Title Act 1993 (Cth).[81] Nonetheless, judicial reluctance to recognize a "property interest" outside the conventional IP sphere has limited wide application of native title as a regime for TK protection.[82]

In *Neowarra v. Western Australia*, the Wanjina-Wunggurr community claimed a right to "use, maintain, protect and prevent the misuse of cultural knowledge of the Wanjina-Wunggurr community" as part of their native title claim to 7,000 square kilometers of land.[83] The court reiterated previous dicta that recognition of such a right would require "a new species of intellectual property right" and could not fall under native title "for want of a connection with land."[84] Indeed, five years earlier, in *Bulun Bulun v. R&T Textiles*, another court had emphasized the "fundamental principle" of Australian law that "ownership of land and ownership of artistic works are separate statutory and common law institutions."[85] Yet, the fiduciary obligations recognized in *Bulun Bulun v. R & T Textiles* suggest that equitable remedies could offer substantial potential for creative protection of Indigenous knowledge without the need to establish in rem property rights.[86] As Henry Smith has argued, there is a role for equity in private law "to counteract the opportunistic misuse of the existing framework of property rights"[87] and to act as a "safety valve" to prevent opportunistic behavior facilitated by the simple structures

---

[79] Australian Law Reform Commission, Serious Invasions of Privacy in the Digital Era: Final Report (2014).

[80] Native Title Act 1993 (Cth) § 223(2).

[81] Marianne Lotz, *Colliding Worlds: Indigenous Rights, Traditional Knowledge, and Plant Intellectual Property*, 21 BUS. & PROF. ETHICS J. 71 (2002).

[82] Christoph B. Graber, *Aboriginal Self-Determination vs the Propertisation of Traditional Culture: The Case of Sacred Wanjina Sites*, 13 AUSTL. INDIGENOUS L. REV. 18 (2009).

[83] Neowarra v. State of Western Australia FCA 1402 (Federal Court of Australia, 2003).

[84] *Id.* at 485–486; Western Australia v. Ward, 213 CLR 1, 59 (High Court of Australia, 2002).

[85] Bulun Bulun v. R&T Textiles Pty Ltd., *supra* note 34, at 524.   [86] *Id.*

[87] Smith, *supra* note 66.

of entitlements established by private law.[88] Moreover, equitable enforcement has historically occurred by demonstrations that a violation of custom evidenced bad faith, without creating a property right or having any kind of in rem effect.[89]

The role of equity in TK enforcement warrants careful study. As a preliminary matter, claims in equity are particularly useful since Indigenous communities largely seek legal entitlements in TK to defend against misuse, rather than a means to strengthen bargaining positions in exchange transactions. In this regard, equity could serve a fairly precise function of redressing harms specific to Indigenous communities whose susceptibility to opportunism is especially severe. In its emphasis on commercial morality, equity also has the added advantage of accommodating broader social interests in weighing the particular TK harm against the needs of a third party who may have a legitimate interest in use of the TK. In short, equity inherently is well suited for precisely the type of remedies, such as injunctive relief, and the types of disparities – including fundamental imbalances in power and access to information – between Indigenous people and external constituencies that make other private law tools much rougher proxies of the harms associated with TK misuse.[90]

IV. Conclusion

A legal framework for the production of creative goods has among its goals helping individuals organize their interests, conceive of their duties, and participate in civic and economic activities. Intellectual property embeds certain underlying assumptions about the creation, ownership, and disposition of knowledge and information goods that do not appropriately represent or fully capture Indigenous duties and values. In some cases, IP rights are directly oppositional to Indigenous interests. Nonetheless, resort to a full (and largely untested) panoply of private law tools may prove costly for Indigenous peoples and the public interest at large. An appropriate legal regime requires as a first step, that private law theories of TK protection be disciplined by the nature of the harms endured. Further, legal protection should support the capacity of Indigenous people to obtain redress for harms that weaken cultural systems of knowledge production. Reinvigorating this capacity should be the immediate focus of regulatory and private law options for the meaningful protection of TK. In so doing, equity could play a key role in balancing competing interests and adjusting for information gaps that plague transactions in TK goods in national and global markets.

It certainly is possible to conceive a framework of protection for Indigenous knowledge goods that includes many overlapping private law claims, whether in addition to or in place of individual property rights. But the costs of TK governance by private law, with no predictable limits and untethered to the type of harms at issue, poses risks for Indigenous communities while also exacerbating the unbridled expansion of IP rights to the detriment of social welfare broadly.

---

[88] *Id.*   [89] *Id.*   [90] *Id.*

CHAPTER 27

....

INSURANCE

....

KENNETH S. ABRAHAM

ONE of the central principles of the New Private Law is that legal doctrine should be taken seriously. In insurance law, a corollary of that principle would seem to be that legal doctrine should take insurance policy language seriously. Insurance law and insurance law scholarship are largely—though not always—consistent with both the principle and its corollary. A contrasting view is that insurance law doctrine is, or should be, a vehicle for covert judicial regulation of insurance, for the purpose of policyholder protection or in order to promote more risk-spreading generally. I will call this view the "regulatory" conception of insurance law.[1]

Insurance law is not only a combination of common law doctrines and federal and state legislative and administrative directives. Insurance law also consists heavily of judicial interpretations of standard-form insurance policy language that has persisted unchanged for so long that the interpretations have the same practical effect as common law doctrines. These interpretations are so heavily anchored to the language of standard-form insurance policies that they are the locus of most insurance coverage disputes.

---

[1] To the best of my knowledge, no scholar or court has expressed this view as a general matter. But there are numerous instances in which the view is either explicit or implicit in positions that scholars or courts have taken regarding particular issues. For what are perhaps the seminal expressions of this view, see Friedrich Kessler, *Contracts of Adhesion—Some Thoughts About Freedom of Contract*, 43 COLUM. L. REV. 629 (1943); Robert E. Keeton, *Insurance Law Rights at Variance with Policy Provisions*, 83 HARV. L. REV. 961 (1970). For a contemporary expression of this view, see Jeffrey W. Stempel, *Enhancing the Socially Instrumental Role of Insurance: The Opportunity and Challenge Presented by the ALI Restatement Position on Breach of the Duty to Defend*, 5 U.C. IRVINE L. REV. 587, 589–590 (2015) ("Reduced deference to the policy text can be justified, not only by public policy concerns or greater appreciation of the limits of language but also by greater appreciation of the other identities of insurance policies . . .").

I. The Scope of Insurance Law

Insurance law governs transactions involving the transfer of risk from one party, the "policyholder" or "insured," to another party, the "insurer," whose principal business is pooling similar risks posed by a sizable number of insureds. Insurance law does not govern a number of other transactions (e.g., product warranties) that bear an economic resemblance to insurance but do not have this feature.

Insurance law is effectively a one-size-fits-all legal regime: the same rules, doctrines, and interpretations of policy language apply to insurance covering both ordinary individuals with little understanding of what they are purchasing, and large entities with the capacity to know what their insurance policies cover. Insurance law sometimes reflects a compromise between what may be optimal for one but not for both types of policyholders. But once that balance is struck, the courts generally apply it uniformly, without regard to the differential benefits and burdens for different classes of policyholders that doing so may generate.

Because insurance law is contract law, most conventional contract-law doctrine applies directly in this field, though sometimes with different emphases depending on the setting. This difference is at least partly because much of insurance law doctrine reflects and reconciles the tension between two forces. On one hand, insurers need to address or combat the three principal challenges to the insurance function: adverse selection, moral hazard, and correlated loss, (discussed later).[2] In doing so, insurers not only protect themselves as contracting parties but indirectly also protect the community of policyholders who depend on the insurer to be available to pay claims when insured losses occur. On the other hand, disputes over coverage usually arise only after a policyholder has suffered a loss. The impulse to protect policyholders against such loss yields pro-coverage legal doctrines and practices that are sometimes in conflict with insurers' efforts to combat these three challenges.

The first threat to the insurance function, adverse selection, is the tendency of those who know (or think they know) that they are at above-average risk of suffering a loss disproportionately to seek insurance against the loss. To combat adverse selection, insurers engage in applicant screening, premium-setting based on the degree of risk posed by an applicant, and they include provisions in their policies that exclude coverage of losses that may be the result of adverse selection. For example, homeowners policies contain "earth movement" exclusions that preclude earthquake coverage, which a homeowner must purchase separately. The threat of adverse selection, however, varies depending on the setting: insurers sometimes know more than individual policyholders

---

[2] Kenneth S. Abraham & Daniel Schwarcz, *Insurance Law and Regulation* 229 (6th ed. 2015).

about the degree of risk they pose, and in any event potential policyholders' risk aversion may neutralize adverse selection.[3]

The second threat, moral hazard, is the tendency of a party with insurance against a loss to exercise less care to avoid the loss than the party would exercise if not insured. The most egregious form of moral hazard—the temptation to destroy or harm insured subject matter—has generated the requirement (often by statute but sometimes by judicial decision) that any party purchasing insurance have an "insurable interest" in the subject matter. The point is to permit insurance only to protect against net loss, not to create the possibility of net gain. In property insurance, for example, the insured must have a legal or meaningful interest in the property insured.

Insurers also employ contractual devices to combat moral hazard. They often experience-rate premiums based on an applicant's past loss experience, thus creating an incentive for even an insured party to avoid losses in order to reduce future premiums; insurers sell only partial insurance, using deductibles, coinsurance, and monetary limits on coverage, so that the insured is effectively a self-insurer of a portion of its potential losses; and insurers exclude coverage of certain kinds of losses that are most susceptible to moral hazard—those that the insured "expected or intended," for example.

Although economists often see adverse selection and moral hazard to be problems of asymmetric information, these problems can be at least as accurately understood to involve fairness among the community of policyholders. A party who is successful at adverse selection is undercharged, to the detriment of those who pay in actual proportion to the risk they pose; a party who exercises less care because of moral hazard will experience more insured losses, to the detriment of those who do not reduce their level of care even after they are insured.

The third threat to the insurance function is correlated loss. The probability that one insured will suffer a loss must not be excessively correlated with the probability that another insured party will suffer the same kind of loss. Otherwise insurers will either pay no claims or pay massive numbers of claims. For this reason, insurance policies typically exclude coverage of loss resulting from war, nuclear hazards, and flood, among other things, which tend to cause loss to large numbers of parties all at once. Here, too, legal doctrine recognizes the validity of such efforts. Other devices are necessary to protect against such losses.

For the most part, the courts do not second-guess the practices, or distort the doctrines or policy language, that implement insurers' efforts to combat adverse selection and moral hazard and to avoid insuring correlated risks, although occasionally (as indicated later), the protection of policyholders is a countervailing consideration. To illustrate the manner in which insurance law largely reflects the tenets of the new private law, the following discussion addresses a number of major areas of insurance law, including the law governing the application process, insurance policy formation and interpretation, general principles regarding the transfer of risk, the claims process, coordination of coverage, and remedies for breach.

---

[3] See Peter Siegelman, *Adverse Selection in Insurance Markets: An Exaggerated Threat*, 113 YALE L.J. 1223 (2004).

II. The Application Process

By identifying comparatively low- and high-risk applicants, insurers can charge the latter higher premiums and neutralize adverse selection. In order to do this, insurers need information about the characteristics of applicants relevant to their risk of loss. The application for coverage serves, among other things, to obtain this information. A material misrepresentation on an application is therefore grounds for rescinding an insurance policy issued in reliance on the misrepresentation, or denying a claim for coverage after a loss occurs.[4] This rule applies not only to fraudulent misrepresentations but also to negligent and innocent misrepresentations.

In addition, the materiality requirement of misrepresentation is satisfied even if the fact misrepresented on the application does not figure in the loss that actually occurred. For example, if an insured states that his home has a metal roof when in fact the roof is made of wooden shingles, but he experiences damage in his basement because of a leaking water heater, the misrepresentation still may be material and be the basis for a misrepresentation defense to a claim for coverage. The courts apply an "increase of hazard" test for materiality, not a "contribute to loss" test, notwithstanding that there may seem to be a forfeiture as a result. This approach is highly similar to the materiality test applied in ordinary contract and tort misrepresentation actions.

The argument for this approach in insurance is that misrepresentations frequently are not discovered until a loss occurs and claim for coverage is made. The insurer then carefully examines the application for inaccuracies on which to base a coverage defense. This strategy has been called "post-claim underwriting," and the pejorative term reflects distaste with the practice. But often it would not be in the interest of policyholders for insurers to invest in vetting the accuracy of statements on applications. Only a tiny percentage of policyholders ever makes a claim for coverage under a particular policy. It is far more cost-effective to investigate the accuracy of statements made only by this comparatively small number of claimants after a loss occurs, than to do the same for a far larger number of applicants prior to loss.

III. Insurance Contract Formation and Interpretation

Most liability and property insurance policies are standard-form contracts prepared in the first instance by the Insurance Services Office (ISO), an independent entity that is heavily influenced by the insurers it serves. These policies are contracts of superadhesion—with few exceptions, every insurer tends to issue a policy with very nearly

---

[4] See *Restatement of the Law of Liability Insurance* § 7 (Am. Law Inst. 2019) [hereinafter RLLI].

the same policy language. This practice facilitates comparison shopping by price, and predictability of application through precedents governing the meaning of standard provisions, although it may to some extent inhibit innovation.

Insurance policies on the life and health insurance side of the market are not standardized in this way. But the principal policy provision in life insurance—the promise to pay on the death of the party whose life is insured—is completely standard anyway. Individual health insurance policies are standard within each insurance company, but group health insurance policies tend to be tailored to the needs of the party arranging them (usually an employer), although these too are to some extent subject to regulation, under the Affordable Care Act[5] or state law, regarding their terms.

Insurance policy interpretation is a matter for the court, although purely empirical questions on which interpretation depends may be decided by the trier of fact. The general rules of contract interpretation apply to insurance policies. One of the most important rules is *contra proferentem* ("against the drafter" or "offeror"), directing that ambiguous language be interpreted against its drafter. In insurance, the drafter is virtually always the insurer. Effectively this is a rule that ambiguous policy language— language that is susceptible to two reasonable interpretations—is to be interpreted in favor of coverage. *Contra proferentem* gives insurers the incentive to draft clear policy provisions, and it breaks interpretive ties in favor of coverage.[6]

But this doctrine is not treated as a blank check for roving judicial regulation. In my experience and based on my reading of thousands of appellate opinions in insurance coverage cases, in the vast majority of instances in which an insured contends that a policy provision is ambiguous, the courts hold that it is not.

The majority of courts follow a plain-meaning rule, under which they determine whether a policy provision is ambiguous only by reference to the material within the four corners of the policy, and such judicially noticeable matters as dictionary definitions. Probably the ease with which the provision in question could have been made more clear also influences the determination.[7] A minority of courts permit the admission of extrinsic evidence to show that a policy provision that is unambiguous on its face contains a latent ambiguity.

Under either approach, if a policy provision is ambiguous, the courts still do not automatically interpret the provision in favor of coverage. Rather, extrinsic evidence is considered in determining the meaning of the provision. Extrinsic evidence may consist of, among other things, trade custom, the past course of dealing between the parties, pre-contract negotiations, or the drafting history of the policy.

Some commentators have argued that, because insurance policies are contracts of adhesion, they should be treated more like products and that consumer insurance

---

[5] 42 U.S.C. § 18001 et seq.

[6] Michelle Boardman has argued, however, that often insurers are content not to redraft ambiguous policy language, because judicial interpretations in favor of coverage render outcomes predictable and make charging increased premiums feasible. Michelle E. Boardman, *Contra Proferentem: The Allure of Ambiguous Boilerplate*, 104 MICH. L. REV. 1105 (2006).

[7] Kenneth S. Abraham, *A Theory of Insurance Policy Interpretation*, 95 MICH. L. REV. 531 (1996).

policies should be construed to provide coverage if the policy is "defective."[8] These proposals reflect the regulatory conception of construction of insurance policies, rather than a private law conception that takes insurance policy language seriously. They are reminiscent of a broader debate about the role of boilerplate in contract law generally,[9] and of an ill-fated episode in the history of insurance law, in which some courts honored what they held to be the "reasonable expectations" of policyholders, notwithstanding contrary policy language.[10] The reasonable expectations principle never garnered widespread support and has little support in contemporary case law. The recently adopted *Restatement of the Law of Liability Insurance* expressly rejects it.[11]

IV. GENERAL PRINCIPLES REGARDING THE RISKS INSURED

With only a very few exceptions, the provisions of insurance policies are simply contract terms that (absent regulatory objection) can be changed when a new contract—in this case a new or renewed insurance policy—is executed. There is a vast array of what are understood to be "rules" of insurance law, but in fact these are rules only in a distinctive sense. They are rules about the meaning and legal effect of provisions that insurers, with the seeming acquiescence of the policyholders who purchase them, have chosen to include in their policies. These are almost all "default" rules: if the relevant policy provisions are changed, then new rules might well apply. Indeed, sometimes policy provisions are modified precisely in order to avoid a prior judicial interpretation that applied to the displaced language. This section highlights some of the key issues for both liability insurance (including automobile and "general" liability insurance) and first-party insurance (including life, disability, health, and property insurance).

A. Liability Insurance

Liability insurance policies typically contain an affirmative grant of coverage, or insuring agreement, a set of exclusions that nonetheless preclude coverage of certain losses that fall within the insuring agreement, and certain conditions and limitations on coverage. In addition, as part of the grant of coverage, most liability insurance policies provide

[8] See Daniel Schwarcz, *A Products Liability Theory for the Judicial Regulation of Insurance Policies*, 48 WM. & MARY L. REV. 1389 (2007); Jeffrey W. Stempel, *The Insurance Policy as Thing*, 44 TORT TRIAL & INS. PRAC. L.J. 813 (2009).

[9] See, e.g., Margaret Jane Radin, *Boilerplate: The Fine Print, Vanishing Rights, and the Rule of Law* (2014).

[10] See generally Symposium, *The Reasonable Expectations Doctrine after Three Decades*, 5 CONN. INS. L.J. 1 (1998–1999).

[11] RLLI, *supra* note 4, at § 3 cmt. *h*.

for a duty on the part of the insurer to defend suits against the policyholder. Courts have ruled that there is also a duty to accept reasonable settlements.

1. *The Affirmative Grant of Coverage*

A. AUTOMOBILE INSURANCE

Auto liability insurance is by far the dominant form of coverage from an economic standpoint. Auto liability insurance is required by law and therefore is widespread. Mandatory auto liability insurance requirements influence the tendency of the courts to find that a liability is covered under an auto policy where they might not otherwise do so. This tendency occurs because these requirements are recognized to be designed not only to cushion the impact of liability on the insured but also to ensure that victims of auto accidents injured by another's tortious conduct have an available source of recovery when the tortfeasor is otherwise judgment-proof.

There are comparatively few contemporary coverage disputes in auto liability insurance, both because the law on most issues has long been settled and because the amount at stake in most coverage disputes does not warrant litigation. The main issues that do arise from time to time involve the scope and limits of the "driver other cars" and "omnibus" clauses that are designed to ensure that anyone driving an insured vehicle with permission has at least one source of liability insurance,[12] what it means to "use" an insured vehicle,[13] and the extent to which exclusions involving suits between family members are valid.[14] In each instance, the policy behind the statutory auto insurance requirement is reflected in the case law. The result is that sometimes the courts do not take policy language as seriously as they do in other areas. For example, some cases have held that the permittee of a permittee may be understood to have "permission" to drive, and therefore be insured under the omnibus clause of standard policies.[15] This rule is an instance in which the regulatory conception of insurance law appears to be influential enough to affect case outcomes.

B. "GENERAL" LIABILITY INSURANCE

General liability insurance primarily covers liability payable as "damages because of bodily injury or property damage." Under the dominant "occurrence" form of coverage, the bodily injury or property damage must occur "during the policy period." In contrast, claims-made policies cover liability arising out of claims made against the policyholder, regardless of whether bodily injury or property damage occurred during the policy period.

Commercial General Liability (CGL) insurance covers businesses against liability for these two forms of physical damage. Individuals are covered by corresponding provisions in homeowners or renters policies. These latter forms of liability insurance are

---

[12] See, e.g., Curtis v. State Farm Mut. Ins. Co., 591 F.2d 572 (10th Cir. 1979).
[13] See, e.g., Farm Bureau v. Evans, 637 P. 2d 491 (Kan. 1981).
[14] See, e.g., Hartline v. Hartline, 39 P. 3d 765 (Okla. 2001).   [15] See *Curtis, supra* note 12.

"general" in the sense that there is no requirement that the liability insured be connected in any way with the property that is separately insured against loss by such policies.

In the CGL context, a host of important issues have arisen over the last four decades, creating a new and important body of insurance coverage law. These issues are mainly associated with the application of occurrence-policy language requiring bodily injury or property damage "during the policy period" to modern products, mass tort, and environmental liability. These issues include whether bodily injury or property damage can "trigger," or activate, more than one policy year's worth of coverage; if so, how to allocate coverage responsibility among multiple triggered policy years; and how to count occurrences for purposes of determining the amount of per-occurrence coverage and per-occurrence deductibles to apply.[16]

The trigger of coverage under occurrence-based policies is critical, because in modern "long-tail" liability for latent injury or damage, a suit against the policyholder may be brought decades after the injury or damage began to occur, and corresponding coverage claims will target the policy or policies that were in force at that time, because of the coverage for harm that occurred "during the policy period." The result has been a series of extended battles over coverage between corporate policyholders and (in each case) dozens, or hundreds, of their historic insurers.

The overall tendency of the case law has been to provide that policyholders held liable for injury or damage that occurred over a period of years, such as through exposure to asbestos, or through contamination of underground water supplies by hazardous waste, have potential access to multiple years of coverage. Even when the policy language governing an issue is incomplete or does not expressly resolve an issue, however, the courts usually have not rested their decisions on the ambiguity of the policy provisions in question. Rather, the courts have constructed a body of doctrine addressing the issue. This development has been most notable in connection with the "trigger" and "allocation" issues mentioned earlier.

This approach takes the challenge of constructing legal doctrine that has integrity much more rigorously than would the alternative of declaring the relevant policy language ambiguous and construing it in favor of coverage. Often a particular interpretation against the drafter (the insurer) would favor the policyholder in some settings but not in others. For example, both deductibles and coverage limits are specified on a "per-occurrence" basis. The number of occurrences that have caused a loss may therefore determine the amount of coverage available, but sometimes coverage would be maximized if an event were considered to involve multiple occurrences, and sometimes such an interpretation would minimize coverage. Interpreting the term "occurrence" in a way that always favored coverage would result in different meanings being attributed to the same term in different cases. There would be uniform language, but nonuniform meaning. Construction of the policy language in such instances would be a form of judicial regulation designed to promote coverage, rather than an effort to develop doctrinal interpretations that can be applied even-handedly regardless of outcome. Instead, the

---

[16] See Abraham & Schwarcz, *supra* note 2, at 469–495.

courts have gone about building their own approaches to the problems that incomplete, imperfect, or overly general policy language has generated, by developing legal doctrines governing such issues. The result is more nearly uniform meaning.

2. *Prominent Exclusions and Coverage of Coverage*

All liability insurance policies contain exclusions precluding coverage of liability for harm that is in substance "expected or intended" by the insured. These provisions are designed to address the most egregious form of moral hazard. Under CGL policies there also is extensive case law addressing the nuances of exclusions precluding coverage of harm caused by pollution, a provision concerned mainly with adverse selection.[17] And general liability insurance policies also exclude coverage of liability for harm to property owned, occupied, or rented to the insured, a provision designed to avoid overlapping with property insurance policies.

There is comparatively little litigation over the scope of exclusions in homeowners and renters policies, largely because so many of these exclusions are designed to avoid duplication of coverage and do so effectively. Thus, there are motor vehicle, aviation, watercraft, aircraft, and business liability exclusions in such policies, and there are only rarely issues about precisely where the boundaries between these forms of insurance lie. The courts honor these boundaries and do not seek to promote coverage by holding that there is coverage under two different types of policies when an exclusion is clearly designed to assign coverage responsibility to only one of them.

In recent years, the most frequently litigated issue under claims-made policies of all sorts is which policy in a series of annual policies provides coverage. This issue arises because claims-made policies were developed at least in part to ensure that only one policy would cover a particular liability. To accomplish this aim, claims-made policies contain a number of variously named exclusions for "related claims," claims related to "prior and pending litigation," claims for loss arising out of "inter-related wrongful acts," and so forth. The point is to identify a single policy or policy year that is solely responsible for a cluster of claims or suits involving the same or a similar liability-generating event. This approach also helps to combat adverse selection and encourages insureds to provide insurers with prompt notice of claims, since all future related claims will thereby be covered (if they are covered) by the policy in force at the time notice is given.

Whether a related-claims exclusion applies is a question of degree, because "relatedness" is exactly that. The dominant test for relatedness is the "sufficient nexus" test, under which the courts make a judgment about how related one claim or suit is to an

---

[17] Perhaps the most salient example of what could plausibly be understood to be judicial regulation of CGL insurance involved the "qualified" pollution exclusion that was contained in CGL insurance policies between 1970 and 1985. This exclusion made an exception for "sudden" pollution. Many courts ruled that the word "sudden" did not necessarily mean "abrupt," and therefore that under some circumstances, coverage of liability for gradually occurring pollution was not excluded. These holdings led to the substitution of an "absolute" pollution exclusion in CGL policies issued after 1985. For discussion, see Abraham & Schwarcz, *supra* note 2, at 516–527.

earlier claim or suit.[18] This test is probably the best the courts can do to apply policy language that is somewhat vague, but the result is that outcomes are sometimes difficult to predict.

In connection with almost all of the issues that arise under CGL and the other forms of liability insurance, the considerable advantage of standard-form policy provisions has been that the courts have been able to interpret these provisions authoritatively, and thus to limit the need for repeated litigation over the meaning of such provisions. For example, once a jurisdiction decides whether the policyholder "expected or intended" injury or damage is to be judged by a subjective rather than an objective standard, the issue has been largely laid to rest.

The principal "condition" in liability insurance policies is that notice of a claim or suit against the policyholder must be given to the insurer "as soon as is practicable." Because of concern to avoid what would amount to a forfeiture of otherwise-provided coverage, the courts have declined to read this provision literally and have added a requirement that is nowhere in the policy language. The quoted phrase tends to be interpreted to mean "within a reasonable time, depending on the circumstances," which may vary. A delay in providing notice of a few months may violate the notice condition under some circumstances but not others.

Even if notice is unduly late, however, the majority of courts hold that coverage is not forfeited unless the liability insurer has been prejudiced by the delayed notice. Prejudice may consist of greater difficulty defending the insured against liability, or greater difficulty proving that there is no coverage. Usually, though not always, these forms of prejudice involve the disappearance, or greater difficulty of obtaining, evidence relevant to either or both of the issues in question. There is no doubt that the grafting of the prejudice requirement onto the timely-notice condition resonates to some extent with the regulatory conception of insurance law. But the courts have shown considerable willingness to grant summary judgment to insurers on the issue, sometimes even by invoking a presumption of prejudice providing that, if enough time has elapsed before notice was provided, then there is prejudice as a matter of law.[19] This willingness suggests that the prejudice requirement is not used to camouflage judicial regulation of the claims process but to recognize that the notice requirement is actually a contractual condition rather than an unconditional promise.

3. The Claims Process: The Duty to Defend and the Duty to Settle

Liability insurance policies contain separate provisions governing the conduct of the insurer once a suit against the insurer is brought. These provisions pertain to the insurer's right and duty to defend and to the settlement of such suits. These provisions are another example of incomplete contracts that require legal doctrines to flesh out their application to a variety of different situations that the policy language does not address. As discussed earlier, the courts have not taken the opportunity to hold that these

---

[18] See, e.g., Federal Ins. Co. v. Raytheon Co., 426 F.3d 491 (1st Cir. 2005).
[19] West Bay Exploration v. AIG Specialty Agencies, 915 F.2d 1030 (6th Cir. 1990).

provisions are ambiguous in order to construe them in favor of coverage when doubts arise about their proper meaning and application. Rather, the courts have developed doctrines that they apply even-handedly to the situations that the doctrines address.

A. THE DUTY TO DEFEND

Most liability insurance policies contain an agreement by the insurer to defend any suit against the policyholder alleging liability that would be covered by the policy if the suit were successful. The insurer not only has a duty to defend but a right to do so. The defense of a suit against the policyholder protects the insurer's money, and the insurer therefore has an interest in defeating the suit, if possible. The duty to defend is covered "outside of limits." That is, sums the insurer spends on defense do not erode the amount of coverage provided.

It is often said that the duty to defend is "broader" than the duty to indemnify. This characterization is accurate in the sense that the insurer has a duty to defend suits containing allegations that are groundless, false, or fraudulent. The insurer must defend such suits even though ultimately there may be no liability for which to indemnify.

The test for the duty to defend is variously described,[20] but the most accurate description is the scope-of-the-pleadings test. This description means that the duty depends on what is alleged, not on what is true. Consequently, the insurer has no duty to defend a suit if a judgment based on the allegations in the pleadings would not be covered. In such a situation, the duty to defend is not broader than the duty to indemnify, but instead depends completely on the existence or nonexistence of coverage according to the pleadings.

When the insurer does defend and wishes subsequently to contest its indemnity obligation, it must reserve its right to do so. This "reservation of rights" must specify the grounds on which it is reserving its rights. In the absence of a reservation, the insurer has waived its right to contest coverage. There is a division of authority regarding remedies, however, for the insurer's breach of its duty to defend. A substantial number of courts hold that if the insurer breaches the duty to defend, it still may assert that it had no duty to indemnify. Another group of courts takes the position that an insurer that breaches its duty to defend waives its right to contest coverage, although it may contest the reasonableness of any settlement that the policyholder enters.

The rules just described reflect the courts' recognition that, for ordinary individuals and small business or other entities, the defense insurance provided by liability insurance policies is of great importance, and sometimes even more important than coverage of liability itself. Having the insurer defend against, and when necessary, settle suits (see later), even groundless or questionable ones, is critical to policyholders without substantial assets. The traditional tendency has therefore been to encourage insurers to defend their policyholders through the scope-of-the-pleadings rule, and a rule (where it applies) that an insurer in breach of its duty to defend has waived its right to contest coverage.

In recent years, however, there has been another trend that is double-edged in this respect. Some courts have permitted insurers to recoup their costs of defense from

---

[20] See RLLI, *supra* note 4, at §13 cmt. *a*.

policyholders when they have defended in the absence of a duty to do so. In one respect the right to recoup encourages insurers to defend claims against their insureds, for insurers who might not otherwise do so are encouraged that if a defense was not required, they may later recover their costs of defending. But this also means that some policyholders who previously would have received a defense without the risk of having to reimburse their insurer for their defense costs find later that they must do so. There is a split of authority regarding the right to recoup,[21] however, and even in jurisdictions that permit recoupment, cases in which an insurer seeks recoupment from an individual policyholder, as distinguished from a business, are rare.

B. THE DUTY TO SETTLE

Liability insurance policies typically give the insurer an unlimited right to settle or not to settle claims against the policyholder. The insurer may settle over the policyholder's objection and may refuse to settle despite the policyholder's strong preference for settlement. As with the duty to defend, the major exception involves directors' and officers' liability insurance policies, which afford the policyholder the right to settle, but only with the consent of the insurer.

The insurer's privilege to settle or not has been universally limited, however, by judicial decisions creating a duty to accept reasonable offers to settle. These decisions arise from recognition of the potential conflict of interest between the interests of the policyholder and the insurer when settlement is possible. When there is an offer from the plaintiff in the underlying suit against the policyholder to settle for a sum that falls within the monetary limit of the policy, it is always in the short-term economic interest of the policyholder to accept the offer, because the result will be that the policyholder is relieved of all risk at no cost.

In contrast, accepting such an offer is not always in the interest of the insurer. If the risk that liability will be imposed on the policyholder is small, it may be in the insurer's interest to reject the offer of settlement, especially if the lion's share of any potential judgment may exceed the monetary limits of the insurer's coverage obligation. In the event that liability is imposed, the policyholder would then be responsible for any sum in excess of that monetary limit.

This possibility may create a conflict of interest between the policyholder and the insurer, because the insurer rejecting a settlement offer will not have to bear all the consequences of that rejection. To reduce this conflict of interest, the courts have created a duty to settle. The liability insurer has a duty to disregard the limits of its policy and thereby to accept offers that a party responsible for the entire judgment that may ensue would accept.[22] If the insurer rejects a reasonable offer to settle—one that an insurer with no monetary limit on its obligation would accept—then the insurer is liable for the entire judgment, including the amount of the judgment in excess of the policy limits.[23]

---

[21] *Id.* at § 21.   [22] See *id.* at § 24 cmt. *c.*

[23] The seminal case on the duty to settle is *Crisci v. Security Ins. Co. of New Haven, Conn.*, 426 P. 2d 173 (Cal. 1967).

Importantly, however, the courts have not accepted the invitation to adopt a regulatory conception of the duty to settle and impose strict liability for rejecting any offer to settle within policy limits. The disregard the limits (DTL) test imposes liability for judgments in excess of the policy limits only when the insurer has wrongfully risked causing such judgments and still allows a liability insurer to reject unreasonable offers to settle.[24]

B. First-Party Insurance

Various forms of insurance protect people and entities against the risk that they will suffer their own losses. These include life, health, disability, and property insurance.

1. *Life Insurance*

One of the major issues in life insurance clearly reflects the tension between insurers' need to combat adverse selection and the desirability of ensuring that policyholders be able to rely on the coverage they have purchased. A provision in virtually all life insurance policies, often as a statutory requirement, is that the policy becomes "incontestable" after a specified period after issue, which is usually two years. Defenses based on misrepresentation cease to be available at that point. The idea here is that life insurance policies often are in force for twenty or thirty years or more and that stale defenses should lapse in order to assure the owner of the policy and its beneficiaries of the reliability of coverage.

Incontestability is in effect a contractual statute of limitations on defenses based on facts that were or were not in existence at the time of the application. Sometimes the courts refer to the test for incontestability as "discoverability," which is an accurate description as long as that is understood not as practical or reasonable discoverability, but rather discoverability in principle. If an applicant for life insurance sends his identical twin to take a physical exam that is a prerequisite to coverage, then a policy issued in reliance on the exam becomes incontestable after two years, even if it would have been a practical impossibility to discover this fraud. Interestingly, in fashioning incontestability doctrine, the courts have declined to create an exception even for outright fraud. They have not seen their role to involve policing fraud at the cost of maintaining the integrity of the incontestability principle.[25]

2. *Disability Insurance*

Disability insurance protects against the inability to work. Moral hazard is a considerable threat here, because different insureds sometimes react differently to comparable injuries and thus sometimes take different views as to whether the injury prevents them from working. In disability insurance, the main legal issue pertains to the meaning of disability. Partly the resolution of this issue depends on the precise language of the particular policy at issue. But most policies require (after a certain point) "total" disability. Clearly this

---

[24] For an argument in favor of strict liability, see Bruce L. Hay, *A No-Fault Approach to the Duty to Settle*, 68 Rutgers U. L. Rev. 321 (2015).

[25] See, e.g., Amex Life Ass. Co. v. Sup. Ct., 930 P.2d 1264 (Cal. 1997).

requirement does not mean that the policyholder must be unable even to sell pencils on a street corner. Exactly how much disability constitutes total disability, however, is likely to be a matter of dispute in marginal cases. Thus, in one case a physician infected with a hepatitis virus was considered unable to work,[26] and in another, a policyholder who was able to drive a bus was not precluded from coverage, notwithstanding policy language providing that the insured "does not engage in any occupation . . . for wage or profit during any such disability."[27] Here, in contrast to many of the doctrines I have been analyzing, apparently the policyholder's need to earn at least some income in order to survive trumps the literal meaning of the policy language in many cases.

3. *Health Insurance*

Even before enactment of the Affordable Care Act,[28] health insurance was partly private insurance but also heavily regulated. After the Act, and even after repeal of the mandate that all individuals purchase health insurance,[29] this form of insurance still is more heavily regulated than most.

The main private law focus of the ACA and of prior, less rigorous state regulation has been ensuring access to coverage, as well as affordability. Without regulation, insurers' efforts to combat adverse selection by imposing preexisting condition limitations on coverage, and by engaging in medical underwriting that charged those who purchased policies in the individual market higher premiums if they posed a higher risk, would mean that high-risk individuals would have little or no access to affordable coverage. The ACA achieved its aims by requiring insurers offering health insurance under the aegis of the Act to take all comers and by limiting medical underwriting to differentials based on age, place of residence, and tobacco use, and even then to a maximum differential of 3 to 1 from highest to lowest premium charged.

This arrangement is effectively a cross-subsidy under which the healthy subsidize the unhealthy, and the young subsidize those who are older. The viability of the arrangement, of course, depends on its being able to combat adverse selection, since the young and healthy, and especially those who are young, healthy, and poor, have much less incentive to purchase health insurance than others. The now-repealed individual mandate was the ACA's method of combating adverse selection, by eliminating selection entirely. It remains to be seen whether the individual and small group health insurance markets will now function effectively.

4. *Property Insurance*

Homeowners and renters insurance, as well as commercial property insurance, cover the risk of physical damage to or loss of use of tangible property, both real and personal. The principal issues under both forms of insurance involve the application of exclusions from and limitations on coverage, because most such insurance covers losses from all

---

[26] Doe v. Great-West Life & Annuity Ins. Co., 208 F.3d 213 (6th Cir. 2000).
[27] Moots v. Bankers Life Co., 707 P.2d 1083 (Kan. 1985).   [28] 42 U.S.C. § 18001 et seq.
[29] 26 U.S.C. § 5000A(c)(3)(A) (Supp. V) 2017.

causes ("perils") except those excluded, or (in the case of personal property) specifies a long list of covered causes.

Among the major, typically excluded causes of loss are earth movement, flood, and deterioration, the latter understood as any quality that causes insured property to damage or to destroy itself. The first two exclusions can be explained by reference to concern about adverse selection. Owners of property in earthquake prone and flood prone areas must separately purchase targeted earthquake or flood insurance.

One of the most litigated issues in recent years concerns concurrent causation, typically when the above-mentioned exclusions are potentially applicable. When a loss is caused both by a covered "cause" and an excluded "cause," the issue is whether coverage is excluded. For example, suppose that negligence by a municipality causes a mudslide that damages insured property. If the owner's policy covers "all risks" of physical loss, then the municipality's negligence is a covered cause of loss; but a mudslide is earth movement and is an excluded cause. The question is answered literally by the "anti-concurrent causation" clause included in most policies, which provides that coverage is excluded under these circumstances.[30] Apportionment issues also may arise, for example, as when hurricane winds (a covered cause) damage part of an insured property, and then a tidal surge (flood, an excluded cause) destroys what remains.[31]

When the standard anti-concurrent causation clause was first introduced, some courts took a regulatory perspective on its meaning, holding that a cause of loss had to be an "efficient proximate cause"[32] before the clause excluded it from coverage. That approach, however, is now the distinctly minority view. Today, most courts apply the clause as written, declining to adopt an interpretation that would promote coverage notwithstanding the language of the clause.[33]

V. Coordination of Coverage

It is fairly common for two sources of insurance, or one source of insurance and another source of compensation, such as a tort recovery, to be available to cover the same loss. For example, a driver who borrows a friend's car is likely to be covered by both his own and the friend's auto insurance. And a person injured by another party's negligent driving is likely to be covered by his own health insurance and to have a cause of action in tort against the negligent driver. The various approaches to coordinating coverage from multiple sources all serve the principle of indemnity—the notion that the purpose of insurance is to protect against loss, not to create the possibility of gain. Allowing net gain would not only be wasteful but at least under some circumstances could promote moral hazard.

---

[30] See Abraham & Schwarcz, *supra* note 2, at 237–242.
[31] See, e.g., Broussard v. State Farm Fire & Cas. Co., 523 F.3d 618 (5th Cir. 2008).
[32] Abraham & Schwarcz, *supra* note 2, at 241–242.   [33] See *id.* at 240.

The question, then, is whether and to what extent each source provides coverage, when multiple sources are available. The answer in the first instance is that the potentially applicable insurance policy or policies may contain provisions governing the issue. In liability insurance these are usually labeled "other insurance" clauses.[34] And in health and similar insurance they are labeled "coordination of coverage." It takes two consistent clauses in the two policies to achieve seamless coordination. For example, the standard auto policy provides that the owner's policy is primary, that is, pays first up to its limits of liability, and that the driver's policy is secondary or excess, that is, pays any excess remaining after the primary policy has paid what it owes.

Sometimes, however, the two clauses are in conflict. The courts then hold that the clauses are to be ignored. At this point it is as if both policies contained incomplete provisions. The courts do not then conclude that the policies are ambiguous and interpret them in favor of coverage, however. Rather, they have developed doctrine governing the construction of the conflicting policies, under which coverage responsibility is prorated, according to different formulas depending on the court. However, the courts will not permit an insured to be worse off because two policies provide coverage than she would be if she had only one policy. In health insurance the matter may be more complicated, both because health insurance policies frequently only partially overlap rather than provide identical coverage, and because a federal statute requires that Medicare always be treated as a secondary payer, regardless of what any other available policy says, except when that policy is provided to a retiree.[35]

The second area in which the coordination of coverage issue occurs is under the doctrine of subrogation. A health or property insurer, for example, may have paid the policyholder, or, in the case of liability insurance, made a payment on behalf of a policyholder for a loss for which the policyholder has a right of recovery (usually in tort) from a third party. Both under traditional doctrine and by virtue of express policy provisions, the insurer is subrogated to the policyholder's rights against that third party. The insurer may therefore bring an action against the third party, if the policyholder has not brought one, to recover the losses it has paid the policyholder. And if the policyholder brings suit and recovers, then under the policy's subrogation provision, the policyholder must reimburse the insurer for the amount previously paid. When the policyholder settles with the third party for less than the full amount of loss, then under the majority approach, the insurer has no right to reimbursement unless the policyholder has been "made whole."

It is worth noting that states may achieve certain kinds of tort reform simply by altering subrogation rights by statute. For example, if health insurers are denied rights of subrogation as against their insureds' tort recoveries, then health insurance rather than tort-and-liability insurance becomes the primary source of compensation for medical expenses associated with tortiously caused bodily injury. Whether that makes sense will depend, among many other things, on the view one takes about the importance of the incentives that are created by channeling primary coverage responsibility through liability insurance, as opposed to health insurance.

---

[34] *Id.* at 679–686.
[35] See, e.g., Harris Corp. v. Humana Health Ins. Co. of Fl., 253 F.3d 598 (11th Cir. 2001).

VI. Remedies

Most of the remedies for breach of an insurance contract parallel contract remedies and need not be separately discussed here. These include compensatory damages measured by the amount due under the policy and recission. In addition, punitive damages may be available in a cause of action in tort for "bad-faith" breach of an insurance policy, when breach is sufficiently blameworthy.[36]

One remedy that is distinctive to insurance, even if not always completely unique, is the cause of action for extra-contractual damages for "bad-faith" breach. Many states, by common law rule or statute, permit such a recovery. The test for bad faith varies, although clearly it does not require a malicious or dishonest state of mind on the part of an employee or agent of the insurer. Rather, the test is something like whether the insurer denied an insured's claim for coverage even though the validity of the claim was not even fairly debatable.[37] When this test is met, then the policyholder may recover not only the amount due under the policy but also compensatory damages for consequential economic losses resulting from the breach, and in some states compensatory non-economic damages for emotional and similar losses. Some statutes provide similar remedies, although a number limit recovery to counsel fees incurred in the breach of contract action. All these causes of action, however, are preempted by the Employee Retirement Income Security Act as to insurance that is provided as part of an employee benefit plan—mainly group health insurance.[38]

There can be little question that part of what lies behind liability for bad-faith breach is a regulatory impulse. But it is also clear that the courts see the doctrine as accomplishing justice between the parties—whether denominated corrective justice or civil recourse—in cases in which an insurer has not merely breached its insurance policy obligations but has done so in an egregiously wrongful manner.

VII. Conclusion

Insurance law takes common law doctrine seriously, and in doing so takes insurance policy language seriously. Doctrine and interpretation are not covert vehicles for the judicial achievement of regulatory goals; they reflect the courts' effort to apply the principles underlying insurance law with integrity and in a largely even-handed fashion.

---

[36] See RLLI, *supra* note 4, at § 50.   [37] See RLI, *supra* note 4, at § 49.
[38] Pilot Life Ins. Co. v. Dedeaux, 481 U.S. 41 (1987).

PART III

CORE PRINCIPLES OF PRIVATE LAW

CHAPTER 28

···

FORMALISM
AND REALISM
IN PRIVATE LAW

···

EMILY SHERWIN

ONE feature of the renewed interest in private law that inspired this collection of essays is a willingness to study legal doctrine and to recognize the role of doctrine in judicial decision-making.[1] In this respect, New Private Law stands in opposition to Legal Realism, which denies or at least minimizes the influence of doctrine on adjudication.[2] New Private Law assumes that legal concepts, categories, and rules play a vital role in defining legal relations between parties interacting with one another.[3]

Yet even those who are open to the idea that doctrine plays a role in adjudication of private rights and duties tend to reject "formalistic" approaches to legal doctrine.[4] Most often, those who believe in legal doctrine but not in formalism take a fairly broad view of

[1] See John C.P. Goldberg, *Introduction: Pragmatism and Private Law*, 125 HARV. L. REV. 1640, 1640 (2012), in *Symposium: The New Private Law, id.* at 1639.

[2] See *id.* at 1643–1644 (discussing Karl Llewellyn). Brian Leiter points out that few of the classic Legal Realists held that judicial references to doctrine are always or entirely pretextual. Brian Leiter, *Legal Realism and Legal Positivism Reconsidered*, 111 ETHICS 278, 298–299 (2001). Nor did Realists deny the existence of law as a social fact. *Id.* at 291–293 (suggesting that in arguing that law did not determine decisions, Realists presupposed a notion of law); Brian Leiter, *Legal Realisms, Old and New*, 47 VAL. U. L. REV. 949, 950 (2013). Realists, however, did maintain that at least in appellate cases, doctrine is indeterminate and consequently incapable of guiding decision-making. Leiter, *Legal Realism and Legal Positivism Reconsidered*, at 295–299.

[3] Goldberg, *supra* note 1, at 1652–1656; Shyamkrishna Balganesh, *Foreword: The Constraint of Legal Doctrine*, 163 U. PA. L. REV. 1843, 1851 (2015) (introducing a collection of essays on the constraint of legal doctrine in various, mostly private, areas of law).

[4] See, e.g., Balganesh, *supra* note 3, at 1846–1847 ("mechanistic" formalism); Benjamin C. Zipursky, *Reasonableness In and Out of Negligence*, 163 U. PA. L. REV. 1231, 1270 (2015) ("rigid doctrinalism"). See also Briane Leiter, *Legal Formalism and Legal Realism: What Is the Issue?*, 16 LEGAL THEORY 111, 111 (2010) ("vulgar formalism").

what legal doctrine comprises.[5] Some hold that doctrine includes not just rules of law but a body of recognized legal concepts such as right and duty and care that guide, limit, and organize legal decision-making.[6] Others say that legal materials must be interpreted in light of their intended purposes or the interests they are understood to serve.[7] Alternatively, legal doctrine consists in the "organizing principles" that have come to define the field of law to which the doctrine belongs.[8]

I endorse the effort to investigate what remains of legal doctrine after the Realist challenges of the last century and to identify what doctrine contributes to legal decision-making. In this chapter, I will go further and present an argument in favor of serious formalism—deductive, mechanistic, vulgar formalism. From the point of view of a legal authority or an individual who imposes a rule on herself, deductive formalism is practically rational in some circumstances, even if it sometimes produces results that are wrong when judged by the purposes of the rule or the rule follower's reasons for action, all things considered.

At the same time, my argument for deductive formalism is qualified in various ways. I do not suggest that all legal doctrine takes or should take the form of general rules stated in determinate language. In many situations, a comparatively indeterminate standard of behavior that invokes norms of fairness or reasonableness is a better mechanism for

---

[5] Fred Schauer helpfully traces the gradual expansion of the notion of "law" over the last several hundred years, beginning with Langdell and ending with Dworkin. See Frederick Schauer, *Law's Boundaries*, 130 HARV. L. REV. 2434 (2017). Schauer includes a number of Realists and successors to Realists in his account, although the Realist position is less an expansion of the notion of legal doctrine than an expansion of nondoctrinal decision-making by judges.

[6] Goldberg, *supra* note 1, at 1652–1653 (citing "conceptualism" as an element of the "inclusive pragmatism" typical of New Private Law); Zipursky, *supra* note 4 (discussing the legal concept of reasonableness).

[7] Lon L. Fuller, *Positivism and Fidelity to Law—A Reply to Professor Hart*, 71 HARV. L. REV. 630, 663 (1958) (purposes); Melissa Murray, *Family Law's Doctrine*, 163 U. PA. L. REV. 1985, 2017 (2015) (functions and interests served); Schauer, *supra* note 5, at 2448–2449 (describing the debate between Fuller and H.L.A. Hart).

[8] This is my reading of Alex Stein's discussion of evidence doctrine. See Alex Stein, *The New Doctrinalism: Implications for Evidence Theory*, 163 U. PA. L. REV. 2085 (2015). Stein argues that evidence law is organized according to principles of case-specific decision-making, minimization of the combined costs of error and error prevention, and equal protection of civil parties, or criminal defendants, against error. *Id.* at 2088. Stein suggests that although radical revision is always a possibility, current evidence doctrine is governed and limited by these principles. *Id.* at 2095.

Possibly Ronald Dworkin's approach to legal decision-making could be characterized as an expansion of doctrine rather than a rejection of doctrine: legal decisions should conform to whatever principles provide the morally best explanation of prior decisions and other legal materials. See Ronald Dworkin, *Law's Empire* 95–96 (1986) (law as integrity); Ronald Dworkin, *Taking Rights Seriously* 82–84 (1978) (legal principles). This depends on how stringently judges adhere to the requirement of fit between principles and prior decisions in the process of constructing legal principles. For an argument that fit plays no part at all, see Larry Alexander & Ken Kress, "Against Legal Principles," in *Law and Interpretation: Essays in Legal Philosophy* 279, 304–306 (Andrei Marmor ed., 1995).

regulating conduct than a determinate rule.[9] In other cases, a determinate rule may be preferable, but current rules may be inadequate because background conditions or underlying norms have changed. In cases of this kind, the role of the judge is to overturn or amend the rule. A further problem is that a rule that provides a determinate answer in most cases may be indeterminate when applied to particular facts.

A premise of my argument for deductive rule-following is that rules can and should be overruled or amended when they are unsatisfactory *as rules*.[10] For this purpose, I distinguish between good rules that sometimes generate bad results and bad rules. A rule is a good rule if, judged according to background moral principles or practical objectives, actors would do better by following the rule in all cases that fall within its terms than they would do by following their own best judgment about reasons for action. Ideally, judges should apply good rules deductively, without assessing reasons for action in the particular case before them. If, however, a rule does not meet the test of a good rule, either because it was poorly conceived at the outset or because social circumstances have changed, then the rule should be amended or overruled. Assuming the rule is a judge-made rule, judges as well as legislatures have the power to change or eliminate the rule.[11]

I. FORMALISM

A. Why Judges Should Enforce Good Rules

A good rule is one that, if regularly followed, will yield a set of outcomes that is superior, by relevant standards of desirability, to the set of outcomes actors would achieve if they judged case by case what to do. Good rules, however, will sometimes yield results that are

---

[9] See Zipursky, *supra* note 4. For discussion of the distinction between rules and standards, see, e.g., Kevin M. Clermont, *Rules, Standards, and Such*, 67 BUFFALO L. REV. (2020); Isaac Erlich & Richard A. Posner, *An Economic Analysis of Rulemaking*, 3 J. LEGAL STUD. 257, 261–271 (1974); Louis Kaplow, *Rules Versus Standards: An Economic Analysis*, 42 DUKE L.J. 557, 560–562 (1992).

[10] For further elaboration of the arguments presented here in favor of rule-following, see Larry Alexander & Emily Sherwin, *The Rule of Rules: Morality, Rules, and the Dilemmas of Law* 53–95 (2001). For an excellent general discussion of rules and rule-following, see Frederick Schauer, *Playing by the Rules: A Philosophical Examination of Rule-Based Decision-Making in Law and Life* (1991).

[11] I am assuming that, subject to the rules of stare decisis, judges have power to make rules, as opposed to simply discovering them in the ether. For discussion of judicial power to make rules, and the related implication that judges have power to amend or eliminate judge-made rules, see Larry Alexander & Emily Sherwin, *Demystifying Legal Reasoning* 40–63 (2008). Toward the end of the discussion last cited, Alexander and I suggested that judicial overruling should be limited to *significantly* flawed rules, to avoid undermining the general reliability of precedent rules. *Id.* at 63. On reflection, I now think overruling must be a matter of unconstrained judgment. That is, judges should overrule whenever a rule slips below the standard defining a good rule, subject only to the qualification that the overruling judge must consider the effect that overruling a particular rule will have on the overall reliability of judicial rules. If overruling will cause more harm (by relevant standards of harm) by undermining the positive effects of other rules than it will avoid by eliminating the negative effects of this rule, then the judge should not overrule.

wrong, measured by the same standards. Errors of this kind are inevitable because effective rules must be both general and determinate.[12] Because rules are formulated in advance of at least some of their particular applications, and because they must be formulated in words that are sufficiently determinate to guide conduct in a range of cases, rules will sometimes prescribe outcomes that are wrong when judged by the motivating reasons for the rule, or wrong, all things considered. This fact about rules does not prevent them from being good rules that judges ought to apply deductively.

General, determinate rules have a number of instrumental benefits.[13] One is to guide conduct: if the rule-making authority has special expertise that its subjects lack, actions prescribed by the rule are likely to conform more accurately to the subjects' reasons for action than actions the subjects would choose on their own. The rule-making authority also may be more impartial than individual actors would be in choosing among possible actions. Even if the rule maker has no special capabilities or attributes that qualify it to assess reasons for action, the rule's authoritative status enables it to serve as a focal point for coordination of conduct.[14] If actors expect that other actors will regularly follow the rule, they can plan their own actions on this basis. Authoritative rules also settle controversy about what to do and cut down on time spent in assessing reasons for action.

As described earlier, however, the various benefits associated with rules come at a cost: because rules are general and determinate, they inevitably will lead to unsatisfactory outcomes in some of the cases to which they apply. This fact about rules does not defeat their instrumental value, as long as they produce better outcomes on average than unconstrained choice of action. Nevertheless, it might seem that the best way to realize the benefits of rules is not to apply them deductively, but instead to treat them as guides to decision-making, with the understanding that judges should not enforce the rule when, all things considered, the actor was justified in breaking the rule. The rule, in other words, would be subject to a general exception for all cases in which the rule gives the wrong result.

One difficulty with a general exception for unsatisfactory outcomes is that the exception cannot simply depend on whether the particular state of affairs that will result from an exception is better than the state of affairs that would result from applying the rule. Instead, the question is whether the benefits of an exception are sufficient to outweigh any harm the exception will cause to the social value of the rule.[15] Each exception made

---

[12] On the generality and determinacy of rules, see Schauer, *supra* note 10, at 53–68. On the problem of determinate meaning, see generally Kent Greenawalt, *Law and Objectivity* 34–89 (1992); H.L.A. Hart, *The Concept of Law* 122–138 (1961); Jules L. Coleman & Brian Leiter, *Determinacy, Objectivity, and Authority*, 142 U. Pa. L. Rev. 549 (1993); Lawrence B. Solum, *On the Indeterminacy Crisis: Critiquing Critical Dogma*, 54 U. Chi. L. Rev. 462 (1987).

[13] Fred Schauer describes a number of benefits associated with rules. Schauer, *supra* note 10, at 135–166.

[14] On the coordination effects of rules, see, e.g., Gerald J. Postema, *Coordination and Convention at the Foundations of Law*, 11 J. Legal Stud. 165, 172–186 (1982).

[15] Schauer calls this "rule-sensitive particularism." Schauer, *supra* note 10, 94–100. His solution to the problems of rule-sensitive particularism is what he calls "presumptive positivism" in which actors and judges presume in favor of deductive application of rules but leave open the possibility of exceptions in strong cases. *Id.* at 196–206. This approach, however, does not completely solve the problem of erosion of coordination value over time. It also fails to eliminate the pressure judges may feel to make exceptions when outcomes seem wrong, but not quite wrong enough to overcome the presumption in favor of enforcement.

will indicate to observers that the rule is not regularly enforced, and so will reduce the coordination benefits of the rule. The effect of each exception is small, but as more exceptions are made the effects will cumulate and the coordination value of the rule will diminish.

The second difficulty with a generalized exception to deductive enforcement of rules within the determinate core of their application is that judges are not perfect reasoners. They are not omniscient, their inferential reasoning may be mistaken, and they are subject to the various cognitive biases that affect all human reasoners.[16] They may also misjudge the extent and effects of their own cognitive limitations. Thus, although an ideal reasoner might be able to calculate the exact detriment to rule values that will result from failure to enforce a particular rule in a particular case, a judge probably cannot and probably will not know when her estimate is incorrect.

If judicial mistakes in applying a general exception for bad outcomes of good rules were evenly distributed between mistaken enforcement and mistaken leniency, results might average out over time with minimal damage to rule values. Cognitive bias in applying rules, however, is likely to skew decisions away from rule-following and toward exceptions. One common type of bias is the tendency to give greater weight in decision-making to salient or emotionally charged features of a situation, as opposed to background probabilities or long-term consequences of the decision.[17] As a result of this cognitive tendency, judges are more likely to be swayed by the immediate circumstances of parties in a case before them, and particularly by circumstances that arouse sympathy, than by potential harm to the capacity of a rule to guide conduct and provide coordination. This suggests that judges will err systematically in favor of proposed exceptions and against deductive applications.[18] Judicial experience and training may reduce some of these biases, but they do not eliminate the problem. Thus, still assuming that the rule in question is a good rule, an exceptionless rule is likely to produce better outcomes over the long run than a rule coupled with a general exception for bad outcomes.

(a) *Example 1: Texting Rule*.[19] D, a working mother, is subject to Texting Rule, which prohibits drivers from using a cell phone while driving. D approves of Texting Rule, believing that drivers, including herself, tend to underestimate risks and overestimate

[16] For overviews of the problem of cognitive biases and studies documenting the availability heuristic and similar patterns of human reasoning, see Daniel Kahneman, Paul Slovic, & Amos Tversky eds., *Judgment Under Uncertainty: Heuristics and Biases* (1982); Daniel Kahneman, Paul Slovic, & Amos Tversky eds., *Heuristics & Biases: The Psychology of Intuitive Judgment* (2002).

[17] See Amos Tversky & Daniel Kahneman, "Availability: A Heuristic for Judging Frequency and Probability," in *Judgment Under Uncertainty, supra* note 16, at 163; Norbert Schwarz & Leigh Ann Vaughn, "The Availability Heuristic Revisited: Ease of Recall and Content of Recall as a Distinct Source of Information," in *Heuristics and Biases, supra* note 16, at 103; Jeffrey J. Rachlinski, *Bottom-Up and Top-Down Decisionmaking*, 73 U. CHI. L. REV. 933, 942–943 (2006) (discussing the effects of affect and availability biases in judicial decision-making); Frederick Schauer, *Do Cases Make Bad Law?*, 73 U. CHI. L. REV. 883, 895 (2006) (observing that judges, as rule makers, are subject to the availability bias).

[18] See Rachlinski, *supra* note 17.

[19] I have used a variation of this example in other work. See Emily Sherwin, "Exclusionary Rules," in *Moral Puzzles and Legal Perplexities: Essays on the Influence of Larry Alexander* 286 (Heidi M. Hurd ed., 2019).

their ability to perform two tasks at once. One day D is driving on a highway in slow traffic when she hears on the radio that her daughter's school has been placed on lockdown. She is currently an hour from the school. D would like to text her daughter to see if she is unharmed and her husband to alert him and tell him to go to the school. There are no exits in sight. Calling is legal, but D knows that both her daughter and her husband keep their ringers off during the day, so D texts.

A nearby officer sees D texting, pulls her over, and issues a ticket for violation of Texting Rule. D later explains her situation to a traffic court judge, hoping to avoid conviction. Conviction carries a large fine and a temporary suspension of her driver's license, which would mean hardship for D because her job requires her to travel by car.

Deductive application of Texting Rule yields an answer: D was caught in the act of texting and therefore must pay the fine and lose her license. Texting Rule appears to be a good rule: it is designed to prevent serious harm in a setting in which individuals often misjudge their abilities. The traffic court judge deciding D's case may sympathize with D's panic over the lockdown and the consequences she faces and may speculate that one act of leniency will not undermine the rule. Yet, given the importance of the rule to safety, the difficulty of drawing lines among justifications, and the effect that a public decision in favor of leniency will have on general obedience to the rule, the better choice may be to enforce the rule against D.

(b) *Example 2: Sophisticated Minor.* P, an actress, lives in Alabama.[20] At age eighteen and ten months, P was approached by Fox Film and signed an exclusive two-year employment contract with Independent. One month later, while still eighteen, she was approached by Independent Film, a smaller company, which offered her a two-year contract for a larger sum of money. After consulting with her lawyer, P signed this contract also. Neither film company was aware of P's negotiations with the other. After she turned nineteen, P repudiated her contract with Independent and affirmed her contract with Independent. Fox responded by threatening to sue Independent and urging Independent to break its contract with P, which it did.

Under the laws of Alabama, the age of majority is nineteen. A person who signs a contract while a minor is entitled, upon reaching majority, to choose either to enforce her prior contract, or to repudiate it without liability. The object of this set of rules is to protect minors against oppressive bargaining and to establish a clear age limit on which contracting parties can rely.

Assume that P sues Fox, seeking legal remedies against Fox for interfering with her contract with Independent. Deductive application of the rules governing the age of majority and the contractual rights of minors will result in a decision for P: P was a minor when she signed with Fox, P was entitled after majority to reject her Fox contract

---

[20] This example is based loosely on the facts of *Carmen v. Fox Film Corp.*, 269 F. 928 (2d. Cir. 1920). In the original case, Carmen lived in California, which at the time of the case set the age of minority at twenty-one. Alabama is now one of the few states that sets the age of majority over eighteen.

The only unusual aspect of the original case is that after the court denied Carmen an injunction ordering Fox to cease pressuring her second employer, Carmen was able to recover damages for interference with contractual relations. See *Carmen v. Fox Film Corp.*, 204 A.D. 776 (N.Y. App. Div. 1st Dept. 1923).

and affirm her Independent contract, and Fox is unlawfully interfering with a valid contract. Like Texting Rule, the Minor Contract Rule appears to be a good rule: age nineteen is a reasonable estimate of the minimum age for legal competence and the rule draws a useful line on which contracting parties can rely. A judge presiding over P's case may suspect that P was a highly sophisticated minor whose claim lies outside the protective purpose of the rule and who is now taking opportunistic advantage of the rule's terms. Yet, given the blatant nature of the P's advantage-taking, the temptation to sympathize with Fox's reliance, and the chance that the judge will undervalue the harm that a single decision will have on the coordination value of the rule, it may be better over the long run to apply the rule strictly to all cases it covers.

(c) *Example 3: Mistake.* S agreed to sell his home, and B agreed to buy it. Negotiations were conducted mainly through S's wife, who spoke accented English. B then drafted a contract stating what B believed to be the agreed price. S signed the contract without reading it, having in mind a price higher than the price stated in the document. In a subsequent suit by B for specific performance of the written contract, the judge finds that although the stated price was low, B did not engage in fraud and did not know that S was mistaken about the price.[21]

Mistake Rule holds that in the absence of fraud, a mistake by one party to a contract does not invalidate the contract.[22] Deductive application of this rule will enable B to enforce the contract against S. A judge presiding over this case may feel that enforcing the contract will impose a hardship on S and allow B to profit from the mistake of an unsophisticated seller. Yet, taking account of contractual practices that have coalesced around the rule, deductive application may be appropriate even if is sometimes results in undeserved gains and losses.

B. The Formalist's Dilemma

If a rule is a good rule in the sense I have described, then from the perspective of an authority overseeing a legal system, it is instrumentally best that actors apply the rule deductively in choosing their actions. If they fail to do so, it is best that judges apply the rule deductively in resolving legal disputes. Another way to put this is that actors and judges should treat good rules as exclusionary reasons for action, providing both a first-order reason to act or decide as the rule requires and a second-order reason not to act or decide based on contrary reasons for action that fall within the general range of reasons the rule maker considered in enacting the rule.[23]

---

[21] This example is based on *Panco v. Rogers*, 87 A.2d 770 (N.J. Ch. Div. 1952).

[22] The Realist-influenced *Restatement (Second) of Contracts* alters this rule by allowing the mistaken party to avoid the contract if "the effect of the mistake is such that enforcement of the contract would be unconscionable." *Restatement (Second) of Contracts* § 153(a) (1981).

[23] On exclusionary reasons for action, see Joseph Raz, *The Morality of Freedom* 57–62 (1986); Joseph Raz, *The Authority of Law* 16–19, 22–23, 30–33 (1979). See also Joseph Raz, "Promises and Obligation," in *Law, Morality, and Society: Essays in Honour of H.L.A. Hart* 221–223 (P.M.S. Hacker & Joseph Raz eds., 1977) (applying the notion of exclusionary reasons to promises).

Judges enforcing the rule in particular cases confront the rule from a different perspective, in which a set of facts has emerged from the general coverage of the rule. The judge may agree that the rule is a good rule, realize that her judgment is imperfect, and understand the reasons why, from the authority's point of view, it is best to enforce the rule in all cases. But she will also understand that all general rules are overbroad and will produce some wrong results. Therefore she may come to believe that her current reasons tally against applying the rule in this case. Because the rule is a good rule, judges who reach this conclusion will be wrong more often than they are right, but the judge has already taken this fact into account and believes that this time she is correct.

For example, consider again the case of Texting Rule. D has been issued a ticket for violation of the rule. The traffic court judge hearing D's case believes that the rule is a good rule. Nevertheless, the judge is sympathetic to D's situation: she has a child herself and believes that the consequences of the rule are too harsh in this case, given the panic induced by a lockdown and the threat to D's job. The judge may be wrong; she may be failing to account for the dangers of texting and consequences of a lenient decision. But it is at least possible that she is correct.

Similarly, in the case of Sophisticated Minor, the judge may believe that the rule governing the age of majority is a good rule that many people act under and that making an exception could impair the reliability of the rule. Yet, the judge is considering only a single exception in a single case and is convinced that P did not rely in good faith but instead quite knowingly used the rule to benefit at the expense of Fox. The judge may be wrong; she may be underestimating the effects of her decision on other cases governed by the rule. But, given the generality and overbreadth of the rule, it is at least possible that she is correct.

Likewise, in the case of Mistake, the judge may believe that rule is a good rule, assigning responsibility in a way that is reasonable in most contractual situations and providing a template for transactions. At the same time, she may think that B should have double-checked or simply that the result is unfair. The judge's assessment may be wrong: a stricter rule may encourage care and reduce litigation. But again, it is possible that the judge is correct.

The dilemma posed by rules can be characterized as a problem of rationality. Practical rationality is rationality in action, judged by how well an agent's choice of action serves her ends.[24] One natural way to understand practical rationality is that an agent's choice of action must conform to her current reasons for action, as they stand at the time of

---

[24] Practical rationality is primarily an instrumental concept, assessing the appropriate connection between an agent's choice of action and her ends. Rationality may also impose limits on the agent's ends; I set this question aside. See Michael E. Bratman, *Intentions, Plans, and Practical Reason* 52 (1987) (doing the same).

Like Bratman, I focus on agent rationality, which turns on whether the agent is rational in performing the act and thus allows for a reasonable assessment by the agent of what her reasons require. See *id.* at 53. By comparison, act rationality may require a more objective fit between reasons and actions.

action.[25] On this view, it is not rational for a judge to apply a rule deductively when she reasonably believes she has reason to make an exception.

Alternatively, it is possible to look at practical rationality as a process that extends over time.[26] In other words, it may be practically rational to form a plan of action at one time and then act on the plan at a later time, if this course of action will better serve the agent's ends. On this view, if a legal rule is a good rule in the sense that over time, regular enforcement of the rule will produce a better sum of results than case-by-case judgment, then it may be practically rational for a judge to apply the rule deductively in every case that falls within the rule's core of determinate meaning.[27]

The difficulty with this argument for the practical rationality of deductive application of rules lies in identifying the cognitive process by which a judge can enforce the rule when she believes that in the particular case before her, the rule is a good rule but the party who broke it acted correctly. In the case of Texting Rule, for example, the judge may believe that overall, regular enforcement of the rule will produce a better sum of outcomes than regular rethinking of whether to enforce the rule. She may understand that her own judgment is unreliable because she is prone to underestimate negative long-term consequences of lenient decisions. But she also understands that in fact, the rule will sometimes produce a bad result, and she believes that it produces a bad result in this case. Long-term consequences will be best if she enforces the rule in all cases, including this one; but immediate consequences appear to be better if she makes an exception now. How is she able to suppress her own current judgment and act on her long-term judgment that the rule is a good rule that ought to be enforced deductively in all cases?

In my view, the most persuasive account of this type of temporally extended practical rationality comes from Michael Bratman.[28] Bratman's interest is not specifically in rule-following but in making and following plans in everyday life. Very briefly, Bratman focuses on the cognitive role of intentions. Intentions, in his view, are not just combinations of belief and desire but independent mental states that carry with them an element of "volitional commitment." Volitional commitment means that if the agent formed her intention rationally and does not reconsider it before the time of action, she can, rationally, proceed to act without further consideration of what to do. Reconsideration is

---

[25] See Edward F. McClennen, *Pragmatic Rationality and Rules*, 26 PHIL. & PUBL. AFF. 210 (1997) (calling this view, which he ultimately rejects, the "Separability" principle). Heidi Hurd appears to take this view, though her position is not explicit. Heidi M. Hurd, *Moral Combat* 69–94 (1999). Hurd's focus is on the rationality of accepting the practical authority of another person or entity; mine is on the rationality of rule-following.

[26] See Bratman, *supra* note 24; David Gauthier, "Intention and Deliberation," in *Modeling Rationality, Morality, and Evolution* (Peter A. Danielson ed., 1998); David Gauthier, *Assure and Threaten*, 104 ETHICS 690 (1994); Edward F. McClennen, *Pragmatic Rationality and Rules*, 26 PHIL. & PUBL. AFF. 210 (1997); Edward F. McClennen & Scott J. Shapiro, "Rule-Guided Behavior," in III *New Palgrave Dictionary of Economics and the Law* 367 (Peter Newman ed., 1998); Scott J. Shapiro, *Legality* 122–124 (2011); Scott J. Shapiro, "The Difference that Rules Make," in *Analyzing Law: New Essays in Legal Theory* (Brian Bix ed., 1998).

[27] Scott Shapiro endorses a view similar to this. See McClennen & Shapiro, *supra* note 26, at 365–366.

[28] See generally Bratman, *supra* note 24.

always possible, but a rational agent will possess a set of reasonable dispositions toward prior intentions that lead her not to reconsider unless some good reason appears to do so. Thus, in many cases, a practically rational agent who has formed a rational long-term intention will just act on her intention, bypassing further reflection about what to do at the time of action.[29] Applying this set of ideas to the case of Texting Rule, the practically rational decision for the traffic court judge is to enforce the rule.[30]

This is not the end of the story, however, because there remains a problem of epistemic rationality, meaning rationality in forming beliefs. Standards of epistemic rationality promote true belief, either by requiring agents to align their beliefs to their evidence or by requiring them to adopt processes of belief formation that are conducive to truth. Either way, epistemic rationality is synchronic in the sense that the objective is to justify the agent's current beliefs, not a course of belief formation over time.[31]

The synchronicity of epistemic rationality means that if practical rationality is defined in the temporally extended sense that Bratman suggests, practical rationality and epistemic rationality can conflict. Returning to the case of Texting Rule: taking into account the fallibility of her reasoning in particular cases and the harm that a public decision not to enforce the rule would have on its overall value as a guide to conduct, the judge has formed a practically rational intention to enforce the rule in all cases. If, in D's case, she forms a reasonable belief that she should make an exception, she must reconsider her intention. In this way, epistemic rationality can undermine practical rationality.

A supporter of temporally extended practical rationality might say that, under Bratman's principles of practical rationality, the problem is easily solved: the judge can simply act on her prior intention to follow the rule without forming any beliefs about her current reasons for action, as long as she is guided by reasonable dispositions toward prior intentions. Because she never consults evidence about what to do, or consults it only to the extent necessary to spot an obvious or overwhelming reason to abandon her intention, epistemic rationality never comes into play, and she is free to do what is practically rational over time.[32] This path to reconciling long-term practical rationality with

---

[29]   Bratman also develops a special principle of rationality of "policies," which seems particularly suitable to rule-following. See *id.* at 88–91. A policy is an intention to perform a type of action in recurrent situations. For this type of intention, Bratman formulates a principle allowing the act unreflectively on the intention if her reasonable dispositions favor both retaining the intention and not blocking its application to the particular case.

[30]   Notice that this is not mindless rule-following. The judge's intention to follow the rule is rational only if she initially concluded that Texting Rule is a good rule that will produce better results over time than further reflection. If this is not the case, she can and should reject the rule at the outset, using whatever techniques of overruling or crafty interpretation she has learned from Legal Realism.

[31]   See Earl Conee & Richard Feldman, *Evidentialism: Essays in Epistemology* 233 (2004); Richard Foley, *The Theory of Epistemic Rationality* 8 (1987); Alvin Goldman, *Toward a Synthesis of Reliabilism and Evidentialism, in Evidentialism and Its Discontents* 275–276 (Trent Doherty ed., 2011).

[32]   Bear in mind that we are not talking about mindless enforcement of draconian rules. Bratman's principles of extended practical rationality require that the agent's intentions must be rational when formed in order to have the volitional force needed to sustain future acts without further reflection. If the rule in question is not a good rule, a rational judge would not form the intention to apply it deductively, but would instead exercise whatever powers she has to amend it or engage in Realist-style avoidance.

epistemic rationality may not, however, be available. Simplifying an otherwise complex subject, the difficulty is that on one very plausible understanding, epistemic rationality includes an element of epistemic responsibility to advert to new evidence, at least when that evidence casts doubt on the agent's current beliefs.[33] If so, then an epistemically rational judge cannot simply rely on her prior belief in the long-term practical rationality of enforcing the rule in all cases, if her current evidence appears to show that the better course is to enforce the rule generally but not in this case.

Judges tasked with deductive application of rules face an intractable dilemma. Good legal rules—those that, if regularly followed, will yield a better sum of actions than case-by-case judgment—provide important social benefits. Therefore, from the general perspective of lawmakers, including judges in their lawmaking capacity, good rules should be applied deductively. Good rules, however, do not always produce good outcomes in particular cases. From the particular perspective of those who act under rules, including judges in their law-applying capacity, it will sometimes seem wrong to apply even a good rule deductively when it appears to produce the wrong result based on the evidence in a particular case.

II. Solutions

A. Traditional Equity

Aristotle is translated as saying that equity consists in "rectification of law in so far as the universality of law makes it deficient."[34] English and American courts once were able, and to some extent are able still, to accomplish something like a rectification of law through the procedures and remedies associated with the English Chancery. Equity courts, and later courts granting equitable remedies in a procedurally merged legal system, used various techniques to soften the consequences of deductive application of legal rules without fully acknowledging that they were making exceptions to the rules.

---

[33] Even strong supporters of the view that epistemic rationality requires only that an agent's beliefs should conform to evidence she has already internalized when she forms her belief have made exceptions when the agent is confronted with new evidence that threatens to defeat her existing beliefs. In this type of case, if the challenge posed by the new evidence is clear, the agent must process the evidence and, if necessary, revise her beliefs. See Richard Feldman, "The Ethics of Belief," in Conee & Feldman, *supra* note 31, at 186–188; Goldman, *supra* note 31, at 23. Technically, it is not quite accurate to say, in the rule-following cases, that new evidence suggesting that an exception is warranted in a particular case defeats the judge's existing beliefs about rule-enforcement. At T_1, the judge believes that Texting Rule is a good rule, that enforcing Texting Rule deductively will yield better results over time than following her own possibly faulty judgment in all cases. Yet she also believes that, due to the generality of rules, there will be some cases in which she would judge correctly that rule requires the wrong result. Her evidence at T_2 does not actually defeat this set of beliefs. But it does suggest that she would do better by following the rule deductively in all cases except this one.

[34] Aristotle, *Nicomachean Ethics* ¶ 1137b25 (C.D.C. Reeve trans., 2014).

This type of rectification relies on several features of equity doctrine that derived from the need to avoid direct conflict between Chancery and the political authority of the law courts.[35] Equity courts purported to accept the authority of legal rules over the legal status of property and contracts and to address only the personal obligations of parties to one another. They characterized their remedial powers as supplemental, to be exercised only when legal remedies were inadequate, and as discretionary. For the most part, these principles carried over to postmerger judicial exercise of equity powers.

One particularly useful vehicle for rectification of the law was the technique of equitable defenses, meaning defenses that apply only to equitable remedies such as injunctions and not to legal damage remedies.[36] Certain defenses, often involving conduct that was unfair in some hard-to-define way, or hardship falling disproportionately on one party, would bar equitable remedies. In this way, courts could enforce a general, determinate legal rule deductively, but only by one form of relief. This technique resulted in rectification of harsh results of the rule because equitable remedies normally were available only when legal remedies were inadequate to protect the claimant's rights. Thus, although the court enforced the rule, the claimant did not realize the full value of the legal right that appeared to be embedded in the rule.

The case of Mistake is an example. Applying Mistake Rule deductively, the judge might conclude that S was bound by the contract he signed and that B was entitled to damages. The judge could then recognize an equitable defense, denying B the remedy of specific performance on the ground that B might have confirmed the price with S and that specific performance will deprive S of his primary asset without adequate compensation. Thus, B wins, but a jury awarding damages may aim low in the circumstances of the case, and B will never receive the home he intended to buy.

Sophisticated Minor is another example. The court denied the claim of P, the technical minor, for an injunction forbidding Fox from pressuring Independent to break its contract with her, relying on the equitable defense known as "unclean hands."[37] In a separate suit, however, P was able to recover damages for Fox's interference with the contract.[38] The damage award may not have been enough to fully compensate for her loss, but it preserved the appearance that courts would apply the Minor Contract Rule deductively.

If all parties, or even all lawyers, were fully aware of the existence and effects of equitable defenses, the advantages of determinate rules would be diminished, if not lost. Equitable defenses, however, play a fairly arcane role in the law. As a result, they are not likely to enter into parties' calculations at the planning stages of a transaction, at least in the ordinary type of transaction in which case-by-case rectification is likely to come into play. Thus, traditional equity doctrine provided a certain amount of cover for occasional judicial rectification of the outcome of rules. The solution may not have been a stable

---

[35] See generally F.W. Maitland, *Equity*; also the *Forms of Action at Common Law: Two Courses of Lectures* 2–11 (A.H. Chaytor & W.J. Whittaker eds., 1st ed. 1909) (describing the development of Chancery).

[36] For an insightful mini-treatise on equitable defenses, see Edward Yorio, *Contract Enforcement: Specific Performance and Injunctions* (1989).

[37] Carmen v. Fox Film Corp., 269 F. 928, 931 (2d Cir. 1920).

[38] Carmen v. Fox Film Corp., 204 A.D. 776 (N.Y. App. Div. 1st Dept. 1923).

one over time, but it was, to some extent, a way to simultaneously apply and soften rules, without amending their determinate terms.

B. Legal Realism

Most American Legal Realists were highly skeptical of the capacity of determinate rules to govern judicial decision-making.[39] Some held that the legal concepts often woven into doctrinal rules were fictitious and therefore had no practical meaning.[40] Some held that rules were indeterminate, mainly because for any given problem, multiple rules could be found supporting opposite practical results.[41] Another Realist theme was that law and legal scholarship should be as transparent as possible: judges should be forthright about the grounds of their decisions, and meaningless phrases should be purged from the law.[42]

Consequently, the Realists proposed that courts should give up the enterprise of applying rules deductively and instead use their own experience and any available social science to determine the best outcome for each dispute.[43] Alternatively, they proposed that fact-specific decision-making should be incorporated into the rules themselves.[44] Relatively determinate language should be replaced by language that forced judges to determine a social and morally appropriate response to the circumstances of each dispute, or at least of each dispute type. For example, in cases like Mistake, courts should

[39] See generally Brian Leiter, "American Legal Realism," in *The Blackwell Companion to Philosophy of Law and Legal Theory* 249 (Dennis Patterson ed., 2d ed. 2010); Brian Leiter, *Legal Realism and Legal Doctrine*, 163 U. PA. L. REV. 1975 (2015).

[40] See, e.g., Felix S. Cohen, *Transcendental Nonsense and the Functional Approach*, 35 COLUM. L. REV. 809 (1935).

[41] See, e.g., Karl N. Llewellyn, *The Bramble Bush: Some Lectures on the Law and Its Study* 2–4, 64–69 (1930) ("every single precedent, according to what may be the attitude of future judges, is ambiguous, is wide or narrow at will") (emphasis omitted); see also Karl N. Llewellyn, *A Realistic Jurisprudence—The Next Step*, 30 COLUM. L. REV. 431, 447–448 (1930) (discussing the difference between "paper rules" and the "real rules" that govern decisions).

[42] Llewellyn said that "Covert tools are never reliable tools." Karl N. Llewellyn, *The Common Law Tradition: Deciding Appeals* 365 (1960), quoting Karl N. Llewellyn, *Book Review*, 52 HARV. L. REV. 700, 703 (1939).

[43] See, e.g., Jerome Frank, *Law and the Modern Mind* 111 (1930) ("The peculiar traits, dispositions, biases and habits of the particular judge will, then, often determine what he decides to be the law); Joseph C. Hutcheson, *The Judgment Intuitive: The Function of the "Hunch" in Judicial Decision*, 14 CORNELL L.Q. 274, 278 (1929) ("I, after canvassing all the available material . . . wait for the feeling, the hunch—that intuitive flash of understanding that makes the jump-spark connection between question and decision . . ."); Underhill Moore & Theodore S. Hope Jr., *An Institutional Approach to the Law of Commercial Banking*, 38 YALE L.J. 703 (1929) (attempting a scientific study of legal decision-making); Herman Oliphant, *A Return to Stare Decisis, Pt. 2*, 14 A.B.A. J. 159, 159 (1928) ("we see that courts are dominantly coerced not by the essays of their predecessors but by a surer thing,—by the intuition of fitness of solution to problem,—and a renewed faith in judicial government is engendered.").

[44] See U.C.C. §§ 1-304 (good faith in performance and enforcement); 2-302 (unconscionability). For critical commentary, see Arthur Allen Leff, *Unconscionability and the Code: The Emperor's New Clause*, 115 U. PA. L. REV. 485 (1967).

adopt a "rule" that allows rescission for unilateral mistake if the mistake has "unconscionable" consequences.[45] This solution, however, simply gives up on the possibility of meaningful doctrine, and thus on the values of governance, coordination, and settlement of controversy that rules promote.

III. Conclusion

The dilemma of rules is an inescapable problem in any legal system in which decisions are open to the public.[46] It is unescapable because judges encounter rules from two different perspectives.[47] One is the general perspective of the rule maker, from which the long-term benefits of strict enforcement are easy to see. The other is the perspective of participants in a particular case, who observe a single application of the rule. From this perspective, long-term benefits may be obscured by the rule's adverse consequences in the case. If the rule is a good rule, then over time, a decision to follow the rule will be correct more often than not; but nothing in the general perspective rules out the possibility that an exception to the rule is currently justified. Accordingly, the particular perspective puts pressure on judges to engage in equitable correction of rules, of the type endorsed by Aristotle.[48]

The Realist response was to call either for an end to doctrine or for changes in doctrine that incorporate equitable correction into the doctrine itself, through terms such as "unconscionable." In some contexts, such as the law of negligence, determinate rules may not work well, and broader standards that invite particularistic decision-making are appropriate.[49] In other situations, however, determinate rules have significant value, which is lost when rules are either abandoned or coupled explicitly with general equitable exceptions to be applied by adjudicators.

The procedural and remedial details that once allowed the legal system to strike a compromise between determinate rules and equitable correction have tended to fade away over time. In the post-Realist atmosphere of clarity about law and legal decision-making, the best way to protect the value of rules is to bring attention to both their costs and their benefits. Rules are not always appropriate tools for regulating conduct. When rules are appropriate, current rules may not be good rules. Even good rules will not

---

[45] *Restatement (Second) of Contracts* § 153.

[46] Jeremy Bentham favored a legal system in which legal rules, in the form of legislation, were made public, but judicial decisions were not. See Gerald G. Postema, *Bentham and the Common Law Tradition* (1989) (assembling, synthesizing, and reviewing Bentham's proposals made for an ideal system of law). This might ameliorate the problem of rules, but is not likely to engender public faith in the system. See also Meir Dan-Cohen, *Conduct Rules and Decision Rules: On Acoustic Separation in Criminal Law*, 97 HARV. L. REV. 625 (1984) (examining the possibility of separate transmission of different rules, one to actors and one to judges).

[47] See Larry Alexander, *The Gap*, 14 HARV. J.L. & PUBL. POL'Y 695 (1991).

[48] See *supra* note 34 and accompanying text.   [49] See Zipursky, *supra* note 4.

always yield the right result. And in any event, the dilemma associated with rules will never disappear.

There is, however, a place for rules, and for deductive application of rules, in law and legal theory. Rather than belittling deductive reasoning, legal scholarship and legal education should pay more careful attention to the values served by determinate rules and the criteria for determining when judges should follow rules. Sometimes the most industrious moral or economic reasoning will not yield the best decision.

CHAPTER 29

....

PRIVITY

....

MARK P. GERGEN

PERCY Winfield once observed that the old privity rules in contract law and negligence law made contract a "perfect circle that must be marred by no indentation or protuberance."[1] By perfect, Winfield meant impregnable. Privity rules in contract law prevented obligations created by a contract from protruding on third parties, while a privity rule in tort law prevented obligations to third parties that might otherwise be imposed by tort law from "indenting" upon a contract. Contract no longer is an impregnable circle of obligation. But contract law still has a privity requirement that prevents a contract from protruding negatively on nonparties. Meanwhile, in tort law the function of preventing negligence law from indenting upon a contract has devolved to rules that preclude a negligence claim for pure economic loss. And there are rules in property law and the law of restitution that perform the same functions as the old privity rules in contract law and negligence. These include bona fide purchaser rules in property law and rules in the law of restitution that preclude claims for indirect enrichment and that preserve the priority of contract as a mechanism for resolving problems of unjust enrichment.

I argue these rules perform two general functions. Rules that prevent a contract from protruding negatively upon a nonparty serve a partitioning function. Because of these rules, when an actor engages in a transaction that is part of a chain or web of contracts she need not worry about a contract to which she is not a party subjecting her to a contractual obligation. Bona fide purchaser rules perform a similar function in property law with respect to property claims arising from upstream transactions. These partitioning rules are largely justified by the concern for information costs. Rules that prevent negligence law and the law of restitution from altering contractual relationships preserve the priority of contract and contract law as the mechanism for determining responsibility for an accidental loss when parties can reasonably be expected to deal with the problem by contract. I will refer to this as a boundary-drawing function. These boundary-drawing rules are justified by a set of concerns that make private ordering through contract preferable to public ordering as a mechanism for determining responsibility for accidental harm.

---

[1] Percy H. Winfield, *The Restatement of the Law of Torts—Negligence*, 13 N.Y.U. L.Q. REV. 1, 15 (1935).

The law of restitution has particularly strong partitioning rules that preclude a restitution claim in cases of indirect enrichment. And it has particularly strong boundary-drawing rules that preclude a restitution claim when there is a possible contractual solution to a problem of unjust enrichment. These strong partitioning and boundary-drawing rules mean that a restitution claim generally is available only in a narrow band of cases in which the plaintiff and defendant are in a direct relationship (which might make it possible for them to handle a problem of unjust enrichment by contract), but they do not handle the problem by contract, and cannot reasonably be expected to do so. I suggest the law of restitution takes this laissez-faire approach to accidents because the accidents at issue involve a shift in wealth between a plaintiff and defendant and not a social loss. A similar phenomenon occurs in the law of economic negligence, which also has particularly strong partitioning and boundary-drawing rules. I suggest this may be justified in a significant subset of economic negligence cases because the losses at issue are private losses and not social losses.

I. Contract and Property

A pair of rules in contract law limit the legal effect of a contract to the parties to the contract. The first rule is that a contract cannot bind a nonparty[2] or "destroy rights of a nonparty."[3] There is no exception to this rule in contract law: other bodies of law must be used to get around it. Property law makes it possible to use a covenant to bind a nonparty. A nonparty may also be liable for tortious interference with contract. And a nonparty may be required to respect a contractual restriction on the use of property by the doctrine of equitable notice.

The second rule is that a nonparty acquires no rights under a contract. Modern contract law does make exceptions to this rule though the common law took some time to come around to this position. Modern contract law allows parties to a contract to bestow a contract right on a nonparty by assignment[4] or as a third-party beneficiary.[5]

---

[2] The rule is described as "elementary," Gambles v. Perdue, 572 P.2d 1241, 1243 (1977), as "so fundamental that it rarely receives mention," FCM Group, Inc. v. Miller, 17 A.3d 40, 54 (Conn. 2011), and as something that "goes without saying." Equal Empl. Opportunity Comm'n v. Waffle House, Inc., 534 U.S. 279, 294 (2002).

[3] Young v. Tri-Etch, Inc., 790 N.E.2d 456, 459 (Ind. 2003).

[4] Assignments had to be done by the workaround of treating an assignment as creating a power of attorney in the assignee to sue on behalf of the assignor. Assignees who could not enforce a claim at law were able to sue in equity. Law courts recaptured the business of enforcing assigned claims when *Winch v. Keely*, 1 Term R. 619 (1787), held that a common law court could "take notice of an equity."

[5] Prior to the rise of classical theories of contract in the late nineteenth century, courts in England and the U.S. regularly recognized third party beneficiary contract claims. But in the late nineteenth and early twentieth centuries courts rejected such claims. In England and some states they were rejected categorically, while in New York they were allowed in a limited category of cases. Melvin A. Eisenberg, *Third Party Beneficiaries*, 92 COLUM. L. REV. 1358, 1360–1371 (1992). U.S. law liberalized in the twentieth century. Today most U.S. courts use the "intent to benefit" test to determine third-party beneficiary status. *Restatement (Second) Contracts* § 302(1)(b). Third-party beneficiary claims have been available in England only since the Contracts (Rights of Third Parties) Act of 1999.

Secondary rules in the law of assignment and third-party beneficiary ensure that a contract defines the obligation owed to a nonparty who acquires a right under the contract. Thus there is a rule that "a third party beneficiary cannot have greater rights than a contract creates."[6]

The rule that a contract cannot bind or destroy rights of a nonparty serves a partitioning function. When three or more persons engage in a complicated project, like a construction project, their conduct is likely to be governed by a chain or web of binary contracts. The rule that a contract cannot bind or destroy rights of a nonparty creates a partition so that a person can generally rely on the binary contracts to which she is a party to determine the full set of her contractual obligations with respect to the project. Similarly, when an asset passes through multiple hands through a chain of transactions, the rule creates a partition so that a downstream holder of an asset need not worry about an upstream contract imposing a contractual obligation on her with respect to the asset.

One aspect of this partitioning function is that the rules of contract law apply to determine people's obligations to each other only when people are in privity of contract.[7] As I explain in an earlier paper, "While contract is a mechanism for private ordering, much of contract law exists to resolve mistakes in private ordering, such as misunderstandings and oversights."[8] When one party to a contract carelessly harms another party, contract law makes it possible for a court to impose liability for the harm, when liability seems appropriate. Similarly contract law makes it possible to prevent unjust enrichment when this seems appropriate. But rules of contract law cannot be used to impose liability or to prevent unjust enrichment when the plaintiff and defendant are not in privity of contract.

The rules on assignment and third-party beneficiary make it possible to endow nonparties with contract rights. But, again, it is impossible under contract law to subject a nonparty to a contractual obligation. Because an assignee acquires rights under a contract but does not assume obligations under the contract, there is a need for a rule outside of contract law so that a person who acquires a lease by assignment assumes obligations under the lease. This rule is found in property law. The obligations of an assignee are said to arise through "privity of estate."[9] The concept of "privity of estate"

---

[6] Doe v. Grosvenor Prop. (Haw.) Ltd., 829 P.2d 512 (Haw. 1992).

[7] The rule is backed up by a rule that applies when a writing formally identifies the parties to a contract. The rule precludes using nontextualist rules of interpretation and construction to establish that a person not formally identified as a party in the writing is a party to the contract. Thus in *Harding Co. v. Sendero Resources, Inc.*, 365 S.W.3d 732 (2012), an owner of a corporation who signed a purchase and sale agreement in his capacity as owner and president of a corporation was held not to be personally bound by a covenant not to compete even though this rendered the covenant meaningless. The purchaser argued the formal capacity in which the owner signed the writing should be disregarded under the general rule that rejects an interpretation of a contract that renders the contract meaningless. The court concluded this rule did not apply because "[a] general rule of contract construction cannot be used to bind a party to a contract it did not sign." 365 S.W.3d at 740.

[8] Mark P. Gergen, *Privity's Shadow: Exculpatory Terms in Extended Forms of Private Ordering*, 43 Fla. St. L. Rev. 1, 35 (2015).

[9] Kelly v. Tri-Cities Broadcasting, Inc., 147 Cal. App.3d 666 (1983).

also appears in the law of covenants. These typically involve restrictions on the use of property that run with the property. Covenants bind and are enforceable by downstream parties only if they are in "privity of estate" with the persons who created the covenant.[10]

These rules reduce information costs. As Merrill and Smith observed in a 2001 paper, the rule that a contract cannot bind a nonparty requires parties to a transaction who want to bind a nonparty to use property law.[11] This brings into play features inherent to the concept of property and rules of property law that reduce information costs. To be imposed on a nonparty a term must "touch and concern" an asset that is capable of being treated as property. Most types of property have clear and distinct boundaries, which reduces information costs. Tying a term to an asset generally caps the potential cost to a nonparty of being subjected to the term at the value of the asset. There is little risk of open-ended liability. And property law has other rules to reduce information costs. These include rules that restrict the permissible forms of property rights; recording requirements; ownership registries; and the rule protecting a bona fide purchaser from a property claim.

Merrill and Smith focus on the savings in information costs when a term that is tied to property may impact potentially numerous nonparties who are remote in time and space from the transaction in which the term is imposed. The rule that a contract cannot bind a nonparty also yields significant savings in information costs when a small number of persons are engaged a multiperson project governed by a chain or web of multiple binary contracts.[12] The rule ensures that each person can look to contracts to which she is a party to determine her contractual obligation and that she need not worry about contracts to which she is not a party subjecting her to a contractual obligation. Her concerns with respect to contracts to which she is not a party are indirect and are always mediated through a contract to which she is a party.[13]

Property law has its own rules that perform the partitioning function with respect to proprietary claims. The most important of these is the rule that a bona fide purchaser of property takes it free of many types of claims that might arise from prior transactions by

---

[10] Runyon v. Paley, 416 S.E.2d 177 (N.C. 1992).

[11] Thomas W. Merrill & Henry E. Smith, *The Property/Contract Interface*, 101 COLUM. L. REV. 773 (2001).

[12] Gergen, *supra* note 8, at 41–43.

[13] Consider a stylized example of a three-person project with a pair of binary contracts between A and B and B and C. A need not worry about the B-C contract subjecting her to a contractual obligation. A may have an indirect interest in the B-C contract because it may affect B's ability to perform the A-B contract, or it may affect A's liability should she breach the A-B contract. But A's interests in the B-C contract can be regulated by a term in the A-B contract. For example, if A is concerned with her potential risk of liability to B for losses on the B-C contract, should A breach the A-B contract, then she can include a liability cap in the A-B contract.

her predecessors in interest.[14] These include agreed terms concerning the use of the property. The bona fide purchaser rule creates a partition so that a person who acquires property can determine her rights with respect to claims covered by the rule without investigating prior transactions by her predecessors in interest. The rules that allow a term that "touches and concerns" property to run when there is a privity of estate are exceptions to the general rule that a bona fide purchaser takes property free of agreed terms concerning the use of property.

The partition created by the bona fide purchaser rule in property law is more penetrable than the partition created by the rule that a contract can neither bind nor destroy rights of a nonparty. Contract law makes no exception to its partitioning rule, though a nonparty who knowingly does an act inconsistent with a contract may be subject to a claim in tort for interference with contract.[15] The bona fide purchaser rule is riddled with qualifications. The rule protects a purchaser only if a seller has record title, the purchaser satisfies the requirements of being a bona fide purchaser, and the seller has at least voidable title in the property.

Contract law has its own bona fide purchaser rule. It is called the rule of "latent equities," and it is part of the law of assignment. The rule applies when a contract right (typically this will be a debt claim) is assigned multiple times. Unless a debt claim is in the form of a negotiable instrument, every assignee takes a claim subject to whatever defenses the debtor might have against the original note holder. For example, if A commits fraud in acquiring a note from T, and A sells the note to B, who sells the note to C, then T can raise A's fraud as a defense to a claim on the note by C even if C is a bona fide purchaser. But when a note is assigned multiple times, a subsequent assignee does not

---

[14] In the United States, bona fide purchaser rules do not protect a purchaser of property from the risk property was acquired from a prior owner by theft or comparable means. For real property, for which there is a title record system, the bona fide purchaser rule applies only if a seller has record title and there are exceptions to cover possibilities like a forged instrument transferring title. See Ralph L. Straw Jr., *Off-Record Risks for Bona Fide Purchases of Real Property*, 72 DICK. L. REV. 35, 39–50 (1967). There is no title record system for most personal property. There the general rule is that a purchaser acquires only the title the transferor "had or had power to transfer," but this is subject to the general exception that "[a] person with voidable title has power to transfer a good title to a good faith purchaser for value." U.C.C. § 2-403(1). There is also an exception that covers "[a]ny entrusting of possession of goods to a merchant who deals in goods of that kind." U.C.C. § 2-403(2). Grant Gilmore, *The Good Faith Purchase Idea and the Uniform Commercial Code: Confessions of a Repentant Draftsman*, 15 GA. L. REV. 605 (1981), briefly tells the history of these rules alongside rules protecting holders of financial assets. Gilmore observes with typical panache:

[t]he moral of the story, as we saw it, was that whenever any kind of property came into the market—that is became the subject of a large volume of transactions either of outright sale or of transfer for security—then that kind of property sooner or later acquired some or all of the attributes of negotiability: commercial property must be freely transferable—no restraints on alienation can be tolerated: the good faith purchaser for value, at least from the time the property comes into his possession, holds it free of both of equities of ownership and of contract defenses; no adverse claims can prevail over the title acquired by good faith purchase. *Id.* at 611.

[15] A nonparty who acquires property with knowledge of a contractual restriction on its use may also be required to obey the restriction under the doctrine of equitable notice.

take the claim subject to defenses involving a prior assignment. These defenses are "latent equities." For example, if B commits fraud in purchasing T's note from A, and B sells the note to C (who is unaware of the fraud), then while A could recover the note from B, he cannot recover the note from C. Basically, a contract right that is assigned is treated like a property right as between assignees.

The rules on assignment and third-party beneficiary limit information costs of contract parties by ensuring that a contract strictly defines the obligation they owe to a non-party. A party to a contract need not worry about a third-party beneficiary or an assignee increasing her obligation. On the other hand, the rules on assignment and third-party beneficiary potentially impose significant information costs on a third-party beneficiary and on an assignee. The rule on latent equities protects a bona fide purchaser of a note from claims arising from midstream transactions, which reduces information costs for purchasers. But an assignee takes an assigned claim subject to whatever defenses the obligor has against the original obligee, including discharge and modification.[16] This rule requires an assignee who is concerned about the value of an assigned claim to investigate the origination of the claim, and it requires the assignee to monitor the obligor and original obligee to ensure the assigned claim is not discharged or modified. Financial markets cannot operate on this basis so most routinely traded financial claims are imbedded in negotiable instruments, which eliminates these risks and reduces information costs. Jan H. Dalhuisen has observed that financial claims that are not in the form of negotiable instruments tend to be treated as negotiable by traders and financial institutions as a matter of practice.[17] This practice reduces information costs.

II. RESTITUTION

The law of restitution has a rule similar to the old privity rule in tort law. The rule applies when the restitution plaintiff and defendant are connected through a chain of contracts and the plaintiff seeks to leapfrog her contract with an intermediary to recover from the defendant for a benefit obtained by the defendant at the plaintiff's expense as a result of the plaintiff's contract with the intermediary. A recurring type claim is brought by a subcontractor who is bilked by a general contractor. The subcontractor brings a restitution claim against the owner of the property seeking payment for work benefiting the owner. Section 25 of the *Third Restatement of Restitution and Unjust Enrichment* addresses this type of claim. Comment *b* explains that "Under a traditional analysis, the restitution claim . . . would often be barred by invoking a test of 'privity.'"[18] Section 25 allows the

---

[16] The rule allowing a downstream assignee to take a claim free of adverse claims arising from an upstream assignment, so long as the downstream assignee is a bona fide purchaser, addresses the concern for information costs with respect to defects in upstream assignments.

[17] Jan H. Dalhuisen, *Dalhuisen on Transnational Comparative, Commercial, Financial and Trade Law*, Vol. I, at 375 (6th ed. Hart 2016).

[18] *Restatement (Third) Restitution and Unjust Enrichment* § 25, comment *b*.

claim in narrowly defined circumstances. Typically restitution is available only when the owner has not paid the general contractor for work done by the sub, so if restitution were not allowed, the owner would obtain for free work for which he had agreed to pay.

Section 25 is a narrow exception to a general rule. The law of restitution generally does not allow a plaintiff to leapfrog a contract to recover a benefit acquired by the defendant at the plaintiff's expense as a result of the plaintiff's contract with an intermediary. *Lincoln Land Company, LLC v. LP Broadband, Inc.*[19] illustrates. The plaintiff leased property to a tenant who breached a term in his lease by entering into an unapproved sublease with the defendant. The sublease was for placing antenna equipment on the rooftop of the leased property, and the rent paid to the tenant on the sublease was well below market. Rather than suing the tenant for breach of the lease agreement, which would have presented a difficult damage issue, the plaintiff sued the subtenant, seeking to recover the difference between the below-market rent paid by the defendant to the tenant and the market rent. The claim failed because the law requires the owner to look to his contract with the tenant for compensation, unless the subtenant had known the lease was a breach of a term in the lease, in which case the plaintiff would have had a claim in tort for tortious interference.

Often the result in cases like *Lincoln Land* is pitched on a rule that precludes claims involving "indirect enrichment." This rule performs the partitioning function mentioned earlier in connection with restitution claims: forcing the parties to rely on their bargained agreements. The law of restitution has other rules that also perform the partitioning function. Thus it has rules to protect a bona fide purchaser and a bona fide payee from a restitution claim.[20] And the law of restitution has rules that draw a boundary between contract and restitution as mechanisms for dealing with unjust enrichment. These rules establish the primacy of contract as the preferred mechanism for resolving issues of unjust enrichment, when there is a possible contract solution to a problem of unjust enrichment. Thus there is a rule that a valid contract displaces possible restitution claims within its scope[21] and a rule precluding a restitution claim for a voluntarily conferred benefit when there was a possibility of a contractual exchange.[22]

The partitioning and boundary-drawing rules in the law of restitution create two concentric circles. The inner circle is defined by the boundary-drawing rules when the plaintiff and defendant are in privity of a contract, or they are in some other type of close relationship in which they can be expected to deal with a problem of unjust enrichment by contract. The outer circle is defined by the partitioning rules that apply when the

---

[19] 163 Idaho 105 (2017).

[20] *Restatement (Third) Restitution and Unjust Enrichment* §§ 66 and 67. The bona fide purchaser rule typically cuts off property-based restitution claims. The bona fide payee rule cuts off a claim when the restitution-defendant receives money as payment of a debt.

[21] *Restatement (Third) Restitution and Unjust Enrichment* § 2(2) ("A valid contract defines the obligations of the parties as to matters within its scope, displacing to that extent any inquiry into unjust enrichment.").

[22] *Restatement (Third) Restitution and Unjust Enrichment* § 2(3) ("There is no liability in restitution for an unrequested benefit voluntarily conferred, unless the circumstances justify the claimant's intervention in the absence of contract.").

plaintiff and defendant do not directly interact. Any enrichment of the defendant at the plaintiff's expense is indirect and typically involves the action of a third person. The partitioning rules that preclude a restitution claim in cases of indirect enrichment eliminate claims outside the outer circle. The boundary-drawing rules that preclude a restitution claim when the parties' contract addresses the matter, or when the parties can be expected to deal with the problem by contract, eliminates claims inside the inner circle. Left for the law of restitution are claims in a narrow band between the two circles where the enrichment is direct but the plaintiff does not address the matter by contract, and cannot reasonably be expected to do so.

The limitation of restitution claims to this narrow band of cases often is ascribed to interests like the interest in finality or the interest in legal certainty. I suggest these interests operate particularly strongly in the law of restitution because much of the law of restitution is concerned with reversing accidental shifts in wealth, the paradigmatic example being a mistaken payment.[23] The law of restitution takes a strikingly laissez-faire approach to what are accidents. I suggest this laissez-faire approach persists and may be justified because it often is in the nature of unjust enrichment that a plaintiff's loss is matched by a defendant's gain and so represents a private loss but not a social loss. While the accidental shift in wealth may seem unfair as between the two parties, from society's perspective it often is best to let the chips fall where they may. It is also in the joint interest of the plaintiff and defendant to let the chips fall where they may.

III. Tort

The old privity rule in tort law served a boundary drawing function that has largely devolved to rules that limit the availability of a negligence claim for pure economic loss. I will take up these rules after situating them within a larger theory of tort law and alongside the torts of interference with contract and deceit, which are shaped by the concerns that shape the privity rules in contract and the law of restitution. The interference tort also is an important qualification to the rule that a contract cannot bind a nonparty. A nonparty who knowingly interferes with a contract can be liable for tortious interference.

Mark Geistfeld has shown that tort law can be conceptualized on two dimensions.[24] One dimension is the balance a rule strikes between the defendant's interest in liberty of action and the plaintiff's interest in security from harm. At one end of this dimension are immunity rules that prioritize the defendant's interest in liberty of action. At the other end are strict liability rules that prioritize the plaintiff's interest in security from

---

[23] Mark P. Gergen, *What Renders Enrichment Unjust?*, 79 TEX. L. REV. 1927, 1929, 1945–1949 (2001). Other parts of the law of restitution provide disgorgement as a remedy for a wrong or help to solve small number collective action problems.

[24] Mark Geistfeld, *Essentials of Tort Law* 15–16 (2008).

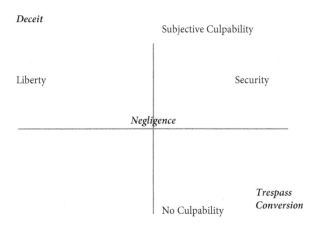

FIGURE 29.1. A Two-Dimensional Map of Private Law

harm. The negligence rule is at the center, for it balances the parties' conflicting interests by making an actor liable for harm she causes when her action creates an unreasonable risk of harm but privileging the actor's conduct when her conduct does not create an unreasonable risk of harm. The negligence rule makes victims bear the cost of accidents that are not worth avoiding, which promotes liberty of action. Geistfeld's other dimension is how a tort rule defines a culpable state of mind. At one end of this dimension are intentional torts that require subjective culpability. At the other end are strict liability rules that require no culpability. "Negligence once again is at the conceptual center," Geistfeld observes, because it is a rule of "objective culpability."[25]

Figure 29.1 situates the major torts protecting economic and property interests on Geistfeld's two dimensions. The liberty-security dimension is the horizontal axis and the culpability dimension is the vertical axis.

The normative concern on the liberty-security dimension is the trade-off between the plaintiff's interest in not being harmed and the defendant's interest in engaging in harmful conduct. The Hand formula for negligence explicitly balances the competing interests of risk bearers and risk creators when action creates a risk of harm. The torts in the upper-left corner also represent a product of interest balancing but with a heavy thumb being put on the scale in favor of liberty of action through the imposition of a scienter requirement. Consistently with this element of the diagram, the *Second Restatement of Torts* explicitly requires courts to balance interests in deciding whether a defendant's intentional interference in the plaintiff's business relationships is improper, and therefore tortious.[26]

The most salient normative concern on the culpability dimension is the morality of the defendant's conduct. Another concern that often is correlated with an actor's moral culpability is the burden a legal rule places on an actor to determine her liability under the rule. This basically is a concern for information costs that an actor must incur to

[25] *Id.* at 16.
[26] *Restatement (Second) Torts* § 767.

identify potential claimants and claims and to estimate her potential legal risk under a rule, if she engages in conduct that injures people protected by the rule.[27]

Rules that require subjective culpability impose relatively small information costs on an actor because liability requires an actor know that she is committing a wrong. To be liable for interference with contract a defendant must know of the plaintiff's contract and know that her action is likely to interfere with its performance.[28] The scienter requirement in the law of deceit reduces information costs when an actor disseminates information that may be false or misleading. The savings in information costs are significant if one compares a rule that makes an actor liable for negligently disseminating false information with a rule that requires for liability that the actor know the information he is disseminating is false, or at least that an actor be reckless with regards to the falsity of information he disseminates. A negligence rule creates broad incentives for an actor to verify the accuracy of information she disseminates and to investigate potential users and uses of the information to ascertain her potential liability if the information is inaccurate.[29]

The torts in the upper-left-hand corner share a feature with the law of restitution. They redress wrongs that often involve a social cost that is much smaller than the private loss inflicted on the plaintiff by the wrong. Interference with contract usually involves appropriation of contract opportunities. Fraudsters take wealth; they do not destroy it. This characteristic feature of fraud helps to explain rules that resolve doubts about the existence of deceit in favor of the accused fraudster.[30] While these rules predictably result in some frauds going uncorrected, a policy of resolving doubts about the existence of fraud

---

[27] In the case of the rule of strict liability for manufacturing defects, the informational burden the rule imposes on manufacturers to determine what losses are worth avoiding is thought to be more than offset by the rule's benefits. These benefits include reducing the administrative cost of determining negligence, creating an incentive for firms to take cost-effective measures to avoid defects that are observable by the firm but not by courts, and spreading the cost of losses that are not worth avoiding. Meanwhile, the foreseeability requirement in a negligence rule limits the burden the rule places on a risk creator to determine her potential liability under the negligence rule.

[28] Liability for tortious interference requires that the defendant have knowledge of the contract with which he interferes and that the defendant have intended to interfere with the contract. See, e.g., Quelimane Co. v. Stewart Title Guaranty Co., 19 Cal.4th 26, 55, 77 Cal. Rptr. 2d 709, 960 P.2d 513 (1998) (stating the two elements as "defendant's knowledge of this contract [and] defendant's intentional acts designed to induce a breach or disruption of the contractual relationship"). The knowledge element can be satisfied by showing "that the defendant had knowledge of facts that, if followed by reasonable inquiry, would have led to the disclosure of the contractual relationship between plaintiff and third parties." Revere Transducers, Inc. v. Deere & Co., 595 N.W.2d 751 (Iowa 1999).

[29] Mark P. Gergen, A Wrong Turn in the Law of Deceit, 106 GEO. L.J. 555 (2018). The paper compares the old scienter requirement of intended reliance with the modern rule in the United States that requires that a plaintiff's reliance on a misrepresentation be reasonable. I argue the rules are roughly comparable with respect to information costs and that the old rule of intended reliance is superior as a matter of fairness. The requirement of intended reliance has been described as a privity rule. This is a mistake. Under the rule, a fraudster can be liable to remote and numerous victims so long as they are intended victims of the fraud. But the intended reliance requirement is similar to a privity rule in that both rules reduce information costs.

[30] These rules include a procedural rule requiring that fraud be pled with specificity and an evidentiary rule requiring that fraud be established by clear and convincing evidence. The rules on justifiable reliance also serve this function by allowing a court to dismiss a fraud claim early in the proceedings when the plaintiff's reliance seems unreasonable.

in favor of an accused fraudster reduces the incentive to take precautions to avoid false accusations and mistaken findings of deceit. They also reduce claim-processing costs by enabling courts to dismiss weak claims early on.[31] If all one cared about was efficiency narrowly defined, then the optimal level of fraud might well be greater than zero, because of the concerns for claim-avoidance and claim-processing costs.

Interference with contract and deceit also share a feature with the property torts in the lower-right corner. All lead to coercive remedies, including an injunction, disgorgement, and punitive damages. Coercive remedies for deceit can be justified as being facilitative of private ordering when there is clear and convincing evidence that the defendant is a fraudster because deceit is destructive of private ordering. The same reason can justify coercive remedies for interference with contract. As Calabresi and Melamed famously observed, strong remedies encourage an actor who plans to violate an entitlement to bargain with the entitlement holder in advance.[32] The premise is that the parties will work out their conflicting interests through bargaining.

Returning to Geistfeld's diagram, contract law logically belongs alongside negligence law in the middle of the diagram. Both bodies of law resolve conflicts of interest in cases in which the parties' interests often are in near equipoise. Both bodies of law also generally take an objective view when it comes to evaluating an actor's decisions and conduct. Obligation in contract generally is a matter of objective assent and liability in negligence generally is a matter of objective fault. Of course, there are major differences between contract law and negligence law. Contract law facilitates cooperation and private ordering and generally resolves conflicts of interest that arise in the execution of what was intended by the parties to be a mutually beneficial transaction or project. Negligence law typically regulates conflicts of interest between strangers that arise when an actor's conduct creates a risk of harm to another. Saul Levmore puts these differences succinctly when he describes contract as the law of "bargained benefits" and tort as the law of "nonbargained harms," juxtaposing these with restitution as the law of "nonbargained benefits."[33]

This brings me to the old privity doctrine in tort law. The doctrine entered tort law in the early nineteenth century when English courts used the doctrine to distinguish between contract and tort as bases for duty under rules of pleading that did not clearly delineate between duties imposed by law and duties created by the will of the parties. *Winterbottom v. Wright*[34] is an important part of this story, although the decision in the case probably did not rest on the rule with which the case is associated. Vernon Palmer argues persuasively that the case only held that a plaintiff who was not a party to a

---

[31] Gergen, *supra* note 29, at 595–597.

[32] Guido Calabresi & A. Douglas Melamed, *Property Rules, Liability Rules, and Inalienability: One View of the Cathedral*, 85 HARV. L. REV. 1089 (1972). Later scholarship adds that property rules are particularly appropriate when the value of an entitlement to an entitlement holder is uncertain because this uncertainty increases claim-processing costs and creates a risk of error by a court in pricing the entitlement. Conversely, there is less need for a property rule when the value of an entitlement to an entitlement holder is certain because a court will be expected to set a price for a violation equal to would be the bargained for price.

[33] Saul Levmore, *Explaining Restitution*, 71 VA. L. REV. 65, 67 (1985).   [34] (1842) 10 M. & W. 109.

contract could not assert a defendant's breach of a contractual duty as a basis for establishing a duty of care for purposes of a tort claim, when there was no precedent for the duty asserted (which there was not because the alleged breach involved nonfeasance).[35] Yet, the decision quickly came to be associated with a rule that treated a contract as a shield that cut off a duty to a nonparty that might otherwise have existed under tort law. A plausible explanation for why this occurred is that courts found the rule a useful tool for cabining the expanding negligence action. While the rule was overbroad, it did perform the function of drawing a boundary between contract and tort. This rule was abolished in tort law for most types of claims involving physical harm early in the twentieth century.[36] When Cardozo refers to the "assault upon the citadel of privity,"[37] he is referring to the overturning of this rule.

The abolition of the old rule led to negligence claims that inappropriately encroach upon contract as a mechanism for allocating risk. *Eaves Brooks Costume Co. v. Y.B.H. Realty Co.*[38] is such a case. A fire sprinkler system in a commercial building malfunctioned, damaging the tenants' property. They sued an inspector for failing to detect the flaw in the system and the fire alarm company for failing to detect the sprinkler system was activated. The old privity rule would have precluded a negligence claim against the inspector and the fire alarm company. The abolition of the rule opened the door to the claim.[39] What is problematic about this is that companies in the position of the inspector and the fire alarm company almost always cap their liability. Indeed the defendants' contracts had damage caps. If the court had allowed the negligence claim (it did not), then it would have defeated a sensible contractual arrangement for allocating this risk.

Eaves Brooks is atypical in that the claim was for physical harm. In the United States, the function of drawing a boundary between contract and tort that used to be performed by the old privity rule has largely devolved to rules that limit the availability of a tort claim for pure economic loss.[40] A rule in the *Third Restatement of Torts* precludes a

---

[35] Vernon Palmer, *Why Privity Entered Tort—An Historical Reexamination of* Winterbottom v. Wright. 27 AM. J. LEGAL HIST. 85 (1983). One of Palmer's targets is the argument that the claim pled in *Winterbottom* was a breach of contract claim, and not a tort claim, and that the case merely held that the absence of privity between the injured carriage driver and the carriage supplier precluded a contract claim. See, e.g., Francis H. Bohlen, *Basis of Affirmative Obligation in the Law of Tort (Part II)*, 53 U. PA. L. REV. 273, 283–284 (1905).

[36] Some subrules persisted for a long time. For example, in Texas the rule relieving a general contractor from a duty of care owed to the public after acceptance of its work by its employer persisted until *Strakos v. Gehring*, 360 S.W.2d 787 (1962). The acceptance rule was still alive in Indiana in 1997, though it was riddled with exceptions. See Bush v. Seco Electric Co., 118 F.3d 519 (1997).

[37] Ultramares Corp. v. Touche, 174 N.E. 441, 445 (N.Y. 1931). It is also to this rule to which Prosser refers to in William L. Prosser, *The Assault Upon the Citadel (Strict Liability to the Consumer)*, 69 YALE L.J. 1099 (1966), and William L. Prosser, *The Fall of the Citadel*, 50 MINN. L. REV. 791 (1966).

[38] 556 N.E.2d 1093 (N.Y. 1990).

[39] These include the establishment of a general duty of reasonable care covering conduct that creates a risk of harm, the elimination of contributory negligence as a defense, the elimination of rules on superseding cause, and the extension of negligence liability to claims for economic loss or emotional disturbance in the absence of physical harm.

[40] Catherine M. Sharkey, *The Remains of the Citadel (Economic Loss in Products Cases)*, 100 MINN. L. REV. 1845, 1849 (2016).

negligence claim for pure economic loss when the defendant's negligence is in the per-formance or negotiation of a contract with the plaintiff.[41] The rule basically precludes a negligence claim when the plaintiff and defendant are in privity of contract.[42] Some states have a general rule that precludes a negligence claim for pure economic loss when the parties can be expected to handle the problem by contract.[43] Other states have a gen-eral rule that conditions liability for negligent misrepresentation on the plaintiff and defendant being in "near privity."[44]

When a negligence action is not available for harmful conduct, it follows that private law provides no redress even though the harm inflicted on the victim(s) may exceed the benefit to the actor from engaging in the harmful conduct. Looked at this way, rules that preclude a negligence action for pure economic loss can seem unjustifiable—how can it be that private law provides no redress when all of the elements of a negligence action could be satisfied (i.e., the defendant acted unreasonably, his unreasonable action was a factual cause of harm to the plaintiff, the risk of such harm was among the risk that made the defendant's action unreasonable, the harm can be appropriately quantified as dam-ages, and neither the plaintiff nor a third person more appropriately bears responsibility for the harm)?

There is a straightforward answer to this question with respect to the rule in the *Third Restatement* that precludes a negligence claim for pure economic loss when the plaintiff and defendant are in privity of contract. Contract law has rules that protect a party from the other party's carelessness, including implied standards of performance, the duty of good faith, the doctrine of promissory estoppel, and the doctrines of waiver and equita-ble estoppel. Some unreasonable conduct that ought to be redressed probably falls through the cracks, but the benefits of having a bright-line rule that takes a negligence claim off the table outweigh the cost of the occasional injustice.

A rule that precludes a negligence claim for pure economic loss when the plaintiff and defendant are not in privity of contract, but can be expected to handle the problem by contract, is more problematic because the rule requires courts to draw a line that cannot be drawn in the abstract. I proposed in an earlier paper that rather than trying to draw a bright line, courts should approach this as a problem of contract construction that is informed by principles of negligence law.[45] When the plaintiff and defendant are con-nected through a chain of contracts that address (or that might address) the conduct and harm in question, a court should ask whether the parties would have agreed to

[41] *Restatement (Third) of Torts: Liability for Economic Harm* § 3, Tentative Draft No. 1 (Apr. 4, 2012), at 21.

[42] There is an exception for professional malpractice. Some states have a "strict privity" rule for a malpractice action against an attorney that precludes a claim by a nonparty. See, e.g., Nobel v. Bruch, 709 A.2d 1264 (Md. 1998).

[43] Berschauer/Phillips v. Seattle School District, 881 P.2d 986, 989, 992–993 (Wash. 1994); BRW Inc. v. Dufficy & Sons, Inc., 99 P.3d 66 (Colo. 2004).

[44] Ossining Union Free School Dist. v. Anderson LaRocca Anderson, 539 N.E.2d 91 (N.Y. 1989).

[45] Gergen, *supra* note 8, at 68–82. The privity rule in contract law prevents treating the problem as one of contract construction in contract law except in cases which the plaintiff argues she is a third-party beneficiary of an exculpatory term in the defendant's contract.

establish a rule of negligence liability, if the parties had thought about the issue when they made the contract. In engaging in this inquiry, a court should consider the strengths of the reasons for imposing negligence liability, applying the principles of negligence law, and a court should examine the contracts that connect the plaintiff and defendant to see if they provide a mechanism for redressing the conduct and harm, or if the contracts suggest the parties would have decided the problem is not worth redressing, had they addressed the issue when they made the relevant contracts.

Often an inspection of the contracts that link the plaintiff and defendant will yield a quick answer to this question. For example, in *J'Aire Corp. v. Gregory*,[46] an inspection of the contract between the airport and the contractor would have revealed that the tenant could recover its lost profits through on a contract claim against the airport, which could then have passed the loss through to the contractor on another contract claim.[47] There was no need for negligence liability. In *Eaves Brooks Costume Co. v. Y.B.H. Realty Co.*,[48] the exculpatory terms in the two contracts, which were ubiquitous in the trade, reinforced the conclusion the court reached by applying principles of negligence law that the defendants owed no duty to the plaintiffs.

A rule that conditions negligence liability on the plaintiff and defendant being in near privity is more difficult to justify.[49] In New York law, the near privity requirement is rooted in two famous Cardozo decisions: *Glanzer v. Shepard*[50] and *Ultramares Corp. v. Touche*.[51] *Glanzer* held that a buyer who overpaid for beans as a result of a bean weigher's mistake could recover from the bean weigher on a negligence claim. *Ultramares Corp.* held that a lender who lost a substantial sum of money relying on inaccurate certified accounts of company could not recover from the auditor on a negligence claim. The near privity requirement comes from Cardozo's explanation that *Ultramares* was unlike *Glanzer* because there was nothing close to privity between the plaintiff lender and the auditor: "[n]o one would be likely to urge there was a contractual relationship, or even one approaching it" between the auditor and "the indeterminate class of persons who, presently or in the future, might deal with the Stern company in reliance on the audit."[52] In *Glanzer*, Cardozo had argued that the contract between the bean seller and the bean weigher offered an alternative basis for the duty he chose to ground in tort. Presumably, this would be on a theory of third-party beneficiary.

---

[46] 598 P.2d 60 (Cal. 1974).   [47] Gergen, *supra* note 8, at 72–73.

[48] 556 N.E.2d 1093 (N.Y. 1990).

[49] The rule produces perverse outcomes when a court fails to examine the contracts that connect the plaintiff and defendant to see if they support allowing the claim. *Ossining Union Free School Dist. v. Anderson LaRocca Anderson*, 539 N.E.2d 91 (N.Y. 1989), may be such a case. The plaintiff school district hired an architect as a consultant for a project. The architect hired two engineers as subconsultants. The district sued the engineers after it incurred an unnecessary expense as a result of a careless error by the engineers. The district had hired the engineers directly in the past. The court allowed the claim, applying the near privity rule, while saying nothing about the terms of the contracts between the district, the architect, and the engineers. If the parties had used the standard AIA contract, then there would be a reciprocal waiver of consequential damages. Gergen, *supra* note 8, at 35–37.

[50] 135 N.E. 275 (N.Y. 1922).   [51] 174 N.E. 441 (N.Y. 1931).   [52] 174 N.E. at 446.

The combination of a near privity requirement for a duty of care and a rule that precludes a negligence claim for pure economic loss when the plaintiff and defendant are in privity of contract creates a band in the law of economic negligence that is similar to the band I described earlier in the law of restitution. A negligence claim for pure economic loss is available only in the narrow band of cases in which the relationship between a plaintiff and defendant "approaches" a contractual relationship but is not a contractual relationship. But it is not clear why the absence of a near-contractual relationship between the plaintiff and defendant should preclude a negligence claim for pure economic loss when the plaintiff is able to establish the elements of a negligence claim, in the absence of countervailing reasons, such as the concern for indeterminate liability. The preclusion of a negligence claim when the parties are not in a relationship approaching a contractual relationship cannot be justified by a preference for private ordering because the attenuated relationship between the plaintiff and defendant impedes a private solution to the problem.

Perhaps the near privity requirement could be justified by a more general argument for why the law should put a heavy thumb on the scale in favor or liberty of action over security from harm when the harm in question is a pure economic loss. The argument is "that private economic losses do not necessarily amount to comparable social losses."[53] Earlier I suggested the fact that many restitution claims involve private losses and not social losses may explain why restitution claims are only allowed in a similar narrow band. Moral sensibilities best explain why negligence and restitution claims are allowed in this narrow band. People who are concerned about possible inefficiencies in indulging moral sensibilities can take some comfort in the fact that the existence of a relationship approaching a contractual relationship lowers the cost of contracting around an undesired liability rule.

IV. CONCLUSION

The concept of privity has gotten a bad name because it is associated with the old rule in negligence law that prevented downstream users who were harmed by defective products from recovering against manufacturers. Privity rules in contract law continue to perform a vital function by preventing a contract from negatively affecting the rights of

---

[53] *Restatement (Third) of Torts: Liability for Economic Harm*, Tentative Draft No. 1 (Apr. 4, 2012), Reporter's Note. Bishop, *Economic Loss in Tort*, 2 OXFORD J. LEGAL STUD. 1 (1981), is an early statement of this point. Victor Goldberg has made this point using *Glanzer v. Shepard*, 135 N.E. 275 (1922). Goldberg explains that a buyer who overpays for goods would typically recover from the seller on a restitution claim, but he infers the claim was barred by a term in the contract making the certified weight "final and binding." Victor E. Goldberg, *Framing Contract Law: An Economic Perspective* 249–250 (2006). Goldberg argues the court was wrong to allow a negligence claim because it defeated the purpose of the clause, which is to eliminate potential litigation. He concludes "[s]hifting the losses around in this way looks like a reasonably expensive proposition for little to show for it in the way of deterrence." *Id.* at 271.

a nonparty. These rules require parties to a transaction who want to bind nonparties to use property law (or the law of equity), where there are rules that make it possible to define the interests of third parties with respect to assets while reducing third-party information costs. Rules associated with the concept of privity in the law of restitution and negligence law also continue to serve the important function of making contract law the mechanism for resolving responsibility for accidental losses when the plaintiff and defendant are in privity of contract. These rules basically create a circle around a contractual relationship in which the law of restitution and negligence law cannot intrude. This generally is unobjectionable, for there are rules in contract law to deal with unjust enrichment and carelessly caused harm that are adapted to the contractual setting. Rules associated with the concept of privity that draw an outer boundary around the law of restitution and negligence are more difficult to justify. The absence of privity (or of near privity) between a plaintiff and defendant is usually not a reason in itself to preclude a restitution or negligence claim that would otherwise be justified under principles in those bodies of law. But, when the plaintiff and defendant are connected through a chain of contracts, a court should examine the contracts that connect the plaintiff and defendant to see if they provide a mechanism for redressing the loss in question, or if the contracts suggest the parties would have decided the problem is not worth redressing.

CHAPTER 30

··

GOOD FAITH IN
CONTRACTUAL
EXCHANGES

··

RICHARD R.W. BROOKS

At the outset it must be noted that hardly anyone, certainly no prudent
man, presumes to give certain and universally adequate rules and
doctrines for recognizing in buying and selling what is precisely in every
case allowable or not allowable, just or unjust.

—Johannes Nider, *On the Contracts of Merchants* (circa 1460)

I. INTRODUCTION

··

GOOD faith (*bona fides*) is an ancient doctrine. Already timeworn when it first appeared
in the formal rules governing sales in Roman antiquity, the contractual duty of good
faith has endured through the fall of Rome in the *lex mercatoria* of the Middles Ages and
later during the early modern period in the development of the civil law and common
law forms now prevalent throughout the world. In our present period, with few notable
exceptions, the doctrine of good faith in contractual exchanges is broadly incorporated
in national regimes, international law, and transnational legal orders.[1] Good faith's early

---

[1] Code and doctrine within the United States, for instance, recognize that "[e]very contract
imposes upon each party a duty of good faith and fair dealing in its performance and its
enforcement." *Restatement (Second) of Contracts* § 205 (Am. Law Inst. 1981). The American Uniform
Commercial Code (U.C.C.) similarly provides, "[e]very contract or duty within the Uniform
Commercial Code imposes an obligation of good faith in its performance and enforcement."
U.C.C. § 1-304. See also the United Nations Convention on Contracts for the International Sale
of Goods, S. Treaty Doc. No. 98-9, art. 7 (1983) ("In the interpretation of this Convention, regard

traces and broad continuing relevance are plainly observable, yet after all this time its meaning remains clouded and indeterminate.[2] Indeterminacy, indeed, may explain the doctrine's prevalence and persistence. With so many available interpretations, almost everyone can agree on the requirement of good faith without having to agree on what, exactly, good faith requires.

Advocates promoting one or another specific interpretation of good faith, however, have little patience for unresolved ambiguity in the doctrine. Their partisan zeal, tending to stake out differences and overlook commonalities, causes an apparent paradox. As each more assuredly advances its view as uniquely correct, together they generate more uncertainty. Recent academic efforts, casting about for the elusive 'proper' understanding of good faith, have only further revealed its indeterminate quality. Contemporary scholars would do well to recall the restraint of certitude expressed by the fifteenth-century theologian Johannes Nider in his treatise on the ethics of contractual exchange among merchants.[3] Today a din of confident assertions makes clarity and consensus difficult to discern.

Still, even in this cacophony, one can vaguely make out a general statement of the doctrine and its purpose. When contractual disputes revolve around latently ambiguous terms or obviously omitted ones (i.e., gaps in a contract) courts are encouraged to avoid literal interpretations that would allow one party to exploit another in a manner too inconsistent with the expectations of their agreement. Nearly all commentators would embrace some version of this anodyne statement of the doctrine. Dissension surfaces over what is or should be the distinctive contribution of good faith in securing those

is to be had to . . . the observance of good faith in international trade"); UNIDROIT Principles of International Commercial Contracts (UNIDROIT) art. 1.7 (1) ("Each party must act in accordance with good faith and fair dealing in international trade"); and Hugh Collins, *Good Faith in European Contract Law*, 14 OXFORD J. LEGAL STUD. 229 (1994). Exceptions are largely limited to some common law countries. For example, English common law has shown notable resistance to explicit incorporation of a doctrine of good faith—notwithstanding Lord Mansfield's well-known observation that good faith underscores all contractual dealings. See Boone v. Eyre [1789] 126 Eng. Rep. 148 (K.B.); Carter v. Boehm [1766] 97 Eng. Rep. 1162, 1164 (K.B.). Instead of good faith, English common law is said to rely on other devices, particularly principles of estoppel and interpretation, to exclude bad faith in exchange settings. See, e.g., John Cartwright, "Protecting Legitimate Expectations and Estoppel: English Law," in *La confiance légitime et l'estoppel, 4 Droit Privé Comparé et Européen* 321 (2007). Canada has only recently recognized a "duty to perform contracts honestly"; to make contractual exchanges "more just and more in tune with reasonable commercial expectations." Bhasin v. Hrynew, [2014] 3 S.C.R. 494 (Can.).

[2] "These words, good faith, have a very broad meaning wrote Cicero." See Bénédicte Fauvarque-Cosson & Denis Mazeaud, *European Contract Law: Materials for a Common Frame of Reference*, at 152 (2009) (quoting *De Officiis*, 3, 17, translated from R.M. Rampelberg, *Repères Romains pour le Droit Européen des Contrats*, L.G.D.J., *Systèmes, Droit* 2005, p. 44). As Cicero also observed "the head of the pontifical college, said that there was the greatest force in all decisions to which the phrase 'in good faith' was annexed," which applied to "the whole system of social transactions[.]" Marcus Tullius Cicero, Cicero De Officiis, translated with an Introduction and Notes by Andrew P. Peabody (1887). https://oll.libertyfund.org/titles/542, at 3, 17.

[3] Johannes Nider, *On the Contracts of Merchants* 3 (Ronald B. Shuman ed., Charles H. Reeves trans., 1966) (1468).

expectations.[4] No one doubts that bad faith is excluded by the doctrine,[5] which limits without seeking to eliminate self-interest.[6] Conflict and confusion arise over the role played by good faith in determining where blind pursuit of self-interest crosses over into the territory of bad faith.

Unyielding self-interest poses a unique threat to contractual exchanges. Contractual exchanges, unlike donative transfers, presuppose a rivalry of interests between parties. A contractual agreement among negotiating parties is reached only if this inherent antagonism is outweighed by the anticipated mutual gains of cooperation. Cooperation in the presence of competing interests is the signature trait of contractual exchanges. In idealized market exchanges there is no pretense of cooperation; just the opposite, as the charade of an invisible hand coordinates buyers and sellers without placing any demands on their cooperation.[7] Contractual exchanges, however, whether idealized or mundane, are impossible without the direct cooperation of buyers and sellers (or their

---

[4] In controversies where good faith is called into question, the case law is "emphatic about its existence," as Judge Posner observed, but "cryptic as to its meaning." Mkt St. Assocs. Ltd. P'ship v. Frey, 941 F.2d 588, 593 (7th Cir. 1991). See also Justice Alito's latest opinion concerning good faith: "While most States recognize some form of the good faith and fair dealing doctrine, it does not appear that there is any uniform understanding of the doctrine's precise meaning." Nw., Inc. v. Ginsberg, 572 U.S. 273, 285 (2014).

[5] Observing that good faith "is a phrase which has no general meaning or meanings of its own," Summers triggered the contemporary U.S. academic discussion of good faith with his "excluder" analysis, proposing that the doctrine principally "serves to exclude many heterogeneous forms of bad faith." Robert S. Summers, *"Good Faith" in General Contract Law and the Sales Provisions of the Uniform Commercial Code*, 54 VA. L. REV. 195, 196 (1968). *See also* E. Allan Farnsworth, *Good Faith Performance and Commercial Reasonableness Under the Uniform Commercial Code*, 30 U CHI. L. REV. 666 (1963).

[6] This is another point on which there has long been broad consensus. As Cicero wrote, the doctrine called for "honest sentiments of a good conscience, *without requiring a scrupulousness which would turn selflessness into sacrifice.*" Fauvarque-Cosson & Mazeaud, *supra* note 2, at 152.

[7] See, e.g., Francis Y. Edgeworth, *Mathematical Psychics: An Essay on the Application of Mathematics to the Moral Sciences* (1881), addressing whether the normative mode of economic exchange is better characterized by the Walrasian competitive market or by contractual relations. While under contract actors remain self-interested (which is a first principle for Edgeworth—"that every agent is actuated *only* by self-interest" *id.*, at 16, emphasis added) they cooperatively contract and "recontract" to reach mutually superior outcomes. Norms of idealized market exchange, however, at least as Edgeworth saw them, have no place for such cooperative contracting and recontracting. "Walras's laboured description of prices set up or 'cried' in the market is calculated to divert attention from a sort of higgling which may be regarded as more fundamental than his conception[.]" 2 F.Y. Edgeworth, *Papers Relating to Political Economy*, at 311 (1925). Not only does this market paradigm dispense with the relational character of exchange but, by stipulation, the fictitious Walrasian auctioneer stands between buyer and seller, preventing any form of intersubjective—much less cooperative—exchange between them. *Cf.* Donald A. Walker, *Edgeworth versus Walras on the Theory of Tatonnement,*13 EAST. ECON. J. 155 (1987); Donald A. Walker, *Disequilibrium and Equilibrium in Walras's Model of Oral Pledges Markets*, 41 REVUE ÉCONOMIQUE, 961 (1990).

agents).[8] Contracts "set in motion a cooperative enterprise,"[9] calling on norms of cooperation, the legal boundaries of which are defined by good faith.[10]

It is unsurprising that contract law would devise doctrines to keep cooperation on track. Contractual misunderstandings often arise even among those who begin with the best of intentions. As time passes, unexpected occurrences may dissipate anticipated gains of exchange for one or both parties. Keeping a "losing contract," i.e., wherein a party's costs of performance exceed the benefits that party captures from performance, or having to carry out a remunerative but still less-profitable-than-imagined exchange can be bitter pills to swallow. In these contexts thoughts of evasion inevitably ensue as self-interest swamps prior cooperative inclinations.[11] Hardship and disappointment, however, are not the only threats to cooperation: even when the gains of exchange remain significant and mutually beneficial, a party may still attempt to exploit terms of a contract in light of realizations previously unknown or unacknowledged. Such strategic uses of contract terms, particularly in the public domain (e.g., when placed before the official scrutiny of judges) subverts much more than the meaning and spirit of any given agreement.

A special burden is placed on the cooperative norms of contractual exchange when the terms of the agreement *themselves* become instruments of bad faith. Without some assurance that these terms of exchange will not be hijacked and used strategically to holdup counterparties, the institution of contract itself would be fundamentally weakened.[12] Absent this baseline assurance, parties would contract less often and spend

---

[8] See Alan Schwartz & Daniel Markovits, this volume.

[9] As Judge Richard Posner observed in *Market Street Associates Limited Partnership v. Frey*, 941 F.2d 588, 595 (7th Cir. 1991).

[10] Because all contracts are necessarily incomplete, parties always have discretion in realized contingencies that were not fully or adequately specified in the contract. In this context of inevitable discretion, the implied duty of good faith does not so much give rise to an independent cause of action, but rather affects the interpretation of *how* a party may legally exercise its discretion. Importantly, good faith is not the only means used to define and police the legal boundaries of contractual exchange. Closely related doctrines include prevention and hindrance—which are often asserted in disputes concerning real estate brokers, see Drake v. Hosley, 713 P.2d 1203 (Alaska 1986), and insurance coverage, see D & S Realty, Inc. v. Markel Ins. Co., 816 N.W.2d 1 (Neb. 2012). Doctrines of prevention and hindrance, like the implied covenant of good faith, require counterparty cooperation and, at a minimum, noninterference with the other party's performance. United States v. Peck, 102 U.S. 64 (1880). A variety of additional equitable doctrines and rules of interpretation may also be enlisted to defeat contractual bad faith conduct, but these approaches should be distinguished from the doctrine of good faith. See *infra* note 42 and accompanying text.

[11] Seeking some way out, parties frequently scrutinize their written agreements looking for exculpatory clauses that might release them from less attractive and losing contracts. See Andrew Kull, *Restitution as a Remedy for Breach of Contract*, 67 S. Cal. L. Rev. 1465 (1994).

[12] As Henry Smith has emphasized, courts of equity relying on principles dating back to Aristotle have long provided assurance to contractual parties, relieving them by way of an equitable "safety value" from exploitation and "opportunism arising from the simple structures of the common law." Henry E. Smith, *The Equitable Dimension of Contract*, 45 Suffolk U. L. Rev. 897, 903–905 (2012); Kenneth Ayotte, Ezra Friedman, & Henry E. Smith, *A Safety Valve Model of Equity as Anti-Opportunism* (Mar. 30, 2013), Northwestern Law & Econ Research Paper No. 13–15. Available at SSRN: https://ssrn.com/abstract=2245098 or http://dx.doi.org/10.2139/ssrn.2245098. See also Carol Rose, pointing to "unconscionability [a]s only one of a number of doctrines, some quite ancient, that

more resources to guard against the risks of knife's-edge exchanges. Trust in the institution of contracts is promoted by the legal presumption, irrefutable in most cases, of a good-faith reading of contractual agreements.[13] A presumption of good faith as such is not an imposition of an independent substantive term, but rather a rule of interpretation over the terms of a contract. By interpreting contractual terms through the lens of good faith, courts disable or at least discourage bad-faith uses of the institution of contracts, and thereby bolster more efficient, fair, and functional contractual cooperation.

Good faith protects contracting parties, but its principal aim is protecting the practice of contracts. How, exactly, does the doctrine of good faith protect these interests? Two competing views on the doctrine—labeled here "consensual rationality" and "contractual morality"—bracket the various approaches to good faith. Both views grant that good faith entails norms of cooperation. It is where the doctrine locates these norms that defines the difference between consensual rationality and contractual morality. Consensual rationality adopts a narrower perspective on the doctrine, restricting good faith to expectations derived from the parties themselves. Cooperative norms here are internal to the agreement, based solely on that to which the parties have, or are imagined to have, rationality consented.[14] Contractual morality, in contrast, expands the legal bounds of good faith to include external standards and norms established outside of any actual or rationally reconstructed agreement between the parties.[15]

These competing views of good faith frame the remaining discussion. Three principal claims are advanced in the chapter. First, consensual rationality and contractual morality may be best seen as extreme points on a common continuum over which courts and most commentators take positions somewhere in the middle. Second, the doctrine of good faith exists to protect *the practice of contracting*, more so than aggrieved parties to

interfere with unequal bargains or exchanges." Carol M. Rose, *Giving, Trading, Thieving, and Trusting: How and Why Gifts Become Exchanges, and (More Importantly) Vice Versa*, 44 FLA. L. REV. 295, 309 (1992). Whereas unconscionability and other equitable doctrines provide assurance to parties from outside their contract, good faith's assurance emanates from (and is part of) the agreement itself. See *infra* note 53 and accompanying text.

[13] While some categories of agreement in some jurisdictions are excluded from the demands of good faith—or so it is claimed (for example, in many, if not a majority of states in the United States, at-will employment agreements are formally not subject to the implied duty of good faith in performance and enforcement)—most types of agreement in most jurisdictions are subject to some mandatory duty of good faith.

[14] See, e.g., *Restatement (Second) of Contracts* § 205 cmt. *a* (Am. Law Inst. 1981). Good faith requires conduct of each party within the contract consistent with "faithfulness to an agreed common purpose and consistency with the justified expectations of the other party"; the Uniform Commercial Code also relies on an internal cooperative morality by calling for "honesty in fact" between the parties. U.Ç.C. § 1-201.

[15] Good faith "excludes a variety of types of conduct [that] violate community standards of decency, fairness or reasonableness." *Restatement (Second) of Contracts* § 205 cmt. *a* (Am. Law Inst. 1981). The Code, too, also looks to external standards: "the observance of reasonable commercial standards of fair dealing." U.C.C. § 1-201. As one advocate of this view put it, not only is it "natural for two parties to assume that each will act in good faith toward the other throughout the course of their contractual dealings" but external norms found in conventional morality legally "obligate them to act this way." Summers, *supra* note 5, at 197–198.

any given contract. Contracting parties are generally assumed to be able to protect themselves, except where the law or special relations invite them to let down their guard.[16] Protecting the practice of contracting, by interpreting contract terms to prevent their bad-faith uses, allows courts to provide assurance to parties engaging in the institution of contracts. Third, efforts to remove morality from the doctrine of good faith are futile. Were it even possible to eliminate morality from good faith, we would be left with a doctrine less able to protect reasonable expectations and support efficient private ordering,[17] which is not to suggest that every moral code is equally adaptive to these purpose. Any functional and practical implementation of the doctrine will imply certain constraints on the operative moral and social forms.[18] An elaboration of these claims follows.

II. Consensual Rationality and Contractual Morality

Good faith as a legal principle governing contractual exchanges derives from cooperative norms of conventional morality. Like a promise, good faith finds its basis in a social practice, which under certain conditions law will recognize and enforce. Promise and

---

[16] This fact distinguishes fiduciary and confidence relations from strictly contractual ones. See, e.g., Daniel B. Kelly, "Fiduciary Principles in Fact-Based Fiduciary Relationships," in *The Oxford Handbook of Fiduciary Law* 3, 18–19 (Evan J. Criddle, Paul B. Miller, & Robert H. Sitkoff eds., 2019); Paul B. Miller, "The Identification of Fiduciary Relationships," in *id.* at 367, 369–374; Henry E. Smith, "Fiduciary Law and Equity," in *id.* at 745, 761–762.

[17] Economists have long recognized the importance of morality in correcting inefficiencies resulting from unbounded self-interest. "Those general rules of conduct," concerning "what is just and unjust in human conduct," Adam Smith observed, "are of great use in correcting misrepresentations of self-love concerning what is fit and proper to be done in our particular situation." Adam Smith, *The Theory of Moral Sentiments* 186 (Knud Haakonssen ed., 2002). See also John Haynes, who emphasized economic importance of "the restraints which morals place upon men so far as they make economic prosperity possible." John Haynes, *Risk as an Economic Factor*, 9 Q.J. ECON. 409, at 438 (1895). Frank Knight, called this restraint as a "beneficent limitation" observable from, "the fact that the human individual has been found normally incapable of wielding to his own-advantage much more industrial power than, aided by legal and moral restraints, society as a whole can safely permit him to possess." Frank Knight, *Risk, Uncertainty and Profit*, at 193 (1921). Kenneth Arrow, too, stressed that ethics and moral principles "are to some extent essential for efficiency." Kenneth J. Arrow, *The Economics of Moral Hazard: Further Comment*, 58 AM. ECON. REV. 537, at 538 (1968). See also the insightful analyses of Amartya Sen and James Buchanan: Amartya K. Sen, *Rational Fools: A Critique of the Behavioral Foundations of Economic Theory*, 6 PHIL. & PUB. AFF. 317 (1977), and Amartya K. Sen, *Goals, Commitment, and Identity*, 1 J.L. ECON. & ORG. 341 (1985); James M. Buchanan, *Choosing What to Choose*, 150 J. INST. & THEOR. ECON. 123, 128 (1994).

[18] As Andrew S. Gold observes in this volume, referring to his co-authored work with Henry Smith, "inclusive functionalism" combined with "inclusive interprestivism" takes moral norms as serious constraints but not unlimited in form. Andrew S. Gold, this volume; Andrew S. Gold & Henry E. Smith, *Sizing Up Private Law*, U. TORONTO L.J. (forthcoming, 2020). See also Alan D. Miller & Ronen Perry, *Good Faith Performance*, 98 IOWA L. REV. 689 (2013), for an axiomatic demonstration of the constraints required for practical implementation of good faith informed by conventional morality.

good faith, in fact, are often inextricably linked. But while the principal test of a promise is *whether* the obligation is kept, good faith is concerned with *how* obligations are discharged. Good faith seeks to maintain the cooperative spirit that underwrites the letter of agreements. By what standard, then, is this spirit or principle of cooperation evaluated? As suggested earlier, academic projects aiming to describe the law and inner logic of good faith have largely revolved around two standards, which we now consider in more detail.

First, a number of commentators have asserted that the doctrine of good faith may be considered only in light of "the intentions of parties."[19] No external consideration, moral or otherwise, ought to be brought to bear on parties' agreement through the implied doctrine of good faith. That is, beyond the limits determined by the parties *themselves* through their agreement, they "remain free to be self-interested within the contract—as self-interested as they were without it[.]"[20] Good faith's limited purpose here is to realize the parties' actual agreement through a searching inquiry of what *they* rationally consented to under the contract. Nothing more.[21] Consensual rationality is the sole principle that guides the doctrine of good faith in the first approach.

Second, other commentators maintain a view of good faith that allows or even invites courts to impose external standards on the parties' exchange.[22] Some support for this view, often called contractual morality, is provided by the *Restatement (Second) of Contracts* and the Uniform Commercial Code, which describe the duty of good faith not only in the language of faithfulness to the parties' actual agreement and justified expectations but also in terms of "community standards of decency, fairness or reasonableness" and "reasonable commercial standards of fair dealing."[23] Looking to norms and expectations beyond the bounds defined by the parties' consensual arrangement, good faith may here imply overriding legal and moral constraints on the parties' exchange.

Skeptics of the contractual morality view of good faith argue that appeals to external norms both undermine the usefulness of the doctrine and are unnecessary for maintaining the moral bounds of contracting. Community standards of fairness and conventional morality are evident in various contract doctrines, including public policy, unconscionability, and promissory estoppel, inter alia, as well as in a number of other equitable remedies and

[19]   Steven J. Burton, *Breach of Contract and the Common Law Duty to Perform in Good Faith*, 94 Harv. L. Rev. 369, 371 (1980).

[20]   Daniel Markovits, "Good Faith as Contract's Core Value," in *Philosophical Foundations of Contract Law* 272, 280 (Gregory Klass, George Letsas, & Prince Saprai eds., 2014).

[21]   Commentators, however, sometimes speak in terms of "justified," "legitimate," or "reasonable expectations" of a bargain or exchange to which the parties have consented. For contractual parties, for instance, Burton says the aim of good faith is "to protect their reasonable expectations." Burton, *supra* note 20, at 371. See also *Restatement (Second) of Contracts* § 205 cmt. *a* (Am. Law Inst. 1981), which "emphasizes faithfulness to an agreed common purpose and consistency with the justified expectations of the other party." One is left to wonder about the additional contribution of the terms "justified," "legitimate," and "reasonable" to the baseline consideration of rational consent under this approach to the doctrine.

[22]   See Summers, *supra* note 5, at 195 (observing the then "growing interest in devising legal standards of contractual morality"). See also Steven J. Burton, *More on Good Faith Performance of a Contract: A Reply to Professor Summers*, 69 Iowa L. Rev. 497, 499 (1984) ("Contractual morality implies a ground for judicial decision that lies outside of and may take precedence over the agreement of the parties.").

[23]   *Restatement (Second) of Contracts* § 205 cmt. *a.* (Am. Law Inst. 1981), and U.C.C. § 1-201(20) (2014).

rules of interpretation.[24] Enlisting good faith to police such well-patrolled territory is gratuitous, insist critics, and in any event doing so would only stretch the doctrine beyond its analytical value. These critics, often with an economics orientation, recall the Holmesian reproach of loose "moral" language in the law, particularly in the law of contracts.[25] Holmes would simply rid law of all "moral phraseology,"[26] but skeptics of contractual morality would unlikely be satisfied with merely stripping away its moralistic veneer.

The debate over whether to cast the doctrine of good faith in moral or amoral terms is not merely a quibble over words. Two distinct claims are discernable in the charge against moralistic language. First is that vague moral usage tends to confound legal analysis.[27] Avoiding such vagaries when applying the doctrine would clarify "the nebulous scope of good faith."[28] Note that this first claim may still give countenance to conventional morality, but it would do so without the verbal excesses thought common to many cases. Second, and more stringent, is the claim that rational application of the doctrine ought to exclude all consideration of external norms and conventional morality. It is doubtful that Holmes would go so far,[29] but it is precisely here, where morality and rationality are set in opposition, that the interests in debates over good faith are best revealed. "Those interests are [the] fields of battle."[30]

Seeking to bring order to the "moral thicket" seeded by high-minded doctrinalism, critics of contractual morality have turned to arguments grounded in the logic of economics.[31] In making this turn they rely on the belief that analyses largely informed by

[24]   As Robert Summers observed, good faith sits among "a family of general legal doctrines, including implied promise, custom and usage, fraud, negligence and estoppel, which . . . supplement, limit and qualify specific legal rules and contract terms." *Id.* at 198. On adopting, instead of good faith, rational rules of textual interpretation, see, e.g., Harold Dubroff, *The Implied Covenant of Good Faith in Contract Interpretation and Gap-Filling: Reviling a Revered Relic*, 80 St. JOHN's L. REV. 559 (2006).

[25]   "Nowhere is the confusion between legal and moral ideas more manifest," observed Holmes, "than in the law of contract." Oliver Wendell Holmes Jr., *The Path of the Law*, 10 HARV. L. REV. 457, 462 (1897).

[26]   "For my own part, I often doubt whether it would not be a gain if every word of moral significance could be banished from the law altogether, and other words adopted which should convey legal ideas uncolored by anything outside the law. We should lose the fossil records of a good deal of history and the majesty got from ethical associations, but by ridding ourselves of an unnecessary confusion we should gain very much in the clearness of our thought." *Id.* at 464.

[27]   "The law is full of phraseology drawn from morals, and by the mere force of language continually invites us to pass from one domain to the other without perceiving it, as we are sure to do unless we have the boundary constantly before our minds." *Id.* at 459–460.

[28]   Clayton P. Gillette, *Limitations on the Obligation of Good Faith*, 1981 DUKE L.J. 619, 620–621. Richard Posner writes the function served by good faith is "explicable in nonmoral terms" and overlaying moral phraseology can only "conceal the actual character of the doctrine." Richard A. Posner, *Let Us Never Blame a Contract Breaker*, 107 MICH. L. REV. 1349, 1361 (2009).

[29]   As Holmes famously wrote, "law is the witness and external deposit of our moral life." Holmes, *supra* note 26, at 459.

[30]   Oliver Wendell Holmes Jr., *Privilege, Malice and Intent*, 8 HARV. L. REV. 1, 7 (1894).

[31]   See, e.g., Posner, *supra* note 29. "A better general description of all contract breach behavior can be constructed from an economic analysis of the traditional view of simple express promises." Burton, *supra* note 20, at 374. "We could of course do without the term 'good faith,' and maybe even without the doctrine. We could," observed Judge Posner, "speak instead of implied conditions . . . [and] . . . whether we say that a contract shall be deemed to contain such implied conditions . . . , or that a contract obligates the parties to cooperate in its performance in 'good faith' . . . [it] comes to much the same thing." Mkt. St. Assocs. Ltd. P'ship v. Frey, 941 F.2d 588, 596 (7th Cir. 1991).

economic reasoning will clarify the doctrine of good faith by pointing judges toward consistent and therefore predictable conclusions. No doubt it may. However, as Holmes long ago saw, there lies an "illusion" at the core of this belief. "You can give any conclusion a logical form. You always can imply a condition in a contract," he observed, "[b]ut why do you imply it?"[32] Whatever the answer, argued Holmes, its ultimate basis must lie beyond the strictly rational and logical. Why have an implied duty of good faith? "It is because of some belief as to the practice of the community or of a class, or because of some opinion as to policy[.]"[33] In other words, community practices, conventional morality, and policy "preference[s] of a given body in a given time and place" are the contingent interests generally concealed in claims of rational or logical necessity.

III. Identifying the Doctrine

Mutual cooperation is the touchstone of good faith under both consensual rationality and contractual morality, but it is not at all obvious what form or degree of cooperation is required by either view. As an abstract obligation, good faith is clarified only in its application to the specific cases, yet resolving its indeterminacies in actual cases under either view is no trivial matter. Even the most capable judges can lose track of the means, if not the principle, animating its application.[34] Much turns on the nature of the task before the court. Courts are asked to invoke the doctrine of good faith either to interpret vague or ambiguous terms in contracts or else to fill in gaps or missing terms in contracts. When gap-filling is called for, consensual rationality takes a particularly restricted approach to good faith.

Any number of considerations may add content to a contract among parties. As Emile Durkheim observed, "in a contract, not everything is contractual,"[35] which is to say contracts contain more than that to which the parties have strictly agreed. Trade usages, for instance, are often invoked to supplement contracts, as well as considerations of public policy, and such. Consensual rationalists do not claim that every consideration beyond the parties' intent and expectations must be excluded from the contract. Rather, their claim is only that the application of the implied duty of good faith cannot be a means to add *content* to the contract outside of the intentions and expectations of the parties to the agreement.

According to Professor Burton, a pioneering figure in applying economic reasoning and consensual rationality to good faith, the doctrine should only be "used to effectuate the intentions of the parties, or to protect their reasonable expectations, through interpretation and implication."[36] Importantly, his claim is not that courts are unwilling or

---

[32] Holmes, *supra* note 26, at 465.   [33] *Id.*

[34] See Rakoff's insightful analysis of Judge Posner's opinion in Todd D. Rakoff, *Good Faith in Contract Performance:* Market Street Associates Ltd. Partnership v. Frey, 120 HARV. L. REV. 1187 (2007).

[35] Emile Durkheim, *The Division of Labor in Society, Free Press: New York*, at 158 [1893] (1984).

[36] Burton, *supra* note 23, at 499.

ought not advance conventional morality in recognizing and enforcing contracts; instead he asserts simply that good faith is an inappropriate doctrine for that aim. Courts may and often do pursue "contractual morality" through doctrines of unconscionability, excuses, estoppel, waiver, or interpretation. However, says Burton, "it is hard to see what justifies a court in disregarding the agreement of the parties on grounds of 'contractual morality' when the intentions of the parties or their reasonable expectations can be reasonably ascertained, and none of the above-mentioned doctrines properly are invoked."[37]

A contractual moralist might counter by saying that good faith places a distinct moral marker on contracts as an institution of exchange, securing a baseline morality in its formation, modification, performance, or enforcement.[38] While a number of other doctrines, such as those based on estoppel or excuses, may be used to relieve one party or another of some unfair burden under the contract, the doctrine of good faith looks to protect the practice of contracting *itself*, rather than the contracting parties per se. Consider, in contrast, the doctrine of unconscionability. Recognizing a duty of contractual good faith is not the same as policing against outlandish contract terms (*pace* price or substantive unconscionability) or egregious processes by which some terms became part of a contract (procedural unconscionability), but rather it is to recognize that a term, which may be neither procedurally nor substantively unconscionable, may still be used in bad faith in contingencies that one or both parties never imagined or simply discounted.

Other doctrines, such as fraud, quasi-contract, promissory estoppel, and the like, may similarly be enlisted to guard against bad-faith exchanges, but these are noncontractual forms, at least as traditionally understood. These doctrines are used to correct a failure of contract. They operate like a safety value, as Henry Smith observed, providing equitable relief through release from oppressive contracts.[39] Good faith, however, vindicates the contract. With good faith, exchanges are assured not through appeals to noncontractual forms but through a doctrine that explicitly recognizes the continuing validity of the contract and the applicability of its terms. In this sense, good faith is more directly concerned with the practice or institution of contracts than the parties themselves. Contractual morality reveals this key point more clearly than consensual rationality.

A strict consensual rationalist applying the doctrine of good faith would not promote the aims of a practice or an institution above the parties to a contract. All aims beyond those determined by actual identified parties to a contract are beyond the pale of good faith under this view, including traditional economic objectives and approaches

---

[37] *Id.* at 498–499.

[38] No suggestion of a universal or uniform baseline of good faith in contract formation, modification, performance or enforcement is intended. Each moment of contractual engagement, from early negotiations to completion, may be subject to different standards of good faith even within a single jurisdiction. There is, for instance, no implied duty of good faith in negotiation and formation of contracts in the commercial code or common law of American states, while modification is subject to standards distinct from the general duty of good faith in performance and enforcement. See U.C.C. § 2-209 and the Restatement, Second, of Contract § 89.   [39] See *supra* note 13.

that seek to import "utopian ideals" into a contract through the doctrine. Making this argument in a recent chapter on the good-faith doctrine, Professor Daniel Markovits offered a robust consensual rationalist critique of intrusive economic ideals drawn into the doctrine—identifying Judge Posner's opinion in *Market Street Associates Limited Partnership v. Frey* "as a clear statement of the utopian approach."[40] Judge Posner would no doubt resist the characterization, and perhaps argue instead that his approach simply seeks to "give the parties what they would have stipulated for expressly if at the time of making the contract they had had complete knowledge of the future and the costs of negotiating and adding provisions to the contract had been zero."[41] Yet that would concede much of Markovits' critique.

Arguments based on rational hypothetical bargains necessarily look beyond the actual parties to given agreements. To see this point, first note that the hypothetical bargain approach applies both to gap-filling (adding content to incomplete contracts) and interpretation (clarifying ambiguous and otherwise inadequately specified contract terms). With gap-filling, the judicial task under this approach is to identify what the parties *would have wanted* had they anticipated and attended to some realized contingency. Yet because the parties to the contract failed to provide for the relevant realized contingency, the court cannot rely on their actual intent or agreement. It must look beyond the parties and their agreement, which would violate the consensual rationality prohibition against drawing on external considerations.

Moving away from gap-filling, the interpretive task becomes identifying what the parties *actually wanted*, yet failed to make clear in their agreement. Here, at least, the court is focused on actual intentions, rather than hypothetical ones. Absent direct admissible evidence showing actual intent, however, some other means must be used to find what the parties actually wanted. There is a common solution suggested by the conventional economics approach. Assume all parties are "rational."[42] They can then only want one thing from an ambiguous or otherwise unclear term: an interpretation of it that would maximize their joint surplus. We arrive at this conclusion (or are rather presented with it) as if it were merely a product of pure logic emanating directly from the parties and their agreement. Yet, the economic hypothetical bargain approach must draw on considerations beyond the parties' actual agreement and intent.

Hypothetical bargains attribute to parties not their actual intent but rather an intent that maximizes the value of their exchange in some realized state of the world. To carry out this exercise a court must make presumptions based on conventional norms, as Holmes observed (e.g., policy and social preferences of a group or class, or what it

---

[40] Markovits, *supra* note 21, at 285.

[41] Mkt. St. Assocs. Ltd. P'ship v. Frey, 941 F.2d 588, 596 (7th Cir. 1991).

[42] While neoclassical economic rationality demands only complete and consistent preferences, the hypothetical bargaining approach adds monotonic preferences—such that more of "good things" are preferred to less—to the rational behavioral assumptions. People with so-called "satisficing preferences" do not provide the clarity imaginable of those with maximizing preferences which is the key to resolving the indeterminacy of good faith, particularly if convexity of preferences is also assumed.

means to be rational in some relevant community or according to some abstract standard, and so on). As such, external factors are always implicit in this approach.[43] Hence, while the economic hypothetical bargaining approach to good faith is usually offered as a strictly rational application of the doctrine, it is in fact more akin to "contractual morality" in terms of its ready willingness to look beyond the parties' manifest intent and expectations.[44]

A strict consensual rationalist looks only to the parties' actual expectations and understandings under their agreement to give content to and interpret the contract. Delaware Chancery recognizes this approach as "subjective good faith."[45] As does the state's supreme court, which has rebuked trial judges who replace actual parties "with hypothetical reasonable people when making the inquiry."[46] Other states, like Wyoming, explicitly embrace community standards of decency and fairness in their formulation of the doctrine.[47] Professor Markovits would seem to favor Delaware's subjective approach, which he sees a "*pedestrian* ideal" (in contrast to the *utopian* ideal he attributes to the

---

[43]   Indeed, not just this approach, but "all major accounts of good faith . . . rely to some extent on the concept of community standards," as observed by Miller & Perry, *supra* note 19, at 725. They call this the "common demoninator" of good-faith accounts. *Id.*

[44]   To assert that the economics approach offers a mode of reasoning akin to other forms of contractual morality is not to suggest that it has no distinguishing qualities. Not all forms of conventional morality are equally compelling. Thomas Carlyle appealed to a widely shared morality when he was first to label economics a "Dismal Science" because it discarded established norms and accepted relations of his time. Today most people would agree that economics offered a more attractive answer to the question posed by Carlyle than the one he advocated. See Thomas Carlyle, *Occasional Discourse on the Negro Question, Fraser's Magazine for Town and Country*, Feb. 1849, at 677. See also John Stuart Mill, *The Negro Question*, FRASER'S MAGAZINE, 1850, reprinted in *Littell's Living Age*, Vol. XXIV, 465–469 (E.D. Littell, ed., Boston, Massachusetts), available at http://www.hetwebsite.net/het/texts/carlyle/mill1850negroquestion.htm.

[45]   "Although occasionally described in broad terms . . . the implied covenant of good faith and fair dealing protects the spirit of what was *actually bargained and negotiated for* in the contract." Fisk Ventures, LLC v. Segal, No. 3017-CC, 2008 WL 1961156, at *10 (Del. Ch. May 7, 2008) (emphasis in original).

[46]   Allen v. Encore Energy Partners, L.P., 72 A.3d 93, 107 (Del. 2013) ("It is essential to ensure, however, that the subjective good faith standard remains distinct from an objective, 'reasonable person' standard."). Delaware, a "four corners" and "plain meaning" jurisdiction, restricts not only interpretation but also content. In fact, it is clear that "a court cannot and should not use the implied covenant of good faith and fair dealing to fill a gap in a contract with an implied term unless it is clear from the contract that the parties would have agreed to that term had they thought to negotiate the matter." Segal v. Fisk Ventures, LLC, 984 A.2d 124 (Del. 2009) (quoting Corp. Prop. Assocs. 14 Inc. v. CHR Holding Corp., C.A. No. 3231 VCS, 2008 WL 963048 (Del. Ch. 2008)).

[47]   Universal Drilling Co., LLC v. R & R Rig Service, LLC, 271 P.3d 987 (Sup. Ct. Wyo. 2012) at 999. Similarly, New Jersey's Supreme Court stresses that "while a commercial party does not have to act with benevolence towards an opposing party, it cannot behave inequitably." Brunswick v. Rout 18 Shop. Center 86 A.2d 387 (NJ 2005) at 399–400. "We are not eager to impose a set of morals on the marketplace. Ordinarily, we are content to let experienced commercial parties fend for themselves[.] But as our good faith and fair dealing jurisprudence reveals, there are ethical norms that apply even to the harsh and sometimes cutthroat world of commercial transactions." *Id.* at 399. A number of American states, though not uniformly, "clearly employ the doctrine to ensure that a party does not 'violate community standards of decency, fairness, or reasonableness.'" Northwest, Inc. v. Ginsberg, 572 U.S. 273, 286.

economics approach). As an example of the pedestrian ideal in operation, he provocatively and interestingly claims that good faith is fully compatible with "the expectation remedy and the associated practice of 'efficient breach.'"[48] Yet the logic behind this claim is neither pedestrian nor, I believe, fully consistent with the strict consensual rationality view he advocates. It is instructive to unpack his claim that efficient breach displays no bad faith, which may in some cases be true, but is only necessarily so by presuming contractual influences beyond the parties and their actual agreement.

On what basis can one align good faith and efficient breach? By Markovits's account, the answer lies strictly within the agreement and the intent of the parties *themselves*, as they bargain "in the shadow of the [expectation damages] remedy." Two distinct bargaining contexts may be imagined here. First, and uncontroversially, when parties anticipate contingencies wherein nonperformance would be efficient, they may explicitly address those contingencies in the written terms of their agreement *or* they may reflect them implicitly in the price term, where the promisee is charged a lower price "in light of the promisor's *right* to retain the gains from the 'efficient breach.'"[49] What might be called "efficient breach" in this context is actually not a breach or a wrong at all, but is in fact the exercise of a right, properly understood.[50] Indeed, in this context, it is the *promisee* who stands to commit a wrong by making a "bad-faith" demand for performance or compensation greater than her expectation damages.[51] It is difficult to argue against these claims, and no one seriously does, when the agreement between the parties reflects an *actual* bargain.

When credible evidence of the bargain thus described is presented, no sensible court should deem nonperformance a "breach."[52] When there is no such evidence, however, Markovits invites us to consider a second bargaining context that is still able to rescue efficient breach from any taint of bad faith. In this alternative bargaining context,[53] how can a promisor's deliberate decision to breach in order to capture greater gains by nonperformance necessarily constitute good faith? According to his

---

[48] Markovits, *supra* note 21, at 280. So long as a breaching promisor "transfers to the promisee an amount equal to the expectation remedy, a promisor who commits such an 'efficient breach' surely displays no bad faith." *Id.* at 281.   [49] *Id.*

[50] The "payment will have been memorialized in a lower price term, which is to say that the promisor's entitlement to the gains from efficient breach is made express in the contract, or at least implied in fact rather than in law." *Id.*

[51] Bad faith follows from the promisee's demand for some or all of the gains from efficient breach through a disgorgement remedy or an action in specific performance, "as this would give the promisee a benefit that he did not pay for and deprive the promisor of one of the benefits that the contract expressly gave her." *Id.*

[52] When there is evidence indicating that the parties *actually* adjusted the price downward to give the promisor an option to not perform in contingencies where nonperformance is (weakly) mutually more valuable, then the court is simply enforcing the agreement.

[53] It is important to note that this is the typical context assumed in debates about efficient breach—and *not* a context where the parties explicitly or implicitly bargain for alternative performances wherein payment of expectation "damages" is treated as sufficient to discharge a duty rather than remedy a wrong.

argument, good faith obtains not only when parties knowingly bargain "in the shadow of the remedy" but also when they transact in the context of a competitive market environment wherein expectation damages are available for breach. Competitive forces (in addition to the parties) determine the terms of exchange, and these forces will take account of the remedy, even if the parties themselves fail to do so, and cause that accounting to be reflected in the price term. So the efficient breacher, again, captures only gains for which ex ante compensation was accorded to the promisee, hence there is no bad faith.[54]

Granting that there is necessarily no bad faith in that context, which is far from established, there is yet another point on which to focus. Turning to market competition to interpret or complete a contract in this context requires looking beyond the actual agreement of the parties. To be sure, were the parties to make explicit their intent to adopt market provisions, as if using a form to avoid needless reproduction of terms, then those terms would be correctly counted among the parties' actual agreement. That would suggest they were bargaining under the first context, however, wherein they simply selected the market's default terms. In the second bargaining context, by supposition, we are in a setting where there is no evidence indicating that the parties *actually* contemplated and reached any such agreement. It is no response to assert that by knowingly transacting within a competitive environment, parties adopt the market's determinations as their own actual intent and agreement. An awareness of competitive market forces, like an awareness of conventional moral forces, does not imply assent to terms dictated by those forces. To satisfy the claim that "an 'efficient breach' *surely* displays no bad faith,"[55] it would seem that one must, at least in some cases, make external appeals (even when the expectation damage remedy is reflected in the contract price).

None of this is to deny Professor Markovits's more general and compelling description of a pedestrian *ideal* in the doctrine of good faith. All that is claimed here is that a 'good faith efficient *breach*' must draw on factors beyond the subjective agreement and intent of contracting parties. It is hard to see how it could be otherwise. What would it mean to exclude all considerations external to the parties' agreement and intent as suggested by the strict consensual rationality view of good faith? An answer to that inquiry is as difficult to imagine as a principled limit to the imposition of a liberal contractual morality in the doctrine of good faith. There is no great worry in any case since these are not questions of practical importance. Consensual rationality and contractual morality are extreme points, ideal types, on a continuum where courts and most commentators occupy mixed and middle positions. To paraphrase Nider, in closing—hardly anyone, and certainly no prudent person, presumes to give certain and universal rules for recognizing in buying and selling what is precisely in every case allowable or not allowable under the doctrine of good faith.

[54] *Id.*   [55] *Id.* at 281 (emphasis added).

IV. CONCLUSION

Though much has been made here, and elsewhere, of the differences between the consensual rationality and contractual morality views of good faith, they in fact have significantly more in common than divergences. When there are clearly specified terms in a contract, courts are encouraged, both under principles of consensual rationality and on grounds of contractual morality, to avoid literal interpretation that would allow one side to exploit another in an unanticipated manner. Consensual rationality and contractual morality are used to screen for ill motives,[56] and both also serve as safety valves.[57] In most cases, as observed by Justice Scalia, then a judge on the D.C. Circuit, "the result is, or should be, the same."[58] Writing at a time when contractual morality was more in favor, Justice Scalia opined that its broader "formulation may have more appeal to modern taste since it purports to rely directly upon considerations of morality and public policy, rather than achieving those objectives obliquely, by honoring the reasonable expectations created by the autonomous expressions of the contracting parties."[59]

Today consensual rationality appears ascendant. The driving "principle," we are told, "is one of freedom of contract, which takes precedence over considerations of fairness or reasonableness."[60] One might predict continuing oscillation between the two views as tastes for formalism and freedom of contract rise and recede as they have before. With the ebb and flow, however, a few things will remain constant. First, practical implementation of good faith will always lie between the extremes of strict consensual rationality and loose contractual morality. Second, the doctrine of good faith, under all interpretations, will operate principally to protect the practice of contracting. Third, notions of conventional morality or community standards and preferences will always play some role, though perhaps unacknowledged, in the doctrine, including those interpretations grounded in economic reasoning. Claims proposing a strict "separation between economics and morals" are, as James Buchanan observed, "an illusion that

[56] Burton, for example, does acknowledge that "noneconomic motives, such as spite or ill will, are likely to run afoul of the good faith performance doctrine," but concludes these "factors so rarely are evidenced in the reported cases, however, that the focus of the theory must be on economic motives." Burton, *supra* note 20, at 387 n.80.

[57] Good faith is "useful in curing unreasonable and unjust results[.]" Dubroff, *supra* note 25, at 596. "It is a kind of 'safety valve' to which judges may turn to fill gaps and qualify or limit rights and duties otherwise arising under rules of law and specific contract language." Robert S. Summers, *The General Duty of Good Faith—Its Recognition and Conceptualization*, 67 CORNELL L. REV. 810, 812 (1982). For more on "safety value," see Summers, *supra* note 5, at 215–216; See Rose, *supra* note 13, at 309; Smith, *supra* note 13, at 903–905.

[58] Tymshare, Inc. v. Covell, 727 F.2d 1145, 1152–1153 (D.C. Cir. 1984).

[59] *Id.* Echoes of Justice Holmes are discernible in Justice Scalia's observations.

[60] Steven J. Burton, *History and Theory of Good Faith Performance in the United States*, UNIV. IOWA LEG. STUD. RESEARCH PAPER SERIES, Number 2017-08, at 7 (2017) (available at: http://ssrn.com/abstract=2742354).

simply cannot be sustained."[61] An economic order based on efficiency without fairness is as plausible as a legal order based on law without equity. As equity promotes compliance with law, so often does morality contribute to efficiency. Indeed, for contractual exchanges, the implied doctrine of good faith and fair dealing is arguably more important for an efficient economic order than it is for an equitable one. It is time to dispense with the false dichotomy between "morality" and "rationality" too often expressed or implied in claims based on economic reasoning.

---

[61] James M. Buchanan, *Choosing What to Choose*, 150 J. INST. & THEOR. ECON. 123, 128 (1994). See also Bruno S. Frey, Matthias Benz, & Alois Stutzer, *Introducing Procedural Utility: Not Only What, but Also How Matters*, 160 J. INST. & THEOR. ECON. 377 (2004). Cf. John Harsanyi, who cleverly (though unsatisfactorily) sought to avoid the critique of separation by treating morality as a subset of rationality: "moral behaviour itself is a special form of rational behaviour." John C. Harsanyi, "Morality and the Theory of Rational Behaviour," in *Utilitarianism and Beyond* 40 (Amartya Sen & Bernard Williams eds., 1982). "[A] rational pursuit of common human and humane interests, which, in my view, is the very essence of morality." *Id.*, at 41.

CHAPTER 31

···

THE RULE OF LAW

···

LISA M. AUSTIN

I. INTRODUCTION

···

IN the famous eighteenth-century British case *Entick v. Carrington*, Lord Camden offered strong words about the value of property: "our law holds the property of every man so sacred, that no man can set foot upon his neighbour's close without his leave; if he does he is a trespasser, though he does no damage at all; if he will tread upon his neighbour's ground, he must justify it by law."[1] But the case was not about upholding property rights as between two neighbors, it was about the rights of an individual as against the state. Entick was accused of seditious libel and his home was broken into and his papers searched by several of the king's messengers. The search warrant purporting to authorize this gave broad authority, on the basis of a unilateral accusation, to search and seize all papers in Entick's premises with no safeguards regarding potential abuse. Lord Camden held that the authorities had no jurisdiction to grant such a warrant, and that if there was such legal justification "it would destroy all the comforts of society."[2] This case has become a canonical statement of common law constitutionalism and the rule of law, affirming that public authorities are subject to the ordinary law of the land and cannot trespass absent legal authorization.[3] But the case also highlights the historical entwining of private law concerns (property) and more traditional public law concerns (abuse of state power).[4]

This chapter argues that the relationship between the private law and the rule of law has been underdeveloped, or ignored, by private law scholarship until recently and that its recovery and reimagining provides us with an important critical lens for the private law problems of the twenty-first century. Political theory has a long history of discussion of the

---

[1] Entick v. Carrington (1765), 95 ER 807.   [2] *Id.*

[3] Within public law it has also come to stand for the broader principle that "public authority must be authorized by law." See Paul Scott, Entick v. Carrington *and the Legal Protection of Property in* Entick v. Carrington: *250 Years of the Rule of Law* 131 (Adam Tomkins & Paul Scott eds., 2015).

[4] This influence was long-lasting on constitutional thinking in relation to search and seizure, which was rooted in trespass notions in American and Canadian traditions until the courts shifted to a "reasonable expectation of privacy" analysis. See Hunter v. Southam, 2 S.C.R. 145 (1984).

rule of law, a history that is not confined to liberal theorists but stretches back to ancient Greece and Rome.[5] Legal theorists write about it in relation to debates about the nature of law and law's moral justification. Sometimes these latter debates discuss private rights as important liberties operating against the state and secured through the rule of law—positions that echo *Entick v. Carrington* and have been variously expressed through thinkers like Dicey and Hayek.[6] But until recently there has been relatively little attention to what the rule of law, as a conceptual and critical framework, could bring to private law theory itself. Does the rule of law apply to the interpersonal norms that regulate relations between private individuals or only to public authorities? Is the rule of law limited to securing private liberties against unjustified state interference, or can it also tell us something important about the content of those liberties and the system of private law that protects them?

Why this lacuna in the literature? I want to offer two speculative reasons that take up some of the themes and concerns of the New Private Law. The first reason concerns the U.S. legal academy. As Goldberg points out, American scholars have often treated the category of private law with skepticism, embracing the view that "all law is public law."[7] If all law is public, and if the major rule-of-law discussions in twentieth-century legal theory have largely been about public law concerns, then one might expect the American legal literature on private law topics to take up rule-of-law principles with more frequency. However, Goldberg also points out that the U.S. legal academy has also embraced the mantra that "we are all realists now."[8] Legal Realism saw the rule of law as bound up with the formalism it opposed.[9] Realism's more critical progeny also took issue with the conservatism of some rule-of-law champions and their resistance to the administrative state. The U.S. legal academy could embrace the idea that law is "public" but not that the rule of law could provide critical insight into law's nature as an instrument of public authority.

The second reason concerns private law theory in the commonwealth, and the problem there is almost the inverse. There is a rich tradition in these jurisdictions of embracing legal formalism—although it is a more sophisticated version than that attacked by Legal Realism.[10] However, there is also a strong tradition within this formalism of understanding private law in terms that are fundamentally distinct from public law. If formalism looks particularly primed to embrace rule-of-law concerns, it resists the "public" nature of the private law.[11]

In this chapter, I will outline the general contemporary view in the legal theory literature regarding the core idea of the rule of law, and also what remains controversial, and then outline some of the recent work that has taken up the question of the relevance of the rule of law to private law theory. In doing so I will outline potential critical pathways for reclaiming a rule-of-law perspective on private law that address some of

---

[5] Brian Z. Tamanaha, *On the Rule of Law: History, Politics, Theory* 7–14 (2004).

[6] A.V. Dicey, *Introduction to the Study of the Law of the Constitution* (1908); F.A. Hayek, *The Road to Serfdom* (1944).

[7] John C.P. Goldberg, *Introduction: Pragmatism and Private Law*, 125 HARV. L. REV. 1640, 1641 (2012).

[8] *Id.*   [9] Tamanaha, *supra* note 5, at 73ff.

[10] See, e.g., Ernest J. Weinrib, *The Idea of Private Law* (1995).

[11] This has changed with Weinrib's landmark essay *Private Law and Public Right*, 61 U. TORONTO L.J. 191 (2011), which I discuss in a later section.

the reasons I have just offered for its underdevelopment. I will then outline how a focus on the rule of law in general, and in relation to some of its specific commitments and virtues, provides an important critical lens in relation to understanding and responding to the way that private power operates in the twenty-first century within what I call the "global data economy."

II. The Rule of Law:
Its Core and Controversies

The rule of law is often contrasted with the rule of people, as an ideal that is regulative of public power. "Rule of law" means that rulers do not rule *by* law but are themselves subject to the law. Although there is a long and rich intellectual tradition associated with the rule of law, in contemporary debates it is often associated with a particular view of the liberal state. For example, the rule of law has been invoked by thinkers like Dicey and Hayek to criticize the administrative state and defend a realm of private rights bound up with a liberal market vision. Something like this—rather than the general idea that law constrains public power—is usually what people have in mind when they label rule-of-law concerns as "legalistic" or "neoliberal." Theorists interested in critiquing liberalism or defending the administrative state have often agreed with their opponents' assumptions about the rule of law (that it is bound up with liberalism, that it is a problem for the administrative state) but choose instead to demote the importance of the rule of law. As Tamanaha describes it: "[w]hile the political right laments the degeneration of the rule of law in the West, radical left theorists encourage this decline."[12]

A key part of the American story regarding the Left's abandonment of the rule of law from their critical toolkit is the legacy of Legal Realism and its attack on legal formalism.[13] It associated the rule of law with an idea of "judicial fidelity to pre-existing law," a view that emphasized rules—a strong distinction between law and politics—and the neutrality of judges.[14] What I would like to do in this section is not recount this story but offer a different critical pathway. Although I consider this pathway to be open to theorists on both the right and the left, my interest here is to persuade the rule-of-law skeptics to consider this path. Because many such skeptics work within traditions that have critiqued formalism and natural law traditions generally, in what follows I will emphasize the perspective of legal positivism and underscore where it differs from some other traditions. As I outline in the following, legal positivists take a very instrumental view of the rule of law, and this is helpful in outlining a critical approach to the rule of law that can both adopt its insights as well as subject its elements to external critique. In what follows, I will sketch the outline of how the general rule-of-law literature answers two main

[12] Tamanaha, *supra* note 5, at 73.   [13] *Id.* at 77ff.

[14] Robin L. West, *Re-Imagining Justice: Progressive Interpretations of Formal Equality, Rights, and the Rule of Law* 18–26 (2001). West discusses this view as the dominant view of legal scholars, but this is not accurate, especially outside of the U.S. Academy.

points: (1) what does it mean for something to be deficient in relation to the rule of law?; and (2) what kind of criticism is it to say that something is deficient in this way?

There is a fair degree of agreement among legal theorists regarding the set of core commitments contemplated by the rule of law.[15] Lon Fuller famously articulated these commitments in his fable of the ruler Rex and the various ways in which he fails to create law. Fuller distills the requirements of the rule of law into eight principles for a system of legal rules: generality, publicity, nonretroactivity, clarity, noncontradiction, possibility of compliance, stability, and congruence between official action and declared rule.[16] These are often referred to as the "principles of legality." Waldron has argued that this list emphasizes the "formal and structural character" of the law and points to the need to also appreciate the procedural demands of the rule of law, which emphasize that the application of rules conform to natural justice and procedural due process.[17] Raz's influential version of the core idea also places a stronger emphasis on procedural elements and institutional requirements such as the role of the courts.[18] However, these differences in emphasis do not amount to a critique of Fuller's basic list so much as a drawing out of some of the implications of principles like congruity with more specificity in terms of its procedural and institutional aspects.[19]

All of these versions of the rule of law coalesce around two main sets of ideas: (1) that law cannot confer or uphold the arbitrary exercise of power, and (2) that law must be able to guide action.[20] Some version of this core has become a familiar starting point in many discussions of the rule of law in the legal theory literature. The discussion then forks into different directions. For example, there are many different positions regarding whether the rule of law is also intrinsically connected to "substantive" norms[21] such as democracy,[22] autonomy,[23] human rights,[24] or ideas of social welfare.[25] These debates often are bound up with broader questions about why the rule of law is, or is not, valuable.

---

[15] Some influential accounts deny this agreement. Fallon argues that the rule of law has "multiple strands" that are "complexly interwoven." Richard H. Fallon Jr., *"The Rule of Law" as a Concept in Constitutional Discourse*, 97 COLUM. L. REV. 1, 1 (1997). Radin has also argued that it is ambiguous and contested. Margaret Jane Radin, *Reconsidering the Rule of Law*, 69 B.U. L. REV. 781, 781 (1989).

[16] Lon L. Fuller, *The Morality of Law* 39 (rev. ed., 1969).

[17] Jeremy Waldron, *The Concept and the Rule of Law*, 43 GA. L. REV. 1, 7–8 (2008).

[18] Joseph Raz, *The Rule of Law and Its Virtue*, 93 L.Q. REV. 195, 201 (1977).

[19] John Gardner, "The Supposed Formality of the Rule of Law," in *Law as a Leap of Faith: Essays on Law in General*, at 204, 210 (2012).

[20] Lisa M. Austin & Dennis Klimchuk, "Introduction," in *Private Law and the Rule of Law* at 1 (Lisa M. Austin & Dennis Klimchuk eds., 2014).

[21] See generally Paul P. Craig, *Formal and Substantive Conceptions of the Rule of Law: An Analytical Framework*, 21 PUB. L. 467 (1997).

[22] See generally Donald Meiklejohn, *Review: Democracy and the Rule of Law*, 91 ETHICS 117 (1980).

[23] See generally Colleen Murphy, *Lon Fuller and the Moral Value of the Rule of Law*, 24 LAW & PHIL. 239 (2005); Jennifer Nadler, *Hart, Fuller and the Connection Between Law and Justice*, 27 LAW & PHIL. 1 (2008).

[24] See generally Evan Fox-Decent, *Is the Rule of Law Really Indifferent to Human Rights?*, 27 LAW & PHIL. 533 (2008).

[25] See generally Nick Barber, *Must Legalistic Conceptions of the Rule of Law Have a Social Dimension?*, 17 RATIO JURIS 474 (2004).

I will take up an important strand of this debate regarding why the rule of law is valuable—the debate about its relationship to morality—for it helps outline the general nature of the critical pathway that the rule of law offers rather than its many winding offshoots. Fuller famously referred to his principles of legality as an "internal" morality of law, and there are many traditions that defend the claim that the rule of law is inherently a moral ideal.[26] However, for positivists like Raz, the virtue of the rule of law "is the virtue of efficiency; the virtue of the instrument as an instrument."[27] Conformity with the rule of law enables the law to achieve its ends—largely because the law must be capable of guiding behavior—but the rule of law is "morally neutral" in relation to those ends.[28] As Gardner argues, the morality of law's ends is "left to ordinary, unspecialized, external morality, the same morality that binds us all."[29]

What is at stake in these differences? Rarely is the issue whether or not one can critique a particular legal state of affairs. For example, an instrumentalist can still critique the law should it pursue evil ends, or argue that the failure to uphold human rights norms is a moral failure. What an instrumentalist cannot argue is that these are rule-of-law failures. This does not mean that the rule of law is neutral in relation to various ideas of political order. As Gardner argues, if liberalism is concerned with freedom, then the fact that the rule of law is consistent with some ideas of freedom is of value. Indeed, many positivists have defended the rule of law for its consistency with ideas of individual agency.[30] The point is simply that we understand this value from the point of view of external political theories, and some political theories will value the rule of law more than others.[31] Put another way, the rule of law itself cannot tell us why it is good to have a legal system; what it tells us is that if we have a legal system, then it should be one governed by the internal morality of law.[32]

Those who disagree with this instrumental account of the rule of law in favor of an approach that argues for a thicker constitutive relationship between law and morality are usually disagreeing about a deeper question about the nature of law.[33] What is at stake is one of two types of conclusions, which are off limits to the positivist/instrumentalist approach. Roughly, the first is that law that fails to conform to the rule of law is not actually law, and the second is that law that aims at evil ends is not actually law. To be clear, positivists can argue that law should conform to the rule of law, and also that law that aims at evil ends should be condemned. The issue is not an inability to gain critical traction but how one identifies a legally valid norm.[34]

I consider the details of the "what is law" debate largely irrelevant for the purposes of retrieving and reimagining a critical rule-of-law perspective on the private law. What is

---

[26] T.R.S. Allan, *The Sovereignty of Law: Freedom, Constitution and Common Law* (2013); Michael Oakeshott, "The Rule of Law," in *On History and Other Essays* (1999); Nigel Simmonds, *Law as a Moral Idea* (2007).

[27] Raz, *supra* note 18, at 208.   [28] *Id.*   [29] Gardner, *supra* note 19, at 211.

[30] Waldron, *supra* note 17, at 28.   [31] Gardner, *supra* note 19, at 216.   [32] *Id.* at 215.

[33] See Simmonds, *supra* note 26. Sometimes an outsider to this debate might be forgiven for thinking that many of its participants are speaking past one another.

[34] John Gardner, "Legal Positivism: 5 ½ Myths," in *Law as a Leap of Faith* 19 (2012).

important is that the positivist tradition shows how the rule of law can intersect with many different theoretical and critical traditions in different ways. The rule of law is not inherently neoliberal, and there are many ways in which one may get on or off the neo-liberal boat, so to speak. A rule-of-law account can also include an argument that a par-ticular position overemphasizes the importance of the rule of law when this is just one virtue that the law should uphold and not the only one. The positivist account of the rule of law is therefore helpful to the project of critical reclamation in that it provides a way of adopting the core rule-of-law ideas into a critical toolkit that does not presuppose a set of political commitments.

However, there is another sense in which the positivist tradition appears less help-ful with at least some of the post-Realist critical projects, and that is in how it con-ceives of the relationship between the rule of law and power. Recall that the core ideals of the rule of law coalesce around the twin ideas of nonarbitrariness and guidance. Different theoretical traditions tend to prioritize one of these over the other, and the positivist tradition has emphasized guidance. For example, according to Raz, the more that the law conforms to the rule of law, the more capable it will be of guiding behav-ior, and the more the law will achieve its purposes.[35] The concern regarding arbitrari-ness is, for Raz, about solving problems that law itself creates. This is why he calls the rule of law a negative virtue: "conformity to it does not cause good except through avoiding evil and the evil which is avoided is evil which could only have been caused by the law itself."[36]

Contrast this with Postema's view that orients the relationship between power, law, and nonarbitrariness differently.[37] Taking the broad view of political theory, Postema argues that the core ideal of the rule of law

> has been rooted in the twofold thought that (1) a polity is well ordered when its members are secured against the arbitrary exercise of power and that (2) law, because of its distinctive features, is especially if not uniquely capable of providing such security.[38]

This (the well-ordered polity) is a political justification for law, which then is thought to have "features" that allow it to constrain arbitrary exercises of power. "Arbitrary" has a specific meaning within the rule of law tradition. It does not mean unreasoned or unpre-dictable but *unanswerable*. Where law rules, according to Postema, "power is systemati-cally rendered non-arbitrary."[39] On a view that places nonarbitrariness at its core, guidance will be understood in terms that support nonarbitrariness.

It is quite significant, then, that Raz has recently backed away from aspects of his account of the rule of law that make guidance central. In his Tang Prize lecture he instead concludes that "the rule of law protects us from arbitrary use of legal power, and from

---

[35] Raz, *supra* note 18, at 207.   [36] *Id.* at 206.

[37] Gerald J. Postema, "Fidelity in Law's Commonwealth," in *Private Law and the Rule of Law* 17 (Lisa M. Austin & Dennis Klimchuk eds., 2014).   [38] *Id.* at 17.

[39] Waldron is a positivist who agrees with Postema on this point. See Waldron, *supra* note 17, at 11.

similar abuses of legal power."[40] Raz acknowledges that one way to understand what unites the core principles of the rule of law is in terms of guidance.[41] However, he points out that this is inadequate as an explanation. A central reason for its inadequacy is that we cannot answer the question of how much guidance is required in order to comply with the rule of law. For example, Raz argues that the idea of guidance does not help us answer the question of the degree to which official discretion should be curtailed in order to comply with the rule of law. This is because "people can plan and organize their affairs on the basis of partial information, and in the face of risk."[42] Instead, he argues that the core idea of the rule of law is that governments conform to the rule of law when "acting with manifest intention to serve the interests of the governed, as expressed by the law and its morally proper interpretation and implementation."[43]

Raz's interpretation of the rule of law as governments serving the interests of the governed broadly conforms to Waldron's understanding of the public nature of law. As Waldron argues, a defining feature of law is that it presents itself "as standing in the name of the public and as oriented to the public good."[44] Waldron denies that this involves a commitment to a more natural law understanding of law and argues that the idea is aspirational: "nothing is law unless it *purports* to promote the public good, i.e., unless it presents itself as oriented in that direction."[45] We might then argue that the rule of law does not simply allow the law to achieve its ends (whatever they might be) but that it helps to constitute the law as the kind of thing that it is, which is an instrument of public authority oriented to the public good.[46] This makes nonarbitrariness central to the rule of law, for the principles that coalesce around nonarbitrariness seek to ensure that authority exercised in the name of law is answerable to public criteria.

III. How Does the Rule of Law Apply to Private Law?

Because of the theoretical literature's dominant framing of the rule of law in terms of constraints on government, the private law most often appears in rule of law discussions in an *Entick v. Carrington*–type of role: property rules like trespass preserve individual liberty against interference from the state.[47] However, as Postema argues, there is a history of also seeing the rule of law as protecting against the arbitrary wielding of nongovernmental power.[48] West, in her project of reimagining a progressive interpretation of the rule of law,

---

[40] Joseph Raz, *The Law's Own Virtue*, 39 OXFORD J. LEGAL STUD. 1, 15 (2019).   [41] *Id.* at 3.

[42] *Id.* at 4.   [43] *Id.* at 8.

[44] Waldron, *supra* note 17, at 31–32. Waldron calls this an "aspirational" ideal rather than a substantive one and so distances his view from the natural law tradition.

[45] *Id.*

[46] See Lisa M. Austin, "The Power of the Rule of Law," in *Private Law and the Rule of Law* 269 (Lisa M. Austin & Dennis Klimchuk eds., 2014).

[47] Richard Epstein, *Design for Liberty: Private Property, Public Administration, and the Rule of Law* (2011).

[48] Postema, *supra* note 37, at 19ff.

argues for a reappropriation of a "Hobbesian Rule of Law" that promotes the role of law in protecting citizens from "the private realm of assault, violence, and private subordination."[49] Taken together, these positions can show us why we could give a rule of law justification for the private law in that private law is important in constraining both public and private power. Working out the details of this in different contexts and in different ways is important and, as I outline in the next section, part of a much-needed research agenda. There is a further important question, however, that recent scholarship has started to address. That question is: To what extent can the rule of law help us understand and critique the specific architecture and doctrines of the private law? As outlined in the introduction section previously, this question is sometimes difficult to raise within a literature that has often sought to emphasize what is distinctly "private" about private law rather than what features it might share with public law, even if expressed differently.

One initial answer to this question is that the core principles of legality provide us with the requirements of the form that private law doctrines should take, but does not tell us anything about its substance. This would roughly track the positivist sensibilities that the rule of law is about the means rather than the ends of law. Indeed, Waldron offers this view in his Hamlyn lectures on property and the rule of law.[50] Another reason one might take this view is that the point of the basic private rights involved in core private law areas like property and contract is that they are exercised in furtherance of one's own self-interest rather than any kind of public interest; the purchase of the principles of legality lies in the more procedural aspects of effectively securing these rights. Fuller himself seemed to suggest that what he called the internal morality of law had limited application in relation to private activity. For example, he writes:

> private economic activity takes place within a restraining framework set by the law and morality of property and contract. At the same time, this activity cannot and should not be conducted in accordance with anything resembling the internal morality of law. It knows but one general principle, that of obtaining a maximum return from limited resources. This remains true even when the restraints surrounding economic calculation are expanded to include, let us say, the obligation to pay a minimum wage, to provide some form of job security, and to submit discharges to arbitration. Obligations like these serve simply to shrink the framework within which economic calculation takes place; they do not change the essential nature of that calculation.[51]

Thus, an individual engaged in contract negotiation, through which she creates new legal obligations, is not in the same position as Fuller's figure of the lawmaker Rex.

All of this might be true, but it is also misleading in a number of important respects. For one, it supposes a strong separation between formal and institutional aspects of the law on the one hand, and substantive norms on the other. Weinrib (working within the

---

[49] Robin L. West, *Re-Imagining Justice: Progressive Interpretations of Formal Equality, Rights, and the Rule of Law*, at 37 (2003).

[50] Jeremy Waldron, *The Rule of Law and the Measure of Property*, at 42–43 (2012).

[51] Fuller, *supra* note 16, at 171.

natural law tradition) offers an elegant argument to show why this separation does not hold. Weinrib argues that any system of private law has two sets of norms—the norms that govern the legal relations as between the parties, and the norms associated with the institutional aspects of adjudication and enforcement.[52] As Weinrib argues,

> Any sophisticated system of private law brings these two aspects together. Yet, in the remarkable proliferation of theoretical scholarship about private law over the last several decades, little has been said of the connection between them.[53]

According to Weinrib, corrective justice and Kantian agency characterize the "bilateral" relations of the former, and "public right" characterizes the "omnilateral" relations involved in the latter, or the relationships among members of the state where everyone is linked to everyone else.[54] Within this framework, public right usually adds the rule of law dimensions of publicness and systematicity to the private law but does not change the nature of the underlying rights. However, at times the demands of either publicness or systematicity can operate to modify those substantive norms, and Weinrib provides numerous examples including new ways to understand a variety of tort and contract defenses and remedies.[55]

Weinrib's approach shows us that a focus on the demands of a *system* of private law brings with it considerations of the rule of law, and that these can shape the substance of the norms that then regulate bilateral relationships. However, one need not adopt Weinrib's formalism or Kantian commitments to make use of this insight, for there are other approaches that are broadly congruent on this general point. For example, working within the very different tradition of law and economics, Smith has argued that we should understand property norms in terms of their general architecture—the system of property—rather than simply in terms of how they operate in any particular dispute.[56] The structure of this architecture, according to Smith, can be explained through a focus on information costs, and the information costs approach tracks many traditional rule-of-law concerns like publicity and predictability. As he explains "property itself implements the rule of law, which reduces the information costs of coordinating the actions of large and indefinite sets of persons with respect to things."[57] A focus on the architecture of property understood as a system, where that system conforms to rule-of-law demands, shows us that the property norms that regulate interpersonal conduct can in substance be shaped by what otherwise look like formal, procedural, and institutional concerns.

Much of private law in the common law tradition is judge-made. I have argued in previous work that common law reasoning regularly adopts the principles of legality as concerns in a manner that shapes substantive doctrine.[58] A focus on the common law

---

[52] Weinrib, *supra* note 11, at 192.   [53] *Id.*

[54] *Id.* at 196.   [55] *Id.* at 202ff.

[56] Henry E. Smith, *Mind the Gap: The Indirect Relation between Ends and Means in American Property Law*, 94 CORNELL L. REV. 959, 973–974 (2009).

[57] Henry E. Smith, "Property, Equity, and the Rule of Law," in *Private Law and the Rule of Law* 224 (Lisa M. Austin & Dennis Klimchuk eds., 2014).

[58] Lisa M. Austin, *Property and the Rule of Law*, 20 LEGAL THEORY 79, 79 (2014).

can help rule of law debates overcome an overly simplistic reliance upon a rules-based account of law and in this way can address the concerns of rule of law skeptics as previously discussed. For example, Postema argues that law should not be conceived of in terms of norms addressed to individuals as it instead guides "by giving shape to, and taking its shape from, the network of informal social practices" individuals who are situated within.[59] For this reason, forms of legal reasoning "open" to social context are not rule-of-law deficient.[60] But some areas of private law concern the conferral and use of legal powers such as contract or transfer of property. Legal powers specify what kinds of actions need to be taken in order to secure specific legal consequences, and these consequences change the normative position of specific individuals. In these cases the law does need to address individuals, and here we do find common law judges elucidating the doctrine with strong concerns to preserve clarity, stability, and nonretroactivity in ways that are different from more "open-textured" areas of the private law, like tort.[61]

One way in which Fuller's comments regarding private activity are actually wrong instead of misleading is that they ignore areas of private law where individuals have what Fox-Decent calls "other-regarding powers."[62] A central example of this is a legal trust, where a trustee's powers as owner are not self-regarding but other-regarding in relation to the trust's beneficiaries. Fox-Decent argues that in such contexts equity imposes "public law" duties similar to those in administrative law that govern the exercise of discretionary power.[63] Although Fox-Decent does not put it in these terms, these "public" duties can be understood in familiar rule-of-law terms of constraining the abuse of power, and it is unsurprising that these considerations appear across the private-public spectrum.

Indeed, the law of equity more generally has become a very fruitful site of rule-of-law theorizing. Some equitable doctrines provide courts with discretion to not enforce various private law entitlements, and this broad discretion would seem to undercut claims regarding rule-of-law compliance. But Smith argues that these equitable doctrines solve the problem of opportunism and therefore, from the perspective of the system of property as a whole, uphold the rule of law.[64] Similarly, Klimchuk argues that equity upholds the rule of law when it "prevents someone from being a stickler in a bad way, by exploiting the generality of a legal rule."[65]

Private law entitlements can give rise to domination concerns in other ways than those tracked by equity. For example, many of the rights associated with private law are ones that can be exercised in a self-regarding way that is arbitrary in the sense of being

[59] Gerald J. Postema, "Conformity, Custom, and Congruence: Rethinking the Efficacy of Law," in *The Legacy of H.L.A. Hart: Legal, Political and Moral Philosophy* 53 (Matthew H. Kramer et al. ed., 2008).

[60] See also Hanoch Dagan, "Private Law Pluralism and the Rule of Law," in *Private Law and the Rule of Law* 158 (Lisa M. Austin & Dennis Klimchuk eds., 2014).

[61] Austin, *supra* note 58, at 88ff. For a discussion of the relationship between the guidance function of the rule of law and nonarbitrariness in the context of property law, see Austin, *supra* note 46.

[62] Evan Fox-Decent, "The Constitution of Equity," in *Philosophical Foundations of the Law of Equity* (Dennis Klimchuk et al. eds., 2020).

[63] *Id.*   [64] Smith, *supra* note 57.

[65] Dennis Klimchuk, "Equity and the Rule of Law," in *Private Law and the Rule of Law* 257 (Lisa M. Austin & Dennis Klimchuk eds., 2014).

unanswerable to another. If I am the owner of Blackacre, then I can exclude anyone for any reason or for no reason at all, and this decision is not subject to review. We might even defend this on rule-of-law grounds for this individual discretion in relation to the use of things that are "mine" is part of the liberty that protects individuals from both social and political power. However, this general rule-of-law defense of ownership starts to run aground when social and economic conditions lead to significant inequalities in relation to ownership. Should a shopping mall owner be able to exclude a tenant's employee who engaged in lawful picketing? Should a grocery store be able to enforce a restrictive covenant prohibiting another grocery store from opening on a sold lot if this creates an inner city food desert? Can a farmer exclude individuals bringing medical and legal information to migrant workers who live on the farmer's property? In all these cases the exercise of legal rights in conditions of social and economic inequality can place the rights holder in a position of power and domination over vulnerable others.

Courts have come up with various answers to these scenarios, and often the debate is thought to be between a narrow, formalistic account of ownership and a broad examination of public policy. From a rule-of-law perspective, these are better understood as cases where it is the law itself and the legal relations it sets up that directly facilitate the exercise of private power over others—a rule of law concern that is more basic than categories of what is "private" versus what is "public." There remain difficult institutional questions of whether the courts rather than the legislature should make the changes needed to address these concerns. As many have pointed out, there are strong reasons why the legislature is sometimes best placed institutionally to effect legal change.[66] The rule of law does not resolve this debate but does show that the terms of the debate in these contexts are not only about private versus public norms.

IV. New Challenges: The Global Data Economy

Entick v. Carrington expressed a particular view regarding power, the private law, and the rule of law. As the previous section outlined, there is still a rich tradition of defending private law norms as revealing "the fundamental point of the rule of law."[67] However, as argued in the previous section, the social and economic conditions within which such rights come to be protected and exercised can change dramatically, and those same rights can come to be tools of private domination rather than a bulwark against such domination. This raises rule-of-law tensions that can show up in particular juridical contexts, like the trespass cases previously discussed. The basic components of the

---

[66] Lon L. Fuller, "The Forms and Limits of Adjudication," in *The Principles of Social Order: Selected Essays of Lon L. Fuller* 101 (Kenneth I. Winston ed., 2001); Thomas W. Merrill & Henry E. Smith, *Optimal Standardization in the Law of Property: The* Numerus Clausus *Principle*, 110 YALE L.J. 1, 59 (2000).

[67] T.R.S. Allan, "The Rule of Law as the Rule of Private Law," in *Private Law and the Rule of Law* 67, 68 (Lisa M. Austin & Dennis Klimchuk eds., 2014).

social-welfare state that came into being in the mid-twentieth century addressed some of those social conditions by seeking a role for the state in providing the positive basis for equal opportunities rather than merely safeguarding a more abstract ideal of freedom as independence. This gave rise to many questions of whether the administrative state was compatible with the rule of law, but this debate often presupposes that the rule of law was coextensive with its previous private-law and court-centric versions. An alternative perspective is that the administrative state's response to non-state power is itself an expression of rule of law values regarding the need for law to constrain private power. And instead of being seen as a rule of law-free zone, the body of administrative law emerged to make the administrative state consistent with the principles of legality while enabling its development. The question of power in the twenty-first century follows different contours and will require different responses. As I outline in this section, the relationship between private law and the rule of law will be central to these responses.

State power in the twenty-first century is bound up with information. Jack Balkin argues that the information state is "a state that tries to identify and solve problems of governance through the collection, collation, analysis, and production of information."[68] Within this broad category, there are special cases such as the "National Surveillance State" in which "the government uses surveillance, data collection, collation, and analysis to identify problems, to head off potential threats, to govern populations, and to deliver valuable social services."[69] The problem with this definition of the information state, both in its broad iteration and its special case, is that it does not really mark out what is distinctive about the information state. Information practices are a way of making individuals, and aspects of the social world, legible. As James Scott so clearly outlined in *Seeing Like a State*, statecraft has *always* been tied to conditions of legibility: "Any substantial state intervention in society to vaccinate a population, produce goods, mobilize labor, tax people and their property, conduct literacy campaigns, conscript soldiers, enforce sanitation standards, catch criminals, start universal schooling—requires the invention of units that are visible."[70] For example, a system of property registration is not simply a "map" of existing land systems but the imposition of a kind of social order that makes it possible to effectively subject individuals to recording and taxation. Legibility is a precondition of governance, one that both influences the forms that governance can take and is, in turn, influenced by that governance.

If state power has always been partially wielded through information, this power has also been constrained. Scott frames these constraints in terms of three factors that are decisive in resisting "authoritarian" versions of what he calls "high modernist planning" and that echo a number of liberal articulations of the rule of law: (1) a private sphere where the state cannot interfere; (2) a strong private sector, where the economy is too complex to be managed; and (3) democracy, because in such settings "high modernist schemes [...] must accommodate themselves sufficiently to local opinion in order to

---

[68] Jack M. Balkin, *Essay: The Constitution in the National Surveillance State*, 93 MINN. L. REV. 1, 3 (2008).
[69] *Id.* at 3.
[70] James C. Scott, *Seeing Like a State: How Certain Schemes to Improve the Human Condition Have Failed* 183 (1998).

avoid being undone at the polls."[71] These are all areas where the control of the state can be resisted, and a kind of respect for the lived experience and values of those subject to state power is protected. All of these constraints are enabled through law, and the first two echo the *Entick v. Carrington* view regarding private law and state power. However, there are good reasons for us to rethink the relationship between private law and the rule of law in the twenty-first century.

In Scott's world it is the state that seeks ways to impose a representation on diverse and complex social phenomena in order to govern. The information state upends this. What the information state does is look at a map that has largely been constructed by mediating technologies provided by the private sector. This is important, for Scott showed that state-mapping exercises are not just about trying to "see" what is already there but are acts of world-making.[72] State-mapping involves abstracting from social reality, and abstraction involves both distorting local knowledge and shaping the world into an "administrative grid" suitable for the particular governance objective. If information intermediaries are the primary mappers, then they are the ones with the primary power of remaking the world. Unlike the administrative goals of the state, the imperatives of intermediaries are largely commercial. Facebook does not try to create a platform for social interaction that maps existing modes of interaction; it seeks to create new possibilities for that interaction, and those possibilities are deeply tied to its commercial interests.[73] But if the private sector is the primary mapper, then in many ways the role of the private sector is to enable, rather than to constrain, state power. We see this in the public/private nexus of state surveillance, where the state gets access to data with fewer constraints than if it collected the data itself.[74] It is also evident in recent controversies regarding election interference based upon data collection, profiling, and political-ad targeting infrastructure all provided through the private sector with few safeguards against abuse.[75]

Major actors within the global private sector also exercise their own kind of power over individuals through their data practices. The inability of private law models to safeguard individual interests—such as through terms of service individuals consent to—has led to a push to think about technology companies as exercising governance functions and to apply public law norms to them.[76] However, if we take up the lessons

---

[71] *Id.* at 102.   [72] *Id.* at 36.

[73] See Shoshana Zuboff, *The Age of Surveillance Capitalism: The Fight for a Human Future at the New Frontier of Power* (2019).

[74] Balkin, *supra* note 68; Lisa M. Austin, *Technological Tattletales and Constitutional Black Holes: Communications Intermediaries and Constitutional Constraints*, 17 Theoretical Inquiries in Law 451 (2016).

[75] Matthew Rosenberg et al., *How Trump Consultants Exploited the Facebook Data of Millions*, N.Y. Times, Mar. 17, 2018, https://www.nytimes.com/2018/03/17/us/politics/cambridge-analytica-trump-campaign.html.

[76] See, e.g., Kate Klonick, *The New Governors: The People, Rules, and Processes Governing Online Speech*, 131 Harv. L. Rev. 1598 (2018). For a broader discussion of global governance models that incorporate private bodies, see Benedict Kingsbury et al., *The Emergence of Global Administrative Law*, 68 Law & Contemp. Probs. 15 (2005).

from the rule-of-law scholarship in relation to the private law, we have another alternative, which is to show that the private sector is *already* subject to rule of law norms and rule of law critiques.

One of the key issues regarding information intermediaries is the question of transparency. Currently this is part of both academic and policy discussions in relation to privacy, as "openness" is one of the fair information practice principles that underpin contemporary data protection legislation. It is also an important aspect of the current debates regarding algorithmic fairness, in which transparency is most often related to ideas of explainability and the sense in which individuals should be able to understand the basis for an automated decision that affects them. But the question of transparency is more fundamental than this, for it goes to the heart of whether the global private sector is one that will be governed by law at all. The immense complexity at the core of new digital technologies, and often their disconnection from corresponding social and physical analogs, makes their workings and effects opaque, even to those responsible for their design and operation. In other words, the private-sector infrastructure that makes our social world legible in new ways that create new power dynamics is itself opaque. And if it is opaque, then all the law on the books will simply remain on the books and private-sector data practices will be practically immune from the law.[77] This broader, systematic rule of law perspective on transparency in the global private sector is sorely needed.

V. Conclusions

In this chapter I have outlined the view that a polity governed by the rule of law is one where, as Postema stated, "power is systematically rendered non-arbitrary."[78] The private law has historically played an important role in achieving this vision, for it provides a sphere of protection against arbitrary state interference, and a sphere of protection against arbitrary non-state power. The rule of law's core features, its requirements of generality, publicity, nonretroactivity, clarity, noncontradiction, possibility of compliance, stability, and congruence between official action and declared rule, constitute law as an instrument of public authority. These principles of legality provide us with a set of critical tools for understanding private law doctrines, for these principles help to shape the substance of the private law in many different ways. They also provide us with a set of tools for the critique of existing laws and for identifying the ways in which they are deficient from a rule-of-law perspective, particularly in cases where the law itself becomes an instrument of private domination rather than a bulwark against it.

---

[77] "Practical immunity" is a term Barber, *supra* note 25, at 485, uses but in the context where inequality in wealth prevents the weak from holding the powerful to account through the courts.

[78] Postema, *supra* note 37, at 19.

At the end of his book about the nineteenth century *Black Act*, which prosecuted those who hunted deer in the royal forests, Marxist legal historian E.P. Thompson controversially defended the rule of law in the following terms:

> I am not starry-eyed about this at all. This has not been a star-struck book. I am insisting only upon the obvious point, [...], that there is a difference between arbitrary power and the rule of law. We ought to expose the shams and inequities which may be concealed beneath this law. But the rule of law itself, the imposing of effective inhibitions upon power and the defence of the citizen from power's all-intrusive claims, seems to me to be an unqualified human good. To deny or belittle this good is, in this dangerous century when the resources and pretension of power continue to enlarge, a desperate error of intellectual abstraction.[79]

Our century requires us to critically engage with the question of arbitrary power in the global private sector. The data economy is one where the information practices of large technology companies work to both augment state power over individuals and limit the state's ability to protect individuals. Its increasing opacity creates the conditions for a digital infrastructure where law does not rule. We need to shift the dialogue away from the very concerns raised by specific areas of private law, like privacy or intellectual property, and to see that there is something much more fundamental at stake.

Acknowledgments

I would like to thank the participants of the Landscape of Private Law conference, Harvard 2019, for their helpful comments on an earlier version of this chapter.

---

[79] E.P. Thompson, *Whigs and Hunters: The Origin of the Black Act* 266 (1975).

CHAPTER 32

....

DEFENSES

....

ROBERT STEVENS

CONSIDERABLE theoretical ink has been spilt grappling with the normative justification(s) for the various claims that arise in private law. This focus on the rights and powers in private law is understandable. After all, without a claim there is nothing much further to discuss. What has gone underexamined are the justifications for the various defenses that exist—the ways of *resisting* otherwise good claims.[1] Defenses pose a challenge to any monist theory of private law. If private law, or a part of it, is all about efficiency or independence or utility or any other single thing, why not deal with all the elements of what justifies the plaintiff's claim as an element of the cause of action? Why do we need defenses at all? Either the claim is justified or it is not. On the monist view of private law—that it is only concerned with One Big Thing—what is the need or role for any separate "defenses" that concern countervailing considerations?

I. WHAT IS A DEFENSE?

....

Practitioners are familiar with defenses from their pleadings. Not everything that is relied upon by a defendant in answer to a claim is a defense properly so called. A plaintiff in her Complaint[2] may assert:

1. The defendant did on May 1, 2018, enter an oral agreement to deliver 1,000 tons of durum wheat to the plaintiff's premises on September 1, 2018, for $100,000.

---

[1] Important recent work includes James Goudkamp, *Tort Law Defences* (2013); *Defences in Tort* (Andrew Dyson, James Goudkamp, & Frederick Wilmot-Smith eds., 2015); *Defences in Unjust Enrichment* (Andrew Dyson, James Goudkamp, & Frederick Wilmot-Smith eds., 2016); *Defences in Contract* (Andrew Dyson, James Goudkamp, & Frederick Wilmot-Smith eds., 2017); *Defences in Equity* (Paul S. Davies, Simon Douglas, & James Goudkamp eds., 2018).

[2] A "Particulars of Claim" in English law. The American terminology seems peculiar. The document is not just a moan or grumble.

The defendant may assert in his Answer:[3]

1. Paragraph 1 is denied.

This is not a defense, but merely a denial of a fact necessary for the making out of the claim.[4]

Similarly, there are many procedural rules by which a defendant may seek to resist a claim (such as that the plaintiff must provide security for costs before the claim is allowed to proceed) that are not defenses as they are not formally pleaded. By contrast, the Complaint may continue:

2. The plaintiff paid the defendant the sum of $100,000 on May 2, 2018.
3. In breach of the agreement, the defendant failed to deliver such wheat on September 1.

And the defendant may assert:

2. On August 1, 2018, the plaintiff orally stated to the defendant, "I know you're having problems on your side, don't worry about getting the wheat to us before December."

This is a defense, at least to any claim for breach for late delivery on September 1. The defendant is asserting that the plaintiff waived her contractual right to delivery on that date. He has asserted a new fact that is not merely a denial, that provides a good reason why the claim should fail. Any fact[5] that the defendant pleads, that can in whole or in part resist the plaintiff's action, that does not constitute a mere denial of an element of the claim, and that raises a new reason why the claim should fail, is a defense.

We can consider a further complexity where the plaintiff replies by alleging new facts that operate to rebut a defense. The plaintiff might reply:

1. On August 15, 2018, the plaintiff sent an email to the defendant stating, "Sorry, we have a large order and so need to have the wheat on September 1 as previously agreed."

The proof of this allegation would rebut the defense, as a waiver (unlike a contractual variation) may always be withdrawn. We could continue the sequence with counter-replies (if the waiver has been detrimentally relied upon by the defendant, the plaintiff may be estopped from reasserting his contractual rights), counter-counter-replies and so on.[6]

---

[3] A "Defence" in English law. The American terminology seems superior as not everything in an Answer is a defense properly so-called.

[4] On the classification of defenses in the criminal law, and the difference between denials and defenses, see Paul Robinson, *Criminal Law Defenses: A Systematic Analysis*, 82 COL. L. REV. 199 (1982).

[5] We plead facts, not law.

[6] In England, the traditional labels are rejoinder, sur-rejoinder, and replication for the sequence.

Illegality is not a defense. If a criminal gang wish to have a dispute over whether one of its members did or did not carry out a contracted-for "hit," a court will not hear the claim, even if both the plaintiff and defendant wish it to do so. Just as a plaintiff's claim may be ruled out for illegality, so may a defendant's defense. If a defendant argues, in response to a claim for the restitution of a mistaken payment, that he has "changed his position" because he spent the sum received on bribing officials to get him an honor, the defense should fail. Illegality is a rule to ensure the coherence of the legal system. Its operation will, and will only, result in injustice as between the parties inter se, so that some judges have proven reluctant to enforce the rule.

II. Pleading and Proof

The general rule in private law is *ei incumbit probation qui dicit*: he who asserts must prove. In practice, the most important effect of characterizing an issue as being a defense is that it will determine who has to prove what as a matter of evidence.

This rule is not logically necessary, however. In the criminal law, when the defendant raises self-defense, it is for the prosecution to adduce sufficient evidence to show beyond reasonable doubt that no such defense applies. There is no necessary reason why the same approach could not apply in private law, with the defendant required to plead defenses but the plaintiff required to disprove their existence. Indeed, in English law this is the approach in the area of limitation of action: it is for the defendant to plead the relevant time-bar but for the plaintiff to show that his claim is still within the relevant period.[7] This is important for a theory of private law because it shows that what constitutes a defense is not determined by practical considerations of which of the litigants is best placed to prove what. Rather, what the defendant pleads are facts showing countervailing *reasons* why a claim should fail.

The formal pleading rules should (and do) track the different *kinds of reason* that make out a claim or a defense. The defendant is not asserting that the plaintiff owes him any obligation, but rather why, exceptionally, he should not be ordered by the court to comply with an obligation. This involves a different range of reasons from the (austere) set that can legitimately justify enforceable legal obligations.

III. Justification and Excuse

In law, whether someone owes another a duty is a conclusion. It is an all-things-considered question, which gives rise to a binary answer: you owe the duty or you do not. This is different from the position that often exists in morality, where there may be

---

[7] Lloyd's Bank plc v. Crosse & Crosse [2001] EWCA Civ 366, [2001] Lloyd's Rep. P.N. 452.

many reasons for or against an action, and where the choice to behave in one way may still be contrary to many reasons even if, overall, it is the right thing to do. In morality, there may be no right conclusion one way or the other in the "weighing up" of reasons on each side of the balance sheet. One of the central points of law is to provide us with the "all things considered" answer on how to act. So, if I punch you on the nose in order to prevent you from killing me with an axe, my action is, in law, justified. All things considered, I committed no crime or tort. I did, however, still act against the good moral reasons for not punching each other on the nose. That these reasons may, in morality, be "outweighed"[8] by other reasons does not wipe them out or destroy them, so that I may have reason to regret punching my "victim" on the nose. In law, unlike morality, if an action is covered by an absolute privilege, no trace of the wrong exists.

In the criminal law it is common, and correct, to distinguish between defenses which justify what would otherwise constitute a crime and excuses that relieve the defendant from punishment, but which do not prevent him from committing a crime. To those who think that the criminal law answers the question "who gets punished?" or think that private law concerns "is civil recourse available?," the distinction may appear obscure, but it is fundamental. An illustration of the practical significance of the difference (in both the criminal and civil law), is where the defendant procures another to commit conduct for which the person acting has the defense of an excuse which the defendant lacks. If I procure a police officer to arrest you by providing him with reasonable grounds for thinking that you have committed an offence, when you have not, he will be excused from both a sanction and liability. But if I know the allegations to be false, I will commit, through his actions, both a tort[9] and a crime. If the grounds for the arrest are in fact true, his actions are justified, and so no tort is committed by either of us. If I did not believe the grounds to be true, when they were, I may commit a criminal attempt, but no tort.

In private law, this distinction between justifications and excuses is, if anything, more important than it is in the criminal law (as the previous example illustrates). Here it reflects the distinction between an *obligation* and a *liability*. Some defenses *justify* the defendant's action, providing a *privilege* (i.e., the defendant is exceptionally not under a duty, or synonymously the plaintiff exceptionally has no right). Examples of justifications include consent, statutory authority, self-defense where the defendant is acting reasonably in response to a real threat, and truth in the law of defamation. A privilege is the exceptional case where the defendant has no duty, of which a liberty is the general case.

Other defenses provide the defendant with an *immunity* (the defendant is exceptionally not liable to be sued, or synonymously the plaintiff exceptionally has no power to sue). Examples of excuses are the expiry of limitation periods, contractual exclusions or

---

[8] The metaphor of "weighing" may be unhelpful. There is no common metric by which to weigh the various reasons in play, as they are all too often incommensurable (unless one believes in the barbarity of reducing everything to the util or the dollar.) A central point of law is to provide us with answers where, as a matter of morality, no right one is possible.

[9] Barker v. Braham (1772) 2 Black W. 866, 96 E.R. 510.

limitations of liability, comparative fault now in England and in most U.S. states, self-defense where the defendant is mistaken as to whether there is a real threat,[10] and immunities that are given to various entities such as trade unions and the state for public policy reasons. Within contract law, formality requirements excuse a contract from being performed, but rarely prevent valid but unenforceable legal obligations from arising at all. An immunity is the exceptional case where the defendant is subject to no liability.

An excuse may be absolute or qualified. If I am starving on a mountainside in a snowstorm, I may have a privilege to break into your log cabin and eat the food stores you have inside in order to save my life. However, this privilege is qualified: in order to stay within the privilege, just as I must not eat more than I need, I must pay for any damage and for the food I have eaten.[11] If I do so, no trace of a wrong is left behind. The law may compel me to pay, not because I am a wrongdoer but in order to ensure that I am not.

More common than absolute excuses are situations where there is no doubt that there is a legal obligation, but the courts refuse injunctive orders that perfectly replicate what the law says ought to be done and instead confine the plaintiff to damages. Examples of these partial excuses travel under homely maxims, for example, "he who comes to equity must come with clean hands" or "he who seeks equity must do equity." The granting of a court order creates a new obligation on the defendant to comply with it, subject to the heavy enforcement mechanism of contempt of court, so that a court may have good reasons not to order direct compliance with the underlying legal obligation.

This range of reasons for denying a court order is greater than those that apply to justificatory defenses. A court may refuse specific performance of a contract for reasons of harshness on the defendant[12] or because the defendant made a unilateral mistake in entering into the deal.[13] Such factors would not be sufficient to allow the defendant to argue that no enforceable contract exists at all, but are sufficient to allow the court to decline a specific remedy. In all cases, where the defendant invokes a reason why a specific remedy should be refused, and the plaintiff is confined to damages, he invokes a partial excuse, a limited defense.

Goldberg (and others) have argued that the law of torts never recognizes excuses.[14] This accords with the view that he and Zipursky have expressed that a core defining feature of the law of torts, and of private law more generally, is civil recourse. But the difference here is merely a semantic one of usage: he wishes to confine the word "excuse" to defenses that excuse *the wrong itself* as opposed to those that excuse the *sanction or court ordered response*.

A more conservative claim is that the excuses recognized by the law of torts are different from those recognized by the criminal law. Excusatory reasons in the criminal law

[10] Unlike in the criminal law, honest but unreasonable mistakes do not suffice: Ashley v. Chief Constable of Sussex Police [2008] UKHL 25, [2008] 1 A.C. 962.
[11] Vincent v. Lake Erie Transportation Co., 124 N.W. 221 (Minn. 1910).
[12] Patel v. Ali [1984] Ch. 283.   [13] Malins v. Freeman (1837) 2 Keen 25.
[14] John C.P. Goldberg, *Inexcusable Wrongs*, 103 CAL. L. REV. 467 (2015). See also Joseph Raz, *Responsibility and the Negligence Standard*, 30 O.J.L.S. 1, 10 (2010); John Gardner, *Offences and Defences: Essays in the Philosophy of Criminal Law* 92 (2007).

often concern the subjective state of mind of the defendant (she was mistaken, subject to duress, or acted out of necessity). Such reasons may operate in the criminal law, but not so as to excuse the payment of *damages* in the law of torts. (They may suffice to relieve from liability to a specific remedy.)[15] If I think you are attacking me, when you are not, this may excuse my punching you in the nose in the criminal law but not in the law of torts. Mistakes made by the defendant should not relieve us from liability for damages in the law of torts, although they do excuse any sanction in the criminal law.

This more limited claim, that some kinds of excusatory reasons do not suffice to relieve from liability to pay damages (but may relieve from criminal sanction), is true. If I walk on your land honestly and reasonably believing it to be mine, I commit a tort. If I take your umbrella reasonably mistaking it for my own, I commit conversion. On this view, the defendant who honestly and reasonably acts in self-defense should still be liable in private law if it turns out that he was mistaken as to whether there was in fact a threat. The reason for the divergence is, I suggest, that the law of torts never has any mens rea element of wrongfulness. The rights and duties that we have one against another are objectively determined; want of virtue or subjective moral blameworthiness is neither here nor there.[16] As whether the defendant is (subjectively) wanting in virtue is irrelevant, in a way that is untrue in the criminal law, excuses that in the criminal law show that the defendant was lacking in moral blameworthiness (e.g., mistake, duress, necessity) also have no role.

In addition to the liability of accessories, three further reasons may be given for the practical significance of the distinction between justification and excuse in private law.

First, as an unenforceable legal obligation is not a nullity, its performance may provide a good justifying reason against a plaintiff's recovery of it.[17]

Secondly, if we ignored the distinction between liability and obligation, contractual exclusions of liability, which constitute a defense, would be incoherent. If legal obligations were synonymous with legal liabilities, a contract which purported to undertake obligations to another, while excluding legal liability for noncompliance, would make no sense. On that view a contracting party could not in the same breath say, "I undertake to deliver the goods to you on Friday, no liability for late delivery is accepted." Just as the parties may make their agreement wholly unenforceable ("Subject to Contract"), there is nothing mysterious about their agreeing to make it partially unenforceable, civil recourse not being a defining feature of what it is to undertake a contractual obligation. The important distinction between terms that define the parties' *obligations*, and those that exclude or limit their *liability* for breach, is also reflected in legislation that controls the latter but not the former.[18]

Thirdly, the availability of different remedies reveals the difference. This is nicely illustrated by the decision of the English Court of Appeal in *AB v. CD*.[19] The defendants were

---

[15] A judge at dockside in *Ploof v. Putnam*, 81 Vt. 471, 71 A. 188 (1908), would not have ordered an injunction to stop the mooring of the boat.

[16] E.g., *Vaughan v. Menlove* (1837) 132 E.R. 490.

[17] *Moses v. Macferlan* (1760) 2 Burr. 1005, 97 E.R. 676 (Lord Mansfield).

[18] Misrepresentation Act 1967 (UK), s 3.   [19] [2014] EWCA Civ 229, [2015] 1 W.L.R. 771.

the owners of intellectual property rights for an internet-based platform for the provision of goods and services relating to the mining business. They granted the plaintiffs a license to market this "eMarketplace" in the Middle East. The defendants purported to terminate the contract, and the plaintiffs sought an interim injunction to restrain them from doing so. At first instance, Stuart-Smith J refused to grant an injunction because the plaintiffs had an adequate remedy in damages. The Court of Appeal allowed the appeal. They did so on the basis that the license agreement excluded *liability* for loss of profits. As a result of this clause, the defendants were, to that extent, immune from a suit to enforce their obligation to pay damages reflecting the actual harm their breach caused. As Underhill LJ stated:[20]

> The primary commercial expectation must be that the parties will perform their obligations. The expectations created (indeed given contractual force) by an exclusion or limitation clause are expectations about what damages will be recoverable in the event of breach; but that is not the same thing.

The effect of the clause was that a court's order of damages ceased to be an adequate remedy, as no longer reflecting the legal obligation to pay compensation. As a result, the court ordered an injunction that it would, absent the exclusion or limitation, have refused.

IV. FORM OF REASONS

Weinrib identifies "the basic feature of private law [as being]: a particular plaintiff sues a particular defendant."[21] This cannot be correct. Civil recourse—the ability to sue in a court—is not confined to private law. Public duties are commonly enforced through civil legal process brought by individuals, such as judicial review. Further, the posited rights of private law would exist regardless of the ability to enforce them (as do the various rights that exist in the public international legal order, but where legal redress is all too often unavailable).

Weinrib's more important, and correct, claim is that private law duties, unlike duties of morality or public duties, are necessarily bilateral in form, and that as a result they require bilateral reasons to justify them. If we thought the reasons why we hold a negligent driver liable to a pedestrian he runs over were the twin concerns of deterring negligent conduct and compensating victims, why not deal with this through a clearing system, where negligent drivers paid a fine into the fund, with a claim upon it by unlucky injured people? Such a system would be better than the one we now have as we could tailor the fine to the degree of deterrence we sought to achieve (unconstrained by the happenstance of whether the driver had hit anyone) and we could target payments out at

[20] *Id.*, [28].   [21] Ernest Weinrib, *The Idea of Private Law* 63 (rev. ed. 2012).

those most in need and not at the lucky few who happened to be able to identify a solvent or insured tortfeasor. By contrast, if we think that what justifies a claim is the wrong done by the defendant and suffered by the plaintiff, private law's bilateral form is understandable.

Similarly, if we thought the law ought to be concerned to give effect to the actual intentions of promisors, why not enforce wholly unilateral uncommunicated vows? By contrast, if we think that what justifies a contract is an agreement for which each is responsible—an offer by the one party, accepted by the other, objectively created by both of them—what either on his own side of the line actually intended is irrelevant to the creation of the contractual rights between them.

Privileges, or defenses which operate as justifications, operate so as to show that there is no right (or no wrong) as between the parties, there is no injustice that requires the law's intervention. Consequently they must, where legitimate, share the bilateral feature of the kinds of reasons that can justify rights in private law. For example, if the plaintiff attacked the defendant with a knife, the defendant's action in punching him to prevent his own death is (overall) nonwrongful. Such self-defense creates a privilege because it concerns what is fair as between the two parties, and does not need to rely upon reasons external to their relationship.

Immunities, or defenses which operate as excuses, operate so as to show that although the plaintiff has a right against the defendant or has suffered a wrong committed by him, there are exceptional reasons why he should not be liable to be sued. Because the plaintiff is seeking to bring to bear state power in his dispute with the defendant, concerns external to their relationship may be of relevance. The immunity of trade unions from suit for the commission of economic torts, for example, is based upon a public policy of allowing collective industrial action by workers in disputes with employers. The conditions that this immunity are subject to (for example, balloting of members) have been adjusted many times over the years. The immunity is not based upon what is fair as between the individual union and individual employer. Similarly, where the defendant argues that he should not be liable because of a consideration that applies to him but not also the plaintiff (for example, he made a mistake as to the plot of land he was buying), this may operate as an excuse, although not one necessarily based upon wider concerns of public policy.

As in the criminal law, the classification of justifications and excuses can be disputed, and whether the positive law is correct in classifying a defense as creating a privilege or immunity may be contested. In the modern law, courts have adopted arguments that there is "no duty of care" owed by accountants to potential investors in preparing a company's accounts on the basis that this would lead to liability of indeterminate scope and amount,[22] or that the police should not be liable for carelessly failing to catch criminals on the basis that this would lead them to be overly "defensive" in the carrying out of their duties.[23] Arguments of this kind are properly nothing to do with whether one party

[22] Caparo Industries plc. v. Dickman [1990] 2 A.C. 605 (HL).
[23] Hill v. Chief Constable of West Yorkshire [1989] A.C. 53 (HL).

owes a duty to another, but are in fact (unpersuasive) arguments for the recognition of an immunity (i.e., exceptionally no civil recourse) for a class of defendants.

V. General Defenses

Some defenses are claim-specific, so as not to warrant detailed consideration in a general overview. Under English law, truth or justification is a defense in claims for defamation, showing that the gist of the wrong is the damage to reputation, thereby setting back our ability to interact in the world, rather than the falsity of what was said. Some defenses are more general, such as res judicata, abuse of process, discharge from bankruptcy, statutes of limitation, foreign state immunity,[24] the immunities of the Crown in the United Kingdom[25] and the far more extensive immunities of the federal government in the United States, and the judicial process immunities of judges, jurors, witnesses, and prosecutors. It may be noted that each of these creates an immunity, not a privilege, and this reflects the fact that each is based upon some kind of public policy unrelated to the reason why the underlying right or wrong exists.

Limitation periods are the creation of the legislature. They have a policy justification: ensuring that we are all able to close the books on the past. They generally operate to create immunities from suit, not as justifications for past wrongs. There is no correct answer for how long individual limitation periods should be or when time should start to run, and these vary between states and between claims. Similar approaches are found across common law systems, however, and this may be contrasted with the criminal law where in a vivid example of American exceptionalism, limitation statutes that do not exist in other common law jurisdictions are applied to serious crimes.[26]

Although the bright lines of limitation statutes are accompanied by exceptions for mistake, fraud, and concealment, this policy-based approach may be contrasted with the equitable doctrine of laches, and its considerations of what is fair as between the parties (Is the plaintiff's delay unreasonable? Has the defendant been prejudiced?)

Some limitation statutes operate to extinguish rights, as with the extinction of title of the owner of converted goods[27] or the (nowadays very rare) loss of title to unregistered land against a trespasser.[28] These operate as exceptions to the first-in-time rule of title, ensuring that all of us can be certain in the title to things we have, and can pass on a good title to others. One person's title (at root based on either his own or another's possession) is eventually lost if unasserted against another who is in possession.

Consent is a defense to all wrongs, but not to the assertion of all rights. The label used seems to vary, but the idea remains the same. Torts are susceptible to the defense *volenti*

---

[24] E.g., State Immunity Act 1978 (UK), s.1(1).

[25] Restricted by the Crown Proceedings Act 1947 (UK), s.2(1).

[26] Daniel W. Shuman & Alexander McCall Smith, *Justice and the Prosecution of Old Crimes: Balancing Legal, Psychological and Moral Concerns* 62 (2000).

[27] Limitation Act 1980 (UK), s 3.   [28] *Id.*, ss.15–17.

non fit iniuria, breach of contract to waiver, and breach of trust may be resisted by pleading acquiescence or authorization by the beneficiaries. Consent does not operate to extinguish rights but holds the right in suspension until the moment it is withdrawn. So, if you consent to my kissing you, I commit no battery if I do so, but if you withdraw your consent, I commit the tort if I then persist. The same applies in contract law where a waiver may (subject to estoppel) be withdrawn, as in the example with which we began.

Consent is also a defense in "unjust enrichment." If, for example, a plaintiff voluntarily discharges another's obligation, being under no compulsion to do so and knowing full well that he is not the proper person to bear its cost, there is no injustice to him that requires correction.[29] Similarly, a person who pays another money for no good reason, and who knows that to be the case, should have no recourse to recovery, unless his consent is vitiated for some reason such as a mistake or duress.

Whether consent operates as a defense, or its nonexistence is something that the plaintiff must plead as an element of his claim, depends upon whether there is a prima facie injustice absent consent. If I punch you on the nose, that is prima facie wrongful without more, so that it would be for the defendant to assert that it was consented to. If I shake your hand, that is not ordinarily sufficient to be prima facie wrongful, but if the plaintiff pleads and proves that it was done without such consent, it would exceptionally be a battery.

Consent probably has two forms (although as a matter of authority this is hard to demonstrate). If the plaintiff subjectively consents to the act the defendant commits (the punch on the nose), it is probable that no wrong is committed. If the plaintiff is responsible for objectively manifesting consent (as where he enters a boxing ring wearing shorts and gloves), and the defendant believes the impression created and acts upon it (by hitting him), there is no wrong, even if the plaintiff's subjective state of mind does not accord with its outward appearance.

Countervailing contractual rights may operate as both justifications and excuses. In relation to property rights (to land, goods, and intellectual property) if a defendant has a contractual license to use, this will prevent the commission of a tort, even where the right holder attempts to withdraw his consent. Licensees are not trespassers. They do not, however, unlike a lessee, acquire property rights good against all others, but merely a privilege as against the right holder (although they may independently obtain *a* title to the land or goods through possession).

It may be doubted whether a contractual right can trump or override other rights so as to provide an irrevocable privilege. A celebrity contracts with a television company to stay in the "Big Brother House" for a season of its run; and he demands to leave after a week, but is kept inside, this would constitute false imprisonment regardless of the contractual undertaking. The scope of contract is greater where it operates as an excuse and not a justification. Agreed exclusions of liability for wrongdoing are generally effective. In the United Kingdom these agreements are subject to statutory controls that do not apply to other agreements.[30] In the United States some courts have adopted a policy of

---

[29]   Norton v. Haggett, 85 A.2d 571, 574 (Vt. 1952).
[30]   E.g., Unfair Contracts Terms Act 1977 (UK), s.2(1).

striking down such clauses in cases of gross negligence and intentional wrongdoing.[31] The reason for the suspicion of such clauses is that they involve a conflict between two general principles: (roughly) that agreements are to be kept and that the commission of a wrong gives rise to civil recourse for damages.

VI. Defenses in Contract

Contract lawyers, unlike torts lawyers, do not tend to think in terms of defenses, but they should. In order to bring a claim for damages for breach of contract, the plaintiff has to plead (and prove) a number of facts that demonstrate the existence of a series of necessary conditions: offer and acceptance, sufficiently certain terms, consideration, intent to create legal relations (in England), and a breach. The defendant may, however, be able to resist the claim by pleading other facts that demonstrate one of a number of alternative sufficient conditions for the defeasibility of what would otherwise be a good claim. Duress, misrepresentation, undue influence, insanity, intoxication, common mistake, waiver, frustration, contractual exclusion or limitation of liability, failure to comply with a requirement of form, or the expiry of a limitation period are all defenses.

Again, we may divide this list into justifications and excuses, those reasons why either there is no contract or no breach of it, and those going to its enforceability. Formality requirements, like limitation periods, traditionally (and correctly) went to enforceability and not validity. We have formality requirements to encourage parties to reflect on the seriousness of what they are doing, to evidence the terms of what has been done, and to show that they meant their agreement to be binding. As a way of encouraging others to employ the formality convention, we only enforce agreements that are in this form, even where we can independently show that these goals are met through other evidence.

The traditional categories the defense applied under the Statute of Frauds 1677 were contracts for the sale of land, contracts for the sale of goods above a certain amount, contracts that cannot be completed in less than one year, and contracts of guarantee. In England, the Statute of Frauds was largely repealed, save in the case of guarantees.[32] Formality requirements for the sale of land were maintained, and today in England problematically render the contract wholly invalid, and not merely unenforceable, when not complied with.[33] Whether this is to be taken seriously, so that fully executed but informal contracts for the sale of land can be unwound without more, remains unclear.

The existence of an agreement and its content are objective matters. They depend upon what the parties have done in the world, not upon what they subjectively intended. For the purpose of defenses, however, the parties' subjective states of mind is often relevant. An agreement may be set aside for a number of reasons related to defects in the subjective intentions of one or both parties. Where there has been a misrepresentation,

---

[31] Novak & Co. v. New York City Housing Authority, 480 N.Y.S.2d 403 (N.Y. App. Term. 1984).

[32] Law Reform (Enforcement of Contracts) Act 1954 (UK).

[33] Law of Property (Miscellaneous Provisions) Act 1989 (UK), s.2.

duress, or undue influence, the party whose consent was as a result defective has the power to avoid the contract. If one subscribes to the view that agreements take place in, or are at least dependent upon, our subjective intention to subject ourselves to obligations, then the true position in all of these cases would be that there is no promise at all. Any putative contract ought as a result to be void.

This latter view does not align with the positive law. A party subject to duress, or acting under undue influence, or to whom a misrepresentation has been made by the counterparty has the power to avoid the contract. It is not the case that no agreement has been made: there has been, regardless of any defects in the promisor's subjective consent. The reason why the contract can be set aside is a quite separate one from what a contract is. In each case the defect in intention is invoked in order to deny responsibility for the agreement created.

It may be objected that there are occasions when a contract is rendered void as a result of a vitiating error, such as mistake, and not just voidable. One example in England is the case of common fundamental mistake:

> A agrees to buy B's horse Dobbin, currently in his stables in East Oxford. Unbeknownst to either party, at the time of the agreement the stables had burnt to the ground and Dobbin was killed.

Under Section 6 of the Sale of Goods Act 1979 (U.K.),[34] a contract for the sale of specific goods where they have perished at the time of contracting without the knowledge of the seller is void. However, if we change the story, the oddity of concluding that no agreement was entered into because of the mistake becomes apparent. If the contract stipulated that title to Dobbin was to pass the following week upon delivery, and the fire had taken place after the contract but before delivery, the contract would have been frustrated. We could not, however, say that no contract had ever been entered into; clearly there had.

The better view is that there is an agreement in both cases, but that the meanings of promises, like words more generally, are not absolute. They run out.

In the law the limits of what has been promised is inevitably a matter of interpretation. Promises do not cover all unforeseeable eventualities, such as the nonexistence of the subject matter. Promises to buy and sell in such a situation are no less real, but they do not bind. It does not matter that the parties never considered this situation, nor does it matter that they never considered this situation's possibility.

That the contract in the common mistake case is not absolutely void may be shown by reflecting upon the fate of terms other than the promises to buy and sell. If the contract for the sale of Dobbin contains a jurisdiction or arbitration clause, the terms of the clause are binding. But they would not be if the contract were indeed a nullity. Rather, all that is no longer binding are the parties' primary obligations to buy and sell, and this is because the promises do not cover the situation where the subject matter of the

---

[34] But see *Restatement (Second) of Contracts* § 152(1), which provides that the agreement is voidable by a party prejudiced.

agreement does not exist. This is so regardless of whether its destruction takes place ten minutes before or ten minutes after the agreement is concluded.

Where the promise made has been obtained through the duress, undue influence, or misrepresentation of the counterparty, the promisor may, at his option, rely upon a countervailing reason of justice that enables him to have the contract wholly set aside. These are all ways of showing that, despite the objective impression of agreement he has created, he is not responsible for that impression because his subjective consent was vitiated, and the counterparty either knew that or was responsible for it. He can rely upon a bilateral consideration of justice that invalidates the duty that there would otherwise be.

That these are defenses is important, as it is all too easy to slip into thinking that, say, undue influence or innocent misrepresentation are freestanding causes of action which sound in damages. What constitutes a wrong and what constitutes a defense to that wrong are not and need not be the same because the reasons justifying them differ.

VII. Defenses to Torts

Many defenses in tort concern the conflict of rights or, more accurately, a conflict between the bilateral reasons why rights exist. If through no fault of mine my football is kicked into your garden, I may have a license to enter to retrieve it, so long as I pay for any damage I cause in doing so. The reason why I have a property right to my football, conflicts with the reason why you have a right to exclude others from your land, creating a privilege. Similarly, abatement of nuisance is a defense to trespass to land.[35] Recapture of land or chattels is a defense to battery, when reasonable force is used to regain possession of land occupied by a trespasser or chattels wrongfully in the possession of another.[36] A plaintiff may have a privilege to detain chattels, such as straying cattle, where they have caused damage to his land under the doctrine of distress damage feasant. All of these circumstances arise because there is a bilateral reason as between the parties as to why, exceptionally, no duty should be owed: a privilege. Each is structurally the same as self-defense in its justificatory form.

The application of the defense of contributory or comparative fault has varied dramatically across time and jurisdiction within the common law. The traditional rule was, and in some jurisdictions still is, "that if there is blame in causing the accident on both sides, however small that blame may be on one side, the loss lies where it falls."[37] This "vicious"[38] rule has nothing to recommend it. The justification appeared to have been that where the plaintiff caused his own injuries he was not the victim of a wrong at all.[39] Of course, at a certain point the plaintiff's own fault may be so great, and the defendant's causal contribution so small, that we can say no wrong has been suffered, but the rule as

---

[35] James Goudkamp, *Tort Law Defences* 108 (2013).
[36] *Id.*, 109.   [37] Cayzer Irvine & Co. v. Carron Co. (1884) 9 App. Cas. 873, 881 (Lord Blackburn).
[38] Tony Weir, *An Introduction to Tort Law* 123 (2d ed. 2006).
[39] Davies v. Mann (1842) 10 M. & W. 546, 152 E.R. 588.

applied seemed, or seems, to operate in a way more generous to the defendant than ordinary principles of causal responsibility would require.

In England and other Commonwealth jurisdictions, statutes reformed the rule rather than abolish it altogether, as a way of reducing proportionately the damages payable by comparing the fault of plaintiff and defendant. In some American states, the same change was introduced judicially. This has transformed the rule from operating as a justification into being one of partial excuse. If one understands the law of torts as concerned with ensuring that the blameworthy bear appropriate responsibility for the consequences of their actions, this change appears to be correct. If, by contrast, one understands torts as concerned with wrongs and the continuity of the obligation not to injure, it may be argued that abolition of the rule altogether would have been the better course.

VIII. Defenses in Unjust Enrichment

By far the most significant defense within the law of unjust enrichment is that of change of position. Whether it is properly so-called a defense, the kinds of claim it applies to, and what its normative justification may be, are questions that are intimately linked to the normative question of what the justification(s) for the underlying claim might be. Consider a variation on one of the examples Burrows gives in his chapter in this volume:[40]

> P pays $1,000 to D by mistake. D, as a result, gives $750 to a charity as a gift, which he would not otherwise have done. Is P entitled to restitution of the $750 from D?

If one takes the view that "enrichment" in claims such as these is constituted by the factual state of affairs of being better off, we might conclude that D should not be liable because he is "disenriched." On this view, D's proof that he gave $750 away is really a denial of enrichment. We might place the onus of proving what has happened to the money after receipt upon him, but we would be doing so because he is presumptively better off and better placed to prove what has happened to the money received than P, rather than because he is asserting a defense properly so-called. However, explaining the "defense" in this way has the advantage of explaining why it only applies to a limited range of claims and not, say, to claims in the law of torts.

On another view, "enrichment" does not bear its ordinary meaning, but instead refers to the payment made by P and received by D. This cannot be subsequently lost. The explanation for the defense may be that we are trying to ensure that a morally blameless defendant is not made worse off by the operation of the claim. Such an explanation faces the problem of accounting for why it does not apply to other claims in private law more generally. Further, it is an explanation that focuses solely on the defendant and does not seem to relate to the reason for the claim itself, meaning that the defense should operate as an immunity not a privilege.

---

[40] See Andrew Burrows, this volume.

The operation of defenses enables us to see whether claims are alike. If the same normative justification underlies a claim, one would expect the same rules, in particular the same defenses, to apply, unless we can come up with a good exceptional reason why not. So:

> P pays D, a builder, $10,000 in advance for repairs to his house. D, fully intending to carry out the work, spends the money on a holiday for himself and his family. D dies while abroad.

If, as is sometimes claimed, this kind of claim is of the same kind as that of the mistaken payment it might be assumed that the same change of position defense should apply. If it does not, this may indicate that the underlying normative justification for the claim is different.

IX. Equitable Defenses

There are many equitable defenses, and most are best now treated as general defenses (such as equitable set-off) or as defenses that are either justifications in contract law (innocent misrepresentation, undue influence) or excuses barring equitable remedies (acquiescence, laches, lack of clean hands).

The defense that has caused most confusion within the common law is that of estoppel. It is possible to be estopped (i.e., barred) from asserting two different things: facts and rights. Where A makes a clear and unambiguous statement of fact to B, intending B to rely upon such statement, and B believes the truth of such statement and acts upon it, A may be estopped from proving that the fact is false. This rule is not, properly speaking, a defense at all, but a rule of evidence. It is neither a cause of action nor a defense, although it may allow a cause of action or a defense that would otherwise fail to succeed. This rule has long applied in both the common law and Chancery courts and is applicable to all private law actions. (Confusingly, it has become common in U.S. law to refer to this form of estoppel as "equitable" estoppel, despite its never having been confined to the courts of equity.)

Quite different is estoppel as it applies to rights. Returning to the example with which we began, where there is a contract for the sale of goods for the delivery on May 1, if the buyer informs the seller in advance that delivery at a later point is fine, and nothing further happens, this should constitute waiver of his right to delivery at that point and so provide a defense to a claim for breach. However, this waiver can at all times prior to the date of delivery be withdrawn, so that the buyer may return to his legal rights. This may be unfair on the seller in certain circumstances. If relying upon the waiver, he had sold his supply elsewhere, he may no longer be able to deliver on the specified date. To overcome this problem, we may bar the buyer from withdrawing his waiver until such time as the seller can return to the position he would have been in if it had never been given. The buyer is estopped from asserting his rights, and the estoppel is promissory in the sense that what he is estopped from asserting is his promissory rights.

Seen in this way, many of the traditional features of promissory estoppel are explicable. It is a shield not a sword. Detrimental reliance is required. A preexisting contractual relationship is necessary. The rule is generally suspensory, not extinctive, of contractual rights.

Estoppel of this form should not be, and is not, confined to contractual rights. We may be estopped from asserting proprietary rights as well, hence "proprietary estoppel," or in principle any kind of rights at all. This latter form of rights-estoppel is genuinely equitable and has the form one associates with other equitable rules. It is a form of meta-law, or a rule about another rule. The right holder is barred, or estopped, from asserting an otherwise valid legal right.

In all common law jurisdictions, however, the label "estoppel" has ceased to describe many of the rules being given effect to. Perhaps we are blind to the problem because it is an archaic French term. Instead of plaintiffs being estopped from asserting facts or rights, "estoppel" has been transformed into a cause of action. This development, as so often, happened earlier in the United States with the adoption by the American Law Institute in 1932 of § 90 of the *Restatement of Contracts* of enforceable promises created by detrimental reliance. This has created an entirely new cause of action, alongside that of contract. In England, the development has been more localized, but even more dramatic. A cause of action called "proprietary estoppel" has been recognized, which, although confined to rights to land,[41] allows a plaintiff to be awarded a fee simple estate in land or other proprietary rights, despite not fulfilling the ordinary rules of acquisition for such rights.[42]

If we are to recognize legal rights created in this way, we need to accept that they are not justified by the more limited reasons for the traditional defense of estoppel. We should at a minimum separate out the two bodies of rules and accept that the rules that apply to the cause of action need not, indeed do not, apply to the defense.[43] A bolder, but more reactionary, view is that this expansion of the role of estoppel is an obvious confusion between claims and defenses, lacks secure normative foundations, and should be reversed or at least confined.

X. CONCLUSION

The agenda of New Private Law has two aspects: the analytic and the normative. This chapter has attempted to pursue both. The patron saint of the first is Hohfeld. We need to take the positive law seriously, to distinguish between the various meanings of "right" employed, and not slide between them. In this chapter, I have sought to distinguish

---

[41] Thorner v. Major [2009] UKHL 18; [2009] 1 W.L.R. 776.

[42] Pascoe v. Turner [1972] 1 W.L.R. 431 (CA).

[43] This is the central thesis of the monumental treatment in Ben McFarlane, *The Law of Proprietary Estoppel* (2014).

privileges and immunities from one another as used in our law in common. On the normative side, it is easier to point to villains than it is saints. Once we have made the necessary analytic distinctions, it should become clear that the underlying normative reasons for the various rules (obligations and liabilities, privileges and immunities) differ and are not, and need not be, of the same form.

Neither task is easy, and this chapter has merely scratched the surface. One reason for the relative dynamism of private law scholarship in the Anglo–common law world is the luck of having interesting people interested in it, notably Birks. His clear and innovative work gained both supporters and passionate opponents. One of his more amusing, if perhaps unfair, statements was that:

> The realists and the post-realists have done a good job of debunking legal science. In the United States, where Jerome Frank and his intellectual successors did their most serious damage, it has never recovered. It now lets in floods of law and economics in the hope of filling the broken vessel. However, if we are to adopt Chesterton's famous dictum upon the Christian way of life, we might say that a rational science of law has not been found wanting but has merely been found difficult and left untried.[44]

Let us try the difficult.

---

[44] Peter Birks, *Equity in the Modern Law: An Exercise in Taxonomy*, 26 U.W.A. L. REV. 1 (1996).

CHAPTER 33

....

EQUITY

....

BEN MCFARLANE

I. OVERVIEW

....

THIS chapter addresses two general questions. The first is what the New Private Law can do for Equity.[1] Equity provides a particularly striking example of the significance of the New Private Law. Indeed, the importance of the movement to the subject may even be existential. It will be argued that recent work on Equity not only exemplifies the New Private Law but is also vital to justifying the continued distinctiveness of Equitable, as opposed to common law, principles. That work is particularly important as Equity has faced a double threat: not only from analyses, often American, that are generally skeptical as to conceptual distinctions, but also from scholars, in other parts of the common law world, who have focused on doctrinal coherence and doubted the wisdom of maintaining separate legal and Equitable responses to apparently identical questions. In response to such challenges, more recent scholarship can be seen as providing three separate, but closely linked, approaches to identifying what is special about Equity. It will be argued that the most promising of those approaches is a formal one, which accepts Equity's second-order role of adjusting the position that would otherwise arise through the operation of first-order law, and focuses specifically on Equity's role in regulating the acquisition and enforcement of rights.

But we should ask not only what the New Private Law can do for Equity. The second general question addressed here is what the subject can do for the movement. If Equity owes much to the New Private Law, the reverse is also true. The distinctiveness of private law lies in the correlative nature of the legal relations it recognizes: for example, a defendant's entry into a contract does not merely mean that she will have to pay a sum of money if she does not honor that contract, nor does it merely mean that she has a duty to

---

[1] In this chapter "Equity" refers to the body of rules developed by the English Court of Chancery, while "equity" refers to a generalized concept defined in contradistinction to law. See *infra* text accompanying note 10.

perform; it rather means that she owes a duty *to the counterparty* to perform and that the counterparty therefore has a claim-right against her, as well as powers that correlate to liabilities of the defendant. This structural aspect of private law creates a risk:[2] by recognizing that duties and liabilities of a defendant correlate to rights of a claimant, it places the claimant in a powerful position. The benefits to the claimant are not only practical (as where the claimant has a power to enforce a duty through the courts) but also normative, in the sense that the existence of a claim-right or power affects the operation of other legal rules, and can do so even in the exceptional cases where the claimant has no power to enforce the underlying duty.[3] If, then, the distinctiveness of private law lies in the bilateral relationship between defendant and claimant, justifying that distinctiveness requires the identification of mechanisms to deal with the risks created by such a relationship. And Equity provides just such mechanisms: indeed, "the first principle upon which all Courts of Equity proceed [is that] . . . the person who might otherwise have enforced those rights will not be allowed to enforce them where it would be inequitable having regard to the dealings . . . between the parties."[4] As will be discussed later, specific Equitable principles play an important role in justifying the operation of key private law rules, such as the rules on the transfer of rights, or the formation of contracts, as those Equitable principles mitigate potential specific injustices, as between claimant and defendant, that would otherwise arise from those primary private law rules. This legitimizing function can, however, be generalized: Equity not only mitigates the risk of injustice, as between specific parties, arising from the operation of particular private law rules, in doing so it also mitigates the risk of injustice, as between specific parties, arising from having a system of private law at all.

Equity is not, however, merely strong on defense, dealing with risks created by private law. As Hanoch Dagan powerfully argues in this volume, private law enhances the autonomy of its subjects "by offering a structurally pluralist repertoire of property types and contract types."[5] Equity has played a pivotal role in providing parties with additional means of structuring their legal relations, and these means have proved to be of great practical value. In some cases, the assistance is indirect—as Henry Smith has argued, the "safety valve" offered by equity (for example in the possibility of rescinding a contract as a result of undue influence or a nonfraudulent misrepresentation, or of allowing rectification of a written document) permits first-order legal rules (such as those relating to contractual formation or interpretation) to operate in a clear, stable manner that facilitates the parties' planning and transactions.[6] In other cases, however, the positive role of Equity is clear, as can be seen from the use made today of the trust,

---

[2] See Anita Bernstein, this volume (exploring nature of this risk). The "domination-potential" of particular private law relations has been most prominently discussed in relation to property law: see, e.g., J.W. Harris, *Property and Justice* 268–274 (1996).
[3] See Robert Stevens, this volume.
[4] Hughes v. Metropolitan Railway Co., [1877] 2 App. Cas. 439, 488 (Lord Cairns).
[5] Hanoch Dagan, this volume.
[6] See Henry E. Smith, "Property, Equity and the Rule of Law," in *Private Law and the Rule of Law* 224 (Lisa M. Austin & Dennis Klimchuk eds., 2014).

which offers parties a flexible and highly customizable means of both managing wealth and structuring commercial transactions.[7] The need to prevent the unconscionable assertion of a right may lie at the origins of the trust concept, as the courts intervened to prevent a party from acquiring property on one basis (that it would be used for the benefit of another) and then using that property on a different basis (for his own benefit). Yet the form of that outcome—of one party holding a right for another—can of course be consensually achieved and has been employed massively[8] to expand the "repertoire of property types."[9]

Before embarking on this short survey of Equity and the New Private Law, three qualifications must be made. All three flow from the fact that, as Frederic Maitland noted, "Equity" can be defined only in historical and jurisdictional terms: as the body of rules which consists of, or derives from later developments of, the body of rules once administered by the English courts known as Courts of Equity.[10] The same approach was taken by Jeremy Bentham, who also cautioned that nothing could be gained in understanding those rules by attempting to define the concept of equity—one might as well try to understand the business of the Star Chamber "by the definition of a star."[11] It is for that reason that "Equity," when referring to the body of rules rather than the general concept, is capitalized here.

The first qualification is that none of the analyses discussed purport to explain *every* aspect of Equitable intervention. There is a great diversity to the doctrines that fall within the scope of Equity, and some operate in a way that places them outside the standard private law model. For example, a charitable trustee owes duties in relation to the trust property, but those duties are not owed to anyone with a power to release them, and they are enforced, in effect on behalf of the public, by public officials or bodies.[12] There are also more recently developed aspects of Equity that are difficult to fit into the standard second-order model: the doctrine of breach of confidence, for example, focused originally on controlling a defendant's ability to make use of a particular asset, but it has been co-opted in the protection of privacy and so now extends to cases where

[7] See John D. Morley & Robert H. Sitkoff, this volume.

[8] There are, of course, modern concerns as to the extent of that expansion. See, e.g., Lionel Smith, *Massively Discretionary Trusts*, 70 CURRENT LEGAL PROBLEMS 17 (2017).

[9] Jeffrey Hackney, *Understanding Equity and Trusts* ch. 1 sec. 3 (1987) ("[T]here are many different kinds of trustee, ranging from the willing manager to the entrapped villain.").

[10] See Frederic W. Maitland, *Equity: A Course of Lectures* 1 (Alfred H. Chaytor & William J. Whittaker eds., 2d ed. 1936). Maitland referred to "Courts of Equity" arguably as mere rhetorical flourish to emphasize the circularity of the definition of Equity. While there certainly were multiple courts of equity, in fact it was the body of rules of only one court—the Court of Chancery—that defined Equity.

[11] 7 *The Works of Jeremy Bentham, Published Under the Superintendence of His Literary Executor John Bowring* 291 n.301 (Edinburgh, William Tait 1843). For discussion of Bentham's views, see Chris Riley, *Jeremy Bentham and Equity: The Court of Chancery, Lord Eldon, and the Dispatch Court Plan*, 39 J. LEGAL HIST. 29, 32–40 (2018).

[12] In England, for example, charitable trusts can be enforced by the Attorney General: see, e.g., Ben McFarlane & Charles Mitchell, *Hayton and Mitchell: Text, Cases and Materials on the Law of Trusts & Equitable Remedies* (14th ed. 2015), ch 6.

the impugned conduct of the defendant does not relate to any discrete right held by the defendant.[13]

The second qualification is that, in arguing that a particular feature is characteristic of Equity, it is not necessary to show that such a feature is *never* present in the body of rules that consists of, or derives from, rules developed by courts of common law. First, even when and where separate court systems are in place, some degree of interaction between the two bodies is inevitable.[14] Second, whether a substantive, functional, or formal approach (or some combination thereof) is taken to analyzing Equity, it would be surprising if there was no evidence for such an approach in the common law.

The final, related qualification is that care must be taken not to fetishize Equity. After all, if it consists merely of a set of doctrines that can be traced to a particular set of English courts, and very many countries (such as all civil law jurisdictions) never had such courts, then it would be rash to assume that a legal system can only function with a similarly defined set of doctrines. An attempt to justify a separate treatment of Equity is not an attempt to justify the bizarre situation in which the nonfederal jurisdiction of England ended up with a dual system of superior courts. Rather, it is an attempt to understand what may be special about a particular set of doctrines, and there is no immediate reason why similar doctrines might not also be found in the law of other countries.

II. SETTING THE SCENE: EQUITY BEFORE THE NEW PRIVATE LAW

Maitland's definition of Equity invites an immediate objection: if our interest is in the content and operation of the law *today*, why should it matter if the historical roots of a particular rule lie with one set of English courts rather than another? Being obvious, this objection is not new;[15] Maitland was of course aware of it, and was suitably apologetic about his definition of Equity.[16] The objection meant that Equity was particularly vulnerable to the Legal Realist attack on meaningless conceptualism, and it is no surprise that, by the time Chafee stated that it would be "absurd" to continue with a distinction

[13] For an English example, see *PJS v. News Group Newspapers Ltd.* [2016] UKSC 26, [2016] AC 1081, where Lord Mance, noting the distinction between rights of confidence and rights of privacy, found at [35] that the latter could be infringed by the publication of material already widely known, where such publication would add "greatly and on a potentially enduring basis to the intrusiveness and distress felt by the claimant."

[14] For discussion of some recent examples of the fluidity of the distinction, see, e.g., John C.P. Goldberg & Henry E. Smith, "Wrongful Fusion: Equity and Tort," in *Equity and Law: Fusion and Fission* 309 (John C.P. Goldberg, Henry E. Smith, & P.G. Turner eds., 2019).

[15] See, e.g., John Austin, *Lectures on Jurisprudence* 38–39 (1st ed. 1863) ("[T]he distinction [between common law and Equity] is utterly senseless. . . .").

[16] See Maitland, *supra* note 10, at 1 ("This, you may well say, is but a poor thing to call a definition.").

"put up by historical accident in 14th century England,"[17] Equity had in effect ceased to exist as an independent subject of study in American law.[18] On one view, separate study was no longer required as Equity's characteristic flexibility came to permeate much of American law.[19] Certainly, in the twentieth century in the United States, there was no shortage of commentators arguing in favor of a general adoption of the fact-sensitive, context-specific approach associated with each of Legal Realism and Equity.[20] To their eyes, the benefits of such a judicial approach, and the possibilities of legal reform inherent in it, far outweighed any possible reasons for maintaining a distinction between common law and Equity.[21] It might even be said that Equity became a victim of its own success: when its particular mode of adjudication was adopted generally, there was no longer a need to treat it as a distinct entity.[22]

Realists are not, however, the only group who might chafe when told that there is an important difference between a common law concept and its equitable equivalent: that, for example, a legal property right differs from an equitable property right, common law estoppel from equitable estoppel, and common law set-off from equitable set-off. Those looking for the possible doctrinal principles (and not just policies) behind the existing rules of Equity can rightly point out, in no less pointed terms than a Realist, that the mere fact of a rule's jurisdictional origin cannot, in itself, justify a difference between that rule and its common law equivalent.[23]

As a result, Equity was also under pressure in other common law jurisdictions less affected by Legal Realism.[24] The diagnosis shared a premise with the Realist critique; yet

[17] Zechariah Chafee, *Foreword to Selected Essays on Equity* 3, 4 (Edward D. Re ed., 1955).

[18] See, e.g., Samuel L. Bray, *The Supreme Court and the New Equity*, 68 VAND. L. REV. 997, 1022 (2015) (noting that the "era of the most systematic treatments of equity," which began with Joseph Story, *Commentaries on Equity Jurisprudence as Administered in England and America* (1st ed. 1836), "effectively ended" with the last edition of Henry L. McClintock, *Handbook of the Principles of Equity* (2d ed. 1948)).

[19] See, e.g., Douglas Laycock, *The Triumph of Equity*, 56 LAW & CONTEMP. PROBS. 53, 54 (1993) (arguing that "the discretion once associated with equity now pervades the legal system").

[20] In the procedural context, see, e.g., Stephen N. Subrin, *How Equity Conquered Common Law: The Federal Rules of Civil Procedure in Historical Perspective*, 135 U. PA. L. REV. 909, 1000 (1987). In the substantive context, see, e.g., U.C.C. §§ 1-304, 2-302 (1977) (describing the use of good faith and unconscionability, respectively, two characteristically Equitable terms).

[21] One such benefit, it was hoped, would be increased transparency as to the real reasons for judicial decisions. See, e.g., Herman Oliphant, *A Return to Stare Decisis*, 14 A.B.A. J. 159 (1928); K.N. Llewellyn, *The Standardization of Commercial Contracts in English and Continental Law*, 52 HARV. L. REV. 700, 703 (1939) (book review).

[22] See, e.g., Roscoe Pound, *The End of Law as Developed in Legal Rules and Doctrines*, 27 HARV. L. REV. 195, 226–227 (1913) (arguing that general legal aims could be seen as developments of what had once been specifically Equitable ideas).

[23] See, e.g., Peter Birks, *Equity in the Modern Law: An Exercise in Taxonomy*, 26 U.W. AUSTL. L. REV. 1 (1996); Andrew Burrows, *We Do This at Common Law But That in Equity*, 22 OXFORD J. LEGAL STUD. 1 (2002).

[24] In England and Australia, in contrast to the United States, specialist works on Equity were (and are still) regularly updated, but they faced a sometimes hostile reception. See, e.g., Jeffrey Hackney, *Snell's Equity*, 117 L.Q. REV. 150, 154 (2001) (book review) (calling for "no more Snells" and noting that the first edition of *English Private Law* (Peter Birks ed., 2001) had no chapter called Equity. That remains true of the current, third edition of *English Private Law* (Andrew Burrows ed., 2013)).

the treatment prescribed was different. The concern for doctrinal scholars such as Peter Birks was not to ensure that the law was reformed so as to allow the clear application of the most appropriate policies; it was rather to ensure conceptual consistency. Further, while the Realist prescription prioritized the flexibility and fact-sensitivity of Equity, the doctrinalists tended to prefer the common law solutions. For example, Birks strongly objected to any idea that a defendant's position should turn on the judge's view of whether it would, on the particular facts, be "unconscionable" for the defendant to retain the benefit of property.[25]

On one side of the Atlantic, then, scholars emphasizing the benefits of fact-sensitive applications of particular policies, and finding such an approach in principles identified with Equity, argued for the wider application of Equitable ideas. On the other, scholars emphasizing the importance of conceptual coherence and clearly stated principles, and thus resistant to Equitable notions such as unconscionability, argued for the wider application of particular common law rules. Two very different starting points, two very different ends, but a common means: the elision of the distinction between common law and Equity.

III. THE DISTINCTIVENESS OF EQUITY TODAY

In considering the legacy of Legal Realist approaches to property, Henry Smith has noted the "persistence of system in property law."[26] The doctrines which, on a Realist critique, might be seen as mere empty labels have endured, and concepts such as "possession" still form a key part of the legislative and judicial approach to resolving disputes. The same point can be made in relation to Equity. For example, as Samuel Bray has shown, the U.S. Supreme Court continues to link particular limits on the availability of certain remedies to the Equitable origins of those remedies.[27] As a result, the requirement that an injunction should not be granted if there is an adequate remedy available at law, rather than falling away,[28] has once again become prominent. Similarly, while the *Restatement (Third) of Restitution and Unjust Enrichment*, like its predecessors, downplays the significance of the divide between common law and Equity, it cannot but, as Lionel Smith has shown, employ that distinction in setting out the current law.[29]

In England and Australia, too, notwithstanding the arguments of scholars such as Birks, the courts have continued both to assume the distinctiveness of Equity and to employ the maligned concept of unconscionability. The argument for following the common law to impose a prima facie strict personal restitutionary liability on the recipient of

---

[25]   See, e.g., Peter Birks, "Receipt," in *Breach of Trust* (Peter Birks & Arianna Pretto eds., 2002).

[26]   Henry E. Smith, *The Persistence of System in Property Law*, 163 U. PA. L. REV. 2055 (2015).

[27]   See generally Bray, *supra* note 18.

[28]   This would have been consistent with the analysis of Laycock. See Laycock, *supra* note 19.

[29]   Lionel Smith, *Common Law and Equity in the Restatement (Third) of Restitution & Unjust Enrichment*, 68 WASH. & LEE. L. REV. 1185 (2011).

trust property, for example, has been expressly rejected by the High Court of Australia,[30] and the Court of Appeal in England has dealt with such cases by requiring that the "recipient's state of knowledge must be such as to make it unconscionable for him to retain the benefit of the receipt".[31] Moreover, in explaining when a mistake by the settlor of a trust may allow the rescission of her voluntary settlement, the U.K. Supreme Court in *Pitt v. Holt* refused to accept that *any* causative mistake could suffice to allow rescission, or to classify mistakes into different categories, instead using "equity's cumbersome but familiar term, unconscionableness"[32] to determine if the causative mistake is sufficiently grave to allow for rescission. In arguing that a court must be free to "form a view about the merits of a claim," Lord Walker drew on his own statement in another vibrant area of modern Equity, proprietary estoppel, that "the fundamental principle that equity is concerned to prevent unconscionable conduct permeates all the elements of the doctrine. In the end the court must look at the matter in the round."[33]

A parallel can be drawn with the approach of the High Court of Australia in *Australian Financial Services v. Hills Industries Ltd.*[34] to the operation of the change of position defense,[35] which is available to reduce or eliminate the prima facie strict liability of the recipient of an unjust enrichment. On one view, favored for example by Birks in his later writing,[36] the defense is primarily enrichment-related: if the defendant wishes to invoke it, she needs to show the extent to which events subsequent to receipt mean that she is no longer enriched. In *Hills*, the High Court rejected such an approach and, like the Supreme Court in *Pitt*, invoked both the concept of unconscionable retention and the analogy with estoppel. Chief Justice French, building on an earlier analysis of Justice Gummow,[37] emphasized the "general application of equitable considerations to restitutionary actions" and stated that "Recovery depends upon whether it would be inequitable for the recipient to retain the benefit. Retention may not be inequitable if the recipient had changed its position on the faith of the receipt and thereby suffered a detriment."[38] He stated that a focus on whether it would be inequitable for the defendant to retain a benefit "does not involve the acceptance of an arbitrary judicial discretion," and its application on a "case-by-case basis. . . . allows for the development of criteria adapted to particular classes of case."[39]

In considering these restitutionary claims, the highest court in each of England and Australia, like their counterpart in the United States when considering the test for an

---

[30] See, e.g., Farah Constructions Pty Ltd. v. Say-Dee Pty Ltd., (2007) 230 CLR 89.

[31] BCCI (Overseas) Ltd. v. Akindele, [2001] Ch 437, 455.   [32] Pitt v. Holt, [2013] 2 AC 108, [124].

[33] *Id.* at [128].

[34] Australian Financial Services & Leasing Pty Ltd. v. Hills Industries Ltd., (2014) 253 CLR 560.

[35] See *Restatement (Third) of Restitution & Unjust Enrichment* § 65 (2011).

[36] See Peter Birks, *Unjust Enrichment* 208–212 (2d ed. 2005).

[37] See Roxborough v. Rothmans of Pall Mall Australia Ltd., (2001) 208 CLR 516.

[38] (2014) 253 CLR 560, [1]. See also *id.* at [65]–[76] (judgment of Hayne, Crennan, Kiefel, Bell, and Keane JJ.).

[39] *Id.* at [21]–[23]. See also *Restatement (Third) of Restitution and Unjust Enrichment* § 65 (2011), where the inquiry is whether it would be inequitable to the recipient to require restitution of the original benefit.

injunction, applied distinctive principles traditionally associated with Equity, rejecting arguments that such tests are out of place in the modern law. Indeed, in each of *Pitt* and *Hills*, the court expressly addressed, and rejected, academic concerns about applying notions such as unconscionability. The practical effect of such reasoning, as Bray has noted in the American context,[40] is to defend a view of Equitable intervention as exceptional and discretionary. The effect of *Pitt*, for example, is that rescission may be denied, even where the claimant made a causative mistake, if the mistake is not sufficiently grave that it would be unconscionable for a party to insist on her rights under the settlement: this means not only that not all causative mistakes will lead to rescission but also that wider factors about the context of the case can be considered.[41] The concern that traditionally Equitable notions such as unconscionability can lead to unchecked and unjustified liability does not, therefore, bite in such contexts.[42]

This very brief survey is not intended to suggest that the academic arguments against the distinctiveness of Equity have had no purchase. In England and Australia, for example, it is still possible to maintain the distinction between an equitable assignment and an actual transfer of a legal chose in action.[43] In the United States, however, that view has long since ceased to be tenable, given early and consistent judicial adoption of the idea that the assignee is to be recognized as "the owner" of the right,[44] at common law as well as in equity,[45] and the adoption of the same approach in the influential New York Field Code. There are also recent examples of the U.K. Supreme Court's limiting the distinctiveness of Equity.[46] When considering the liability of solicitors who had held money on trust for the claimant bank as part of a conveyancing transaction, and had then (apparently through inadvertence) paid that money away without authority, that court rejected the claimant's attempt to bypass limits applied in contract and tort claims by instead relying on the solicitors' duty, as trustee, to account to it, as beneficiary.[47] Lord Toulson stated that, in such a case, "the extent of equitable compensation should be the same as if damages for breach of contract were sought at common law" as such compensation is "intended to make good a loss."[48] This argument draws on two ideas familiar from the

[40] See Bray, *supra* note 18.

[41] Pitt v. Holt, [2013] 2 AC 108, [135] ("In some cases of artificial tax avoidance the court might think it right to refuse relief.").

[42] The same is true where the court limits the personal liability of a recipient of trust property transferred without authority by asking if it would be unconscionable for the defendant to retain the benefit of trust property, rather than by recognizing a prima facie strict liability. See the cases cited in notes 30 and 31, *supra*.

[43] As made clear in the comprehensive analysis by Chee Ho Tham, *Understanding the Law of Assignment* (2020). See too James Edelman & Steven Elliott, *Two Conceptions of Equitable Assignment*, 131 L.Q. REV. 228 (2015).

[44] That view is sometimes taken in England too. See, e.g., First Abu Dhabi Bank PJSC v. BP Oil International Limited [2018] EWCA (Civ) 14, [37].

[45] See, e.g., Wardell v. Eden, 2 Johns. Cas. 258, 260 (N.Y. Sup. Ct. 1801); Colbourn v. Rossiter, 2 Conn. 503, 508 (Conn. 1818).

[46] See Makdessi v. Cavendish Square Holdings BV, [2016] AC 1172, where the rule against contractual penalties was analyzed as now being a common law doctrine; see also *infra* text accompanying note 50.

[47] AIB Group (UK) v. Mark Redler & Co., [2015] AC 1503.

[48] AIB Group (UK), [2015] AC 1503, [71].

analysis of scholars such as Birks: a different approach cannot be justified simply by noting its Equitable origins; and a unified approach should be modeled on that of the common law. On a conceptual level, there is thus a tension with a case such as *Pitt*, where the distinctiveness of the Equitable rules is emphasized; although on the practical level, the result is again to limit the availability of Equitable relief.

Three main points arise from this necessarily brief survey of the courts' current approach. First, notwithstanding academic criticism from both Legal Realist and doctrinal scholars, concepts and language traditionally associated with Equity have persisted. Second, there is no single consistent approach, even within a particular jurisdiction, to maintaining or rejecting the distinctiveness of Equity. There is a good deal of commonality, for example, between England and Australia, but the highest courts there have taken different approaches in areas such as the nature of a trustee's liability to account for trust property,[49] and to the basis of the rule against penalties.[50] Third, while there is variety as to how such practical outcomes are reached, many cases have shared a preference for limiting the availability of particular relief. Indeed, in some cases the limiting cart has been put before the Equitable horse, and a remedy has been wrongly characterized as Equitable simply in order to emphasize restrictions on its availability.[51]

IV. The Significance of the New Private Law for the Distinctiveness of Equity

A. The Importance of Means

Debates about the distinctiveness of Equity reflect debates about the distinctiveness of private law. Just as it may be argued that there is no room for distinct Equitable and legal rules within one system, it could be said that there is nothing distinctive about the mode of analysis that should apply when considering private as opposed to public law, as all law can be seen as simply an application of governmental power to citizens.[52] As John Goldberg has pointed out, part of the attraction of such an argument is that it appears to push "past the surface to get to what is 'really' at stake."[53] So, for Holmes, for example, the concept of a contractual duty of performance can be seen as hiding the reality that, in practice, the consequence of such a duty is simply that a party can be ordered by a court

---

[49] Youyang Pty Ltd. v. Minter Ellison Morris Fletcher, (2003) 212 CLR 484 (maintaining the traditional irrelevance of questions of causation to a claim based on a misapplication of trust assets).

[50] Andrews v. ANZ Banking Group Ltd., (2012) 247 CLR 205 (emphasizing the continuing Equitable basis of the rule against penalties). But see Makdessi v. Cavendish Square Holdings BV, [2016] AC 1172 (regarding the rule instead as now part of common law).

[51] See, e.g., Great-West Life & Annuity Ins. Co. v. Knudson, 534 U.S. 204, 215, 234 (2002) (inaccurately characterizing mandamus as an Equitable remedy).

[52] See generally Thomas W. Merrill, this volume.

[53] John C.P. Goldberg, *Pragmatism and Private Law*, 125 HARV. L. REV. 1640, 1642 (2012).

to pay a sum of money if she acts, or fails to act, in a particular way.[54] Casting aside the language of duty not only more clearly distinguishes legal from moral reasoning; it also allows a focus on practical outcomes: on ends rather than means. Exactly the same point can be made, of course, in relation to Equity, and it is no coincidence that scholars who influenced Holmes, such as Austin[55] and Bentham,[56] were similarly skeptical as to the role of Equity.

In responding to such arguments, John Goldberg and Benjamin Zipursky[57] have drawn on H.L.A. Hart's response to an Austinian or Holmesian analysis of contract law and tort law, with its key point that a statement of legal duty is distinct from a prediction of a sanction.[58] Such an analysis does not necessitate equating legal with moral duties, but it does pay attention to a significant aspect of the *means* by which law attempts to regulate behavior. Indeed, focusing on such means, and in particular the fact that a duty correlates to a claim-right of a specific other party, is crucial to defending the distinct existence of private law.

B. Three Approaches

Where scholarship on Equity can be seen as an example of the New Private Law, it emphasizes the importance of means as well as ends. At the risk of oversimplification, three general strands of such scholarship can be identified. The strands are nonexclusive: much recent work includes elements of all three.

The first approach is substantive. The claim is that Equity embodies a distinctive normative approach, and its preservation matters chiefly as such norms should be retained and applied by the courts. For example, in considering cases where a cause of action in proprietary estoppel can arise as a result of a promise, Irit Samet[59] has argued that Equity gives effect to a specific moral principle.[60] As the focus is on the substance of the law, it could be argued that it does not require the preservation of Equity, as such a moral principle might just as well be applied at common law, or in a wholly fused system. Indeed, Samet's discussion of the "clean hands" defense is a general one of how a court should best respond to illegality,[61] and thus, like the U.K. Supreme Court's recent approach to the issue,[62] seems to assume that there is no distinct Equitable defense. Her point is

---

[54]   See Oliver Wendell Holmes, *The Path of the Law*, 10 HARV. L. REV. 457 (1897).

[55]   See *supra* note 15.   [56]   See *supra* note 11.

[57]   See John C.P. Goldberg & Benjamin C. Zipursky, *Seeing Tort Law from the Internal Point of View: Holmes and Hart on Legal Duties*, 75 FORDHAM L. REV. 1563 (2006).

[58]   H.L.A. Hart, *The Concept of Law* 84 (2d ed. 1994).

[59]   Irit Samet, *Equity: Conscience Goes to Market* ch. 2 (2019).

[60]   See T.M. Scanlon, *What We Owe to Each Other* 300 (1998) (identifying the principle as the "loss prevention" principle).   [61]   Samet, *supra* note 59, at ch. 4.

[62]   Patel v. Mirza, [2017] AC 467. For a persuasive attempt to identify, instead, a distinct role for an Equitable "clean hands" defense, separate from a general illegality defense, see Nicholas J. McBride, "The Future of Clean Hands," in *Defences in Equity* (Paul S. Davies, Simon Douglas, & James Goudkamp eds., 2018).

rather as to the substance of the principles applied: if they are based directly on morality, and allow for "ex-post, particularistic, and principle-led methods of adjudication,"[63] they can be seen as part of Equity's contribution.

The second approach can be described as functional, as it aims to uncover specific functions played by characteristically Equitable doctrines. For example, Henry Smith has argued that "a major theme of traditional equity was to counteract opportunism. To do so equity needs to go beyond *ex ante* bright line rules, because it is difficult to anticipate all the avenues of evasion."[64] Rather than providing a general means for the application of moral principles, Equity is seen as dealing with a specific problem of opportunism. On this view, for example, fiduciary law is characteristically Equitable, as it responds to the risks of exploitation inherent in the relationship of fiduciary and principal.[65] It is also possible for a claimant to try opportunistically to exploit Equitable rules, and so the "clean hands" defense, for example, can deal with that risk. The correspondence of at least some Equitable principles to moral values, a key aspect on the substantive view, is also relevant to the function of Equity, in at least two ways. First, as has been argued, for example, by Irit Samet[66] and by Matthew Harding,[67] the role of Equity in avoiding obvious injustices assists in encouraging an attitude of respect for the law, and thus "contribute[s] to the conditions under which citizens are likely to form and maintain a disposition to engage with law."[68] Second, as Andrew Gold and Henry Smith have argued more generally,[69] if a basis for the court's intervention tracks a commonly understood moral idea, it may cause less uncertainty in its application, thereby reducing information costs for parties who wish to avoid being exposed to such intervention.

The third approach is a formal one, as it focuses on the form of the parties' legal relations. It can be closely linked to a functional approach, as can be seen in Henry Smith's argument that Equity has a distinct second-order character,[70] plugging loopholes in the first-order rules. Adopting a formal approach, it is also possible to take a narrower view of the second-order character of many Equitable doctrines: they regulate, in favor of the claimant, the acquisition or enforcement of rights by the defendant.[71] If, for example, a contract has been entered into following a misrepresentation, even if innocently made,

---

[63] Samet, *supra* note 59, at 2.

[64] Smith, *supra* note 6, at 232–233. See too Henry E. Smith, *Equity as Meta-Law*, YALE L.J. forthcoming, where Smith identifies Equity's particular role in dealing with problems of polycentricity and of conflicting rights, as well as with opportunism.

[65] See Henry E. Smith, "Why Fiduciary Law Is Equitable," in *Philosophical Foundations of Fiduciary Law* 261 (Andrew Gold & Paul Miller eds., 2014).

[66] Samet, *supra* note 59, at ch. 1.

[67] Matthew Harding, *Equity and the Rule of Law*, 132 L.Q. REV. 278, 297 (2016).   [68] *Id.*

[69] Andrew S. Gold & Henry E. Smith, *Sizing Up Private Law* U. TORONTO L.J., forthcoming (https://www.utpjournals.press/doi/abs/10.3138/utlj.2019-0038).

[70] See Henry E. Smith, "Equitable Defences as Meta-Law," in *Defences in Equity* 17 (Paul S. Davies, Simon Douglas, & James Goudkamp eds., 2018).

[71] Ben McFarlane, "Form and Substance in Equity" in *Form and Substance in the Law of Obligations* (Andrew Robertson and James Goudkamp eds., 2019); Ben McFarlane & Robert Stevens, "What's Special About Equity? Rights About Rights," in *Philosophical Foundations of Equity* (Dennis Klimchuk, Irit Samet, & Henry E. Smith eds., 2020).

Equity, while acknowledging the validity of the contract, can control its enforcement by offering a party the power to rescind the contract. Similarly, where equitable estoppel arises following a promise of forbearance made to a contractual counterparty, Equity does not claim that the contract has been varied, so that the contractual right no longer exists; it rather regulates the enforcement of that right. On this view, the structure of the parties' legal relations prior to any Equitable intervention can be crucial in determining the applicability of Equitable doctrines.

C. Analyzing the Three Approaches

The variety of modern Equity and the willingness of common law also to employ open-ended standards pose a challenge to any attempt to defend the distinctiveness of Equity. It would seem, for example, that a purely substantive account may have difficulties in dealing with important areas of Equity that do not rely on an "ex post, fact-intensive" method of adjudication. The trust is, of course, a key contribution of Equity, and many aspects of its operation are determined by tightly defined rules which have a rigidity characteristic of "hard-nosed property rights"[72] rather than of discretionary decision-making. As Lionel Smith has pointed out, there is, for example, little remedial flexibility when considering the beneficiary's basic claim that the trustee account for the trust property:[73] if the trust property is available, the trustee must provide that very property and cannot argue that a money payment will be an acceptable substitute. Indeed, important remedies against the trustee can be available even without the beneficiary needing to show a breach of trust: in requiring the trustee to account for the trust property, for example, the beneficiary is seeking to enforce a primary duty. When an account is taken, the beneficiary may choose to disqualify the trustee from relying on a disposition made contrary to the terms of the trust: this is not in itself a sanction for a breach of trust, but is rather a result of a disability of the trustee, as against the beneficiary. The same argument can be made when considering the position of a fiduciary who acquires property when acting in an area covered by the scope of her fiduciary duties: where a trust of such property is imposed, it is not a discretionary sanction for a breach of duty, it is rather a product of the fact that, *as against the principal*, the fiduciary is disabled from acquiring such property.[74] Such cases thus provide excellent examples of the crucial Hartian point that a statement of legal relations (whether they involve a duty or a disability) is more than a prediction as to a possible sanction.

The example of the trust can be used in support of a formal analysis which emphasizes the second-order nature of Equity, and can thus be linked to a functional analysis which

---

[72] Foskett v. McKeown, [2001] 1 AC 102 (HL) 109 (describing rules allowing a beneficiary of a trust to assert a claim to traceable proceeds of the trust property in the hands of a third party).

[73] See Lionel Smith, "Equity Is Not a Single Thing," 157 in *Philosophical Foundations of Equity* (Dennis Klimchuk, Irit Samet, & Henry E. Smith eds., 2020).

[74] See Lionel Smith, *Constructive Trusts and the No-Profit Rule*, 72 CAMBRIDGE L.J. 260, 262 (2013) (discussing this disability as reflecting the fact that "the fiduciary acts in the sphere of fiduciary management *for* the beneficiary"); Lionel Smith, *Prescriptive Fiduciary Duties* (2018) 37 UNIV QUEENSLAND L. R. 261.

characterizes Equity as often concerned with responding to opportunistic conduct. Indeed, some recent analyses of the trust depend on this formal view:[75] in protecting a beneficiary, both against the trustee and at least some third parties,[76] Equity does not deny that the defendant holds various rights: it simply imposes duties on the defendant, owed to the beneficiary, in relation to those rights. Adopting a two-level analysis shows that the trustee and beneficiary do not have competing claims to a single asset. In fact, it is to the beneficiary's advantage that the trustee has valid rights, provided that the trustee is under a duty to use those rights for the benefit of the beneficiary.

Three points arise from this analysis. First, in understanding the role of Equity, it would be a mistake to focus simply on the single level of outcomes and not look more deeply at how those outcomes are reached. If, for example, one were to look simply at how the "bundle of sticks" of proprietary enjoyment are distributed as between trustee and beneficiary, the picture is of their competing entitlements. This would wholly over- look the point that the beneficiary in fact depends on the trustee's rights and so does not deny their existence, but rather takes their benefit indirectly, through a claim on the "conscience" of the trustee. The existence of the trustee's duties to the beneficiary, and the fact that the beneficiary thus takes the economic benefits of the trustee's rights, does not alter the fact that the trustee in fact holds those rights; in the same way, the fact that a claimant may have a contractual duty to pay over to a third party sums obtained from an action against the defendant is not inconsistent with the fact that the claimant holds a right against that defendant.[77]

The second, related point concerns the *in personam* nature of Equitable intervention. On the substantive or functional approaches, this can be related to the limited, fact- intensive nature of Equity; on the formal view, it can also assist in understanding the relationship of Equity and common law. If, for example, a trustee transfers property to a stranger in breach of trust, or a fiduciary acquires property in breach of fiduciary duty, it is not accurate to say that, in general, the trustee or fiduciary has no power to act in that way. Rather, in the first case, the property *does* pass from trustee to recipient, and in the second, the property *is* acquired by the fiduciary. The question asked by Equity is whether the trustee or fiduciary has power *as against the beneficiary or principal* to act in that way. Equity does not deny that a particular dealing with rights has occurred, but rather seeks to regulate the effect of such a dealing on a specific claimant. Similarly, where the claimant mistakenly transfers a right to the defendant, the claimant does not deny the validity of the primary legal rules that state that the transfer has occurred; the claim is rather that, as a result of the circumstances in which it occurred, the defendant should now be under a liability to the claimant.[78] The protection of third parties may, for

---

[75] See, e.g., Ben McFarlane & Robert Stevens, *The Nature of Equitable Property*, 4 J. EQUITY 1 (2010).

[76] As for the position of third parties, see, e.g., Sinéad Agnew & Ben McFarlane, "The Paradox of the Equitable Proprietary Claim," in *Modern Studies in Property Law: volume 10* 303 (Ben McFarlane & Sinéad Agnew eds., 2019).

[77] See, e.g., Sprint Comm. Co. v. APCC Servs. Inc., 554 U.S. 269 (2008).

[78] See, e.g., Stephen Smith, "The Restatement of Liabilities in Restitution," in *The Restatement Third, Restitution and Unjust Enrichment: Critical and Comparative Essays* 227 (Charles Mitchell & William Swadling eds., 2013).

example, explain why a subjective mistake does not invalidate the transfer of a right; but it does not prevent the recognition of a liability of the recipient, to the particular claimant, to return a gain made at the expense of the claimant.[79]

The third point, related to the previous two, again concerns form. It is notable that a number of significant Equitable claims may arise even where it is impossible to say that the defendant has breached a preexisting duty to the claimant. For example, the innocence of the defendant at the moment of receipt, or at the moment of making a precontractual misrepresentation, does not in itself prevent a restitutionary claim or a claim for rescission. An equitable estoppel does not require the defendant to have made a promise intending not to honor it, and, when operating as a cause of action, equitable estoppel does not always impose on the defendant a duty to perform a promise.[80] Similarly, a beneficiary may claim the trust property or its traceable proceeds from a third-party volunteer even if that recipient knew nothing of a breach of trust when receiving the property. A substantive view, or a functional view based on responding to opportunism, may perhaps apply in such cases, but only if a formal point as to timing is noted. The point, reflected in the courts' language, is that the conscionability of the defendant's conduct is assessed not at some earlier point, but rather at the point when the claim is made (or, if earlier, when the defendant has knowledge of the claim). In the context of restitution, rescission, or innocent receipt of trust property, for example, the question often asked is whether it would be unconscionable for the defendant to *retain* the benefit;[81] in the context of equitable estoppel, the question is not whether the defendant breached a duty to perform a promise, but rather whether, given what has occurred since the making of the promise, it would *now* be unconscionable for the defendant to leave the claimant without a remedy.[82] As a result, the work of Stephen Smith on the importance of liabilities[83] (as opposed to immediate duties) in private law has particular significance to our understanding of Equity.

V. Conclusion

Reports of the deaths of legal concepts are notoriously vulnerable to exaggeration. It has been suggested here that, thanks in part to recent academic work, Equity, like private law itself, retains some life. While this means that the lectures of those such as Maitland remain worth reading, the New Private Law cannot simply be the Old Private Law. It must add to the wealth of older writing by learning lessons from criticisms of such

[79] See, e.g., Ben McFarlane, "Unjust Enrichment, Rights and Value," in *Rights in Private Law* 581 (Donal Nolan & Andrew Robertson eds., 2012).
[80] See, e.g., *Restatement (Second) of Contracts* § 90 (1981); Jennings v. Rice, [2002] EWCA (Civ) 159.
[81] See *supra* section III.
[82] See, e.g., Grundt v. Great Boulder Pty Gold Mines Ltd. (1937) 59 CLR 641; Walton v. Walton (CA, 14 April 1994).
[83] See, e.g., Stephen A. Smith, *Duties, Liabilities, and Damages*, 125 HARV. L. REV. 1727 (2012); Stephen A. Smith, *Rights, Wrongs, and Injustices* (2019); see also *supra* text accompanying note 79.

scholarship. This requires consideration of the function and practical effect of Equitable doctrines within a wider legal system; determination to break down broad concepts such as unconscionability into more specific principles;[84] and willingness to ask whether apparent differences between common law and Equity can really be justified. It has been argued here that a focus on form reveals two vital functions of Equity. First, Equitable doctrines assist in legitimizing the operation of other legal rules and in dealing with a key risk of private law: the risk that a party may take advantage of her position as the holder of rights and powers that correlate to duties and liabilities of another. Second, Equitable doctrines increase the options available to individuals when entering into legal relations, particularly in relation to property. The flexibility and practical value of the trust, for example, depends on a formal innovation: the notion that one party (a trustee) can hold a right, yet at the same time be under a duty to another (a beneficiary) in relation to that specific right.

This raises an important question as to the nature of Equity: Can it perform these roles while functioning within the distinctive bilateral private law structure, or must Equity instead have a stronger flavor of public or general law? Two points can be briefly made here. First, consistently with the idea that Equity "acts *in personam*," many key Equitable principles are based precisely on the idea that a particular use of A's rights would, for a specific reason, be unconscionable *as regards B*, and the structure of the consequent intervention is consistent with private law, as it is B, and only B, whose practical and/or normative position then changes as a result. So if, for example, B enters a contract with A following A's innocent but material misrepresentation, the contract is not void: rather, B has a power, as against A, to rescind the contract. As an aside, this means that there may be a recursive aspect to Equitable intervention: in such a case, as Equity replicates the characteristic private law structure by giving B rights (such as a power to rescind) against A, it may also be necessary to limit, this time in A's favor, B's acquisition or enforcement of such rights. To that extent, then, such Equitable principles can be seen as remaining squarely within the private law paradigm.

Second, a more public law element may be introduced when considering the issues of timing and of the role of the court. To keep to the example of rescission for innocent misrepresentation, B does not argue that A, when making the misrepresentation, breached a duty to B; the point is rather that, given the misrepresentation and what has occurred since (including B's expressed desire to rescind) it would *now* be, in a specific sense, unconscionable for A to insist, as against B, on enforcement of the contract. The court, rather than simply establishing, for example, whether a duty existed and was breached, may therefore undertake a broader inquiry into the parties' relations and conduct. Further, historically at least, it is a court order, and not B's mere expression of

---

[84] See Lord Briggs of Westbourne, *Equity in Business* 135 L.Q. REV. 567 (2015) 583: "defining the underlying equitable principle too broadly, or at too high a level of abstraction, helps no-one, even if it may generate a comfortable glow of legal uniformity in the mind (or heart) of the writer and of the incautious reader."

desire, that effects rescission in Equity.[85] The role of the courts in such cases (and in making orders that concretize liabilities into duties) may add an extra ingredient into the standard private law mix. Yet, if such a dash of public law is necessary to allow Equity to fulfill its role of legitimizing and enhancing core areas of private law, such as the law of contract and the law of property, it should please the palate of even the most committed supporter of the Old Private Law.

Acknowledgments

I am grateful for the support provided by the UCL Global Engagement Fund.

---

[85] See Dominic O'Sullivan et al., *The Law of Rescission* 3.34–3.36 (2d ed. 2014) (noting *id.* at 3.53–3.54 the "difficulties" caused by the contrary suggestion of Lord Hatherley LC in *Reese River Silver Mining Co. Ltd. v. Smith* (1869) LR 4 HL 64). See too A Reilly *Is the "Mere Equity" to Rescind a Legal Power? Unpacking Hohfeld's Concept of "Volitional Control"* 39 Oxford J. Legal Stud. (2019) 779.

CHAPTER 34

....

REMEDIES

....

SAMUEL L. BRAY

I. INTRODUCTION

LIKE the law of procedure, the law of remedies emerged relatively late in common law systems. The old writs melded together what would now be called substance, procedure, and remedy; only with the retreat of the writs have these fields taken on independent lives.

Yet that very claim of independence may be misleading. Although the law of remedies is trans-substantive, seemingly independent of the substantive law, there is ample remedial discretion, and that discretion is to be exercised in accord with the aims of the substantive law. Moreover, in equity there is sometimes no sharp differentiation of equitable substantive law and equitable remedies, especially in fiduciary law.[1] It is an inevitable weakness of a survey such as this chapter that it will highlight points of commonality—here is what is true of injunctions generally, for example—while slighting the differences large and small that emerge from the interaction of a remedy with a particular body of substantive law.

Nevertheless, despite the influence of the substantive law on remedial choice, it remains the case that the law of remedies has an independent and relatively coherent existence. It is available to be cross-referenced by the substantive law. This characteristic of remedies as a relatively cohesive body of law, which can be accessed by other bodies of law, is not unusual but is rather an aspect of law's systematicity.[2] Indeed, the cohesiveness and modularity of remedies law provides a rationale for one aspect of how judges read statutes: they tend to read statutes as incorporating, but not changing, the law of remedies, unless there is a clear statement to the contrary.[3]

---

[1] See Samuel L. Bray, "Fiduciary Remedies," in *Oxford Handbook of Fiduciary Law* (Evan J. Criddle, Paul B. Miller, & Robert H. Sitkoff eds., 2019).

[2] See Paul B. Miller, this volume; Henry E. Smith, this volume; Jeremy Waldron, *"Transcendental Nonsense" and System in the Law*, 100 COLUM. L. REV. 16 (2000).

[3] E.g., eBay v. MercExchange, 547 U.S. 388, 391 (2006) (equitable remedies); Nken v. Holder, 556 U.S. 418, 433 (2009) (stays).

Here the focus is on the main outline of the remedies available in private law in the United States.[4] Attention is given to several themes that are developed in the New Private Law, including the systematicity of law,[5] the distinctiveness of private law,[6] the use of internal and external perspectives on the law,[7] the centrality of the judicial process in the award of a remedy,[8] and the continuing significance of the law of equity.[9]

This chapter proceeds as follows. Section II canvasses the competing rationales offered for private law remedies, emphasizing as primary that the defendant is restoring the plaintiff to his rightful position. Section III sketches how contract and tort achieve that goal, primarily through the development of measures and limiting principles. Section IV shifts from how private law remedies restore losses to how they transfer gains. Section V introduces the panoply of remedies offered by equity, such as the injunction, specific performance, equitable rescission, accounting, and constructive trust. Once equity has been introduced, the basic structure of private law remedies has been outlined: the pursuit of the primary goal of having the defendant restore the plaintiff to his rightful position, the doctrines that limit that pursuit, and the additional remedies provided by the second-order system of equity. Section VI extends the basic structure, or, depending on one's perspective, introduces anomalies: statutory damages, punitive damages, and declaratory judgments. Section VII concludes.

II. THE RATIONALE(S)
OF PRIVATE LAW REMEDIES

The rationale for remedies in private law is disputed. The question of rationale is important, however, because it orients judicial practice. Several rationales have been suggested. The most common include compensation for the plaintiff's loss, deterrence of socially costly behavior, punishment of wrongdoing, adjustment of unjustified gains, and prevention of private revenge. Which rationale, or rationales, one advances will tend to depend on one's view of law and its purposes.

Some of these rationales may have once been more important in the development of monetary awards, such as the avoidance of revenge.[10] But for present purposes there are two widespread approaches to the question of remedial goal.

The first is to say the primary goal is the plaintiff's rightful position, typically achieved with substitutionary relief but sometimes with specific relief. This primary goal is largely

---

[4] With due recognition that each legal system is particular, see Nathan B. Oman, this volume, it is also the case that many of the points made here are broadly true of remedies throughout the common law world.

[5] See Henry E. Smith, this volume.   [6] See Thomas W. Merrill, this volume.

[7] See Andrew S. Gold, this volume.

[8] See Stephen A. Smith, *Duties, Liabilities, and Damages*, 125 HARV. L. REV. 1727 (2012).

[9] See Ben McFarlane, this volume.

[10] See William Ian Miller, *Eye for an Eye* (2006); cf. Scott Hershovitz, "Tort as a Substitute for Revenge," in *Philosophical Foundations of the Law of Torts* 86 (John Oberdiek ed., 2014).

characteristic of the black letter law, and it also resonates with corrective justice and civil recourse scholarship (although that scholarship will tend to emphasize not just that the plaintiff is restored but that the *defendant* must do the restoring[11]).

The second is to say the primary goal is optimal deterrence. In some formulations, the primary goal is said to be the minimization of social costs;[12] or, more positively, the maximization of social welfare. This goal is then achieved by using remedies to adjust the incentives of various actors. This approach is characteristic of law and economics scholarship.[13]

There are ways to assimilate these approaches. For example, the assimilation could be undertaken through eclecticism about remedial purposes, perhaps unprincipled eclecticism. That is, we might say that sometimes the goal is achieving the plaintiff's rightful position, but sometimes it is deterrence or punishment.

Or there could be a measure of assimilation by deploying the is/ought distinction. That is, we could say that the goal *is* the rightful position, but the legal system *should* have as its goal the maximization of social welfare.

Or, perhaps most persuasively, there could be assimilation of the different goals by means of a goal/constraint distinction. That is, we could say that the goal of remedies is the restoration by the defendant of the plaintiff's rightful position,[14] even while recognizing that there are efficiency-related constraints on a legal system's pursuit of that goal. In effect, then, there would be a compensatory core with a periphery of punishment and the adjustment of incentives for primary conduct and litigation conduct.

Note, however, that regardless of which view one adopts, it is undeniable that even though one rationale may best explain the structure of private law remedies, those very same remedies might also have the effect postulated by some other rationale. A remedy that compensates, for example, may also deter.[15] But the rationale question remains useful: although a remedy may have the effect of both compensating and deterring, there may be a rationale that better explains the remedy's design, incidence, and stopping points.[16]

Each of these ways of approaching the goal of private law remedies has its adherents, and each can be the right answer depending on what question is being asked. These different approaches are not neutral, however, on the question of whether private law exists as a useful category. In particular, the use of "private law" as an organizing category tends to comport with the view that the restoration or vindication of the plaintiff's rightful position is the goal of remedies (perhaps with some room for punishment and for efficiency constraints). By contrast, to see the goal of remedies as more directly maximizing

[11] E.g., Arthur Ripstein, this volume; Benjamin C. Zipursky, this volume.

[12] E.g., Robert D. Cooter & Ariel Porat, *Getting Incentives Right: Improving Torts, Contracts, and Restitution* 187 (2014).

[13] On law and economics and the New Private Law, see Daniel B. Kelly, this volume.

[14] Douglas Laycock, *Modern American Remedies: Cases and Materials* 14–15 (4th ed. 2010).

[15] Darryn Jensen, "Compensation for Breach of Trust—The Remoteness Impasse," in *Justifying Private Law Remedies* 205, 218 (Charles E.F. Rickett ed., 2008) ("There can be no doubt that deterrence is often a by-product of private law, insofar as the possibility of being sued provides rational people with an incentive to behave in a way so as to reduce the probability of being sued, but deterrence is not always part of the structure of private law responses.").

[16] On internal perspectives on the law, see Andrew S. Gold, this volume.

social welfare will lead all but the most hardy doctrinalists to blur the distinctions between the criminal and the civil, as well as between the legal and the equitable.[17]

If the question is which goal best explains, as a descriptive matter, the structure of private law remedies, it is submitted that the best answer is the restoration or vindication of the "rightful position" of the plaintiff, that is, the position that the plaintiff would have been in if the defendant had not violated the plaintiff's legal rights. This single goal broadly explains the remedies of tort, contract, and restitution.

This goal can be achieved with movement forward or backward, to use figurative language. In tort, the rightful position is typically achieved with backward movement: awarding damages that put the plaintiff *back* in the position he would have been in if the defendant had not violated his rights.[18] In contract, the rightful position is often achieved with forward movement, as when expectation damages put the plaintiff *forward* to the position he would have been if the defendant had not violated his rights. Reliance damages, in contrast, are meant to put the plaintiff back to the precontractual position.[19]

These compensatory remedies no doubt have deterrent effects, and that consequence is welcome. But the basic principles of damages in tort and contract, as well as the basic principles of legal restitutionary awards and of equitable remedies, are largely not explicable in terms of reduction of social costs. To take one example, tort damages are not increased when detection is difficult—this is certainly true of compensatory damages, and it is even largely true of the punitive damages taken up in section VI.[20]

III. Measures and Limits in Tort and Contract

The rightful position is a good statement of the goal of private law remedies. But like most general maxims, it does not decide concrete cases. Instead the quantum of damages is typically determined by two kinds of doctrinal categories: measures of damages and limiting principles.

There are multiple measures of damages within each major area of private law, such as tort, contract, and restitution. In tort, there is one measure of damages for destroyed

---

[17] For a case in point involving the representation of equitable remedies in Guido Calabresi & A. Douglas Melamed, *Property Rules, Liability Rules, and Inalienability: One View of the Cathedral*, 85 HARV. L. REV. 1089 (1972), see Samuel L. Bray, *Remedies, Meet Economics; Economics, Meet Remedies*, 38 OXFORD J. LEGAL STUD. 71, 75–78 (2018).

[18] For numerous reasons, including incommensurability and judgment-proof defendants, the restoration is partly fictive. Cf. Smith, *supra* note 8, at 1753 (describing the law's attempt not "to make the world as if the wrong never happened, but instead to make it clear to the world, or more precisely to the two parties, that the wrong was a wrong and should never have happened").

[19] E.g., Sullivan v. O'Connor, 296 N.E.2d 183 (Mass. 1973).

[20] The likelihood of detection is, however, a theme in opinions about punitive damages written by Judge Richard Posner, e.g., Mathias v. Accor Economy Lodging, Inc., 347 F.3d 672 (7th Cir. 2003); and in the scholarly literature, e.g., A. Mitchell Polinsky & Steven Shavell, *Punitive Damages: An Economic Analysis*, 111 HARV. L. REV. 869 (1998).

property, namely, the fair-market value of the property at the moment of its destruction. There is another measure for damaged property: the diminution in value or the cost of repair, whichever is lower. (And measures of damages can vary from jurisdiction to jurisdiction: some use the diminution in value or the cost of repair, whichever the plaintiff chooses.[21]) The measure of damages may also be tailored to a particular kind of property, such as a special measure of damages for used telephone poles.[22]

In contract, the most common measure is "expectation damages," that is, the damages that would put the plaintiff in the position he would be in if there had been no breach. Conversely, damages might try to put the plaintiff back into the precontract position ("reliance damages"), or, less commonly, restore to the plaintiff any payments made to or other benefits conferred on the defendant ("restitution damages").[23] Here, too, there are specialized measures of damages, such as the special measures used for fluctuating assets such as stocks.[24]

The measure of damages provides a more specific way of saying what the rightful position is. The pursuit of the rightful position is bounded, however, across private law. Some of the constraints belong not to the law of remedies but to other areas of the law, such as evidence or statutes of limitation. Some of the limiting principles apply to both tort and contract, such as the reasonable-certainty requirement for lost profits. Many of the limiting principles, however, are specific to tort or contract (or to restitution, discussed in section IV; or to equity, discussed in section V). An example is the exclusion of damages for emotional distress in contract.

Note that some aspects of the substantive law of tort or contract can be seen, from a remedies perspective, as remedial constraints. For example, the contemplation-of-parties limit on contract damages and the reasonable-foreseeability limit on tort damages both operate to constrain damages that might otherwise grow beyond the reach of the imagination,[25] even though both are firmly rooted in the substantive law of each domain, each has different principles, and they differ in severity (the contract restriction is more strict).

In addition to contract law having its own measures of damages and limiting principles, contracting parties may customize the remedies for breach. Two especially common ways of doing this are with liquidated damages and with limitations on consequential damages.[26] There is a gap between the doctrine on liquidated damages (which requires judicial scrutiny to ensure the amount is not a "penalty" relative to the actual costs of

---

[21] Badillo v. Hill, 570 So. 2d 1067, 1068 (Fla. Dist. Ct. App. 1990); J & D Towing, LLC v. Am. Alternative Ins. Corp., 478 S.W.3d 649, 656 n.28 (Tex. 2016).

[22] Portland Gen. Elec. Co. v. Taber, 934 P.2d 538 (Or. Ct. App. 1997).

[23] The language of expectation, reliance, and restitution can be found in the influential work of Lon Fuller and William Perdue. L.L. Fuller & William R. Perdue Jr., *The Reliance Interest in Contract Damages: 1*, 46 YALE L.J. 52 (1936), and *The Reliance Interest in Contract Damages: 2*, 46 YALE L.J. 373 (1937). For trenchant criticism, see Richard Craswell, *Against Fuller and Perdue*, 67 U. CHI. L. REV. 99 (2000).

[24] Broadwater v. Old Republic Surety, 854 P.2d 527, 531–532 (Utah 1993).

[25] See Emily Sherwin & Samuel L. Bray, *Ames, Chafee, and Re on Remedies* 75–88 (3d ed. 2019).

[26] These customizations alter the existing contract remedy rules, more as *bricolage* than creation *ex nihilo*: "Contracting parties cannot create the foundations of remedy law. . . ." Alan Schwartz & Daniel Markovits, this volume.

breach) and the economic justifications for liquidated damages, such as reducing litiga-tion costs, protecting secret information such as product designs and supply chains,[27] and encouraging efficient investment.[28] These rationales for liquidated damages either depend on the parties *not* having to prove the actual costs of breach (litigation costs, secret information) or else suggest that the quantum of liquidated damages might not even be meant to approximate the actual costs of breach (risk allocation). Perhaps there will be more sustained thinking about the history of the penalty-clause doctrine, and its roots in equity, with the result that courts will relax the strictures of this doctrine, at least when there has been bargaining between the parties to the contract.

IV. From Restoring Losses to Transferring Gains

Although compensatory damages are the default remedy in tort and contract, they are not the only monetary remedy in private law. In restitution the typical award is meas-ured not by the plaintiff's loss but by the defendant's gain. The field of restitution has for decades been a subject of intense interest in the United Kingdom, Canada, and Australia,[29] and there has been a revival of interest in the United States,[30] largely due to the scholarly labors of Andrew Kull.

Legal restitutionary awards (i.e., recovery in quasi-contract[31]) are also meant to achieve the plaintiff's rightful position.[32] Various measures are used for determining the rightful position in quasi-contract, including the following:

(a) the value of the benefit in advancing the purposes of the defendant,
(b) the cost to the claimant of conferring the benefit,
(c) the market value of the benefit, or
(d) a price the defendant has expressed a willingness to pay.[33]

---

[27] Omri Ben-Shahar & Lisa Bernstein, *The Secrecy Interest in Contract Law*, 109 YALE L.J. 1885 (2000).

[28] Aaron S. Edlin & Alan Schwartz, *Optimal Penalties in Contracts*, 78 CHI.-KENT L. REV. 33 (2003).

[29] See, e.g., Graham Virgo, *"All the World's a Stage": The Seven Ages of Unjust Enrichment* (U. Cambridge Faculty of Law Res. Paper, No. 51/2016), https://ssrn.com/abstract=2845462.

[30] On the earlier history of restitution in the United States, see Andrew Kull, *James Barr Ames and the Early Modern History of Unjust Enrichment*, 25 OXFORD J. LEGAL STUD. 297 (2005). For two views of U.S. exceptionalism on restitution, compare Chaim Saiman, *Restitution in America: Why the US Refuses to Join the Global Restitution Party*, 28 OXFORD J. LEGAL STUD. 99 (2008), with Dan Priel, *The Law and Politics of Unjust Enrichment*, 63 U. TORONTO L.J. 533 (2013).

[31] Equity also developed restitutionary claims and remedies, initially for wrongdoing by fiduciaries. For discussion of accounting and constructive trust, see *infra* section V.

[32] The plaintiff's rightful position is especially salient in restitution cases explicable in property terms, while the rightful positions of both parties tend to be salient in restitution cases that are contract-mimicking.

[33] *Restatement (Third) of Restitution and Unjust Enrichment* § 49 (2011). The *Restatement* also supplies measures of recovery for conscious wrongdoers and defaulting fiduciaries in Section 51, which are best considered under the heading of equity. *See infra* section V.

When a plaintiff seeks legal restitution, again there are principles that will limit the pursuit of the rightful position. For example, in cases of mistaken payments, the plaintiff's claim for restitution might be limited by a defense of change of position.[34]

V. THE PANOPLY OF EQUITY

The legal remedies just described do not exhaust the range of private law remedial responses. Critically, there are also equitable remedies in private law. There are two sources for such remedies.

First, some of the equitable remedies were responses to the imperfection of the law's typical remedy of an award of money. For many familiar reasons, such an award can be imperfect and inadequate.[35] With this fact held firmly in mind, the English chancellors created a number of supplemental equitable remedies. The most commonly used today is the *injunction*, an order by the court for someone to take or not take certain actions. The injunction is an all-purpose equitable remedy that can prohibit a single definite act or even commit the court to a long process of overseeing the defendant's efforts at remediation. Other equitable remedies are specific to the contract context, and they respond to the relational problems from breach that cannot be cured with an award of damages. These contract-focused equitable remedies include *reformation, equitable rescission,* and *specific performance.*[36] Such remedies also allow judicial oversight of the parties, as well as subsequent modification or dissolution of the court's decree. That oversight or revision is often more theoretical than actual, especially in private law, but it remains available to the parties should it be needed.

Second, other equitable remedies were developed within trust law and the modern body of law traceable to trust law, namely, fiduciary law.[37] The paradigm remedy in trust

[34] On the change of position defense, see *Restatement (Third) of Restitution and Unjust Enrichment* § 65 (2011). Note, however, contra the *Restatement,* change of position is not a defense in "restitution" or "unjust enrichment" generally: it is a defense to certain kinds of legal restitutionary claims. If a trustee were to unwittingly receive benefits that belonged to the trust, thus breaching her fiduciary duties, she would not be able to invoke a change of position defense to avoid the equitable remedy of accounting for profits.

[35] As a historical matter, "[t]ailoring specific relief requires factual investigation and raises issues of supervision and adjustment of the decree that are beyond the administrative capability of a jury of laypersons convened for a one-time sitting at an itinerant *nisi prius* trial court." John H. Langbein, Renée Lettow Lerner, & Bruce P. Smith, *History of the Common Law: The Development of Anglo-American Legal Institutions* 274 (2009). For contemporary reasons, see Douglas Laycock, *The Death of the Irreparable Injury Rule* (1991); Samuel L. Bray, *The System of Equitable Remedies,* 63 UCLA L. Rev. 530, 551–553 (2016).

[36] In addition, there is a legal remedy of rescission, which has fewer requirements but also does not involve the same judicial oversight of the parties. Bray, *supra* note 35, at 555–556. It more closely approximates the easy to get but less generous remedy of rescission urged in Richard R.W. Brooks & Alexander Stremitzer, *Remedies on and Off Contract,* 120 YALE L.J. 690 (2011).

[37] See generally Bray, "Fiduciary Remedies," *supra* note 1.

law is an accounting, which compels a trustee to perform a duty that is at the heart of the trust relationship: the duty to account. That duty and the corollary remedy of accounting were not first developed in equity.[38] But equity made them its own, and the modern accounting is descended from equity.[39] In addition to the remedy of accounting, the equitable remedies pertaining to trust and fiduciary law include the *constructive trust*[40] and *equitable lien*.[41] These remedies are now used beyond the fiduciary context and can be used for many kinds of conscious wrongdoing (e.g., a constructive trust may be used, at least in the United States, as a remedy for a tort). Thus, although there was once a strong distinction between these two sources of equitable remedies—equity's addition of its own remedies to the available legal ones, and equity's operation in the areas that it developed exclusively—there has now been some confluence.

Nevertheless, distinguishing these two sources of equitable remedies in private law is useful, because it helps clarify the theoretical basis for equity's intervention. In equity's concurrent jurisdiction, the essential principle is that equity is a second-order corrective to deficiencies in the first-order system of law.[42] The deficiency in the legal remedies might be case-specific, or it might be categorical (e.g., damages are presumed inadequate for contracts to convey real property[43]). But either way, equity's intervention happens against the backdrop of law; one cannot justify the equitable remedy without making a comparative argument. Thus, even where equitable remedies are statistically commonplace (e.g., intellectual property, intentional torts), because of this requirement of comparative justification they remain conceptually exceptional.[44]

By contrast, in equity's exclusive jurisdiction, no deficiency need be shown. Although judicial decisions vary in how they approach the question, the best conclusion is that all of the remedies in the exclusive jurisdiction are equitable.[45] That has implications especially for the design of awards of money for breach of trust or breach of fiduciary duty. Such awards are best seen as equitable, which means they may operate on distinct principles. For example, "equitable compensation" (or "equitable damages") may require a less rigorous showing of causation, may allow offsets for services rendered by the fiduciary, may allow appreciation damages, and may not allow recovery for nonpecuniary losses.[46]

Whatever the source of an equitable remedy, or however far it might have traveled from its deployment by the chancellors, the fact that it is equitable has a number of significant consequences. These include the availability of the equitable defenses, such as

---

[38] See generally Joshua Getzler, "Fiduciary Principles in English Common Law," in *Oxford Handbook of Fiduciary Law* (Evan J. Criddle, Paul B. Miller, & Robert H. Sitkoff eds., 2019).

[39] See S.J. Stoljar, *The Transformations of Account*, 80 L.Q. REV. 203 (1964).

[40] *Restatement (Third) of Restitution and Unjust Enrichment* § 55 (2011).   [41] *Id.* § 56.

[42] See Ben McFarlane, this volume; Henry E. Smith, "Fusing the Equitable Function in Private Law," in *Private Law in the 21st Century* 173 (Kit Barker, Karen Fairweather, & Ross Grantham eds., 2017).

[43] On shifting presumptions in equity, see Mark P. Gergen, John M. Golden, & Henry E. Smith, *The Supreme Court's Accidental Revolution? The Test for Permanent Injunctions*, 112 COLUM. L. REV. 203 (2012).

[44] Samuel L. Bray, *The Supreme Court and the New Equity*, 68 VAND. L. REV. 997, 1037–1039 (2015).

[45] See Bray, "Fiduciary Remedies," *supra* note 1.   [46] See *id.*

laches and unclean hands; the unavailability of a civil jury; and the enforcement of the remedy with contempt.

In addition to these fairly hard-edged juridical consequences, there are further implications of the equitable classification that are more fluid and thematic. One is equity's flexibility and freedom in shaping the remedy to the particular facts. Another is equity's attention not only to the rightful position of the plaintiff but also to the rightful position of the defendant.[47] Closely related to this concern with the defendant's rightful position is the long-standing principle (now sometimes honored in the breach) that equity will not punish.[48] Still another is equity's concern with the broader public consequences of the awarding or tailoring of the equitable remedy.

✳   ✳   ✳

The equitable remedies complete the basic structure of private law's remedial responses. When A infringes a right of B, the standard remedial response is that A must pay a quantum of money to B that will place B in his rightful position. In tort and contract, that remedial response travels under the name of "damages." In legal restitution, although the term "damages" is not typically used, the standard remedy is also an award of money meant to achieve the plaintiff's rightful position. These standard remedies are not always suitable, however. Sometimes, therefore, resort must be had to the second-order system of equity to supplement the standard legal remedies. These equitable remedies allow the court to achieve a greater measure of justice and judicial effectiveness than could be achieved with legal remedies alone.

VI. At the Edge of Private Law Remedies

This basic structure does not include all of private law remedies. In particular, there are three additional remedies that can be seen as extensions of this structure, or as anomalies that are in tension with it. These are statutory damages, punitive damages, and the declaratory judgment.

Statutory damages are an award of money that is fixed ex ante for an entire class of cases. For example, a federal statute prohibits businesses from printing a customer's full credit card number on a receipt, and the remedy is a fixed quantum of money per violation.[49] Statutory damages share features of ordinary compensatory damages: they are measured in money, and they are legal and thus may be given by a jury. The

---

[47] Richard Hedlund, *The Theological Foundations of Equity's Conscience*, 4 Oxford J.L. & Religion 119, 124–126 (2015).

[48] E.g., Tull v. United States, 481 U.S. 412, 424 (1987) ("[W]hile a court in equity may award monetary restitution as an adjunct to injunctive relief, it may not enforce civil penalties."); see generally Samuel L. Bray, "Punitive Damages Against Trustees?," in *Research Handbook on Fiduciary Law* 201 (D. Gordon Smith & Andrew S. Gold eds., 2018).

[49] Fair and Accurate Credit Transactions Act of 2003, 15 U.S.C. § 1681 (2006).

interesting variations from compensatory damages are the shift from a case-specific remedy to a categorical one, the difference in institutional choice (i.e., statutory damages are set not by a judge or jury but by a legislature, or at the least the legislature sets the range), and the potential untethering of the award from whatever quantum is needed to achieve or approximate compensation. That is to say, the amount of statutory damages might be set because of some other public purpose, such as deterrence. It is this feature especially that makes statutory damages somewhat anomalous within private law remedies.

Another extension or anomaly is punitive damages. This remedy has a long history in private law, though in older usage it was often called "exemplary damages" and no sharp distinction was drawn between it and compensatory damages.[50]

Punitive damages are central to many economic accounts of private law remedies, because they allow a supracompensatory award that can ameliorate the problem of underdetection and consequent underenforcement.[51] Nevertheless, punitive damages cannot usually bear the weight of optimal deterrence, because there are many limits on them.[52] The main driver of punitive damage awards does not appear to be the chance of detection, as required in optimal-deterrence models. Nor do these awards seem well calibrated to incentivize private enforcement when the public benefits of suit exceed the private benefits. Rather, the main driver of punitive damages appears to be the jurors' sense of outrage, as well as perhaps the size of the compensatory award.[53]

Even so, punitive damages also sit uneasily with corrective justice accounts of private law, a tension which has led some scholars to describe punitive damages in terms redolent of public law, as if the plaintiff receiving punitive damages were in part acting as a private attorney general.[54]

In short, no matter what theory one adopts about private law remedies, there is something anomalous about punitive damages. But they undeniably have deep roots in the history of the common law, and they may serve a variety of valuable functions.

Finally, the declaratory judgment allows a court to make a legal determination that is binding on the parties—such as a determination about who owns this real property or this patent—without immediately issuing any further relief. It is especially useful in circumstances where the parties know how to order their behavior, as long as they can have a determination of some threshold matter, such as ownership.[55]

---

[50] See John C.P. Goldberg, *Two Conceptions of Tort Damages: Fair v. Full Compensation*, 55 DePaul L. Rev. 435 (2006).

[51] E.g., Polinsky & Shavell, *supra* note 20, at 874 ("In summary, *punitive damages ordinarily should be awarded if, and only if, an injurer has a chance of escaping liability for the harm he causes.*").

[52] E.g., State Farm Mut. Auto. Ins. Co. v. Campbell, 538 U.S. 408 (2003).

[53] The regularity of punitive damage awards, and their strong association with the level of compensatory awards, is a theme in numerous articles by Theodore Eisenberg and coauthors. E.g., Theodore Eisenberg et al., *The Predictability of Punitive Damages*, 26 J. Legal Stud. 623 (1997). For a cautionary note, see A. Mitchell Polinsky, *Are Punitive Damages Really Insignificant, Predictable, and Rational? A Comment on Eisenberg et al.*, 26 J. Legal Stud. 663 (1997).

[54] For a hybrid account, see Benjamin C. Zipursky, *Theory of Punitive Damages*, 84 Tex. L. Rev. 105 (2005).

[55] See generally Samuel L. Bray, *Preventive Adjudication*, 77 U. Chi. L. Rev. 1275 (2010).

VII. Conclusion

The remedies of private law give teeth to the substantive law. These remedies are largely trans-substantive, and they generally exhibit a primary goal of having the defendant restore or vindicate the plaintiff's rightful position. Yet this core point about the remedial goal would be misleading by itself. The rightful position is determined differently for specific kinds of entitlements. There are many limiting principles that give reasons to stop short of the rightful position. There are extensions or anomalies, such as punitive damages. And equitable remedies are available as a second-order system when there are deficiencies with the legal remedies.

There was no founding moment for the law of remedies, and it bears few marks of conscious design. It resembles the streetscape of Boston, not that of Washington, D.C. Yet for all of its happenstance and contingency, it offers the thoughtful judge a powerful—yet also relatively parsimonious—set of tools for righting wrongs and adjusting incentives.

Acknowledgments

I am grateful for comments received at the Oxford Handbook of New Private Law Conference held at Harvard in March 2019.

CHAPTER 35

....

PRIVATE AND PUBLIC
LAW

....

THOMAS W. MERRILL

ANY consideration of private law must come to terms with its relationship to public law. In civil law countries, the public-private distinction serves as an organizing principle of the entire legal system. In common law jurisdictions, the distinction is at best an implicit design principle and is used primarily as an informal device for categorizing different fields of law. Even if not explicitly recognized as an organizing principle, however, it is plausible that private and public law perform distinct functions. Private law supplies the tools that make private ordering possible—the discretionary decisions that individuals make in structuring their lives. Public law is concerned with providing public goods—broadly defined—that cannot be adequately supplied by private ordering.

When we look more closely at the American legal system, where the public-private distinction is not recognized as a general design principle, we nevertheless find that the distinction turns up in a variety of contexts. The judicial performance in each of these areas has been widely criticized and borders on the incoherent. This reflects the lack of intellectual attention given to the distinction in the United States. An interesting feature of the doctrine in these areas, however, is that judges are at pains to preserve a meaningful domain for private law, notwithstanding their inability to articulate a general case for its functional importance.

A possible explanation for this state of affairs is that different jurisprudential perspectives have dominated at different times in the evolution of both civil law and common law systems. During the post-Enlightenment period up through the nineteenth century, natural rights thinking, with the assumption that all individuals are endowed with rights that roughly correspond to those protected by private law, was ascendant. In the twentieth and twenty-first centuries, various schools of thought derived from utilitarianism have denied the existence of natural rights and have assimilated both private and public rights to the same general criterion of aggregate welfare analysis. The result of this incompatible layering of legal theory has left judges with no clear conception of the distinction between private and public law. Yet because the distinction is critical in many legal contexts, it also means that judges are uneasy about denying the existence of a distinctive realm of private law.

A final problematic feature of modern legal thought is a curious inversion in which scholars who focus on fields of private law have turned increasingly to law and economics, one of the derivatives of utilitarianism, whereas scholars who concern themselves with public law are increasingly drawn to new versions of natural rights thinking, in the form of universal human rights. This makes it increasingly difficult to preserve the autonomy of private law as a distinct body of legal principles that sustains private ordering.

I. The Public-Private Distinction

Like much else, the distinction between private and public law originates in Roman law. Private law in Rome was that which concerned the interests of individuals; public law addressed matters of public concern, "such as the powers of magistrates and the state religion."[1] Perhaps because of the great influence of Roman law in the development of European and Latin American legal systems, the public-private distinction has long been of central importance in the civil law. As John Henry Merryman has written:

> The main division of law in the civil tradition is into public law and private law. The distinction seems to most civil lawyers to be fundamental, necessary, and on the whole, evident. Treatises, monographs, and student manuals all contain discussion of the dichotomy, often in confidently dogmatic terms that put to rest incipient doubts.[2]

The dichotomy plays no equivalent role in English and American law. Merryman concluded that the distinction "is not taken seriously in the United States."[3] Perhaps with the emergence of the New Private Law this will change. Until recently, however, explicit use of the dichotomy has been largely confined to the classification of different fields of law. Property, contracts, torts, and restitution are generally agreed to be private law. Constitutional, administrative, criminal, and tax law are regarded as public law. The proper categorization of other topics, such as corporation law, is more debatable. And other fields of law, such as evidence and conflicts of law, inhabit both sides of the divide. The public-private distinction is also replicated within fields of law, such as in the division between private and public international law.

Without regard to its status as a legal concept, what is the basis for the classification of different fields of law as either public or private? The most widely invoked factor is the presence or absence of the government as a party. If a dispute involves only

---

[1] Peter Stein, *Roman Law in European History* 21 (1999).

[2] John Henry Merryman, *The Civil Law Tradition* 91 (2d ed. 1985).

[3] John Henry Merryman, *The Public Law-Private Law Distinction in European and American Law*, 17 J. Pub. L. 3, 4 (1968).

nongovernmental actors, the matter is governed by private law; if a government actor is either the moving or responsive party, the matter is regarded as a type of public law. This maps reasonably well onto the conventional classification. Actions for trespass to land, breach of contract, personal injury, and unjust enrichment—actions generally regarded as being part of private law—typically involve nongovernmental parties as both plaintiff and defendant. In contrast, claims of constitutional right or arbitrary agency action are brought against a governmental actor or agent; criminal charges and demands for payment of taxes nearly always involve the government as the moving party. The presence or absence of the government as a party also presumably explains the internal division between private and public international law.

There are, perhaps inevitably, exceptions where this factor fails to explain the classification. Contemporary governments own property, enter into contracts, and subject themselves to tort suits. When disputes arise between the government and a nongovernmental party about these matters, questions may arise about whether the government has waived its sovereign immunity. Still, if the action is permitted, the law that applies will generally be the same or at least closely similar to that which applies in disputes between nongovernmental parties.[4] And some disputes between nongovernmental actors, such as actions between injured workers and their employers, are adjudicated by administrative agencies, and these actions are generally classified as public law.

The distinction between private and public law carries other connotations, yet these seem to work less well in explaining the conventional classification. A second factor sometimes thought to be important is the source of law. Private law is thought to have its source in customary or common law or the *jus commune* derived from Roman law; public law is grounded in positive law enacted by the sovereign. This factor has some explanatory force as a matter of intellectual history. But specialists in fields generally considered private law can point to the importance of legislation in the development of that law. Property scholars, for example, can cite statutes such as Quia Emptores, the Statute of Wills, the Statute of Frauds, statutes of limitations for the recovery of property, and recording acts as fundamental to the development of property law. On the other side of the divide, some areas of law that have their source in enacted law are now dominated by judicial glosses on the original text, largely because of the infrequency with which the original text has been amended.[5]

A third factor sometimes invoked to explain the distinction concerns the number of persons affected by individual applications of the law. Criminal prosecutions, which are invariably classified as a species of public law, are said to reflect the general interest of society in preserving peace and stability. Tort actions, regarded as part of private law, reflect the need to vindicate more particularized interests.[6] Clearly, however, many crimes like murder and assault implicate both the general interest in social order and individual interests, and can be charged as both crimes and torts. This is as it should be,

---

[4] The Federal Torts Claims Act is a good example. See 28 U.S.C. § 2674.

[5] Thomas W. Merrill, *Interpreting an Unamendable Text*, 71 VAND. L. REV. 547 (2018).

[6] Randy E. Barnett, *Four Senses of the Public Law-Private Law Distinction*, 9 HARV. J.L. & PUB. POL'Y 267, 268 (1986).

but makes it difficult to have the public-private distinction turn solely on the number of persons affected. Here, as elsewhere, the presence or absence of the government as a party provides a better explanation for the classification.

If we put aside the quest for defining traits and consider the distinction from a functional perspective, greater coherence may be possible. In functional terms, private law can be said to be the law that supports private ordering; public law is the law that generates public goods that must be collectively supplied because they cannot be adequately supplied through private ordering. In Dagan and Dorfman's spatial metaphor, private law concerns the horizontal relations among individuals; public law governs the vertical relationship between the individual and the collectivity.[7] To be sure, persons seeking to plan their individual affairs will have to take public law constraints into account in doing so; but the tools they use in effectuating their personal aspirations vis-à-vis other individuals will be those provided by private law.

From this perspective, private law is the law that persons use to structure their lives in relation to others: where they live, what things they acquire and how they use them, what they buy and sell including their labor, whether to form or dissolve a business organization, who to marry, how to raise their children, what religion to profess, and so forth. This explains why property, contract, tort, and restitution are by general consensus the core of private law: these are the tools that persons use when they engage in these forms of private ordering. Although legal advice may be sought in making some of these decisions, litigation will ordinarily be avoided. The law serves primarily as a backdrop against which individuals shape their lives. This suggests that private law will draw from and reinforce social norms, will evolve slowly and incrementally, and will at any point in time enjoy a high degree of consensus about its content. These features also explain why private law tends to be anchored in history, whether through custom, settled precedent, or the *jus commune* derived from Roman law.

Public law, to continue the functional account, exists to provide public goods—understood broadly to include not just conventional public goods like roads and national defense but also the regulation of public bads such as crime and pollution and the provision of a social safety net. These sorts of general benefits cannot be readily provided by a system of private ordering because of insuperable transaction costs and collective action problems. Instead, we need some mechanism of collective governance and the use of coercion to promote compliance with collectively determined norms. This explains why constitutional law, administrative law, criminal law, and tax law are by general consensus regarded as forms of public law: these are the instruments for creating and funding governments and exercising coercion to promote compliance with its mandates. One can also see why newer forms of regulation, such as environmental law, consumer safety law, banking regulation, and so forth are readily assimilated to the category of public law.

Public law, like private law, could hardly exist without a significant degree of voluntary compliance by persons subject to its mandates. Nevertheless, given that its content is collectively determined, it can deviate more sharply from social norms than private

---

[7] Hanoch Dagan & Avihay Dorfman, *Just Relationships*, 116 COLUM. L. REV. 1395, 1400 (2016).

law, it is subject to more avulsive changes than private law, and often elicits sharper disagreement relative to private law. Given that public law has the power to trump private law (in nearly all legal systems), these features pose a threat to private law, devoted as it is to the facilitation of private ordering where the predictability and stability of legal norms is critical. This means, in turn, that private law must be insulated to a significant degree from public law. Such insulation can be achieved in a variety of ways, including specialization within the legal profession, the assignment of jurisdiction to different courts, distinct doctrinal traditions, or constitutional limitations on the scope of public law.

II. The Judicial Performance

Puzzles about classification are one thing, actual legal interpretations are another. Even in the United States, where there is no general doctrinal division between private and public law, the distinction pops up in a number of legal contexts. I will offer five examples. Generalizing, the doctrine in each context is unsatisfactory. There is no consistent intuition about how the public-private distinction should be drawn. The general pattern over time has been an expansion of the sphere of the "public" and a corresponding shrinkage of the "private." But the intuition that there remains a domain of private law that must be preserved refuses to go away.

A. The Article III Public Rights Doctrine

One prominent point of controversy in American law concerns the right to have one's dispute heard by a tribunal that enjoys a high degree of independence from the political branches. Under the U.S. Constitution, Article III federal judges are highly independent; they serve for life and have secure compensation. Other tribunals, including state courts, certain specialized federal courts, and administrative adjudicators, enjoy lesser degrees of independence. A recurring question generated by this institutional arrangement is whether a claimant is entitled to have her dispute heard by an Article III court, as opposed to a tribunal of lesser independence.

One prominent understanding that has emerged in resolving this question is that matters of "private right" must be heard by an Article III court (if there is federal jurisdiction over the matter), whereas matters that involve "public rights" may be heard by specialized courts or administrative tribunals. The doctrine thus affords greater protection to private rights relative to public ones. The Supreme Court has acknowledged that its decisions have never "definitively explained" why private rights are privileged in this context, and it has admitted that its decisions are not "entirely consistent."[8] Historically, the general understanding was that public rights involve "privileges" extended by the

---

[8] Oil States Energy v. Greene's Energy Group, 138 S. Ct. 1365, 1373 (2018) (citations omitted).

government, which can be adjudicated by tribunals within the political branches, whereas private rights are entitlements to life, liberty, and property of the sort that existed before the adoption of the Constitution.[9] More recently, some Justices have suggested that public rights are those in which the government is a party, which appears to differentiate public and private according to the presence of the government in the action.[10] Still other Justices have suggested that private rights are those that were enforced by "the courts at Westminster,"[11] invoking the source of the rights as the defining factor. Pursuing this latter line of thought, the Court has held that suits for breach of contract and tort that affect the size of a bankruptcy estate must be heard by an Article III court rather than a specialized bankruptcy court that lacks Article III protection.[12]

In its latest foray into the matter, the Court decided that previously issued invention patents can be canceled by an administrative tribunal, on the ground that patents are a "public franchise."[13] This hearkens back to the privileges-rights distinction, but by classifying what the Court suggested would otherwise be regarded as a property right as a type of public right, it sows further doubt about the future path of the doctrine. Whether or not this particular decision is sound, it is consistent with a longer-range pattern, in which the sphere of "public rights" gradually has expanded and that of "private rights," where claimants are entitled to an adjudication by an independent Article III court, has correspondingly shrunk—but has not disappeared.

B. The Public Use Requirement in Eminent Domain

Another controversy that has left many dissatisfied with the judicial performance involves the constitutional requirement that private property may be taken by the government only for a "public use."[14] The requirement has long been understood to mean the government may not take the property of A and transfer it to B, even if A is compensated for the market value of the property taken. That is, compulsory exchanges are not permitted merely to augment the holdings of one private party at the expense of another. In this sense, the doctrine is designed to provide a measure of protection for private rights against compulsory transfer.

The controversy concerns the meaning of "public use." Some nineteenth-century courts (and one sitting Justice) have insisted that public use means that the property taken must either be held by the government or the public must have a legal right to use it.[15] This interpretation would limit takings followed by a transfer to a nongovernmental

---

[9] Caleb Nelson, *Adjudication in the Political Branches*, 107 COLUM. L. REV. 559 (2007).

[10] Northern Pipeline Co. v. Marathon Pipe Line Co., 458 U.S. 50, 69 (1982) (plurality opinion).

[11] *Id.* at 90 (Rehnquist, J., concurring).

[12] Stern v. Marshall, 131 S. Ct. 2594 (2011) (tort claim); *Northern Pipeline*, 458 U.S. 50 (contract claim).

[13] *Oil States*, at 1373–1374.   [14] U.S. CONST. amend. V.

[15] See, e.g., Thomas Cooley, *A Treatise on the Constitutional Limitations Which Rest upon the Legislative Power of the States of the American Union* 531–536 (2d ed. 1871); Kelo v. City of New London, 545 U.S. 469, 521 (2005) (Thomas, J., dissenting).

entity to takings for facilities open to the public, such as stadiums and common carriers. The dominant construction, however, has been the broader view that public use means "public purpose." But once the functions of the government expand to include things like economic development, it is hard to see that interpreting public use to mean public purpose imposes much of any limit at all.

The most recent decision by the U.S. Supreme Court held that a public use can include a compensated taking of property from A for retransfer to B, provided the taking is projected to create additional jobs and tax revenues for the local community.[16] In response to the dissent's observation that this would permit any taking that would result in an "upgrade" in the market value of the property, the majority responded that eminent domain cannot be used when it is a pretext for a "private use."[17] But the Court offered no definition of private use in this context. The decision triggered a public uproar and widespread adoption of reforms at the state level designed to restrict the use of eminent domain.[18] But no clear consensus has emerged about how to give content to the public-private distinction in this context. At least at the level of federal constitutional doctrine, the pattern over time, once again, has been a large expansion of the range of takings that qualify as a public use, and a corresponding shrinkage of the circumstances in which forced exchange of property rights is impermissible.

C. Public and Private Nuisance

A third area of controversy involves the distinction between public and private nuisance. Here we find the distinction between private and public law directly reflected in legal doctrine. Historically, public nuisance was a public action, typically brought by public authorities seeking to abate a condition inimical to the public as a whole.[19] Private nuisance was a tort, brought by a landowner seeking damages or injunctive relief against action of a defendant that impairs the use and enjoyment of the plaintiff's land. Thus, the distinction was defined in significant part by whether a government actor was the moving party. In addition, however, the conditions that would qualify as a public nuisance were typically identified by legislation. Indeed, commentators up to the latter part of the twentieth century could confidently assert that a public nuisance is always a criminal offense.[20] Private nuisance, in contrast, did not involve the government as a party, and the conduct that would give rise to liability was defined by courts in a common law process, emphasizing a variety of variables such as the nature of the locality and the balance of benefits and burdens between the parties.

The division between public and private nuisance began to collapse with the adoption of the *Restatement (Second) of Torts*, which recharacterized public nuisance as a species

---

[16] *Kelo*, 545 U.S. at 483–484.
[17] Compare *id*. at 503 (O'Connor, J., dissenting), with *id*. at 477–478 (majority opinion).
[18] Ilya Somin, *The Grasping Hand*: Kelo v. City of New London *& the Limits of Eminent Domain* (2015).
[19] See generally Thomas W. Merrill, *Is Public Nuisance a Tort?*, 4 J. Tort L. Issue 2, at 1 (2011).
[20] William L. Prosser, *Private Action for Public Nuisance*, 52 Va. L. Rev. 997, 997 (1966).

of tort liability and largely assimilated the standards for identifying a public nuisance to those for finding a private nuisance.[21] The result was that public nuisance could now be identified by a judicial balancing test, without regard to legislative action. The *Restatement* also approved a line of cases that allowed private plaintiffs to prosecute a public nuisance action, provided they could show "special injury" beyond that suffered by the public at large. Little came of this revisionism until sometime around the turn of the twenty-first century, when plaintiffs' law firms, often acting in concert with state attorneys general, began invoking the *Restatement*'s version of public nuisance liability in an effort to recover large damage awards from corporate defendants for various widespread social harms, such as smoking-related illnesses, greenhouse gas emissions, poorly regulated gun sales, lead paint residue in apartments, and opioid addiction.[22] The results have been mixed, but there has been enough success in some contexts to yield settlements for large amounts of money.

Whether the traditional understanding of the difference between public and private nuisance was more protective of private rights than public rights is debatable. Stepping back, however, the larger pattern is clear. At least as traditionally understood, public nuisance was hedged in with various constraints—public enforcement was the norm, the conditions proscribed were those that would constitute a crime, and relief was limited to orders of abatement. With the *Restatement*'s revisionism and the recent outbreak of entrepreneurial litigation, public nuisance has re-emerged as a kind of "supertort," in which massive damages can be sought for various social conditions perceived to be inadequately regulated by conventional legislation. Meanwhile, private nuisance has largely but not entirely been displaced by public regulation in the form of land use planning and environmental law. The net effect is similar to what we see in other areas of law where the public-private distinction has wobbled, namely, an expansion of public law and a corresponding eclipse of private law.

D. The Public Trust Doctrine

Yet another controversy concerns the scope and content of what is called the public trust doctrine. The public trust doctrine applies to certain resources deemed to be of critical importance to the public, such that the public's right of access must remain unimpaired. The doctrine incorporates the distinction between private and public, insofar as the creation of exclusive private rights in a public trust resource is subject to revocation without compensation. This is because the public status of the resource—the "trust" assuring open access—is embedded in the title to which the resource is held.

The doctrine has its roots in Roman law, but was given its canonical formulation in the *Illinois Central* case in 1892.[23] The paradigmatic resource at issue in these early

---

[21] Merrill, *supra* note 19, at 20–29 (recounting history).

[22] See Donald G. Gifford, *Suing the Tobacco and Lead Pigment Industries: Government Litigation as a Health Prescription* (2010).

[23] Illinois Central R. Co. v. Illinois, 146 U.S. 387 (1892).

sources was navigable water. Public access to navigable water had to be assured because this was by far the best way to transport goods and people from one place to another. Thus, the public trust doctrine, in its early incarnation, was focused on the bed and waters of navigable harbors and rivers. This posed a relatively small incursion on private rights. For example, no claim was made that riparian land bordering navigable waters was impressed in any kind of trust assuring public access. Notwithstanding its limited scope, the public trust doctrine posed a number of puzzles that have yielded conflicting judgments by courts. It is unclear who serves as the "trustee" of public trust resources, who has standing to enforce the trust, what standard of review should be applied by courts in reviewing alleged violations of the trust, and whether an action to enforce the trust can be barred by principles of estoppel or laches.

A law review article published in 1970 urged that the doctrine be reformulated to cover any type of publicly owned resource subject to potential privatization, including parks and wilderness areas.[24] This cut the nexus between the public trust and navigable waters, and expanded the purpose of the doctrine to include the preservation of recreational opportunities and the conservation of natural resources more generally. A number of states followed suit in endorsing this expanded conception of the doctrine.[25] Academic commentators have repeatedly endorsed further expansion to encompass a variety of favored resources, ranging from wildlife, to cyberspace, to the atmosphere itself.

We thus see in the public trust doctrine the common pattern of expansion of the "public" at the expense of the "private." Interestingly, however, a recent state-by-state survey confirms that the judiciary has shown considerable reluctance to extend the doctrine to resources that have no connection to navigable waters.[26] The doctrine has been applied to non-navigable tributaries of navigable water, to dry sand beaches bordering on navigable water, and, in a handful of states, to wildlife.[27] But no court has had the temerity to extend it to the vast inland holdings of the federal government devoted to national parks and forests, wilderness areas, and wildlife refuges.

E. State Action

A final area of controversy involves the state action doctrine. The U.S. Supreme Court has interpreted the Constitution and many other legal protections to apply to government actors but not to nongovernment actors. This requires courts to distinguish

---

[24] Joseph L. Sax, *The Public Trust Doctrine in Natural Resource Law: Effective Judicial Intervention*, 68 MICH. L. REV. 471 (1970).

[25] E.g., Paepcke v. Public Building Comm'n of Chicago, 263 N.E. 2d 11 (Ill. 1970) (applying the doctrine to a city park).

[26] Robin Kundis Craig, *A Comparative Guide to the Western States' Public Trust Doctrines: Public Values, Private Rights, and the Evolution Toward an Ecological Public Trust*, 37 ECOL. L.Q. 53 (2010) [hereinafter Craig, *Western States*]; Robin Kundis Craig, *A Comparative Guide to the Eastern Public Trust Doctrines: Classifications of States, Property Rights, and State Summaries*, 16 U. PA. ENVTL. L. REV. 1 (2007).

[27] National Audubon Society v. Superior Court, 658 P.2d 709, 728–731 (Cal. 1983) (tributaries of Mono Lake); Raleigh Ave. Beach Ass'n v. Atlantis Beach Club, Inc., 879 A.2d 112, 121 (N.J. 2005) (foreshore of Atlantic Ocean); Craig, *Western States*, *supra* note 26.

between "state action" and private action. The doctrine implicitly rests on the belief that the government poses a greater threat to individuals than does private action. Hence the need to cabin government with special legal constraints, such as constitutional checks and balances and guarantees of individual rights. The doctrine assumes that these constraints are less necessary in the case of nongovernmental action. Private action is thus implicitly favored in the sense of being comparatively unfettered with constitutional and legislative constraints relative to public action.

One particularly problematic application of the state action concept involves judicial enforcement of rights of property, contract, and torts. The judiciary is a branch of government, and it is uncontroversial that constitutional provisions directed at what happens in court constrain judicial behavior. For example, the guarantee of trial by jury in the Seventh Amendment would clearly be violated if a federal court refused to hold a jury trial in a common law action.[28] What is more controversial is the application of constitutional limits directed at government more generally to judicial proceedings involving common law disputes between nongovernmental actors.[29] A notable example is provided by *Shelley v. Kraemer*,[30] where the Court held that judicial enforcement of a racially discriminatory covenant—essentially a contract entered into by a group of nongovernmental homeowners—would violate the Constitution's Equal Protection Clause. Commentators have generally approved of the decision but continue to disagree about its proper rationale or how it might be cabined to prevent judicial enforcement of all private law from being deemed a form of state action subject to constitutional limitations on the government.[31]

Another expansion of the state action doctrine involves action by nongovernmental entities that perform functions equivalent or analogous to traditional governmental functions. Older precedent holds that company towns, in which all facilities are owned and operated by a single private corporation, can be regarded as state action.[32] In the 1970s, the Court extended this reasoning to large shopping centers, but then changed its mind and reversed course.[33] Recent concern has centered on the increasingly widespread use of contracts with private corporations to perform functions traditionally undertaken by government entities. Private prisons, private security firms protecting government facilities, charter schools, and firms that process requests for government reimbursement of health care claims are examples.[34] Commentators have argued that these sort of privatization efforts should be deemed state action.

Overall, the pattern of evolution with respect to the state action doctrine is similar to what we see with respect to the other illustrations. There has been some expansion of the scope of public law at the expense of private law, yet we also see judicial resistance to

---

[28] U.S. Const. amend. VII.

[29] The First Amendment, by its terms, applies only to Congress. U.S. Const. amend. I. The Due Process Clauses are expressed either in the passive voice: "no person shall" (U.S. Const. amend. V); or apply to government generally: "nor shall any state" (U.S. Const. amend. XIV).

[30] 334 U.S. 1 (1948).

[31] For an overview, see Mark D. Rosen, *Was* Shelley v. Kraemer *Incorrectly Decided? Some New Answers*, 95 Cal. L. Rev. 451 (2007).   [32] Marsh v. Alabama, 326 U.S. 501 (1946).

[33] Lloyd Corp., Ltd. v. Tanner, 407 U.S. 551 (1972), effectively overruling Amalgamated Food Employees Union v. Logan Valley Plaza, 391 U.S. 308 (1968).

[34] See Gillian E. Metzger, *Privatization as Delegation*, 103 Colum. L. Rev. 1367 (2003).

obliterating the distinction. Most notably, there is a lack of any clear definition of the line of demarcation between public and private, and a near-complete absence of any understanding of the rationale or purpose for maintaining such a distinction.

III. Jurisprudential Views

Perhaps the lack of any clear conceptual understanding of the distinction between public and private law can be attributed to changing jurisprudential views. Simplifying greatly, we can identify two schools of thought relevant to the divide between public and private law. The first, which can be called liberal individualism, prevailed from the last part of the eighteenth century through the end of the nineteenth. The second, which can be called utilitarianism, emerged in the legal canon in the latter part of the nineteenth century and became dominant in the twentieth. Perhaps the doctrinal confusion about the division between public and private law is attributable to the shifting influence of these different jurisprudential views.

A. Liberal Individualism

One theory that bears on the distinction between private and public law can be called liberal individualism. It manifested itself in different ways in different countries. But the unifying theme was the importance of protecting the individual from overbearing forces of absolutism, class hierarchy, or majoritarian bias. Private law, from this perspective, is the law that is anchored in the natural rights of individuals and protects individuals from having these rights taken without their consent.

The connection between liberal individualism and private law can be seen most clearly in the civil law systems that emerged in Western Europe in the nineteenth century. The German scientific school that unfolded around 1800 conceived of private law as an autonomous body of law having no connection to public law or the state. The function of private law was "to assign a sphere of individual freedom; private law had no social responsibilities beyond that at all, and private autonomy should be kept strictly free of any interference by the state."[35]

The civil codes developed in the nineteenth century in France and Italy and later in Germany were grounded in a similar conception of the role of private law. As Merryman has written:

> The dominant legal concepts in all of these codes were individual private property in land and individual freedom of contract. The codifiers believed these rights to be the natural rights of man. In the legal thinking of that century the statement and elaboration of these rights in the codes served as legal guarantees against intrusion

[35] Hans-Peter Haferkamp, *The Science of Private Law and the State in Nineteenth Century Germany*, 56 Am. J. Comp. L. 667, 684 (2008).

by the state into areas properly left to individual autonomy. . . . Private law meant that area of the law in which the sole function of government was the enforcement and protection of these rights.[36]

In England, liberal individualism emerged somewhat earlier, and was not grounded in any conception of private versus public law. Instead, the theories of Hobbes and especially Locke gave rise to the celebration of property and freedom of contract as natural rights enjoyed by all persons. These natural rights were packaged by Blackstone as core principles of the common law, which in turn was depicted as a distillation of custom that existed from time immemorial.[37] The judges who applied and enforced the common law enjoyed increasing independence throughout the eighteenth and into the nineteenth centuries. Parliament was acknowledged to exercise sovereignty, but there was little legislation seeking to modify the common law. The net result, by the beginning of the nineteenth century, was a highly individualistic jurisprudence that regarded private property as nearly inviolate and freedom of contract as a fixed principle of interpretation.[38]

In the United States, liberal individualism took the form of Lockean natural rights adopted as constitutional rights. These were the rights said by the Declaration of Independence to be "inalienable" and were further referenced as the life, liberty, and property protected by the Due Process Clauses of the Constitution. Decisions of the Marshall Court, especially those interpreting the Contracts Clause, included renditions of the Lockean story about the pre-political nature of natural rights.[39] The jurisprudence of "liberty of contract" that emerged later in the nineteenth century can be seen as one that privileged private rights grounded in consensual exchange relative to public legislation designed to modify the balance of wealth and power generated by private exchange.[40] As reflected in the most famous decision in this genre, *Lochner v. New York*,[41] this jurisprudence was explicitly hostile to what it regarded as redistributive legislation.[42] Somewhat paradoxically, therefore, although American law recognized no generalized distinction between private and public law, American jurisprudence "found protection for property and contract rights in public law—in a constitution—rather than in private law."[43]

B. Utilitarian Theory

A very different conception of law traces its roots to utilitarian theory, as expounded by Jeremy Bentham and John Stuart Mill. The point of departure here was also with the individual, but focused not on rights but welfare. All social policy must be justified by

---

[36] John Henry Merryman, *The Italian Style II: Law*, 18 STAN. L. REV. 396, 403 (1966).

[37] 1 William Blackstone, *Commentaries* 67.

[38] See generally P.S. Atiyah, *The Rise and Fall of Freedom of Contract* 256–501 (1979).

[39] Ogden v. Saunders, 25 U.S. (12 Wheat.) 213, 318–331 (1827) (opinion of Trimble, J.); *id.* at 345–357 (Marshall, C.J., dissenting).

[40] See David E. Bernstein, *Rehabilitating* Lochner: *Defending Individual Rights Against Progressive Reform* (2012).   [41] 198 U.S. 45 (1905).

[42] Morton J. Horwitz, *The History of the Public/Private Distinction*, 130 U. PA. L. REV. 1423, 1425 (1982).

[43] Merryman, *supra* note 3, at 14.

the criterion of collective social welfare—the greatest good for the greatest number—
taking into account both aggregate wealth and distributional considerations. An
extreme version of the collectivist perspective was developed by Marx and his followers,
who sought to abolish capitalism. A less extreme version crystalized in the progressive
movement, which shared with the Marxists a deep skepticism of laissez-faire economics, but did not advocate the abolition of capitalism. Robert Hale, an American economist and lawyer who taught at Columbia, was an exemplary thinker in this tradition.[44]

The progressives in particular debunked any notion of natural rights. Bentham had
argued that without law there would be no property.[45] This idea was extended by Hale
and others to include contracts and torts. It followed that all law is public law, and private rights of property and contract exist only "at the sufferance of the state."[46] Private
law is simply a historically contingent version of public law that delegates special privileges to particular individuals over particular resources. From this perspective, inaction
by the state—failure to regulate—is as much a collective decision to confer power on
particular persons as is a decision to regulate.[47]

Hale and like-minded progressives were selective in their assault on individual rights.
Following the classic utilitarians, they generally supported civil liberties like freedom of
speech.[48] Their central argument was that greater collective regulation of property and
contract would improve social welfare by rectifying the inefficiencies and distributional
inequalities they associated with capitalism and laissez-faire.

The jurisprudential offshoot of progressivism was legal realism.[49] Although realism
came in different flavors, all realists accepted the central tenet of the progressives in
rejecting the idea of natural law. In its place, the realists advocated a kind of nominalism
about common law entitlements, especially property and contract. Property, in particular, came to be characterized as a "bundle of rights." One could add or subtract various
sticks in the bundle, such as the right to exclude, use, alienate, inherit, pledge, and so
forth, and still call the bundle "property" if it was convenient to do so.[50] The critical
point in terms of legal analysis was that it was appropriate to consider the proper mix of
sticks in any context, and this would be determined, following the progressives, by
considering which mix would best promote aggregate welfare.

A major implication of realism was that legal doctrine should be shaped by facts
rather than normative commitments. This opened the door to modeling legal doctrine after the actual practice of actors on the ground (Llewellyn), evaluating legal
doctrine in terms of its consequences as shown by empirical investigation (Brandeis),
and incorporating the insights of social science (Frank).[51]

[44] See generally Barbara H. Fried, *The Progressive Assault on Laissez Faire: Robert Hale and the First
Law and Economics Movement* (1998).

[45] Jeremy Bentham, *The Theory of Legislation* (C.K. Ogden ed. 1931) (1830).

[46] Fried, *supra* note 44, at 87.

[47] Morris Cohen, *Property and Sovereignty*, 13 CORNELL L.Q. 8 (1927).

[48] E.g., J.S. Mill, *On Liberty* (1989) (1859).

[49] On the emergence of realism and its relationship to the progressives, see Neil Duxbury, *Patterns of
American Jurisprudence* 65–159 (1995).

[50] Tom Grey, "The Disintegration of Property," in *NOMOS XXII: Property* (1980).

[51] See Duxbury, *supra* note 49.

Realism, in turn, had multiple heirs. One particularly influential offshoot in the realm of public law was the idea of "preferred freedoms." This idea effectively subdivided the world of Lockean natural rights, putting liberty on one side and property and contract on the other. Liberty was a preferred freedom; property and contract were not. This became the orthodox position of public law scholars in the postwar era. This view privileged certain liberties, such as freedom of speech and religion and equal protection of historically disadvantaged groups, while continuing to regard rights of property and contract in nominalist terms that rendered them subject to any plausible form of legislative and administrative regulation.[52]

Soon other offspring of realism appeared. One was the law and economics movement, which followed realism in rejecting any essentialist conception of common law rights and embracing a welfarist approach to evaluating these rights.[53] Law and economics also shared with realism its preference for assessing legal doctrine in terms of empirically demonstrated consequences, and its receptivity to social science, in this case microeconomics. Where law and economics departed from realism, in addition to its singular focus on one type of social science, was in its indifference to distributional considerations (at least outside discrete areas like tax policy) and its relative hostility to legislative and regulatory revisions of the common law. Indeed, early versions of law and economics reversed the hierarchy of the preferred freedoms position, valorizing the common law as efficient (in a Kaldor Hicks sense) and disparaging most public law intervention as misguided.[54]

Another offshoot of realism was the critical legal studies movement and its several "critical" derivatives. The "crits" embraced an extreme form of realism, in which all law was seen as a form of power politics in which the privileged sought to subordinate the underprivileged. The idea of private law, as a distinct body of law, was treated with scorn.[55]

C. The Sedimentary Stratification Hypothesis

We are now in a position to offer a simple hypothesis that may explain the failure of modern judges, at least in common law jurisdictions, to develop a coherent conception of the distinction between private and public law. The explanation is that modern legal doctrine consists of a foundational layer in which liberal individualism was dominant, covered over by a layer influenced primarily by utilitarian/progressive/realist thought. In effect, the foundation of the public-private distinction was laid at a time when the liberal view was ascendant, with its strong intuitive understanding of private rights as the

---

[52] The original expression in a judicial opinion came in *United States v. Carolene Products Co.*, 304 U.S. 144, 152 n. 4 (1938).

[53] See Thomas W. Merrill & Henry E. Smith, *Making Coasean Property More Coasean*, 54 J. LAW & ECON. S77 (2011).

[54] E.g., Richard A. Posner, *The Economics of Justice* 48–115 (1981).

[55] Duncan Kennedy, *The Stages of the Decline of the Public/Private Distinction*, 130 U. PA. L. REV. 1349 (1982).

rights of individuals grounded in natural law. That foundation still exits, but is submerged under a thick stratum of utilitarian theory, with its central assumption that there is no such thing as natural rights, and hence no meaningful distinction between private and public rights.

The hypothesis explains why contemporary American judges have no clear or consistent conception of the public-private distinction in law. All judges currently sitting on the bench were schooled during an era when the utilitarian theory and its various off-shoots dominated legal education. A root assumption of utilitarian theory is that all law is public law, and the decision to allow nongovernmental actors to call upon the law is one of social policy, to be determined by considerations of aggregate welfare. This perspective provides no meaningful basis for defining a sphere of private law distinct from public law.

The hypothesis also explains why the public-private distinction has not disappeared and why judges have instinctively resisted the notion that private law should be swallowed up by public law. Liberal individualism is hardwired into the foundational structure of our legal system. This is quite clear with respect to the U.S. Constitution, with its explicit protections of property and contract and its state action requirement, for example. But it also extends to more general social norms about the importance of protecting rights of property, contract, and bodily integrity. To adopt the assumptions of progressive theory wholesale would be to reject the most fundamental presuppositions of the legal order, something that judges, who engage in "interstitial" lawmaking but not root and branch revisionism are not in a position to do.

IV. The Modern Methodological Divide

The difficulty of developing a coherent approach to the public-private divide has been compounded in the contemporary world by a curious inversion in the methodological approaches to questions of private and public law. The most influential intellectual legacy of legal realism is the modern law and economics movement. In its early incarnation, law and economics appeared to offer a universal metric for evaluating questions of law.[56] Over time, its practitioners have increasingly retreated into specialized subjects generally classified as private law. This is especially true if one regards business law subjects like corporation law, securities, and corporate finance as private law. But law and economics also continues to play a significant role in scholarship on traditional private law subjects like contracts, torts, and property.

The irony here is that law and economics rests on the same premise that animated utilitarian theory and its offshoots like legal realism, namely, the denial of any meaningful conception of private as distinct from public law. Thus, to the extent that the primary expositors of private law today approach their subject through the lens of law and

---

[56] E.g., Richard A. Posner, *Economic Analysis of Law* (1st ed. 1972).

economics, one would not expect them to develop a robust conception of private law as distinct from public law.

When we turn to the realm of public law, we find to an increasing degree that scholarship is guided by ideas expressed in the vocabulary of natural rights. The rights in question have their roots not in Lockean theory but in the natural law tradition associated with Grotius and Pufendorf, grounded in international consensus. Unsurprisingly, this perspective has taken hold most strongly in public international law. But it has spread to various transnational conventions on human rights, informs the drafting of modern constitutions, and is beginning to affect at least scholarly commentary about the proper interpretation of the U.S. Constitution.[57]

The universal human rights version of natural law, like the Lockean tradition, is grounded in concern for the individual. All individuals have rights to equal respect, dignity, and basic civil liberties. The new human rights version of natural law would go further, however, and insist that all individuals have positive rights—to shelter, food, housing, education, medical care, and so forth. The basic problem of social order from this perspective is assuring that states—or perhaps international or multinational organizations—provide a robust package of goods and services to every individual, in order to guarantee a fulfilling life to all. Thus, although the concern has returned to the individual, the rights in question are seen as flowing from a process of collective action. The law of greatest significance is public law, although it derives from a transnational consensus about universal rights, not from the commands of the state. This perspective, whatever its merits, is also unlikely to sustain a close engagement with private law, viewed as a distinctive form of legal inquiry, or to develop a clear distinction between public and private law.[58]

V. CONCLUSION

Today, the idea of private law as a distinct body of law faces formidable challenges from all sides. On the one hand, the law and economics tradition, which increasingly dominates scholarship about private law, views each legal issue in isolation and is quick to suggest alternatives that are claimed to improve efficiency. On the other hand, scholars influenced by the human rights tradition demand that private law be infused with greater concern for mutual respect and equality. This sounds appealing in the abstract, but in practice would seemingly require situation-specific judgments by some authoritative third party, which would undermine the role of private law as a tool for planning.[59]

---

[57] See, e.g., Jamal Greene, *A Private Law Court in a Public Law System*, 12 LAW & ETHICS OF HUM. RTS. 37 (2018) (urging a reconceptualization of American constitutional law to make it conform more to the reasoning of the European Court of Human Rights).

[58] Which is not to say that concepts originally developed in private law do not infuse modern theories of public law, as for example in the "fiduciary" theory of the state.

[59] See, e.g., Dagan & Dorfman, *supra* note 7; Hugh Collins, *Private Law, Fundamental Rights, and the Rule of Law*, 121 W. VA. L. REV. 1 (2018).

Both perspectives ignore the critical role private law plays in facilitating private ordering. Private law allows individuals to shape their affairs, exercise initiative, and plan for the future. But to perform this critical role, private law needs to be highly stable and predictable. This means private law must be rooted in history, evolve slowly, and respond to existing social norms. The "meta-justification" for preserving a distinct sphere of private law could be framed either in aggregate welfare terms or in terms of human rights. But the content of private law, if it is to perform its critical function, must be highly conventional. It must be developed from the bottom up, reflecting existing practice among social actors, rather than the top down—whether it be the judgments of administrative "experts" or judges who regard themselves as moral authorities.[60] The task of the New Private Law is to develop a defense of private law along these lines—at once "pragmatic" but at the same time more "doctrinal" and even "conceptual" than either the economists or the human rights lawyers would have it be.[61]

---

[60] See, e.g., Robert C. Ellickson, *Order without Law: How Neighbors Settle Disputes* 137–155 (1991).

[61] See John C.P. Goldberg, *Introduction: Pragmatism and Private Law*, 125 HARV. L. REV. 1640 (2012).

INDEX

Note: Footnote material is indicated by an "*n*" and note number following the page number. Figures are indicated by an "*f*" following the page number.